Ernst Kantorowicz

Ernst Kantorowicz

a Life

Robert E. Lerner

PRINCETON UNIVERSITY PRESS
PRINCETON AND OXFORD

Published by Princeton University Press, 41 William Street,
Princeton, New Jersey 08540
In the United Kingdom: Princeton University Press,
6 Oxford Street, Woodstock, Oxfordshire OX20 1TR

press.princeton.edu

Jacket art: Ernst Kantorowicz in Copenhagen, summer 1925
(courtesy of the Lerner archive)

ISBN 978-0-691-17282-8

British Library Cataloging-in-Publication Data is available

This book has been composed in Minion Pro and Birch Std

Printed on acid-free paper. ∞

Printed in the United States of America

1 3 5 7 9 10 8 6 4 2

For Callum, Minna, Theo, and Till

Contents

Figures

Acknowledgments

One of the rewards of working on this book has been that it allowed me to get to know a large number of scintillating people who granted me interviews. Sadly, because much time has elapsed since I started my project, many of them are no longer alive. I mention the deceased first, with reverence for their memories: John W. Baldwin, Robert L. Benson, William M. Bowsky, Donald Bullough, William A. Chaney, Walter D. Fisher, Horst Fuhrmann, Arianna Giachi, Felix Gilbert, Ralph Giesey, Gordon Griffiths, Walter Gross, Erich Heller, Harry Jaffa, Alice Kahler, Howard Kaminsky, Ursula Küpper, Gerhart Ladner, Gertrude Meyer, Charles Muscatine, Margarete Ohlig, Vera Peters, Felix Rosenthal, Beate Salz, Ihor Ševčenko, Margaret Bentley Ševčenko, Lacey Baldwin Smith, Sir Richard W. Southern, Homer Thompson, Joseph Tussman, Donald Weinstein, Kurt Weitzmann, and Josefa Weitzmann-Fiedler. Lucy Cherniavsky, so sound and sensible, was a particularly valuable "research source" over the telephone. Her death just as this book was sent to the publisher deprived me of a friend whom I had never met. Others who generously consented to interviews are Beata Alden, Wilder Bentley, Jr., Michael Hauck, Eva Peters Hunting, Ellen Hurwitz, Norman Rich, Bernard Rosenthal, and Katherine Whild. Another list comprises people who have aided me with information of various sorts. They are Dauril Alden, Margaret Anderson, Sonja Asal, Hartwig Graf von Bernstorff, Thomas Bisson, Eva Cherniavsky, David d'Avray, Thomas Gruber, Henry Hardy, Peter Hayes, Peter Jelavich, Arnd Kerkhecker, Thomas Kuehne, Andrea Meyer Ludowisy, Karl F. Morrison, R. I. Moore, Elisabeth Müller-Luckner, Ute Oelmann, William A. Percy, Jr., Tom F. Peters, Johanan Petrovsky-Shtern, Carl F. Petry, Martin Ruehl, Kaya Sahin, Korinna Schönhärl, Elizabeth Sears, Walter Simons, Randolph Starn, and David H. Wright. And then there was a marvelous number of women who gathered evidence for me near and far: Catherine Arney, Christina Bobek, Stephanie Di Notto, Deborah Gerrish, Fiona Robb, and Kim Setze. Ariane Phillips not only authorized me to publish passages from her granduncle's letters but transmitted to me a hitherto unknown cache of letters, dating from the period of the First World War. A project aimed at publishing an annotated edition of Kantorowicz's letters is still under way. The de facto editors, Janus Gudian and Jost Philipp Klenner, and I were always exchanging information and evaluating evidence. John Van Engen helped to improve the book with a careful reading. I have deeply appreciated my acquisitions editor Ben Tate's confidence in me, and I express my deep appreciation as well to Jill Harris, who gets the message to Garcia, and to Anita O'Brien, expert "which" hunter. Eckhart Grünewald and Harvey Shoolman provided unflagging encouragement and crucial advice for writing this book over many years; aside from my wife, my debt to them is the greatest. Yes, my wife Erdmut. Indeed, yes.

Abbreviations

Baethgen papers	Archiv A246, Monumenta Germaniae Historica, Munich
Becker papers	Nachlass Carl Heinrich Becker, Geheimes Staatsarchiv Preussischer Kulturbesitz, Berlin
Benson papers	Robert L. Benson Papers, Charles E. Young Research Library, University of California, Los Angeles
Bolton papers	Herbert Eugene Bolton Papers, Bancroft Library, University of California, Berkeley
Bowra papers	Sir Maurice Bowra Papers, Wadham College Archive, Oxford
Brackmann papers	Nachlass Albert Brackmann, Rep. 92, Geheimes Staatsarchiv Preussischer Kulturbesitz, Berlin
Cherniavsky papers	Michael Cherniavsky Papers, AIS.1974.15, Archives Service Center, University of Pittsburgh
Curtius (Ernst Robert) papers	Nachlass Ernst Robert Curtius, Deutsches Literaturarchiv, Marbach
Curtius (Ludwig) papers	Nachlass Ludwig Curtius, Deutsches Kunstarchiv, Germanisches Museum, Nürnberg
CV	Ernst Kantorowicz, curriculum vitae of 1938, Ernst Kantorowicz Collection, AR7216, Leo Baeck Institute, New York, box 1, folder 2
DLA	Deutsches Literaturarchiv, Marbach
EG	Eckhard Grünewald, *Ernst Kantorowicz und Stefan George. Beiträge zur Biographie des Historikers bis zum Jahre 1938 und zu seinem Jugendwerk "Kaiser Friedrich der Zweite"* (Wiesbaden, 1982)
Emergency Committee papers	Emergency Committee Papers, New York Public Library, box 17: Ernst Kantorowicz
Frankfurter papers	Felix Frankfurter Papers, Library of Congress, Washington, DC

GA	Stefan George, Gesamt-Ausgabe der Werke (Berlin, 1927–34)
Gundolf Archive	Gundolf Archive, Institute of Germanic and Romance Studies, University of London
Hampe papers	Nachlass Karl Hampe, Heid. Hs. 4067, Universitätsbibliothek Heidelberg
Hepner papers	1206 Hepner and Cahn Family Papers, Wiener Library, London
Hicks papers	John D. Hicks Papers, BANC MSS 69/132, Bancroft Library, University of California, Berkeley
IAS	The Shelby White and Leon Levy Archives Center, Institute for Advanced Study, Princeton, New Jersey
Kahler papers	Nachlass Erich von Kahler, Deutsches Literaturarchiv, Marbach
Kennan papers	George F. Kennan Papers, Seeley Mudd Manuscript Library, Princeton University
KFII	Ernst Kantorowicz, Kaiser Friedrich der Zweite (Berlin, 1927)
K2B	Ernst Kantorowicz, The King's Two Bodies. A Study in Mediaeval Political Theology (Princeton, 1957)
Kuttner papers	Stephan Kuttner Papers, Stephan Kuttner Institute of Medieval Canon Law, Munich
Langlotz papers	Nachlass Ernst Langlotz, Universitätsbibliothek Bonn
LBI	Ernst Kantorowicz Collection, AR7216, Leo Baeck Institute, New York
Lorimer papers	Emily Overland Lorimer Papers, MSS Eur F177/56 1930–48, British Library, London
Lowie papers	Robert Harry Lowie Papers, BANC MSS C-B 927, Bancroft Library, University of California, Berkeley
Nef papers	John Ulric Nef, Jr., Papers, Special Collections Research Center, University of Chicago
Olschki papers	Leonardo Olschki Papers, Special Collections, Getty Research Institute, Los Angeles.
Princeton Press papers	Collection CO728, Box 262/F2, Archives, Princeton University
Salin papers	Nachlass Edgar Salin, C34, Universitätsbibliothek Basel

Saxl papers	Fritz Saxl Papers, Warburg Institute Archives, London
Schramm papers	Familie Schramm, L 230, Bd. 6, Unterakte Ernst Kantorowicz, Staatsarchiv Hamburg
Stein papers	Nachlass Wilhelm Stein, StGA
StGA	Stefan George Archiv, Stuttgart
UCSC	Special Collections Research Center, University of Chicago

Ernst Kantorowicz

Figure 1. Ernst Kantorowicz in Copenhagen, summer 1925. (Lerner archive)

Introduction

A MEDIEVAL HISTORIAN APPEARS AS A CHARACTER in a German novel of 1960, *Die Rolltreppe* (The Escalator). He is the author of a biography of the Hohenstaufen emperor Frederick II and a member of the esoteric circle around the poet Stefan George. During the First World War he had served in Anatolia on the staff of General Liman von Sanders. One scene in the novel is set in 1928 in an elegant Roman restaurant, "Ranieri." The director of the Prussian Historical Institute is hosting a dinner for a small group consisting of a museum director, a prominent industrialist, and the noted historian. They dine off baked scampi, breast of turkey with artichokes, red endive salad ("particularly fine for the season"), a cheese soufflé ("specialty of the house"), fruit, and coffee. The courses are accompanied by a Barolo, a Frascati, and an Asti Spumante.[1] The historian, here called "Witkowski," is transparently Ernst Kantorowicz (pronounced "Kantor-Ovitch"), who did live in Rome in 1928, did patronize the restaurant in question, and did greatly enjoy Rome's "sensational Frascati bianco."[2] Later in the novel "Witkowski" appears wearing "a white tropical suit and off-white shirt with a red velvet tie,"[3] and a photo taken in the same period (fig. 1) shows Kantorowicz in similar attire, with the addition of a white bucket hat and white gloves.

Few twentieth-century historians deserve a full-scale biography more than Ernst Kantorowicz (1895–1963) on the basis both of "work" and "life." More than fifty years after his death Kantorowicz remains one of the most influential of all medieval historians, perhaps the most influential. To be sure, the work of others might count as equally great: the names of Henri Pirenne, Marc Bloch, R. W. Southern, Charles Homer Haskins, and Joseph R. Strayer come to mind. But while their scholarship was pathfinding and while some of their books continue to be read, nothing written by any of them continues to sell as well as Kantorowicz's *The King's Two Bodies*. This book has been kept in print

[1] Friedrich Viga (pseudonym for Friedrich Glum), *Die Rolltreppe* (Munich, 1960), 246–48. Glum, *Zwischen Wissenschaft Wirtschaft und Politik: Erlebtes und Erdachtes aus vier Reichen* (Bonn, 1964), 392, 737, indicates that he met with Kantorowicz for evening discussions during this period and specifies that 90 percent of his novel rested on personal experience or that of acquaintances or friends.

[2] "Rainieri": Erich Rothacker, *Heitere Erinnerungen* (Frankfurt, 1963), 67; "Frascati bianco": to Fine von Kahler, 29 August 1928, StGA, Kahler papers, III:6568.

[3] Viga, *Die Rolltreppe*, 393. Here and throughout this book, translations from German are my own.

by Princeton University Press since its first appearance in 1957; it has been translated into German, French, Italian, Spanish, Portuguese, Polish, Slovenian, and Japanese. The steady sales and numerous translations reflect the fact that Kantorowicz's book has had extraordinary resonance in several disciplines: not only in history but in art history, literary criticism, and political thought. Fifty years after the book's publication, Stephen Greenblatt wrote that it "remains a remarkably vital, generous, and generative work." Giorgio Agamben has called it "unquestionably a masterpiece" and "one of the great texts of our age on the techniques of power."[4]

Although Kantorowicz's reputation rests primarily on *The King's Two Bodies*, substantial claims can be made for his other works. His first book, published in German in 1927 as *Kaiser Friedrich der Zweite* (Frederick the Second), was one of the most discussed history books in Weimar Germany. Establishment academic historians attacked it because of its alleged "mythical view" of the Hohenstaufen emperor, but others welcomed it as marking a liberation of historiography from positivism. Whereas the book appeared without footnotes, leading many to suppose that the author was inventing things, Kantorowicz embarrassed his critics in 1931 by publishing a "supplementary volume" that documented most of what he had written. Although other biographies of Frederick II have superseded it, the work remains a historiographical monument, and the supplementary volume remains basic for scholarship. ("You don't want to go into thirteenth-century Italian history without your Kantorowicz.")

Then there is *Laudes Regiae*, written over the course of a decade but first published in 1946. Whereas the main methodological claim for the importance of *Friedrich der Zweite* lay in its use of literary sources (poems, prophecies, panegyrics), and that for *The King's Two Bodies* its use of legal sources, the claim for *Laudes Regiae* lies in its use of liturgical sources. As Kantorowicz remarked in his preface, he hoped it soon would no longer be possible for scholars "to deal cheerfully with the history of mediaeval thought and culture without ever opening a missal." *Laudes Regiae* has attracted less attention than the two other books, but it remains important for its substantive contributions to the history of kingship and for its strategies for studying "medieval political theology." Finally one cannot neglect to mention Kantorowicz's articles, many of which are scholarly gems ("cabinet display pieces"). Lynn White once sent him thanks for one of these: "This is certainly one of the most extraordinary feats of contemporary scholarship. I am proud to know you!"[5]

Among Kantorowicz's distinctive traits was his versatility. One might imagine showing his collected articles to a group of beginning students without revealing his name and asking them to identify the author's specialty. Some

[4]Stephen Greenblatt, "Fifty Years of *The King's Two Bodies*," *Representations* 106 (Spring 2009), 63; Giorgio Agamben, *Homo Sacer: le pouvoir souverain et la vie nu* (Paris, 1997), 101–2.

[5]Lynn White, Jr., to Kantorowicz, 3 January 1944: LBI, box 7, folder 5.

might say he was an art historian, others that he was a theologian with extensive knowledge of canon law, others that his fascination with the derivation of words points to a philologist. Ultimately they might conclude that the author's vast knowledge of patristics and Byzantine history, medieval philosophy, and medieval literature revealed him to be a broad-gauged medievalist. But then they would be in for a surprise if told that this particular medievalist had never taken a course in medieval history.

All this said, the lives of scholars are seldom stuff for engrossing reading. "Stay close to your desk and you may be the winner of an endowed chair." Yet the life of Ernst Kantorowicz is an exception. Born of a wealthy Jewish liqueur manufacturing family in Posen (now Poznań), in his early career Kantorowicz was an ardent German nationalist. He volunteered to fight for the Kaiser in the First World War, winning an Iron Cross for his service on the western front (he was wounded during "the hell at Verdun"), and an Iron Crescent from the Ottoman Empire for his service in Anatolia. At war's end he took up arms three times in the space of a few months: against the Poles in his native city, against the Spartacists in Berlin, and against the "reds" of the short-lived Soviet Republic in Munich. Supposedly Kantorowicz said in the postwar period "right of me is only the wall"; in 1922 he wrote that German policy should be dedicated to the destruction of France. Closely connected to his politics was his membership in the elitist circle of the German poet-prophet Stefan George. Widely considered at the time to be Germany's greatest living poet, George was a riveting cult figure who espoused antirationalism, antimodernism, hero-worship, and faith in the country's subterranean resources (the "Secret Germany"). George dedicated himself to grooming a coterie of handsome and clever young men: they were expected to address him in the third person, hang on his every word, and propagate his ideals by their writings and example. The goal was to transform Germany into a land of truth and purity. Kantorowicz was one of the most prominent "youths" in the George circle (another was Claus von Stauffenberg, later Hitler's near assassin), and he wrote his biography of Frederick II with the "Meister's" encouragement.

After the Nazis took power Kantorowicz spoke against them courageously as a full professor from the lecture platform to an overflowing crowd in Frankfurt in November 1933. (This may have been the only time that a German professor expressed himself publicly against the regime.) Unable to continue teaching because of Nazi student boycotts, he was forced to "retire" and become a private scholar. In 1938 he barely escaped Kristallnacht and fled first to England and then the United States, where in the fall of 1939 he took a one-year position at Berkeley. This was succeeded by further interim appointments there until 1945, when he finally gained a full professorship. He would have been happy to stay in Berkeley for the remainder of his career, but the loyalty oath controversy at the university prevented that. Kantorowicz, of course never a communist, immediately became a leader of faculty opposition to the oath and remained a stalwart "nonsigner" until he was fired in August 1950. Then he "fell up the ladder" by an appointment at the Institute for Advanced Study in Princeton, where he pursued his scholarly interests while maintaining friendships with a considerable number of the most noted intellectuals of his day.

Kantorowicz had a fascinating personality. He was urbane and witty (and sometimes nasty). He was a natty dresser, a noted wine connoisseur, and a flamboyant cook. He flourished at night and resented being called in the morning before ten. From 1934 until his death his closest friend was the Oxford don Maurice Bowra, widely thought to have been the wittiest man in Oxford. The two traveled together through Europe in the mid-1930s and summered together in Greece in the 1950s. Other friends included a roll call of Weimar intellectuals and Institute notables. Kantorowicz was a brilliant lecturer and a renowned teacher at Berkeley. He could be seen on campus surrounded by one group of students, who delivered him to another group, who then escorted him further. He had girlfriends and boyfriends. He was transferred out of the German Fifth Army in Turkey because of an affair with the mistress of the commanding general. In the early 1920s he had affairs successively with the wife of one his good friends and an aristocratic young man in the George circle. Shortly afterward he entered into a relationship with the half-sister of the young aristocrat, and then he and Bowra became lovers. In the United States he had a long-term intimate relationship with his first cousin.

Hitherto there has not been an adequate biography.[6] Among the reasons are that one needs fluency in German and English, and familiarity with the respective German and English scenes. Furthermore, the enormous documentation in two languages is intimidating. Kantorowicz often said that he was "Schreibfaul," a lazy letter writer. Yet something on the order of fifteen hundred outgoing letters are known to survive. (I have located two hundred letters in private hands that were donated to me in originals or copies, and which I refer to for the purposes of this book as being in the "Lerner archive.") In addition come many surviving incoming letters, perhaps five hundred. Kantorowicz gave instructions in his will that his executor "gather all [his] letters and correspondence and burn them," but this mandate was discreetly ignored. His close relatives who had the authority to review the letters that lay in his possession did destroy two sets, letters written by his one-time lover, Lucy von Wangenheim, and letters written by Maurice Bowra. But the widow of another close friend,

[6]Eckhart Grünewald, *Ernst Kantorowicz und Stefan George* (Wiesbaden, 1982), is superb but has been rendered somewhat outdated by the subsequent discovery of many new sources and is limited to Kantorowicz's life up to 1938; Alain Boureau, *Histoires d'un historien: Kantorowicz* (Paris, 1990) (translated as *Kantorowicz: Stories of a Historian* [Baltimore, 2001]), is a slight assemblage of "stories"; Adelaide D'Auria, *La vicenda umane e intellettuale di Ernst Hartwig Kantorowicz* (Rome, 2013), is the work of someone who apparently cannot read German; and Janus Gudian, *Ernst Kantorowicz: der "ganze Mensch" und die Geschichtsschreibung* (Frankfurt, 2014), is reliable but short and sketchy.

Leonardo Olschki, was allowed to retrieve a large number of her husband's letters, so that a nearly complete exchange is now available. Similarly, a graduate student, Robert Benson, saved his carbons together with the letters he received, allowing for the existence of another set. Not least, Kantorowicz himself saved numerous incoming letters, mostly of an official nature, which recently have made been made accessible digitally by the Leo Baeck Institute in New York.

The documentation does not stop there by any measure. Kantorowicz's unpublished scholarly writings, handwritten addendums to his published articles, and many complete texts of his undergraduate lectures at Berkeley are all available in the Baeck Institute (and also digitally). Since he was a fascinating personality he often was mentioned in other people's letters and memoirs. The documentation is so thick that it can be reported with certainty that a lunch Kantorowicz once ordered on September 27, 1957, while he was in a hospital in Philadelphia, consisted of soup, beef brisket with horseradish sauce, mashed potatoes, brown bread and butter, fruit, and coffee with cream. (The patient skipped the broccoli and baked squash.) In 1938, after a flurry of correspondence regarding the Munich crisis, he wrote jocularly to Bowra that their "future biographers" would be grateful for the documentation.[7] This is no longer so funny.

It goes without saying that no end of documentation can ever allow full entry into a subject's mind. In Kantorowicz's case a fundamental question is why he turned from being the author of a highly rhetorical, politically charged biography written for a large audience in the grand style without footnotes into being the author of a methodical, distanced analysis of a political theology ("the cold searchlight of fact and reason") rammed with footnotes and designed for a small scholarly audience. Similarly, why did he move from the right of Hindenburg to the left of Kennedy? One can document steps on the way but to account for motives is hazardous. This book follows a rather strict chronology for the purpose of seeing its subject's development and also to note continuities as well as changes. As for motives, it does the best it can.

People ask whether I was a student of Ernst Kantorowicz, but I was not. In April 1961, when I was a first-year graduate student at Princeton in medieval history, my professor, Joseph Strayer, hosted a faculty cocktail party to which graduate students were invited. I can hardly say that I felt as if I belonged: I had recently turned twenty-one. But there I was, talking with Strayer, who soon was joined by the noted French historian on the faculty, R. R. Palmer. The two came to discuss plans for a meeting of the Society for French Historical Studies, soon to be held in Princeton, and although I had nothing to contribute they did not seem to mind my presence. Then another guest entered the room and strode over to Strayer and Palmer. I had no idea who he was, but his presence announced "great man." I had never seen anyone like this. His natty tailoring,

[7] Bowra papers, 1 October 1938.

replete with vest-pocket flair, suggested Savile Row, perhaps Beau Brummell. I had never heard such remarkable speech: a weird sing-song that communicated a message that "nobody else speaks like me." Next to Strayer and Palmer this person seemed to have arrived from a different world, for their suits were drab and their speech was flat. Yet all three were jovial with each other, and the team of two and party of one knew how to poke fun at each other's habits. The third man wished know when a protégé of his was scheduled to speak at the upcoming meeting since he wanted to be there. When Palmer announced that the student was slotted for a morning session, the third man expostulated that such was entirely out of the question, for, as the other two well knew, he lived according to the maxim that dawn was the time when men of clear reason retire to bed. Palmer and Strayer played it straight, proposing that the night owl must suffer. After several volleys, with an outcome I do not remember, the group dispersed, as people do at cocktail parties. As for me, I located a more advanced graduate student to inquire who the great man was. The answer was: "Ernst Kantorowicz."

The incident marked the beginning of a fascination that grew when I read *The King's Two Bodies* and when I learned that Kantorowicz had been a member of the bizarre circle around the poet Stefan George. And it grew still more after I was in his house for an hour or two. By the time of Kantorowicz's death in September 1963 I had come to know Ralph Giesey, the protégé who had been the subject of the conversation at Strayer's party. Ralph was one of the two literary executors of Kantorowicz's will and was on the scene since he was then on leave at the Princeton Institute. Somewhat earlier Strayer had passed along to Kantorowicz a paper I had written in order to see what he thought of it, so I asked Ralph whether he had ever noticed it among Kantorowicz's belongings. (I was curious as to whether he had scribbled any comments.) No, he hadn't, but he had a key to the house and I could come over with him and look around. I did not find the paper but there was compensation. After we left, we drank a bottle of Kantorowicz's Rhine wine, for Ralph had inherited the famous cellar and was opening bottles that would not keep.

Ernst Kantorowicz's life and work became an ambitious research project for me in 1988. In the fall of that year I was asked to participate in a conference on "German-Speaking Refugee Historians in the United States after 1933" to mark the opening of the German Historical Institute in Washington. Because my assignment was to speak on prominent medievalists, I decided to choose Kantorowicz. Coincidentally in that academic year I was holding a membership at the Princeton Institute, and accordingly I was able to talk with a considerable number of local eminences who had known Kantorowicz well. That did it. After I gave my Washington lecture I resolved to gather materials "toward a biography." Around that time I came to thinking of Kantorowicz as "EKa" (from the German for his initials and pronounced to rhyme with "Hey, Ma") because that was the way he asked to be called by his friends. I follow that usage here. One might say then that I have been working at this biography for twenty-five years, but that is not entirely true because I began the actual work of writing four years ago. But because EKa was someone who "combined depth of mind with abundance of spirit" (I borrow the phrase from his friend Felix Frankfurter[8]), the long engagement has never ceased to be rewarding.

[8] Felix Frankfurter to Murray Gartner, 24 May 1950: LBI, box 6, folder 1.

CHAPTER 1

Old Posen and Young Ernst

AROUND 1835 AN ARTIST FROM POSEN PAINTED A CANVAS representing a scene in Posen's market square (fig. 2). A carriage bearing two aristocratic ladies is rushing through. It is drawn by galloping thoroughbred horses and accompanied by a hussar on a rearing steed. Behind the carriage stand several prosperous men, probably local eminences, and a less prosperous group has its attention fixed on the carriage. The artist seemed intent on portraying various elements of the city's society, and he also depicted Jews. Three shabbily dressed men can be seen in a corner of the painting who appear as if they could have played in *Fiddler on the Roof*. Indifferent to the commotion, they are engaged in a business transaction that apparently concerns the sale of cloth and pots and pans. Ernst Kantorowicz's grandfather, Hartwig Kantorowicz (1806–1871), was born to this milieu. He and his wife Sophie (the granddaughter of a rabbi) sold home-produced liquor from a stand in the market when they were young, around the time of the painting just described.[1] But Hartwig was a remarkable entrepreneur; by 1845 he had gained the means to build a two-story distillery with the most technologically advanced copper apparatus. Well before his death in 1871 he had become one of the two entrepreneurs in Posen with the largest amount of capital.[2] A grandniece remembered years later that when he relaxed in his home he wore a red fez with a black tassel.[3] An inscription written

[1] H. P. Kent, "The Kantorowicz Liqueur Business," in Kent, "To the Members of the Kalahora, Kantorowicz, Landsberg, and Related Families: Follow-Up Information II, Aug.–Oct. 1989," in H. P. Kent Collection, AR6186, LBI. Kent was a grandson of Hartwig Kantorowicz by adoption and married Judith Salz, EKa's niece. Ruth Wolff (another member of the Kantorowicz family—a great-granddaughter of Hartwig) is the source of his understanding that Hartwig and his wife kept a stand in the market. Implicit confirmation comes from the fact that Hartwig Kantorowicz began to distill liquor in 1823 from his home at "Old Market 10": see Stanisław Nawrocki, "Die Geschichte der Familie Kantorowicz und deren Firma," in *Ernst Kantorowicz [1895–1963]: Soziales Milieu und Wissenschaftliche Relevanz*, ed. Jerzy Strzelczyk, 75–90 (Poznań, 1996), at 86.

[2] Nawrocki, "Die Geschichte der Familie Kantorowicz," 86–87.

[3] Anna Kronthal, *Posner Mürbekuchen: Jugend-Erinnerungen einer Posnerin* (Munich, 1932), 26, first noted in EG, 6, n. 7.

Figure 2. Market Square in Posen, circa 1835. (Courtesy Salomon Ludwig Steinheim-Institut für deutsch-jüdische Geschichte an der Universität Duisburg-Essen)

over the entrance to the main building of his firm bore the words "Alles durch eigene Kraft": everything through one's own power.[4]

Details of Hartwig's rise "through his own power" are scanty. But the main outlines can be discerned. The Prussian province of Posnania was heavily agricultural, aside from manufacturing in or near the prosperous city of Posen. (In 1850 the population of Posen was 38,500; by 1895 it had almost doubled to 73,000.) This meant that a talented businessman could negotiate advantageous deals to purchase grain for distillation into spirits. Hartwig Kantorowicz was talented in that regard, but his true genius lay in recognizing the possibility of branching out from schnapps (hard liquor) into liqueurs. As German

[4]Nawrocki, "Die Geschichte der Familie Kantorowicz," 87.

prosperity grew during the nineteenth century, a penchant for luxury items grew with it. Hence a market opened for more refined alcoholic beverages than schnapps—herb-flavored or fruit-flavored and suitable for serving at home (rather than in taverns) as aperitifs or after-dinner drinks. A document of 1862 referred to two of Hartwig Kantorowicz's products: "Kümmelliqueur" and "Goldwassercrême."[5] The first, otherwise known as "Allasch," was made primarily from caraway seeds, the second from an essence based on a mixture of herbs such as anise, cinnamon, nutmeg, cloves, and peppermint (and always plenty of sugar). The same document reveals that Hartwig's products already were being exported beyond Germany to lands as distant as Australia and America.

The founding father and his wife had seven sons and a daughter (five other children died in infancy). The three sons that concern us were Max (1843–1904), Edmund (1846–1904), and Joseph (1848–1919).[6] These assumed joint management of the firm after Hartwig's death in 1871: the eldest as director, the other two as junior partners. Max Kantorowicz possessed the enterprising genius of his father. Sometime in the 1880s he traveled to the United States to arrange for the regular exporting to Posen of fruit juices, which made for a more varied range of liqueurs. On the same trip he arranged for the regular purchase of California wines, which were extremely cheap, in order to introduce the sale of wines as a sideline to the Kantorowicz business. So far as is known, Max was the first to introduce California wines to Europe.[7]

A description of the Kantorowicz enterprise that appeared in a Posen newspaper in 1895 offers a good impression of what Max and his partners had accomplished. In addition to an unspecified number of workers who tended to the machinery in the factory, thirty people were assigned to packing, twenty more to sorting and shipping, and fifteen to keeping accounts (including three stenographers). Products included not only liqueurs but bitters. One hundred thousand liters were stored in the cellar for eventual domestic sale, and exports were sent to France, Denmark, Southwest Africa, and Japan. A cherry press was deemed to be the best in Europe; every day tons of sour cherries were pressed hydraulically. The firm even owned its own small factory for manufacturing seals for its crates.

In addition to being a gifted businessman and manager, Max Kantorowicz was a greatly admired human being. A nephew by marriage, Wilhelm Wolff, reminisced in 1945 about the relative who had died forty-one years earlier: "Max Kantorowicz, what an exemplary man, intellectually sharp and acute,

[5] Kent, "Kantorowicz Liqueur Business."

[6] Details about the descent, names, and dates of the many members of Ernst Kantorowicz's family (extending back to 1495 on the maternal side) can be found in an invaluable family tree drawn up by EKa in 1936 during a period of enforced leisure: LBI, box 5, folder 6.

[7] Max's trip to the United States is reported in a letter of 26 March 1958 by his grandson, Ernst Milch, to a director of the Leo Baeck Institute. Kantorowicz Family Collection, AR 439, LBI, box 1, folder 1.

honest and aware of his inner worth, and so simple and modest, and always ready to help others."[8] Max's granddaughter, Ellen Fischer, wrote a memoir in which she stated that he was a "liberal democrat, successful businessman, respected citizen and benefactor, city counselor [and] father to his employees in the factory."[9] Fischer reported that when she lived in New York after the Second World War a Russian lady, visiting her mother on West End Avenue, saw a portrait of Max who she insisted had been a link in an underground chain that smuggled young Jewish men out of Russia at a time of the czarist draft. Fischer supposed that her grandfather gave them money and perhaps a boat ticket before they made their way to America. When Max died "his funeral cortège wound for hours through streets and streets."

Max's wife Rosalinde (1854–1916) presided over a household that would have been visited often by the young Ernst Kantorowicz. Wilhelm Wolff described Rosalinde as "lovely, always obliging and cheerful, and dedicated to higher and nobler things." Ellen Fischer used similar language, calling Rosalinde "sociable, gracious, and lively." Rosalinde "dressed beautifully (never wore too much jewelry)," had a tasteful salon, and enjoyed playing the piano, especially Chopin. At an advanced age she took delight in playing *à quatre mains* with a granddaughter. She was one of the muses of the cultural life of Posen. When a student of Richard Wagner came to live in the city, she engaged him to speak in her home about Wagner's new style of music. A prominent portrait painter, Reinhold Lepsius, spent a month in 1897 in the Kantorowicz house working on a portrait of Rosalinde.[10]

Very little is known about the middle partner, Edmund, who was a bachelor. But one well-documented story serves as compensation. In 1880 Edmund was in Berlin and there became party to a cause célèbre. Bernhard Förster, a high school teacher soon to marry the sister of Friedrich Nietzsche, was a rabid antisemite. On the day Edmund was in town Förster had attended an antisemitic rally in a tavern and was returning home on a horse-drawn tram with some like-minded friends. Fired up from the meeting, Förster continued spouting his rancid opinions, talking loudly of "Jewish impudence," complaining of "the Jewish press," mocking Jewish intonations, and warning that Jews would soon be hit by "German blows." As he spouted he caused a stir, and when he left the tram with his companions another passenger got off as well. According to the language of the subsequent police report, this was a "respected Jewish merchant"—our Edmund Kantorowicz. On the street Förster and the

[8] Wilhelm Wolff to Franz Kantorowicz (Max's son); letter in German dictated from Montreal, 13 July 1945: Lerner archive. (Here and throughout, translations from the German are my own.)

[9] A copy of Ellen Fischer's (née Milch) unpublished memoirs was generously given to me by Chris Barkan (Max's great-great-great-grandson); Ellen Fischer's daughter, Constance Sattler, allowed me to quote from her mother's work. I have deposited the memoirs in the Leo Baeck Institute.

[10] Letters from Reinhard Lepsius to his wife Sabine Lepsius, 3, 4, 6, 12, 13, 23 1897: Lepsius papers, DLA.

thirty-four-year-old Edmund had words. A crowd gathered and Kantorowicz demanded to know the unruly antisemite's name. When the reply was, "Why should I tell you? You're only a Jew," he responded—again according to the official report—by punching Förster so hard that the latter's hat fell to the ground. An ensuing melee had to be broken up by the police. The newspapers soon publicized the scuffle and Förster was brought to court. The judge then ruled that he pay a fine and as a teacher in the public schools be placed on probation because of his "unworthy extra-official behavior."[11]

The third partner was EKa's father, Joseph. Ellen Fischer wrote that "we children called him 'uncle Juju' and loved him."[12] EKa had a strong bond with Joseph, displayed in exchanges of letters between the two about the political situation right before and during the First World War.[13] In the United States EKa told people that he "loved his father," unusual language for him, and he kept a photograph of him on his bedroom dresser.[14] A glimpse of the father-son relationship appears in a reminiscence found in a letter of 1961 to Elise Peters, EKa's favorite relative from the Posen days. He wrote that when he was in his teens he had a brief flirtation with "Clärchen," the daughter of one of Joseph's younger brothers. She was very pretty, and, as he could not resist adding, "she wore the most elegant underwear in Berlin." (He was told this by another female relative Clärchen's age who had reason to know.) But his father called him into his study (the "Herrenzimmer") and said, "My son I do not wish that you start anything with Clärchen. Do not forget that she is your first cousin." EKa recalled that he "was somewhat taken aback by the arbitrary nature of the argument" but decided not to pursue the matter.[15] (At the time he wrote this he was having an affair with another first cousin.)

EKa's mother, Clara Hepner, was born in 1862 in Jaraczewo, a town of barely a thousand people, thirty-five miles from Posen.[16] The Hepners had drawn on farming to found a large distillery. Joseph probably met Clara in the course of business transactions with the Hepners. Coming from a rural environment, she lacked the sophistication characteristic of the Kantorowiczes. The picture that EKa portrayed of her was one of the beaming Jewish mother. In a letter of 1956

[11] Erich F. Podach, *Gestalten um Nietzsche* (Weimar, 1932), 137–38. Podach does not name Förster's Jewish antagonist, but he is identified as Edmund Kantorowicz in Kurt Gassen and Michael Landmann, eds., *Buch des Dankes an Georg Simmel* (Berlin, 1958), 276.

[12] See also the affectionate words about Joseph in a letter from Eva Kantorowicz, Joseph's niece by marriage, to Vera Peters, 13 October 1943: Lerner archive.

[13] Joseph to Ernst, 29 July 1914; Ernst to his parents, letters of 1918: collection of Ariane Philipps.

[14] Interview with Lucy Cherniavsky, 3 March 1991; interview with Vera Peters, 1 August 1989. Ralph Giesey to Maurice Bowra, 29 September 1963: Bowra papers.

[15] Kantorowicz to Elise Peters, 21 October 1961: Lerner archive.

[16] "Stammliste von Familie Hepner" (LBI, box 5, folder 4—in Clara's handwriting), born 5 July 1862. The population of Jaraczewo is given in Felix Hepner, "Erinnerungen": Hepner papers, 1206/2/1/1, p. 1.

to Elise Peters he wrote that Clara, "thoughtful as always," had gilded his first baby tooth and given it to his father as a birthday present to wear on his watch fob; this strengthened EKa's ego but still had him wondering, "with a certain degree of modesty" why this tooth was so important even though every day it was getting dirtier.[17] The doting on an only son (called by his mother "Ernstl") also emerges from a playful remark in a letter of 1958 in which EKa reported that he had recovered so well from a recent operation that his doctor was terribly proud of him: "as proud as only my mother would have been—and that's saying something."[18]

When Joseph Kantorowicz's two older brothers died in 1904 he became co-manager of the firm with Max's son, Franz Hartwig (born in 1872). Franz had attended universities even though other business families would have considered that an untenable waste of time. After studying political science and philosophy at the Universities of Lausanne, Munich, and Berlin, Franz received his doctorate in 1896 at Göttingen in political economy with a dissertation on "The Ruble Exchange Rate and Russian Grain Export."[19] Dr. Kantorowicz then spent a while in the United States strengthening the family firm's commercial ties. In San Francisco he developed a close relationship with Arthur Lachman, a California wine grower. (On the latter's death in 1916 he wrote a condolence letter—in German—to Lachman's wife that included greetings to her children.[20]) Franz became a partner of the Kantorowicz firm in Posen in 1902, and in 1907 director-in-chief. [21] Nevertheless, Joseph continued to play an important role until his death in 1919. Evidence of the collaboration between uncle and nephew appears in a letter that Franz sent to his wife while interned by the Polish government in Posen in February 1919: "Today, the sixteenth day! Who would have suspected this, and now the tragedy of uncle's death just at this moment when his advice would have been of the greatest value."[22]

During the early years of the twentieth century the Hartwig Kantorowicz firm continued to burgeon.[23] The year 1907 saw its reorganization as a joint stock company and the opening of an enormous new factory. This was on the

[17] 30 November 1956: Lerner archive.

[18] Kantorowicz to Leonardo Olschki, 7 September 1958: Olschki papers. The original German has more flavor: "mein tüchtiger Arzt hier war so stolz auf mich, wie es sonst nur meine Mutter gewesen wäre—und das will etwas heissen."

[19] Franz Hartwig Kantorowicz, *Rubelkurs und russische Getreideausfuhr. Eine Währungsstudie* (Jena, 1896).

[20] Franz Kantorowicz to "Frau Ab. Lachman," 17 March 1916: Lerner archive. The letter, written from the Russian front, was mailed from Posen on 1 April and then returned to the sender.

[21] For biographical data on Franz Kantorowicz, *Reichshandbuch der deutschen Gesellschaft* (Berlin, 1930), 880.

[22] Franz Kantorowicz to Eva Kantorowicz, 13 February 1919: Lerner archive.

[23] For the following paragraph I rely on Nawrocki, "Die Geschichte der Familie Kantorowicz," 87–88, a letterhead of the firm of 1917 (Pannwitz papers, DLA), and a clipping from Hamburg Nachrichten, 3 September 1914, at http://www.zbw.eu/beta/p20/company/42961/about.en.html.

outskirts of Posen on a large campus with attractive appurtenant residences for the workers. (The firm was noted for its benevolent paternalistic policies.) Although the factory was in Posen, Berlin had become the commercial hub of the business. A warehouse and branch office were located there, and also retail stores on the Friedrichstrasse in the heart of the city and the Joachimsthalerstrasse in the newly built upper-class neighborhood of Charlottenburg. A branch devoted to imports and exports was located in Hamburg. Products of the firm ranged from spirits and cordials to fruit juices (cherry and raspberry), and retail sales extended to wines. In September 1914 stockholders received a 12 percent annual dividend.

It can be seen, then, that Ernst Kantorowicz was born in the most comfortable of circumstances. It is useful to know for all that follows that he grew up entirely as a German. Posen had a Polish majority. The percentage can only be estimated because the Prussian census counted by religion rather than ethnicity. Thus we know that in 1900, 73,403 Catholics, 37,232 Protestants, and 5,988 of the "Mosaic faith" lived in Posen, but the best we can do is translate the first two figures into roughly 65,000 Poles and 50,000 Germans because about 10 percent of the Catholics were Germans.[24] The numerical predominance of Poles should not be surprising because the province of Posen lay within the borders of the Kingdom of Poland until 1793, when it was annexed by Prussia. (The cathedral of Posen was the burial place of the earliest Polish monarchs, and the town hall, the architectural gem of the city, dated from the Polish era.) With Prussian ascendancy many Germans arrived as officials, merchants, and professionals, but until 1871 little or no hostility existed between Germans and Poles. The nationalities lived apart in their own neighborhoods and patronized separate restaurants and theaters, but Germans shopped in Polish stores where they were greeted in German, and Poles shopped in German stores where customarily at least one employee spoke Polish.[25]

Yet in the last quarter of the century Poles steadily became estranged. After the unification of Germany in 1871 the government of the new Reich, dominated by Prussia (vastly the Reich's largest state in a federal system), began to pursue a policy of advancing *Deutschtum* (Germanness) in the eastern border regions.[26] Chancellor Otto von Bismarck worried about a Catholic threat, which for him was inseparable from a national threat. Germany had been unified as the result of the victory of Protestant Prussia over Catholic Austria, and Bismarck continued to view Austria as a potential enemy. He believed that he

[24] Census figures according to religion for the years for 1871 through 1910 are in Gotthold Rhode, *Geschichte der Stadt Posen* (Neuendettelsau, 1953), 144.

[25] Kronthal, *Posner Mürbekuchen*, 12–13.

[26] For Prussian policy in Posnania in the late nineteenth century, Piotr S. Wandycz, *The Lands of Partitioned Poland, 1795–1918* (Seattle, 1974), 233–37. On population, Richard Blanke, *Prussian Poland in the German Empire (1871–1900)* (New York, 1981), 41–42.

needed to guard against the possibility of Austria using Catholic Poles as a fifth column, with an additional concern that Poles were multiplying more quickly than Germans in Posnania. Aside from that, he despised Catholics and considered their separate educational system and loyalty to Rome to be divisive. (Papal infallibility was proclaimed in 1870, one year before the creation of the Reich.) Thus the Prussian government in Posen ruled in 1872 that German be the sole language of instruction in the elementary schools and replaced Polish priests with Protestant German schoolteachers. Legislation followed in 1876 making German the sole language of administration, thereby forcing many Polish officials out of positions. The ruling of 1876 went so far as to require Poles to speak German at the windows of post offices and railway stations. In the 1880s all teaching of Polish was eliminated in the schools attended by Germans—Polish was not even offered as an optional subject in the gymnasia (high schools). In 1870 roughly seventy Poles taught in the gymnasia of the province of Posen; by 1918 the number had fallen to ten, of whom one taught Latin and Greek and the remaining nine were priests teaching religion.[27] Understandably the Polish Catholic hierarchy inveighed against these measures and encouraged Poles to improve their lives and resist the Germans by founding their own small businesses and "buying Polish." As tensions increased, the Prussian government created a "colonization commission" in 1886 for the province of Posen whose object was to buy land from large-scale Polish landowners and parcel it out to Germans. In short, by the end of the century Posen was rent by an intense nationality struggle.

During this period, and continuing through the First World War, the Jews of Posen identified with *Deutschtum*. For at least a century the first language of Posen's Jews had been German; thus they now all attended German schools where they were inculcated in the greatness of German culture. Educated Jews assumed that Germany was a Parnassus of "poets and philosophers." (Rosalinde Kantorowicz's uncle assembled his nine children every morning to read them ballads by Schiller.[28]) Jews generally felt uneasy about Polish Catholics; every Easter priests told their parishioners that Jews were "Christ killers," and Catholics might even spread rumors of Jewish host desecrations. In contrast Jews felt more comfortable with Protestant Germans who spread no Easter hatreds and who, if they were antisemites, generally kept such feelings to themselves. A relation of the Kantorowiczes by marriage, Georg Pietrkowski (later George Peters), born in Posen in 1874, recalled that prosperous Jews would often meet "humane, often well-educated administrators" (*humanen, oft fein gebildeten Beamten*) in the evenings for a glass of beer, and that the

[27] Witold Molik, "Der Einfluss der preussischen Politik auf die Gesellschaftsstruktur des Grossherzogtums Posen," in *Preussen in der Provinz*, ed. Peter Nitsche, 63–79 (Frankfurt, 1991), at 74.

[28] Ellen Fischer memoirs: "The Grandparents in Posen," 10.

presence of a Prussian officer at such gatherings was "not rare."[29] (After 1871 Posen had become a garrison city.) Jews of Posen availed themselves of easy railroad travel westward to Berlin that took only three hours on a direct route. And they had only to look slightly to the east to view the oppression of Jews in Russia or the backwardness of Jews in Austria-Hungary to be reminded of the benefits of being German.

German Jews certainly felt as if they "belonged." In the late nineteenth century Victor Klemperer's father, a rabbi in Landsberg an der Warthe, seventy miles from Posen, listed himself in a public document as "preacher," the point not being to hide, since every gentile knew he was a rabbi, but to his express his own sense of being German.[30] Reinhard Bendix's father, who came to maturity in Berlin around 1900, later recalled that "we did not live as aliens who wanted to become natives, but rather as natives who did not understand, and objected strongly when they were looked on and treated as aliens. We in no way felt we were assimilated *Jews*, but Germans like other Germans."[31] Jews in Posen (many of whose families had come from Galicia a few generations earlier) shuddered at the thought of being associated with "disreputable" eastern Jews (*Ostjuden*) located on the other side of the Prussian border.[32] A stunning token of identification with *Deutschtum* in the Kantorowicz family is that when a son was born to Max and Rosalinde in 1877 they named him Otto Siegfried, "Otto" having been the founder of the first German Reich, and "Siegfried" Wagner's prototypic blonde, brawny German hero.

A commitment to *Deutschtum* eroded a commitment to Judaism among the Kantorowiczes. Ellen Fischer wrote that "no Jewish tradition was kept up in our family." As late as the Nazi years, Ellen's mother, Else, asked her what the difference was between Rosh Hashanah and Yom Kippur.[33] In Else's household the very word "Jude" was avoided; if someone absolutely had to refer to a Jew, it was "Juif" in French.[34] In the Kantorowicz family it was somewhat different. The Kantorowiczes held seders in their home during Passover and read the Haggadah in Hebrew. Since Ernst was the youngest child he intoned the "four questions" and still remembered in 1962 that they began with "Mane shtane."[35] The fact that Joseph served on the board of representatives of

[29] The unpublished memoirs of Georg Pietrkowski, who died in Berkeley in 1953, were passed on to me by his grandson, Tom F. Peters.

[30] Victor Klemperer, *Curriculum Vitae: Erinnerungen 1881–1918*, 1 (Berlin, 1996), 16–17.

[31] Reinhard Bendix, *From Berlin to Berkeley: German-Jewish Identities* (New Brunswick, 1986), 81.

[32] Steven E. Aschheim, *Brothers and Strangers: The East European Jew in German and German Jewish Consciousness, 1800–1923* (Madison, 1982), esp. 4–5, 43.

[33] Fischer memoirs: "The Grandparents in Posen," 5; "The Milchs," 21.

[34] From the memoirs of Gertrude Meyer (née Milch), "Gertrude's Life Story," graciously given to me by the author, now LBI ME 1651.

[35] Kantorowicz to Vera Peters, 19 May 1961: Lerner archive.

the Posen synagogue congregation from 1905 to 1916[36] makes it certain that the family attended services on the High Holidays. Moreover, Clara took her Judaism seriously enough to send Rosh Hashanah greetings to her brother in 1931.[37] On the other hand, nothing here is truly "devout," and Ernst did not take his Judaism seriously at all. His recollection of "Mane shtane" was connected with his recollection of a children's song, "ring little bell, klingelingeling," which he thought was "either a Christmas song or a Chanukah song, or an Easter song or a Passover song," when in fact it was a Christmas song. It is quite certain that Yiddish was not spoken in the Kantorowicz home except for the occasional use of Yiddish words and phrases. (Kantorowicz's voluminous correspondence is sprinkled with Yiddishisms in letters to other Jews, but these are standard ones like *meschugge*.) And it is quite certain that he was not Bar Mitzvahed.[38] Toward the end of his life he referred to himself as being of "Jewish descent, not Jewish belief."[39]

Born in 1895, Ernst was the youngest of three siblings, not counting a boy born in 1884, who died at the age of two.[40] He had two sisters, Sophie, known as "Soscha" (born in 1887), with whom he was close, and Margarete, known as "Grete" or "Gretel" (born in 1888), with whom he was not. The family lived on the Berlinerstrasse in the elegant Neustadt (new city).[41] One of Ernst's earliest memories was that of a maid delighting him by striking a match and teaching him the Polish word for "matches" (*zapalki*).[42] He never learned more Polish, but his parents believed that teaching him English was essential, based on the presumption that he would be engaged in trade. Thus they gave him to the care of an English governess until he was twelve, and he learned to speak English well enough to be able to lecture in that language at Oxford in 1934 without having spent any previous time in the country.[43] When Ernst was ten years old the family moved to the newly built "villa quarter," a neighborhood

[36] Information from a series of Posen directories (Adressbücher der Residenzstadt Posen) communicated to me by Eckhart Grünewald. ("Stellvertreter in der Repraesentanten-Versammlung der Synagogen-Gemeinde," 1905 bis 1910; "Mitglied der Repraesentanten-Gemeinde," 1911–1916.)

[37] Clara to Felix Hepner, 2 October 1931, referring to having sent the "New Year's" greetings earlier: Hepner papers, 1206/1/14/8, 9.

[38] Interview with Eva Hunting, a close relative, 22 February 2013.

[39] To Vera Peters, 14 October 1961: Lerner archive.

[40] The child, "Otto Hartwig," is not on the family tree that EKa drew up in the 1930s and hence was unnoticed in Kantorowicz scholarship until the discovery of the birth and death record by Adam S. Labuda, "Ein Posener Itinerar zu Kantorowicz," in *Geschichtskörper: Zur Aktualität von Ernst H. Kantorowicz*, ed. Wolfgang Ernst and Cornelia Vismann, 73–91 (Munich, 1998), at 81.

[41] For Joseph Kantorowicz's succession of residences, see ibid., 80–82.

[42] Ihor Ševčenko, email message, 22 November 2008.

[43] CV: "I had an English governess for the first twelve years of my life." (According to William A. Chaney, one of Kantorowicz's students at Berkeley, he said that he intensely disliked this woman.) Kantorowicz refers to "having spoken English from childhood" in a letter of 10 October 1939 to Robert H. Lowie: Lowie papers.

of luxury dwellings on Posen's western periphery that had just been created by the razing of walls. The Kantorowiczes resided in an enormous ten-room apartment (fig. 3) that ran the length of an entire story in a large house on a street named for the Prussian royal family: Hohenzollernstrasse.[44] Not far was the imposing new Wilhelmssplatz, and running off it, the Wilhelmstrasse, a wide boulevard on which stood a range of elegant shops. Jews of the villa quarter lived and shopped among Germans and watched patriotic parades that issued into the Wilhelmssplatz. Years later EKa reminisced in a letter to Elise Peters (née Pietrkowski) about how often he met her "in Miethe's or Appel's," both specialty shops (the one for desserts, the other for delicatessen) located on the Wilhelmstrasse.[45]

EKa's schooling is well documented. In the spring of 1901, when he was six, he entered a local municipal "middle-school for youths," which he attended for three years. His courses were in religion (probably Bible stories), German, arithmetic, geography, singing, and penmanship, and he received good grades in all of them except penmanship, in which his endeavors were deemed barely passing.[46] From the middle school he proceeded to the Royal Auguste-Viktoria Gymnasium. This institution, named for the reigning queen of Prussia and empress of Germany (nevertheless, it was an all-male school), was of recent construction in the villa quarter and meant for the city's elite. It was a "humanistic" gymnasium that required the intensive study of Latin and Greek plus one modern language, which in EKa's case was French. The Classics curriculum was demanding. In EKa's last semester the set texts included Horace and Tacitus, Thucydides and Sophocles. Selections from Livy and Xenophon were to be translated off the cuff.[47] He saved his diploma (*Abiturzeugniss*) because it was necessary for Germans to present the high school diploma as documentation for further study or employment. Thus it exists today among the Kantorowicz papers in New York. The diploma shows that he attended the gymnasium for eight and a half years, from the spring of 1904 until the spring of 1913. In the spring of 1907 he was not promoted to the next class. Because of that he withdrew for half a year to gain private tutoring and was readmitted in the fall.

The last fact indicates that after performing satisfactorily in the middle school, EKa had become a poor student in the gymnasium. The splendors of Prussian record keeping yield knowledge of his entire record for all his years there. Kantorowicz never received the highest possible grade in any of

[44] Jan Skuratowicz, "Im Kreis der Kantorowicz's, Jaretzkis und Samters. Die Residenzen des jüdischen Bürgertums in Posen vor 1918," in Strzelczyk, *Ernst Kantorowicz*, 91–102, at 98–99.

[45] Kantorowicz to Elise Peters, 23 May 1949: Lerner archive. I thank Eckhart Grünewald for identifying the shops of Miethe and Appel.

[46] Witold Molik, "Ernst Kantorowicz's Schuljahre in Posen," in Strzelczyk, *Ernst Kantorowicz*, 65–73, at 67.

[47] Paul Schulze, *Königliches Auguste Viktoria-Gymnasium in Posen: Jahresbericht über das Schuljahr 1912/13* (Posen, 1913), 11–12. (My thanks to Eckhart Grünewald for obtaining this title for me.)

Figure 3. The apartment building where the Kantorowicz family resided in Posen, now Poznań. (Photo Erdmut Lerner)

his courses, not even in history; most of them were either "barely passing" (*genügend*) or "failing." Nor did he care much for doing homework; teachers frequently wrote in this regard "needs much improvement."[48] After his half-year absence he performed slightly better. But even so he graduated by a hair's breadth. As his *Abiturzeugniss* reveals, he failed in handwriting. Although that was a minor subject, he failed his written exams in both Latin and Greek and was saved only by grades on his orals—"good" in Greek and "barely passing" in Latin. History? The future author of historiographical classics received the lowest possible passing grade in that subject too.[49]

Actually the dismal grades are not proof of Kantorowicz being one of the weakest students in the school. Prussian grading was tough, and many of EKa's classmates received grades that were comparable to his.[50] Some forty-eight students had been in his class in 1904, but by 1913 the number had dwindled to fifteen who managed to graduate, and of these, three had been left back for different periods of time.[51] Still, it remains perplexing that his grades were as low as they were. After all, not much later he knew Latin and Greek just as well as an

[48] Molik, "Ernst Kantorowicz's Schuljahre," 68–69.
[49] LBI, box 5, folder 4.
[50] Molik, "Ernst Kantorowicz's Schuljahre," 69.
[51] Schulze, *Königliches Auguste Viktoria-Gymnasium*, 16.

accomplished classicist. In a letter of 1920 he wrote that he was reading much Horace, "whom [he] always loved greatly, and knew very well, but who was now saying more to [him] than ever before."[52] In other letters of the period he inserted Greek quotations written in Greek characters, as he was to do afterward throughout his life. (When typing he left spaces for the Greek to be inserted by hand.) EKa was also an avid reader when he was in the army. Another soldier who knew him reported that he amazed his comrades by the number of books he carried around and by his display of an astonishing range of erudition.[53] One is forced to conclude, then, that his poor grades in the gymnasium did not stem from indifference to learning, let alone incapacity. The school instruction emphasized learning by rote, and EKa may have been nurturing a disregard or contempt for authority that we will see on subsequent occasions. (A rare anecdote about his youth in Posen has it that once at a family gathering he was obliged to dance with a distant relative, and when she said, "You know, you really don't have to," he abruptly walked off.[54])

Perhaps too he was somewhat distracted by social activities. The Royal Auguste-Viktoria was the most fashionable of Posen's four gymnasia. Only about 20 percent of the students in the lower classes were Polish, and few of those continued to graduation. (It should be born in mind that Poles were required to do all their classwork in German and were allowed to speak Polish only during recess; there were two Poles among the fifteen in EKa's graduating class, both studying for the priesthood.) The German students were mostly sons of administrators, officers, or professionals; in a sample from 1904 to 1907 there were twenty-five sons of administrators, six of officers, seven of physicians and architects, and only one of a manual worker. To this it may be added that in EKa's own class of some fifty students, he and one other alone were of the "Mosaic faith."[55]

Clearly this was an environment in which one could mingle with the elite, and EKa appears to have done so with enthusiasm. The earliest known photograph depicts him in a group portrait taken in a studio among seven formally dressed young men, evidently constituting the membership of a club. All look stiff, with the exception of Kantorowicz, who is leaning over toward the camera from the top row in a more relaxed pose (fig. 4).[56] The president of the club (who sits in the middle of the group on a chair not too different from a throne) reappears in the first extant piece of mail sent to Ernst Kantorowicz.

[52] Kantorowicz to Josefine von Kahler, 26 April 1920: StGA, Kahler papers, III:6513.

[53] EG, 17.

[54] Horst Fuhrmann to Eckhart Grünewald, 7 June 1991, reporting a story recounted by Eva Kuttner, the dancing partner in question. I am obliged to Eckhart Grünewald for showing me this letter.

[55] Molik, "Ernst Kantorowicz's Schuljahre," 70.

[56] The photo, which EKa obviously treasured enough to save, today is in the Cherniavsky papers, box 8, envelope 3.

Figure 4. Student club, Auguste Viktoria-Gymnasium, circa 1912. Kantorowicz is second from left, leaning forward. (University of Pittsburgh, Michael Cherniavsky papers: AIS.1974.15)

This is a postcard of May 22, 1913 (two months after he graduated from the gymnasium), addressed by "Kurt N." from Potsdam to Ernst Kantorowicz in Hamburg.[57] The sender was now attending a military school for Prussian junior officers. His message to "Ernst" states that in a few days he will be traveling with the military school to Thorn-Marienburg, an outpost in West Prussia; the reverse shows a photo of him in military uniform. The group portrait and postcard, both saved by Ernst Kantorowicz for the length of his life (who knows whether "Kurt N." was killed in battle during the First World War?), are noteworthy for revealing a penchant for socializing with the upper class. This trait, like contempt for authority, was to prove a constant.

Aside from the young men's club, young Ernst brushed up with a different society while he was a gymnasium student. In 1911 his sister Soscha was auditing courses in Heidelberg and lived there in the same pension that was inhabited by two junior faculty members—a young economist named Arthur Salz and a student of German literature named Friedrich Gundolf. Both were intensely serious young intellectuals who had fallen under the spell of Germany's most famous poet, Stefan George. During the Easter vacation of 1911

[57] A copy of this postcard was given to me by Lucy Cherniavsky.

the sixteen-year old Ernst traveled to Heidelberg to visit his sister and during his stay went on an outing with her and the two men to Wimpfen, a nearby picturesque town. There they sent Easter greetings on a postcard to Josefine Sobotka, a former Heidelberg student with whom they were close. (We will be hearing a great deal more of her later.) The card, with a caricature of Josefine by Gundolf, bore the initials "A.S.," "F.G.," "S.K.," "E.K," making it clear that she was understood to know who "E.K." was.[58] The postcard interrelates with a passing remark made by Gundolf in a letter he wrote to her shortly thereafter. There he reported that the "Kantorowna's" brother had been in Heidelberg for a time, and that he was "an endearing youth," possessed of "a touching elegance, which led us often to tease him."[59]

EKa also came to know in Heidelberg a friend of Gundolf's, a student of literature named Ernst Robert Curtius.[60] The name may be familiar because Curtius was to become one of Germany's most prominent men of letters. Of interest here is that Curtius, like Gundolf and Salz, was then an ardent admirer of Stefan George. It may be reasonable therefore to infer that the teenage Kantorowicz was infected with the same enthusiasm. Certainly his own dedication to the poetry and worldview of George, whenever it began, was to be an influence that would shape the course of his life.

After graduating EKa entered an apprenticeship for what then seemed to be his foreordained career. In a later curriculum vitae he wrote: "As my father suggested to me that I should join him in his business, I went to Hamburg in order to become acquainted with the world of trade, finance, and economics."[61] He served in the Hamburg branch of the Kantorowicz firm and dealt with such matters as an order from Tanganyika for fruit juice.[62] His residence was on the Isestrasse, a street in a newly built quarter lined with stately houses in the art nouveau style. In June 1914 he received money from his parents to finance expenses for a two-week vacation at a beach hotel on the Atlantic between Nantes and La Rochelle.[63] In later years his memory of the stay was largely blotted out by the Great War.[64]

[58] StGA, Kahler papers, III:4055. (Soscha Kantorowicz was soon to marry Arthur Salz.)

[59] Klaus Pott, ed., *Friedrich Gundolf/Erich von Kahler Briefwechsel 1910-1931. Mit Auszügen aus dem Briefwechsel Friedrich Gundolf-Fine von Kahler*, 2 vols. (Göttingen, 2012), 2:309: Gundolf (in Heidelberg) to Josefine Sobotka, April 1911.

[60] Kantorowicz to Ilse Curtius, 21 May 1956 (Universitätsbibliothek, Bonn), mentions having known Ernst Robert Curtius "since 1910"; Curtius was present in Heidelberg in that year.

[61] CV.

[62] Kantorowicz to parents, 8 June 1914: Ariane Phillips collection.

[63] Ibid.

[64] Kantorowicz to Lucy von Wangenheim, 2 August 1939, communicated to me by Eckhart Grünewald.

CHAPTER 2

"With Rifle and Gun"

Ernst Kantorowicz wrote in his curriculum vitae of 1938: "When war broke out in August 1914, I immediately volunteered and joined the colours, and was sent to the front in France in September 1914." The first entry in his military identification card yields specificity.[1] The nineteen-year-old volunteered for Posen's first field artillery regiment on August 8, six days after Germany's declaration of war on France. Patriotism had been inculcated in the Auguste-Viktoria Gymnasium.[2] In his last year the school celebrated the birthdays of the Kaiser and the Kaiserin with declamations and choruses—also "Sedan Day" commemorating the great Prussian victory in the Franco-Prussian war, and the centennial of the "rising of Prussia" in the Napoleonic Wars. The set essay for graduation was: "Can we as Prussians agree with the saying of Virgil, 'Nulla salus bello' (there's no safety in war)?" EKa's paper does not survive, but the loaded formulation suggests the likelihood of an answer that "Prussians always have been obliged to find safety in war."

Kantorowicz's speed in enlisting was typical. Tens of thousands of young German men, Jews by all means included, stormed the recruiting stations. The mood is communicated vividly in letters written by EKa's cousin Gertrud. On August 2, 1914, she headed a letter "first day of mobilization" and wrote: "The times are momentous; it is inconceivable that we can be fainthearted." On the tenth she wrote: "The war itself is pure greatness and people are now greater than they've ever been"; and on the nineteenth: "I am attached to the reality of this war with my entire being . . . my being that relates to Germany as a life's breath relates to the body out of which it arises. . . . I do not ask how right this war is; I know only that it *is*."[3]

[1] For the framework of Kantorowicz's military career and details that are not otherwise specified, I draw on EG, 18–22.

[2] Schulze, *Königliches Auguste Viktoria-Gymnasium*, 17, 9.

[3] Robert E. Lerner, "The Secret Germany of Gertrud Kantorowicz," in *A Poet's Reich: Politics and Culture in the George Circle*, ed. Melissa S. Lane and Martin A. Ruehl, 56–77 (Rochester, N.Y., 2011), at 61.

Posen's first field artillery regiment was among the so-called 1-A-Troops—meaning units whose soldiers had a high degree of education and were preferred for engagements that demanded great reliability. The officers were upper-class men from the city and province of Posen; some of the volunteers were graduates of the gymnasia; others came from a wide variety of walks of life. Many probably knew the saying of Frederick the Great that "artillery lends dignity to what otherwise might be a vulgar brawl," and also that the Prussian field artillery was "the king's final argument" (*ultima ratio regis*).

EKa was sent on September 17 to join his regiment on the western front. This was part of a force that stormed the heights of the Meuse south of Verdun between September 21 and 24. Immediately thereafter the French halted the Germans on the right bank of the Meuse and initiated a war of attrition. Aside from a furlough that allowed him to spend Christmas 1915 with his family in Posen,[4] Kantorowicz fought on this front from September 1914 until he was sent to a hospital in Bavaria with an unspecified illness in April 1916. After recuperating for a few days he was attached to a reserve unit in Posen until the summer, when he was sent back to where he had been before. His period of fighting in this region ended when he wounded in the battle of Verdun.

He received successive promotions. He entered the army as a private (*Soldat*) and moved up by steps from private first class, to corporal, to sergeant (*Vizewachtmeister*), a noncommissioned officer rank he attained in October 1915. A soldier who fought with him stated in 1978 that his "excellent military behavior and his courage were well known." In June 1915 he received the Iron Cross, second class. An evocative photo, taken at the front in March 1916 (fig. 5), shows him with a cigarette dangling from his mouth and wearing his Iron Cross ribbon.

A cache of wartime letters that Kantorowicz sent home to his parents has just come to light which allows us to view him in action and gain a sense of his thoughts on the basis of his own words.[5] On October 20, 1914, he took delight in reporting about his situation in his "firing position." His battery was behind the infantry in the trenches. One needed to be ready to shoot at any moment. Throughout the night there was firing on both sides; the French sent up signal flares, and the commander of EKa's unit was badly wounded. This was the first time he was under fire, but he reported that he did not feel himself in any danger and that "the battle was *very* interesting" (emphasis his). A year later, on October 12, 1915, he wrote of his "real happiness" about his promotion to the rank of sergeant. He was very proud, especially since he was the only volunteer in his battery who had attained this. Now he would wear a special lanyard (*portepée*)

[4] Kantorowicz to parents, 12 October 1915: Ariane Phillips collection; Soscha Salz to Friedrich Gundolf, 29 December 1915: Gundolf Archive.

[5] From the archive of Ariane Phillips, granddaughter of EKa's sister Soscha. I am deeply indebted to Mrs. Phillips for informing me of this collection and for sending me a complete set of copies.

Figure 5. Kantorowicz on the Western Front, March 1916. He is wearing the ribbon awarded for his Iron Cross, second class. (Copyright © Archiv Dr. Eckhart Grünewald, Frankfurt am Main)

and carry a sabre. Granted that he also would be obliged to invite all the corporals to a cask of beer, which "would not be entirely cheap," he would have been disappointed had he not been made sergeant after his full year of service.

The soldiers were regularly granted rest days, and EKa's letters convey news about these too. He wrote home requesting extra stores of food and—the Kantorowicz specialty—drink. His list included not only sausage, bacon, and anchovy-paste but also "Podbipieta" (a liqueur made by the family firm), rum, and brandy (fig. 6). All these items were meant not just for himself but for regaling the battery officers with whom the troops "shot the breeze" behind the lines. These officers asked daily when the wonderful packages would be arriving. He also had time for reading. In July 1915 he requested English books together with a little dictionary and the Odes of Horace, in the original and in translation. On rest intervals he could travel to Metz, a distance of some 80 kilometers from the front. There he could shop (as he wrote home) and engage in other activities (about which he did not write home).

On July 5, 1916, Kantorowicz joined a field artillery regiment that was in the midst of the battle of Verdun. The fighting already had raged for several months with enormous carnage: tens of thousands dead and many more wounded. EKa

Figure 6. "Liqueur at the Front": a 1915 postcard bearing an advertisement of the Kantorowicz firm. (Courtesy Eckhart Grünewald)

entered the thick of it. On July 8 he wrote home in pencil scrawl—"from the field"—that he had experienced "a few wild days." His company was put on a march from ten at night until two in the morning when it finally halted in a forest to rest until six. Surrounded by filth, he dozed for a half an hour and then had to march again in order to bivouac. Later the order came that by evening the company needed to reach a firing position, but "the weather gave its blessings with some cloudbursts." EKa's raincoat helped for nothing against the downpours. He wrote that he never had seen soldiers being so cowardly and corporals so helpless, even though he recognized that for most of them this was their "baptism of fire." As for himself, he was happy that he had maintained his reputation and also that he had felt indifferent to the firing from the very beginning. With perfect sang froid he added: "What I earlier thought was warfare was merely a maneuver compared to this, it pleases me very well."

On July 17 he responded to his father's admonition that he should not be "indifferent" by saying that this should not be confused with brashness, and that there were moments in the fighting when only indifference could help see one through. He thought that the firing where he had been in the previous years (Dompierre, Combres) might have been heavier, but the current terrain was dreadful. He added that he expected to be able to go to Metz soon for a four-day rest. But that was not to be. One can do no better than to let him tell the story of how he was wounded on July 21:

> I was lightly wounded last night: right side of the head, directly right of the right eye. Fortunately the eye is unscathed. I'm doing well, aside from some pains, wild hangover, and a little bit of fever. Today I go with a hospital train to Montmédy, and from there probably to Germany. As soon as I know my address I'll let you have it. But you can rest easy—it's not so bad. I rode while wounded for two hours. That is, yesterday I had to go into position unusually with munitions and we were already on the way back when we suddenly ran into rounds of fire. The third round was a direct hit on the column. Aside from me—I rode in front—a lieutenant and two horse attendants were wounded. I fell in a high arc off of my horse and realized immediately that I had been wounded. So. A bound and into the nearest abandoned tunnel. Still, there came shot after shot. My horse was off and running. I located my bandage pack and made an emergency dressing and then crawled out when the firing stopped in order to go back on foot. After a short while I found one of my men with my horse and rode to the nearest first-aid station, let myself be bandaged etc., and was almost at the camp when, last not least, four aerial bombs exploded right nearby. Well, it's all come to a good end and I've gotten away with a literally blue eye.

"Getting away with a blue eye" is a German expression for "getting off lightly." And EKa did get off lightly, given the rate of deaths and crippling wounds of July 1916. After a period of time his wound healed and he never said anything more about it. Nor did he ever regale people with accounts of his military experiences, let alone vaunt his bravery. That was not his manner. But now that we have his war letters we can see that coolness under fire was a consistent trait.

EKa recuperated from his wound in a military hospital for three weeks. Then, after being stationed with replacement troops in Germany until early January, he was dispatched to the Russian front. He served from January 5, 1917, until February 19 with a field-artillery regiment in Volhynia, a region in northwestern Ukraine where fighting had come to a standstill for a "winter sleep." All we have by way of "texture" is a stamped document he carried with him on his return certifying that he had been deloused.[6]

The next stage of Kantorowicz's war service comes as a surprise: after a mere ninety days in the Ukraine he was sent to Asia Minor. The record in his military pass states that he was transferred to Constantinople to be attached to "special railway company five." This company was engaged in extending a railway line running through Asia Minor toward Aleppo, but the notation was made in advance and it is certain that after EKa passed through Constantinople he never worked with a railway detachment. Instead we have his statement of 1938: "After my recovery, I was sent to Russia and, in 1917, to a German staff in

[6]EKa saved two documents from his time on the Russian front: a permit to travel from Lezachow to Kolonia Zurawiec, and a "delousification" certificate, issued in Kolonia Zurawiec on 18 February 1917; Ariane Phillips collection.

Turkey."[7] He gave more detail to the chairman of the Berkeley History Department in 1940 who introduced him for a lecture: "As a very young man he spent four years in the World War, seeing service in France, Russia, and Turkey. His linguistic attainments are illustrated by the fact that on the Turkish front he was interpreter in the Fifth Army of Liman von Sanders."[8]

What caused the quick transfer? All but certainly EKa owed it to the influence of his brother-in-law, Arthur Salz, who had held a position as an economic advisor in the Austro-Hungarian Embassy in Constantinople since January 1916.[9] Proof that Salz was able to arrange things for friends exists in the fact that when he was on mission in Germany in February 1917 he managed to have Friedrich Gundolf transferred from service on the western front to a desk job in Berlin.[10] Given that EKa was transferred in February 1917 as well, this hardly could have been a coincidence. For an adventurous young man to serve in exotic Turkey instead of the snows of the Ukraine was an easy choice. Moreover EKa had already developed an interest in the history of the "Orient." According to the fellow soldier on the western front interviewed in 1978, he carried books on this subject in his baggage and particularly loved the *Arabian Nights*.[11]

Chronological uncertainties exist concerning EKa's whereabouts in Turkey. The most plausible reconstruction for the first half year is that he arrived in Constantinople in March, spent perhaps two months there in Turkish language training, and then went to the small city of Panderma on the Sea of Marmara, where he stayed until early September. The dating evidence for Panderma consists primarily of several photos he saved of Turkish friends.[12] The earliest is a snapshot, probably taken in Panderma, of a proud-looking Turkish officer, mounted on horseback. It is inscribed on the reverse "A M^{er} Kantorowitz" (the signer's name is difficult to decipher) and is dated May 8, 1917. EKa certainly

[7] CV.

[8] 9 April 1940: Bolton papers.

[9] EG, 23, supplemented and slightly corrected by a letter of Josefine von Kahler to her husband Erich, 10 January 1916: "der Arthur . . . ist am 4ten nach Constantinopel gefahren an die Gesandtschaft. Nur durch Zufall u. Chuzpe" (Pott, *Gundolf-Kahler Briefwechsel*, 2:401–2). Salz wrote from Constantinople to Gundolf, 21 February 1916, describing his activities: Gundolf Archive C36012072309420. (My thanks to Andrea Meyer Ludowisy for locating this document for me.)

[10] Gundolf to Friedrich Wolters, 18 February 1917: "nach zweimonatlichem Schippertum bin ich, durch Vermittlung von Arthur Salz, zum Generalstab an die Abteilung für kriegswirtschaftliche Transporte befohlen worden," in Christoph Fricker, ed., *Friedrich Gundolf—Friedrich Wolters: Ein Briefwechsel aus dem Kreis um Stefan George* (Cologne, 2009), 157. This is supplemented by Josefine von Kahler to Friedrich Gundolf, 1 and 8 February 1917: Pott, *Gundolf-Kahler Briefwechsel*, 2:402–3.

[11] EG, 17.

[12] EKa gave or lent four photos of Turks, apparently all officers, to his student Michael Cherniavsky; today they are in the Cherniavsky papers. Copies of two snapshots, one of EKa together with one of the officers, and another of him on a white horse leaping over a hurdle, were given to me by Lucy Cherniavsky.

Figure 7. Kantorowicz with Turkish friend Lufti Schoukri, summer 1917. (Lerner archive)

was in Panderma six weeks later, for a photo inscribed to him there by a Turkish officer is dated June 20, 1917. After that other photos of Turkish friends inscribed in Panderma are dated August 3 and September 1.

The city, conveniently accessible to Constantinople by boat, was the site of the headquarters of General Otto Liman von Sanders, the commander of the Ottoman Fifth Army.[13] EKa seems to have been a liaison officer between Turks and Liman's staff. His much later friend Ihor Ševčenko reported that "he was in Turkey as a member of the corps of translators."[14] Certainly he developed close friendships with Turks. The photo dated June 20, 1917, was inscribed in German by one Lufti Schoukri "to dear Kanto, as a memento of wonderfully spent summer days in Panderma"; an undated snapshot shows EKa and Lufti sitting together outdoors with arms interlinked (fig. 7). The photo inscribed on August 3 is of a Turk in the dress of a prince who had a formal portrait taken in a studio in Constantinople. This person wrote in French, "to my very dear friend Kantorowicz, as a memento of a very sincere and intimate friendship."

The use of German and French is not surprising given that members of the Turkish elite knew Western languages. It is more noteworthy that a fourth photo (fig. 8) of a Turkish friend is inscribed in Turkish in Perso-Arabic script: "I am presenting this to my dear Kantorowicz as a memento of our parting,

[13] [Otto] Liman von Sanders, *Fünf Jahre Türkei*, 2nd ed. (Berlin, 1920), 149.

[14] Email message, 11 March 2008.

1 September 333 [i.e., 1917], Nedjib."[15] Thus a friend assumed that EKa could make his way in Turkish after he was in the Ottoman Empire for roughly half a year. Certainly he knew sufficient Turkish to register for a second-level course at the University of Munich in 1919.[16] Much later, in the 1940s, he exchanged Turkish words and phrases with the Hungarian-speaking Lucy Cherniavsky, seeking to test the supposed relations between Turkish and Hungarian; in Princeton he once said that "Turkish is a very difficult language to learn and a very easy one to forget."[17]

As early as May 28, 1917, Kantorowicz was awarded the Iron Crescent, the Ottoman counterpart to the Iron Cross. Bestowed "in the name of the Sultan," the document was signed (actually rubber-stamped) "Liman von Sanders."[18] But later Kantorowicz incurred the general's wrath. According to Maurice Bowra, EKa's closest friend from the 1930s onward, his service in Asia Minor "came to an abrupt end [because] he had an affair with a nurse who was the mistress of the German general."[19] Kantorowicz referred to his having "taken the commanding chief in Turkey" in a letter to Bowra of 1939,[20] and the affront to Liman von Sanders is confirmed by a passage from a letter to EKa of 1956 by Arthur Salz. At the time Salz was irked by an article EKa had sent him. He complained:

> After I read the whole piece, a question forced itself on me: is the subject—the world as seen through the feet of the apostles—really worth the printing expense, the laborious work, the sweat, and the erudition? . . . How you have changed! Earlier, in your younger years, you were fully disposed to the heroic and behaved yourself heroically. Just to mention one episode from your life story, didn't you stand up to your military commander-in-chief? . . . Didn't you tell him what's what? Tell him where he gets off? Didn't he come up short in the endless battle between the Davids and the Goliaths? That was courageously conceived and bravely handled. That was . . . as if the noted Joe Smith put horns on the President of the United States. You had the courage to leave behind the whole Panderma-box (or was it Pandora's box?) with a bang. Those were the days![21]

Salz's use of the term "horns" implies cuckoldry and hence implicitly confirms Bowra's report of an affair with Liman's mistress. If such conduct seems daring, telling von Sanders "what's what" is astonishing. Liman was

[15] I owe the translation to Professor Kaya Sahin.

[16] EG, 33.

[17] Interview with Lucy Cherniavsky, 16 September 1990; statement in Princeton made to William A. Percy, Jr., and reported to the author.

[18] LBI, box 7, folder 7.

[19] C. M. Bowra, *Memories 1898–1939* (London, 1969), 288; in a letter to Felix Frankfurter, 1 November 1963, Bowra specified that EKa was proud of what happened: Frankfurter papers.

[20] 13 March 1939.

[21] Salz to Kantorowicz: 3 December 1956: LBI, box 4, folder 11. The letter is in German, but Salz moves at one point into English: "Tell him what's what? Tell him where he gets off?"

Figure 8. "I am presenting this to my dear Kantorowicz as a memento of our parting, 1 September 333, Nedjib." (University of Pittsburgh, Michael Cherniavsky papers: AIS.1974.15)

short-tempered[22] and EKa was merely a sergeant. The open insubordination is one of the many items on the list of Kantorowicz's bravado.

We have seen that EKa parted with "Nedjib" on September 1, 1917. To help us from there we have Maurice Bowra's statement that he served as "interpreter with the German troops in Istanbul and Smyrna," and this is confirmed by a letter EKa sent from Turkey to his uncle Felix Hepner before his departure that

[22] Ulrich Trumpener, *Germany and the Ottoman Empire: 1914–1918* (Princeton, 1968), 85. (I thank Margaret Anderson for this reference.)

refers to English planes bombing while he was in Constantinople and Smyrna.[23] (The letter was sent from yet another location, unspecified.) Somewhere in Turkey he bought two kilim rugs that became part of his furnishings in Germany until 1938.[24] The letter to Hepner is missing its first page and hence its date. But it does say that the heat was holding and indicates that it was written shortly before EKa's departure. Thus he must have left Turkey toward the end of the year.

The Turkish interlude had a profound effect on Kantorowicz's career. We will see that in 1921 he completed a doctoral dissertation in Heidelberg on "The Nature of Muslim Artisan Associations." Shortly after that a professor remarked that Kantorowicz was "best suited for material that links Orient and Occident."[25] Thirty years later he was on the same track, planning a volume of "West-Eastern Studies." By that time "Eastern studies" meant primarily Byzantine studies, but even so the Byzantine Empire was centered on Asia Minor.

EKa's locations and activities remain uncertain between his departure from Turkey and May 3, 1918. At that time we find him on the basis of a letter from Berlin to his parents formally attached to a translator's school. Yet he does not seem to have had any duties. He was living in the heart of West Berlin and wrote that he had just registered for lectures at the university "at least to have something to do."[26] He explained that this would count as his "war semester," a concession for soldiers then granted by the German government. The three lecture courses he chose were determined by his assumption that he would be assuming a directorial position in the family firm—he wrote in the letter that he believed himself to be the most promising heir. Accordingly the lecture courses were in economics: two given by the famous historian of capitalism, Werner Sombart, and the third by another historically oriented economist, Ignaz Jastrow. Supplementary evidence indicates that Kantorowicz took another course, one given by the most famous classical Greek philologist of the day, Ulrich von Wilamowitz-Möllendorff.[27] (The gymnasium student who did so poorly in Greek was obviously determined to pursue a literature he loved.)

After the summer semester in Berlin came to an end, Kantorowicz returned to the western front in August.[28] Initially a bureaucratic mix-up left him ignorant about where he would be stationed and he found himself with time on his hands for a few days in the drab northeastern French city of St. Quentin. But soon he was sent to a unit in Guise, where his duties were to decode enemy

[23] Bowra, *Memories*, 288; Hepner papers 1206/1/14/10.

[24] Household inventory: LBI, box 5, folder 3.

[25] EG, 48.

[26] The envelope with a return address survives: "F.A. 20 (Dolm. Schl), z.Z. Berlin Prinzregentenstrasse 75. The "Field Artillery Regiment 20" was headquartered in Posen but apparently had a "translators' school" in Berlin.

[27] William A. Chaney to David Spear, 6 August 2001, reporting a statement by Kantorowicz; Lerner archive.

[28] Kantorowicz to parents, 2 September 1918, points to a departure date of 18 August.

telegraph messages and translate them from French or English into German. Life there was comfortable. Guise, at the edge of France's northeastern border, was picturesque and quiet. EKa took his meals with the officers. He needed to be on duty only two hours in the morning and two in the afternoon. Otherwise he read what he liked at his leisure and studied "his diverse grammars" (probably including Turkish). Entertainment was provided by a movie house and even some theater. He could not resist writing to his parents about the hilarity when there was a kiss on the stage: the audience had not seen any kissing for months "and everyone smacked along."[29]

But the situation of the German Army was dire. American troops had joined the war and the German defenses on the western front were collapsing. While EKa was in Guise the regiment with which he had served in the Ukraine passed through. There was a happy reunion. His former comrades were delighted by the coincidence of seeing him. But their numbers had been decimated. Five batteries had been wiped out.[30] A month later the Germans evacuated Guise, and by October 8 Kantorowicz had found private quarters in a village, Dorengt, twenty kilometers to the east. Retreating troops flooded the roads. Meanwhile he had come down with an intestinal infection that brought diarrhea. He wrote to his parents that his landlady was being very good to him—"just like a mother." She made him chamomile tea, strong coffee [*sic*], and waffles and sent him to bed with a hot brick. She was spoiling him so much that he hardly wished to get well.[31]

EKa did not get well. On October 21 he was in a military hospital in central Germany, near Halle. Then, on the twenty-ninth, he was sent to Berlin, with the recommendation of a four-week recovery furlough. On November 9 he wrote from Berlin to his parents that the recommendation had been accepted and that he probably would no longer be called to arms. By then, two days before the armistice, everyone knew that the war was over. Consequently he registered for a second semester at the university. Once more he concentrated on economics, signing up for three courses in that field. To pursue his fascination with Islam he signed up additionally for a course with the prominent Islamicist Carl Heinrich Becker: History of the Caliphs.[32] He wrote that if he were called to service he would present excuses, but in the event that was unnecessary.

If one asks what Kantorowicz thought of the war during his four years of service, the first set of letters—those from 1914 through 1916—offer an answer only indirectly. Never do they express enthusiasm for fighting for his country's cause, but never do they express outrage about needless loss of life. Full

[29] Ibid.

[30] Kantorowicz to parents, 28 August 1918.

[31] Kantorowicz to parents, 8 October 1918.

[32] Kantorowicz to parents, 9 November 1918 (the economics courses were given by Ignaz Jastrow, Rudolf Eberstadt, and Heinrich Herkner); EG, 26.

of descriptions of battles, including a close call with death, they were written as if the author were performing a self-evident task. The first explicit opinions appear in the letter of May 3, 1918. Now he refers to "this unhappy war" and shares his parents' hopes for peace. But the reference to the war as "unhappy" appears in the context of a personal consideration: it was robbing him of years in which he could be preparing for his career with the family firm. In a bitter aside he complained about an antisemitic rant made by a member of the Prussian Parliament: "Why has one sacrificed one's self these years if only to be set upon by such people?"[33] Nevertheless, he said nothing about the purpose of the fighting itself here or in the subsequent letters written again from the front. He was dejected that the war was continuing and wrote that it was too early for his parents to think of vacationing on the Riviera. Apparently he thought that whenever the war might be over peacetime conditions would not be much different from those before August 1914. The vastly different reality was to be his major preoccupation from the time of the armistice until the early 1930s.

When EKa wrote to his parents on November 9 he assured them that he now was going to dedicate himself seriously to his studies. But events intruded. The situation in Posen for German business owners was dire.[34] On November 11, the day of the armistice, Poles announced the formation of a "supreme people's council" under Polish leadership to speak for the province of Posnania. Germans formed their own provincial "people's council" on November 14, and local German councils came into being on December 12. Among the prominent members of the Posen council was Franz Kantorowicz. Soon a delegation of the Prussian government in Berlin (now run by Social Democrats) arrived to treat with the Poles, but the negotiations broke down. Then the pianist and Polish patriot Ignace Jan Paderewski arrived in the city on December 27 and gave a fiery speech in favor of the incorporation of Posnania into the Polish state that had been founded in Warsaw. The speech catalyzed an armed uprising. Street fighting ensued, and by January 5, 1919, the Germans were overwhelmed.

Toward the end of November Ernst Kantorowicz left Berlin for Posen.[35] Whether he was motivated by the tense political situation or by the grave illness

[33]"Wofür opfert man nur diese Jahre? Damit ein Kerl wie Heins im Abgeordnetenhause so gegen einen loszieht, ein Mann, der der Typ für die Denkweise unseres gesamten Mittelstandes ist—von den Konservativen noch garnicht zu reden. . . . Ich fühle mich tatsächlch so jeder Verpflichtung bar diesen Leuten gegenüber!" I am grateful to Professor Thomas Kuehne for identifying Wilhelm Heins, an elementary school teacher from a rural district with a strong antisemitic tradition who joined the Prussian Parliament in 1913.

[34]EG, 27–28, partially superseded by Dariusz Matelski, "Nationalbeziehungen in Grosspolen in den Jahren 1918–1920," in Strzelczyk, *Ernst Kantorowicz*, 43–63. (But Matelski errs in having Ernst Kantorowicz fleeing Posnania in 1920 and gives a mistaken date for Franz Kantorowicz's internment.)

[35]Clara Kantorowicz to Felix Hepner, c. 25 November 1918 (Hepner papers, 1206/1/13/10). (The approximate date of the letter is fixed by a reference to the recent pogrom in Lemberg.)

of his father is unclear.[36] In either case he stayed in Posen throughout December: his father's birthday was on the fourteenth and soon after came Christmas. Immediately afterward he engaged in some fighting. In letters of 1933 meant to defend his nationalist record, he referred to his participation in "defense against Polish encroachments" as one in a sequence of paramilitary activities. He could not have fought for more than two or three days, for a letter to his parents of January 3 indicates that he had returned to Berlin by train on New Year's Day. Otherwise all that is known is that he took a precipitous flight, destroying his identification papers. The letter to his parents tells of his relief that there was no control of papers on the train.[37]

Conversing in Berkeley with his student William A. Chaney, Kantorowicz remarked that he was "sorry he had fought against the Poles."[38] By then he must have appreciated that Poles had a right to rule in a city that historically had been theirs and where they were in the majority. But during the time of the uprising he had reason to be concerned about the safety of his family home and family factory. His cousin Franz, who had not been involved in the street fighting, paid some price for being on the wrong side. On January 29 the new Polish government interned him in a castle fortress as a hostage; a few days later Franz wrote to his wife in Berlin that he was permitted to walk outdoors under guard for fifteen minutes per day.[39] He was released on June 14.[40]

Once back in Berlin, EKa found a situation which, as he wrote to his parents, he found "much, much worse than in Posen." Since December Berlin had been exposed to strikes and demonstrations directed by far leftists, most of whom called themselves "Spartacists."[41] (They took this name from Spartacus, the leader of a great Roman slave revolt.) Germany had had a "revolution" in November when moderate Social Democrats took power in Berlin and proclaimed a republic. These men were gradualists, careful not to offend the Prussian ruling class, whereas the Spartacists supported the idea of a communist revolution along the lines of the recent revolution in Russia. Because the Spartacists had no large following and lacked heavy military equipment, they had little chance of accomplishing their goals. But the Social Democrats, playing on the specter

[36] Joseph Kantorowicz died on 8 February 1919. On 8 October Kantorowicz wrote home about his happiness that his father again was feeling well, but on 2 December 1918 Clara wrote to her nieces: "Uncle is feverish and lies in bed": Hepner papers, 1206/1/13/1.

[37] Kantorowicz to the Kuratorium of the University of Frankfurt, 15 April 1933 (LBI, box 5, folder 5): "Für meine Teilnahme an der Abwehr polnischen Uebergriffe in Posen errichteten Deutschen Volkswehr vermag ich dokumentarische Unterlagen nicht beizubringen, da ich bei meiner fluchtartigen Abreise aus Posen alles etwa belastende Material wie Ausweiskarten vernichtet habe." Letter to parents, 3 January 1918 [*sic* for 1919].

[38] Chaney to David Spears, 6 August 2001.

[39] Franz to Eva Kantorowicz, 4 February 1919, letter headed "Wilde Interniert als Geisel": Lerner archive. The date of Franz's internment is established by his letter to his wife of 13 February 1919.

[40] Matelski, "Nationalbeziehungen in Grosspolen," 36.

[41] A detailed account is Pierre Broué, *The German Revolution 1917–1923* (Leiden, 2005), 228–58.

of bolshevism to the east, were resolved to eliminate them and to do so made an alliance with leftover units of the former imperial army and newly formed units constituted by far-right volunteers known as Freikorps (Free Corps) that were camped around the city.

Events came to a head in early January. The Social Democrats had deposed the far-left police chief of the city, and in protest an alliance of leftist Socialists and Spartacists called for a mass demonstration. It was a Sunday and the turnout was much larger than had been expected: crowds of demonstrators swelled the city on both sides of the Brandenburg Gate. This emboldened some of the Spartacists to believe that the time was ripe for the real revolution. On the night of January 5 some ill-advisedly seized several buildings in Berlin's "newspaper district" to silence the hostile press, while others seized some buildings in the downtown government area. Street fighting followed, but the government soon gained the upper hand by calling in its army and the Freikorps. Army units secured the heart of the city and established headquarters in the downtown Reichskanzlei (Reich Chancellery). On January 11 a Freikorps contingent assaulted the main Spartacist bastion in the newspaper district by using flame throwers and howitzers, soon overrunning the building. Defenders who survived were taken away and shot. A day later other Freikorps fighters arrived in the same neighborhood where desperate Spartacists were still trying to hold out and went about clearing houses and summarily executing the inhabitants. By January 13 the city was quiet.

It has long been supposed that Kantorowicz fought against the Spartacists with the Freikorps, but the recent discovery of a letter to his parents on January 14 proves this to be mistaken.[42] He was living at the time in Charlottenburg, not near any real fighting. Still he felt that the situation in Berlin was "threatening" and on January 12 decided to volunteer for service with the forces of order. To do this he reported to the civilian militia in Charlottenburg, where he ran into an acquaintance from Posen who also had come to volunteer. The two then received orders to report in the evening before midnight to the Reichskanzlei. EKa had arrived in his uniform but was told to change into civilian clothing to avoid suspicion when he went to the city's center.

His description of what happened next is colorful. He and his companion had been given a password, but this was not recognized by guards when they left the downtown train station. So they were marched from checkpoint to checkpoint until they reached the Reichskanzlei, where their password was accepted. There they found soldiers stretched out on the "blue velvet rococo furniture" and every inch of space used for camping out. (By coincidence the

[42] From the Ariane Phillips collection. The letter is dated "13 January 1918," but it describes events of 1919 and must have been written on the fourteenth of the month because Kantorowicz wrote that he had just learned on the previous evening of the birth in Posen of Franz Kantorowicz's son (Max Hartwig), which happened on the thirteenth.

diarist Harry Graf Kessler was in the Reichskanzlei on the same night and noted the same scene: "The impression created in the large congress hall of the Reichskanzlei palace was remarkable: a camp of soldiers, some with machine guns, some bivouacking on carpets set up for the night, all slack and unkempt."[43]) Because he "needed to," Kantorowicz went to use the toilet. As he wrote to his parents, he sat down where "Bülow, Bethmann Hollweg, and perhaps even the Kaiser, had found relief from their cares." But disappointingly "there was no leather upholstered seat." Then, after a while, he and his companion were sent to the nearby Reichstag building, received guns and hand grenades, and were instructed to stand guard on a street in proximity to a post office building that was being stormed by government troops. They kept their position for four hours, but it turned out that the building under attack was actually held by other government soldiers.[44] (He wrote, "Of course there were losses.") Afterward they waited for another assignment and finally decided that everything there was "too unmilitary." So they went to Dahlem in the far West to report to the headquarters of the government army.[45] (This would have been on the morning of the thirteenth.) But even then they were not dispatched but loitered around until they found the waiting "too dumb" and went home. In concluding his narrative, EKa wrote, "Now the affair has come well to an end without me, and so there you have the story of my second military period."

In an official statement of April 20, 1933, explaining his right to remain as a professor at the University of Frankfurt, Kantorowicz referred to having been a "postwar fighter against Spartacus," and in a letter of 1933 to a colleague he called himself a "Spartacus victor."[46] But the evidence of his letter of 1919 indicates that he hardly had been a "fighter" or "victor," although not for lack of trying. He discussed with William Chaney and Lucy Cherniavsky in Berkeley his motives for volunteering.[47] He told them independently that he had not been interested in politics and only wanted to get on with his studies. As Chaney reported, "EKa said to me that . . . he couldn't get any work done in Berlin with riots going on in the streets daily"; according to Lucy Cherniavsky he said that "he just wanted to do his own thing, 'but when they turned off the lights [he] got angry.'" Yet one must wonder whether this stance was disingenuous.[48] While we

[43] Angela Reinthal, ed., *Harry Graf Kessler. Das Tagebuch, Siebter Band 1919–1923* (Stuttgart, 2007), 89.

[44] The morning edition of the *Vossische Zeitung* for 13 January reported the "retaking" of the postal building during the night. I thank Eckhart Grünewald for the clipping and the reference in the following note.

[45] Gustav Noske, *Von Kiel bis Kapp: zur Geschichte der deutschen Revolution* (Berlin, 1920), 71.

[46] EG, 114; letter to Percy Ernst Schramm of late May 1933: "alter Kriegsknecht und Spartakussieger": Schramm papers.

[47] Chaney to David Spears, 6 August 2001; interview with Lucy Cherniavsky, 16 September 1990.

[48] His friend Erich Kahler wrote to Friedrich Gundolf on 18 January describing the left-wing revolutionaries as "rabble and debris" (Gesindel und Geschiebe): Pott, *Gundolf-Kahler Briefwechsel*, 1:207.

know nothing of Kantorowicz's political views at that time, we do know that a few months later he volunteered to fight against the "reds" in Munich and that thereafter he stood with the far right. Thus taking up a gun and grenades does not seem to have been a matter of dissatisfaction with the electric supply.

Throughout the winter EKa continued attending lectures at the university. Then, when the semester was over toward the beginning of February, he transferred to the University of Munich. Although he told Chaney that he did this because he thought he could get more work done in Munich, there was a different motive. He had fallen in love with a fascinating woman. That story will be told in the following chapter; here we may pursue his activities in the Bavarian capital outside of the bedroom. He was able to profit from the fact that the university was offering a supplementary semester during the winter and early spring, designed to help returning veterans compensate for lost time. EKa matriculated on February 20 and continued his studies in economics, taking a course in finance, as well as "principles of international economics" and "general economics." As previously in Berlin, he complemented his economics regimen with courses that evidently really interested him: German history from 1648 to 1806, logic, and a course entitled Basic Political Questions of the Present.[49]

Political questions of the present interrupted Kantorowicz's life at the beginning of the next semester. The local situation had been in flux since the assassination of Kurt Eisner, the left-wing Socialist premier of the "Republic of Bavaria," on February 21, 1919. Opposing factions of far leftists competed for control of the city, forcing a moderate Socialist premier to retreat to Bamberg where he struck an alliance with the Social Democrats in Berlin who had eliminated the Berlin Spartacists. On April 13 a "soviet republic" was proclaimed in Munich, but this government lacked authority any further than the city, and the Bamberg government gathered superior military forces, including troops sent from Prussia, to overthrow it. Turmoil prevailed in Munich as the leftists turned on those they thought were traitors. Reactionary troops reached the suburbs in the last days of April. Meanwhile some of the "reds" had seized several leading members of the murderous far-right "Thule society," and on April 30 they made a disastrous mistake by executing them. Once the word went out, volunteers calling themselves "the people's defense" (*Volkswehr*) organized themselves within the city to wreak vengeance. These fighters and those who were arriving in Munich from the outside then crushed the red revolution by the end of the day of May 2.

"Herr Ernst Kantorowicz has attached himself to the *Volkswehr*." These were the words on an identification card issued on May 1, 1919, showing that EKa was one of the volunteers who rushed to fight after the executions of the day

[49]EG, 31–32.

before.[50] The card was issued at counterrevolutionary headquarters in the former residence of the Bavarian monarchs on the edge of downtown Munich. (EKa was living in a pension nearby.) Unfortunately at this point we have no letter describing his activities. It may be inferred, however, that on the first or second of May he fought in the "Stachus" (roughly Munich's Times Square).[51] The fighting in Munich was intense because the leftists had had time to arm themselves and knew that they were fighting for their lives. At some point EKa was wounded. As he reported in his curriculum vitae of 1938: "In 1919 I took up arms again: against the communists, then in power in Munich, and I was wounded once more."[52] He repeated that he had been wounded in a statement he made in regard to the loyalty oath controversy in Berkeley in 1950, and in conversation with a Berkeley colleague he alluded to his scars.[53] But his wounds were not severe enough for him to be hospitalized.

A contemporary German historian has written that "the 'liberation' of Bavaria contradicted any rationale of military necessity. . . . [T]he atrocities committed by the Freikorps in the name of the national government far outstripped any justified recompense for the deeds or misdeeds of the Soviet regime. The six hundred dead in Munich alone make it impossible to defend the action against the Soviet republic as a constitutional act."[54] Although EKa did not actually engage in the fighting in Berlin, in Munich he not only fought but almost certainly killed. The evidence consists of two statements reported during the loyalty oath controversy. According to the chair of the Berkeley History Department, Kantorowicz once said to him: "John, I have been shot at by Communists and I have shot Communists"; according to a colleague in the department he said, "I have *killed* Communists, but I shall never take the oath."[55] Moreover, he fought side by side with death's head warriors, many of whom would become Nazis two decades later. Perhaps the best comment comes from a statement Kantorowicz made in a letter of October 4, 1949, to the president of the University of California. Explaining that he was not, nor had ever been a Communist,

[50] EG, 28. EG, 28, n. 111, referring to an interview with Beate, the daughter of EKa's sister Soscha, is misleading. According to this, Beate Salz claimed to remember seeing EKa in Munich at Eastertime, when he played "Easter Rabbit" with her and her sister (she would have been six years old and her sister five) and was "in uniform." But Easter fell on 20 April, which would have been too early for EKa to have been committed to military action.

[51] EG, 126.

[52] CV. A second CV, of 1939, omits this sentence. Perhaps the omission was designed to avoid giving the impression of militant anticommunism for American readers, but it may simply have been omitted for purposes of streamlining.

[53] Ernst H. Kantorowicz, *The Fundamental Issue: Documents and Marginal Notes on the University of California Loyalty Oath* (San Francisco, 1950), 13; interview with Joseph Tussman, 3 March 1992.

[54] Ulrich Kluge, *Die deutsche Revolution, 1918/1919* (Frankfurt, 1985), 135.

[55] John D. Hicks to Robert G. Sproul, 12 July 1950, quoted by Randolph Starn, "Kantorowicz in the Archives," 8 (unpublished paper). (I am grateful to Professor Starn for permitting me to draw on his work.) Lawrence A. Harper, "Shall the Professors Sign?" *Pacific Spectator* 4 (1950): 21–29, at 25.

he wrote: "My political record will stand the test of every investigation. I have volunteered twice to fight actively, with rifle and gun, the left-wing radicals in Germany; but I know also that by joining the white battalions I have prepared, if indirectly and against my intention, the road leading to National-Socialism and to its rise to power."[56]

[56]The letter is reprinted in Kantorowicz, *The Fundamental Issue*, 6–7.

CHAPTER 3

Fine Fever

THE MOST ARDENT AMOROUS ATTACHMENT IN EKA'S LIFE was with the beautiful and fascinating Josefine von Kahler (fig. 9). "Fine" (pronounced "feenah") was born Josefine Sobotka (accent on first syllable) of Jewish parents in 1889. In 1884 her father had moved with his family from Bohemia to Vienna, where he cofounded a fabulously successful malt manufacturing business. Brewer's malt, produced from barley, was required for brewing beer and baking bread. By around 1900 the firm of Hauser and Sobotka, using new techniques, had become the largest brewer's malt concern in Europe.[1] Fine, the eighth of nine children, grew up in Vienna. Her parents sent her to a girls' school aimed at preparing "higher daughters" for dignified wifehood. But when a doctor announced that she would not be able to bear children, Fine decided that a Miss Manners school was irrelevant.[2] Instead she gained parental consent for transferring to a humanistic gymnasium for girls. There she learned Latin and Greek. Breaking off an engagement at the age of eighteen with a young lawyer suitable to her family, she made some intellectual male friends. One was her future husband, Erich Kahler, from a rich Jewish family (Kohn until 1894) that had relocated itself from Prague to Vienna, and another, Arthur Salz, also a German-speaking Jew from Bohemia from a wealthy background. Salz had studied in Berlin and Munich from 1900 to 1903 (at Munich he received a doctorate in economics from the noted Lujo Brentano) and then assumed management of his family's malt business in the Bohemian town of Staab until 1906, which explains the connection to the Sobotkas.[3] Then he returned to his studies in economics, first in Vienna, where Fine met him, then in Prague. The intellectual engagements of Kahler and Salz contrasted with what she

[1] The company still exists. See http://www.teletrader.com/us/stadlauer-malzfabrik-ag/stocks/profile/tts-399945. On the business and on Fine's youth, Valentin Sobotka, *Ways & Issues Retraced* (Berkeley, 1980).

[2] Sobotka, *Ways & Issues Retraced*, 209, n. 18, with no explanation of the grounds for the doctor's prognosis.

[3] For biographical information about Salz: Korinna Schönhärl, *Wissen und Visionen: Theorie und Politik der Ökonomen im Stefan George-Kreis* (Berlin, 2009), 58–61.

considered to be her family's philistinism. Both were enchanted by Fine. Salz, "knightly in height and manners,"[4] was the more forward, and she was not averse to his advances. In 1908 he followed his professor, Max Weber's brother Alfred, to Heidelberg, and in 1909 "habilitated' (the qualifying hurdle for becoming a professor), which meant staying on in the capacity of Privatdozent. With Salz in Heidelberg, the young woman who was probably his girlfriend took the opportunity of joining him.

Fine Sobotka matriculated at the historic university in the *Weltdorf* (world-town) on the Neckar in April 1909 at the age of twenty. Female attendance at German universities was still rare. (Soscha Kantorowicz was auditing courses in Heidelberg at the same time but not following a degree program.) Only in 1900 were women first allowed to matriculate. Fine opted to study medicine, a field favored at the time for career-seeking women because of the social acceptability of pediatrics. But she recognized quickly that medicine was not her calling; she hated her anatomy classes and left Heidelberg in the winter of 1911.[5] Yet she was very much noticed during her short time there. Not only were women a seldom presence, but she signaled her independence by wearing her hair short, and she was quite attractive.[6]

Of the many who noticed Fine, one was Friedrich Gundolf, who was "set aflame" when he first laid eyes on her in Heidelberg's castle park in May 1910.[7] We have met him earlier as the writer of a postcard and letter sent to Fine in 1911. Now he should be properly introduced. At the time Gundolf met Fine in 1910 he was the most prominent younger disciple of Germany's most famous poet, the charismatic Stefan George, and would himself soon emerge as one of Germany's most noted men of letters. He had been friends with Arthur Salz since 1901 when the two had been together in Berlin. Attracted by Salz's presence in Heidelberg, Gundolf came there in April 1910 to work for his habilitation and stayed with Salz in the same pension—the Pension Neuer, on the castle hill. He was astonishingly handsome: "a beautiful young person"; "of almost Greek beauty."[8] In Heidelberg he engaged intensely on his "Habilitationsschrift," the large work required for the habilitation, writing 490 manuscript pages in two months.[9] Brought out in 1911 by Stefan George's house publisher as *Shakespeare und der deutsche Geist* (Shakespeare and the German Spirit), it became an instant success. A revered contemporary authority in the history of

[4] Ludwig Thormaehlen, *Erinnerungen an Stefan George* (Hamburg, 1962), 90.

[5] Fine Sobotka to Friedrich Gundolf, [27 May 1911], in Pott, *Gundolf-Kahler Briefwechsel*, 2:315.

[6] Rothacker, *Heitere Erinnerungen*, 66: "*bildschön*" (pretty as a picture). In an interview with the author of 18 March 1989, Erich Kahler's second wife Alice ("Lilly") Kahler referred to her husband's first wife as "a well-known beauty."

[7] Gundolf to Fine Sobotka, 16 December 1911, in Pott, *Gundolf-Kahler Briefwechsel*, 2:325.

[8] Marie Luise Gothein, *Eberhard Gothein: Ein Lebensbild* (Stuttgart, 1931), 199; Ludwig Curtius, *Deutsche und Antike Welt: Lebenserinnerungen* (Stuttgart, 1950), 368.

[9] Robert E. Norton, *Secret Germany: Stefan George and His Circle* (Ithaca, 2002), 271.

Figure 9. Fine von Kahler. (Deutsches Literaturarchiv, Marbach)

ideas, Wilhelm Dilthey, wrote that for him it opened a view "from the mountain into the Promised Land"; Eberhard Gothein, another senior authority, declared that "with one step he has placed himself among the masters—or even more—for where is there anyone now who would be able to write such a book?"[10] Even today George's American biographer Robert Norton writes of the "almost incandescent flare of [Gundolf's] language"—of a prose "lucid, poised, shimmering with intelligence and enlivened by dramatic turns of phrase so finely crafted that they almost sound like aphorisms."[11]

Gundolf was not only incandescent in writing about Shakespeare; he was the same in declaring his love for Fine Sobotka. About a month after he was set aflame in the castle park, he wrote to her: "Fine, dearest being . . . I love and honor you with all my heart; I thank you for your mere existence, for the joy

[10] Lothar Helbig [pseudonym for Wolfgang Frommel] and C. V. Bock, "Friedrich Gundolf," in *On Four Modern Humanists*, ed. Arthur R. Evans Jr., 54–84 (Princeton, 1970), at 77–78.

[11] Norton, *Secret Germany*, 463.

of summer, for the fullness that you have brought to my life."[12] A few months afterward Gundolf indulged in some baroque prose in a letter he sent to Fine at a time when she had gone away from Heidelberg to return home for the summer.

> If you are sad and feel lonely ("in the midst of the magnificent alpine world!"), and if it can comfort you to know that the most grateful, most tender, often fist-thick and with a span of up to twenty meters thoughts of a person in love with you who is in his best years, of esteemed standing, engaging appearance, and faultless character, constantly from mornings at eight to evenings at ten dwell on you, if this, I say, touches you positively, then know herewith that such is the case. This is not, as disinterested people might think, a concealed marriage proposal, but an open declaration of love—two entirely different poetic genres, which unfortunately are so often confused as the ode and the hymn.[13]

But Fine did not feel sad only occasionally; she was severely depressive. Perhaps the early gynecological prognosis was a cause. To Gundolf she wrote of her "pain" and of a "burden" that was "too great for her shoulders." She wrote of her "dullness" and "internal desolation," of feeling "pressured," and of needing "so terribly much sleep."[14] In 1911 Gundolf stayed for the Christmas holidays with Fine and her family in their Alpine house in Strobl near Salzburg. Perhaps he was moving to the marriage proposal he earlier had disavowed; perhaps he even made it. But a marriage was not to be. In early January, after the two had left in different directions, she wrote to him: "I would like you not only to know but also to understand that you cannot entirely help me." Then she moved to talk of her old friend Erich Kahler, who she said "suffers under my suffering." Thus she could "do no other than follow him—and even if he hides."[15] Gundolf bore his rue and immediately wrote to Kahler that he could not free Fine of her constant depressions; consequently he was not the right man for her. Instead he told Kahler: "the sole person who *really* can help her, who really *can* help her, is you."[16]

Which of course brings us to Erich Kahler. His father was an insurance magnate, rewarded for services to the Austrian Empire with ennoblement in 1914.[17] The Kahlers moved to Vienna when Erich was fifteen. He received his *Abitur* (diploma) from a humanistic gymnasium in 1903 and a doctorate in

[12] Pott, *Gundolf-Kahler Briefwechsel*, 2:25.

[13] Ibid., 268.

[14] Ibid., 299, 303, 306.

[15] Ibid., 327–28.

[16] Ibid., 508.

[17] On Kahler's early years, ibid., 1:297, 2:503–5. Since his father had been ennobled he was "Erich von Kahler" during his years in Germany, but he dropped the particle in the late 1930s when he came to the United States. German authors refer to him as "Erich von Kahler" but I follow the American usage, although retaining the "von" for his wife.

1911 from the University of Vienna. (The dissertation was "On Law and Morality"; thereafter Kahler remained oriented to "cultural philosophy.") In 1912 he declined a proposal by Alfred Weber that he work toward habilitation in Heidelberg on the grounds that he had sufficient financial resources to pursue scholarship independently and did not wish to take a scarce university position away from another.[18] But he did visit Heidelberg often between 1910 and 1912 in order to be with his friend Arthur Salz, and also with Gundolf, whom he met through Salz and with whom he became close. The presence in Heidelberg of Fine Sobotka was another attraction. Already in 1909 in Vienna Erich and Fine had adopted the familiar *Du*.[19] Kahler was shy. As Fine recognized, he was also depressive. In 1910 he wrote to her that he had his "gray side"—that he knew "a spiritual tiredness that presses so heavily and shuts off everything that one thinks that one cannot live a minute longer and wishes nothing else than sleep."[20] He had failed his doctoral orals in July, and after passing them on a second try in March 1911 he spent June and July in a sanatorium.[21] He thought he was incapable of marriage. After Gundolf's letter to him of January 1912, he agonized for months. In a letter to Fine of May 1912 he reported that he had just spoken with the poet Stefan George who thought "what now I myself may be permitted to believe—that if both sides are agreed, the wedding then can take place."[22] The wedding took place in November.

But the marriage was not carnal. For the first few years the couple spent most of their time together but then saw each other less and less often: "The marriage was conducted in letters of which 1,250 are extant."[23] Erich insisted from the start that the two lead independent lives.[24] Almost clinically, he kept a record of his wife's depressive sayings: "I go my own un-ways"; "I am enough for myself—no, I am too much for myself"; "Most of what I do I don't do gladly, but what I'm glad at I leave"; "If I could only croak, so that all will laugh."[25] (Kahler's second wife, it is good to report, was of a very jovial disposition.)

Fine's rejection of Gundolf only seems to have fanned his flame. A month after he gave her up he wrote to her that he and Erich had spent two days "from eleven to seven," talking without interruption about practically nothing other

[18] Gerhard Lauer, *Die verspätete Revolution. Erich von Kahler: Wissenschaftsgeschichte zwischen konservativer Revolution und Exil* (Berlin, 1995), 228.

[19] Pott, *Gundolf-Kahler Briefwechsel*, 2:455.

[20] Ibid., 507.

[21] Ibid., 1:296–97, 2:329

[22] Kahler to Fine Sobotka, 18 May 1912, StGA, Kahler papers, III:5276.

[23] Pott, *Gundolf-Kahler Briefwechsel*, 2:518.

[24] StGA, Kahler papers, III:5514: Kahler to Fine 5 February 1919: "Erinnere Dich wie ich die ganze erste Zeit nach unser Heirat darum gekämpft habe, ein beiderseits selbstständigeres Leben durchzusetzen."

[25] Michael Landmann, *Figuren um Stefan George: Zehn Porträts* (Amsterdam, 1982), 90; Lauer, *Die verspätete Revolution*, 173.

than "Fine, Fine, Fine" and outdoing each other in "longing, admiration, tenderness, and willingness to help."[26] Around the same time he wrote to Stefan George of Fine's "beauty, nobility, and purity."[27] In 1916 Gundolf dedicated his most famous book, *Goethe*, to "Fine von Kahler." The two continued to correspond with each other, using terms of endearment. In 1917 they adopted the familiar "Du."[28] They also were together for stretches of time without Erich. As for Arthur Salz, he once had proposed to Fine, but she had rejected him with "a straight out no."[29] Even so, Gundolf wrote to Fine that Salz continued to love her as much as ever three days before his marriage to EKa's sister, Sophie Kantorowicz, in 1912.[30] Gundolf and Salz were never constrained by conventional societal norms: Max Weber thought that his own mistress Else Jaffé had had successive sexual relationships with the two of them.[31] Nor was Fine constrained herself. In 1917 when Salz was on leave from service in Turkey she met with him in Munich without either of their spouses present.[32] In May 1919 the two were close enough to collaborate in sheltering Eugen Leviné, a defeated leader of the Munich red revolution who once had been Salz's student in Heidelberg.[33] In 1920 Fine wrote to Gundolf that "Erich was her "beloved head," Arthur "her beloved heart," and Gundolf her "most beloved soul."[34] If that were not enough, we are well in a world of merry-go-round when we learn that for a period of time before the end of 1916 Gundolf was conducting an affair with his

[26] Pott, *Gundolf-Kahler Briefwechsel*, 2:344.

[27] Robert Boehringer and Georg Peter Landmann, eds., *Stefan George—Friedrich Gundolf Briefwechsel* (Munich, 1962), 241.

[28] Pott, *Gundolf-Kahler Briefwechsel*, 2:402–3.

[29] Fine von Kahler to Ernst Kantorowicz, 22 June 1919, StGA, Kahler papers, II:6501; "Ich sehe so deutlich . . . wie absolut richtig mein jugendlicher Instinkt war, der ihm, als ich auf Ihrer Altersstufe stand, ein glattes 'nein' entgegensetzte."

[30] Gundolf to Fine Sobotka, 31 March 1912, Pott, *Gundolf-Kahler Briefwechsel*, 2:356. (At the time of the marriage Max Weber wrote to Salz of his favorable impression of Soscha: M. Rainer Lepsius and Wolfgang J. Mommsen, eds., *Max Weber: Briefe 1911–1912* [Tübingen, 1998], 428.)

[31] Joachim Radkau, *Max Weber: A Biography* (Cambridge, 2009), 312.

[32] Fine von Kahler to Gundolf, 8 February 1917, Pott, *Gundolf-Kahler Briefwechsel*, 2:402–3. A year later she made a copy for herself of Salz's war diary: StGA, Kahler papers, I:8050.

[33] Schönhärl, *Wissen und Visionen*, 64. It appears that the two sheltered Leviné and his wife at the instigation of Salz's friend, the exiled Turkish leader Ahmed Djemal Pasha, who hoped to strike a deal with the Bolsheviks in order to return to power. Salz sheltered Leviné at the home of a friend and Fine sheltered his wife in the Munich apartment of her brother Valentin. Djemal Pasha was living incognito in Fine's apartment at the time (at Salz's behest), and Valentin Sobotka tells in his memoirs of his intriguing "in the hope of returning to the political scene in Turkey": Sobotka, *Ways & Issues Retraced*, 114–15. Salz's sheltering of the communist Leviné has puzzled scholars because he was conservative in politics. Beate Salz stated in an interview (28 June 1990) that she was puzzled herself about her father's action and could only conclude that he was a "Don Quichotte." But the Djemal Pasha connection seems a better explanation.

[34] Pott, *Gundolf-Kahler Briefwechsel*, 2:434–35.

friend Salz's wife, Soscha.[35] And just a few years later Fine took up with Soscha's brother, Ernst Kantorowicz.

Although EKa initialed a postcard to Fine in April 1911, he did not meet her then. But he would have heard about her from his sister. In 1910 and 1911 Soscha was living in the Pension Neuer together with Fine's admirers, Gundolf and Salz, and she came to know Fine directly in July 1910.[36] In March 1917 the two stayed together in a rented dwelling in the Bavarian Alps. At that time Soscha wrote to Gundolf that his ears must be getting red because she and Fine were continually talking about him, adding that for the first time she was really getting to know Fine and to love her.[37] EKa met Fine in Berlin in the autumn of 1918 through his sister and brother-in-law. The Salz family was living in Berlin, and Fine came to see them in October.[38] Erich joined her at the end of the month, and the two remained in Berlin until November 16 or 17.[39] EKa and Erich struck up a friendship as indicated by a reminiscence of the latter. It was a time of tumult in Berlin, and Kahler remembered that he was walking together with Kantorowicz along Unter den Linden when revolutionary soldiers rushed up and ripped the shoulder straps off of Kantorowicz's uniform.[40] EKa and Fine also first met then: "in Berlin, at the time of the outbreak of revolution."[41]

But they were not yet intimate, for in a later letter to Fine EKa referred to "our very earliest time in the Franz-Josephstr.," meaning an apartment that Erich and Fine had rented in Munich.[42] The question of why Kantorowicz transferred from the University of Berlin to that of Munich is thus answered with "cherchez la femme." Roughly by the middle of April EKa and Fine had come to know each other well enough that Fine visited EKa while he lay in a Munich clinic after an operation for appendicitis. And shortly after that came their "earliest time." In a letter of April 17, 1920, EKa reminisced about the visit to the clinic and wrote about how dearly he wished that he could go driving again with Fine

[35] This fact, hitherto unnoticed, emerges from letters from Soscha to Gundolf in the Gundolf Archive. E.g., 14 June 1915: "schreibe mir einmal, mein Herz, um zu zeigen dass du nicht bös bist"; 27 November 1915: "meine Treue und [. . .] unverändlerliche Liebe"; 24 November 1916; 20 July 1917: "was *war* kommt nie wieder, ebenso diese Jahre lassen sich nicht vergessen [. . .] mein geliebtes Herz." It is unclear whether this relationship began before Soscha's marriage to Arthur Salz.

[36] Pott, *Gundolf-Kahler Briefwechsel*, 2:274, 281, 458.

[37] Soscha to Gundolf, 5 March [1917], Gundolf Archive.

[38] StGA, Kahler papers, II:5063. For the context, Pott, *Gundolf-Kahler Briefwechsel*, 1:476.

[39] Pott, *Gundolf-Kahler Briefwechsel*, 2:489–90, 1:423; StGA, Kahler papers, III:5511. See also Gundolf to Kahler, 8 January 1919: "ich zehre noch von den kuriosen Tagen im Bristol [Kahler was staying in the hotel Bristol] wo die Revolution noch ein Säugling war." (Pott, *Gundolf-Kahler Briefwechsel*, 1:206.)

[40] EG, 26.

[41] Fine to Erich von Kahler, 4 June 1926, StGA, Kahler papers, II:5213.

[42] Letter of early February 1921: ibid., 6544. On the Munich apartment, Pott, *Gundolf-Kahler Briefwechsel*, 2:428.

in Munich's English Garden.[43] An undated message he left for Fine at the Munich apartment reads: "first payment for the accompaniment of the debt, your 'despairing' Ernst."[44] There is also a mention in a later letter of the consternation about Fine on the part of Djemal, who was living in the Kahlers' Munich apartment before their lease ran out in the middle of May. The pasha, who spoke no German, inquired of EKa: "Tante Fine, est-elle gaie maintenant?"[45] Erich seems to have been away often—Erich and Fine had an open marriage.

We have seen that EKa fought against the revolutionaries in Munich on the first and probably the second of May. Lectures began at the university on May 6, but probably he disregarded them. Certainly he paid his student fees in July with the excuse that he had had an operation at the beginning of the semester.[46] But on May 1 he had been fit enough to bear a rifle. The real reason he did not pay his fees on schedule must have been that he was planning other things. After Fine gave up her apartment in Munich around May 15,[47] the two went off together to Heidelberg. The fact is established by a note of May 25 that EKa left for "Frau v. Kahler" at a Heidelberg pension.[48] What made them go to Heidelberg? The presence there of Fine's younger brother Valentin, who had recently arrived for his studies,[49] as well as that of Friedrich Gundolf must be the answer.

EKa's note of May 25 read: "Heavens, *must* I have been in despair??" The meaning now is inexplicable but the intensity is evident. The couple spent much of the month of May together, for in a letter of June 22 Fine referred to having "gotten along so well for a few weeks."[50] EKa traveled by himself to Munich on the second or third of June.[51] Although he now really may have meant to attend lectures, he was in far-away Constance in the middle of June. The rationale for that trip is a mystery, but we know that he was engaged there in learned conversations with his brother-in-law Salz and none other than Erich

[43] StGA, Kahler papers, III:6511. This letter presents the grounds for the April datings: "[es] wird jetzt bald ein Jahr sein und jetzt etwa vor einem Jahr hast Du mich bei Krecke besucht [Albert Krecke, a surgeon who had a private clinic in Munich]. Himmel, himmel, was gäbe ich drum, wenn ich wieder mit Dir an einem Sonnen-Vormittag durch den engl Garten fahren könnte." For the appendicitis, EG, 32, n. 11.1.

[44] StGA, Kahler papers, III:6500.

[45] K. to Fine, 1 January 1921: ibid., 6538.

[46] EG, 32, n. 11.1.

[47] Pott, *Gundolf-Kahler Briefwechsel*, 2:428.

[48] To "Frau v. Kahler, b. Volk, Schlossberg 17" (StGA, Kahler papers, II:6501). In a letter from Heidelberg to Fine of 25 December 1920, EKa refers to her brother Valentin's contact with "Frau Volk" (ibid., III:6537).

[49] Sobotka, *Ways & Issues Retraced*, 155–56.

[50] Fine from Postalm, near Strobl, to EKa in Berchtesgaden: "jener Ernst . . . mit dem ich mich einige Wochen lang so gut vertragen habe": StGA, Kahler papers, II:6501.

[51] The Kantorowicz papers in the LBI include a "one-time permit": "Herr Ernst Kantorowicz ist berechtigt die Linien der Regierungstruppen Hoffmanns am 2. u. 3. Juni von 6°° Uhr früh bis 11°° abends zu passieren. Muenchen 2.6.1919." (I thank Eckhart Grünewald for calling this to my attention.)

Kahler.[52] Evidently, however, he had exhausted himself too much after his appendicitis operation and now needed to be confined to bed. Thus sometime before June 22 we find him in a recuperation clinic in Berchtesgaden.[53] This was very far from Constance, and quite far from Munich, where he may have stopped again, but not far from Strobl, the location of Fine's family home to which she had returned.

We may now put the hectic travels to the side and view the flood of passionate letters that EKa and Fine exchanged from late June 1919 until the relationship cooled in the spring of 1921. Many are missing but 114 survive: 69 written by Fine and 45 by EKa. A striking trait is the inversion of customary male-female modes of expression. Fine, six years older than EKa (in 1919 she was thirty and he twenty-four), took the dominant role. Her nickname for him was "foal." She ended her first letter, written from an Alpine hilltop hamlet, with the words, "Horses are grazing here, even mares with tiny, lovely foals, so I'm ever reminded of you."[54] EKa accepted the role and signed "your foal."[55] He also accepted being addressed as "child."[56] None of this precluded ardent endearments. In April 1920 he wrote that he loved Fine so much with "every fiber, every nerve" that he "almost was in physical pain"; if he did not at least get a letter from her he would be "as unhappy as a sow."[57] In May he expressed his longing "to caress and kiss [her], and to be caressed and kissed." He continued: "You Fine, my dearest, sweetest life! Ach, I'm not silent now, only crazy, crazy with the maddest longing for you."[58] The two dreamt of each other. In November 1920 he wrote: "I have a raging longing for you; I dream of you almost every night"; she wrote: "Dearest child . . . I think about you so much, too much. I even suppose I dream about you every night, otherwise why would I always waken with thoughts of you?"[59]

There are aspects of rapport and times of frustration. The writers exchange Yiddishisms (*deiges, tachles, naches, meshugass*). EKa is solicitous about Fine's dark moods and wants to cheer her up at least a little bit.[60] He is jealous of the time she spends with Gundolf and even with her husband ("can't you fit me

[52] For EKa in Constance on 13, 15, 17 and 18 June, Pott, *Gundolf-Kahler Briefwechsel*, 2:498, StGA, Kahler papers, II:6501, 6502. For Salz and Kahler in Constance: Kantorowicz to Erich Kahler, 12 October 1919: DLA, Kahler papers, 8.60/1, Fine from Postalm, near Strobl, to EKa in Berchtesgaden, 28 June 1919: StGA, Kahler papers, II:6503, Pott, *Gundolf-Kahler Briefwechsel*, II:498.

[53] Fine addressed a letter from Postalm on 22 June to EKa in "Berchtesgaden, Kurhaus," and this was forwarded to "Vorderbrand" (an inn in the town), indicating that he had been released: StGA, Kahler papers, II:6501. By 28 June EKa was in Berchtesgaden's "Grand Hotel": ibid., 6503.

[54] Ibid., 6501.

[55] Ibid., 6502.

[56] Ibid., 6501, 6553, 6570.

[57] Ibid., III:6511.

[58] Ibid., 6502.

[59] Ibid., 6535; II:6553.

[60] Ibid., III:6538.

in?").[61] After he has moved to Heidelberg (as of the fall of 1919) he chronicles daily events, expresses opinions of his courses and teachers, tells about his reading. (One night he reads Hölderlin's short novel *Hyperion* from beginning to end to distract himself from his longing.) He briefs Fine assiduously about his work on his dissertation and sends a draft copy for her corrections. He writes that "less than ever could he endure people in numbers more than one."[62] A recurrent subject is the need for discretion in their meetings since Fine after all was a married woman. Erich knew about their affair, and so did Valentin and Soscha. But others did not need to know. Would they meet in a hotel in Munich? If so a business hotel would be best because there they would be least noticed. But Fine does not care for this boudoir-farce strategy of stealth. From time to time EKa sends news about the fortunes of the family firm. But he never mentions current events. For her part Fine tells of her innermost thoughts and sometimes her darkness. ("Ach Ernst! I've brought much trouble and confusion into your life!") She recounts dreams. She offers advice about how to handle people. She enjoys poking fun at her husband's intense intellectual seriousness. ("Stefan George says that when there is no longer anyone on the face of the earth Erich will still be writing about past, future, and present"; "[Erich] began a new work, 'Gens, Natio, Status,' but suddenly interrupted it in the recognition that he first needed to write another much more far-reaching one and is now at work on that. It is entitled simply 'Foundations of a New Universal Theory.'")[63]

Returning to the course of events, five days after Fine reached Strobl in June 1919, she ascended ten kilometers higher to "Postalm," little more than a pasture endowed with a few primitive huts. She wanted to be alone with nature. As she wrote to her husband on June 20, "We must find our way back to the eternal things—they are so near—to the ever-unchanged things: heaven and love, animal and plant, bodily need, and divine knowledge."[64] But this did not mean that she put "young Ernst" out of her mind. In a letter of the twenty-second she confessed to her lover that "of all who I might wish to be here in truth it would be *you* who, though unbidden, one day would appear out of the forest below and leap over the brook that borders the meadow, and then, a little bit merry, I would do nothing other than cry out: 'heavens *you* must never have been in despair!'"[65]

Given the proximity between Berchtesgaden and Strobl, it was convenient for Fine to meet with EKa after he was fit. Sometime during the next three weeks

[61] Ibid., 6502, 6505, 6510.

[62] 21 July 1925, ibid., 6563: "Ich konnte weniger als je Menschen die die Zahl von Einem überschreiten aushalten."

[63] Ibid., II:6540. A further sense of the letters is offered by Barbara Picht, "Verliebt–verglaubt–verhofft: Fine von Kahler," in *Frauen um Stefan George*, ed. Ute Oelmann and Ulrich Raulff, 213–31 (Göttingen, 2010), at 219–21.

[64] Pott, *Gundolf-Kahler Briefwechsel*, 1:498.

[65] StGA, Kahler papers, II:6501.

she interrupted her communing with the eternal for a tryst.[66] EKa returned to Munich only on July 15; on July 17 he paid his long-overdue fees for the semester.[67] By then the semester was practically over, but he needed to display a certain number of attested seminars before he could sit for a doctoral examination at any German university. Paying for the semester guaranteed this because there was little or no record keeping concerning actual attendance. Accordingly the transcript showed registration for several courses in economics, as well as another in sociology, and another in Turkish.[68] But all this was fiction. The swindling was the mark of a young man who was not too fastidious about conventions.

A day after the dues payment EKa displayed his indifference to conventions in another way by signing his name ostentatiously, "Ernst Hartwig Kantorowicz," in the guest book of the Kahlers' villa near Munich.[69] Erich was then staying in the villa without his wife, and EKa was not going to let his affair stand in the way of his friendship with Fine's husband. Following his own sense of correctness, he duly informed Erich of his relations with Fine, and Erich was unruffled. On the contrary, he wrote to his wife, who was still in Postalm, "Fine, Fine, now there'll again be amorousness! Well, but you'll also have to be a bit motherly there." Playfully Fine sent this to EKa with the remark: "Am I? I really have no idea."[70] The guestbook shows that EKa again was at the villa on August 7 and 21. On September 8 he was vacationing (without Fine) in Graubünden, Switzerland.[71]

Around that time the lovers made decisions respectively about their plans for the year. EKa intended to pursue his studies at Heidelberg; Fine planned to obtain a license in horticulture from a gardening school on Lake Constance. Since they were headed in the same direction they traveled together by train. Fine's account to her husband was lively. "Ernstchen" (little Ernst) picked her up by car. Then at Munich's main train station she "cuddled (*schmuste*) with Arthur [!]" while Ernstchen, "famous as he is for illegal ways," sneaked into the train before the barrier opened and held two seats.[72]

We will follow EKa's career in Heidelberg in the next chapter; here we will see his affair with Fine to its end. At Christmas 1919 the couple spent some

[66] EKa to Fine, 28 April 192o (ibid., III:6515), referring to his summer in Munich "between Strobl [and some other words canceled.]" Also EKa to Fine, 31 December 1930 "now, eleven years ago on the Bürgl" (the Sobotka family property in Strobl): ibid., 6571.

[67] Ibid., II:6504:16 July1919; military pass for 31 July: LBI, box 7, folder 7. EKa's address in Munich was Pension International/ Von der Tannstr. 22

[68] EG, 32–33.

[69] The guest book is preserved today in StGA, Kahler papers, IV:0035.

[70] Fine to EKa, 18 July 1919: "Unter anderen steht auch drin: 'Fine, Fine, da wird's wieder Verliebtheit geben. Na ja, aber Du must auch ein bisschen mütterlich sein, da.' Bin ich? Ich hab wirklich keine Ahnung." I owe this citation, which I have been unable to locate in the unpublished correspondence, to Barbara Picht.

[71] StGA, Kahler papers, II:6509.

[72] Fine to Erich Kahler, 30 September 1919: ibid., 5077.

wonderful days in EKa's rooms at the university, walking along the Neckar on Christmas Day.[73] On New Year's Fine wrote: "Let me thank you for these beautiful days. They were perfect—from the lovingly set, brightly lit table that greeted me until the end. There was nothing wrong."[74] (This letter is the first that survives in which she uses the intimate "Du.") The couple then had an assignation in the winter in a large home rented by the Salzes in Oberstdorf in the Bavarian Alps.[75] EKa traveled to Lake Constance to see Fine on Good Friday, but the meeting lasted for only a few hours because of her schedule ("Himmel, Himmel, Fine!"). Soon they made it up by mail ("Fine, Fine, Fine!!!),[76] and in the second half of May Fine came to Heidelberg, where they spent some more perfect days.[77] Immediately afterward EKa wrote ecstatically that the time had been "*without* restrictions, *without* a 'nevertheless,' *without* an 'although.'"[78]

But afterward the steam began to run out. After May 1920 the couple saw each other rarely. In March or April 1921 EKa wrote to Fine that he was depressed about their relationship.[79] He was developing a much firmer sense of himself (a photo, figure 10, shows that he had taken to wearing elegant bow ties), whereas she was continuing to play mother. Indeed a letter of hers of February 12, 1921, continues to address her "dearest child" and to refer to what she "always wanted to teach him."[80] This was the wrong way to talk. In April EKa wrote about "changed circumstances."[81] Then the couple fell almost entirely out of touch. The following November EKa wrote to Fine that he had not heard from her since July and was not even sure where she was.[82] A month later they saw each other in Heidelberg, but the meeting was brief and EKa wrote that it left all questions open. Not wishing to leave it that way, he added that it was impossible for him to return to their old terms: he had reached the point where he could no longer be "educated" by her. He thought that another sort of relationship might be possible, one that "would seem desirable" to him, but added that "you are not light-blooded and light-minded enough for [this other] sort of relationship—and quite rightly, for otherwise you would not be you."[83]

Silence followed for a year and a half. During this period Fine had entered into an affair with her brother-in-law, Jascha Marschak, who was three years

[73] EKa to Fine, 25 December 1920: ibid., III:6537.

[74] Ibid., II:6513.

[75] EKa to Fine, c. 29 March 1920: ibid., III:6504. On Oberstdorf, Friedrich Gundolf to Stefan George, 17 November 1919, in Boehringer and Landmann, *Stefan George*, 333.

[76] 15 April 1920: StGA, Kahler papers, III:6510.

[77] EKa to Fine, 3 May 1920: ibid., III:6517.

[78] EKa to Fine, 27 May 1920: ibid., 6520. Also Fine's report to Erich about the trip to Heidelberg: Pott, *Gundolf-Kahler Briefwechsel*, 2:476.

[79] StGA, Kahler papers, III:6550.

[80] Ibid., II:6570.

[81] Ibid., III:6551.

[82] Ibid., 6554.

[83] Ibid., 6555.

Figure 10. Ernst Kantorowicz with bow tie, roughly at age twenty-six. (Stefan George Archiv, Stuttgart)

younger even than EKa.[84] Valentin had married Franja Marschak in August 1922, and Fine met Jascha the following May. On July 28 she wrote to Erich: "What to do? I love him." From January to April 1924 the two took an extended trip to Italy. This may not have ended well, for on her return to Germany she broke the silence with EKa by sending him a birthday letter.[85] After that came a trickle of exchanged birthday greetings and mild civilities until the flame suddenly flared up again in September 1926. EKa was in Dalmatia and Fine was heading for a stay in Italy when they met in the Dalmatian coastal town of Zara. Immediately afterward EKa wrote from Trieste: "Our time could not have been more perfect than it was—halcyon days, about which I can say no more than Fine!"[86] And a few days later he wrote from Heidelberg:

[84] On Fine and Marschak, Pott, *Gundolf-Kahler Briefwechsel*, 2:146, 151, 495.

[85] Reference to the letter: StGA, Kahler papers, III:6556. Fine also socialized with EKa in Heidelberg in October 1924 when he had become involved with a male lover: Pott, *Gundolf-Kahler Briefwechsel*, 2:156.

[86] EKa from Trieste to Fine in Naples, 28 September 1926: StGA, Kahler papers, III:6564.

> I steal some time for myself for thinking of you—pressed in a corner of my bed before falling asleep; mornings on awakening and while shaving. But I'm not at all melancholy: the entirely frictionless repose of our time together . . . this day and night of only loving each other—without problems before or after—all of that still is a happy afterglow, all of that without a drop of wormwood (not "Vermouth") was rare for me . . . the gods meant it well with us this time, and you, dearest, I thank you with my entire soul. Keep on thinking of me with love as I think of you![87]

Between EKa's break with Fine in 1921 and this rendezvous of 1926 came a homosexual relationship with Woldemar Count Uxkull-Gyllenband. Many who have written about Kantorowicz have wondered about his sexual orientation, and most have assumed that it was exclusively homosexual. But it takes no effort to see the alternation of affection from woman to man to woman again. And such alternations would be repeated.

Regarding Fine, the meeting in Zara did not mark the reestablishment of an intimate relationship. Very shortly afterward EKa found another woman, about whom more will be heard later. Over the next four years he wrote merely newsy letters to Fine at intervals. In February 1931, while he was vacationing at a ski resort, he wrote to apologize for being late with birthday greetings.[88] His excuse was that he was exhausted from slaloming. Soon after he wrote that they should try to get together again. He said he was sure it would happen,[89] but apparently it never did.

[87] 30 September 1926: ibid., 6566.
[88] Ibid., 6575.
[89] Ibid., 6576.

CHAPTER 4

Heidelberg

Ernst Kantorowicz arrived in Heidelberg in late September 1919 and matriculated at the university on October 3.[1] The choice was obvious. Heidelberg was where he belonged. Already as a teenager he had visited the picturesque university town on the Neckar where his sister Soscha was one of a group of committed young intellectuals: Friedrich Gundolf, Arthur Salz, Fine Sobotka, and Erich Kahler. That group maintained its ties in the intervening years, and by the autumn of 1918 EKa was becoming a junior member. The cameo of his walking along Under den Linden with the decade-older and already well-published Erich Kahler shows that he was being taken seriously.

Gundolf's presence in Heidelberg alone would have been a magnet. In the spring of 1919 he had returned there as professor of German literature and had become a celebrity. His book of 1916 called simply *Goethe* was the most discussed literary biography of the day: it offered a new approach to the genre by fixing itself boldly on the subject's *Gestalt*—the essence of man and work without attention to development.[2] For Gundolf every word and action of Goethe was an expression of his being, and he was convinced that he had become the imprint of his subject's stamp. Professional scholars had reservations (the book lacked footnotes and made no mention of specialized literature), but general readers, caught up in the German religion of Goethe, were awed by Gundolf's verbal virtuosity and apodictic judgments. (Fine, with her own verbal virtuosity, said that "wherever Gundolf pronounced, no grass grew."[3]) The young René Wellek found that because Gundolf's work was "free of pedantry and dazzling by the boldness of its generalizations and the authoritative tone of its judgments

[1] Heidelberg University, matriculation lists, winter semester 1920–21. Kantorowicz gave his "faculty" as "Cam" (viz. "Kameralwissenschaft" or economics) and listed his religion as Jewish.

[2] Carola Groppe, *Die Macht der Bildung. Das deutsche Bürgertum und der George-Kreis 1890-1933* (Cologne, 1997), 302–9. On the Goethe book, Rainer Kolk, "Von Gundolf zu Kantorowicz: Eine Fallstudie zum disziplinären Umgang mit Innovation," in *Literaturwissenschaft und Wissenschaftsforschung*, ed. Jörg Schönert, 195–208 (Stuttgart, 2000); Norton, *Secret Germany*, 583–85, and Helbig and Bock, "Friedrich Gundolf," 70.

[3] Curtius, *Deutsche und Antike Welt*, 369.

it . . . held up a new hope for what literary history could be."[4] Consequently *Goethe*, more than 800 pages long, was a huge success. EKa's sister wrote that everyone she knew was reading it and could speak of nothing else.[5]

Gundolf gave a series of lectures in Heidelberg during the summer semester of 1919 devoted to the German Romantics and immediately attracted crowds. Addressing an audience that included many recently returned war veterans and looking like a presence from the Romantic age himself, with broad cravat and windswept hair (fig. 11),[6] he told of how a new kind of poetry had awakened German spirits during the Napoleonic era. The implication was that the contemporary poetry of Stefan George, Gundolf's master who often stayed in Heidelberg, would be the means for a second German awakening.[7] EKa had already met Gundolf; soon after his arrival he was on close enough terms with him to borrow books.[8]

A second contact for the young Kantorowicz was Max Weber's younger brother, Alfred.[9] Known by the Gundolf group as "Walfred" and occasionally by students as "Minimax," he was a professor of economics whose real interest lay in cultural sociology. Perhaps his greatest claim to fame lies in his having been the professor who granted Franz Kafka a doctorate in Prague in 1906. Arthur Salz came under Weber's influence in Prague; when Weber moved to Heidelberg in 1907 Salz followed him. After Erich Kahler turned down Weber's offer to work with him at Heidelberg he still kept up his contacts.[10] Fine's brother Valentin studied with him (he completed his dissertation under Weber in 1921); and inevitably Fine von Kahler was a friend.[11]

If Kantorowicz already knew Gundolf and could count on knowing Alfred Weber, he could at least hope to lay eyes on Stefan George. For EKa this would have been something close to the beatific vision. To say that all those closest to him worshipped George would be quite on the mark. Soscha was a devotee who knew all George's poetry. In 1912 she and her husband hosted the poet

[4] René Wellek, "The Literary Criticism of Friedrich Gundolf," *Contemporary Literature* 9 (1968): 394–405, at 394.

[5] Letter to Gundolf from Posen, 24 November 1916 (Gundolf Archive). By 1932 the book had sold over 45,000 copies: Helbig and Bock, "Friedrich Gundolf," 77.

[6] A woman who wrote about Heidelberg when she was a student there in 1919 wrote: "Above all there was Friedrich Gundolf. I can still see him climbing down from the Schlossberg, hatless, with his hair and black scarf blowing in the wind." Rosie Goldschmidt, *Prelude to the Past* (New York, 1934), 88–89.

[7] A description is in Sobotka, *Ways & Issues Retraced*, 117.

[8] Hans Cymorek, "Momentaufnahmen eines Mythos: Heidelberg 1919, Heidelberg 1931: Zwei unveröffentliche Briefe von Ernst Kantorowicz und Heinrich Zimmer," *Mitteilungen der Ernst-Troeltsch Gesellschaft* 16 (2003): 64–102, at 75.

[9] Martin Green, *The von Richthofen Sisters* (New York, 1974), 225–36.

[10] See the memorial he wrote after Weber's death: Erich Kahler, "Alfred Weber (1868–1958)," *Social Research* 25 (1958): 361–64.

[11] Sobotka, *Ways & Issues Retraced*, 113, 118, 123; Pott, *Gundolf-Kahler Briefwechsel*, 2:396.

Figure 11. Friedrich Gundolf. (Deutsches Literaturarchiv, Marbach)

for two weeks in their apartment in Heidelberg.[12] Three years later she wrote to Gundolf, "How is George, and is he with you? I think of him often and it does me good to picture his presence"; in 1916 she wrote, "I long to have an hour with him, not for any particular reason, only just to *see* him."[13] (One of Soscha's daughters remembered seven decades later how her mother would read George's poem's aloud with George's prescribed intonation.[14]) Gundolf apostrophized George as "the way, the truth, the life."[15] And in this reverence EKa's Fine was in no way behind. In 1912 Gundolf wrote to George about a letter he had just received from Fine during a time of her depressions. To console

[12] Erich Kahler from Heidelberg to Fine Sobotka, 16 May 1912: "George ist da, wohnt bei Salz": StGA, Kahler papers, III:5274; H.-J. Seekamp et al., *Stefan George: Leben und Werk: Eine Zeittafel* (Amsterdam, 1972), 234.

[13] Soscha to Gundolf, 14 June 1915; 25 December 1916: Gundolf Archive.

[14] Interview with Beate Salz, 28 June 1990.

[15] Thomas Karlauf, *Stefan George. Die Entdeckung von Charisma* (Munich, 2007), 521.

her he had sent a photo of the poet, and she thanked him profusely: "Ach Gundolf, how much am I under his spell! . . . Such a picture is really too much!"[16] In 1914 her words to Gundolf were "That *is* poetry. So inexorably rigorous, and so deeply comforting . . . so strictly directed to the Highest and hence directed to everything *eternally* human. Here are all the answers to all the questions."[17] In 1918 when George and Gundolf stayed with Fine in her villa near Munich while Erich was away, she wrote afterward that George had relieved her of her "vegetative, painful soddenness," made her feel "the eternity of the present" by means of "the incredible concentration of his *Da-sein* [being there/existence]," had "lighted up a yet undiscovered world."[18] Given that all around him were stricken with a fever too high to be measured by a thermometer, EKa must have had hopes for a meeting of his own, although even seeing the great life-transformer from a distance might have been satisfactory.

Kantorowicz took a room in Heidelberg in the Pension Friedau, a boarding house favored by the Gundolf circle.[19] Edgar Salin, a friend of Gundolf's with whom EKa would have much to do in future years, had lived there before the war, and Gundolf himself inhabited the pension for two semesters: winter 1915–16 and summer 1916.[20] A plaque could be placed in front of the house because in August 1915 Stefan George and Max Weber lived in the pension together.[21] In the winter of 1918–19 the proprietress, Klara Bezner, took in refugees from Strassburg, including the widow of Georg Simmel. Known familiarly as the "Beznerei," the pension was located on the western outskirts of the university area, fifteen minutes away from the main classroom building. Boarders took lunch (the main meal of the day) with Frau Bezner and her daughter, Magda, to whom Gundolf addressed several poems and many letters.[22] (Gundolf's middle name was Lothario.) Klara Bezner was a warm and capable woman: once she told EKa that he was so skinny that he seemed undernourished.[23] Meals were served in a large room on the ground floor. The second floor had six rooms,

[16] Boehringer and Landmann, *Stefan George*, 240.

[17] Pott, *Gundolf-Kahler Briefwechsel*, 2:381.

[18] Lothar Helbing et al., eds., *Stefan George: Dokumente seiner Wirkung* (Amsterdam, 1974), 145.

[19] Hans-Martin Mumm, "'Die sieghafte Jugend der Neckarfluren': Die Pension Friedau, Gaisbergstrasse 16a, als Ort Stefan Georges und des Georgekreises," *Jahrbuch der Stadt Heidelberg* 15 (2011): 127–43. (Thomas Gruber kindly called my attention to this article.) Mumm relies primarily on university documents, and these can be supplemented. Viz. Fine addressed a postcard to EKa at the Pension Friedau on 30 September 1919: StGA, Kahler papers, II:6511.

[20] Edgar Salin, *Um Stefan George: Erinnerung und Zeugnis*, 2nd ed. (Munich, 1954), 31, 98; Arthur Salz, postcard to Elli Salomon, at Gaisbergstrasse 16a, 18 March 1915; Seekamp et al., *Zeittafel*, 260; Lothar Helbing and Claus Victor Bock, eds., *Gundolf Briefe, Neue Folge* (Amsterdam, 1965), 153.

[21] Radkau, *Max Weber*, 295. (Mumm, "'Die sieghafte Jugend der Neckarfluren,'" 137, points out the lack of evidence that they lived door to door.)

[22] Pott, *Gundolf-Kahler Briefwechsel*, 1:401. Letters to Magda Bezner are in the Gundolf Archive.

[23] Salin, *Um Stefan George*, 98; Kantorowicz to Erich Kahler, 19 January 1920 (DLA, Kahler papers, 8.60/3).

two of which were taken by the proprietress and her daughter, the others by boarders; more rooms were above, including quarters for servants.[24] Discussions at the lunch table could be earnest: one might talk of Ernst Troeltsch's views on the philosophy of religion.[25]

EKa's main field of studies remained economics. Evidently he was still preparing for a career in the family business, or at least holding that out as an option. More indicative of his real interests were his "special subjects": "history of economics, geography, and Arabic philology."[26] His courses during his first two semesters are ascertainable.[27] He attended lectures in finance, which he found "deadly" but could not avoid because the subject was a requirement. Alfred Weber's lecture courses in economics, every day for an hour, were a requirement too, and EKa was by no means delighted by them. In his second semester he wrote scathingly to Fine that they were "splendid" so long as one took "major points as minor ones, and minor ones as major ones"; they were "lovely" even though "[Weber] stumbles over all that's proper without ever seeing it."[28] A semester later he had entirely lost patience with Weber and now complained to Fine that his lectures were "always the same"—"dreadful."[29] A third lecturer in economics—actually "social politics"—was the left-leaning Emil Lederer. EKa took a course with him in his first semester with no surviving comment, and the fact that he registered for no further courses with Lederer may speak for itself.[30] Then came Eberhard Gothein, a vastly learned author of thousands of pages on both economic history and cultural history. Gothein's weakness, however, was spewing information without processing it. EKa found attending his daily lectures a chore, complaining that "Gothein always gives one a bit of a stomachache: he talks too much, granted that's his job."[31] Finally there was Gothein's assistant, Edgar Salin. (The name was shortened from Salinger.) EKa took a seminar with him on John Stuart Mill and Classical Economics and liked it well enough to regret that he had no room on his schedule for another.

[24] Sobotka, *Ways & Issues Retraced*, 120–21.

[25] EKa to Fine, 17 April 1920: StGA, Kahler papers, III:6511.

[26] CV.

[27] I rely on a letter to Erich Kahler of 16 December 1919, published by Cymorek, "Momentaufnahmen eines Mythos," 78–80, and one to Fine of 5 May 1920 (curiously Kantorowicz misdated this to 5.3.20 instead of the surely correct 5.5.20): StGA, Kahler papers, III:6502.

[28] StGA, Kahler papers, III:6502.

[29] 6 November 1920: ibid., 6530. Many years later EKa contributed to a Festschrift on the occasion of Weber's eightieth birthday and wrote to Edgar Salin that this constituted "belated thanks, which [Weber] truly earned much earlier because of his humanity": 4 March 1948: Salin papers.

[30] Valentin Sobotka reported: "There were two main groups within the Department of Economics at Heidelberg: one centered on two senior members, Eberhard Gothein and Alfred Weber, both of whom had contact with George-circle, and the other around Emil Lederer" (Pott, *Gundolf-Kahler Briefwechsel*, 1:579).

[31] StGA, Kahler papers, III:6502.

The economics courses did not prevent EKa from following Gundolf's lectures: "German Literature from Opitz [a poet of the early seventeenth century] to Lessing" and "Founders of the Romantic School." It was unthinkable that he would not attend the lectures of Fine's dear friend who also was offering him occasional intellectual guidance.[32] Moreover, everyone went to hear Gundolf. In the summer semester of 1919 his lecture course drew 138 students; two years later the number had doubled to 275 when Heidelberg had only about 500 students in all fields of the humanities.[33] Gundolf had become a cult figure partly because his looks could have made him a matinee idol, partly because he was seen as the alter ego of Stefan George, and partly because of his own noted books. Moreover, his subject was compelling. Students who a few years earlier had been in the trenches or had experienced the German "starvation winter" of 1916–17, and who now felt "the shame of Versailles," were easily persuaded that the transcendent powers of German poetry could be a rallying point for the future.

In fact, however, although Gundolf was a powerful literary stylist he was a poor lecturer.[34] He read in a monotone from a script meant to be published, without seeking eye contact with his audience and occasionally looking out the window. He seldom paused for punctuation. When he lost his place he was capable of reading the same line twice or skipping a page without realizing it. And when he gave a lecture series a second time he ran into additional trouble: he customarily marked where he had left off for the day in order to continue from there on the next, but on the second round he confused his old marks with the new. Nor did he make any concession to accessibility by means of any prefatory information, and he chose to lecture after the heavy midday meal. Bored or baffled students sometimes left the hall after the first ten minutes. On one occasion Gundolf locked the door to halt the flow. The subsequently prominent playwright Carl Zuckmayer came to all his lectures in 1919 but "slept through most of them and learned what Gundolf said only after the lectures came out in print."[35] Yet students tend to flock to celebrities. Sitting with Kantorowicz in Gundolf's audience in the summer of 1920 was Joseph Goebbels, as yet unperturbed about listening to a Jew.[36] EKa reported to Fine that Gundolf was lectur-

[32] EKa to Fine, 28 April 1920, ibid., 6515, complains that Gundolf earlier had thought unfairly that he had been looking for a dissertation topic indiscriminately yet tells of how he had sought out Gundolf to discuss new theories regarding the topic he had chosen.

[33] Groppe, *Die Macht der Bildung*, 318–19. Gundolf exaggerated the figures in his own correspondence: e.g., Pott, *Gundolf-Kahler Briefwechsel*, 1:210.

[34] Groppe, *Die Macht der Bildung*, 319, n. 154; Hermann Glockner, *Heidelberger Bilderbuch* (Bonn, 1969), 32.

[35] Carl Zuckmeyer, *A Part of Myself* (New York, 1966), 208. Gundolf acknowledged privately in 1919 that he had heard complaints, yet this did not seem to make any difference: Fricker, *Friedrich Gundolf/Friedrich Wolters*, 199.

[36] Claus-Ekkehard Bärsch, *Der junge Goebbels* (Munich, 2004), 20.

ing at a rostrum surrounded by potted laurel trees, "with all Heidelberg there." A large bouquet of roses had been placed on his desk as a token of appreciation for his having just declined a professorship in Berlin. He noticed that Gundolf was visibly moved, but he himself felt correspondingly miserable, apparently because he knew of Fine's doting.[37]

EKa wrote to Erich Kahler in December 1919 that he often did not attend lectures.[38] This certainly was not owing to a lack of intellectual commitment. During the summer he had wrestled with Bergson and Nietzsche, delighted by his ability to understand philosophy and "radiating Bergson" in his letters to Fine.[39] When he was with her in the winter of 1920 he wrote a paper on "the four-dimensional world," and a letter of April 1920 is full of metaphysics and his decision to read Plato's *Phaedo*.[40] (Plato was de rigueur for anyone who followed Stefan George.) EKa also attended the biweekly "sociology evenings" organized by Alfred Weber to hear and discuss papers.[41] But he was taking mostly required courses that did not interest him, and none of his lecturers were gifted. The same letter to Kahler displays the talent for irony that was to become a Kantorowicz trademark. Mocking academic fads and pretentiousness, EKa wrote that when he arrived in Heidelberg he had to get used to "Heidelbergisch"—he had only been able to understand "every third word." Initially such talk seemed enormously wise, but he soon realized that the speakers knew just as much or as little as he did, which was a comfort. Nevertheless, he remained puzzled by all the "combinations, permutations, and variations" that characterized the intellectual environment. Everything began with the letters "s.o.z.": a dissertation was on "The Soziologie of the Intimate Theatre"; a lecture on Matthias Grünewald's Isenheim Altar revealed "Grünewald's Sozial Ethic." But the same letter expresses his own commitment to studying Islam. Here one notices real enthusiasm. He wrote that he was looking for a dissertation topic in Islamic history, "plowing through the entire Orient." He was borrowing books from Gundolf (a book collector) concerning anything that "smelled of the Orient."

Driven by his intention to write a dissertation on "Orientalistik," EKa opted to study Arabic. At the beginning of the summer semester of 1920 he was weighing the choice of Turkish, Persian, or Arabic as a minor field and soon chose Arabic as the most practical.[42] He had started studying the language sometime earlier on his own and wrote to Fine that he had forgotten much of his Arabic grammar. Now he continued, taking courses at Heidelberg for

[37] StGA, Kahler papers, III:6502. In a letter of 29 September 1919 to his beloved Elli Salomon, Gundolf still referred to "the divine Fine": Gunilla Eschenbach and Helmuth Mojem, eds., *Friedrich Gundolf-Elisabeth Salomon Briefwechsel (1914–1921)* (Berlin, 2015), 199.

[38] Cymorek, "Momentaufnahmen eines Mythos," 78–79.

[39] EKa to Fine, 28 April 1920: StGA, Kahler papers, III:6515.

[40] Ibid. The same letter also refers to the paper written in Oberstdorf.

[41] Ibid.: "beim Soziologen-Abend wo Wolters *sehr* schön gesprochen hat."

[42] Eka to Fine, 5 May 1920, ibid., 6502.

two successive semesters (summer 1920 and winter 1920–21).[43] In the winter semester of 1920–21, when he was all but finished with his dissertation, he followed a lecture course in Political and Economic Geography of the Earth. EKa wrote to Fine that he was enthralled by this course given by the geographer Alfred Hettner and that it was showing him how much he did not know.[44] In his dissertation he thanked the professor for pointing out that Islam in its origins had spread over an "oasis-culture."[45]

EKa settled on a dissertation topic, "Muslim Artisan Associations," soon after December 1919. This was suggested to him by Arthur Salz.[46] After serving as an economic advisor in Turkey during World War I, Salz maintained a professional interest in Islam. The 1920–21 volume of the *Archiv für Sozialwissenschaften und Sozialpolitik*, Germany's leading journal for the social sciences, contained a thirty-five-page article by Salz on "The Problem of 'Decadence' in Islam," in which he took issue with Max Weber's argument that Islamic religion lacked qualities supportive of the development of capitalism.[47] Had Salz's career worked out differently he might have become EKa's supervisor, for he had been in line for an economics professorship in Heidelberg early in 1918. But this professorship did not materialize, and Salz's once-promising career ran aground in the following years; he lacked any regular position from the time of his return from Turkey until 1924, when he took a job at the business institute (Handelshochschule) in Mannheim.[48] EKa, who had no great love for his brother-in-law, still lamented his absence. After he started writing he was frustrated about the lack of competent guidance and wrote to Fine: "I have no expert, an Orientalist who isn't only a philologist, with whom I can talk—Arthur, to be precise.[49]

EKa turned to Eberhard Gothein (1853–1923) to be his dissertation supervisor *faute de mieux*. Gothein had a well-deserved reputation for omnicompetence, but EKa's remark that his lectures "gave one a bit of a stomachache" gibes with the judgment of others. Max Weber, who knew Gothein well, envied his storied memory but thought him a "great idiot" (*Rindvieh*) because he could do nothing with all his learning.[50] Heidelberg wits said that he was a micro historian—he studied only one planet. Gundolf called him "a specialist for universalism."[51] By the time EKa chose him for his supervisor he had pub-

[43] Ibid., 6502, 6529, 6534, 6540.

[44] Ibid., 6529.

[45] EG, 48, n. 102.

[46] EG, 54, n. 127, citing a verbal communication from Salz's daughter.

[47] Schönhärl, *Wissen und Visionen*, 63.

[48] Ibid., 63–67.

[49] StGA, Kahler papers, III:6511.

[50] Folker Reichert, *Gelehrtes Leben: Karl Hampe, das Mittelalter und die Geschichte der Deutschen* (Göttingen, 2009), 223. The standard biography is Michael Maurer, *Eberhard Gothein (1853–1923)* (Cologne, 2007).

[51] Karlauf, *Stefan George*, 420.

lished four brobdignagian volumes: *The Cultural Development of Southern Italy* (1886: 600 pages); *The Economic History of the Black Forest Region* (1895: 896 pages); *Ignatius Loyola and the Counter-Reformation* (1895: 795 pages); and *The Constitutional and Economic History of the City of Cologne in the First Century of Prussian Rule* (1916; 707 pages). Added to this were scores of pages on subjects as diverse as "Political and Religious Movements before the Reformation," "The Christian Socialist State of the Jesuits in Paraguay," "The Breisgau under Maria Theresia and Joseph II," "Plato's Political Thought in the Renaissance," and "War and Economy."

Despite all this, Gothein lacked credentials in Islam. EKa could come to him as a supervisor pro forma only because Gothein did work in both economic and cultural-religious history, the general areas in which EKa's dissertation lay. Fortunately the old man (he was sixty-eight at the time of EKa's choice) was amiable and not likely to present difficulties. Those who knew him lauded his modesty, good nature, and generosity to students.[52] EKa never took a seminar with Gothein but had easy access to him because he was friends with Gothein's assistant Salin and also with Gothein's son Percy. There also was a connection via Fine, who socialized with Gothein and his wife, Marie Luise, Heidelberg's premiere bluestocking.[53] (Fine wrote to EKa that she considered his sister Soscha to be the smartest woman she knew, "aside from Frau Gothein, who really did not count because she wasn't a woman."[54]) Once EKa overcame his stomachaches he developed an affection for the old man. In 1939 he reminisced nostalgically about the presence of "old Gothein as a midday guest in the Beznerei."[55] But Gothein could not have been of any scholarly help and only read the dissertation after its submission. Then he wrote to his wife that his "reading material" had been "Kantorowicz's work" and a book cited in the dissertation whose author's name he misspelled.[56]

EKa accordingly proceeded on his own. Toward the end of April he wrote to Fine that he had attended Alfred Weber's discussion group the night before and that the talk had been extremely lively—so much so that afterward he dreamt "about Islam, you, religion generally, and historical materialism—all in wild

[52] EG, 52–53; Curtius, *Deutsche und Antike Welt*, 362–63.

[53] Salin, *Um Stefan George*, 104–5; Curtius, *Deutsche und Antike Welt*, 363. See also Michael Maurer, "'Weibliche Kultur' oder 'Aristokratie des Geistes'? Marie Luise Gothein," in Oelmann and Raulff, *Frauen um Stefan George*, 195–212.

[54] StGA, Kahler papers, II:6507.

[55] Robert E. Lerner, "Letters by Ernst Kantorowicz Concerning Woldemar Uxkull and Stefan George," *George-Jahrbuch*, 8 (2010/2011): 157–74, at 168.

[56] Letter of 1 March 1921 published in Michael Maurer et al., eds., *Im Schaffen geniessen: Der Briefwechsel der Kulturwissenschaftler Eberhard und Marie Luise Gothein* (Cologne, 2006), 547. EG, 49–53, 56, assumes that Gothein exercised a dominant influence on Kantorowicz but offers no specific evidence.

confusion."[57] Still, he was euphoric; he wrote in the same letter: "I'm so happy with this work that I can hardly express it!" He believed that he had developed his own conception of Islam and was pleased and astonished that he had been able to formulate it by himself. In particular he had seen suddenly that there were no "guilds" in Islam—guilds were purely a Western phenomenon conditioned by Catholic Christianity. Seeking to pursue his theory, he rushed to have a discussion with Edgar Salin, an expert on the social thought of Christianity. In June EKa was still wrapped up in his work; in August he wrote of his intention to use the Berlin library; by the end of October he had written a nearly complete draft.[58] The dissertation was finished by Christmas; on January 13 he sent a copy to Fine, and by January 17 he was preparing to submit it to Gothein.[59]

It would have been best had EKa actually found a conscientious scholar to criticize his work. The dissertation was only 104 pages long, and while this length was typical for German dissertations of the day, such dissertations usually were based on original research while this one was not. Almost all of Kantorowicz's references were to secondary sources written in German or French; on the rare occasions when he drew on primary sources, he cited them from German or French translations. A reader might have suspected that he knew no Arabic were it not for the presence of a few Arabic terms hand-penciled in Arabic script. (In 1922 he did confess that his knowledge of the Arabic language, and especially of Arabic sources, was limited.[60]) Equally troubling was his uncritical use of secondary sources; the dissertation lacks an introduction treating the state of scholarship, draws frequently on dated surveys, and never questions veracity by challenging any given author by means of reference to another. Instead its method resembles that of a bird taking twigs and bits of string from wherever they might be found in order to build a nest.

The dissertation's goal, never stated, can be inferred from its title: "The Nature of Muslim Artisan Associations."[61] Perhaps influenced by Gundolf on Goethe, Kantorowicz sought the essence of an institution without reference to change over time. Nor did he even note differences according to region: the dissertation adduces examples from Arabic and Turkish realms indiscriminately. The primary mode of analysis is to contrast "Oriental" with "Western": Islam vs. Christianity. Islam lacked the respect for labor found in the medieval West; it tolerated labor because it kept the laborer from poverty, but for

[57] StGA, Kahler papers, III:6515.

[58] Ibid., 6523, 6525, 6529.

[59] Ibid., 6537, 6540, 6541.

[60] Letter to Carl Heinrich Becker, 16 September 1922, cited in Cymorek, "Momentaufnahmen eines Mythos," 74, n. 30.

[61] *Das Wesen der muslimischen Handwerkerverbände*: LBI, box 3, folder 9. Passages quoted in the present paragraph: pp. 21, 15, 81–82. Kantorowicz's own summary of the contents of his dissertation, included in the yearbook of the Heidelberg Philosophical Faculty for 1921–22, is reproduced in EG, 54–55.

Muslims "speed is the work of the devil and delay the work of God." Kantorowicz's central proposition was that Islam lacked *guilds*. Muslims sought prestige in a concept of nobility and concentrated on religious ceremonies influenced by Sufism; guilds that aimed at certifying technical accomplishments or creating monopolies did not exist. For Kantorowicz Islam valued multiplicity rather than monopoly: "if the West says 'unity brings strength' the Orient says 'multiplicity brings strength.'" The members of artisan associations were indifferent to price fixing, for "it is a known fact that bargaining inheres in the blood of the orientals." In support of that proposition Kantorowicz quoted the words of an imam: "At buying and selling there should be bargaining until sweat runs down the foreheads of both bargainers." The dissertation presents no trends; the only explanation it offers for the disappearance of the institution it treats was the presumed replacement of local artisanal production by Western manufactured goods. All told it was a piece of juvenilia. It was bold in antitheses; powers of imagination and a gift for phrase-making were plainly there. But concern for proof by evidence and the weighing of sources were absent. Nuance was not even a goal. To say that this doctoral dissertation equals a good American undergraduate senior thesis probably would be giving it too much credit.

When EKa was registering for his winter semester courses in November 1920, he wrote to Fine that he "was glad to be finished with Islam for a while."[62] And indeed he soon ceased concerted work in the area. After completing his course in Arabic during that semester he no longer pursued the language and stopped referring to Islam in his correspondence. In the spring he devoted most of his time to preparing for his doctoral oral examination—the *rigorosum*. The membership of his committee is unknown, but economics, still his main field, was the main subject. He passed the exam in June and thereupon received his doctorate. The notation, referring both to the quality of the dissertation and performance in the *rigorosum*, was magna cum laude—short of summa.[63]

After gaining his degree EKa remained enrolled in Heidelberg for the winter semester of 1921–22. We will see later that the Kantorowicz firm, endangered briefly by the Polish takeover of Posen, had recouped its fortunes. Because the firm was being directed with skill by his cousin Franz, EKa now could think of an academic career without hesitation and decided to change his subject. In October 1921 he wrote to Fine that he was thinking of transferring; Berlin and Munich were the only possibilities, but meanwhile he was staying on in Heidelberg for the winter.[64] He now matriculated in the philosophical faculty, evidently intending to gain a second doctorate. All indications are that this was

[62] StGA, Kahler papers, III:6529.

[63] Friedrich Gundolf from Heidelberg, 21 June 1921: Pott, *Gundolf-Kahler Briefwechsel*, 1:259. For a point of comparison, Herbert Grundmann's Leipzig degree of 1926 was a summa.

[64] StGA, Kahler papers, III:6553.

to be in the field of Roman history. He had taken a course on the subject during the previous winter semester, and a reference in a letter to Fine of April 1920 shows that the Roman Empire was on his mind.[65] Soon after he submitted his dissertation he wrote to Fine that he was excited about starting a new project concerning ancient religion: "late antique cults, Roman tombs, inscriptions."[66] So far as is known nothing came of that, but in the winter of 1921–22 he took a course in ancient history that was perhaps more important for his intellectual development than any other.

This was a seminar given by Heidelberg's ancient historian, Alfred von Domaszewski who then was one of the most prestigious men in his field. Domaszewski, much unlike Eberhard Gothein, was a dedicated specialist. His areas were Roman military history, Roman religion, and the careers of the Roman emperors.[67] He lived apart from Heidelberg's intellectual world and did not play to crowds. As a result of malnutrition during the "starvation winter" of the First World War, he was suffering from bone degeneration that made him lame. But when he spoke about Roman warfare it seemed that he was in the midst of a camp on the Roman frontiers. He had studied with the great Theodor Mommsen, who had called him *perspicax et strenuus et peritus* (sharp-sighted and vigorous and expert). Johannes Haller, a well-informed contemporary, considered him to have been Mommsen's best student. As an exemplary professional he inherited Mommsen's commitment to epigraphy (the study of inscriptions), and this was just one manifestation of attention to detail for the goal of obtaining the larger picture.

Domaszewski's seminar, given in his home, was on Alexander the Great. Along with EKa the other seminar members were Edgar Salin, a man of wide-ranging interests; Josef Liegle, a George disciple and friend of EKa's who was preparing for a degree in classical philology; and EKa's closest friend, Woldemar Uxkull. We will hear much more about the last named in succeeding chapters; here it suffices to say that he had opted to work in Roman history and had just gained Domaszewski's willingness to be his doctoral supervisor.[68] In a memoir about EKa written after his death, Salin described the seminar.[69] Ernst Kantorowicz was the star. After the other members began speaking on report topics chosen from a list, Domaszewski usually interrupted them by interjecting details about inscriptions and bibliography. Then he discoursed on battles from the tactical and strategic points of view, becoming so engaged in what he was saying that it seemed as if he were a commander telling of his own

[65] Ibid., 6515; EG, 48, with n. 101.

[66] Monday [14 February] 1921: StGA, Kahler papers, III:6547.

[67] I rely on EG, 46–47; Curtius, *Deutsche und Antike Welt*, 369–70; and Johannes Haller, *Lebenserinnerungen* (Stuttgart, 1960), 119–20.

[68] EKa to Fine, 31 October 1921 (StGA, Kahler papers, III:6553). "Uxkull, der übermorgen zu Domaszewski hinzieht u. das Semester hier bleibt."

[69] [Edgar Salin], *Ernst Kantorowicz 1895–1963* (private printing, 1963; Lerner archive), 3.

plans, decisions, and successes. But Domaszewski did not interrupt Kantorowicz when he gave his report. EKa treated "the divine honors of Alexander" and held the professor riveted. Afterward Domaszewski showered praise. Salin later asked him whether he finally had found his long-sought successor. "No," came the answer, "this young man is not suitable for ancient history, for most of it would be too sober for him; after all there was only one Alexander. He should work on material that links the Orient and the Occident." Supposedly EKa himself asked Domaszewski whether he had a particular subject for him in mind, and Domaszewski replied, "Maybe Byzance. Or write a history of the Jews—there isn't a good one yet since at present they're all either philo-Semitic or anti-Semitic. You can unite salvational history and world history."

In a revised version of his memoir Salin added another detail. According to him, after Domaszewski heard EKa's paper on the divine honors of Alexander he told him that he should have paid attention to ceremonial acclamations—extremely important throughout Roman antiquity and the Middle Ages.[70] Since Salin connected this with the composition of EKa's second book, *Laudes Regiae*, which dealt entirely with acclamations, one must wonder whether he may have been projecting backward. Nevertheless, acclamations play a signal role in Kantorowicz's biography of Frederick II, written not long after the Domaszewski seminar.[71] The remark about working on material that links East and West might also seem slightly suspicious since that later was one of Kantorowicz's major concerns, but it is tempered with the advice about working on a history of the Jews, a subject that Salin would have known was shunned by EKa. At any rate it is difficult to believe that Salin invented the seminar topic of "the divine honors of Alexander." Taking that as true is almost eerie, for not only was deification of rulers to become one of Ernst Kantorowicz's major themes, but he referred specifically to the deification of Alexander in two of his important articles.[72]

Above all one must note Domaszewski's methodical training. Here was a professor who taught one to be critical and to be alert to all the relevant sources. Domaszewski was EKa's only teacher in the field of history, and the training he offered comes as a bridge between EKa's student career in Heidelberg and his career as one of the most noted historians of the Weimar era.

[70] Edgar Salin, "Ernst H. Kantorowicz. 1896–1963," *Historische Zeitschrift* 199 (1964): 551–57, at 554.

[71] KFII, 186.

[72] "Gods in Uniform" and "The Quinity of Winchester," in Ernst H. Kantorowicz, *Selected Studies* (Locust Valley, NY, 1965), 10, 114.

CHAPTER 5

St. George

THE ENTRANCE OF STEFAN GEORGE (1868–1933) has been delayed in this book, but let him now enter with a flourish. In the spring of 1919 an eyewitness in Heidelberg reported:

> A university professor [Gundolf] was giving a lecture on Goethe before an audience of students, many of whom were still in their field-gray uniforms. The hall was full. The lecturer delayed. He was looking at the door as if he were expecting someone. And indeed, while the impatient were beginning to shuffle, the door opened and in came a man with white hair and a countenance that seemed of another time. The power of his appearance and the purity that surrounded him was so gripping for the young people from the trenches that silence reigned. Then most rose and honored with solemn emotion the poet STEFAN GEORGE.[1]

If that does not suffice, here is Edgar Salin's account of the first time he viewed the poet on Heidelberg's main thoroughfare:

> The viewer stood numb, spellbound. A breath from a higher world grazed him. He no longer knew what had happened. He hardly knew where he was. Was this a human who stepped through the crowd? But he was different from all the nearby humans because of an indefinable grandeur and effortless force such that all the pedestrians next to him seemed like pale masks, soulless shadows. Was it a god who divided the bustling crowd and hastened with lightness of foot to the other shore? But he was wearing the clothing of humans. . . . And then it dawned: if a human, then it was Stefan George.[2]

Americans of a certain generation might recall "It's superman!!" But the quoted authors were deadly serious. Berthold von Stauffenberg, who was executed in 1944 with his brother Claus for attempting to assassinate Hitler, wrote without irony that Stefan George had "been sent as the savior of this world."[3]

[1] Theodor Dschenfzig, *Stefan George und die Jugend*, 2nd ed. (Munich, 1935), 23.

[2] Salin, *Um Stefan George*, 11–12.

[3] Norton, *Secret Germany*, 657.

Kurt Singer, by profession an economist, wrote in memory of the poet, "You were to us more than savior . . . under the lightning of your eagle's glance, death became life."[4]

Stefan George (pronounced "gay-ohr′-guh") (fig. 12) was one of Germany's dominant cultural figures in the first third of the twentieth century. Some critics rank his poetry next to that of his contemporary Rainer Maria Rilke; others disagree. Either way large numbers of Germans by the time of the Great War had come to look on him not only as poet but as prophet. The earlier George had fallen under the influence of Mallarmé to become the country's first and most important Symbolist poet. German poetry was in need of a jolt. Since the days of Hölderlin and Heine the country had lacked a poet of distinction; second-rate versifiers drew on a tired neoclassicism that had lost power to inspire; a few others wished to apply naturalism to poetry, a rather unpromising assignment. Hence Symbolism, an innovative style marked by lushness and compressed obscurity, replete with novel coinages and archaisms, offered a shimmering and captivating alternative to prevailing norms.

The Symbolist George believed in art for art's sake and wrote poetry that aimed to transport his readers into a realm of beauty suffused by the scent of musk. To heighten the effect he assumed the role of messenger from another world. The description of a reading he gave in 1897 in a private home in Berlin conveys the atmosphere. When the guests arrived, some twenty of them, they were led into a darkened living room illuminated only by one lamp veiled in red. An adjoining room, adorned with flowers and laurel branches, was kept clear, "because that is where the poet will be." And suddenly the poet emerged like an apparition, his face illuminated by two bright lamps. Although George then was only twenty-nine, his gaunt visage made him seem timeless. A guest recalled that he seemed to be "part Liszt, part Dante—but more Dante since he seemed to have returned from the Inferno."[5]

George read his lush esoteric poems from a music stand to a gathering that remained hushed and enthralled, as if at a séance. He recited in a strange, chant-like monotone entirely unlike the contemporary style of declamatory reading. Comprehension was difficult because he eschewed aural punctuation, omitting emphases even on endings in order to make it appear as if his poems were a litany drawn from the void. "Pindar," it was said, "might have recited like that."[6]

The aesthetic stance entailed rejection of bourgeois culture, and as time passed George evolved from fin de siècle aesthete to cultural critic. A volume, *The Seventh Ring*, published in 1907, included a poem, "City-Square," that

[4] Schönhärl, *Wissen und Visionen*, 2.

[5] Sabine Lepsius, *Ein Berliner Künstlerleben um die Jahrhundertwende: Erinnerungen* (Munich, 1972), 171; Marie von Bunsen, *Die Welt in der ich lebte* (Leipzig, 1929), 153.

[6] Edith Landmann, *Gespräche mit Stefan George* (Düsseldorf, 1963), 11; Kurt Breysig, *Stefan George: Gespräche, Dokumente* (Amsterdam, 1960), 9.

Figure 12. Stefan George cameo. (Stefan George Archiv, Stuttgart)

alluded to Berlin's hub, the Potsdamer Platz, and excoriated the racing after the idol of cash or "tinsel." Full of sadness—"my people I weep"—the poet foresees that crass materialism would be atoned for by "poverty, trouble, and disgrace."[7] An equally searing poem in the same volume is "The Antichrist." Here the title figure laughs at how he catches the credulous in his nets. His miracles are false but only by a "hair's breadth"; they suffice to make his thralls believe that he is conjuring gold and wine even though the gold is clay and the wine is juice.[8] Set against this is George's vision of himself as educator. He teaches "first on meager soil," but through his tutelage the chosen few ultimately will "dance naked on heather."[9]

What George was saying in difficult poetry his spokesman Friedrich Gundolf proclaimed outright. Gundolf actually had been born "Gundelfinger," but since George did not approve of that unattractive name the bearer changed it to "Gundolf," thereby prompting a wit to remark that he was like the Minnesinger who cut off his finger to honor his beloved.[10] Gundolf had become transported by George's poetry at a young age. In 1899, the first year he came to know George personally (he was eighteen), he already addressed him as "Meister" (master) and expressed his "veneration."[11] In 1910 he emerged as publicist. In an article

[7]GA, 6/7, 207. For commentary, Ernst Morwitz, *Kommentar zu dem Werk Stefan Georges* (Düsseldorf, 1960), 332.

[8]GA, 6/7, 57; Morwitz, *Kommentar*, 248.

[9]GA, 6/7, 54; Morwitz, *Kommentar*, 246–47.

[10]Hermann Glockner, *Heidelberger Bilderbuch: Erinnerungen* (Bonn, 1969), 24.

[11]Boehringer and Landmann, *Stefan George*, 28–29.

that bore the title "Allegiance and Discipleship" (*Gefolgschaft und Jüngertum*), he called for subservience to a führer who must be regarded as more than merely human: "The pride of the disciples is that the master is unique . . . they must absorb into their being his blood and his breath, his light and his warmth, his music and his motion, and pass them on into the frozen or empty world."[12] Gundolf specified the identity of the führer in a second essay, "George's Image." Here he wrote: "George sings of an emerging day for humanity that is already reality for him, although for us still a challenge or a longing. . . . No one has taken up the battle more decisively against today's superficial tendencies and the merely temporal than Stefan George. . . . He is the leader in a no longer avoidable war of the spirit. . . . Stefan George is the most important man in Germany today."[13]

George's collection of poems published in 1913, *The Star of the Covenant*, featured lines wherein the poet was obsessed with the need for "cleansing":

> Speak not to me of the Highest Good
> Before you are punished
> You make it base the way you think and are.
>
> Ten thousand must be struck by holy madness
> Ten thousand must be carried off by the holy pestilence
> Ten thousands by the holy war.[14]

But there would be a saving remnant—those of the "covenant" (*Bund*). These will "spit the rotten from their mouths"; they will know each other "from the true ardor of their eyes"; their *Bund* is a "bond of ore."[15]

Who would not want to think himself one of the *Bund*? When the Great War broke out many soldiers took *The Star of the Covenant* with them into battle. In October 1914 Paul Wittek, a young Austrian, fell wounded: "he still saw that the sky was blue and recited George's latest poems to himself, one by one, until he lost consciousness."[16] Edgar Salin had two extra pockets sewn into his military uniform, one for a volume of Hölderlin, the other for *The Star of the Covenant*.[17] A Swiss observer wrote at the end of 1914 that *The Star of the Covenant* had been written as "a mystery play before the dark solemn night of these times" and hence was a "national German event."[18] Marie Luise Gothein, who lost a son in 1914, later wrote that *The Star of the Covenant* and a subsequent poem by George "were *the* works which throughout the war gave consolation

[12] Norton, *Secret Germany*, 409–10.

[13] Gundolf, "Das Bild Georges," *Jahrbuch für die geistige Bewegung* 1 (1910): 19–48, at 21.

[14] GA, 8, 31, 33.

[15] GA, 8, 93.

[16] Fine von Kahler to Gundolf: Pott, *Gundolf-Kahler, Briefwechsel*, 2:385.

[17] Salin, *Um Stefan George*, 28.

[18] Norton, *Secret Germany*, 526–27.

to herself and her husband, and allowed them to gain meaning from the terrible things that had happened."[19] George rightly observed at the end of the war that German soldiers had carried his book of 1913 as if it were a "war breviary" but warned that the war of his poetry was not the war that had just been fought.[20]

Frau Gothein added a crucially important point. In 1919 her husband had spoken with the poet and was startled to learn that he was not pessimistic in what then seemed Germany's darkest hour because he had great faith in the youth; she herself found it consoling that after all the loss of life the poet had "a wonderful certainty that a new youth would grow up around himself."[21] Indeed, in 1919 George published the following lines:

> If ever this volk awakens from cowardly sleep
> And remembers itself, its election, its calling
> Then will be revealed to it the divine understanding
> Of unspeakable horrors [. . .]
> Then the royal standard with true emblem flutters in the early wind
> And is greeted, bowing, by the Sublime Ones, the Heroes.[22]

George shunned conventional self-promotion: he never accepted invitations to speak in public and never wrote for newspapers or magazines. Aside from his poetry (the production of which declined sharply in the 1920s), his strategy for gaining influence was to gather around him clusters of carefully selected young men. Trespassers were prosecuted. By means of his teaching and "drilling," these would partake of his wisdom and become vehicles for the arduous but inevitable triumph of a wonderfully transformed Germany. The term most often used for his disciples is the "George circle" (*George-Kreis*). The poet was not averse to it, and the disciples used it themselves: Ernst Kantorowicz once referred to someone as being "encircled" (*angekreist*)[23] Although the term will be retained for convenience, it should be noted that it is not entirely accurate because George preferred to keep groups of his disciples in separate locations. Rootless himself, he made circuits like a traveling medieval ruler, holding court with clusters of the chosen in the locations he favored. As one of his most prominent associates later wrote, "George was always proud of never having a permanent home, of not depending on worldly possessions, and of leading a wandering life with only one aim: the search for men to share his views and his form of being."[24] The "Meister" was always at the center, but his "circle" could be thought of as an Alexander Calder mobile with varying numbers of disciples

[19] Marie Luise Gothein, *Eberhard Gothein: Ein Lebensbild* (Stuttgart, 1931), 205.

[20] Salin, *Um Stefan George*, 28.

[21] Gothein, *Eberhard Gothein*, 206.

[22] GA, 9, 114.

[23] EG, 69.

[24] Ernst Morwitz, *Stefan George: Poems Rendered into English by Carol North Valhope and Ernst Morwitz* (New York, 1967), 16.

revolving in clusters at different proximities and heights. After the war George's favored locations were Berlin, Marburg, and Heidelberg; in all three he had senior lieutenants who were favorably placed to help recruit handsome and elite "youths" for the mobile.

A gathering of disciples took place in Heidelberg on Pentecost weekend of June 1919 in a villa George was sharing with Gundolf near Heidelberg's romantic ruined castle.[25] Pentecost was when the Holy Spirit descended on the apostles and George may have had that in mind, but the model was the Platonic Symposium. George "drilled" his ideals by means of dialogue, and everyone took turns reading his poetry in the required mode of delivery. Percy Gothein, whose parents were so elated about George's faith in the German youth, was one of the number. Although Percy was twenty-three, George called him "child." He was extremely handsome and so was Erich Boehringer, another young man in the group, then twenty-two. Since George took beauty to be the expression of spiritual excellence, he chose these two to stand naked before the others as models for a sculptor.[26] Gothein recalled: "We disrobed quickly. It was not easy to stand next to Boehringer without covering and to hold one's ground with him. . . . The swelling of the slender hip began well above the flank, and as he placed his arm around my shoulder and his hair flowed beyond his neck to his back, everyone was full of awed admiration."[27]

There is no record that Ernst Kantorowicz ever stood naked as a model before Stefan George. Nor did his close relationship with George begin in the customary way of being brought to the poet by a senior lieutenant. Uncertainty has previously reigned about the route by which he came to George's attention. Some speculated that his cousin Gertrud Kantorowicz, a friend of George's before the war, was an intermediary; others thought of Arthur and Soscha Salz. But neither of these alternatives is correct, for EKa's correspondence with Fine von Kahler tells the story.[28] The initial point of contact was the Pension Friedau—"the Beznerei." After EKa had been there for two semesters, new boarders moved in—Woldemar Uxkull, a young aristocrat who had been at the Heidelberg Pentecost gathering, and Stefan George. Although George's normal

[25] Karlauf, *Stefan George*, 479–90.

[26] On "the beautiful body" as a Georgian ideal, Groppe, *Die Macht der Bildung*, 415.

[27] Karlauf, *Stefan George*, 488.

[28] Berthold Vallentin, *Gespräche mit Stefan George, 1902–1931* (Amsterdam, 1961), 53, contains a mistake that has contaminated the secondary literature. Supposedly "Friedrich Wolters and Ernst Kantorowicz" visited George at a spa in Hesse between 31 July and 2 August 1920, making it seem as if EKa already was in the inner circle. But Frau Ute Oelman of the Stefan George-Archiv informs me that two typescripts of the Vallentin diaries, both made by Vallentin's son, contain the reading "Wolters and Captain Elze are visiting here." Aside from the fact that Wolters and Kantorowicz did not know each other in 1920, whereas Wolters and Elze did, the printed version is surely mistaken because of the evidence in EKa's letters to Fine that date his first encounters with George to November.

practice was to avoid living anywhere for more than a few weeks, there were special circumstances. He had been suffering from urinary tract infections that caused painful bladder stones and damage to his kidneys. In June 1920 his afflictions had led him to undergo an operation in a Heidelberg clinic; then, after recuperation at a spa during the summer, he returned to Heidelberg to be near his physician, and the dependency was such that he stayed at the Beznerei for sixth months, from September 1920 until February 1921.

George told Edgar Salin that so long as he was in Heidelberg he looked forward to being near his "youngest friends" so that he could have the opportunity to "further" them.[29] He was thinking of Percy Gothein and Woldemar Uxkull, but soon he was "furthering" Ernst Kantorowicz. George took two rooms in the Beznerei from which he could look out on two streets (the house was on a corner); Uxkull and Kantorowicz lived on either side.[30] The poet removed the pictures on his walls because he demanded "the purest simplicity."[31] Although he was fifty-two, the stress of his operation had made him look older—"an aged visionary."[32] One of the most decisive days in the life of Ernst Kantorowicz was November 6, 1920, when George came into his room for a visit. As he wrote to Fine that evening, George had been there before, but the two had merely exchanged commonplaces. Now, however, George unexpectedly engaged him in serious conversation. EKa wrote with unfeigned amazement that the impetus had come from the poet. First they talked of comparative linguistics, then they entered into a discussion—"a really great discussion"—about Zionism.[33] EKa could not bridle his excitement: "It was all so wonderful—more than I have ever experienced." He explained to Fine that the discussions were intense without being heated. George was able to convince "without using formulas and forcing them, as is so often the case with Gundolf. . . . He never offered a rational or metaphysical 'proof' but only the plainest exposition of reality. . . . The outcome was an incredible comfort. One could suddenly see what was right without straining for it but thinking one had seen it long before." From that moment on, Ernst Kantorowicz was an acolyte.

A letter to Fine of two days later is particularly vivid:

> George asked me yesterday whether I could prepare tea. He wanted to try a new variety and came to me after the evening meal; today it was the same again. Goodness! What can I say about these two meetings? It was perhaps less about what we discussed, although that in itself was wonderful! Yesterday we talked about

[29] Salin, *Um Stefan George*, 52.

[30] Sobotka, *Ways & Issues Retraced*, 120–21, describes the layout; also Salin, *Um Stefan George*, 31–32.

[31] Salin, *Um Stefan George*, 32.

[32] Ibid., 46.

[33] StGA, Kahler papers, III:6530.

languages and Islam! Regarding the latter he completely shared my views, which of course was extremely important to me. Today it was geography, prehistory, and creation myths, all matters that lie close to my heart. Each evening was a whole, was so completely "without edges," if one can say that, and in no way scattered; so fully coherent and harmonious in the noblest sense of the word. The manner of giving—tea, cake, or whatever—turns the most simple offering into a treasure, and the giving as well as the taking—for example an offered cigarette—somehow becomes most obviously a consecrated, almost holy act, purely through the wonderful way it happens—through the art of *being able* to give and receive. It is all so difficult to describe, my love, and it might sound exaggerated. But you yourself know best that it's not an exaggeration. It's remarkable that given all my veneration, and indeed real fear, I felt free to speak, and absolutely without inhibition, as I perhaps never have before. It was as if everything that I wanted to say immediately came to me, and things fitted together as I never had realized before.[34]

The reader well may be wondering whether George harbored sexual designs on the awestruck twenty-five-year-old who lived next to him. The answer is certainly not. George's poetry contained many lines of startlingly explicit homosexual eroticism. In one, "Conception," he wrote, "take and consecrate me as a vessel!/fill me: I lie and listen."[35] (The voice is that of a passive recipient of a "storm that overpowers.") But it is mistaken to affix George's poetry to George's practice with his disciples. There is plentiful evidence that many or perhaps most of his disciples had affairs with one another, and some went looking for handsome boys to introduce to the Meister so that he could "educate" them.[36] In 1920 two of them visited the elite Odenwald boarding school for "inspection" purposes, and in the same year Woldemar Uxkull did the same in the streets of Heidelberg.[37] But for George such disciples were cruising in behalf of a noble cause, that of extending his society, and he preferred not to think that any lustfulness was involved. Whatever George might have practiced in an undisclosed world of his own, he adhered strictly to the principle of high-minded relationships between educator and protégés on what he understood to be the basis taught by Plato. As Socrates resisted carnal relations with Alcibiades, so George had no intention of succumbing to the charms of, say, Ernst Kantorowicz.

[34] Ibid., 6531.

[35] GA, 6.7, 146.

[36] Groppe, *Die Macht der Bildung*, 418–32.

[37] Uxkull to Percy Gothein, 9 September 1920: "Beide Ernste [Ernst Morwitz and Ernst Gundolf] kamen an, von einer Inspektion der Süssenschaften in der Odenwald-Schule. Funde hatten sie keine gemacht. . . . Nun muss ich aber schliessen, da ich d. M. der sich noch einmal umgelegt hat wecken mussen und mich selbst zum Inspektionsgang für die Heidelberger S-schaft rüsten muss." StGA, Gothein papers, III:3104. (I am indebted to a transcription made by Eckhart Grünewald.)

To return to the Beznerei, EKa's descriptions to Fine of his meetings continued. Three days after the one just quoted he wrote, "The coming-to-me-for-tea has now become a set program."[38] On November 20 he reported not only that George came frequently into his room but that he was frequently in George's—an extraordinary privilege. The meetings had taken a new turn, for now George was "lecturing": "He has a wonderful way of sensing how far someone is coming along and how far what he says is appropriate for the listener."[39] George lavished so much attention on his young admirer that he reviewed his dissertation with him "chapter by chapter."[40]

In January the poet broached a new topic: "why girls (*Mädchen*) are kept at a distance from the Circle." The reader of EKa's letters to Fine is tantalized but left hanging.[41] As if in compensation, however, EKa reported in almost novelistic detail a meeting of two weeks later:

> D.M. [the Meister] came yesterday in the late afternoon into my room. The light was not on and I was lying on the sofa. Ach, you can imagine my condition. He noticed this immediately and pressed me to tell him all. I was evasive, despite your permission, and only after the evening meal (the others were sitting downstairs with carnival pastries), when D.M. asked me again and again, and seemed to suspect something "unlawful." I told him in two words that you were *the woman* who had carried me away, etc., and that now, suddenly, it's not going well. "Ja, Ja, Fine," he said, "no man has it easy with her. Her demands etc. And then she sets things a bit in order because she can see incredibly clearly. She and Gundolf constantly talk past each other. But she will think it all over." Ach, he is wonderful. . . . And yesterday evening he came here again for reading . . . and asked whether "the hermit"—me—noticed a visitor. Ach ja, it is all so splendid and I can't possibly imagine after these four month how it will be without the Meister.[42]

The last recorded conversation from this period comes from a letter to Fine of February 12, 1921, shortly before George's departure:

> I had a *very* long, entirely principled talk with the Meister about you and me in the course of a long walk while we passed your red house on the Neckar. He asked me how things were going and I told him "well" and that in the last analysis I had good reason to say that. And then I asked him whether he disapproved of our relationship, especially because of your position, for you of course are married, etc. To which he responded: no, because this relationship has deep meaning for both parties. He then spoke generally of the danger that lay in a relationship with

[38] StGA, Kahler papers, III:6532.
[39] Ibid., 6534.
[40] 25 December 1920, ibid., 6536.
[41] 21 January 1921, ibid., 6542.
[42] 9 February 1921, ibid., 6545.

> an older woman: 1.) that she would take the one concerned solely to be a toy for a season; 2.) that the young man, God knows, possibly might flatter himself that he has found grace from a "baroness or sultana" and thus no longer find it fitting that the Meister occasionally trims him into shape. "But with Fine that does not come into consideration since she doesn't support any megalomania." And then, after much talk in general: "You are lucky and are less in danger than others with their appendages [*Anhängseln*]. You are very well taken care of there, for Fine is a smart woman with an entirely solid position and won't work against you." It is all very much seen from the point of view of the "state," which is entirely explicable.[43]

This letter is worthy of comment for two reasons. First, it shows that George laid down no laws against his young men having relationships with women. What they did in their private lives was their own affair; so long as it did not interfere with their subordination to him he had no trouble with "appendages." It is true that at that very time he was raging against Gundolf's passionate love for a woman, Elli Salomon, he wanted to marry. But not only did George hold Elli in utter contempt—he thought her an unworthy tramp—but he feared that she, as a "Kundry," would try to lead Gundolf away from the fellowship of the grail.[44] On the other hand, he knew that Fine revered him and was confident that she presented no threat. Second, EKa's reference to the "state" is telling. Starting around this time, George and his followers spoke of their "state," meaning those who represented Germany's millennial future and who never wavered in their obedience to their leader. Not every aspirant could gain admission, but EKa now knew that he had.

To say that he had come under Stefan George's thrall seems the right expression. Just as Gundolf had "cut off his finger" for the Meister, so Kantorowicz changed his handwriting (fig. 13), which surely must have taken great powers of will. Earlier George had developed a new form of script—"George-Schrift"—as part of his determination to alter accustomed ways and impose his personality. EKa conformed. In the winter and spring of 1921 he switched to making his "E's" according to the George formula: previously they had been looped at the top, now they were formed by a semicircle with a horizontal line coming out from the middle. Similarly he altered his majuscule and minuscule "t's." Anyone viewing the handwriting "before and after" would wonder whether they were written by the same person. He also conformed to the Meister's prescribed way of making ellipses. The whole world used three dots, but George preferred two, and sure enough EKa became a two-dot man . .

[43] 12 February 1921, ibid., 6546. Most of this letter is reproduced in Picht, "Verliebt–verglaubt–verhofft," 213–31, at 227.

[44] EKa later played up to George's hostility toward the woman Gundolf by then had married against George's will by calling her a "whore" and a "piece of dirt": Kantorowicz to Stefan George, 2 December 1931: StGA, Kantorowicz papers, I.

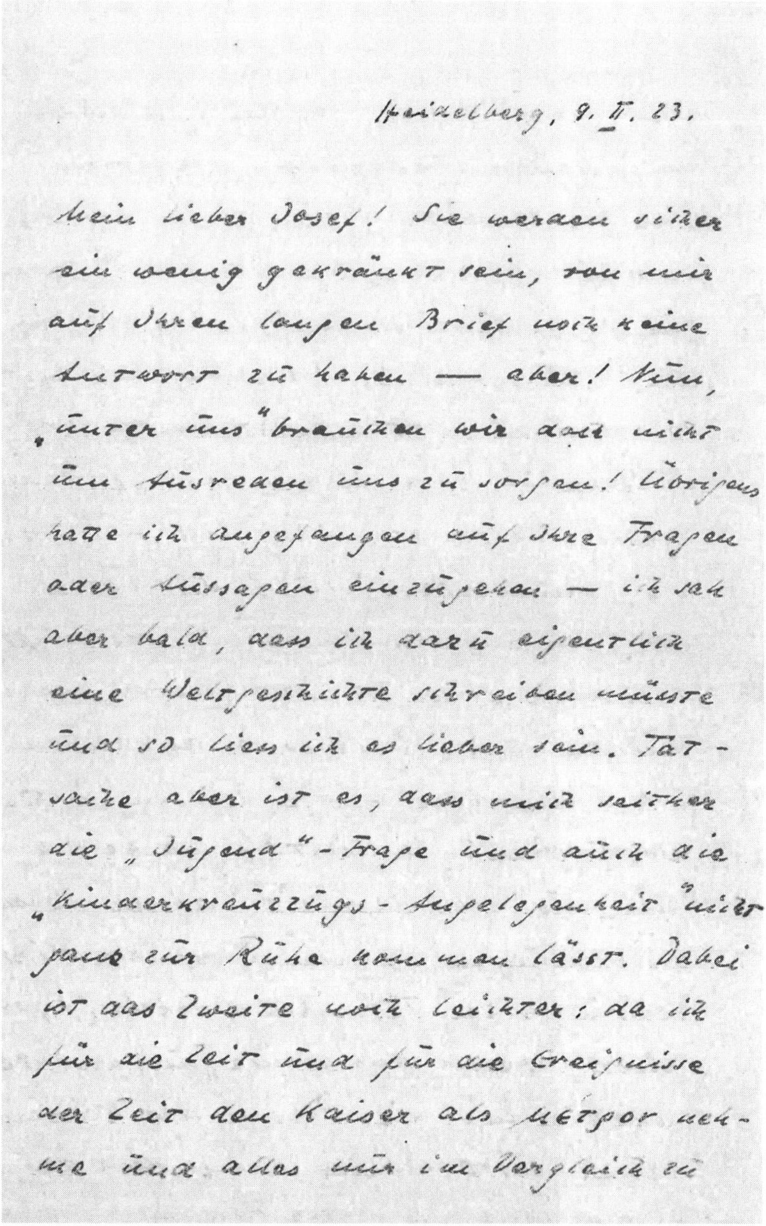

Heidelberg, 9. II. 23.

Mein lieber Josef! Sie werden sicher
ein wenig gekränkt sein, von mir
auf Ihren langen Brief noch keine
Antwort zu haben — aber! Nun,
„unter uns" brauchen wir doch nicht
um Ausreden uns zu sorgen! Übrigens
hatte ich angefangen auf Ihre Fragen
oder Aussagen einzugehen — ich sah
aber bald, dass ich dazu eigentlich
eine Weltgeschichte schreiben müsste
und so liess ich es lieber sein. Tat-
sache aber ist es, dass mich seither
die „Jugend"-Frage und auch die
„Kinderkreuzzugs-Angelegenheit" nicht
ganz zur Ruhe kommen lässt. Dabei
ist das Zweite noch leichter: da ich
für die Zeit und für die Ereignisse
der Zeit den Kaiser als μέτρον neh-
me und alles nur im Vergleich zu

Figure 13. Ernst Kantorowicz's handwriting specimen, letter of February 9, 1923. Kantorowicz's "t's" (as line 4: "Antwort") are made according to Stefan George's prescriptions. (Courtesy Frau Martha Rohde-Liegle)

Perhaps most important, he adopted the correct form of address. When he first wrote to Fine about his meetings with the poet he referred to him as "George," but before the end of the year he switched to "der Meister" and thereafter used that or the abbreviations "D.M." or "d.M." As astonishing as it may seem, when he addressed George directly in writing he customarily employed the honorific in the third person: "During these weeks, there was hardly a day, hardly an hour in which I didn't think of telling about this or that beautiful thing to the Meister."[45] At his boldest Kantorowicz wrote directly: "I believe, Meister."[46] Although we lack transcripts of conversations, he surely used "Meister" in them as well. Indeed the George literature indicates that disciples customarily used not just "Meister" but the third person in conversation: "Would the Meister like to take some tea?"[47]

Ernst Kantorowicz was not a religious personality. He squirmed when duty obliged him to attend religious services and poked fun at religious converts. He was so ironic that he would have been ironic in saying his prayers. Thus when one reads worshipful passages such as those quoted above, one is driven to ask: "Is this a parody?" But it isn't. Kantorowicz's total obeisance to the wishes of Stefan George seems "insanely weird."

How can one explain it? EKa revered his father; his father died in 1919. A year later when EKa conversed with George it was as if he had found a new father. In the United States he placed photos of his father and Stefan George together on his dresser.[48] But are we to say that EKa would not have come to worship Stefan George in 1920 had his father been alive? That seems dubious. In lieu of placing Ernst Kantorowicz on the couch (something he truly would have ridiculed), one can point to three of the most plausible explanatory factors: the poetry, the politics, and the person.

EKa was a fervent admirer of George's poetry; by the time of the meetings of late 1920 he may have known the oeuvre by heart. His decision in April to read Hölderlin's *Hyperion* must have been motivated by his reading of George's poem of the same name. In the letter to Fine describing his first engagement with the poet he evoked lines from a poem of George's that they both knew: "there—without wish or signal—breaks a sheer silver streak through a crevice in the dungeon."[49] Fine herself, as we have seen, was inebriated by the poetry, and enthusiasm for it was not limited to the Gundolf coterie. Germany's renowned turn-of-the century philosopher Georg Simmel compared Stefan

[45] EG, 65.

[46] EG, 68.

[47] Landmann, *Gespräche mit Stefan George*, 7; Werner Vortriede, *Das verlassene Haus* (Munich, [1975]), 296.

[48] Ralph Giesey to C. M. Bowra, 29 September 1963: Bowra papers.

[49] EKa to Fine von Kahler, 6 November 1920: StGA, Kahler papers, III:6530. The poem is "Vorspiel XI" of George's *Teppich des Lebens.*

George to Goethe.[50] Walter Benjamin placed some of George's poems in the realm of epics that come only once every thousand years, allowing "a view into the gold of the mountain."[51] Expressions such as these make it easier to understand how EKa would have felt when Stefan George came into his room and listened his opinions.

Second, one cannot neglect the politics. In the 1920s the poems by George that were on most lips were the later ones—those in which he was invoking a "New Reich." (This was the title of his final collection of poems, published in 1928.) These poems were not explicitly political, but they clearly excoriated the "slumbering" of the present and called for the greatest exertion on the part of an elite to prepare the way for an awakening of Germany to the call of truth and beauty. George was firmly antidemocratic and wrote of a leader who would lead "heroes" under his banner. In conversation he said that the modern world was like a row of zeros: one could add as many zeros as one liked, but no value would ever come until a "one" was placed before them.[52] EKa, having fought for the Reich and then against Poles and "reds," was patriotic and, like most Germans of his day, suffered under a sense of national humiliation as a result of the Versailles Treaty. We will have occasion to see how bitterly he reviled the French occupation of the Rhineland in 1922. George was the prophet of "the secret Germany," and Kantorowicz wanted to be one of its number.

Finally comes George's personal charisma.[53] Overwhelming for many was the sight of the Master's "mighty head." When the painter Reinhold Lepsius was working on a portrait of George he wrote to his wife, "He's becoming more and more head."[54] On reviewing a volume that contained a large number of photographs of George, Friedrich Sieburg wrote that "from these pictures we meet the mightiest head that has ever been carried by a German in human memory."[55] George's head not only was large but seemed "mighty" because of a mane of thick hair, high cheek bones, and sunken eye sockets. The cheek bones seemed Dantesque—indeed George once posed as Dante, complete with laurel wreath and ghost-like white sheet, for a strangely earnest masquerade tableau.[56] As George's eye sockets became ever more sunken with age they recalled Tiresias (fig. 14). In a roman à clef characters are unsure whether the person they see is Stefan George or a man wearing a mask; they think it could be either because

[50] Norton, *Secret Germany*, 214–16.

[51] Karlauf, *Stefan George*, 595.

[52] Friedrich Wolters, *Stefan George und die Blätter für die Kunst* (Berlin, 1930), 116.

[53] For George as a model for Max Weber's invention of the concept of "charisma," Karlauf, *Stefan George*, 410–18; Radkau, *Max Weber*, 394.

[54] Ulrich Raulff, "Im Lapidarium des George-Kreises," in *Das geheime Deutschland: Eine Ausgrabung*, ed. Raulff and Lutz Näfelt (Marbach, 2008), 13.

[55] Ibid., 22.

[56] Robert Boehringer, *Mein Bild von Stefan George: Tafelband* (Düsseldorf, 1967), 90, 91.

Figure 14. Stefan George, 1928, at the age of sixty. (Stefan George Archiv, Stuttgart)

the real George preferred to seem masked in order that ordinary mortals might be left in doubt about whether he was made of flesh and blood.[57]

George enhanced his aura of otherworldliness by appearing and disappearing with little notice, a trick facilitated by his practice of living out of a suitcase. His disciples' letters are sprinkled with the query: "Do you know where the Meister is?" Everyone who visited the Kahlers' villa near Munich signed their names in the guest book but not George. He preferred to leave no traces. No recording of his voice exists. Whoever came into his room by permission found his writing desk bare: "One must work, but only for oneself; one does not exhibit the preparation of the meal or the dirty dishes to the guests."[58] But his presence exerted "a powerful current that transformed all those who came under its influence."[59] Edgar Salin thought he was "living poetry."[60] Kurt Singer

[57] Karlauf, *Stefan George*, 313–14.

[58] Salin, *Um Stefan George*, 32.

[59] Fritz Cronheim, *Deutsch-Englische Wanderschaft. Lebensweg im Zeichen Stefan Georges* (Heidelberg, 1977), 44.

[60] Cited by C. Stephen Jaeger, *Enchantment: On Charisma and the Sublime in the Arts of the West* (Philadelphia, 2012), 277.

said that "his eye was that of the biblical prophets . . . his knowledge and ability rested on the divine ground of then, and now, and tomorrow, and always."[61] When George died in 1933, Gertrud Kantorowicz wrote: "It is like the end of the world; the firm earth shakes; what remains when he does not guide?"[62] An early associate, Henry von Heiseler, compared George to Plato, John the Baptist, St. Paul, Dante, and Meister Eckhart: "He is the voice in the wilderness, he is the messenger of God, he has never in his life been anything else, and with that all is said."[63]

Again one asks, "Is this parody?" But none of these speakers were parodists, and even sober contemporaries distant from veneration knew of the charisma. Arnold Zweig, a socialist who had no sympathy for George's elitist views, wrote that if one saw a man climbing up Heidelberg's castle hill "with eyes, chin, and curve of forehead radiating a magical possession," one would know him to be the living Stefan George.[64] People stood under George's window in the hope that they might gain sight of him when he came to the balcony.[65] Walter Benjamin recalled that when he was in Heidelberg in 1921, "hours were not too long for me to sit, reading on a bench in the castle park, waiting for the moment when [George] might pass by."[66]

Granted, not everyone was caught up in the mystique. Erich Kahler kept his reserve even though his wife and his friend Gundolf were worshippers. Although Kahler knew George personally and even listened to advice from him about whether to marry, he had independent ideas on subjects that were part of George's package and never became a disciple.[67] Erich Rothacker, an instructor in philosophy at Heidelberg in the early 1920s, wrote that he never became a "Georgeaner." Despite his "thirst for beauty and capacity for great enthusiasm," he was "free from any inclination to submit to hierarchy" and found it impossible to attach himself to a "sect" without reservation.[68] Similarly the poet Alexander von Bernus wrote that he remained immune to George: "The blind idolatrous veneration and humbling attendance on the Meister of those devoted to him lay contrary to my entire nature."[69] Walter Ehrlich, a student of literature who was acquainted with EKa, Percy Gothein, and Woldemar Uxkull,

[61] Kurt Singer, "Aus den Erinnerungen an Stefan George," *Das neue Rundschau* 68 (1957): 298–310, at 310.

[62] Lerner, "The Secret Germany of Gertrud Kantorowicz," 69.

[63] Henry von Heiseler, *Stefan George* (Munich 1933), 10.

[64] Karlauf, *Stefan George*, 480.

[65] Michael Buselmeier, *Heidelberg Lesebuch* (Frankfurt, 1986), 141, citing Hermann Glockner, *Heidelberger Bilderbuch*.

[66] Buselmeier, *Heidelberg Lesebuch*, 595.

[67] Kahler to Michael Landmann, 6 January 1963 (DLA, Kahler papers): "Ich bin gewiss niemals ein Jünger im orthodoxen Sinne."

[68] Rothacker, *Heitere Erinnerungen*, 65.

[69] Alexander von Bernus, "Sommergäste auf Stift Neuburg," in Buselmeier, *Heidelberg Lesebuch*, 183.

once was sitting in the anteroom of a pension in Heidelberg (it could have been the Beznerei) and reading *The Star of the Covenant* when two disciples entered and recognized the book. When they asked, "Are you too reading in these holy volumes?," Ehrlich saw from their earnest expressions that they were not joking and thought to himself, "Is this then a new religion? In that case I will separate myself from it."[70]

Max Kommerell was a precociously gifted student of German literature who was taken up by George in 1920 at the age of eighteen. Kommerell became one of the Meister's favorites and remained devoted to him until 1930. But then he decided to make a break. As he wrote in his diary, "The entire way of living rested on a complete surrender of personal identity that can only be fitting and endurable for a youth but never for a man."[71] Kommerell made this decision when he was twenty-eight. EKa was only a little younger when he moved in the opposite direction, and afterward he never made a break.

[70] Walter Ehrlich, *Kulturgeschichtliche Autobiographie* (Tübingen, 1961), 77.
[71] Christian Weber, *Max Kommerell: Eine intellektuelle Biographie* (Berlin, 2011), 59–61.

CHAPTER 6

The Castle Hill

THE MOST MEMORABLE SIGHT IN HEIDELBERG is of the ruined Renaissance castle looming on a hill overlooking the city from a height of three hundred feet. The city had been the principal residence of the princes who ruled the southwestern territory of the Palatinate; in the sixteenth century they had built the grandest castle-palace then known in Germany. But a century later the French king Louis XIV laid claim to the Palatinate, and in 1689 during the War of the Grand Alliance French troops took Heidelberg and destroyed most of the castle. The ruins were left standing and offered a haze of romantic nostalgia for some and a memento of national humiliation for others. In the 1920s when French troops occupied the Rhineland the sense of humiliation predominated. Ernst Kantorowicz dwelled in a villa right above the ruined castle for most of the decade and wrote a book that showed the influence.

Kantorowicz's move to the castle hill ushered in a new phase in his life. He lived there initially with Woldemar von Uxkull, who replaced Fine von Kahler as his amorous attachment, he oriented his personal goals toward pleasing Stefan George, and he began writing his biography of the emperor Frederick II. Late in 1920 he became tired of living in the Pension Friedau, finding that it was too full of bustle. He wrote to Fine that the "trampling [overhead] of Berufeld, junior" (presumably the offspring of a servant) made Uxkull's room impossible for conversation, and another time he wrote that he longed to be alone.[1] But even had Kantorowicz not been thinking of moving, the Meister issued orders that he do so. As EKa wrote to Fine in February, "D.M. demands categorically, actually has led it to be understood *clearly*, that he by no means wishes that either Woldi [Uxkull] or I stay with Bezner for the summer semester."[2] George was leaving Heidelberg for an unstated length of time but would be returning. His custom had been to reside with Gundolf, but by this time he had come to loathe him because of his unswerving devotion to Elli Salomon. Because Gundolf occasionally appeared at the Beznerei, George would have wanted to shun

[1] 20 November 1920; 1 January 1921: StGA, Kahler papers, III:6534, 6538.
[2] 20 February 1921: ibid., 6548.

it, and he would not have wanted his two young protégés to be there either, especially when he might be able to see them in a less public space.

EKa became an apartment hunter and succeeded in finding ideal quarters. These were in the Haus Schlosspark on Wolfsbrunnenweg, above the castle. EKa described his find enthusiastically to Fine: "the upper story of a villa, three rooms, covered veranda, maid's room, kitchen."[3] He and Uxkull were ensconced there by April.[4] A window overlooked the castle park; in May one could breathe the fragrance of flowers.[5] EKa wrote his biography of Frederick II in Haus Schlosspark in a room crowded with books.

George assumed that Kantorowicz and Uxkull would be moving together, for by that time they were a pair. In a letter of January 1921 EKa wrote to Fine that he was learning to cook, for, unbeknownst to Frau Bezner, he and Uxkull were preparing risotto in Uxkull's room.[6] Perhaps they had not yet become lovers—EKa was still sighing over Fine—but certainly they became such after they moved into the house on Wolfsbrunnenweg. Moritz August Woldemar Graf von Uxkull-Gyllenband traced his descent from German Baltic aristocracy back to the thirteenth century. His father, Woldemar Viktor Rudolf Konrad Gustav Graf von Uxkull-Gyllenband, retired captain in the army of the kingdom of Württemberg and honorary knight of the Protestant Order of St. John, belonged to a southwestern German branch of the family. His sister Karoline married Alfred Schenk Graf von Stauffenberg, and her three sons by this marriage all became fervent disciples of Stefan George. (The most famous was Claus, the main architect of the plot to assassinate Hitler in 1944.) Uxkull's mother, Lucy Ahrendfeldt, was a wealthy American heiress of Scandinavian descent, previously married to a German baron.[7] (Her daughter by her first marriage takes a prominent place in our story later on.) "Woldi" came to the attention of Stefan George at an astonishingly early age.[8] In 1906, when he was eight years old and his brother Bernhard was seven, were walking with their governess in the Tiergarten (a park in central Berlin) when one of George's associates, Ernst Morwitz, spotted them. Morwitz was an unmarried student of law (later a judge) who spent his leisure time looking for boys who might

[3] 9 February 1921: ibid., 6545.

[4] Josef Liegle to Elli Salomon, 9 April 1920: "Ernst ist täglich nach Mittag bei mir": Gundolf Archive. (Liegle lived on the same street.)

[5] Boehringer, *Mein Bild von Stefan George*, 169; EKa to Fine, 8 May 1923: StGA, Kahler papers, III:6556.

[6] 4 January 1921: StGA, Kahler papers, III:6539.

[7] Lucy Ahrenfeldt's American birth is unknown to the biographical reference works; I learned of it from her granddaughter, Arianna Giachi: interview of 18 July 1994.

[8] For the following, Groppe, *Die Macht der Bildung*, 441–53; Eckhart Grünewald, "Uxkull-Gyllenband, Moritz August Woldemar Graf von," in *Stefan George und Sein Kreis. Ein Handbuch*, ed. Achim Aurnhammer et al., Band 3 (Berlin, 2012), at 1724–25. The detail of the children walking with their governess in the Tiergarten comes from unpublished papers of Ernst Morwitz as reported to me by Eckhart Grünewald.

please the Meister. Much taken with the children, he followed them to their home. Soon he gained entrance and permission from their mother, Countess Lucy, to see them almost daily in order to "tutor" them. The mother at first was uneasy, but when she learned of Morwitz's connection with the poet George she found the situation flattering. Morwitz then introduced Woldemar and Bernhard to the Meister, who "conversed with them gladly." In an ode of 1913 the poet addressed Woldemar as "longed for little promise" (*ersehnte kömmling*), "born under the song of the waves."[9] Four years later the latter wrote to George, "Through You, Meister, I learned to see."

Three and a half months before the end of World War I, Bernhard Uxkull committed suicide; he had attempted to desert from the army together with another young man, was caught, and chose to kill himself rather than face court martial.[10] George felt "as if both of his legs had been shot off." He wrote a poem in Bernhard's memory, "Du schlank und rein wie eine flamme," that sighed for a young man who was "slender," "pure," "tender," and from "noble race."[11] The reverence put some burden on Woldemar, and he could hardly carry it. He was one of the young men who had attended the Pentecost gathering of 1919 in Heidelberg, but because he was not physically attractive the Meister paid him little attention.[12]

Most likely EKa did not know Uxkull (fig. 15), who was three years younger, before the latter moved into the Beznerei in the fall of 1920.[13] Whatever the case, by the late fall or winter of 1921 they were a couple. EKa later wrote of how they were continually carrying around and exchanging outlines of their projects; how they were "inseparable."[14] To some degree his friendship with the young aristocrat seems unaccountable. Uxkull was rather ugly. His skin was pale and he had glassy eyes that gave him a fish-like appearance. He was tall but height for him was not an advantage: he was gangling and "every time one met him he seemed taller and more awkward."[15] The Meister now took to mocking

[9] GA, 9, 22; Morwitz, *Kommentar*, 414–17.

[10] Karlauf, *Stefan George*, 473–79.

[11] GA 9, 28; Morwitz, *Kommentar*, 483.

[12] Karlauf, *Stefan George*, 485.

[13] Uxkull's niece, Arianna Giachi, told me in interviews of 1993 and 1994 that EKa first saw Uxkull in a student dining hall (*Mensa*) and, noticing his "aristocratic hands," decided to befriend him. But it is difficult to know what to make of this, since it is difficult to place the two together in any *Mensa*. EKa did notice hands: see his letter to Stefan George, cited by Groppe, *Die Macht der Bildung*, 429, which refers to a winning young man "mit schönen händen und gelenken." But photos of Uxkull that show his hands do not reveal them to be particularly noteworthy.

[14] Kantorowicz to Edgar Salin, 22 October 1939, in Lerner, "Letters by Ernst Kantorowicz Concerning Uxkull and George," 168. Kantorowicz to Vera Peters, 16 April 1956: Lerner archive.

[15] Two independent verbal portraits by contemporaries correspond in their details: Ludwig Thormaehlen, *Erinnerungen an Stefan George* (Hamburg, 1962), 182; [Salin], *Ernst Kantorowicz*, 2–3. It is true that Thormaehlen and Salin both disliked Uxkull. Gerhart B. Ladner, *Erinnerungen* (Vienna, 1994), 33, calls attention to the height more positively: "tall like a Viking."

him. George called Uxkull "the princely one" and "the princely greyhound."[16] Uxkull was probably a "greyhound" because he was wealthy enough to own a sports car and liked to drive at fast speeds. The Meister said: "The only love affair that the princely one has is with his automobile—he even caresses it."[17] In the winter of 1921 George left the Pension Friedau to reside for a few days in the Villa Lobstein, located toward the top of the castle hill. (Gundolf had been living there but was temporarily away.) EKa accompanied him but the ascent was steep and George became dizzy, holding on to him for support. After they reached their destination, EKa was extremely worried and asked George whether he and Uxkull should stay with him there to make sure everything would be alright. But the Meister dismissed this by saying Uxkull would be of no help.[18] Uxkull's doctoral supervisor, Domaszewski, was like-minded: "Don't bother me with your Count," he once told Edgar Salin.[19]

What then attracted EKa to "the Count"? One factor must have been that he was indeed "princely" in terms of lineage. EKa was flattered to consort with aristocracy and did not neglect to include Uxkull's title in the dedication for his biography of Frederick II. Moreover, Uxkull's habits were princely. Not only did he drive a luxurious automobile, but he dressed in expensive, up-to-the minute modish clothing. His cousin Alexander von Stauffenberg found this excessive and wrote that Woldi would do best to abandon his scholarly ambitions and travel around in automobiles as the exhibitor of men's styles and fashions.[20] Stauffenberg himself was an aristocrat who could look down on such, but EKa, from a manufacturing family of Posen, was impressed by lordly ways and may even have picked up his taste for natty dressing from his friend. Uxkull also was noble in another sense, for there could be no denying that he had been dubbed into Stefan George's fellowship at an early age. How many had been recognized by George with published poetry as teenagers: "born under the song of the waves"? A member of the fellowship, Uxkull understood what the Meister wanted him to know. In a twelve-page introduction to a book of photos, *Archaic Greek Sculpture*, published in 1920, he was attuned enough to George's ideals to write the following: "When all Greece was gathered for the Olympic Games, Orsippos from Doric Megara appeared as the first to fight naked before the eyes of the Hellenic clans. And disrobing then became customary, for Thucydides relates that before long contestants took off the loincloth that covered their private parts, something that non-Greeks, that is Asiatics, never

[16]From unpublished papers of Ernst Morwitz reported to me by Eckhart Grünewald.

[17]Thormaehlen, *Erinnerungen an Stefan George*, 183. Golo Mann, *Reminiscences and Reflections: A Youth in Germany* (New York, 1990), 217, reports that in his days in Heidelberg—between 1929 and 1932—only two students own automobiles.

[18]EKa to Fine, shortly before 1 March 1921: StGA, Kahler papers, III:6549.

[19][Salin], *Ernst Kantorowicz*, 4.

[20]Groppe, *Die Macht der Bildung*, 475.

Figure 15. Woldemar Uxkull around 1920. (Stefan George Archiv, Stuttgart)

did."[21] To this he added that the nakedness interrelated with statuary, and that "the shaping of the naked youth [is not meant] to make to us think of god in the form of man, but to see the man as god." Uxkull's essay heralded a new George circle practice: the production of full-length statues of boys and young men scantily clad or naked.[22] Quite fittingly, Uxkull had dedicated the picture

[21] Woldemar von Uxkull-Gyllenband, *Archäische Plastik der Griechen* (Berlin, 1920), 7.
[22] Raulff, "Im Lapidarium des George-Kreises," 31.

book to Percy Gothein, the youth who had stood naked for modeling at the Heidelberg Pentecost gathering.

Yet another reason why EKa developed a bond with Uxkull was their mutual interest in ancient history. This was the academic field that Uxkull had decided to pursue by the time he had come to live in the Beznerei. EKa then was finishing his dissertation on Muslim artisan associations and contemplating work on topics other than Islam. We have seen that already in the previous spring the Roman Empire was on his mind. A letter to Fine of January 1921 brings Uxkull into the picture. EKa tells of how the evenings were passing quickly because he, Woldi, and the Meister were reading a new book on the origins of Christianity by the ancient historian Eduard Meyer. George looked on as EKa and Woldi engaged in "endless disputes and exchanges of opinion."[23] EKa's participation with Uxkull in the seminar on Alexander given by Uxkull's dissertation supervisor was the culmination of a participation in a common enterprise.

Edgar Salin, who saw the two young men often in this period, describes the relationship. Uxkull was a "born partner" for Kantorowicz because he continually asked questions. George sometimes groaned about Uxkull's "prattle" (*Gedibber*),

> [b]ut Kantorowicz, himself happy to talk, and always in quest of knowledge, answered every question, at first composed, then with greater vehemence, and sometimes going over to shouting, especially when other discussion partners were present. Then he might suddenly put the matter off. But a few days later he had read all the relevant literature, gave a definitive answer according to his opinion, and was immediately confronted by a new question from his friend.[24]

At this time EKa's inamorata Fine was still trying to play the role of "teacher." Fine was his senior and the role had seemed suitable for a while. But now EKa had found someone three years his junior and was becoming educator instead of educatee, dropping his girlfriend for a boyfriend. In a letter to George of 1924 he wrote of Uxkull as being "touchingly attentive, dear and sincere as ever . . . the lovely, tender bashfulness that he's always possessed has now perhaps increased."[25] Possibly it was Uxkull who made the first homosexual move, for he previously had had a same-sex affair with Percy Gothein: the published dedication of his book on Greek sculpture is to Gothein and takes a line from a verse that Uxkull's deceased brother had written to his own same-sex lover: "We rarely had a rich day when love did not course through our blood."[26] (Gothein was arrested several times during the Nazi era for engaging in homosexual acts.) Although George did not engage in carnal relations with his

[23] 22 January 1921, StGA, Kahler papers, III:6542.
[24] [Salin], *Ernst Kantorowicz*, 4.
[25] Groppe, *Die Macht der Bildung*, 470.
[26] Karlauf, *Stefan George*, 473.

"youths," many of them lived in pairs. In a letter of 1924 to Wilhelm Stein, another member of the circle, EKa wrote that Woldi was the most important person in his life, and in an open postcard of early 1925 he referred to "W." as "table companion and playmate in bed" (*Tischgenoss' und Bettgespiel*).[27] Kantorowicz expressed himself unreservedly in a letter to Stefan George of October 1924, telling of his "marriage" with Woldi as having been "absolutely happy from the first hour."[28]

Despite the "marriage," the partners kept house together only for little more than a year—from April 1921 until June 1922—because Uxkull left Heidelberg after he received his doctorate. He wished to pursue his academic career with the intention of gaining a professorate in ancient history and consequently went to Berlin and then to Oxford and London for further study. After he returned from England in the late spring of 1924, he became *Privatdozent* at the University of Halle in 1925 and remained there until he was called to a professorship in Tübingen in 1932.[29] Passages in EKa's letters from the period indicate that he and Uxkull maintained their intimacy until at least 1927. Thus we learn that before Uxkull left for England in the fall of 1923 the pair had made plans to read their way together through "world literature."[30] When EKa traveled to Italy in the spring of 1924 he wrote to Wilhelm Stein that he thought of Woldi when he saw noteworthy sights and was annoyed that he preferred to stay in London rather than join him. ("What are ten Beazleys [an English expert on Attic Vases] against one Bacchic relief in Naples!")[31] Later Uxkull stayed with him in the apartment in Haus Schlosspark for short periods. In October 1924 Fine von Kahler was there for tea "with Ernst and Uxkull."[32] In the spring of 1925 EKa wrote to Stein that he hoped Woldi was coming soon, and later that his "spouse" had left and that he was now a "grass widow."[33] In the summer of 1926 EKa, on his way from Heidelberg to his mother's home in Holstein, made a considerable detour to see Uxkull in Halle; in October he looked forward to seeing Uxkull in Heidelberg after the latter's return from Italy.[34] The dedication to Uxkull "in reciprocating thanks" that appeared in March 1927 on the title page of *Kaiser Friedrich der Zweite* is the ultimate testimony to the bond.

If nothing kept Uxkull in Heidelberg after June 1922, the question is what kept EKa there? One answer is that he had decided to dedicate himself to writing a biography of the emperor Frederick II, and Heidelberg, where he had a

[27] 15 May 1924; 22 February 1925: Stein papers.

[28] EG, 42; full citation in Groppe, *Die Macht der Bildung*, 470.

[29] Grünewald, "Uxkull-Gyllenband," 1724.

[30] EKa to Wilhelm Stein, 15 May 1924: Stein papers.

[31] Ibid.

[32] Fine to Erich Kahler, Pott, *Gundolf-Kahler Briefwechsel*, 2:156.

[33] EKa to Stein: Stein papers.

[34] EKa to Stein, 27 July 1926: Stein papers; EKa to Fine von Kahler, 2 October 1926: StGA, Kahler papers, III:6566.

quiet, spacious apartment, offered ideal working conditions. A second answer is that Stefan George liked most to live with Kantorowicz in Haus Schlosspark when he stayed in Heidelberg, which turned out to be two or three months of spring and early summer every year between 1923 and 1927. (In June 1928 George stayed with EKa in Heidelberg as well, albeit more briefly and in a different apartment.)

Kantorowicz spent long periods of time with George alone. He described this relationship in 1956 in a letter he wrote to a one-time circle member, Ludwig Thormaehlen, in response to a request for reminiscences.[35] (Thormaehlen had belonged to George's Berlin set and hence knew little about circular activities in Heidelberg.) From this we learn that Kantorowicz saw himself as a "manservant" (*Kammerdiener*), a stance that he said made the relationship easy for the two of them and simplified the daily living together. They did, however, have long discussions about "the Meister's conception of history." (EKa was then engaged in writing a history book.) Also, after a visitor had come the two of them would spend a pleasant hour discussing the details of the visit.

EKa's self-designation as "manservant" seems excessive, but independent evidence indicates that it was apt. In May 1927, when he was already the author of an imposing published book, he sent a postcard to Friedrich Gundolf's brother Ernst, who lived in Darmstadt (an hour's trip from Heidelberg), with a brief message: "DM is here in H. and would be pleased to see you here. Any day is equally welcome after advance notification."[36] Another letter to Ernst Gundolf is in the same secretarial vein: "DM is still here for only a few days and would be pleased to see you. He would like to know whether Tuesday—that is the day after tomorrow—would be suitable for you to come to Heidelberg. In that case d.M. can expect you at the usual hour for the midday meal or already before then."[37] Ernst Gundolf did come on that occasion as he was bade, and most likely EKa and the Meister spent a pleasant hour afterward discussing the visit.

As Kantorowicz took orders from Stefan George in sending out peremptory invitations, it is virtually certain that he took orders in deciding to write a biography of a medieval emperor. The Meister, who favored a cult of "heroes," encouraged the writing of dithyrambic biographies devoted to his favorites. When Kantorowicz's biography of Frederick II appeared in 1927 it followed Friedrich Gundolf's *Goethe* (1916); Ernst Bertram's *Nietzsche* (1918); Berthold Vallentin's *Napoleon* (1922); and Friedrich Gundolf's *Caesar* (1924), all in a series devoted to "Works of Science" (*Werke der Wissenschaft*) published by the firm of Bondi, George's house publisher. No document proves that George indicated to Kantorowicz that he should write a heroic biography, but Ernst

[35] 10 March 1956: StGA, Kantorowicz papers, II:2201.
[36] 22 May 1927, StGA, E. Gundolf papers, III:3402.
[37] 17 June [1928], ibid., 3403.

Morwitz, with whom EKa discussed plans for his book in its early stages and who was on the closest terms with George, later wrote categorically that "it was the poet who urged that [Frederick's] history be newly written."[38]

A gap of a year and a half in EKa's letters to Fine puts us at a disadvantage in determining exactly when he made his decision to write a hero book, but a letter to Josef Liegle of late August 1922 makes clear that it was sometime before the summer of 1922.[39] (George was in Heidelberg in April and May.) EKa wrote that he was "returning to work." He wondered whether he really could bring off a study of Frederick II and whether he was the right person to do it. He thought that the answer was "yes" but was seized by fear about the enormous task, especially when he saw how he could be drowned by relevant new material streaming in from all sides. Indicating that he was going ahead "whether he wanted to or not," he used language suggestive of being called by a higher power: "It would be treachery to work on something only for pleasure and self-procreation, and I would have a bad conscience forever."[40]

Why the medieval ruler Frederick II in particular? Stefan George considered Frederick to have been "the most important of the medieval German emperors."[41] In "The Graves in Speier," a poem written shortly after 1900, George had evoked the presence of "the Greatest Frederick," thereby placing Frederick II above Frederick "the Great," the hero of the Prussian second Reich.[42] Closer in time to EKa's decision to undertake his biography was George's poem of 1919 that told of the "sublime ones" bowing to a royal standard fluttering in the wind. An apocalyptic cleansing precedes the fluttering. The poet-prophet foresees the "driving on clouds" of a "loudly droning army" and the roaring of "the most frightful terror—the third of the storms: the return of the dead ones."[43] Cognoscenti would have known that "the third of the storms" echoed

[38] Morwitz, *Kommentar*, 230. EKa to Josef Liegle, 27 August 1922, Katharina Roettig and Robert E. Lerner, "Briefe von Ernst Kantorowicz und Woldemar von Uxkull-Gyllenband an Josef Liegle," *George-Jahrbuch* 11 (2016–17), 323–55, at 333: "habe es auch mit E.M. besprochen." According to Kantorowicz's American student and friend Ralph Giesey, Kantorowicz originally obtained the idea from having taken a course on the influence of Islam on other cultures and having chosen Sicily as his topic. (See Giesey, "Ernst H. Kantorowicz," LBI, box 1, folder 1.) Although the report has some plausibility it is difficult to determine what course that could have been, and at any rate the move from a seminar paper on Islamic influences in Sicily to choosing to write a book on Frederick II would have been a considerable leap.

[39] As opposed to EG, 65, and Karlauf, *Stefan George*, 549. EKa bought a book by Franz Kampers, *Die Deutsche Kaiseridee in Prophetie und Sage*, that concerned Frederick II as an eschatological figure, and he inscribed "1922" as the purchase date: this is now in the library of the Institute for Advanced Study, Princeton.

[40] Kantorowicz to Josef Liegle, 27 August 1922: Roettig and Lerner, "Briefe von Ernst Kantorowicz," 333.

[41] Morwitz, *Kommentar*, 230. (Morwitz was thoroughly versed in George's opinions.)

[42] GA, 6/7:23.

[43] GA, 9:114.

a passage in Dante (*Paradiso* III: 118–20) telling of Frederick II's mother as "the great Constance who by the second storm of Swabia [Henry VI] bore the third and final power."[44] An allusion in George's poem to the myth of the emperor Frederick who would return with a "loudly droning" ghostly army to destroy the corrupt is unmistakable.[45] (In his biography Kantorowicz repeated "droning" in the context of Frederick II's supernatural afterlife.[46]) It follows too that the "Sublime Ones, the Heroes" who kneel to "the royal standard with true emblem flutter[ing] in the early wind" are the company of those who pay homage to a once and future emperor.

Initially EKa conceived of his research on Frederick II as a "habilitation" project—a major step on the road to a professorial career. This emerges from the letter to Liegle of late August 1922 and another of the same time to Wilhelm Stein. EKa wrote that he had just been in Tübingen, where he had seen the medievalist Johannes Haller. He and Haller had "understood each other extremely well." (It may be noted that Haller was an outspoken German revanchist.) Nevertheless, it was doubtful that he would "go to him" (meaning "go" to habilitate) because his area was distant from Haller's.[47] Evidence of another search for a habilitation overseer appears in a letter of September 16, 1922, written from Heidelberg to Carl Heinrich Becker in Berlin.[48] Becker, then state secretary (second in rank) in the Prussian Ministry of Culture, was Germany's foremost expert on Islamic culture and was known to be sympathetic to the George circle.[49] Earlier he had been a professor in Berlin, at which time Kantorowicz had followed his lectures on the "History of the Caliphs." EKa wrote of his enthusiasm for Becker's recent article on "Islam in the Framework of a General Cultural History" and informed Becker that he had written a dissertation in the same area. (Somewhat cheekily he emphasized that it was about artisans' "associations," not "guilds," even though Becker had used the term guild in his article.[50]) He admitted that his knowledge of Arabic and the relevant sources had been small and went on to say that since writing his dissertation he had neglected both. Instead he now was working on the Sicilian legislation of the emperor Frederick II. Thinking that Becker might be interested in this project,

[44]In his translation of Dante, George gave "sturm" for "vento" (GA, 10/11:168), and Kantorowicz followed this in his subsequent biography: KFII, 19. The influence of George/Dante as background for Kantorowicz's engagement with Frederick II was first noticed by EG, 61.

[45]An extensive treatment of the myth is Hannes Möhring, *Der Weltkaiser der Endzeit* (Stuttgart, 2000), 209–60.

[46]KFII, 613.

[47]26 August 1922: Stein papers. (Eckhart Grünewald called my attention to this passage.)

[48]Becker papers.

[49]In 1920 he supported calling Friedrich Gundolf to Berlin: Groppe, *Die Macht der Bildung*, 535–37, 546–60, for this and other efforts.

[50]C. H. Becker, "Der Islam im Rahmen einer allgemeinen Kulturgeschichte," *Zeitschrift der deutschen Morgenländische Gesellschaft* 76 (1922): 18–36, at 33.

EKa requested an audience to gain some advice and signed his name "Ernst Hartwig Kantorowicz" to signal that he came from a well-known family. EKa and Becker did meet in Berlin, but nothing seems to have materialized from the visit.

It is natural to wonder why EKa did not approach Karl Hampe, who held the chair of medieval history at Heidelberg and was unrivaled as Germany's foremost student of matters surrounding Frederick II. Perhaps he was resisting the idea of remaining in Heidelberg, or else he may not have wanted to go to a traditional scholar who would not look kindly on a treatment of the emperor as "the most frightful terror, the third of the storms."[51] But it is just as likely that Hampe was unwilling to take on a flaming George disciple. Whatever the case, after the trips to Tübingen and Berlin EKa proceeded to write a full-scale biography of Frederick II without any academic connection.

He was able to abandon the goal of habilitating because he possessed sufficient wealth to do as he wished without concern for a money-earning career. His finances call for a short digression. The Kantorowicz firm did well during the war. Foreign trade was limited but domestic fruit-juice sales compensated. In October 1919 the firm announced a satisfactory fiscal year and offered an 18 percent dividend.[52] In the same month EKa directed that a shipment of liqueurs be sent to Erich Kahler and wrote to him that the products were "again thoroughly drinkable."[53] A forced sale of the Posen factory to Polish buyers in November 1920 appeared to constitute a disaster.[54] EKa described the terms in a letter to Fine of January 4, 1921: the sum, however large, was in Polish currency that at the time was nearly valueless, and at any rate the currency could not be exported; thus he was financially strapped.[55] Yet the situation was turned around, owing to the business talents of his cousin Franz. The new Polish owners used the valuable name "Hartwig Kantorowicz," and their factory continued to produce liqueurs—now also vodka—from 1920 until 1939. But Franz directed a German "Hartwig Kantorowicz" firm with a new factory and the old Berlin administrative office and retail outlets.[56] The financial report for the German company for the fiscal year 1920–21 indicated that it prospered to the extent of being able to grant a 30 percent dividend.[57] In 1922 the firm

[51] Hampe kept his distance from the George circle: Folker Reichert, *Gelehrtes Leben: Karl Hampe, das Mittelalter und die Geschichte der Deutschen* (Göttingen, 2009), 181–83.

[52] *Nachrichten für Handel, Industrie und Gewerbe*, 20 October 1919, http://www.zbw.eu/beta/p20/company/42961/about.en.html.

[53] 12 October 1919: DLA, Kahler papers.

[54] Nawrocki, "Die Geschichte der Familie Kantorowicz," 88.

[55] StGA, Kahler papers, III:6539.

[56] Interview with Vera Peters (daughter of Franz Kantorowicz), 29 July 1991: she thought the new factory was in Hamburg but was not certain.

[57] *Deutsche Allgemeine Zeitung (Berlin), Weltwirtschaft*, 25 January 1922; *Industrie und Handelszeitung (Berlin)*, 25 January 1922.

commissioned a charming animated cartoon, "The Miracle," to be played in movie theaters, showing two men having an argument until a bottle of liqueur miraculously appears; golden liquid then flows down their throats; they smile and make up; then a caption appears: "Kantorowicz: Famed throughout the World."[58] EKa was sufficiently flush in June 1922 to be able to surprise his friend Josef Liegle, who was just managing to survive financially, with a generous transfer of cash.[59]

Nothing in EKa's correspondence indicates how he may have been affected by the German inflation of 1923. But at worst it could only have been a blip of inconvenience, for throughout the 1920s he lived on a grand scale. From the spring of 1921 until the early summer of 1922 he and Uxkull were the only two residents (with the exception of a maid who also did the cooking) in the upper story of a luxurious villa. After Uxkull's departure, EKa kept the second room free because he knew that it was suitable for periodic visits by Stefan George, who, after November 1922, no longer spoke to Gundolf. And we have seen that the Meister did stay there regularly for two or three months every year. In 1924 EKa referred to George's presence as his "summer residence."[60] Otherwise, aside from occasional other guests, he lived by himself and had no difficulty paying the rent. He also had no difficulty in financing frequent travel. Aside from traveling between Heidelberg and Berlin regularly, he journeyed to Italy in the spring of 1924, to Copenhagen in the summer of 1925, and to Dalmatia in the autumn of 1926. And every summer he treated himself to extended vacations. In 1918 his father had bought a palatial villa in Malente-Gremsmühlen, which was in a region of eastern Holstein known as "Holstein Switzerland." When Joseph died the following year, EKa's mother Clara inherited the property, and she lived there after leaving Posen.[61] Since the house was surrounded by a park and located near a lake, it offered a summer haven for EKa, who relaxed there for weeks at a time. EKa, who always appeared in the best-tailored clothing, never attempted to hide his wealth.[62] The story is told that when he was dining at a restaurant and someone in his group was complaining about the burden of

[58] Walther Ruttman, *Das Wunder*, in "Walther Ruttmann: Berlin, die Sinfonie der Großstadt & Melodie der Welt" (Edition Filmmuseum 39, 2013). I thank Jost Philipp Klenner for calling my attention to this cartoon.

[59] Liegle to Lucy Heyer Grote, 27 June 1922, Roettig and Lerner, "Briefe von Ernst Kantorowicz," 331: "eine rätselhafte Geldanweisung sich als unerwartete Arznei meiner diesbezüglichen Sorgen herausstellte (unter uns!): ich hätte sonst mutig dem finanziellen Zusammenbruch in die Augen sehen müssen." (The context leaves no doubt that the donor was Kantorowicz.)

[60] EG, 67.

[61] *Chronik von Malente-Gremsmühlen* (Husum, 2008), 105. I am grateful to Thomas Gruber for informing me of this publication.

[62] The clothing, both in Germany and later in the United States, was always tailor-made: Kantorowicz to Vera Peters, 11 February 1963: Lerner archive.

carrying a famous family name, he turned to the waiter and asked, "Could you please bring me a Kantorowicz?"[63]

We can now follow the steps in the composition of the biography of Frederick II (henceforth KFII). Kantorowicz wrote to Josef Liegle in his letter of late August 1922 that he had just visited Mainz, Worms, and Speyer as part of his "program." This would have been a program for visiting sites associated with the career of his protagonist. Then in December he wrote to Liegle that he was making good progress with his work and looked forward to reading to him aloud what he had written in order to have his criticism.[64] An entry in Liegle's diary for January 4, 1923, and Kantorowicz's letter to him of February 9 indicate that when the two were together in Heidelberg in early January they discussed interrelated concerns, which for Kantorowicz involved the young Frederick II's appearance in Rome in 1212 and the Children's Crusade of the same year, both topics treated in his biography's second chapter.[65] Writing to Fine in May 1923 after a long interval, EKa reported that he had not made any progress with his work for two months because of the recent stay of the Meister.[66] Early in the following February he wrote to Fine to send her his birthday greetings, and now he expatiated on his progress.[67] He was very pleased to be living in the mansion of Franz Kantorowicz in Steglitz, a district of West Berlin. Franz and his family were away, meaning peace and solitude for his writing. Steglitz was a fortunate location because it was near Dahlem, the site of the Prussian State Archives, which temporarily housed the vast collection of publications on Italian history of the Prussian Historical Institute in Rome. Being able to draw on this collection was ideal because it meant that he could save himself from working in any Italian library, and he was excited by studying materials that had never been studied before. In conclusion he apologized for boring Fine with so much "Bonzeness" on the grounds that he had nothing else to write because he was postponing all other activities until he finished his book. (Customarily meaning "big shot," the term *Bonze* was used for stuffy professional academics within the George circle.)

Although he felt no need to work in Italian libraries EKa did feel a need to see the Italian sites associated with Frederick II's career. This inclination arose from his friendship with Wilhelm Stein, who had published a book-length study of Raphael at the end of 1922. Thanking Stein for sending him a copy, EKa wrote with awe about how Stein had awakened him to the fact that "not only Word and Deed produce an idea but also Picture (*Bild*)," and to the importance of "pictorial seeing" (*bildhaftes Sehen*).[68] Stein also had taught him that

[63] John Van Engen heard this story from the Heidelberg medieval historian Peter Classen,

[64] 14 December 1922: Roettig and Lerner, "Briefe von Ernst Kantorowicz," 335–36.

[65] Liegle papers.

[66] 8 May 1923: StGA, Kahler papers, III:6556.

[67] 5 February 1924: ibid., 6557.

[68] Kantorowicz to Stein, December 1922: EG, 58.

"there actually was a seeing next to the thinking."[69] EKa spent most of April 1924 in mainland Italy and Sicily.[70] Traveling alone, he boarded a steamer in Venice that made zigzag stops at many ports and allowed him to spend time wherever he landed. The first stop was Ancona, allowing him to visit nearby Jesi (Frederick II's birthplace) and its vicinity. Never having been to Italy before, he was overwhelmed with the beauty of the landscape. Later he wrote to Stein that it was as if he had been in "Djahiligga," the Muslim term for the time of ignorance before the revelation of the Koran.

The next stop was in Apulia, where EKa viewed the "majesty" of Castel del Monte, Frederick II's famous castle on a windswept plain. Afterward the steamer took him to Palermo, where Frederick had spent his youth. He reached the city at Eastertime and there joined a contingent of George disciples who had convened to lay a wreath on the emperor's porphyry tomb.[71] As readers of KFII will know, this bore the inscription "To its Emperors and Heroes, the Secret Germany." After a few days in Palermo the steamer took him Naples, where he visited the archeological museum and made expeditions to Pompeii and Paestum. In Naples he also attended the celebration of the seven hundredth anniversary of Frederick II's founding of the university.

EKa sent a detailed report from Naples to Stefan George, saying that he never would have *seen* certain things had it not been for the Meister's training. Two other detailed accounts appear in letters to Josef Liegle and Wilhelm Stein (May 7). What stands out from all three is how deeply EKa was impressed by the remains of ancient Greece. He had gone to Italy to "see" things for his book on a medieval ruler, but when he got there he became a Hellenophile. He termed Paestum a "holy" site and marveled at the Roman copies of Greek statuary in Naples, being particularly impressed by a sarcophagus depicting a procession with a drunken Bacchus. As he wrote to Stein, "all the golden wonders of the Middle Ages pale in comparison"; the "Frederican things" were "merely interesting—at best they provided scholarly excitement, but they [were] not gripping." One of George's poems had exalted those who carried a banner with the words "Hellas our eternal love." From 1924 until his death Kantorowicz was one of this number. His publications would be about the Middle Ages, but he was a medievalist whose emotional commitment lay elsewhere.

By early May he was back in Heidelberg and working unflaggingly on his book. He wrote his account of Frederick II's Crusade, amounting to forty pages in the published biography, in less than two weeks. As he wrote to Stein, "I go

[69] Kantorowicz to Stein, 15 May 1924 (Stein papers): "ich von Ihnen s.Z. [probably the summer of 1922] in Würzburg zum erstenmale hörte oder es vielleicht nur spürte dass es überhaupt ein Sehen gäbe neben dem Denken."

[70] The following account is based on letters to Stefan George, 30 April 1924: StGA, Kantorowicz papers, I; to Josef Liegle, 7 May 1924, Roettig and Lerner, "Briefe von Ernst Kantorowicz," 341–42; and to Wilhelm Stein, 15 May 1924; Stein papers.

[71] EG, 75, and, with some additional data, Karlauf, *Stefan George*, 557.

to sleep with an Emperor and wake up with him, and write quasi love-letters to him or read the same, so there's no room for anything else."[72] In November 1924 he remained so hard at work that he did not answer letters: Gundolf remarked that Kantorowicz was "bewitched" by Frederick II.[73] By the beginning of July 1925 he had completed a draft of the entire book.[74] Writing to Fine he stated: "The conclusion of my work was somewhat trying; I was pursuing a truly tragic human life down to its ruin and I felt choked up in my throat and breast as if separated from one who is very dear."[75] After working so diligently he felt able to take some time off. In July he indulged himself for two weeks in swimming, tennis playing, and rabbit hunting in his mother's home in Holstein—all for "narcotic effect."[76] Then he traveled to Copenhagen and to a Danish resort hotel.

EKa's description to Fine of his trip to Denmark prompts another digression. The two of them were again on excellent terms, allowing him to write to her expansively about his recent experiences while he was soaking up sun at the resort. He had been in Copenhagen for three days and found the city unexpectedly beautiful. There had been magnificent weather—a cloudless blue sky and wonderful clarity of light. He declared that Copenhagen was "a piece of Hellas." (In a postcard to Fine's husband Erich he wrote: "a really southern city, far in the north."[77]) "Hellas" led him to write that he had been to the Glyptothek, a sculpture museum, where he saw an ancient bust of a boy that was "inconceivably beautiful." The boy had "a breath of youthful sadness that Socrates could have helped him get over." And this led him to write about his impressions at a Copenhagen beach. There sunburned men and boys "swam, and dived, and exercised naked" and all this was "surprisingly easy as a possibility." The modern commentator looks to see whether Plato had ever written about naked swimming.[78]

Kantorowicz returned to Heidelberg in August to dictate his chapters to "the typing girl" so that he would have a typescript with carbon copies that he could send out for criticism.[79] Two chapters were ready in September; two more in October.[80] One set went out in installments to the Meister; another (after the Meister's approval) to Wilhelm Stein, whom EKa alternatively called

[72] 15 May 1924: Stein papers.

[73] To Magda Bezner, November 1924: Gundolf Archive.

[74] Kantorowicz to Stein, 7 July 1925: Stein papers; to Stefan George, 12 July 1925: EG, 69.

[75] 21 July 1925: StGA, Kahler papers, III:6563.

[76] Stein papers.

[77] 30 July 1925: DLA, Kahler papers.

[78] In a letter to Ernst Langlotz of 3 September 1936 (Langlotz papers), Kantorowicz writes of being on a beach in Belgium, "seldom having seen so many bewitching children," and being struck with the beauty of boys between the ages of eight and ten.

[79] Kantorowicz to Wilhelm Stein, 17 August 1925: Stein papers; "Tippmädchen": to Stein, (undated: early 1926).

[80] Kantorowicz to Stefan George, 7 September 1925, as EG, 72; Kantorowicz to Stein, 15 October 1925: Stein papers.

"Cerberus" and "state's inquisitor." EKa also solicited criticism from an academic specialist, Friedrich Baethgen, who was then a junior faculty member in Heidelberg.[81] He intended to shock the "Bonzes" with his method of writing—and we will see that he certainly did—but he did not want it to be said that he had gotten his facts wrong. Baethgen, roughly his contemporary, was the ideal person to guard against this. He had written his dissertation under Karl Hampe on Innocent III's regency for Frederick II and was very well versed in the material. The two also had developed a rapport: Baethgen was EKa's earliest friend in the field of medieval history, and they remained close until EKa's death in 1963. Chapters 5 and 6 were ready for Stein to read in February 1926.[82] In early April the author had reached the penultimate chapter and by July, somewhat more than four years after he had begun his work, he reached the end.[83]

In July Stefan George wrote to his publisher Georg Bondi in Berlin that he was recommending a book manuscript written by "a closely connected person."[84] He had read and commented in detail on the polished typescripts and now was willing to exert his authority on EKa's behalf. In fact George took such an interest in the biography in the last stages of its production that he nearly was a collaborator: after having read the typescripts he read the page proofs. EKa later told Edgar Salin that without the Meister's encouragement he probably would have lost the courage to continue. According to Salin, those who knew George's voice could hear it in some of the book's phrases.[85] The degree to which George engaged himself is remarkable. In reviewing the page proofs he proposed "the first real 'conclave'" instead of "the first real Conclave."[86] The published book (525) shows that the Meister had his way.

George decided to support publication right after he read the final pages. EKa wrote to Wilhelm Stein on July 10, 1926, that he was unable to send him these pages until they had passed muster with "the reviewer," meaning George, who was scheduled to arrive in Heidelberg on the eleventh. And it was on the twelfth that George wrote to Bondi to propose publishing the manuscript.[87] The recommendation was not a routine matter. EKa's biography was the most scholarly book that George had ever supported and was written by a thirty-one-year-old who as yet was unknown to the public. But when Bondi read the manuscript he wrote to George that he was fully caught up by the "magic of the presentation" and was happy to publish. He and George then entered into details about the contract. To speed things along George offered to cover half of

[81] EKa to Fine, 14 October 1926: StGA, Kahler papers, III:6567.

[82] Kantorowicz to Stein, 23 February 1926: Stein papers.

[83] Kantorowicz to Stein, 9 April 1926, 10 July 1926, 27 July 1926: Stein papers.

[84] 12 July 1926, as EG, 73.

[85] [Salin,] *Ernst Kantorowicz*, 5.

[86] Karlauf, *Stefan George*, 561.

[87] The following account of the contract negotiations and publication procedures relies on EG, 150–55.

the production costs. Bondi then inquired if he could deal directly with the author, whose name had not been mentioned, but George demurred, saying that an inexperienced person should not undertake contract negotiations. Perhaps the real reason for his resistance was that he was considering whether the book should be published anonymously or perhaps under a pseudonym. He may have thought that the name "Kantorowicz" was problematic. All the contract details were ironed out in October with a stipulation that pseudonymous authorship would not be excluded. Typesetting then began, and George divulged the name of Ernst Kantorowicz in November, driven by the realization that it would be inefficient for EKa and Bondi not to correspond about the proofs directly. Nevertheless, he remained fully engaged in reading the proofs himself; at the end of the year he expressed his willingness to alter his travel plans in order to avoid possible delays. When Bondi complained of proofreading delays in January, George responded testily that such was unavoidable when proofs were being read by many. He insisted that "regarding [Kantorowicz's] own good will and diligence there can be no doubt, nor, if I may say so, regarding mine." The decision to put the name of Ernst Kantorowicz on the title page was made around that time.

Meanwhile in late September 1926 EKa was in Dalmatia, where he had his passionate tryst with Fine. Then, right after the contract was signed on October 12 (between Bondi and George!), he traveled from Heidelberg via Berlin to his mother's home in Holstein in order to read galley proofs.[88] He wrote to Stein on November 14 that "up here the flags are fluttering." (In German "flags" puns on "galley proofs.") The next step was the page proofs. Stefan George read them first in early January and then sent them to Kantorowicz who reviewed his markings and returned the proofs to him. At that point George sent them to the printer.[89]

Kaiser Friedrich der Zweite appeared at the end of March with a run of 2,600 copies—300 more being reserved for gratis distribution. EKa recently had sat for two portrait busts done by different sculptors.[90] Could it be that he knew instinctively that he would soon be a celebrity?

[88] EKa to Fine von Kahler, from Malente-Gremsmühlen, 14 October 1926: StGA, Kahler papers, III:6567.

[89] Karlauf, *Stefan George*, 560.

[90] He sat for a bust by Alexander Zschokke in the fall of 1926 and January 1927: Kantorowicz to Wilhelm Stein, 23 November 1926: Stein papers. On his sitting for a bust by Max Fueter: Thormaehlen, *Erinnerungen*, 227. Zschokke's bust (now in the Historical Seminar of the University of Frankfurt) serves as the frontispiece for Robert L. Benson and Johannes Fried, eds., *Ernst Kantorowicz: Erträge der Doppeltagung: Institute for Advanced Study, Princeton; Johann Wolfgang Goethe-Universität, Frankfurt* (Stuttgart, 1997). Fueter's was used for the advertisement of the second printing of EKa's biography in 1928; its current whereabouts are unknown.

CHAPTER 7

Frederick II

A FLYER ADVERTISING THE SECOND PRINTING IN 1928 of Ernst Kantorowicz's *Kaiser Friedrich der Zweite* indicated that three thousand copies had already been sold and carried several enthusiastic reviews of the first printing. Among them was this from the *Neue freie Presse* of Vienna, a liberal outlet reviled by Hitler as a "Jew paper": "One reads this as if it were the most suspenseful novel. The brilliant, artful-hot-blooded style of the author identifies him as a member of the circle of Stefan George and Gundolf. . . . Breath-taking." The reviewer was not a professional historian, but the one for the *Schlesische Zeitung*, Franz Kampers, held the chair for medieval history at the University of Breslau. Kampers was a Catholic who would not have been expected to praise a work with an antipapal bias, yet he wrote: "A historian, unknown until now, has dared to take on what is probably the most difficult biographical problem in medieval history. . . . The entire structure of the book is marvelous in its coherence. It fascinates in all its details. The seemingly insignificant is taken up lovingly and harmoniously integrated into the whole. The overwhelming wealth of ideas and also the artistic beauty of the work cannot be conveyed by any summary."[1] The publication of a 632-page book on a medieval ruler by an unknown author had been a gamble, but it had paid off.

Several qualities mentioned in the reviews account for the attractiveness of KFII for large numbers of readers. Not least was the book's "brilliant" style. Kantorowicz was a forceful writer, taken to employing high-flown rhetoric, alliteration, and sometimes archaic diction for dramatic effect: "After the calling and the proving [*Berufung und Bewährung*] came the consecration and the vow" (71); "[He] had reigned, ruled, and raged [*gerichtet, gewaltet und gewütet*] in Italy for more than a decade" (611).[2] The work's penultimate sentence sums up Frederick II's qualities: "the fiery lord of the beginning, the seducer, beguiler, the radiant, merry, the ever-young, the severely powerful judge, the scholar and

[1] The flyer was included by Kantorowicz in a letter to Fine von Kahler, 28 August 1928: StGA, Kahler papers, III:6568.

[2] Numbers in parentheses refer to pages in the original German edition.

wise man, the helmeted warrior leading the round-dance of the muses" (632). Half a century after its publication the work was excerpted in a French literary magazine for its literary qualities.[3]

KFII offers memorable portraits. Frederick's father Henry VI "[had a] body lean and frail, his ever-earnest countenance—fully dominated by a mighty forehead—was pale with a wispy beard" (12). Pope Gregory IX, "already an old man, was still vigorous and handsome, [he] was a priest who loved and understood how to heighten the impression of his presence by means of shining brilliance and majestic pomp" (157). Regarding Frederick's favorite son Enzio: "With his long, flowing golden locks and his supple, mid-sized figure he may well have renewed the image of the *Puer Apulie* [Frederick] so that one would not forget it: slender, lightfooted, and agile—some even called him '*falcanello*,' the falcon-youth" (427). The king of England, Henry III, was "slack and shabby" (521); the villainous Charles of Anjou is never named but only mentioned icily as "the Angevin" (619, 620).

In addition to portrait sketches, the book painted brightly colored scenes:

> All the forces of the East and the West were represented in small Sicily—a selection of all the powers of the contemporary world. They scuffled and tumbled on the island and in Apulia; they surged with the most primitive compulsion through and over each other as if in primeval chaos. There were the Germans of the Emperor Henry, the French of the counts of Brienne, Sicilians and Apulians, Saracens, Pisans, and Genoese. Papal legates appeared recurrently with Italian troops, and finally even Spanish knights took action. (29)

> With full imperial panoply and accompanied by his retinue and friends the banned and hence no longer in the community of the faithful Emperor entered the Church of the Holy Sepulchre. . . . Here, without intermediary of Church, without bishop, without coronation mass, Frederick II, proud and unabashed, reached for the royal crown of holy Jerusalem. Striding to the altar of the Sepulchre he took up the crown and placed it upon his head. (183)

> The remaining retinue of the Chamber aroused the curiosity of the world no less than the exotic animals. For it included Saracen girls and eunuchs, as was often enough noted when the imperial train passed through the cities of Italy. It did seem very likely, even without the help of papal missives, to see these veiled maidens as the favorites of the Emperor's already legendary harem. The uncertainty itself was provoking. For whether these maidens actually served like the ropedancers, jugglers, and acrobats who frequently followed the Emperor merely for the diversion their grace provided—as the Emperor maintained with astounded innocence against constant papal reproaches—or whether Frederick II

[3]Peter Schottler, "Ernst Kantorowicz in Frankreich," in Benson and Fried, *Ernst Kantorowicz*, 144–61, at 147.

occasionally used the Saracen girls for other purposes—"swept away by their allurements" as the pope portrayed it—could of course not be ascertained. . (287)

Added to color were literary allusions. First came Dante. Not only was *il poeta* one of Stefan George's favorites, but his cast of characters often were integral to Kantorowicz's narrative. Thus the biography adduces lines from Dante when it tells of Frederick's mother, the empress Constance (10), Frederick's minister, Piero della Vigna (274), and Frederick's most prominent court scholar, Michael Scot (313). In following Dante, Kantorowicz reconceived Saint Francis—the saint was not the familiar "tender, loving, childish enthusiast," but one who according to Dante (*Paradiso* XI: 91–92) was "regal" when he came before Pope Innocent III (152). Dante serves too for the purpose of sly wit: Frederick II's scores of bastards made him the ancestor of many princes of Renaissance Italy, thus vindicating Dante's line about "Italy . . . lady of bordellos" (450).

Wolfram von Eschenbach, medieval Germany's greatest epic poet and Frederick II's contemporary, comes well after Dante but still is very present. Kantorowicz counted on his audience's familiarity with Wolfram's *Parzival* from their days at school. Allusions to Wolfram serve in KFII as a condiment, enhancing the flavor of heroic knighthood attached to Frederick and his milieu. Thus Kantorowicz sprinkles in references to "Herzeloide" (Parzival's mother) (10), to "Klinschor" (an evil magician, said to have descended from "Virgil of Naples") (25), and to "Feirefiss" (Parzival's "particolored" half-brother) (174). Toward the same goal Kantorowicz piles up eclectic references in a single passage: to "the epic of Firdausi," to "Ornit's helper," to "the wise heathen Zacharias," and to "the Medor of Ariosto" (174). Most readers probably could not have identified these names, but the author liked to show off and the effect of exoticism was all that mattered.

References to classical Latin literature and mythology also served for flavor. When Conrad of Hildesheim accompanied the infant Frederick from the Italian mainland to Sicily he sailed "not without some fear between Scylla and Charybidis" (24). When Frederick returned from the Holy Land and began transforming his Sicilian kingdom into an absolute monarchy it was as if a hero had become aware of his divine origin as a "son of Zeus Ammon" or "grandson of Venus Genetrix" (recondite allusions to Alexander and Julius Caesar) (195). A single direct reference to Greek literature is stunning. In the context of Frederick II's patronage of scholars dependent on Arabic learning, Kantorowicz explains that the Arabs were engaged with Greek philosophy and Greek science—but "never a historian or poet." Yet there was a single line from Homer that Kantorowicz assures his readers that the Arabs considered to be of value: "είς κοιρανος έστώ είς βασιλεύς." No translation is given, and nothing more is said. The present author sought help and learned that "heis koiranos estō heis basileus" (*Iliad*, 2.204–5) means "let there be one ruler and one king" and is the only statement of a monarchical principle in Greek epic.

The Viennese reviewer said that he read Kantorowicz's biography "as if it were the most suspenseful novel." Doubtless this was an exaggeration. The biography dwells on Sicilian poetry for three pages, for many more on scholars at the emperor's court, and for many more still on Frederick's legislation and administrative achievements. Nor did the lack of running heads facilitate skipping. Still, the statement that "the entire structure of the book is marvelous in its coherence" has much justification. Certainly the biography has a plot: the life of a mighty but ultimately tragic hero comparable to Caesar and Napoleon. It opens with a contemporary panegyric of Frederick II's birth as that of a messiah and portrays the young hero advancing from strength to strength as "marvel of the world." Frederick's self-crowning as king of Jerusalem in the Church of the Holy Sepulchre provides a biographical pinnacle. At the height of his powers Frederick boasted that "all the animals tremble at the lion's track" (501). But he was foiled by two popes and his last years were stressful. Granted that he died "in the full brightness of his imperial power" (628), his career beyond life was tragic because of the frightful extermination of his heirs. No one had ever told this story with anything like Kantorowicz's brio.

Although not mentioned by the reviewers, another explanation for the biography's popularity was its celebration of authoritarianism. We have seen that Kantorowicz cited Homer's, "Let there be one ruler and one king"; to this comes Goethe: "On the highest level there is no freedom" (235).[4] Celebration of authoritarianism is most pronounced in the biography's fifth chapter, "Tyrant of Sicily," which the author considered most "central."[5] The thesis appears in the first sentence: "[Frederick II] founded the first absolute monarchy of the West" (195). The following 154 pages (a monograph in itself) consist of extended explanation and applause. Frederick founded in his Kingdom of Sicily (the southern Italian mainland as well as the island of Sicily) "the first purely secular state, freed from the Church." He proclaimed in his law code, the *Liber Augustalis*, that the people bequeathed to the ruler the right to make law.[6] As Kantorowicz commented, "by means of this appeal to the decisive procedure at the beginning of the Roman Empire, Frederick II—as last Caesar equal to the first—puts aside the people's own law-giving power and authority, or more exactly absorbs it" (212). As for the Catholic faith, the state by no means dispensed with religion, for it supported the imperial person and his license to make laws (220–22). Hence the preamble to the *Liber Augustalis* asserted that "the King of King and Lord of Lords demands this above all in the hands of the ruler that he should not allow

[4]Kantorowicz calls this a "Goethe word" as if quoting scripture, but he actually tinkered with the passage. He gives "dass es auf der höchsten Stufe keine Freiheit gebe," whereas Goethe wrote (in a letter to Schiller): "dass es dem Vortrefflichen gegenüber keine Freiheit giebt als die Liebe" ("for the excellent there is no freedom other than love.")

[5]To Wilhelm Stein, 15 October 1925: Stein papers.

[6]English translation by James M. Powell, *The Liber Augustalis or Constitutions of Melfi Promulgated by the Emperor Frederick II for the Kingdom of Sicily in 1231* (Syracuse, NY, 1971), 32.

the most holy Roman Church . . . to be bespattered with the secret faithlessness of those who distort the faith and should protect her by the might of the secular sword." Accordingly the first chapter deals with the extirpation of heresy, declaring it to be treason and punishing it with death. Kantorowicz scornfully rejects the possibility that a "liberal Hohenstaufen only persecuted unfortunate heretics under the pressure of the Church" (243). Rather, the emperor who called himself "the God of vengeance who punishes the guilt of heretics to the second generation" took the initiative for reasons of state (243). Kantorowicz insists that Frederick's tolerance of Jews and Muslims was driven by political considerations and bore no relationship to any policy that would turn Frederick into a liberal ruler. Indeed, Frederick II "was probably the most *intolerant* [Kantorowicz's emphasis] Emperor that the West had ever produced" (247).

Throughout, the book is virtually a treasury of antiliberal expressions. It celebrates aristocratic culture; it lauds the combination of two expressions of nobility—the knightly and the monastic—in the foundation of the Teutonic Knights (77–88). The first grand-master of the Knights, Hermann von Salza, was unfailingly loyal; for him "loyalty" was a driving force—"since the dawn of time possible only among Germans" (85). Kantorowicz defends the actions of his hero even at their most ruthless. When Frederick beheads prisoners daily before the walls of besieged Parma, "the reign of terror was no mania but frightful necessity" (598). The ethnic cleansing of thousands of Sicilian Muslims—their deportation to an isolated town in Apulia—was "wisdom." The Saracens in question had "a joy in being slaves"; by turning them into a private fighting force Frederick evoked their "fanatic devotion" and displayed his skill in "handling human material" (123).

Amazement accompanies an awful anecdote Kantorowicz relates in order to illustrate Frederick's stern commitment to the principle of hierarchy (320). The emperor once had a favorite falcon that "he loved more than a city." One day he released this bird to attack a crane. The falcon was in the air above the crane when it spotted a young eagle below, swooped down, and killed it. When Frederick saw this he commanded a lieutenant in fury to behead the falcon, *perk' avea morto lo suo signiore* (because he had murdered his lord—the words are left in Italian). With implicit approval Kantorowicz comments that "the king of birds," a young eagle, was of a higher order than the falcon and that the hierarchy of all creatures determined by providence would never see it as "good" (the author's irony is dripping) that a lion would lie down with a lamb.

A national fixation was Kantorowicz's outrage against the French. For background we may look at hitherto unpublished passages in letters he wrote to his George circle friends Wilhelm Stein and Josef Liegle in August 1922 upon returning to Heidelberg after a tour of the French-occupied middle Rhineland:

> I found your letter here yesterday morning after a depressing excursion to the occupied territory (Speyer, Worms, and Mainz); the enclosed little picture [of the

> Adoration of the Magi] will at least let the revolting grimaces of the colored and colorless French recede a bit. No, good dottore, I agree with you less than before about the qualities of the French soldier: the coarsest and slowest Pomeranian grenadier is a hero compared to the depraved riff-raff whose outer uncleanliness points only too surely to his inner infection. But the worst is that the Germans—above all in Mainz—are by no means immune. . . . Mainz today has the smell of a French provincial city like St. Quentin or Courtrai. Just now was the time of "final sales" that drew thousands of French petty bourgeois to come for shopping with the result that the entire picture was not only that of a military but also a bourgeois enemy invasion.[7]

> The occupied territory is so depressing, especially during the current "final sales" that draw French, Belgian [and] Dutch vulgar-bourgeois-bluebottles in the myriads. I was happy to flee to my nook, away from everything revolting, where one is spared from the foolish or nauseating grotesqueness of the colored and colorless French. It is very indicative that the French induce complete physical nausea because of their sordidness and the faces that reveal the infection they carry; one never sees this among the English, Americans, or even the Italians. No no, there is no longer any bridge, never, and only a single ceterum censeo, namely Franciam esse delendam.[8] Every German policy today that does not base itself in the last analysis on the destruction of France is reprehensible.[9]

The connection between these remarks and the description of Charles of Anjou's beheading of Frederick II's grandson Conradin in KFII is inescapable:

> The Frenchman ordered the death sentence to be executed in his presence in the marketplace of Naples before a pressing crowd that had never yet seen a royal beheading. But as the head of the last Staufen king rolled to the ground, an eagle, so it was said, swept down from the skies, skimmed its right wing in Conradin's blood, and, stained with the blood of the saint [Divus], swept, swift as an arrow, up into the ether. "How can the Germans," sang a Venetian troubadour, "how can they bear to live when they think of this? They have lost their best and have harvested shame! If they don't take revenge soon they are dishonored!" But the Germans did not feel the trembling of the earth that followed on the night of Conradin's death and they did not think of vengeance. . . . They have never cleansed the blood-stained eagle nor have they ever let the Sicilian Vespers be followed by a German Vespers. (620)

Stefan George said that this passage gave him "hot and cold flashes."[10] Shivers must have come to other German readers as well, and even more shivers

[7] 26 August 1922: Stein papers.

[8] Cato the Censor: "*Ceterum censeo Carthaginem delendam esse*" ("Furthermore, I consider that Carthage must be destroyed").

[9] 27 August 1922: Roettig and Lerner, "Briefe von Ernst Kantorowicz," 332–33.

[10] Edith Landmann, *Gespräche mit Stefan George*, 174. The passage echoes George's line: "If ever this people cleanses itself from shame": GA, 9, 114.

must have attended the portentous conclusion of the biography: "The greatest Frederick—he who his Volk neither grasped nor gratified [*weder fasste noch füllte*]—until today is not redeemed. 'He lives and lives not' . . the Sibyl's saying applies no longer for the Kaiser but for the Kaiser's Volk" (632). The author's reapplication of the Erythrean Sibyl's paradoxical words, "he lives and lives not," was clear enough: "the Kaiser's Volk" needed to be awakened and unshackled. He was addressing numerous readers who shared his deeply antirepublican, anti-Enlightenment, and revanchist sentiments.

Kantorowicz did not mean to write for scholarly specialists but knew that his book would attract their attention. It was the first extended serious biography of the emperor Frederick that had been written. Even though German scholars of the nineteenth century had become engaged with the history of their medieval rulers, they had left Frederick II largely aside. The reason was that he fell between two historiographical camps. Historians of a "Prussian," "small-German" outlook disapproved of him, not only because he was half-Norman and loved southern Italy more than Germany but above all because he effectively sacrificed German unity by granting near sovereignty to the German princes. For them the shame of *Kleinstaaterei* (the jigsaw map of Germany before unification) had been Frederick's responsibility. He perhaps could have been a hero for historians of the "Austrian," "large-German" persuasion. This school, prizing Austria's holdings south of the Alps and the ideal of a unified empire comprising large communities of Catholic Germans, might have favored the one medieval ruler who had laid claim to part of the "large Germany" they had in mind. But even for them Frederick's "selling off" of Germany proper was a stumbling block, and even worse was his "Ghibelline," antipapal policy, which they understood as anti-Catholic. The outsiders Jacob Burckhardt and Friedrich Nietzsche did write favorably about Frederick II—Burckhardt for his forward-looking statecraft; Nietzsche for his "genius"—but they had no scholarly followers.

By the early twentieth century scholars started paying Frederick more attention, especially as the Prussian-Austrian disagreements faded. After all for good or ill he was the last great medieval German emperor, and for good or ill his reign was central for German and also Italian medieval history. But while many spoke of the need for a full-scale biography, the task was intimidating and no one wrote one. And then came along the thirty-one-year-old Ernst Kantorowicz, who had never taken a university course in medieval history but carried off what no previous scholar, young or grizzled, had ever tried. Anyone could see that the 632-page book was comprehensive. Not only did it follow the protagonist year by year from birth to death, but it offered copious detail about numerous aspects of his reign such as legislation, court personnel, artistic life, even his engagement in falconry. Moreover, while it was true that the book lacked documentation (the author promised that such would come in a supplementary volume), anyone could see that it was based on extensive research.

But the book was deeply controversial from the historiographical point of view because it presented a bold challenge to the reigning historiographical positivism. For one, it heroized its protagonist—"the radiant, the merry, the helmeted warrior"—in a way that was objectionable to an academic guild that avoided exaggerations or even bright colors. Friedrich Gundolf was right to call Kantorowicz "Frederick's herald."[11] Here is Frederick II in Aachen in 1215:

> Directly after the Coronation Mass, scarcely having received the diadem, the proud and ardent lad dedicated himself to God and the Empire in the noble devotion of youth by means of his crusading vow. And he himself wished this vow to be understood as a sacrifice, as a dedication to his imperial office and to his calling—"with pure and spotless heart he not only dedicated his body and his abilities to God, but offered them humbly in an all-consuming sacrificial flame." (71)

Clearly this author had no intention of muffling his enthusiasm but adhered to Gundolf's maxim that "enthusiasm enkindles historical writing." Moreover, for him the worthiest enthusiasm was the outpouring of hero worship. Gundolf (Stefan George's mouthpiece) had declared that "the first task and consequence of all culture is to keep alive reverence—the sense for the worthiness and greatness of men," and that "the veneration of great men is either religious or it is worthless."[12] Academic historians, on the other hand, were trained not to be "religious."

KFII was controversial secondly because of the range of sources on which it drew. Until then German methodology preferred "objective" to "subjective" sources with the aim of re-creating events "as they really happened" (*wie es eigentlich gewesen*). Academic historians combed the archives for documents—letters, treaties, wills—that could testify most reliably to the "facts." In lieu of sufficient documentary evidence medieval historians were obliged to draw on chronicles, but when they did they endeavored to subject them to tough-minded criticism, comparing one to another and discounting palpable exaggerations and improbabilities. Kantorowicz, on the other hand, upheld an ideal of "visualization." "Vision" and "shape" (*Gestalt*) were watchwords of the George circle, and he himself had written to Wilhelm Stein in 1922 about having been awakened to the importance of "pictorial seeing". In his biography of Frederick II he sought to implement this ideal. In practice "pictorial seeing" meant word painting based heavily on designedly noncritical use of chronicles. For him it was the exaggerations and inventions of chronicles that created "shape." This was controversial enough, but even more so was his frequent use of "nonpositivistic" sources: legends, prophecies, manifestoes, panegyrics, and ceremonial chants.

To take a few examples, toward the beginning of his account Kantorowicz told of how the empress Constance, said to be beyond the age of childbirth, was

[11] Gundolf to Magda Bezner, December 1924: Gundolf Archive.

[12] Friedrich Gundolf, *Anfänge deutscher Geschichtsschreibung von Tschudi bis Winckelmann* (Frankfurt, 1992), 122, 129. (Originally published in 1938.)

delivered of the infant Frederick in a market square in order to allay any doubts that a nonroyal baby had been smuggled in. And then she displayed her milk-filled breasts for all to see (10–11). The entire story was false, but Kantorowicz told it anyway because it enhanced the aura of a supernatural birth. In this case he did signal to the reader that he was recounting a legend, but a few pages later he wrote without qualification: "Some people along the Moselle were frightened by an apparition: they had seen Dietrich von Bern on a gigantic black steed who had come to announce misery and woe to the Roman Empire" (17). And so it goes. The author tells of a meeting between Frederick II and Saint Francis that never took place (151). According to him the sweetest tones of angelic music flowed out of the throat of the dying Elisabeth of Hungary; her corpse exuded oil that Teutonic Knights collected and sent to churches (385). Toward the end of KFII the author refers with a straight face to Manfred's "magic ring with which he could conjure devils" (618).

Kantorowicz was anything but a religious believer, but he sometimes came close to implying that the hand of God was part of his story. An example is his naming of the scene of Frederick II's birth in Ancona as a "holy region" partly because the Virgin Mary's house from Nazareth where she had received the annunciation had been deposited there miraculously (11). The miracle had transpired in 1294, almost half a century after Frederick II's death in 1250. Yet it showed that God loved Ancona; moreover, 1294 was "exactly one hundred years after the birth of the Staufen youth."

Kantorowicz's most frequently cited prophet was Joachim of Fiore, who wrote in southern Italy during the time of Frederick's childhood and later was celebrated by Dante as "endowed with the spirit of prophecy." He quoted Dante's epithet implicitly in his first mention of Joachim and then provided an epithet of his own, "the John of Saint Francis" (10). Kantorowicz introduced Joachim as a voice for making the newborn Frederick a coming "world chastiser," but in fact Joachim never prophesied about specific personalities; at best he was referring to a "pseudo-Joachite" work, one or another of the many pseudonymous texts fathered on Joachim decades after his death. Similarly we hear of "Joachim of Fiore" announcing the coming of St. Francis and Frederick II—"power and antipower"—decades before their appearance (150). Only later does Kantorowicz admit that "where Joachim with his sayings did not suffice, further Joachite promises and interpretations were invented," yet he still uses them, along with "true and false sibyls, Merlin, prophecies of Michael Scot, oriental oracles, and Spanish predictions," to demonstrate the widespread expectation of imminent apocalyptic events and the Last Judgment (363). Toward the end of his book Kantorowicz brings in the paradoxical saying of the "Erythrean Sibyl": "He lives and lives not" (628). This offered the sense felt by many of Frederick's contemporaries that the emperor, who had more or less disappeared out of nowhere as a result of his sudden death, would return supernaturally to complete his work. In 1905 a German scholar, Oswald Holder-Egger, set himself to editing several pseudo-Joachite prophecies, including the "Erythrean Sibyl," and apologized for wasting time on such "childlike" works; his only excuse was that they were prerequisites for annotating a thirteenth-century chronicle.[13] Two decades later Ernst Kantorowicz was not apologizing.

One other variety of nonpositivistic source material, ceremonial acclamations, may be considered here because Kantorowicz's use of them connects most directly with his subsequent historiographical work. Ceremonies and the words used in ceremonies were of scant interest to professional scholars before he wrote; they assumed that when a king was crowned he was crowned and that was that. But Kantorowicz found not only that evocation of ceremonial details and words gave texture to his story but that the expressions of awe and reverence that were chanted during solemn ceremonies magnified his hero's superhuman qualities. Thus when he tells of the events surrounding Frederick II's coronation as "king of the Romans" in Aachen in 1215, he explains how Frederick drew on the prestige of Charlemagne and on that of his grandfather, Frederick Barbarossa, who had seen to Charlemagne's canonization (70).

Kantorowicz's description of Frederick's Roman coronation in 1220 as Roman emperor is particularly full:

> Near the baths of Diocletian Frederick received the homage of the Roman clergy who led him in solemn procession, with crucifixes and censers, to the church of Saint Peter. . . . Clothed in imperial vestments Frederick now stepped through the silver gate into Saint Peter's, where cardinals intoned blessings and prayers. He paid reverence before the tomb of Peter and was anointed by a cardinal before the tomb of Saint Maurice. And now he climbed up to the altar of Peter to make confession and to receive the kiss of peace from the Pope . . . who crowned him with mitre and crown and then passed to him the sword that Frederick had to brandish mightily three times to indicate that he now was a "knight of Saint Peter." Then he received the orb and sceptre, and now the choir responded: "To Frederick, the undefeated Emperor of the Romans, the ever exalted, Victory and Salvation [*Sieg und Heil*]." (100–101)

Frederick's celebration of his victory over an enemy force at the battle of Cortenuova in 1237 provided another opportunity for "pictorial seeing." After the battle the emperor retired with his troops and many prominent prisoners to his base of Cremona and celebrated a "triumph" in imitation of an ancient Roman imperial event:

> The Milanese carroccio [the enemy's ceremonial battle wagon], the noblest of trophies, was drawn by an elephant behind the great victor through the streets of Cremona, accompanied by the joyous shouting of the people. The yellow imperial

[13] Oswald Holder-Egger, "Italienische Prophetien des 13. Jahrhunderts," *Neues Archiv der Gesellschaftt für ältere deutsche Geschichtskunde* 30 (1904–05): 323–86, at 323.

> banner, adorned with Roman eagles, waved down from the back of the animal, while trumpeters on a wooden tower made known the triumph of the new Divine Caesar Augustus. . . . All the ostentatious Roman titles for Caesar were justified by this victory: the formulaic, mindlessly used "unconquered Emperor" again meant what it originally meant. (401)

Many bits and pieces of the foregoing passages were to be rearranged in Kantorowicz's later scholarly publications. But most striking is his fixation in KFII with the acclamation "Christus vincit, Christus regnat, Christus imperat," for this was to become the subject of an entire book, *Laudes Regiae*. Toward the opening of his biography, Kantorowicz recounts how his hero was brought to Palermo at the age of three and a half for a pro forma coronation as king of Sicily, and how on Pentecost he was led in a "splendid ceremony borrowed from the Byzantine court while the people greeted him according to ancient usage . . . with the cry 'Christ is victorious; Christ is King; Christ is Emperor!'" (20).

Although the chant was not used when Frederick crowned himself king of Jerusalem in 1229, Kantorowicz evoked it again. Christ and Frederick were the first and last kings of Jerusalem: "Savior and Emperor are here seen together as the successors of David, as the sons of God, the angel-like geniuses that mediate between God and men. These implications were lacking for Godfrey and his successors on Jerusalem's throne who were not, as the Roman Emperor, modeled as rulers of the world. But 'Christ is victorious; Christ is King; Christ is Emperor!' was already the age-old acclamation for the Sicilian Kings" (186).

Perhaps the author thought that the three-part acclamation needed to be mentioned thrice for symmetry, for he came back to it yet again at the end of his book: "In accordance with the words that the people of Palermo once showered on the three-year-old at his first coronation, 'Christ is victorious; Christ is King; Christ is Emperor!' the life of the Emperor would not lack glory even in his final struggle" (622).

Moving beyond Kantorowicz's reliance on a range of sources that hitherto had been belittled or shunned, it remains to mention two other features of KFII that made the book controversial. One was a tendency to portray Frederick as a creature of fate. An extreme example is when the author maintains that "Frederick II did not attempt to derive his direct relationship to God as Emperor so much from doctrines and theories as from the obvious miracles of his career that were known to all and that proved more than anything else the chosen nature if not of his imperial rank then of his imperial person" (183). Elsewhere the portentous locutions "it was to happen" and "it would be" occur repeatedly. One misses human psychology and earthbound explanations grounded on political, let alone economic, determinants.

Finally comes Kantorowicz's obsession with the theme of Roman imperial revival. Doubtless he had evidence for his view that Frederick II's ambitious claims to rulership rested on his imperial title as seen from the vantage point of its ancient Roman antecedents. But the difficulty was that Frederick was most "Roman imperial" in his capacity as king of Sicily rather than as ruler of Germany. For Kantorowicz the ideal of the Roman Empire was world rule (Frederick II appropriated the motto "Roma caput mundi"), but in Germany Frederick surrendered power, trading off rights to the German princes in order to have greater leeway for advancing his goals as Sicilian king. Furthermore, from the point of view of political realities it was during the period of Frederick's reign that France was becoming the dominant power in Europe. The many manifestoes and slogans, legends and myths that Kantorowicz adduced could do nothing to alter this. In other words, he allowed exalted claims to overshadow realities and tended to express an overheated imperial mysticism. His work was not teleological. Far from it, for he knew that Germany's Second Reich was entirely different from the medieval German Empire and even the Second Reich was no more. But he was still holding forth imperialism as a worthy goal.

At this point readers unfamiliar with the book may be wondering whether it has any traditional substance at all. The answer is by all means yes. Kantorowicz's progress beyond his amateurish dissertation of 1921 is stunning in terms of the thoroughness of his research and analysis. Among other enduring historical contributions are KFII's analyses of Frederick's legislation, creation of a protobureaucratic state, and founding of the first secular medieval university. The work is a landmark concerning Frederick's patronage of a circle of translators and natural scientists and his own work in falconry. Thus the book was as useful for scholars as it was engaging for nonscholars. And for both it was its uniqueness that was most riveting.

One can do no better than quote from the memoirs of two younger German contemporaries, Gerhart Ladner and Felix Gilbert, to appreciate what was at stake. Ladner wrote that when he first met Kantorowicz in 1929 "he was a heroic example, for he had accomplished a great success—he had created in his biography of the Emperor Frederick II a widely visible monument of a heroic figure in history; his book was history writing in the grand style."[14] Gilbert believed that "Kantorowicz's work on the Emperor Frederick II . . . demonstrated that a different kind of medieval history, one that revealed the ideas and values that motivated the rulers of the Middle Ages, was possible and might have a wide appeal. Even if one did not share the political and literary views and values of Kantorowicz . . . one admired his book for overcoming the rigidification that had set in in medieval history because of an overemphasis on historical techniques."[15]

But hardly anyone reads KFII today. Not only has the relevant scholarship advanced, but Kantorowicz's rhetoric and exaggerations are uncongenial.[16]

[14]Ladner, *Erinnerungen*, 32.

[15]Felix Gilbert, *A European Past: Memoirs, 1905–1945* (New York, 1988), 106–7.

[16]Today the biography of choice is Wolfgang Stürner, *Friedrich II*, 2 vols. (Darmstadt, 1992–2000): exhaustive and sober.

Above all the politics stick in one's throat. A commentator of the 1990s called the book "aesthetically ennobled fascism."[17] A marginal note in a copy from the Edinburgh University library reads: "Just wait, matey. Give it a couple of years and you'll probably like Hitler."[18] At a conference devoted to the career and work of Ernst Kantorowicz held in Frankfurt in 1993 a prominent medieval historian, Otto Gerhard Oexle, had this to say: "Ernst Kantorowicz's *Friedrich der Zweite* and the image of the Middle Ages propagated in it was . . . a weapon in the political struggle over the Weimar Republic. . . . I think that *this* book by Kantorowicz does not really have anything to offer us today. I would like to add the wish: may such a political and social situation to which a book of this kind would have something to say never again be imaginable or realizable in Germany."[19]

In concluding this chapter I would like to pursue Oexle's remarks. When one reads the passage about Germans "having harvested shame" or the biography's concluding words, "'He lives and lives not' . . . the Sibyl's saying is no longer for the Emperor but for the Emperor's Volk," one cannot help but think of the Nazi fight-song: "Germany awaken!" For many a connection with Nazis seems even clearer because of the stylized swastika on the cover and title page of Kantorowicz's book. Those who handle the book today are understandably unnerved, for it is difficult to look at the swastika without shuddering. But in this regard an excursus is necessary.[20]

The swastika on the cover and title page of KFII was the signet for a series of books published by Georg Bondi as a "scientific" (*wissenschaftlich*) supplement to Stefan George's poetry and literary magazine, *Leaves for Art* (*Blätter für die Kunst*). Melchior Lechter, an art nouveau designer favored by George, chose a swastika for the signet because he leaned toward Hindu mysticism and considered the swastika to be a tantric symbol of auspiciousness.[21] The signet first appeared as a logo for a Bondi publication in 1910; in 1916 Lechter encircled it with the words "Blätter für die Kunst." In those years the swastika signet was no more charged with political or racial meaning than a dolphin with an anchor. But obviously once the Nazi Party began gaining notoriety in the

[17] Gustav Seibt quoted in Olaf B. Rader, "Der Bernstein und das Insekt. Die Aktualität der Arbeiten Kantorowicz' aus der Perspektive eines Monumentisten," in Ernst and Vişmann, *Geschichtskörper*, 59–71, at 68.

[18] Communicated to the author by Professor David d'Avray.

[19] Otto Gerhard Oexle, "German Malaise of Modernity: Ernst H. Kantorowicz and His *Kaiser Friedrich der Zweite*," in Benson and Fried, *Ernst Kantorowicz*, 33–55, at 55. A longer and more polemical version of this piece appears as "Das Mittelalter als Waffe," in Oexle, *Geschichtswissenschaften im Zeichen des Historismus* (Göttingen, 1996), 163–215.

[20] For the following, EG, 151, n. 11.

[21] Michael Landmann, *Figuren um Stefan George*, 18. It must be said that the swastika had been appropriated around 1897 as a heathen device standing against the cross (deemed "a castrated swastika") by the proto-Nazi Alfred Schuler: Gerd-Klaus Kaltenbrunner, "Zwischen Rilke und Hitler—Alfred Schuler," *Zeitschrift für Religions—und Geistesgeschichte* 19 (1967): 333–47, at 336–37. But Landmann, whose mother was close to Lechter, rejects a Schuler connection.

1920s the signet took on a different aspect. Bondi (himself Jewish) thus offered a clarification in his annual catalog of 1928. He protested that he had come first. Moreover, he declared that those who knew the books in his "scientific" series even fleetingly knew that they had "nothing to do with politics." Accordingly he was not going to abandon the signet. Well and good? Hardly, for even if Melchior Lechter had chosen the swastika before Adolf Hitler, by the twenties its association with Nazism should have been sufficient reason to abandon it. Kantorowicz had no responsibility in this matter, but one must suppose rather sadly that he did not even think of it.

The larger question is whether Bondi was warranted in asserting that his series—"Works of Science from the Circle of Leaves for Art"—"had nothing to do with politics." Presumably he meant to say that the books in question disregarded daily or party politics. Indeed Stefan George shunned such matters and expected his disciples to do the same. Kantorowicz saluted. A letter of his of October 1926 expresses his view clearly.[22] He had seen that Friedrich Wolters, one of George's most militantly right-wing lieutenants, was lending his name to *völkisch* manifestoes and responded by writing to Ernst Morwitz that such open political activity was "impossible." As he wrote, "One is at liberty to have private views *in politicis*, but one cannot actively serve two states; matters that should stand above all parties should not be dragged into the dirt of one party."

But if Bondi's books indeed had nothing to do with party politics, his unqualified statement that his series "had nothing to do with politics" was disingenuous. George himself often said privately that the series in question was political.[23] By this he meant politics as *Weltanschauung*, which was all that he and his circle cared about. Unfortunately many of the views of which he approved were not far away from those of the Nazis. Returning to Kantorowicz, how uncomfortable is the assertion "loyalty [*Treue*]—since the dawn of time possible only among Germans" (85). In 1931 Hitler praised a member of the SS with the words "Your honor is loyalty," and this subsequently became the motto of the Waffen SS as well as an inscription over the gate to Hitler's Alpine residence in Berchtesgaden. In reaction Alfred Brendel wrote in 1976 about musical *Werk Treue*: "I have been made immune to blind faith by the years I spent under the Nazi regime. In the slave mentality of that era, not only words like 'faith' and 'fatherland,' but also the word 'fidelity' suffered shameful abuse."[24]

Accounts of Kantorowicz's career written after the Second World War often repeat the following: KFII lay on Himmler's nightstand; Göring presented the

[22] EG, 72. The dating to "Summer 1925" can be corrected on the basis of internal references.

[23] Salin, *Um Stefan George*, 253: "'Geistbücher sind Politik'—wie oft hat George diesen Satz gesagt." Norton, *Secret Germany*, 586–87, observes wryly that "nothing to do with politics" really meant "nothing to do with anyone else's politics but [George's] own."

[24] Alfred Brendel, *Musical Thought and After-Thoughts* (Princeton, 1976), 26. The manifestations and valences of the slogan "German loyalty" are explored in several contributions to Nikolaus Buschmann and Karl Borromäus Murr, eds., *Treue: Politische Loyalität und militärische Gefolgschaft in der Moderne* (Göttingen, 2007).

book with an inscription to Mussolini; Hitler himself read it twice.[25] None of these statements are verifiable, although it is certain that the book was reprinted in Germany in 1936 despite its having been written by a Jew.[26] Moreover, in 1942 a Nazi historian, Karl Ipser, evoked Kantorowicz's last lines, as if everyone knew them: "The greatest Frederick is now redeemed. . . . His work is now secured and has found its radiant fulfillment through Adolf Hitler."[27] (Actually Hitler died at fifty-six, just like Frederick II.) Kantorowicz later regretted having written KFII. In the same year when Ipser wrote, Norman Rich, a graduate student who was in EKa's entourage in Berkeley, took his German-born mother to listen to one of EKa's lectures. She had been reading KFII and brought it to him after the lecture to sign. But he declined, saying "the man who wrote that book died many years ago."[28]

Still, however much he may have been a sorcerer's apprentice, "the man who wrote that book" was never a Nazi. We will take this question up in a later chapter, but regarding KFII one finds balanced against the quoted passages others that uphold the virtues of courtliness and a cosmopolitan ideal. A noted one makes Frederick II a "Renaissance man" *avant la lettre*:

> Frederick II, statesman and philosopher, politician and warrior, leader of armies and jurist, poet, diplomat, architect, zoologist, mathematician, the master of six or perhaps nine languages, who collected ancient works of art, guided sculptors, inquired independently into nature, and organized states was in this many-sidedness entirely the Genius of the Renaissance on the imperial throne. (613)

Moreover, this particular "Genius of the Renaissance" had an intimate knowledge of Islam. Kantorowicz's earlier study of the subject allowed him to determine that Frederick used an Arabic formula in his treaty with the sultan, swearing "to eat the flesh of his left hand" if he broke the pact (176). When Frederick was in Jerusalem he noted the architecture of the Al Aqsa mosque (176–77). No Nazi is speaking when Kantorowicz proposes that Frederick II had "an unlimited admiration for the Arab intellect" (176–77).

Most centrally Kantorowicz believed that Frederick's cosmopolitanism was intrinsic to his having been a "Sicilian-Italian Hohenstaufen" (76) imbued with

[25] EG, 165, and repeated widely. The basis of the reports about Himmler and Göring is a letter of 1963 written by Kantorowicz, who seems to have heard such rumors. The source for Hitler is Percy Ernst Schramm, EG, 165, n. 36. But it is counterintuitive to imagine Hitler reading a difficult six-hundred-page work by a Jewish author not once but twice.

[26] EG, 156.

[27] The passage is quoted by Martin A. Ruehl, "'Imperium transcendat hominem': Reich and Rulership in Ernst Kantorowicz's *Kaiser Friedrich der Zweite*," in *A Poet's Reich: Politics and Culture in the George Circle*, ed. Melissa S. Lane and Martin A. Ruehl, 204–47 (Rochester, NY, 2011), at 225–26; and by Marcus Thomsen, *"Ein feuriger Herr des Anfangs . . ." Kaiser Friderich II. in der Auffassung der Nachwelt* (Ostfildern, 2005), 269.

[28] Interview with Norman Rich, 14 January 2010. Marion Dönhoff once reported that in later life EKa thought it better had he never written the biography: Klaus Harpprecht, *Die Gräfin: Marion Dönhoff* (Reinbek, 2008), 188.

allegiance to the ancient Roman Empire. Kantorowicz represented Frederick II "not as a Teutonic hero, but as a Roman emperor, in Dantesque rather than Wagnerian terms."[29] Frederick was "the most Roman" of German emperors (352). He wished to build a world empire that would not be based on the domination of a single people but rather on a "community of all kings and princes, lands and peoples of Christendom under one Roman Emperor who belonged to no nation"; Frederick was "hardly a Swabian duke, indeed not even a German king, but solely Roman Caesar and Emperor and Divus Augustus" (353). Writing to Josef Liegle, Kantorowicz maintained that the question of "Germanness" should not be left between "Potsdam or Weimar" but should be answered by "Bamberg."[30] In his biography he then proposed that the renowned "Bamberg Rider" displayed French and Roman-antique influences that were drawn on by a German sculptor who had envisaged "a beautiful and knightly-noble human type that must have lived in Germany" to create an equestrian statue with worldwide appeal (77). Such passages lack any tinge of Nazi racial thought.

[29] Ruehl, "Reich and Rulership," 205.
[30] 27 August 1922: Roettig and Lerner, "Briefe von Ernst Kantorowicz," 332.

CHAPTER 8

Center of Attention

AFTER KFII APPEARED KANTOROWICZ BECAME A MAN OF PROFILE, much like a character in a novel. We have seen that an acquaintance remembered his appearance in 1928 so well that he indeed placed him in a novel. Otherwise the distinctive impression that he made on many is widely attested. Erich Rothacker, a philosophy professor who saw him in Heidelberg and Italy, found that he seemed like "an Italian or Spanish aristocrat."[1] The Indologist Heinrich Zimmer wrote to Friedrich Baethgen in Rome in 1928: "Send my best regards to our unforgettable bel Kanto."[2] The most detailed description appears in the memoirs of Gerhart Ladner, who first came to know EKa in Berlin in 1929 and afterward maintained close contacts with him in Germany and the United States:

> Initially he made a strange impression. He was a dandy in dress and bearing, elegant and even perfumed.... His entire appearance was fascinatingly exotic.... The large nose[3] and firmly set but by no means ascetic mouth lent his face something classical.... He was of medium height, very erect and taut, and moved with great liveliness. He had an almost captivating amiability. From the first word it was clear that he was "cosmopolitan" and not "professorial."[4]

Ladner's memoirs also refer to EKa's strange manner of speaking: "an almost singing manner of speech"—what later became famous in America as his "third Chinese tone." A student who heard EKa lecture in Berkeley called it "a

[1] Rothacker, *Heitere Erinnerungen*, 67.

[2] 15 February 1928: DLA, Heinrich Zimmer papers.

[3] Kantorowicz himself referred to his "very Jewish nose." (Letter to Elise Peters, 29 April 1963: Lerner archive.)

[4] Ladner, *Erinnerungen*, 32–33. Ladner originally wrote the section "In memoriam Ernst Kantorowicz" after EKa's death as a eulogy. A version appears in EG, 88, but Ladner afterward made some changes, deleting a reference to Kantorowicz's "more Latin than Jewish appearance." A pen portrait of Kantorowicz at age fifty appears in Yakov Malkiel, "Ernst H. Kantorowicz," in Evans, Jr., ed., *On Four Modern Humanists*, 146–219, at 181, n. 18.

curious sing-song Talmudic chant."[5] Poorly informed Americans thought that the quirky speech was an imitation of the recital style of Stefan George, but George read in a severe monotone. Instead, the likelihood that EKa developed it as a conscious affectation is strong. It was another way for him to cut a figure.

Pleasing himself with his persona, sometime around the beginning of 1927 Kantorowicz started requesting that friends and acquaintances call him "EKa" instead of "Ernst" or "Kantorowicz."[6] (Family members continued to call him Ernst.) We have seen that he posed for two portrait busts in Berlin in the winter of 1926–27. Both of the sculptors, Alexander Zschokke and Max Fueter, were in the ambit of the George circle and friends of Wilhelm Stein. EKa preferred Fueter's more idealized version and had it photographed with chiaroscuro lighting from different angles. One of these photos adorned the advertisement flyer for the second printing of KFII, lending the author a certain aura.

After vacationing in his mother's home in Holstein in the summer of 1927 and a brief stay in Heidelberg,[7] Kantorowicz went off for a memorable stay in Rome. In principle he went there to work on the documentation volume that was to serve as an accompaniment to his biography of Frederick II. But he hardly needed to be in Rome for any length of time to do that; instead, he evidently wanted to steep himself in the eternal city. He had already come to know the southern half of the peninsula and Sicily; now, with his biography finished, it was time for Rome. He left Heidelberg on October 10; stopping in Baden-Baden (to see his sister), Lugano, Milan, and Bologna, he reached Rome by the end of the month.[8] After finding an apartment—on the via Bocca di Leone, a street in the most fashionable part of Rome close to the Trevi Fountain and the Spanish Steps[9]—he thought at first that he would work just as he would have done in Germany. But he could accomplish little on his volume of documentation because the resources pertaining to Frederick II owned by the Prussian Historical Institute of Rome were still in Berlin. (He probably knew this already.) So he began work on an unrelated project for which unpublished documents were located in Rome—the mid-fourteenth-century campaigns of Cardinal Albornoz to regain central Italy for the Papal States.[10] Yet this research did not capture his attention enough for him to stay with it. Instead, after a few weeks, the city itself "suddenly sprung up," and he threw himself into "seeing."

[5] Grover Sayles Jr., "The Scholar and the Loyalty Oath," *San Francisco Chronicle*, 8 December 1963, 28.

[6] His letters to Wilhelm Stein move from "E.K." in November 1926 to "EKa" in September 1927.

[7] Kantorowicz to Wilhelm Stein, 22 September 1927: Stein papers.

[8] With exceptions noted, the following account of EKa's time in Italy is taken from his detailed report in a letter to Fine von Kahler, 29 August 1928: StGA, Kahler papers, III:6568.

[9] The address appears on a postcard to Wilhelm Stein, 19 December 1927: Stein papers.

[10] To Karl Hampe, 20 December 1927: Hampe papers.

Throughout the fall Kantorowicz dined regularly in the evenings with Friedrich Baethgen. On one occasion the two were joined by Percy Ernst Schramm, another young Heidelberg medievalist.[11] (Schramm's use of unconventional sources for the study of medieval rulership linked him to EKa; more on this later.) After Christmas the Roman social season began and Kantorowicz joined in. Although Baethgen, then second secretary of the Prussian Historical Institute, was his point of entrance, he soon became part of the scene independently because of his striking personality. Furthermore, the fame of his biography of the emperor Frederick was reaching Italy. (The second printing of early 1928 was of 4,400 copies.[12]) He was on many guest lists—invited to breakfasts, teas, dinners, and "countless times" to soirées. Ludwig Curtius, a leading classicist who assumed direction of the German Archeological Institute in Rome in 1928 and who succeeded EKa in the apartment on the via Bocca di Leone, wrote that "Roman 'Society' of the time consisted of the Roman aristocracy which mingled only with members of the diplomatic corps, and to which foreign scholars were more likely to gain access than Italian ones."[13] This confirms EKa's subsequent report to Fine that during the social season of early 1928 he met ambassadors and aristocrats with intellectual leanings, and that the gatherings he attended were held in the "beautiful palazzi" of these aristocrats.

At the same time he received a visitor from Germany: Woldemar Uxkull's half-sister, the Baroness Lucy von Wangenheim, known as "Baby." An interruption in the narrative to introduce her is necessary because she was to be the second of the three main heterosexual attachments in EKa's life. Her father was Hans Freiherr von Wangenheim, a career diplomat who had served the German imperial government in numerous capitals before being posted to Constantinople in 1912. There he helped engineer the Ottoman Empire's entry into the First World War.[14] In 1915 he died of a heart attack. Von Wangenheim was a notorious philanderer, a circumstance that contributed to his divorce from Baby's mother, the American-born heiress Lucy Ahrenfeldt. The latter, not wishing to be outdone, had been carrying on with Count Uxkull (senior), and when her husband learned of this he challenged the count to a duel with pistols. In comic opera fashion both were wounded but survived. Lucy then gained a divorce from the one and immediately married the other—all in the

[11]David Thimme, *Percy Ernst Schramm und das Mittelalter* (Göttingen, 2003). Schramm, who was in Heidelberg from 1921 until 1929, mentions a long evening in Rome with Kantorowicz and Baethgen in *Erasmus* 18 (1966): 455. See also Kantorowicz to Schramm, 9 January 1956: "Es war höchst erfreulich, Sie in Rom wieder gesehen zu haben, und unser Zusammensein mit Baethgen war im 'Zueinander' genau wie vor 30 Jahren": Schramm papers.

[12]Kantorowicz to Hampe, 6 January 1928: Hampe papers; EG, 156.

[13]Curtius, *Deutsche und Antike Welt*, 503.

[14]Walter von Hueck, ed., *Genealogisches Handbuch der freiherrlichen Häuser: A Band XII* (Limburg/Lahn, 1980), 432; Frank G. Weber, *Eagles on the Crescent: Germany, Austria, and the Diplomacy of the Turkish Alliance, 1914–1918* (Ithaca, 1970), 18.

year 1897.[15] Baby (Lucy Olga Varia Sophie von Wangenheim—born in 1892[16]) stayed with her mother, which meant that she grew up in Berlin and became the older half-sister of EKa's "Woldi" (born in 1898). As an adult she knew English well, probably having learned the language from her mother.

In 1916 Baby married an Italian, Nino Giachi, whom she met in Davos.[17] He was suffering from tuberculosis and had been living in a sanatorium. For a while Giachi tried to make a living in Basel, but he was too weak, returned to the sanatorium, and died there in 1921. But not before he sired three daughters: Lucia, Arianna, and Isotta (fig. 16). The names reflect Baby's style. According to Italian custom Lucia should have been named Anna, after her paternal grandmother, but Baby overruled this and had her named after her own mother (and herself). Then it was Giachi's turn, and that should have meant the choice of Anna. Yet the mother balked: "Anna was a name for serving girls." Accordingly "Arianna" (a variant of Ariadne, the bride of Dionysus) was chosen as a compromise. And when the third child was born after her father's death the mother decided to call her Isotta (Isolde), after a famous tragic adulterous heroine.

Baby was married briefly, from 1924 to 1926, to a former Prussian cavalry officer and landowner, Adolf von Arnim, a marriage that ended in divorce. At the end of 1926 she became intimately involved with Ernst Kantorowicz in Berlin, whom she met through her half-brother, and they saw each other every day for four months.[18] When he went off to Rome in the fall of 1927 he made plans to spend some time with Baby there in the winter of 1928. Anticipating her arrival he bought a Fiat in December and took driving lessons.[19] Baby arrived in Rome with her brother in February. Woldi stayed in EKa's apartment but she appeared regularly for midday meals.[20] EKa gained a driver's license at the end of February and at the beginning of March he and Baby drove south for ten days, experiencing a "fantastically beautiful trip" through the blossoming countryside to Naples and nearby sites.[21] At the end of the month they went off together again, now to Umbria and Tuscany for a trip that lasted until the

[15] Interview with her granddaughter, Arianna Giachi, 18 July 1994.

[16] Von Hueck, *Genealogisches Handbuch*, 433.

[17] Where not otherwise indicated personal information about Baby comes from interviews with Arianna Giachi, 16 December 1993 and 18 July 1994.

[18] Kantorowicz to Lucy von Wangenheim, 24 April 1927, communicated to me by Eckhart Grünewald.

[19] Kantorowicz to Woldemar Uxkull, 19 December 1927, communicated to me by Eckhart Grünewald.

[20] In his letter to Fine von Kahler of 29 August 1928, EKa writes that Woldi was prevented from coming to Rome, but this is contradicted not only by Arianna Giachi, who reported midday meals, but by Rothacker, *Heitere Erinnerungen*, 67, who tells of having seen EKa and Uxkull together "at Ranieri" in Rome.

[21] To Fine, 29 August 1928, for this and what follows. The driver's license is dated 27 February 1928: LBI, box 1, folder 3.

Figure 16. Lucy von Wangenheim with her daughters Isotta (*left*) and Arianna (*right*) on the Kurfürstendamm, Berlin, May 19, 1927. (Lerner archive)

middle of April.[22] After Clara Kantorowicz came to Rome for a week at the end of April, EKa and his mother went back to Germany together.

The Italian episode solidified a long-term relationship with Baby. The romance seems unexpected. Fine von Kahler came from EKa's world. She was connected to his friends and relatives, she knew Stefan George's poetry by heart, and she shared EKa's engagement with the life of the mind. Baby, on the other hand, was not an intellectual; her daughter Arianna reported that she did not read books except those that EKa gave her. EKa and Fine also exchanged Yiddishisms, but the gentile Baby's attitude toward Jews before she met EKa had been ambivalent. Her two husbands had been gentiles, and Arianna remembered that her mother distinguished between German Jews, who were acceptable, and "Ostjuden" (eastern European Jews), who were not. When Arianna was invited to a birthday party in Berlin by a boy named Herbert Cohen, her mother forbade her to accept even though Herbert was a German Jew.

Baby was also mannish. She played golf and smoked cigars.[23] Some people referred to the couple as "the battle-ax Baby and the tender Jew EKa."[24] Arianna stated that her mother was attractive to gay men, a view confirmed by the fact that the bisexual Maurice Bowra "fell at once for her" when he met her in 1934.[25]

[22] A postcard from Perugia to Wilhelm Stein is dated 4 April 1928: Stein papers.

[23] Golf: interview with Michael Hauck: 16 December 1993. Cigars: interviews with Lucy Cherniavsky, 5 September 1990, and with Margaret Bentley Ševčenko, 12 August 1996. (Both women reported EKa's reminiscences.)

[24] Interview with Arianna Giachi, 16 December 1993. Michael Hauck's first remark about Baby was that she was mannish.

[25] Bowra, *Memories*, 291.

Her attractiveness to EKa may have borne some relationship to this. (She was also three years his senior.) Yet Baby surely was not a "beard," chosen to mask homosexual activities, for she and EKa were an amorous couple. Soon after their time in Italy they vacationed together in the summer of 1928 in the posh resort of Timmendorfer Strand on the Baltic Sea together with Baby's half-brother Woldi. [26] From the fall of 1928 until the spring of 1931 they lived separately but saw each other constantly in Berlin. When EKa moved to Frankfurt early in 1931 Baby moved to Heidelberg because she did not want to be too public about her liaison and Heidelberg was near enough so that the two could visit each other often. (Baby drove an expensive car; see fig. 17.) The affair ended sometime in the mid-1930s, but the friendship endured until the early 1960s.

What did Kantorowicz see in Lucy von Wangenheim? The sketch of her that appears in C. M. Bowra's memoirs offers help in accounting for the attachment.[27] According to Bowra she was "strikingly handsome, intelligent, and well educated." He reported that her stories of her earlier life were fascinating: she had stayed with the Kaiser on Corfu, "where she had seen the German generals doing Greek dances for their master." All told, "she belonged to an aristocratic world and kept its independence and distinction." Baby's daughter reported that she enhanced her aura of independence by letting people think she was a widow, even though she had had a second marriage that ended in divorce.[28] (Bowra, who came to know her intimately, was ignorant of this.) Probably because of Baby's lively personality and because she radiated upper-class bearing and independence, she was the one woman whom EKa thought he might marry. He told this to two young confidantes in the United States. He said "he could have had a fine marriage [with Baby]—he living on one side of the house and she on the other" and admitted that he wanted to marry the "German Baroness," but that she did not want to marry him.[29]

Returning to the narrative of EKa's professional career, after the appearance of his biography of Frederick II in the spring of 1927 he was considering "habilitation" and becoming a junior instructor (*Assistent*) at Heidelberg. In this he had the encouragement of Karl Hampe, with whom by this time he had developed a warm and mutually respectful relationship. (EKa's letters to Hampe from this period end with greetings to his wife.) Hampe had even agreed in 1926 to read the proofs for KFII, but circumstances had prevented that from happening before the book came out. (Kantorowicz had made so many corrections on the galley proofs that they had become illegible to all but

[26] Interview with Arianna Giachi. See also EKa to Percy Ernst Schramm, 27 August 1928, Schramm papers; and EKa to Fine von Kahler, 29 August 1928.

[27] Bowra, *Memories*, 290–91.

[28] Arianna Giachi to Robert E. Lerner, 13 February 1994. (She commented that her mother liked to pose as a tragic heroine, which was easier to do as a widow.)

[29] Interviews with Margaret Bentley Ševčenko, 12 August 1996, and with Lucy Cherniavsky, 5 September 1990.

Figure 17. The Baroness Lucy von Wangenheim in her Fiat 15/70 PS Cabriolet, 1929. (By the company of Karl A. Klein. Photograph, 1929. Zander & Labisch - ullstein bild / Granger, NYC)

the typesetter.) While EKa was in Rome he wrote to Hampe that he had been gathering sufficient material for seminars.[30] This and his reference in the same letter to his project of studying documents pertaining to Cardinal Albornoz are the first pieces of evidence that he was planning to become a professional medieval historian. When he returned to Heidelberg in the late spring of 1928 he received an offer from Hampe to habilitate under him and take a junior position, but he turned it down with the explanation that it entailed too many restrictions. Actually, as we learn from a letter to Fine, everything in Heidelberg had seemed so "grotesquely unreal and ghostly" to him after Rome that he was glad to find an excuse for leaving definitively.[31] But he told Fine that this did not necessarily mean the abandonment of plans to habilitate.

Somewhat depressed, he let himself be distracted by means of an extended summer vacation.[32] For two months, interrupted only by two weeks with Baby and Woldi on the Baltic Sea, he occupied himself with athletics at his mother's estate in Holstein. This meant not only swimming and tennis but duck hunting and target practice with bow and arrow. The Olympic Games were being held that summer in Amsterdam and he was pursuing his own "Olympiade," timing

[30] 20 December 1927: Hampe papers.

[31] EG, 84; to Fine von Kahler, 29 August 1928.

[32] To Wilhelm Stein, 8 August 1928: Stein papers; to Fine von Kahler, 29 August 1928; to Percy Ernst Schramm, 27 August 1928: Schramm papers. Passages from the letter to Schramm are quoted in Robert E. Lerner, "'Meritorious Academic Service': Kantorowicz and Frankfurt," in Benson and Fried, *Ernst Kantorowicz*, 14–32, at 15, n. 4.

himself at swimming, measuring how far he could throw a javelin, running the hundred-meter dash in a remarkable twelve seconds. He ran about naked. He went to bed "dead tired" at 10:30 and rose between 7:00 and 8:00 to begin again. His reading related to his archery: *On Lion Hunt with Bow and Arrow* (*Mit Pfeil und Bogen auf Löwenjagd*), an American adventure novel that recently had been translated into German. He joked that he was relapsing to the level of boys' reading that his Heidelberg existence had forced him to repress.

But the documentation volume was weighing on him. The biography of 1927 had promised such a volume—"to appear shortly"—and reluctantly he felt obliged to honor his promise. Scholars had already written to him independently asking for references for one or another passage. (EKa wrote to Baby with a smirk that he dolloped these out "politely and graciously."[33]) Consequently he moved to Berlin at the beginning of September because he wanted to get the job done and Berlin had the best resources.[34] The library of the Monumenta Germaniae Historica (MGH), Germany's research institute for medieval history, had a comprehensive collection of books in the field; moreover, since it was installed in the Prussian State Library it was easy to resort to the collections of the latter for anything missing or not strictly medieval. Choosing to live in comfort as usual, EKa rented an apartment in a villa in Charlottenburg within convenient reach of the MGH by public transportation. But the job of preparing the supplementary volume took much longer than anticipated.

One reason for the delay was that he became embroiled in an extended controversy regarding KFII. This was launched with éclat by Albert Brackmann, one of Germany's most prestigious senior medieval historians, in a paper delivered at a meeting of the Prussian Academy of Sciences in May 1929. Kantorowicz engaged in print with Brackmann a few months later, and exchanges continued until the following April. Brackmann, *Ordinarius* (senior chair-holder) in Berlin when he gave his talk (in the fall he became general director of the Prussian State Archives) and coeditor of the *Historische Zeitschrift*, Germany's premier historical journal, criticized Kantorowicz's method in a paper entitled "Kaiser Friedrich II in 'Mythical View.'" This argued that Kantorowicz had dwelled improperly on myth rather than writing legitimate history.[35] Brackmann began by referring to a generational divide: older historians had dedicated themselves to technical labors—editions of sources and source criticism—and now it was time for others to harvest these achievements by writing synthetic works. Kantorowicz's biography did this by "uniting thorough learning with a gripping manner

[33] Letter of 27 May 1927, communicated by Eckhart Grünewald.

[34] To Fine von Kahler, 29 August 1928.

[35] Originally published in *Historische Zeitschrift* 140 (1929): 534–49; reprinted in Albert Brackmann, *Gesammelte Aufsätze* (Weimar, 1941), 367–80, and Gunther Wolf, ed., *Stupor mundi: zur Geschichte Friedrichs II. von Hohenstaufen* (Darmstadt, 1966), 5–22. Numbers in parentheses refer to pages in the *Historische Zeitschrift*.

of presentation." But the book's enthusiastic reception prompted great reservations because it proceeded along lines that were "methodologically false" (534).

Brackmann's central charge was that Kantorowicz portrayed Frederick II's personality and actions on the basis of preconceived notions stemming from the "dogma" of the George circle. In so doing the biographer confused myth with reality and ignored the "facts" of specific situations. Brackmann concentrated on Kantorowicz's assertion that Frederick's self-crowning in Jerusalem was a turning point in his self-conception as world-ruler, responsible only to God. For Kantorowicz Jerusalem was both the meeting place between East and West and the holiest place where a Christian could be crowned, and the self-crowning demonstrated Frederick's independence of the papacy. Brackmann opposed this by arguing that Frederick was not crowning himself as emperor (he already was emperor) but only as king of Jerusalem, then a small territory, and that the self-crowning was not a gesture of independence from the papacy but an acknowledgment of the papal ban under which the emperor had then been placed. According to him, Frederick purposely avoided an ecclesiastical coronation while under ban to avoid antagonizing the pope, and his immediately subsequent manifesto showed that he wished only to return to the pope's good graces (536–39). Brackmann conceded that a decade later the emperor's supporters compared him to Christ, but he insisted that this was only in the heat of battle (545–47). One needed to look at context and even then not be seduced by the exaggerated language of the sources; especially in the case of Frederick II one should not "overpaint with contemporary dyes" (548).

Brackmann's peroration was virtually a cri de coeur (547–49). For him Kantorowicz proceeded in exactly the wrong direction: he "experienced" the emperor and then based his portrayal on his feelings rather than working from the evidence without preconceptions: "The *imagination créatrice* that today is beginning to appear in our historical work is stronger with him than the hard sense of reality. It exhibits itself here in the attempt to bring historical science and myth close together, and there of course lies a great danger for the recognition of the truth." Brackmann had no hesitation in referring to his own "positivist ideal of knowledge" and steadfastly wished to defend it against "fantasy, aesthetics, or religiosity in the broadest sense." Kantorowicz's biography was symptomatic of "the very grave situation" facing current historiography. One should proceed on the basis of working hypotheses not "dogmas"; one should uphold "the idea of truth and the spirit of truthfulness"; and one should not write history "either as a George disciple, or as a Catholic, Protestant, or Marxist, but only as a truth-seeking human being."

The attack gained notoriety in early June as the result of an article in the *Vossische Zeitung*, one of Berlin's most widely circulated newspapers, that bore the heading "Academy against Mythical View."[36] EKa could hardly ignore the

[36] EG, 86.

challenge, nor did he want to. (A clipping of the article remains today in the Kantorowicz papers now in New York.) Immediately he wrote to Stefan George that a fine opportunity for stating principles had arisen.[37] The *Vossische Zeitung* had quoted Brackmann's criticism that he had "overpainted the emperor with contemporary dyes," and EKa quipped to the Meister that "the contemporary dyes so readily rejected by the guild historian are at any rate more laundry-fast than the modern I. G. Farben [*Farben* means "dyes"] with which he is associated." Brackmann sent EKa proofs of the paper he now was going to publish in the *Historische Zeitschrift* at the end of the summer, together with a letter proposing that they discuss it. Apparently he wished to ward off the possibility that Kantorowicz would insist on publishing a rejoinder, but in this he was deluded. EKa responded that a meeting was inappropriate because of "the fundamental divergence of our historiographical views," adding that "our dispute is of too principled significance that it should be withheld from the public." Thus he requested space in the next issue of the *Historische Zeitschrift* to present his side, and Brackmann was obliged to comply.[38]

Kantorowicz's rejoinder was as polemical as that of his opponent, but he wrote with wit and an ironical style inflected with arrogance that differed greatly from Brackmann's plainspoken earnestness.[39] He opened by saying that whereas his opponent had charged him with following a methodologically incorrect path he could allude to those Austrian generals who claimed that French victories at the battles of Montenotte and Lodi had been gained in methodologically false ways (457). (Knowledgeable readers would have recognized that Kantorowicz was comparing himself to Napoleon.) But he did want to engage in exploring supposed methodological error, as well as answer Brackmann's complaints about specific issues surrounding Frederick II's self-crowning. Regarding the latter, he maintained that the manifesto issued after the event drew for the first time on biblical language that applied to the savior (464), and he produced a poem written by a German soon after the manifesto that hailed Frederick in the terms "here is God, here is the devoted and wise imitator of God" (470). By these means he wished to demonstrate that the central place he had awarded to the self-crowning in Jerusalem did not come from preconceived notions but from the sources.

Still, methodological issues remained the most important. According to Kantorowicz, Brackmann revealed his own "dogma" in writing that history should not be written from the point of view of any partisan camp, and he

[37] EG, 87.

[38] To Brackmann, 15 September 1929: Brackmann papers; see also letters of 5 August 1929 and 27 October 1929.

[39] Ernst Kantorowicz, "'Mythenschau': Eine Erwiderung," *Historische Zeitschrift* 141 (1930): 457–71; reprinted in Wolf, *Stupor mundi*, 23–40. Numbers in parentheses refer to pages in the *Historische Zeitschrift*.

rejected this because it would exclude writing history as a *German* or as a person with *convictions* or *passions* (his emphases) (458). He himself did not wish to prove things but to present a *picture* of a person within his time (460n). Thus he purposely selected vivid contemporary sources instead of documents toward the goal of gaining "thought-colors." He was engaged in history writing, as opposed to historical research, and in this regard wished to create visual pictures and creative moments that had their own reality. He too was a "truth-seeker" yet engaged in *imagination créatrice* as opposed to those who sought "pure facts" and hence were mired in *réalisme déstructeur* (471).

Being the coeditor of the *Historische Zeitschrift*, Brackmann awarded himself the privilege of a surrebuttal, which he printed directly after Kantorowicz's rebuttal.[40] Aside from debating details, he held to his insistence on scholarship that was not driven by poetry (477). But he extended an olive branch. He had learned that Kantorowicz had been seen often in the MGH, an institution famously dedicated to traditional research. Accordingly he wondered whether he did not have a "quiet love" for that sort of thing and "whether at the end of his development he will be standing with Stefan George or Paul Kehr" (the director of the MGH).

The controversy did not end there but was taken to a higher level as a result of EKa's acceptance of an invitation to speak at a German historians' congress scheduled for April 1930. As he wrote to Fine in late January, his work on the supplementary volume had been slowed by his exchange with Brackmann and now he had to interrupt it. He intended to set forth his position regarding the "methods controversy" before a "phalanx" of specialists, all of whom were bound to be against him. The situation would be difficult but he was not going to avoid it; thus he had gone to his mother's home in Holstein for several weeks in order to write his paper without distractions.[41]

EKa was right about a "phalanx."[42] Some 140 history professors and junior faculty attended the meeting held at the University of Halle from April 22 to 26, 1930, as well as 250 others—students, librarians, archivists, and publishers. Among the professors were some of the most prominent historians of the day. Kantorowicz was the main attraction. His personal presence alone was a sensation since he was not yet thirty-five and held no academic position. As always he dressed to be noticed. A reporter from the *Vossische Zeitung* described "a slender young man in choice attire." Although he had been scheduled to speak in a large lecture hall, because of the crowd his talk was moved to the largest.

[40] "Nachwort: Anmerkung zu Kantorowicz' Erwiderung," *Historische Zeitschrift*, 472–78; reprinted in Wolf, *Stupor mundi*, 41–48.

[41] 25 January 1930: StGA, Kahler papers, III:6570.

[42] For a detailed and vivid account of the meeting and reactions to Kantorowicz's address, Eckhart Grünewald, "Sanctus amor patriae dat animum—ein Wahlspruch des George-Kreises? Ernst Kantorowicz auf dem Historikertag zu Halle a.d. Saale im Jahr 1930 (Mit Edition)," *Deutsches Archiv für Erforschung des Mittelalters* 50 (1994): 89–125. Grünewald, 90–125, edits the talk from the manuscript in the LBI, box 2, folder 1.

Delighted to be the center of attention, he also was nervous: he took a sedative before he spoke and a stiff drink after.[43] Certainly his presentation, delivered in his high rhetorical style and with its contents fully undomesticated, was calculated to have the halls buzzing after it was finished.

The talk stands as the most coherent expression of the historiographical views of what Kantorowicz was happy to call the "George School." His title was "Limits, Possibilities, and Duties in the Representation of Medieval History," and he took each point in turn. The "limits" in the representation of history (and not just in that of medieval history) meant a fundamental distinction between historical research and historical writing. Referring to Brackmann's call for objectivity, Kantorowicz granted that no reasonable person would quarrel with the position that historical research should strive to be objective. "Or," as he qualified, "nearly so," for choices inevitably had to be made in research that were determined by subjective judgments; even an index had to rest on choices if it were not to be a simple word concordance. But historical writing by necessity was different because no one would want a work that did nothing other than narrate events hour by hour. On the contrary, the great German historical works of the nineteenth century, those of "Ranke, Droysen, Giesebrecht, Sybel, Mommsen, Treitschke," were outstanding specimens of historical writing: works of literature. (The list was that of the most famous "positivists.")

The distinction between research and writing led the speaker to his topic of "possibilities," that is, appropriate topics in writing, or what he preferred to call "representation" (*Darstellung*). He excluded the search for origins. For him obsession with this question reduced the historical subject to being a mere product of a predecessor, who was the product of a predecessor, and "crablike" so on backward. Ultimately, then, one could say that the German emperors strode into their temples just like the pharaohs or that the kiss exchanged by pope and emperor already was in the Gilgamesh epic. Purposely provocative, he insisted that writers of history should not strive to explain what *became* in a causal nexus but maintained in the classic Rankean formulation that they should write about "what really was."

His main point in this regard was that historians should respect "the individual worth of a person, a people, an epoch, a culture" (112). Paraphrasing Ranke, he said that God would be unjust if he devised one generation merely as the preparation for another; quoting Ranke directly he said "all generations are equal in the eyes of God and so must the historian too view the matter" (116). One had to "drive time out of history," and the pursuit of causality could not serve the goal of seizing a historical subject in its own terms. Indeed one had to appreciate the inevitability of "the irrational moment"; one had to prefer the "in spite of" instead of the "because." Taking an example from his own repertoire, Kantorowicz explained that most historians thought that a long discussion held

[43] To Vera Peters, 15 January 1955: Lerner archive.

between Frederick II and the mathematician Leonardo Fibonacci concerning geometry and algebra could not have transpired in Pisa in 1226 because the emperor then was on the march and needed to keep moving. But if one recognized Frederick's uniqueness and his continual "playing with fate," one could picture him finding leisure for a learned conversation "in spite of" the situation. And for that one had to employ *imagination créatrice* (114–15).

Of course such imagination had to have some relation to the sources. In this regard Kantorowicz insisted on the urgency of using nondocumentary sources for the representation of history—for gaining a "true" picture however "unreliable" such sources might seem to the benighted. Precisely because representation had to be subjective, the historian needed to draw on the greatest number and widest range of contemporary sources in order to "see" his subject as contemporaries did. Among such sources were not only "the thousands of individual observations" of the chronicles but also formularies for letter writing, invented letters, and (the positivists' bête noir) forgeries. Nobody could ever know what Karl or Otto really looked like, but one could know how they presented themselves and how they were perceived by their times (118–19). If this was "Mythical View" so be it.

But even in drawing a picture based on sources of the past one had to position oneself in the present and write with a point of view. Kantorowicz pilloried the "colorless, neutral type," such as the reporter who was ready to convey the views of any of his subjects regardless of party, nationality, or Weltanschauung. The same colorless neutrality was present in the current popular history that addressed the international "half-educated rabble (*Halbbildungspöbel*)" (122). To write good history one could not possibly be neutral. According to Kantorowicz, "Sober positivism today faces the danger of becoming Romantic when it maintains that it is possible to find the Blue Flower of truth without preconceptions" (120). (The "Blue Flower" was a symbol among German Romantics for the transcendental holy miracle of nature.) As Goethe wrote, "Is the truth an onion from which one only peels away layers? What you do not place within you will never pull out."

The current *task* was that of writing history informed by dedication to the nation. Kantorowicz asserted that the great German historians of the nineteenth century, among them Ranke and Mommsen, were inspired by a sense of the nation in danger. Now becoming incendiary, he proclaimed that this was all the more necessary at the present time: one had to write with "a real belief in something like a German mission"—not with "nationalistic tub-thumping" but with "yes, a fanatical belief in today's threatened Nation" (123). And at this juncture he cited a stunning "confession of faith" from Friedrich Schiller, written under the impress of the humiliating peace of Lunéville, which had awarded the entire left bank of the Rhine to France: "Every people has its day in history, but the day of the German is the harvest of all time." In view of the present danger and Germany's mission, historical representation had to be governed by "the dogma of the worthy future of the nation and its honor" (124–25). In concluding Kantorowicz called on his nineteenth-century oath helpers a final time. Alluding implicitly to Brackmann's remark about whether he did not really have a "quiet love" for the positivist work associated with the MGH (an institution founded in the early nineteenth century), he drew an ace from his sleeve and quoted the motto imprinted on the MGH's publications: "Holy love of the fatherland gives life" (*Sanctus amor patriae dat animum*).

How did the historiographical controversy play out? The senior academic establishment displayed no sympathy for the *enfant terrible*'s call for the abandonment of objectivity, a principle to which academic professionals had always held firm, however much some of them may have abandoned it in practice. A short discussion followed EKa's talk, but not a single prominent historian supported him.[44] Brackmann had not been in Halle, but Robert Holtzmann, newly appointed as his successor at the University of Berlin, informed him that although the talk was well organized and studded with piquant remarks, it was "a complete washout" from the point of view of content.[45] Werner Frauendienst, a student of Brackmann's, thought that the great nineteenth-century German historians were "turning over in their graves when they heard how Herr Kantorowicz fancied himself as their like-minded successor."[46]

Certainly he also had his admirers. Putting aside followers of George, some were younger historians who applauded his daring in challenging old-fashioned methods such as Gerhart Ladner and Felix Gilbert, mentioned in the previous chapter, and Theodor E. Mommsen, to be mentioned in the next. Yet none of them were inclined themselves to step out of line methodologically. Konrad Burdach, a prestigious senior scholar of late-medieval German literature, approved of the use of nonpositivistic sources in principle. Brackmann had sent Burdach offprints of the *Historische Zeitschrift* exchange, and the latter responded by saying that "the Heidelberger Georgiast" had "answered with great arrogance." But then he added his reservations about Brackmann's position regarding sources: "One cannot deny—you yourself certainly would not wish to—that the effect of political manifestoes on contemporaries is a very important subject for historical research."[47] EKa's only practicing ally was Percy Ernst Schramm, recently made Ordinarius for medieval history at Göttingen. Unlike Kantorowicz, Schramm wrote in straightforward scholarly prose, but his two-volume work on the emperor Otto III, *Kaiser, Rom und Renovatio* (1929), had been influenced by the Warburg school of art history in exploring imperial Roman symbolism as a form of propaganda in the Ottonian era. Appropriately

[44] EG, 97.

[45] To Brackmann, 27 April 1930: Brackmann papers.

[46] To Brackmann, 30 April 1930, Brackmann papers. This letter was generously called to my attention by Martin Ruehl, who learned of it from his student Sebastian Ullrich,

[47] Burdach to Brackmann, 17 March 1930: Brackmann papers.

Kantorowicz cited his book in his response to Brackmann in the *Historische Zeitschrift* (470n). Schramm was present in Halle, and the two discussed their research agendas in a wine tavern.[48]

As if uncannily plotted, the paths of Kantorowicz and Brackmann later crossed in opposite directions. Not only did EKa present himself as a "fanatical" nationalist in his Halle talk, but afterward he saw to the publication of the incendiary final section in two different far-right publications. One, the *Deutsche Allgemeine Zeitung*, was financed by antirepublican Rhineland industrialists; the other, *Der Ring*, was directed by a far-right-wing propagandist.[49] Yet Kantorowicz moved away from his "nationally oriented position" after 1933 and gradually became a man of the left. As for his historical writing, as the 1930s progressed he abandoned the rhetorical mode of KFII as well as his Halle principle that history had to be founded on "dogma." Instead, he began to concentrate on microanalysis and avoidance of *parti pris*.

As for Brackmann, who had argued against mixing politics with scholarship, already in 1932 he established a "publication center for Eastern research" with close connections to the German government.[50] "Eastern research" (*Ostforschung*) inevitably meant partisanship for Germany against the Slavs, and that became much more obtrusive once the Nazis took power in 1933.[51] Brackmann retired from his administrative position in 1936, but when Germany invaded Poland in 1939 he engaged in supporting Nazi aims from the stance of a historian. In a book commissioned by the SS, *Crisis and Reconstruction in Eastern Europe*, he cited "the Führer of the new Germany," who wrote in *Mein Kampf*, "we will stop the German turn to southern and western Europe and set our sights on the land in the East." Then he concluded: "What other Volk can claim to have accomplished as much for eastern Europe as Germany? When England and France demand today that nothing should happen in eastern Europe without their willing it, we must ask what accomplishments do they have to show to justify their demand? . . . Germany, the dominant power in Middle Europe

[48]Kantorowicz to Schramm, 28 September 1932: Schramm papers.

[49]"Geschichsforschung und Geschichtsschreibung," *Deutsche Allgemeine Zeitung*, 26 April 1930; "Ueber Grenzen, Möglichkeiten und Aufgaben der Darstellung mittelaltericher Geschichte," *Der Ring*, 4 May 1930. A clipping of the former made by the Tübingen legal historian Hans Erich Feine, a far-right-winger who became an enthusiastic supporter of the Nazis, was passed on to me by the late Hans Martin Schaller. On the nature of the two publications, Grünewald, "Sanctus amor," 94–95.

[50]On Brackmann's pre-Nazi right-wing politics, Kaspar Elm,"Mittelalterforschung in Berlin: Dauer und Wandel," in *Geschichtswissenschaft in Berlin*, ed. Reimer Hansen and Wolfgang Ribbe, 211–59 (Berlin, 1992), at 224.

[51]This is emphasized in Michael Burleigh, *Germany Turns Eastwards: A Study of "Ostforschung" in the Third Reich* (Cambridge, 1989). The book has some value but verges on caricature in portraying Brackmann as a scheming villain, endowed with "low-cunning and vindictiveness" (149). In October 1933 Brackmann wrote a generous letter of recommendation for his student Helene Wieruszowski when she was unable to remain employed in Germany on racial grounds.

and the sole carrier of culture in the East for centuries, has this right alone."[52] Two years later Brackmann went so far as to insist that German government officials needed to be present at scholarly meetings: "The politically oriented scholarship that we represent is dependent with inner necessity on the help of officialdom."[53] The irony would be amusing had not the effects of "Eastern research" been so frightful.

[52] Albert Brackmann, *Krisis und Aufbau in Osteuropa. Ein weltgeschichtliches Bild* (Berlin, 1939), 65, 68.

[53] Frank-Rutger Hausmann, "'Auch im Krieg schweigen die Musen nicht': Die 'deutschen wissenschaflichen Insitute' (DWI) im zweiten Weltkrieg (1940–1945)," *Jahrbuch des historischen Kollegs* (2000): 123–64, at 157.

CHAPTER 9

Becoming a Professional

THE APPOINTED SCRIPTURAL LIFESPAN FOR HUMANKIND is "three score years and ten." By this measure Ernst Kantorowicz was "halfway through life's journey" in 1930 when he reached the age of thirty-five. (He did not live for the appointed seventy years but came close, dying at the age of sixty-eight.) Fittingly Kantorowicz's Berlin period around 1930 marked a change in his engagements. The author of the biography of 1927 was a *littérateur*. He had called it a *Geistbuch*, a term that could be translated either as "intellect-book" or "spirit-book." But his supplementary volume published in 1931 was conceived entirely as scholarship. He worked on it in the library of the MGH, a sanctuary of traditional research, and made arrangements to become a professional academic. Granted that he had not swayed from his devotion to Stefan George or abandoned his George circle friends, he had left Heidelberg figuratively as well as literally.

Already by the time EKa wrote his surrebuttal late in 1929, Albert Brackmann had gained wind of his working in the MGH and used the fact, as we have seen, to wonder whether Kantorowicz was manifesting a "quiet love" for that prototypically scholarly institution and whether he would end up "closer to Paul Kehr than to Stefan George." To clarify the allusion it serves to quote from the memoirs of Felix Gilbert:

> The Monumenta Germaniae Historica [was] a research institution founded in the nineteenth century for the purpose of editing and publishing medieval sources. During the nineteenth century the Monumenta had developed into a model of scholarship at its most organized and institutionalized form; in the twentieth century under Paul Kehr, who knew how to get along with emperors, popes, and Prussian socialist ministers, the Monumenta dominated the field of medieval studies more than ever before.[1]

[1] Gilbert, *A European Past*, 105.

In writing about the colorful Paul Kehr (1860–1944), one has to guard against going on at too great a length.[2] Kehr was a pluralist in heading research institutions. He assumed the directorship of the Prussian Historical Institute in Rome in 1903, the directorship of the Prussian Archives in 1915, and the directorship of the MGH in 1919. It might have been thought that he would resign one position after taking the next, but while he did cede his directorship of the Prussian Archives in the fall of 1929, he retained the other two directorships until his retirement in 1936 at the age of seventy-six. Ironically he was not a very conscientious administrator. Living in Berlin after World War I, he traveled to Rome only twice a year to check up on his Roman institute and left the daily administrative work to a deputy (from 1927 to 1929 this was Friedrich Baethgen). In Berlin he appeared at the offices of the Prussian Archives for only two half days a week. That left the MGH, his favored location, but even there his appearances were sporadic. Yet Kehr compensated for his managerial negligence by successfully lobbying for financial support for his institutions in the highest places. Aside from that, he was tireless as a research scholar.

Kehr was overbearing and generally feared. Supposedly he hired people at one o'clock in the afternoon and fired them at four. He had a nasty wit. He called an archivist named Santifaller "Sündenfaller"—one who fell by original sin—because of a mistake in transcription. A shy female researcher was "barren in body and mind." He loved gossip and accordingly appreciated Ernst Kantorowicz, who brought him gossip about the George circle. When Kehr was at the MGH and EKa arrived, Kehr often would open the door of his office and the two—one seventy, the other half that age—would closet themselves together for an hour.[3] The two had a common butt in Brackmann, whom Kehr called "the offended liverwurst." Kehr told his assistants at the Monumenta it was ludicrous that some people who themselves could not write history criticized Kantorowicz. "He [Kehr] could not write it either and did not even want to, but he recognized [Kantorowicz's] achievement."[4] Kehr agreed with EKa on the distinction between historical research and historical representation, dedicating himself exclusively to the former. Asked once why he was a historian he answered disarmingly, "Some gather plants, others beetles, others butterflies; I gather papal documents even though the papacy for me is a highly unsympathetic institution."

Kantorowicz was relaxed and genial at the Monumenta. A young woman who had a desk there herself described him as "a witty, charming, many-sided conversationalist, completely lacking in that stiffness which vitiated the work

[2] Except where noted, the following account relies on Horst Furhmann, "Paul Fridolin Kehr: 'Urkundione' und Weltmann," in Fuhrmann, *Menschen und Meriten: Eine persönliche Portraitgalerie* (Munich 2001), 174–212.

[3] Ladner, *Erinnerungen*, 29.

[4] Gerhart Ladner to Robert E. Lerner, 15 January 1992; similar in Ladner, *Erinnerungen*, 29.

and twisted the personality of some of his friends."[5] Presumably she was referring to some of his George circle friends, for while working in the MGH he made lifelong friendships with two younger men who lacked commanding presences and worked very hard. These were underlings of Kehr, full-time assistants engaged in their own text-editing assignments. For the most part they talked shop, but EKa, located on the spectrum "between Stefan George and Paul Kehr," was now pleased to talk shop himself. One of the two was Gerhart Ladner, born in 1905 to wealthy Viennese Jewish parents.[6] Ladner began his career by studying art history in Vienna. But while working on a doctoral dissertation on eleventh-century Italian painting, he received a stipend from the Austrian Institute for Historical Research in the spring of 1929 to pursue a documentary project that took him to Rome. There he did research in the Prussian Historical Institute during one of the rare times when Paul Kehr was present. Kehr noticed his diligence and hired him for a junior position in the MGH beginning in the fall. When Ladner arrived EKa already was working there and accepted him as a luncheon partner. They would have good collegial relations until EKa's death in 1963.

EKa viewed Ladner with benign tolerance, for he was intensely serious and could give the impression of being a drudge. Whereas EKa's custom was to make his appearance at the MGH at eleven and go out an hour or two later for "breakfast," Ladner was there at the opening at nine. He was so diligent that he completed his Viennese art history dissertation in his first months in Berlin by working on it in the evenings from eight until midnight after finishing his Monumenta day at seven. Ten years younger than EKa, he looked up to him as a "heroic model." When he first met him he asked, "Are you really the author of *Frederick II*?" In addition he was enthralled by the poetry of Stefan George and longed to gain admission into the circle. To this end EKa brought him to the Meister in Berlin in December 1930. With the laconic words "this is Ladner," he left the two alone (EKa must have been skeptical), but the hesitant twenty-five-year-old failed miserably under George's merciless grilling and left, feeling "fully destroyed as never before in his life." (Ladner later translated many of George's poems into English but failed to find a publisher; fortunately he was much more successful in his scholarship and ended his career at UCLA as a highly regarded expert on Church history.)

The other young scholarly assistant whom EKa befriended at the Monumenta was Theodor Ernst Mommsen.[7] This young man, the same age as Ladner,

[5] Raïssa Bloch, a student of Brackmann's, as quoted by Malkiel, "Ernst H. Kantorowicz," 151.

[6] For the following two paragraphs, Ladner, *Erinnerungen*, 29, 33, 41–46.

[7] The following sketch relies primarily on Gilbert, *A European Past*, 102–8. On Mommsen's career, Robert E. Lerner, "Ernst Kantorowicz and Theodor E. Mommsen," in *An Interrupted Past: German-speaking Refugee Historians in the United States after 1933*, ed. Hartmut Lehman and James J. Sheehan, 188–205 (Washington, DC, 1991).

belonged to the highest scholarly nobility: he was a grandson of the great Roman historian Theodor Mommsen, a nephew of Max and Alfred Weber, and a nephew of the renowned classicist Ulrich von Wilamowitz-Möllendorff. But far from vaunting his lineage, he felt oppressed by it. When he made a mistake in a high school Latin class the heartless teacher chided him with "Your grandfather would be turning over in his grave," to which Mommsen responded, "In that case he'd be back in place because you said the same thing yesterday." Later, when he was doing research in Italy, he wrote ahead to an archive in Orvieto to announce his coming, and when he arrived he found the mayor and town councilors welcoming him at the station because someone thought that this was *the* Theodor Mommsen.[8] Amusing as such stories may be to us, the young man suffered depression because of feeling unable to live up to his great ancestor. Indeed he seems purposely to have tortured himself. When he was in America he sent for a portrait of his grandfather done by the leading nineteenth-century portrait painter Franz Lenbach that made the aged Mommsen look particularly severe. He then hung this in his living room, almost as if to increase his dread.[9]

Mommsen arrived at the Monumenta in 1930, after gaining a doctorate in medieval history at the University of Berlin. Although troubled, he was highly intelligent and a very gifted scholar. Like Ladner, he looked up to EKa. He probably took some delight in watching him needle Albert Brackmann, who had been his doctoral supervisor. But above all EKa radiated the self-confidence that he lacked and had written a brilliant book. Mommsen himself was still largely in the editing mode and felt ambivalent about it. This can be seen in a witty but self-deprecatory inscription for Kantorowicz he wrote on an offprint of an article, "On the Transmission of Freising Documents," in 1932: "Sedative sample. Dosage: one to two pages weekly! Warning! Do not exceed! Otherwise danger of lethal yawning seizure."[10] But Mommsen not only possessed a trove of knowledge but also enjoyed exploring ideas. Around 1930 EKa was ready for a firm friendship with such a person even though Mommsen lacked any George circle finesse, and the fact that the younger man admired him was no detriment. The connection was to prove extremely important for EKa's future: Mommsen helped prepare the way for his emigration to America, later helped gain him entry into the Institute for Advanced Study, and later still made a great contribution to the making of *The King's Two Bodies*.

From the fall of 1928 until the winter of 1931 Kantorowicz worked on his supplementary volume, continually groaning or apologizing about it. Early on

[8]Orvieto: interview with Kurt Weitzmann, 3 May 1989.

[9]Kurt Weitzmann, *Sailing with Byzantium from Europe to America: The Memoirs of an Art Historian* (Munich, 1994), 95; the late Lacey Baldwin Smith, who studied with Mommsen in Princeton, remembered the portrait decades later.

[10]The offprint of *Zeitschrift für bayerische Landesgeschichte* 5 (1932): 129–39, is in the Kantorowicz collection, archive of the Institute for Advanced Study, Princeton.

he wrote to his friend Stein that he was laboring "with little pleasure" and that he "typed and typed numbers, footnotes, and pseudo-wisdom."[11] The following summer he wrote to George that he hoped to be finished soon and that "then the learned carping [would] really begin."[12] In January 1930 he referred to "that foolish supplementary volume," and in 1931 he called the book that had finally appeared a "bastard."[13] The last remark was part of an extended apology to the Meister that made sense in terms of his discipleship. The supplementary volume was an obtrusively scholarly work and, necessarily as the companion to the biography of 1927, was published by the firm of Bondi in the same format as all the books in the series "from the Circle of Leaves for Art." EKa felt sure that this was the only one in the series that the Meister had not read and never would since it was nothing other than a display of "scholarly industriousness" and lacked "explosiveness." He only hoped that the volume would do no harm to the reputation of George's "state."[14]

Granted that Kantorowicz felt genuinely ill-at-ease about violating the ideals of Stefan George, he did persevere with the project for two and a half years and produced a remarkable volume. Writing to Karl Hampe, he called it "Frederick II, volume two."[15] Nowadays only dedicated specialists look at Kantorowicz's *Kaiser Friedrich der Zweite: Ergänzungsband: Quellennachweise und Exkurse* (hereafter *Ergänzungsband*), but if one does one can see that it is considerably more than an assemblage of footnotes placed between hard covers. Kantorowicz wrote pugnaciously in the preface that even the most extended display of documentation would not affect what was really essential—the basic conception of the book and the resulting "historical picture." Nevertheless, he had decided that it would be useful to offer access to the sources and relevant publications by means of cross-references to the original pages for the sake of nonspecialists and to pursue certain matters in excursuses that otherwise could not be treated briefly.

Despite disavowals, Kantorowicz surely was writing for experts. This is clear not only from his remark about expecting more "learned carping" but from thickets of technical entries such as "BREVE CHRON. SICUL. in HB I p. 892; RYCCARD, ed. GAUDENZI p. 68; COLLENUCCIO, GÜTERBOCK, RIES loc. cit.; BAETHGEN, Zu Mainardino von Imola. NA XXXVIII p. 685f, who here with justice points to GESTA INNOCENTI III. cap. 21 in MIGNE-PL 214 p. XXXI as the source for COLLENUCCIO." Carl Heinrich Becker, recently retired as the Prussian cultural minister, assumed that the purpose of the book had been to allay any doubts within the "guild."[16]

[11] Kantorowicz to Wilhelm Stein, 23 November 1928, 23 January 1929: Stein papers.

[12] 8 July 1929, EG, 87.

[13] To Fine von Kahler, 25 January 1930: StGA, Kahler papers, III:6570; to Stefan George, 8 July 1931: EG, 105.

[14] To George, 8 July 1931.

[15] 6 March 1931: Hampe papers.

[16] Becker to Kantorowicz, 25 June 1931: Becker papers.

In fact Kantorowicz really could not offer satisfactory proofs for many statements and innuendoes in the biography that did not concern concrete events. He had written (531) that Pope Innocent IV's motto was "Sedens ago" (I act while seated), but his documentation (225) indicated that this was the motto of the pope's family. He ran into his greatest difficulties documenting his book's allusions to prophecies and legends. In some cases he simply was silent. Whereas the biography had maintained that Joachim of Fiore had identified the newly born Frederick II as the coming Antichrist (10) and had foretold a meeting of Frederick and St. Francis (150), the *Ergänzungsband* simply ignores these statements.

When Kantorowicz did produce supposedly supporting evidence, it often was weak. In KFII he frequently introduced legends with an "it was said." In principle there was nothing wrong with that if the purpose was to re-create impressions of contemporaries, so long as what "was said" was said around the time in question. But very often the documentation he produced dated from much later periods. For example, the *Ergänzungsband* blithely adduces support from sources such as the Venetian chronicle of Andrea Dandalo and Benvenuto da Imola's commentary on Dante, both of which dated from well over a century after the time with which the biography was concerned. To be sure, he occasionally admitted that he could not satisfy scholarly demands. In the biography he had written (without an "it was said") that Frederick II's son Enzio had tried to escape from his dungeon by being smuggled out in an enormous barrel but was detected by his resplendent blonde hair that had not been sufficiently tucked in (621), but in the *Ergänzungsband* he conceded (247) that this was a late legend. Similarly, in the biography he had written of natural prodigies occurring in 1246: "The sun and moon did not shine, the stars became pale, it rained blood, the earth was shrouded in thick darkness, and sea waves rose high amid thunder and lightning." But after identifying the source for this as a passage written by a Neapolitan court poet and teacher of rhetoric, he granted that it could have been an exaggeration since such lines were intrinsic to court style (237). In thanking Karl Hampe for a generally complimentary review of the biography and supporting volume, he wrote, "All told you have seen from the annotation volume that I myself [now] am skeptical of certain unconditionalities and exaggerations and today would look more carefully at a number of formulations or express things differently."[17]

That the supplementary volume was no mere collection of footnotes can be seen from its unrestrained expressions of praise and blame. Kantorowicz was awed by the scholarly achievements of the American medieval historian Charles Homer Haskins and did not hesitate to let that be known. Referring

[17] To Hampe, 15 September 1932: Hampe papers. The review is Karl Hampe, "Das neueste Lebensbild Kaiser Friedrichs II," *Historische Zeitschrift* 146 (1932): 441–75, reprinted in Wolf, *Stupor mundi*, 62–102.

to Haskins's *Studies in the History of Mediaeval Science* (1924), he wrote: "This important work by the American scholar, which became known to me just in time, contains such an excellent and exhaustive account of the entire learned life and activities of the Staufen court . . . that I can limit myself to referring to it all but exclusively in the following, except for more recent supplements by the same scholar and his students" (149). On the other hand, he expostulated about the lack of commitment to the German nation in contemporary German scholarship: "It remains humiliating that one can find editors and publishers in Germany for Old-Tibetan marriage hymns and miniature sculptures of Tierra del Fuego but not for this uncommonly interesting work [Frederick II's *Art of Hunting with Falcons*] by the man who after all was the most important monarch of the German Middle Ages" (156).

An equally clear indication that the new volume intended to do more than merely document what had been written earlier is that it continually presented new information, often obtrusively arcane. Sometimes this was the mere display of superfluous learning. Out of nowhere the *Ergänzungsband* reports that the first two Hohenstaufen emperors who ruled Sicily (Henry VI and Frederick II) diverged from their Norman predecessors by taking the Greek title of *Basileus*, meaning emperor, for their Sicilian rule (77) and that Frederick II had struck close relations with the rump Byzantine empire of Nicea (133). A choice display took its departure from a papal propagandist's complaint that Frederick II had said that the soul is not immortal but is "tossed like a breath and consumed like an apple." The word "apple" provoked Kantorowicz to adduce the Pseudo-Aristotelian "*De pomo*" (On the Apple), translated from the Hebrew into Latin at Frederick's court, even though this work aimed at demonstrating the immortality of the soul, exactly the opposite of what Frederick II was supposed to have said. And then, almost as if Kantorowicz were writing an "all you ever wanted to know about the apple," he proffered a statement from Hippocrates that "the apple is a friend of the soul" (229).

Numerous instances pursue themes that particularly absorbed the author and would be developed later in his career. His discussion of the motto "Christus vincit, Christus regnat, Christus imperat" (14) is a link between his evocation of that triad in KFII and the central content of his book *Laudes Regiae*. A three-page disquisition concerns the relationship between the medieval concepts of "divine law" and "positive law," with special relation to the role of the prince as the intermediary between the two (81–84). Here one finds an emphasis on the pivotal position of the influential late-thirteenth-century scholastic political thinker Aegidius Romanus, whom Kantorowicz deemed to be the first to argue that the "king or prince is a kind of law." In this case a line runs from the supplementary volume of 1931 to *The King's Two Bodies* of 1957 (134–35). An egregious digression concerns the crowning of poets (144). Poets were the preeminent geniuses according to the wisdom of Stefan George; hence their apotheoses, as in Virgil's crowning of Dante in the *Purgatorio* or Robert of

Naples's crowning of Petrarch on the Capitoline Hill, was a theme that absorbed Kantorowicz throughout his scholarly life. Although the crowning of poets had no bearing on the career of Frederick II, he introduced it with a weak pretext into the *Ergänzungsband*, and it appears again in *The King's Two Bodies* (491) as well as in the late article "The Sovereignty of the Artist."[18]

Ultimately the clearest manifestation of the supplementary volume's status as a semi-independent work of scholarship lies in its ten formal excursuses, a few of which could have stood as independent articles. A treatment of Frederick II's gold coins pursues their likely Roman models, the question of whether their representation of Frederick had portrait quality, the symbolism of the eagle on their reverse, their worth, and the extent of their circulation and influence on other coins. Another excursus treats Frederick's march into papal territory in 1240. Here the issue was whether the emperor was arrogating to himself priest-like ceremonial qualities in blessing and having a cross born before him. The recommended reading included Marc Bloch's book of 1924 on the "thaumaturgical kings" of France and England. Three of the excursuses were annotated lists: one was a list of all the identifiable teachers at the University of Naples during the Hohenstaufen period, another of the students, and the third all the known "valets" of the emperor Frederick. In regard to all these individuals the author offered as much information about each as he could find. Who would be served by such minutiae? Surely not the general reader for whom the book supposedly was meant, and surely not even the vast majority of professional medievalists. But they did "fill a gap," and Kantorowicz must have gained satisfaction from compiling his lists.

We may stand back, then, and ask whether his continual protesting about "typing and typing numbers and pseudo-wisdom" was mostly a pose. Those to whom he issued these protests were Stefan George and his followers. Kantorowicz was aware that in proceeding with his supplementary volume he would not be ingratiating himself with these men who sniped continually against professional scholars. Consequently he wanted it to be known that he was doing so only against his will. But nothing really forced him to produce the supplementary volume, and the excuse that he earlier had promised one still would not explain the ten excursuses. Evidently, for all his ironies about pettifogging scholarship, Kantorowicz's inclination toward minute research was becoming ever more pronounced.

The extent to which he was heading in this direction around 1930 is apparent as well from another indicator. We have seen that in 1927 he had worked briefly in the Vatican archives on the mid-fourteenth-century Italian military campaigns of Cardinal Albornoz, a project unrelated to his biography (or to German "national" concerns). Although nothing came of that, he remained intent on beginning new scholarly projects. He wrote to Fine in the summer of

[18] Kantorowicz, *Selected Studies*, 362–63.

1928 that he had some in mind but needed to finish his supplementary volume first.[19] That commitment held him back, but in letters to both Fine and Hampe of January 1930 he specified the nature of the projects and seemed keen to begin working on them.[20] One was a critical edition of a thirteenth-century chronicle, the *Annales Placentini Ghibellini* (Ghibelline annals of Piacenza); the other a volume of supplements and corrections for the *Regesta imperii* (a standard set of documents of Frederick II in abbreviated form). He told Hampe that the second project would be laborious but still very necessary. Of course he did not mention either plan to Stefan George.

The edition of the chronicle appears to have been first on his list. One of the responsibilities of the president of the Monumenta was to enumerate projects that were under way in an annual report published in the institution's journal for medieval history. Thus we find an impish entry for March 1930 by Paul Kehr: "A long overdue new edition of the *Annales Placentini Ghibellini* on the basis of the London manuscript will be undertaken by Herr Dr. Kantorowicz so that he may give open expression to his 'quiet love' for the Monumenta."[21] A year later Kehr reported that the edition was currently in preparation, but two years later the director of the Monumenta series in which the edition had been scheduled to appear reported that because of Kantorowicz's assumption of an academic position his work on the *Annales Placentini Ghibellini* had come to a standstill.[22]

The reference to the academic position must take us to the steps by which the onetime man of leisure became a full-time professor. It may be recalled that in the late spring of 1928 EKa turned down an offer to habilitate in Heidelberg and proceed along the academic track. But he wrote to Fine that this did not necessarily mean he was giving up plans to habilitate; first he needed to finish his supplementary volume and then "time would tell."[23] In reality he knew that he might very well be able to habilitate at the University of Frankfurt because toward the end of June, before he went off for his summer vacation, a meeting with Kurt Riezler, the university's *Kurator* (chief academic administrator), presented that possibility.[24]

Let Kurt Riezler, a notable actor in early-twentieth-century German history and subsequently to become one of Kantorowicz's closest friends, now enter

[19] 29 August 1928: StGA, Kahler papers, III:6568.

[20] EKa to Fine von Kahler, 25 January 1930: ibid., 6570; to Karl Hampe, 2 January 1930: Hampe papers.

[21] *Neues Archiv der Gesellschaft für ältere deutsche Geschichtskunde* 49 (1932): iv. (Kehr borrowed the joke from a letter to him by Kantorowicz of 15 March 1930: Peter Th. Walther and Wolfgang Ernst, "Ernst Kantorowicz: Eine archäo-biographische Skizze," in Ernst and Vismann, *Geschichtskörper*, 222.)

[22] Rader, "Der Bernstein und das Insekt," 63.

[23] StGA, Kahler papers, III:6568.

[24] The meeting emerges from a letter to George of late June: EG, 83

the stage.[25] Riezler was once described by Theodor Heuss (the first president of the German Federal Republic) as being "on leave in our midst from the court of Lorenzo di Medici." Some people thought that "he looked like a lion."[26] Riezler had begun his career by gaining a doctorate in classical philology, but rather than pursuing scholarship he entered the German Foreign Office and rose to become a leading advisor to Chancellor Bethmann Hollweg and then a shaper of policy toward Russia during the First World War.[27] It may have been Riezler who devised the idea of putting Lenin on the famous "sealed train" from Zürich; certainly he met with Lenin in Stockholm before the latter's passage to Petrograd's Finland Station. In 1919 he represented the new German government in helping to repress the leftist revolution in Bavaria, and then with an even hand he helped put down the rightist Kapp Putsch in Berlin in 1920. In the same year he resigned from government service because of his disapproval of the Versailles treaty and disagreements with some of the governing Social Democrats. A debonair man of means, married to the beautiful and lively Kaethe, daughter of the wealthy painter and art collector Max Liebermann, he spent the years until 1928 in Berlin devoting himself to writing books on political philosophy with such titles as *Outline for a Metaphysics of Freedom* and *On Restriction and Freedom in the Present Age*. He was both a man of action and a man of intellect.

Once Riezler was named chief administrator in Frankfurt in April 1928 he became determined to make the university one of Germany's foremost institutions of learning. He oversaw the hiring of the psychologist Max Wertheimer, the sociologist Karl Mannheim, the philosopher Max Horkheimer, and the theologian Paul Tillich. He was an admirer of Stefan George, as were two senior Frankfurt professors of classics, Karl Reinhardt and Walter F. Otto, with whom he developed close ties,. Reinhardt's brother-in-law was the ardent George disciple Kurt Hildebrandt; Otto was a patron of George's brilliant disciple Max Kommerell, whose father-in-law he became in 1931. All three were enthusiastic about gaining Kantorowicz for Frankfurt despite his lack of traditional academic credentials. Riezler and Kantorowicz were distantly related: Riezler's brother had married Edith, née Pauly, who was a cousin of EKa's by marriage.[28] Very likely, then, the two already knew each other before their meeting in late June 1928. In any event, the meeting must have gone off well, for they were well matched for lively conversation. Riezler seems to have understood that

[25] My account draws on Lerner, "'Meritorious Academic Service,'" 18–22. See this article for documentation, aside from a few pieces of new evidence.

[26] Interview with Harry Jaffa (a colleague of Riezler's at the New School in New York City): 28 April 2010.

[27] Wayne C. Thompson, *In the Eye of the Storm. Kurt Riezler and the Crises of Modern Germany* (Iowa City, 1980).

[28] I was informed of "Edith Riezler" being a cousin of EKa's aunt, Rosalinde, née Pauly, by Gertrude Meyer; Sonja Asal informed me that Riezler's brother, Walter, was married to an Edith, née Pauly.

Kantorowicz would never accept a lowly teaching position as *Assistent* and thus proposed that he could be habilitated swiftly on the basis of his biography, thereby becoming a *Privatdozent.*

EKa regarded Riezler's proposal as a standing offer and early in 1930, when he thought that the completion of his supplementary volume was imminent, he contacted Riezler about it. The latter then sounded out the Frankfurt philosophical faculty in April about the habilitation he thought he could arrange but met firm resistance. This should not have surprised him. Although he had allies on the faculty, the chair for medieval history was held by Fedor Schneider, a friend of Albert Brackmann's. Schneider had criticized Kantorowicz's biography of Frederick II in a public lecture given in Frankfurt in November 1929. Then, after Brackmann's surrebuttal to Kantorowicz appeared in the *Historische Zeitschrift*, he had written to congratulate him for taking the superior position against the "cheeky and quibbling tone of the *Puer Posnaniae*" (Boy of Posen—a play on Kantorowicz's designation of the young Frederick as *Puer Apuliae*).[29]

Unfortunately for Schneider, he was soon to hear much more about the *Puer Posnaniae*. In early May he wrote again to Brackmann, now to report in distress that Riezler was trying to push through an appointment for Kantorowicz. According to this letter, Schneider had recently managed to rally enough members of the Frankfurt philosophical faculty to block a habilitation, but Riezler, supported by the Prussian Ministry of Culture and Education, was proposing another strategy, that of appointing Kantorowicz as "honorary professor." For Schneider this was an insult to Brackmann and additionally inappropriate because the long-promised supplementary volume had yet to appear. He wondered whether Brackmann could do anything to "prevent the disgrace" but recognized that the battle was probably lost.

In this he was realistic. In fact Riezler had persuaded the Prussian culture minister, the ultimate overseer of the University of Frankfurt, to advance Kantorowicz's cause. (Whether Paul Kehr, a friend of the Prussian minister-president, had played a role cannot be established, although this seems probable.) At the end of April the minister proposed that Kantorowicz be named honorary professor in Frankfurt and solicited the faculty's reaction. Walter F. Otto, the philosophical faculty's dean for the year and a Kantorowicz supporter, chaired a meeting to consider the case, and on May 21 he issued a positive report. This stated that the appointment to a teaching position of an "as yet still unproven younger scholar" was unusual, but that the faculty's reservations were outweighed by the unusual accomplishment demonstrated by KFII, a book that proved its author's "art of representation based on able scientific research." (This was drawing on language from Kantorowicz's Halle address without succumbing to its main argument.) Otto added that the faculty believed that Kantorowicz's teaching responsibilities would be "conducive to his scholarly

[29] 16 March 1930: Brackmann papers.

development." A month later EKa wrote to George with satisfaction that he had received an official letter from the Education Ministry indicating that a letter of appointment would soon follow.

Given that the Great Depression was ravaging the German economy in 1930, it is reasonable to ask whether Kantorowicz had an economic motive to seek a paying job after so many years of living from private wealth. But until the autumn of 1931, when disaster indeed struck, he was not in economic straits. In the winter of 1931 he treated himself to a skiing vacation for several weeks in the posh resort of Hofgastein in the Austrian Alps.[30] Moreover he took the position as honorary professor in Frankfurt even though it paid no salary. (Riezler expressed his satisfaction in a letter to the mayor of Frankfurt by saying that he considered the hiring of Kantorowicz "a special gain, costing nothing.") Thus it was not economics but a turn to traditional scholarship that made an entry into academia now seem fitting. After visiting Frankfurt to look for an apartment, EKa wrote to Stefan George that he thought he would be staying in there for "quite a while."[31]

[30] Letters to Fine von Kahler, 25 January, 30 January, 7 February, 18 February 1930: StGA, Kahler papers, III:6573–75, 6577; EG, 105.

[31] EG, 104.

CHAPTER 10

Frankfurt

Heidelberg and Frankfurt lie less than fifty miles from each other, but in the Weimar years the cultural distance between the two cities was vast. Heidelberg for most of its existence had been a princely residence, best known for its tradition-rich university. It was picturesque, cozy, and suffused with romantic atmosphere. Wherever one stood one could see the ruined castle. Frankfurt, on the other hand, was a large city of about half a million people, driven by finance and trade. The Middle Ages were marginally visible because it had never been a bishopric or a princely residence and hence lacked a cathedral or an ancient castle. It did have a stock exchange, third in importance after those of London and Paris, and one of Europe's largest trade fairs. Frankfurt's most famous native son was Johann Wolfgang Goethe, but he left his native city early in life. Second in fame was Mayer Amschel Rothschild, born in Frankfurt's ghetto five years before Goethe, a man who remained mostly in the city where he built his fabulous fortune. Unlike Heidelberg Frankfurt was not surrounded by hills. Thus in the nineteenth century it built out, creating a district, the "Westend," featuring stately villas. The enormous chemical conglomerate IG Farben was founded in Frankfurt in 1925. Its administrative building, completed in 1931, was the largest office building in Europe.

Frankfurt lacked a university until 1914. There was no real need for one because Heidelberg was nearby and the University of Giessen was closer. But the prosperous citizens, many of them Jews, thought of prestige; hence they raised funds to found the first "endowment university" in Germany.[1] This is to say that Frankfurt was the first German university not founded by a monarch, bishop, or prince. Initially it was self-governing. At the time of the founding a representative of the Prussian Ministry of Education attended meetings of the university's governing body (Frankfurt had been annexed by Prussia in 1866), but although he was allowed to speak, he was not allowed to vote. Only in the

[1] Two exhaustive histories are Paul Kluke, *Die Stiftungsuniversität Frankfurt am Main, 1914–1932* (Frankfurt, 1972), and Notker Hammerstein, *Die Johann Wolfgang Goethe-Universität, Band I* (Neuwied, 1989). Parts of this and the following chapter appeared in my "Ernst Kantorowicz's Decision" in *"Politisierung der Wissenschaft": Jüdischer Wissenschaftler und ihre Gegner an der Universität Frankfurt am Main vor und nach 1933*, ed. Moritz Epple et al., 173–91 (Göttingen 2016).

early 1920s, when funds had been depleted by the era's economic woes, did Prussia take full control. Nevertheless, the unusual circumstances of the university's foundation created a culture of intellectual innovation. It is unlikely that the philosophical faculty of any other contemporary university would have granted the controversial outsider Ernst Kantorowicz a professorial position, even an honorary one, as this one did in 1930.

By special arrangement EKa was permitted to remain in Berlin during the second half of 1930 to finish his remaining work for the *Ergänzungsband*. Then he moved to Frankfurt on the first day of April 1931 to assume his new duties.[2] He chose an apartment on the Bockenheimer Landstrasse, an elegant tree-lined boulevard in the Westend. The wealthiest people in Frankfurt resided there: bankers, factory owners, wholesalers, and rich pensioners.[3] Germany was in the throes of the Great Depression, but EKa went about his life with no apparent concern, moving into a spacious apartment which he furnished expensively.[4]

A cousin of Kurt Riezler's wife wrote in memoirs of 1936 that those who had only known Berlin and not Frankfurt had missed out on much—indeed that Frankfurt, with its much older traditions, had always stood higher than Berlin in matters of taste, simple solidity, and domestic refinement.[5] EKa and Baby (who lived in Heidelberg but was in Frankfurt often) entered into the world of the Frankfurt patricians. They socialized with Hans Lothar, publisher of one of Germany's leading newspapers, the *Frankfurter Zeitung*,[6] and also spent time with members of the prominent banking firm of Georg Hauck and Son. The banking director's son Michael, born in 1927, remembered in 1993 how EKa played electric trains with him and once appeared dressed up as "Nikolaus" (the German Santa Claus).[7] EKa spent time as well with the banker Albert Hahn, who, like him, was made an honorary professor at the university through the initiative of Riezler.[8]

Of course he had come to Frankfurt to be a history professor, and he immediately took up his duties. During his first semester he offered a two-hour seminar in medieval history for beginners (topic unknown) and gave an inaugural public lecture. His celebrity status had been fixed by an entry of 1931

[2] To Carl Erdmann, 28 April 1931: Archive of German Historical Institute, Rome; to Edgar Salin, 18 April 1931: Salin papers.

[3] Michael Hauck, *Albert Hahn: Ein verstossener Sohn Frankfurts* (Leipzig, 2009), 25.

[4] Interview with Walter Gross, a student protégé of Kantorowicz's in the Frankfurt period, 13 August 1994: the apartment was very comfortable—"Grossbürgerlich."

[5] Willy Ritter Liebermann von Wahlendorf, *Erinnerungen eines deutschen Juden, 1863–1936* (Munich, 1988), 172.

[6] Interview with Lothar's wife, Anita Lothar Alexander, 27 August 1996.

[7] Interview with Michael Hauck, 16 December 1993.

[8] Marion Dönhoff, "Ernst Kantorowicz," in Benson and Fried, *Ernst Kantorowicz*, 11–13, at 11; Hauck, *Albert Hahn*. In 1950 Hahn, then living on Park Avenue in New York, sent EKa a check for $50 (now worth almost ten times that amount) so that he could drink some decent wine. Hahn to Kantorowicz, 5 November 1950: LBI, box 6, folder 3.

on "Ernst Kantorowicz, Historian" in the *Grosse Brockhaus*—Germany's equivalent of the *Encyclopedia Britannica.* Knowing that he was likely to attract a crowd for his public lecture, he did his best not to disappoint. According to an eyewitness, "the inaugural lecture of the biographer of the last and most brilliant Hohenstaufen . . . was such a modish event that . . . students took seats hours in advance."[9] (Because it was a Saturday, classes were not in session.) The speaker appeared at the podium in formal dress, as if going to the opera. His topic, clearly chosen to show that he was not limited to the emperor Frederick, was "The Problem of Nobility in the Later Middle Ages."[10]

"What is Nobility?" Most of the lecture reviewed a range of positions taking the view that it was not a matter of blood lineage but rather of "spirit" (*Geist*). The papacy called for the election of emperors on the basis of their qualities rather than their blood, and the Italians introduced the concept of *virtú.* Kantorowicz displayed his own virtuosity by treating the troubadours, Dante and Petrarch, and then less well-known Renaissance writers on "true nobility" such as Poggio Bracciolini. All led up to Castiglione, whose dialogue on the "Courtier" maintained that the essence of nobility lay not in blood and not really even in "spirit," but rather in the quality of "picture"—being a model for imitation—a model for princes. So much for the speaker's task as historian. But he wanted to move into the present to ask, "What is Nobility today?" For him, the answer had to rise above the dichotomy of "blood" as substance and "spirit" as intellect. He vehemently rejected a "tired liberalism" that identified nobility with "mere intellect," as well as an alternative that applied "the ancestors' test." (Stefan George had written: "The new nobility that you seek comes not from shield and crown.") Rather, it was example, it was picture itself. Doubtless meaning to be provoking, Kantorowicz ended by quoting Nietzsche, who paradoxically rejected lineage but still proclaimed: "There is only nobility of birth! Intellect [*Geist*] alone does not ennoble; something is necessary first that ennobles intellect. What is that? Blood."[11] Nietzsche's "blood" was a new elitism, a Stefan George–style elitism of heroes, and Kantorowicz felt impelled to communicate this message.

After his customary annual vacation at his mother's estate in August he returned to Frankfurt to resume his academic responsibilities. In the winter of 1931–32 he offered a lecture course (two hours a week) on The Age of Humanism. This was a subject that had become of interest to him in connection

[9] Karl Korn, *Lange Lehrzeit. Ein deutsches Leben* (Frankfurt, 1975), 142.

[10] Unpublished text in LBI, box 2, folder 9.

[11] "Es gibt nur Geburtsadel! Geist allein adelt nämlich nicht; vielmehr bedarf es erst etwas, das den Geist adelt. Wessen bedarf es denn dazu? des Geblüts." Kantorowicz's citation is a slightly emended version of Nietzsche's fragment "aus dem Nachlass des Achtziger Jahre," Karl Schlechta, ed., *Friedrich Wilhelm Nietzsche, Werke*, 5th ed. (Munich, 1966), 3:466. Kantorowicz probably found the quotation in Ernst Bertram, *Nietzsche. Versuch einer Mythologie* (Berlin, 1918), 20, a book that was required reading in the George circle.

with a new interest in Petrarch, who wrote on nobility and had been crowned with laurel. He also offered a seminar for advanced students that met every other week on the political thought of Aegidius Romanus, whose importance he had noted in the *Ergänzungsband*. Kantorowicz's third course for the winter semester was a seminar on History Writing of the Thirteenth Century. This was listed as being offered together with Fedor Schneider, the Ordinarius for medieval history who had wanted to keep EKa away from Frankfurt. But the team-teaching was a bureaucratic cover-up. Kantorowicz was taking over for Schneider because the latter, only fifty-two years old, was deathly ill; he had contracted malaria during his years of research in Italy and was unable to leave his home.[12] Consequently EKa had three new courses to prepare on different subjects and wrote to George that "my lectures and seminars give me much to do."[13]

To make matters more trying he also was preoccupied by the realization that his financial position was collapsing. In 1927 Hartwig Kantorowicz AG had merged with another manufacturer of alcoholic beverages, C.A.F. Kahlbaum, to become the largest such company in Germany.[14] Upon the merger, the members of the Kantorowicz family sold their holdings and converted them into Berlin real estate. Everything seemed fine until July 1931 when Germany's second largest bank declared bankruptcy and the government proclaimed a month-long bank holiday. EKa may not yet have felt personally concerned, but in late September he learned that he was not immune. The agent who managed the Kantorowicz properties was a certain Alfons Goldstein, who since 1927 had fulfilled his functions reliably.[15] But overnight he lost his own money and tried to recoup by swindling the Kantorowicz's, which was easy enough to do because nobody had kept an eye on him.

Some details of the calamity remain unclear, but others can be established from a series of letters that EKa's mother, then seventy, wrote in October to her brother Felix.[16] Goldstein had appropriated all of Clara Kantorowicz's liquid funds as well as those of her children, Ernst and Grete. (For some reason Clara did not mention Soscha, but her fortune was wiped out too.) Clara initially

[12]Interview with Margarete Ohlig, a doctoral candidate then working with Schneider, 24 October 1993.

[13]Kantorowicz to George, 2 December 1931, EG, 106. Also interview with Walter Gross, 13 August 1994: "er musste schrecklich schuften." (Gross participated in the seminar on Aegidius Romanus.)

[14]Entry for Franz Kantorowicz, *Reichshandbuch der deutschen Gesellschaft* (Berlin, 1930), 880; EG, 4–5, n. 3.

[15]EKa refers to Goldstein implicitly as his financial agent in a letter to Lucy von Wangenheim of 19 December 1927, communicated to me by Eckhart Grünewald.

[16]The fact of the swindle first became clear to the family on 23 September 1931: letter from Eva Kantorowicz to Vera Peters, 23 September 1941 [*sic*]: Lerner archive; Clara Kantorowicz to Felix Hepner, 2, 4 (?), 5, 8, and 19 October 1931: Hepner papers 1206/1/14/4, 5, 6.

estimated the losses of the liquid funds as coming to 30,000–40,000 marks, amounting to some $110,000 today. Goldstein also had neglected to pay taxes due on her Holstein estate, coming to 10,000 to 15,000 marks, and he had sold off the first mortgage on the Holstein estate to a Berlin bank, meaning that she owed interest on it. She needed to pay the taxes immediately and without a loan from her brother (which never came because he too was in financial straits) she could raise the funds only by auctioning the houses from which she and her children drew interest. She had pawned her grand piano and was prepared to pawn her jewelry. She had dismissed the employees on her estate, aside from a couple that stayed without salary. Her greatest fear was that she would need to auction off the estate itself, a nightmare because her husband was buried on its grounds.

After Clara's initial estimate, she found that Ernst's loss in ready money was 20,000 marks—the equivalent of over $50,000 today. He canceled a planned trip to England when he received the news and spent at least a week in Berlin conferring with a lawyer uncle.[17] Then he continued trying to find redress by writing from Frankfurt. In early December 1931 he wrote to George of the "endless letters and negotiations" caused by "the financial collapse of my relatives and me."[18] Yet all attempts were fruitless. The mortgages he held had to be surrendered. Franz Kantorowicz, who had remained on the governing board of Kantorowicz-Kahlbaum, also lost much, but he continued to have means until the Nazis began expropriating Jewish property in the later 1930s.[19] EKa, on the other hand, experienced, a "total loss of assets."[20] (As for Goldstein, at some point he committed suicide.[21])

It is difficult to determine how EKa supported himself after the disaster. He had no salary. It is true that the royalties from KFII at first were substantial. He earned roughly $13,000 in current U.S. value from the initial printing of 1927 and $20,000 from the second printing of 1928.[22] Nevertheless, Stefan George mentioned that Kantorowicz ran through the first sum quickly,[23] and it is likely that he did so for the second. That left the third printing of 1931, which netted him roughly $11,000, and maybe a few more thousand from the publication of the *Ergänzungsband*. (Sales figures are lacking, but they could not have been high.) Possibly a small amount may have come for the rights to the English translation that appeared in 1931. But such bits and pieces would not have been

[17] To Emily O. Lorimer, 24 October 1931: Lorimer papers; Ernst Asch to Clara Kantorowicz, 5 October 1931: Hepner papers 1206/1/13/4.

[18] 2 December 1931, cited in EG, 106.

[19] Interview with Eva Peters-Hunting (Franz's granddaughter), 7 August 2001.

[20] To Ernst Bertram, 17 June 1933, as EG, 106.

[21] Interview with Beate Salz, 28 June 1990.

[22] Figure from 1927 based on a statement by Stefan George, EG, 106, n. 223; the succeeding figures are extrapolations.

[23] EG, 106, n. 223.

sufficient for EKa to continue living in his grand style. Remarkably, however, in March 1932 he treated himself to a skiing vacation during the Frankfurt intersession.[24] Nor is there any evidence that he began to seek any paid employment. The mystery may never be solved.

In any event, fortune smiled when a well-paid full-professorial position (roughly $80,000 per annum in today's money) became available at Frankfurt owing the death of Fedor Schneider in February 1932.[25] A six-man search committee, chaired by Paul Tillich, then dean of the philosophical faculty, was constituted on April 18. Around May 20 the committee settled on a rank listing of names and presented it to three nonvoting historians at the university (all *Privatdozenten*) for the purpose of having a complete record. The response of one, Ulrich Noack, indicates that three of the names were men who not only knew one another but had spent an evening together in Rome in 1927: Percy Ernst Schramm, Friedrich Baethgen, and Ernst Kantorowicz. Although other names were on the list, Noack thought that these were the three who should be considered. For him they were the most prominent medievalists of the younger generation, and if there were objection to any—he clearly was thinking of Kantorowicz—it would need to be supported with proof.

The final list that Tillich sent to the Education Ministry in Berlin on May 31, 1932, after a vote taken the day before by the entire full-professorial membership of the philosophical faculty, would not have pleased Noack.[26] Tillich's letter began by stating that the first choice would have been Schramm, but the faculty doubted that he could be lured away from the position of Ordinarius he had recently obtained in Göttingen. Instead its first choice was Harold Steinacker, Ordinarius at Innsbruck. Second came Baethgen, and tied for third were Paul Kirn, associate professor (*ausserordentlicher Professor*) at Leipzig, and Ernst Kantorowicz. Steinacker comes as a surprise, for he was a fifty-seven-year-old lackluster journeyman who had been in his chair at an undistinguished university for fourteen years. His specialty was "auxiliary sciences," meaning paleography and the formal analysis of documents such as charters and wills; in keeping with this his only books were *The Records of the Counts of Habsburg until 1281* (1905, 128 pp.) and *The Ancient Foundations of Early-Medieval Private Documents* (1927, 117 pp.). The search committee, staffed primarily by historians who had been allied with Schneider in his desperate attempt to hold off Kantorowicz two years earlier, was opting for just the kind of old-fashioned technical historian that EKa scorned, and the philosophical faculty went along with this recommendation unanimously.

[24] To Ernst Robert Curtius, 19 March 1932: Ernst Robert Curtius papers.

[25] Most of the following account of Kantorowicz's appointment to the medieval chair at Frankfurt draws on Lerner, "'Meritorious Academic Service,'" 23–25. I reiterate my thanks to Frau Katarina Becker for her research in my behalf in the Frankfurt University Archives.

[26] Tillich to Ministerium für Wissenschaft, Kunst und Volksbildung, Berlin, 31 May 1932: Frankfurt University Archive, Akten der philosophischen Facultät, II 6, 2.

Baethgen's ranking was also unanimous. The only debate concerned whether Kantorowicz should be ranked in second place together with Baethgen or in third place together with Kirn. A vote was taken on the question of second place and resulted in a tie—seven to seven. That meant that it failed because among the votes in the negative was that of the faculty's dean, Paul Tillich, which had the effect of breaking the tie. It is impossible to know what Tillich's motives were. (In the United States EKa outwardly had good relations with Tillich but told a confidante that he "despised" him.[27]) Kantorowicz then was listed as tied for third, but since he was placed behind Kirn in violation of alphabetical order that effectively meant that he was fourth. Yet it was remarkable that he was on the list at all, for, aside from the controversial nature of his work, he had never habilitated, and making someone a full professor without habilitation was unheard of.

The habilitation issue went unmentioned in the letter to the ministry. Instead the paragraph explaining the grounds for listing Kantorowicz went into pros and cons. It stated that initial concerns that his biography of Frederick II might have been based too heavily on the "play of fantasy" were allayed by the supplementary volume that had appeared the previous year. Further, even those who did not approve of Kantorowicz's overall approach had come to recognize his work as a significant accomplishment because of its "comprehensive mastery of a wide variety of materials, its intellectual energy, its wealth of ideas, and its unusual power of presentation that succeeded swiftly in capturing an extraordinarily large readership." But it was true that he had only taught for three semesters with a relatively light load and had never taught auxiliary sciences. Thus he was not as well tested as the others on the list. Moreover his real strength lay in the "scientific-literary area." Yet all told, his book was such an outstanding accomplishment that the faculty had "held back its obvious concerns in recognition of his overall scientific personality."

Startlingly, despite the equivocal recommendation and Kantorowicz's effective placement as last on the list, he was named to the medieval chair by the Prussian Ministry of Education on August 18, 1932.[28] (The official position included serving as "director of the Historical Seminar.") Given the short interval between the submission of the letter from Frankfurt and the ministry's announcement, the possibility of negotiations having taking place with any of the higher-ranked candidates is remote. Instead someone evidently was pulling strings. The most likely suspect is Paul Kehr, who had delighted in EKa's company when he was at the MGH. Kehr was in Berlin when the Frankfurt letter would have been considered at the ministry, and he was on very close terms with the Prussian minister-president. One of Kehr's honorific titles was "privy counselor" (*Geheimrat*), and he otherwise is known to have lived up to this by

[27] Interview with Margaret Bentley Ševčenko, 27 August 1996.

[28] EG, 111. A postcard from Kantorowicz to Wilhelm Stein, 3 September 1932: Stein papers, thanks Stein and Alexander Zschokke for their congratulations and best wishes on his "Bonzitis."

whispering into highly placed people's ears. The hypothesis that Kantorowicz owed his appointment to the influence peddling of Kehr is strengthened by the fact that the two were in regular correspondence.[29]

The announcement of EKa's appointment in Frankfurt, made at the university in the fall, came to some as a shock. The fact that Kantorowicz was fourth on the nominating list probably was not widely known, but everyone knew that he had not habilitated and everyone knew that he was a Jew. Actually Frankfurt had a considerable number of Jewish professors, but having one as a full professor of history was very unusual, for history was a "national" field. According to the memoirs of Jacob Katz, who was studying at the university at the time, a professor, Georg Künzel, arrived late for his class one day, explaining that he had been delayed by a faculty Senate meeting but was pleased to announce that the Senate had just approved the appointment of Ernst Kantorowicz as Ordinarius. To this he added that the decision had been based strictly on professional merits which outweighed any "extraneous considerations"—implicitly meaning that Kantorowicz had been chosen despite the fact that he was Jewish. According to Katz, "It was clear from the awkward unease that filled the hall and from the expressions of those present that displeasure ran high."[30]

EKa himself affected an ironic stance in writing to Stefan George on November 3, 1932.[31] His induction at the first meeting of the philosophical faculty was "an intellectual circumcision in which the best little piece of brain was nicked off." To this he added, "At any rate I'm now an old bigshot (*Bonze*), which was as little sung to me in my cradle as many other things. But I prefer the many other things since they are true, whereas the bigshot-condition (*Bonzesis*) is an 'economically determined' swindle." The meaning of the last phrase is obscure, possibly referring to the economic necessity of taking a paying academic job. But the meaning of "intellectual circumcision" is clear enough—academics were those with "the best little pieces of brain nicked off." This was exactly what the Meister wanted to hear, and EKa never failed in denigrating the "bigshot-condition"—implicitly a disease. Yet he was remarkably quick to order new stationery that had his name preceded by "Prof. Dr."[32]

Moreover, he dedicated himself to his full professorship very conscientiously. Teaching took first place. Shortly after he learned of his appointment he wrote to Percy Ernst Schramm that even though he was captivated by the idea of a new scholarly project, he would hardly have time for it because he had to concentrate on preparing lecture courses; others who moved up the ladder

[29] Walther and Ernst, "Ernst H. Kantorowicz," 214, 215, 221, 222. (The "Prussian Coup" that forced the minister-president out of office on 20 July 1932 did not entail any dismissals in the Education Ministry.)

[30] Jacob Katz, *With My Own Eyes: The Autobiography of an Historian* (Hanover, NH, 1995), 88.

[31] EG, 112.

[32] To Edgar Salin, 30 November 1932: Salin papers.

had already lectured as *Privatdozenten*, but he lacked any backlog.[33] (Writing lectures was particularly time-consuming for Kantorowicz because he read from scripts.) After preparing three new series in his two semesters as honorary professor—The Age of Humanism (winter semester 1931–32); Imperial History from the Interregnum until the Reign of Charles IV (summer semester 1932); Sources of Medieval Germany History (summer 1932)—he added another, The Normans in European History, for his first semester as Ordinarius (WS 1932–33).[34] The new course on the Normans took its title from a book by Charles Homer Haskins and was a working out of ideas he had inherited from Haskins, enriched with his own research on Sicily.

In addition to the lecture series came two seminars, generically titled Problems of the Late Middle Ages and History Writing of the Thirteenth Century. Very often published course announcements gave seminars generic titles because they were printed well in advance of the new semester and allowed the teacher leeway in deciding what was to be taught. Consequently the only more exact seminar title we have for Kantorowicz's regular period of service at Frankfurt is Aegidius Romanus (winter 1931–32). But certainly his method was to choose a text or set of texts for the closest analytical reading, with papers assigned to offer different background angles. In his Aegidius Romanus seminar he asked a student to present a paper on Franciscan Spirituals;[35] Aegidius was violently opposed to the Spirituals and EKa presumably wanted his class to learn of both sides of the issues.

Teaching text-based seminars was a technical challenge in the age before easy photoduplication. How could a class of some fifteen students be expected to read the same treatise that often was unavailable in a modern edition? Presumably copies of texts had to be passed around in advance. (The memoirs of Johannes Haller report that seminar students rarely had the set text under their eyes during class meetings.[36]) Whatever the case, we do know that seminars were intense, lasting for two hours without interruption. Interviewed in November 1993, sixty years after the event, Gudrun von Nida remembered the few meetings of her seminar with "Kanto" (winter 1933–34) on texts related to Frederick II and how she and her classmates flitted about seeking to prepare thoroughly.[37]

EKa liked to establish contacts with younger people and made himself available outside of the classroom. After Schneider's death he took over the direction of Schneider's dissertation advisee, Margarete Ohlig. In 1993 she remembered

[33] Letter to Percy Ernst Schramm, 25 September 1932: Schramm papers; EG, 112.

[34] EG, 112.

[35] In 1955 Ruth Kestenberg-Gladstein sent Kantorowicz an offprint of her article, "A Joachimite Prophecy Concerning Bohemia," with an inscription reminding him that she had been in a seminar of his in 1931–32 and had written a seminar paper on Franciscan Spirituals: IAS: Kantorowicz offprint collection.

[36] Johannes Haller, *Lebenserinnerungen* (Stuttgart, 1960), 243.

[37] Interview with Katharina Becker, 10 November 1993, reported to me by Frau Becker.

EKa's interest in angelology without knowing that this had persisted to become an important topic in *The King's Two Bodies*. They came to know each other well enough so that when Ohlig was in the United States in 1952 EKa took her out to dinner in a New York restaurant.[38]

Walter Gross, a Jewish student who began his work for a doctorate in Heidelberg under Karl Hampe, came to know EKa better.[39] When Hampe became ill Gross spent the summer semester of 1931 taking courses in Berlin and was given a desk at the MGH where he met Kantorowicz. In the following semester he was in Frankfurt to take EKa's seminar on Aegidius Romanus and did so well that EKa wrote to Hampe that Gross was "extraordinarily gifted."[40] Then he was awarded his doctoral degree in Heidelberg in the fall of 1932 and EKa read the dissertation—"Revolutions in Rome, 1219–1254" (published in 1934). Gross returned to Frankfurt for the summer semester of 1933 after the Nazi takeover: his intention now was to gain a license for high school teaching, which he was told might be useful to him if he emigrated to Palestine. Maintaining his contacts with EKa, he visited his home and joined his private seminar—to be discussed presently. Later, in 1936 and 1937, he saw Kantorowicz in Berlin; EKa again invited him to his home and discussed his current work with the younger man. The pattern of combined role of teacher and friend was to be repeated often with favored students in the United States.

Kantorowicz soon began to attract a coterie. In the spring of 1933 he was on a leave of absence for the summer semester because of the Nazi takeover. But at the request of some students he offered a private seminar in his home.[41] The topic was medieval Roman urban revolutions (Arnold of Brescia to Cola di Rienzo), which must in part have derived from his interest in Walter Gross's dissertation and in part from his interest in Petrarch. Nine students took the course. One was a visitor from Spain, Angel Ferrari, who afterward became a professor at the University of Madrid. EKa kept up his contacts with Ferrari, who hosted him in Spain in the summer of 1958. Then there was Hildegard Coester, who later wrote a paper on "The Cult of Kingship in France around 1300" that EKa cited in *The King's Two Bodies*.[42] Ferrari and Coester both enrolled in one of the seminars that EKa began to give in the fall but could not see to its end, as did four others who had been in the private seminar.[43] Particularly

[38] Interview with Margarete Ohlig, 24 October 1993.

[39] Interview with Walter Gross, 13 August 1994. (Gross then was chairman of the editorial board of the Israeli newspaper *Ha'aretz*.)

[40] Kantorowicz to Hampe, 23 May 1932: Hampe papers.

[41] For the private seminar and the complete list of students, Lerner, "'Meritorious Academic Service,'" 27–28.

[42] K2B, 238, n. 138. "Hilde" Coester wrote a long letter to EKa, 5 December 1935, reporting on her work: LBI, box 5, folder 3.

[43] EKa saved class lists for two seminars that began in the fall of 1933, Über Friedrich den Zweiten and Das Zeitalter Gregors VII. They are now in LBI, box 1, folder 5.

remarkable is the fact that after Kantorowicz was forced to stop teaching in December 1933 because of a Nazi student boycott, four courageous admirers took it on themselves to write to the Nazi minister of education in Berlin to inform him that those who had picketed Kantorowicz were "uninterested in serious work."[44] The four went on to declare that they thought it improper "to surrender to such disruptions for the sake of apparent calm" because this would make it impossible for them to continue their studies "under the direction of a born teacher." The students were promptly disciplined with suspension for the semester because of their "political insensitivity" and were saved from expulsion only because of the intervention of Professor Karl Reinhardt, who threatened to resign over the incident.

Although EKa's dedication to his teaching gave him little time for original scholarship, 1932 was still an important year in terms of his scholarly evolution. In December 1931 he wrote to Ernst Robert Curtius that he was planning an article, "The Plebeianization of Germany in the Later Middle Ages."[45] This was related to plans for a new book, the details of which he presented in a letter of May 22, 1932, to Stefan George.[46] It was to be on the German Interregnum following the death of Frederick II in 1250; the book's title would simply be *Interregnum*. As Frederick II represented the one "eternal German possibility," so the Interregnum represented the other. Whereas Frederick and his contemporary Louis IX of France belonged to the supranational world of the Middle Ages, national alternatives presented themselves in their most egregious forms under Charles of Anjou and Conradin (Frederick II's grandson executed by Charles in Naples in 1268). From there on "deadly enmity ruled." The work would be political history rather than biography and would resonate with conditions of the present. Kantorowicz wrote to George that he hoped it would be "breathlessly fascinating."

Interregnum of course was never written. In his letter to George Kantorowicz wrote that he planned to start work on it at the end of the semester. But when he learned that he had been made Ordinarius he had no time to do that because of class preparations. In November he informed George that although the publisher Bondi wanted "new merchandise" he was unable to "deliver."[47] In retrospect this may have been fortunate because he was in a black mood regarding the current German political situation, and had he written the planned book it probably would have dripped with bile. But he did not abandon the project, taking it up again when he was not teaching in the summer of 1933.[48] After

[44]Greater detail in Lerner, "'Meritorious Academic Service,'" 31.

[45]9 December 1931: Ernst Robert Curtius papers.

[46]EG, 110–11.

[47]EG, 113.

[48]Letter to Stefan George, 5 June 1933, as EG, 122 (the letter is there misdated to 4 June); letter to Konrad Burdach, 23 July 1933: Berlin-Brandenburgische Akademie der Wissenschaften Berlin, Burdach papers. (Martin Ruehl kindly called this letter to my attention.)

another interruption caused by tumult in his life he returned to it in 1934, and it thence became the basis of some of his most important work—"interregnum" now not as political history but as "political theology."

Aside from teaching and planning a new book, EKa engaged collegially in Frankfurt with members of a small "Riezler Kreis." He became good friends with Kurt Riezler himself, calling him "Riezi." The two had much in common in addition to their debonair manners. Both revered the ancient Greeks. Riezler was working on a book on the pre-Socratic thinker Parmenides, which he published in 1934, and he maintained that the pre-Socratics were the "gold of philosophy."[49] Kantorowicz and Riezler explored ideas in long conversations. In 1939 EKa wrote to his friend Maurice Bowra, "Riezi is as he always was, rather mad, but delighted to read about things nobody understands."[50]

Closely associated with Riezler were the university's leading classicists, Walter F. Otto and Karl Reinhardt. Their commitments as ardent Hellenists resonated with Riezler's interests in the pre-Socratics and EKa's own Hellenism derived from the Platonic and pedophilic predilections of Stefan George. Otto's friendship with EKa led him to make a special appearance in his private seminar in the summer of 1933. In the same year Edgar Salin wrote to Kantorowicz regarding a newly published book by Otto, "Here someone speaks of gods who has the right to do so because he has seen them himself."[51] EKa felt close enough to Reinhardt to contribute to a Reinhardt Festschrift in 1952. Reinhardt's civil courage was stunning. In April 1933 he defied the newly installed Nazi rector of the university who had written to the faculty asking them to join in Nazi student demonstrations that were to culminate in a ceremony of book burning. Reinhardt responded: "I must inform your Magnificence that I cannot obey your order of 28 April. Because my participation in the planned processions would be equivalent to an expression of agreement with the proclamation 'Against the Un-German Spirit,' I cannot reconcile it with my conscience and my conception of academic deportment and dignity to obey your direction."[52]

Another friend of EKa's in the Frankfurt years was a very young woman. This was Marion Gräfin von Dönhoff, who later became so famous as a newspaper editor and public personality in Germany after the Second World War that a commemorative €10 coin was struck in her honor. Gräfin (Countess) Dönhoff journeyed from her castle home in East Prussia, where she was an accomplished horseback rider, to Basel in the winter semester 1930–31 to study economics with the recently appointed Edgar Salin.[53] She then returned home

[49] Thompson, *Eye of the Storm*, 232.

[50] 25 February 1939: Bowra papers.

[51] 11 November 1933: Salin papers.

[52] Kantorowicz kept a retyped copy of this statement in his papers: LBI, box 5, folder 5.

[53] The following is based on Christian Tilitzki, "Das 'Alte Preussen' gegen die Moderne: Otto Weber-Krohse und Marion Gräfin Dönhoff," *Jahrbuch für die Geschichte Mittel- und Ost-Deutschlands* 49 (2003): 301–23, esp. 315; Klaus Harpprecht, *Die Gräfin: Marion Dönhoff* (Reinbeck,

but set out again in the fall of 1931, this time to resume her studies in economics in Frankfurt, where she remained until the early spring of 1934. A banker in whose house she was living introduced her to Kurt Riezler, and through him she met EKa. Soon the two began to spend much time together. Marion Dönhoff radiated aristocratic manners as well as youthful beauty. EKa awarded the twenty-two-year-old the nickname of "Stüdchen" (little student). She opposed the Nazis, tearing down their placards, and preferred the Communists because they were most firmly on the other side. As she later recalled, she brought EKa along when she attended Communist rallies. He never was favorable, but the fact that he accompanied her shows how much he was willing to please.

Observers thought that Kantorowicz was "very interested in [the countess] even though she was too young for him" and that Marion Dönhoff had "fallen for him."[54] But they did not have intimate relations, either in Frankfurt or in the later 1930s when Gräfin Dönhoff visited EKa in Berlin and joined him in visits to the country estate of an aristocratic friend. EKa told people in America that he had once considered marrying the Gräfin but matters never went further than that.[55] (It is worthy of remark that of the two women he might have married one was a baroness and the other a countess.) After the war the two reestablished contact. In 1951 they met in New York and Washington and EKa wrote, "We hadn't seen each other for thirteen years, but the conversation picked right up where it broke off in 1938."[56] In 1962 Dönhoff visited him in Princeton. Afterward he sent her a letter in which he reminisced about their earlier years and signed with "a very heartfelt embrace and a no less heartfelt kiss."[57]

2008), 136–48; and Dönhoff, "Ernst Kantorowicz," 11–13. See Joachim Kersten, "In vino dignitas: Der Chevalier und Die Comtesse," in *Mythen, Körper, Bilder: Zwischen Historismus, Emigration und Erneurerung der Geisteswissenschaften*, ed. Lucas Burkart et al., 104–23 (Göttingen, 2015).

[54] Interview with Margaret Bentley Ševčenko, 4 November 1994, who reported words of Hans Rosenhaupt about Kantorowicz's interest in Dönhoff. (Rosenhaupt, who later became director of the Woodrow Wilson Fellowship program in the United States, was then at Frankfurt.) On Dönhoff "falling" for EKa even though she knew she had a rival in the Baroness von Wangenheim, Harpprecht, *Die Gräfin*, 139.

[55] Interview with Margaret Bentley Ševčenko, 27 August 1996. (EKa joked that had they married they might have seen each other somewhat more often than otherwise: Kersten, "In vino dignitas," 121.)

[56] Kantorowicz to Vera Peters, 16 April 1951: Lerner archive.

[57] 16 June 1962: Archiv der Marion Dönhoff Stiftung.

CHAPTER 11

Year of Drama

THE FORTUNE THAT SMILED ON ERNST KANTOROWICZ when he gained a full professorial position in the winter of 1932 frowned when the Nazis took power in Germany in the winter of 1933. After having taught only one full semester, his situation as a Jewish professor became precarious, and by the end of the year it was too precarious for him to continue holding his chair. The year 1933 was full of drama and pain.

Although EKa was content in Frankfurt before the Nazi takeover, he did worry about the political situation. In a letter of October 1931 to Emily Lorimer, the English translator of KFII, he referred to the "unhappy" circumstances in which Germany was finding itself.[1] Two months later he thanked Ernst Robert Curtius for sending him an essay in which Curtius lambasted the anti-intellectualism (*Geistfeindschaft*) of current "nationalism" and warned that it would lead to barbarism. EKa wrote that he found the piece "excellent—unfortunately."[2] When Curtius sent him his book, *Deutscher Geist in Gefahr* (*German Spirit in Danger*), in March 1932, he again expressed his substantial agreement. His main difference was that not just the "spirit" of Germany was in danger but also the "soul"—indeed Germany itself.[3] Premonitions of disaster appear in a letter of September 1932 to Percy Ernst Schramm.[4] The latter's wife had given birth, and EKa wrote that it took optimism to father a child at such a time. He also wondered how long universities would continue to exist.

Kantorowicz mentioned the Nazis directly once in his correspondence before 1933. In October 1932 he had occasion to thank an acquaintance, Kasimir Edschmid, for sending him a copy of his book called *Germany's Fate*. In so doing he congratulated Edschmid for taking a position that steered between

[1] To Emily Lorimer, 24 October 1931: Lorimer papers.
[2] 9 December 1931: Ernst Robert Curtius papers.
[3] 19 March 1932.
[4] 25 September 1932: Schramm papers.

"pacifism on the one hand and saber-rattling on the other," that was "beyond war and peace, liberalism and Nazism."[5]

As noted earlier George disciples avoided referring to party politics. The Meister chose to stand above the mêlée and he expected his followers to do the same. But in a letter to George of December 29, 1931, Kantorowicz did come close to expressing a political stance.[6] He stated that earlier he had been "swimming against the current." But suddenly the current had reversed itself "crazily" and while swimming with it he was being overtaken by others who were swimming faster. Now if he wished to swim once more against the current he would first have to pass through "a teeming mass of rabble, corpses, and vomit" which would make the swimming difficult and present the danger of drowning. So his only option was to find a riverbank and wait to see what was passing until there might be clear water in which he could swim again. The oblique language calls for some glossing. It is said frequently that Kantorowicz would have been a Nazi had he not been Jewish, but the letter belies this. His previous "swimming against the current" meant his outspoken calls for a "national" reawakening. Now the Nazis were swimming so rapidly in the direction he had once taken that it seemed as if the current had changed. But he did not want to swim with them; they were the "rabble, corpses, and vomit." Whatever one may think of the language of elitism, it does indicate that Kantorowicz was revolted by "rabble." (At the time he was writing about the meaning of "nobility.") The issue was not antisemitism but the stench of vomit. Nevertheless, as the letter of late 1931 indicates, Kantorowicz had no intention of speaking against the Nazis but preferred to wait things out.

The Nazis achieved their monopoly of power in the spring of 1933. After Hitler had become chancellor as the result of behind-the-scenes maneuvering, the Reichstag fire of February 27, 1933, led to President Hindenburg's issuance of an emergency decree on Hitler's prompting that suspended civil liberties and resulted in the arrest of large numbers of Communists on charges of complicity in setting the fire. In new Reichstag elections held on March 5 the Nazis gained the largest number of seats but still not the necessary majority to pass legislation without parliamentary alliances. Therefore Hitler called for the passage of an "enabling act" that would grant him dictatorial powers. On March 23 he received more than the necessary two-thirds vote because the Communists by then had been excluded from the Reichstag and the Catholic "Center" party caved in. The passage of the enabling act was the real turning point. The "Nazi spring" blossomed. Claiming that German Jews had influenced the foreign press to manufacture lies about crimes perpetrated by Nazi storm troopers, Hitler struck at them "in defense" and called for boycotts. On the first day of April

[5]Letter of 12 October 1932, published in Lutz Weltmann, ed., *Kasimir Edschmid: Der Weg, Die Welt, Das Werk* (1955), 94–95. (Eckhart Grünewald called my attention to this item.)

[6]29 December 1931, EG, 107–8.

brown-shirted sentinels stood menacingly in front of Jewish shops as well as the offices of Jewish doctors and lawyers with signs reading "Don't patronize!"; "Germans! Defend yourselves!"; "The Jews are our misfortune!"

In Frankfurt the Nazis moved to take control of the university. On the same day as the boycotts, two SS men arrested Kurt Riezler on the grounds that "his safety could not be guaranteed" and sat beside him in an open Mercedes as they drove through central Frankfurt to the main police station so that bystanders could see what was happening. Effectively held prisoner, by the end of the day Riezler was pressured into resigning his curatorship and released.[7] Concurrently the university Senate met to discuss ways of forcing out Jewish faculty members. To this end it requested that Ernst Kantorowicz take an immediate leave of absence for the sake of "avoiding disruptions of his classes." Kantorowicz saved a draft of a response, dated April 3, addressed to the dean of the philosophical faculty for forwarding to the newly installed Nazi commissar for education in the province of Hesse.[8] Instead of asking for a leave, he astonishingly requested suspension of his professorship for the indefinite future, albeit with continuing pay. The grounds were not that he agreed his classes were likely to be disrupted, for he considered his "national" orientation to be well known. But he maintained that the recent antisemitic actions made it impossible for him to demonstrate his national commitment without seeming to curry favor by continuing to teach.

Kantorowicz's insistence on his "national" commitment in this draft letter of April 3 reveals that he had not moved from the views he had held throughout the 1920s. What are we to say? If we replace the term "national" with "patriotic," his statement becomes somewhat more palatable. But nothing can rescue the fact that the letter refers positively to the "again nationally oriented Germany"—evidently referring to the Nazi government—and then goes so far as to maintain that the author's "fundamentally positive view toward a nationally governed Reich" was "not even shaken by the latest measures of the NSDAP." These expressions bring to a head the question of whether Norman Cantor was right when he asserted that "beyond doubt, Kantorowicz was a Nazi" and that "Kantorowicz's Nazi credentials were impeccable on every count except his race."[9] Yet Kantorowicz never had any "Nazi credentials" and never associated himself with Nazis. (The canard that he was friendly with Hermann Goering will be dealt with in a later chapter.) We have seen that in a letter of October 1932 he explicitly opposed Nazism and that earlier he implicitly reviled

[7] Hammerstein, *Die Johann Wolfgang Goethe-Universität*, 199–202.

[8] For this and all the successive drafts and documents concerning the events of spring 1933: LBI, box 5, folder 5.

[9] Norman F. Cantor, *Twentieth-Century Culture: Modernism to Deconstruction* (New York, 1988), 311; Cantor, *Inventing the Middle Ages* (New York, 1991), 95.

the Nazis as "vomit."[10] But he did not hate the Nazis enough to reconsider his "nationally oriented" views.

As for continuing to teach, Kantorowicz explained that the Nazi antisemitic policies had placed him in a bind concerning his "honor." In a yard-long sentence driven by anaphora, his draft letter of April 3 listed all the reasons why as a Jew he felt himself unable to continue in his position:

> So long as every Jew without distinction is regarded as a traitor to his country or is under such suspicion, so long as every Jew as such is considered inferior and placed in a second class of humanity, so long as the fact of having Jewish blood in one's veins presumes a defect in one's beliefs, so long as the indiscriminate attacks on the honor, dignity, and legal status of every Jew brings the daily privation of his basic civil honor and rights without the possibility of gaining personal or legal redress, so long as every Jew who fully says yes to a national Germany must inevitably fall under the suspicion that by proclaiming his views he is merely seeking advantage in hunting for benefices or wishing to ensure his economic livelihood, so long as every German-national oriented Jew must shamefully hide his national convictions in order to avoid such a suspicion, I consider it inappropriate to hold a public office until there comes a public restoration of my diminished honor.

Even if the grounds for the intended withdrawal from service rested on a personal consideration of not wishing to be suspected of opportunism, this excoriation of Nazi antisemitism in a letter to a Nazi official was boldly defiant.

For whatever reason EKa held off from submitting the foregoing letter, and soon an edict issued on April 7 dictated the need for a new one. By the Law for the Restoration of the Professional Civil Service, all professors "not of Aryan descent" were to be dismissed immediately. But there was a qualifying clause—all "non-Aryans" who had fought for the Reich in the recent war and all who had fought against Spartacists or "other enemies of the national movement" after the war could remain in their positions. In a draft letter of April 15 Kantorowicz responded by stating that he passed both tests and thus was exempted from dismissal. But he went on to explain with much of the same language that he used in his draft of April 3 that the Nazi antisemitic measures—and now with specific reference to the Nazi boycott measures—would place him in the position of seeming opportunistic if he invoked his fighting record to accept the terms of the new law. Indeed the draft is stronger on that point in its final words than that of April 3, for now Kantorowicz called for his "honor and authority" to be restored before he could teach. On the other hand, the new draft backed away from asking for an indefinite release from duties and replaced this with a request for a leave of absence "provisionally" for the summer semester.

[10] Marion Dönhoff recalled that he "invariably heaped abuse" on the Nazis: Ruehl, "Imperium transcendat hominem," 224.

Any attempt to make Ernst Kantorowicz a hero in April is vitiated by the fact that on the same day he sent a letter to the administrative office of the University of Frankfurt specifying his activities as a postwar fighter in Posen, Berlin, and Munich. If he did not intend to make use of the qualifying clause, why was he doing this? Worse, he misrepresented his paramilitary activities in Berlin, as is clear from the recently discovered letter he wrote to his parents in 1919. We have seen from this that he reported to the Charlottenburg citizens militia, then went without arms to the Reichskanzlei to join regular troops, then stood guard, and then went to Dahlem to obtain another assignment from the headquarters of the regular troops before he "loitered around" and subsequently went home. But in his letter of April 15 he stated that he joined "the Garde-Kavallerie-Schützen-Division," inscribing himself in Dahlem and obtaining arms in a gymnasium in Charlottenburg.[11] Thus he was trying to create the false impression that he had fought with the Freikorps (viz. the Garde-Kavallerie-Schützen-Division). And at any rate he was going out of his way to overdo things because he did have documentary proof, which he submitted, of having reported on May 1, 1919, to fight the revolutionaries in Munich. Evidently he was padding his paramilitary record to aid in the possibility of using the qualifying clause to remain teaching if he ultimately decided to take that course. (The Nazi Kurator of the university responded to EKa on May 18 that upon inquiry it was established that his name did not appear on the lists of the Garde-Kavallerie-Schützen-Division and that no other records documented any postwar military action by Kantorowicz in Berlin: German bureaucracy was not to be underestimated.)

As of the time of his bogus claim Kantorowicz was not really planning to use his record to remain teaching, as shown by a letter of April 16 to Karl Hampe in which he wrote: "I see for the present no possibility of taking up my teaching so long as every self-evident documentation of one's 'national sentiment' must inevitably awaken the suspicion of merely seeking one's own advantage."[12] Yet he did not mail the letter requesting leave that he wrote on April 15. There was no rush, for the fifteenth was the day before Easter and no official would have read it until April 18, the day after Easter Monday. Meanwhile EKa wished to confer with Stefan George, and to that end he traveled to Berlin to see the Meister on April 17.[13] All that we know of what transpired appears in a letter he wrote to George on June 5 that referred to the meeting.[14] It seems that a lively discussion

[11] Kantorowicz to the Kuratorium of the University of Frankfurt, 15 April 1933, LBI, box 5, folder 5.

[12] To Hampe, 16 April 1933: Hampe papers.

[13] EG, 115, dates the meeting with George "16/17 April," but the letter to Hampe of 16 April was written in Frankfurt, and the source—EKa's letter to George of 5 June 1933—refers to a meeting loosely "at Easter."

[14] Much of the letter to George is reproduced in EG, 121–22 (with misdating to 4 June: for the correct date, Groppe, *Die Macht der Bildung*, 665).

took place among George and some of his disciples concerning the role of the Jewish members of the circle now that Jews were under attack. EKa wrote in June that he had long expected the present "disaster" and had no intention of "denying his blood," but he also did not want to be in a position of standing in the way of "the mission and office" of the Meister. In view of this he was determined to maintain his unswerving loyalty and was overjoyed by George's "tone" of support. From this it seems as if George gave his approval for the leave-of-absence letter but proposed some changes.

Upon returning, Kantorowicz was driven to action by a ukase issued by the Kurator's office on April 19 that Jewish professors who led academic units (which would have included himself as "director of the Historical Seminar") were obliged to participate actively in antisemitic actions. Obviously he could not contemplate being forced into such an intolerable role and hence could no longer delay asking formally for a leave of absence. Still, he agonized about getting the language right, for his papers include four draft letters dated April 20, all of which preceded the one he submitted on the same day.[15] Most of the changes in the succession of drafts are minor but two significant omissions, most likely determined by his meeting with George, appear in all of them. One is the lack of specific mention of the Nazi Party, thereby making the indictment of the current antisemitic measures to some degree less outspoken than it might have been. The other is the omission of the call in the draft of April 15 for the author's honor and authority to be restored.

All told, the final letter was weaker than its predecessors of April 3 and April 15.[16] Instead of requesting to be relieved indefinitely (but with pay) from his professorial positions until wrongs were righted, Kantorowicz requested a leave of absence solely for the summer semester without indication of what might follow. The letter contains a long string of indictments of the recent antisemitic measures but does not specify that they were the work of the National Socialist Party. And the list ends by expressing the author's determination not to seem opportunistic by expressing nationalistic views he had always held and by posing the impossibility of maintaining his dignity as a university professor under the listed circumstances without any explicit call for redress. Yet, whatever the weakening, the letter was still principled: its excoriation of antisemitic actions was searing and its concept of the dignity of a university professor was grand. The letter as finally sent to the Prussian Ministry of Education on April 20 was not a general call for toleration or "the safeguarding of human dignity" as EKa's

[15] Of the seven draft letters in the LBI, one is dated 3 April, another 15 April, and four 20 April. Another is undated and incomplete.

[16] For the German text, Ralph E. Giesey, "Ernst H. Kantorowicz: Scholarly Triumphs and Academic Travails in Weimar Germany and the United States," *Yearbook of the Leo Baeck Institute* 30 (1985), 191–202, at 197, n. 17. (In his English translation, 198, Giesey replaces "national gesinnte" and "nationale Gesinnung" with "patriotic" and "patriotism" and misunderstands the meaning of "Seminar Leiter.") A carbon copy of the typescript of the definitive version is in the Salin papers.

devoted American student Ralph Giesey maintained.[17] Nevertheless, it can still stand as an expression of courageous integrity.

The request for a leave of absence was approved and left Kantorowicz free to occupy himself academically in ways other than formal teaching during the summer semester. Now he had time for writing and did some work on his Interregnum project. Although he was "on leave" he did not neglect his administrative responsibility of directing the university's "Historical Seminar," proposing to Schramm in late May that the Seminars of Frankfurt and Göttingen exchange copies of their doctoral dissertations.[18] And, as already mentioned, he acceded to the request of some of his students to teach a private seminar in his home. He reminisced in a letter of 1962 that his colleague Walter F. Otto participated because of "protest and friendship" and contributed with an interpretation of some odes by Horace and Virgil's Fourth Eclogue.[19] He remembered too that he hosted a garden party at the end of the course. As the evening progressed, Kurt Riezler arrived with his wife in evening clothes since they were coming from an elegant dinner. The summer party against the backdrop of dread is one of the many novelistic scenes in the life of Ernst Kantorowicz.

The dread, however, and the uncertainty of what to do next, was always present. At first EKa seemed confident that in staying out of the classroom he had made the right decision. He wrote mordantly to Schramm of the difficulty a medieval historian faced in lecturing under the present circumstances: it would be easier to be a mineralogist "because the dodecahedron remains a dodecahedron and under no regime can be forced [*gleichgeschaltet*] into being an octahedron."[20] Using a similar image he wrote to Paul Kehr: "If I were a pharmacologist or mineralogist I would not have any insuperable problem. [But] as a historian, as a representative of a so-called 'convictions science' [*Gesinnungswissenschaft*], I can see, at least at the present moment, no other possibility for activity other than acting in the smallest and most private circle."[21]

Kantorowicz's letter to George of June 5 includes the fullest statement of his political views at the time. He was dismayed at hearing the ever-louder shouting of such words as "hero" and "leader," which had had so much meaning for him as a George disciple and now were being abused and "so-to-speak secularized." He expressed concern about the apparent direction of Nazi foreign policy in regard to Austria and the Saarland. Regarding the universities, "sentiments and mystical 'feeling'—based on the so-called volks-consciousness—will be replacing ability, knowledge, and learning." He wrote that "Germany simply becomes ugly as it de-Mediterranianizes itself." In sum he could see "very very

[17] Giesey, "Ernst H. Kantorowicz," 198.

[18] Letter of late May, in Lerner, "'Meritorious Academic Service,'" 27.

[19] Ibid., 28–29.

[20] Ibid., 27.

[21] Letter of 6 June cited in Walther and Ernst, "Ernst Kantorowicz," 215.

little" that was truly constructive. But he was not going to deny his blood and was happy to maintain his dignity and his loyalty to the Meister.[22]

Yet it was this loyalty that led to a painful letter (painful for him at the time and for us today) written to the Meister on July 10. At this point it should be explained that George never made a public statement about his view of the Nazi takeover and seldom (if ever) discussed it with his intimates. But one revealing incident is documented. In early May the Nazi minister of education for Prussia offered George the honorary presidency of the poetry section of the Prussian Academy of Arts. (Heinrich and Thomas Mann and Alfred Döblin had just been expelled.) George's lieutenant Ernst Morwitz drafted an answer for him explaining that George would not accept this position because he never accepted any public office and "had overseen Germany poetry now for nearly half a century without any Academy." The draft went on to say that the poet nonetheless was pleased that the Academy of Arts now "stood under the national sign," to which George required him to add the statement "I absolutely do not deny my paternity [*Ahnherrschaft*] of the new national movement and do not put aside my spiritual involvement."[23] The letter was mailed with George's signature on May 10; on the evening of that day bonfires of books burned all over Germany.

EKa probably did not know the "paternity" statement, but he might not have been surprised had he learned of it. His resignation appears in the letter of July 10 in the context of congratulating George on his imminent sixty-fifth birthday (and penned strictly in accordance with the Meister's handwriting prescriptions) (fig. 18):

> Let Germany be what the Meister has dreamt of! And if current events are not merely the grimaces of that ideal but actually the true way to that fulfillment, let that all work out for the best. And in that case it makes no difference if the individual can stride along—or rather is allowed to—or steps aside instead of rejoicing. Frederick II said "Imperium transcendat hominem" [the empire transcends the individual] and I would be the last one to contradict that.[24]

Kantorowicz had always prized *Treue*—loyalty—and at this moment his loyalty was to George to the exclusion of all else. Yet one can feel the pain. Certainty that EKa did not consider the Nazi regime to be "the true way to the fulfillment" of George's ideals can be established by his reaction to the public speeches of two other of George's disciples. Ernst Bertram, professor of German literature at the

[22] Groppe, *Die Macht der Bildung*, 665, Engish summary in Ruehl, "'Imperium transcendat hominem,'" 221–22.

[23] For the events and full text of the letter, Karlauf, *Stefan George*, 620–22.

[24] EG, 122. The words "Imperium transcendat hominem" are taken from a letter of Frederick II to Louis IX of France quoted in KFII, 501. Michael Rissmann, "'Imperium transcendat hominem': Ernst Kantorowicz, das 'Geheime Deutschland' und der Nationalsozialismus," in *Deutsche Autoren des Ostens als Gegner und Opfer des Nationalsozialismus*, ed. Frank-Lothar Kroll, 451–75 (Berlin, 2000), is a competent review of the subject of Kantorowicz and Nazism that breaks no new ground.

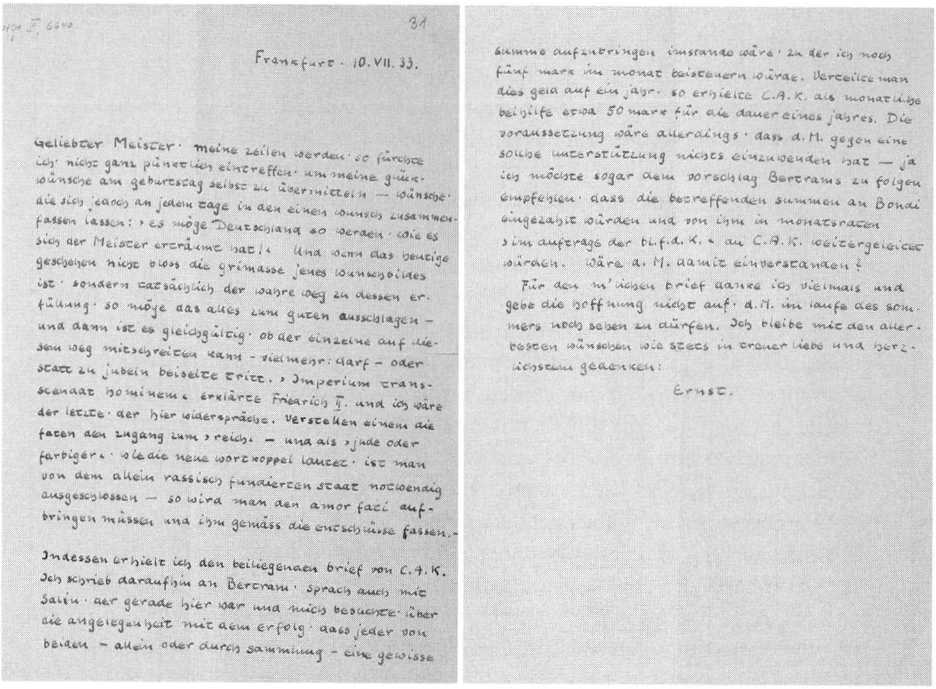
Frankfurt · 10. VII. 33.

Geliebter Meister · meine zeilen werden · so fürchte ich · nicht ganz pünktlich eintreffen · um meine glückwünsche am geburtstag selbst zu übermitteln — wünsche die sich jedoch an jedem tage in den einen wunsch zusammenfassen lassen: › es möge Deutschland so werden · wie es sich der Meister erträumt hat! ‹ Und wenn das heutige geschehen nicht bloss die grimasse jenes wunschbildes ist · sondern tatsächlich der wahre weg zu dessen erfüllung · so möge das alles zum guten ausschlagen — und dann ist es gleichgültig · ob der einzelne auf diesem weg mitschreiten kann - vielmehr: darf — oder statt zu jubeln beiseite tritt. › Imperium transcendat hominem ‹ erklärte Friedrich II. und ich wäre der letzte · der hier widerspräche. Verstellen einem die faten den zugang zum › reich ‹ — und als › jude oder farbiger ‹ · wie die neue wortkoppel lautet · ist man von dem allein rassisch fundierten staat notwendig ausgeschlossen — so wird man den amor fati aufbringen müssen und ihm gemäss die entschlüsse fassen.

Indessen erhielt ich den beiliegenden brief von C.A.K. Ich schrieb daraufhin an Bertram · sprach auch mit Salin · der gerade hier war und mich besuchte · über die angelegenheit mit dem erfolg · dass jeder von beiden — allein oder durch sammlung - eine gewisse summe aufzubringen imstande wäre · zu der ich noch fünf mark im monat beisteuern würde. Verteilte man dies geld auf ein jahr · so erhielte C.A.K. als monatliche beihilfe etwa 50 mark für die dauer eines jahres. Die voraussetzung wäre allerdings · dass d. M. gegen eine solche unterstützung nichts einzuwenden hat — ja ich möchte sogar dem vorschlag Bertrams zu folgen empfehlen · dass die betreffenden summen an Bondi eingezahlt würden und von ihm in monatsraten › im auftrage der bl. f. d. K. ‹ an C.A.K. weitergeleitet würden. Wäre d. M. damit einverstanden?

Für den m' lieben brief danke ich vielmals und gebe die hoffnung nicht auf · d. M. im laufe des sommers noch sehen zu dürfen. Ich bleibe mit den allerbesten wünschen wie stets in treuer liebe und herzlichstem gedenken:

Ernst.

Figure 18. In his letter of July 10, 1933, to "the Meister," Stefan George, Kantorowicz fully employs "George-Handwriting." (Stefan George Archiv, Stuttgart)

University of Cologne, gave a speech at the University of Bonn on the occasion of George's birthday on July 12 that hailed "[the one] whose knowing poetic word helped call forth the mighty realities of today and the future, those which we profess today with such high hopes."[25] Walter Gross brought EKa a copy of a Nazi publication that covered the speech and remembered that he angrily expressed his disapproval.[26] Even worse for EKa was a similar speech, "Stefan George's Revolutionary Ethos," delivered on George's birthday at the University of Tübingen by none other than EKa's former roommate and lover, Woldemar Graf Uxkull. This proclaimed that "the upheaval of 1933 lies determined in the work and life of Stefan George"; further, Uxkull stated that it remained to be seen whether the "New Reich" lay solely in the "New Reich" of George's poetry or would be the transcending of George's "Ethos" in the "Third Reich."[27] He also

[25] Cited by Eckhart Grünewald, "'Übt an uns mord und reicher blüht was blüht!' Ernst Kantorowicz spricht am 14 November 1933 über "das Geheime Deutschland," in Benson and Fried, *Ernst Kantorowicz*, 57–93, at 62.

[26] Interview 13 August 1994.

[27] Cited by Grünewald in "'Übt an uns mord,'" 63.

referred to "the great danger of Jewish influence in the German press."[28] Uxkull sent a copy of his speech to EKa "in constant and most cordial friendship," but EKa had already obtained one on his own and littered the margins with expostulations such as "completely irresponsible," "jargon of the party press," "insulting in every degree of exaggeration and shabbiness," and "Bertram is a hero in comparison."[29]

By the early fall he was faced with the necessity of deciding what action to take for the semester that began in November. By then he had resolved not to apply for another one-semester leave that would settle nothing. Two other choices presented themselves. The first had dropped out of the clouds. The Fellows of New College, Oxford, had decided in September to offer "Common-room Hospitality" to a needy German visitor for the academic year. News of the opportunity made its way to the art historian Fritz Saxl, the director of the Warburg Institute of Hamburg, who was in London negotiating for the transfer of the institute's vast library. Saxl in turn passed the information on to Raymond Klibansky, a young historian of philosophy who had known EKa in Heidelberg, and Klibansky wrote a strong letter supporting Kantorowicz for the visiting position.[30] On September 30 the general secretary of the Academic Assistance Council in London passed this recommendation on to the warden of New College, and within a week the latter reported that "the College has elected Professor Ernst Kantorowicz to be an Honorary Member of the Senior Common Room for one year." After an interval necessitated by the challenge of locating Kantorowicz's address, the office of the Academic Assistance Council sent him the news and a formal invitation followed soon.[31] Accordingly on November 9 EKa submitted a request to the ministry for a leave (with pay) for the winter and summer semesters in order to take the position offered by an institution as prestigious as Oxford. The philosophical faculty of Frankfurt recommended in favor the next day, and the ministry issued its formal approval on December 5.[32]

But while the letters were passing back and forth EKa had decided on a different course of action, evidently leaving open the Oxford possibility for

[28] Cited by Wolfgang Schuller, "Altertumswissenschaftler im George-Kreis," in *Wissenschaftler im George-Kreis*, ed. Bernhard Böschenstein et al., 209–24 (Berlin, 2005), at 215.

[29] Cited by Grünewald in "'Übt an uns mord,'" 63.

[30] Bodleian Library, Oxford, MS SPSL 508/2, file 1, ff. 286–87. (By permission of the Council for Assisting Refugee Academics—as applies to all the following documents from Bodleian SPSL 508/2.) The letter was unsigned, but Klibansky had to have been the author since he had visited EKa in Frankfurt in July and was the only possible link between Kantorowicz and Saxl. (Percy Ernst Schramm falls out of consideration because the letter was produced on a typewriter with an English keyboard: Schramm was in Germany at the time; Klibansky had just moved to England.) On Klibansky's visit in Frankfurt with Kantorowicz, see his letters to Gertrud Bing of 5 and 7 July, as treated in Jost Philipp Klenner, *Bildhistoriker: Ernst Kantorowicz und die Kulturwissenschaftliche Bibliothek Warburg* (Humboldt University Berlin, Master's thesis, 30 May 2003), 12.

[31] Bodleian Library, Oxford, MS SPSL 508/2, file 1, ff. 288–93.

[32] EG, 125–26.

insurance. This was to return to teaching in Frankfurt, an option for which he needed no permission because his leave had been for the summer semester alone and his name remained on the official list of the faculty.[33] He announced two seminars—The Era of Gregory VII and On Frederick II—and a lecture series on the German Interregnum, repeating a topic he had previously offered. Although it was daring for students to register for courses given by Jewish faculty, fifteen enrolled for the first seminar and thirteen for the second.[34] Kantorowicz explained his motives for returning to his chair in a letter to George of November 26. Disregarding what the Meister may have thought about the Nazis, he wrote: "After overcoming the initial nausea, shock, and pain, now hate is beginning to make me productive. Indeed the necessity of marking oneself off with every step against right as against left and to hack away at all sides keeps one . . . on a royal road." He added that entering into a fight brought "real fun [*Spass*]—it rejuvenates."[35]

The fight was launched on November 14 by a "reinaugural" lecture Kantorowicz delivered as the first in his "Interregnum" series. In 1993 Eckhart Grünewald interviewed a woman who had been in the audience: "The lecture hall was overflowing. The audience was in suspense. Those who opposed the Nazis held themselves back, but on such an occasion it could be seen who was on which side. The speech was thought to be very courageous . . . Kantorowicz seemed entirely unperturbed."[36]

At the start the speaker explained the grounds for a new "inaugural."[37] He had been away for only one semester, but "the enormous events of the last months" made it necessary for him to reintroduce himself to his audience. He was going to offer a profession of faith (*Bekenntis*)—"and why does one carry the title of 'professor' if one does not have the courage in a decisive hour to offer a 'profession'"? He was going to speak clearly for the sake of the present and future Germany "with an unshakable faith in the immortality of this land and in its promise" (77–78).

His title was "The Secret Germany" (*Das Geheime Deutschland*), which everyone would have known was a slogan of the George circle.[38] It was the title of one of George's poems; in the preface to KFII Kantorowicz had written that a wreath had been laid on the sarcophagus of the emperor Frederick in 1924 by those of "the Secret Germany."[39] (George had once said that he would rather be

[33] EG, 123. On 5 October Kantorowicz already wrote to the Nazi administrator of the university of his intention to return to teaching: a copy is attached to a letter to Edgar Salin of 10 October: Salin papers.

[34] LBI, box 1, folder 5.

[35] EG, 126.

[36] Dorothea Hölscher-Lohmeier, quoted in Grünewald, "'Übt an uns mord,'" 64.

[37] The lecture is printed in ibid., 77–93. I cite by page numbers.

[38] EG, 74–80.

[39] In February 1925 Elisabeth Salomon wrote to Friedrich Gundolf from Rome that she had just seen the tomb of the German emperor Otto II in the Vatican grottos adorned with a laurel wreath

"Kaiser of the Secret Germany than President of the unsecret Germany."[40]) The speaker indicated at the start that he was conveying the substance of George's ideal, and the talk stands as its only systematic presentation. No one had ever come forth to do that earlier because of the implicit esotericism. But after Ernst Bertram and Woldemar Uxkull had greeted the Nazi Reich as the realization of George's hopes, Kantorowicz was determined to emphasize the difference. Afterward he wrote to Edgar Salin that he had judged it necessary, after Bertram and Uxkull, to "call things by their right name," and he wrote to the Meister that he gave the speech "in order to cover over with a layer of earth the embarrassing manure that friends (above all Woldi) manufacture so that it will stop stinking and gradually become compost."[41]

Ulrich Raulff has written aptly that "Kantorowicz's lecture is subversive, but not denunciatory."[42] It never mentions the Nazis or alludes to their excesses. Instead, Kantorowicz presents a countermythology: "Whoever has eyes to see and ears to hear knows that . . . until the present day there has been another Germany, having life beyond the public visual Reich" (80). This "Empire of Souls" (*Seelenreich*) was the one of his "profession." He broached three questions: How does the Secret Germany exist? Who are its bearers? What are their distinguishing traits? His answers were expressed with sonorous rhetoric; implicit quotations from Stefan George ran through the talk.

The Secret Germany was neither a conspiratorial society "located somewhere" nor a figment of the mind "located nowhere." It is ever near and "deathly factual": "It is a godly empire like Olympus; a spiritual empire like the medieval state of saints and angels; a human empire like Dante's "human society" (*humana civilitas*)"; it is "the world of heroes of the present, the future, and the eternal Germany." It was "like all mysteries"; "it has never taken placed, never occurred, but [it] *existed* everlasting and eternal." Related to the present German space, "it reaches far over it" (80). As if Kantorowicz were a sibyl he told his audience that this Reich was "of and not of this world; there and not there" (81).

Transcendental providence had made the Secret Germany the fourth and eschatologically ultimate spiritually supreme society in a historical series, following "the divine Hellas," the Christian "City of God," and the secularized humane culture of the Renaissance heralded by Dante (82). (Old Testament Judea plays no role.) The Secret Germany returned to the model of Hellas in being located in a certain space, namely, Germany, but it was a society of men

bearing the inscription: "Kaiser Otto II.—Das geheime Deutschland." On inquiry the custodian reported that "two young Germans" had brought it in. One must conclude that they were Ernst Kantorowicz and Woldemar Uxkull, for both were in Rome at that time. For the letter see *Friedrich Gundolf-Elisabeth Salomon Briefwechsel*, 530–31.

[40] Karlauf, *Stefan George*, 554.

[41] Grünewald, "Übt an uns mord," 64.

[42] Ulrich Raulff, "Apollo unter den Deutschen: Ernst Kantorowicz und das 'Geheime Deutschland,'" in *"Verkannter brüder"? Stefan George und das deutsch-jüdische Bürgertum zwischen Jahrhundertwende und Emigration*, ed. Gert Mattenklott et al., 179–97 (Hildesheim, 2001), at 181.

that exceeded even Hellas in its "richness of life" and its "all-encompassing 'allness' of 'deepest-human being'" (83). The rulers and nobility of the Secret Germany, although humans, could belong to the fellowship of Zeus, Apollo, or Dionysius (84). Kantorowicz did not wish to proceed by enumerating the specific membership—he did not think of writing a "Divina Commedia teutsch" (82)—but he emphasized (implicitly versus Nazi propagandists) that many of its greatest representatives, although German, were accused of being "un-German." This was the case with Frederick II, this was the case with Goethe and Hegel, who congratulated Napoleon, this was the case with Stefan George, who shunned the "bourgeois world of the official Germany" (86). As Nietzsche had said, "In order to be more German, one must de-Germanize oneself" (87). The German nation was the core of "all Europe and the Mediterranean lands." It was this that underpinned Schiller's assurance that "the day of the German is the harvest of all time" (88).

The traits of the membership of the Secret Germany grew out of "reverence and love" for the gods of Hellas. It was this discipleship that ennobled them rather than any biological succession from father to son. Some were "Dionysians," such as Frederick II, Matthias Grünewald, and even Rembrandt, who "needed to create a world of darkness for a ray of light" (89). Others, mere youths—Otto III, Conradin—were ready to sacrifice themselves for dreams. Yet other denizens of the Secret Germany, for example, Mozart, were "ennobled by grace" (90). (The mention of a composer was highly unusual; Kantorowicz abhorred classical music and once averred that he could not distinguish a drum from a violin.[43]) All told, one did not measure the "heroes, poets, and wisemen" of the society by specific deeds but by "nobility, beauty, and greatness." German youth might be trained in this triad to become the "Kalokagatoi" (handsome and brave Greek heroes) for the current German state and people (92). Kantorowicz concluded that someday the Secret Germany might become identical with the real Germany, but until then one needed to stand guard. The rulers of the Secret Germany call out to the internal and external enemy in the language of Stefan George: "Impede us! Indelible is the word that blooms!/Listen to us! Take us! Despite your favor it blooms!/Murder us and more richly blooms what blooms!" (93).[44]

For anyone, let alone a Jew, to have delivered a speech such as this against the tide of Nazi enthusiasm in 1933 took bravery. Kantorowicz's presentation was devoid of racism and although centered on Germany not limited to it; the youth who were called to serve the ideal were given a name from the Greek; the "empire" was not one of military might but of beauty. Granted that the quotation from Schiller connoted Germany's "chosen" eschatological role, the speech was not triumphalist. The hour for emergence from the depths had not yet struck, and the speaker offered no assurance as to when it might. A comparison may be

[43] To Vera Peters, 18 April 1954: Lerner archive.

[44] Quoting GA, 8, 94.

made with a quotation from an address of November 3, 1933, to the students of the University of Freiburg by Martin Heidegger celebrating "the complete upheaval of our German existence": "Not theorems and 'Ideas' are the rules of your Being, the Führer himself and alone is the present and future German reality and law."[45] No German professor other than Ernst Kantorowicz spoke publicly in opposition to Nazi ideology throughout the duration of the Third Reich.

Although the content and language of the Secret Germany address seem as distant to us today as that of an Old Norse Saga, EKa was very pleased with it and believed that it had worked its intended effect. In the last of his letters to Stefan George, dated November 26, he wrote that he had spoken in "the great, deadly still auditorium that first was brown and then turned red until at the final words it stamped its feet."[46] He had given a "sketch of the true divine heaven that is eternal and that laughs all the more heartily at every attempt to level it with propaganda." Thus he now had "more students who listen breathlessly to his lectures than ever."

But he was deluding himself. The Nazi-controlled league of students was determined to put an end to his lecturing and imposed a boycott.[47] Young men in brown uniforms stood at the door of the hall and asked those who intended to enter why they wanted to listen to a Jew. When the audiences began to dwindle, Kantorowicz petitioned the university administration to intervene. But a senior colleague in the History Department advised him to stop teaching in order "to preserve quiet." Soon he had little choice but to capitulate, and on December 11 he broke off his classes.

By an eerie concurrence of events Stefan George had died in a small town in Switzerland near Locarno on December 3.[48] Kantorowicz canceled a seminar to rush to the scene when he heard the news. He arrived on the evening of the fifth and kept the death watch with other disciples by an open coffin. The burial followed the next day and EKa stood by the coffin as it was set down. According to Edgar Salin he later said that when he mounted the train to return to Germany he noticed another disciple giving the Heil Hitler salute from a window to two others on the platform who returned it in kind.[49]

[45] Bernd Martin, ed., *Martin Heidegger und das "Dritte Reich": Ein Kompenium* (Darmstadt, 1989), 177.

[46] EG, 127–28.

[47] Lerner, "'Meritorious Academic Service,'" 30.

[48] For a vivid account of George's death and the ensuing obsequies, Ulrich Raulff, *Kreis ohne Meister* (Munich 2009), 31–40.

[49] [Salin,] *Ernst Kantorowicz*, 7. Raulff, 38, is inclined to doubt the veracity of Salin's account, but Salin is specific in saying that EKa told it to him "in Berlin," and it seems difficult to believe that Salin had the imagination to invent it. Certainly George in his last days surrounded himself with young men who were Nazis.

CHAPTER 12

Oxford

As a result of the events in Frankfurt, EKa took the fellowship that was offered him at Oxford. When he arrived in January 1934 he entered an entirely different cultural universe from the one in which he had lived. Intense seriousness was discouraged. Oxford dons would never have dreamt of obeying the dictates of a self-important "Master"; anyone who wanted to talk of a "never occurring, but always existing Secret England" would have been ridiculed. In 1932 an English reviewer of the translation of KFII criticized its "exaggerated and in places almost hysterical tone."[1] EKa's six-month stay in England affected him in a variety of ways. When he wrote his biography his view of the English—Germany's war enemies—was hostile. Writing of the half-English Otto IV, he told of his "stinginess," "strikingly limited education," and "intellectual poverty" (64). But once across the Channel Kantorowicz became an Anglophile. This change in attitude affected aspects of his scholarly subject matter in both the short and long term—ultimately being most evident in *The King's Two Bodies*. In addition, the six months in England offered him the opportunity to engage in new research endeavors that issued into his second book, *Laudes Regiae*. Another advantage was that he had to speak English. Without the fluency he attained he would not later have been awarded a position in Berkeley. Not least, in Oxford he struck up a close friendship with the classicist Maurice (C. M.) Bowra, creating a bond that was to endure for all the years to come. Until 1919 EKa's hero was his father; from 1920 until 1933 he was beholden to Stefan George; from 1934 until his death his closest bond was with Bowra. Photos of all three were on his bedroom bureau when he died in the United States.[2]

EKa's opportunity to be a guest in New College, Oxford, as "Honorary Member of the Senior Common Room" not only spirited him away from Nazi spite for half a year but fulfilled a desire to travel to England. More than three years earlier he had planned to edit the Ghibelline Annals of Piacenza, of which the

[1] Cited by David Abulafia, "Kantorowicz, Frederick II and England," in Benson and Fried, *Ernst Kantorowicz*, 124–43, at 135.

[2] Ralph Giesey to Maurice Bowra, 29 September 1963: Bowra papers.

sole manuscript was in London, and also to provide summaries of hitherto unknown documents pertaining to Frederick II. As he wrote to Fine von Kahler, both of these projects necessitated his being in England, which for him was a "very nice fringe benefit."[3] His Frankfurt appointment had obliged him to hold these projects in abeyance but they remained on his mind. Thus in June 1931 he wrote to Emily O. Lorimer, who had just completed a translation of KFII, that he was planning a trip to London in the late summer or early fall and would happily accept her invitation to visit her at her home in Hertfordshire, although in October he wrote that he had found himself forced to cancel his trip because of "political and economic conditions."[4] (This was when he was trying to retrieve his swindled fortune.)

Mrs. Lorimer had been hired as translator in 1930 by the publishing firm of Constable & Company. The originator of the project was Helen Waddell, the author of a semipopular book on the medieval goliards—*The Wandering Scholars*—who held an editorial position with Constable. In November 1930 she wrote to EKa to express her satisfaction that the firm had undertaken the translation of his "great book" and to propose that it be made the first volume in a new series, Makers of the Middle Ages, aimed at general readers.[5] The book appeared in October 1931 with the translator's name given as "E. O. Lorimer."[6] Lorimer, a woman of diverse accomplishments,[7] set Kantorowicz's extremely difficult prose into English with great accuracy and even with a rhetorical punch similar to that found in the original. (In the finale, Frederick II "slumbers not nor sleeps.") EKa acknowledged Lorimer's accomplishment by writing to her that it was "marvelous" and that she had matched his tone to such a degree that he was astonished.[8]

We have seen that Kantorowicz learned of the new opportunity at a difficult time in the fall of 1933. The letter of recommendation written by Raymond Klibansky was well informed.[9] It stated that he had learned English in his youth and that he already had wished to pursue research in English archives (perhaps exaggerating in saying that he intended a volume of "English Historical Studies"). With great praise for Kantorowicz's accomplishments—his Frederick

[3] 25 January 1930: StGA, Kahler papers, III:6568.

[4] 27 June 1931; 24 October 1931: Lorimer papers.

[5] Helen Waddell to Kantorowicz, LBI, box 5, folder 5.

[6] For the contemporary reviews, Abulafia, "Kantorowicz, Frederick II and England," 132–38.

[7] On her career, too multifarious to be detailed here, Penelope Tuson, *Playing the Game: Western Women in Arabia* (London, 2003); and *Oxford Dictionary of National Biography* (Oxford, 2004), s.v. But it should be mentioned that although the translation of KFII gives the impression of a woman who was supportive of the author's German-national stance, Lorimer's book, *What Hitler Wants* (Harmondsworth, 1939), is a searing indictment of Nazism and the Conservative Party's policy of appeasement.

[8] 24 October 1931: Lorimer papers.

[9] Bodleian Library, Oxford, MS SPSL 508/2, file 1, ff. 286–87.

biography, his appointment at Frankfurt without habilitation, and his "exceptional success as a teacher"—Klibansky concluded by stating that he was particularly suitable for an English grant on the grounds of his "excellent manners, cosmopolitanism, and good knowledge of the English language and English history."

Fortuitously, Klibansky's addressee, the warden of New College, was H.A.L. Fisher, one of Oxford's leading senior historians. Although Klibansky wrote in German and his letter thus might not otherwise have gotten very far, Fisher read German and evidently was impressed: he influenced his colleagues to select EKa for the fellowship without considering other candidates. A story has cropped up that Kantorowicz's invitation to Oxford resulted from confusion with the legal historian Hermann Kantorowicz, whom the dons really wanted to invite.[10] The picture is of bumblers rivaling Winston Churchill's gaffe in inviting Irving Berlin to lunch instead of Isaiah Berlin. But the documents show that Fisher certainly knew the candidate to be Ernst Kantorowicz. Granted that Maurice Bowra wrote in his memoirs that "some of his hosts confused him [EKa] with the legal scholar, Hermann Kantorowicz," Bowra was telling only of confusion in the minds of some dons after EKa's arrival.[11]

When EKa was forced to give up teaching in Frankfurt in December, approval of his request for a leave of absence with pay for two semesters came just in time. He waited until after Christmas, reached England on January 21, and arrived in Oxford before the twenty-seventh.[12] The fact that the leave of absence came with pay facilitated matters financially since all he received from New College was room and board. Although the original terms of his invitation included provision for a house in North Oxford, he preferred to live in the college so that he could take part in its social life. Bowra's memoirs report that "he talked English fluently with many mistakes and bold improvisations on the principle that most French words can be used in English if they are pronounced suitably; thus he would speak of 'my brother-in-law the medicine' or of physicists as 'physicians.'"[13] Bowra goes on to say that "though he was a professor at Frankfurt, he was not in the least professorial, had an excellent sense of humour, and picked up our atmosphere with extraordinary speed." Among the stories Bowra tells is one of EKa returning from a visit to Cambridge "very

[10] Barbara Picht, *Erzwungener Ausweg* (Darmstadt, 2008), 108; Wolfgang Graf Vitzthum, "Ernst Kantorowicz als Rechtshistoriker," in Burkart et al., *Mythen, Körper, Bilder*, 125–47, at 141, n. 7. Geoffrey Barraclough told people about the supposed New College mistake with relish: Howard Kaminsky to author, 20 June 1998. Dietrich von Bothmer, at first a friend and then an enemy of EKa's, was another: when I called him for a telephone interview in 2001 he was curt but could not resist passing on the news of Ernst Kantorowicz's presence in Oxford because of his being mistaken for Hermann Kantorowicz.

[11] Bowra, *Memories*, 286.

[12] EG, 136; Kantorowicz to Fritz Saxl, 27 January 1931: Warburg Institute Archives, London.

[13] Bowra, *Memories*, 286.

depressed": "I asked him why, and he said to my surprise, 'It is so behind the times.' I ventured that Oxford too was behind the times, but he dealt with that summarily, 'Cambridge is a week behind the times, and that's awful, but Oxford is a hundred years behind, and that's splendid.'"[14] A fellow of New College, J. L. Myers, found EKa brash, but another fellow, H. L. Henderson, wrote in 1938 that Kantorowicz "took part truly in general conversation in Senior Common Room" and "made himself extremely popular during his stay."[15]

Shortly after his arrival Kantorowicz sought to solidify contacts with H.A.L. Fisher. Thirty years his senior, Fisher was a brother-in-law successively of Frederick William Maitland and Francis Darwin (son of Charles); he also was a nephew of Leslie Stephen and a first cousin of Virginia Woolf. He had served as education minister under Lloyd George and was liable to begin sentences with "when I was in the Cabinet."[16] When EKa was in Oxford Fisher was working on a three-volume history of Europe; since he had written a book at the beginning of his career on medieval German history, EKa could talk shop with him. A note from Fisher dated February 8, 1934, that EKa tucked away in an offprint on "Imperial and Papal Banners in the High Middle Ages" written in German reads: "Dear Professor, very many thanks for allowing me to see this paper which I have read with interest."[17] EKa always retained fond memories of the older man. In 1949 he wrote to Bowra that one thing that might lure him to Europe would be to "visit the tomb of Warden Fisher."[18]

Oxford historians of his own generation whom he got to know were Austin Lane Poole and T.S.R. ("Tom") Boase. Neither was a fellow of New College, but both had published in areas related to his. Poole had done work in medieval German history, having written his first book on the Welf Henry the Lion. Poole was interested in EKa's research and was happy to profit from his oenophilic expertise. (When EKa later requested a recommendation from Poole for a position in the United States, he wrote that he could omit "[his] knowledge of Hocks which would give too many inferiority complexes to American Dons."[19]) Boase had a common fund of interest with EKa insofar as he had just published a biography of Boniface VIII (in the same series as the English KFII) and was working on a book on St. Francis. This probably was why Maurice

[14] Ibid., 287.

[15] Myers to Walter Adams, 28 March 1938: Bodleian Library, Oxford, MS SPSL 508/2, file 1, f. 309; Henderson to Walter Adams, 25 March 1938: ibid., f. 312. From this and Bowra's memoirs it can be seen that the rancorous account of Kantorowicz in Oxford purveyed in Cantor, *Inventing the Middle Ages*, 97, is fiction.

[16] Bowra, *Memories*, 151.

[17] The offprint was of Carl Erdmann, "Kaiserliche und päpstliche Fahnen im hohen Mittelalter," *Quellen und Forschungen aus italienischen Archiven und Bibliotheken* 25 (1934–35): 1–48, with a dedication to Kantorowicz. IAS: Ernst Kantorowicz: Correspondence found in his offprints.

[18] 27 April 1949.

[19] To A. L. Poole, 8 August 1938: LBI box 5, folder 3.

Bowra brought the two together. But while Bowra made an outward show of friendship for Boase he detested him. Behind his back he spoke of his "cerebral thromboasis."[20] And EKa, here at his worst, picked this right up, exhibiting friendship to Boase and then joining Bowra in mocking "Tombo" privately. Boase was later to be of great service to EKa, yet EKa never abandoned the mocking tone when he referred to him in his letters to Bowra.

EKa became good friends with Alic Smith, a philosopher whom Bowra liked. As dean of chapel at New College, Smith dispensed with Sunday chapel requirements for those "who could not be bothered to come."[21] EKa admired his "delightful detachment and good humor" and shared an enthusiasm with him for outdoor swimming. The two would go together to "Parson's Pleasure," a secluded area on the River Cherwell reserved for male nude bathing (women went to nearby "Dame's Delight"), where Smith did high dives. [22] (In a letter to Bowra of 1939 EKa writes, "With an almost Smithish somersault I dived into the depth of the Middle West."[23]) Another philosopher EKa met and befriended was the young Isaiah Berlin, then serving as a lecturer at New College while holding a fellowship at All Souls. The two maintained warm contacts until the time of EKa's death.[24] And it was Berlin who introduced EKa to Maurice Bowra (1898–1971) at a lunch at All Souls in April 1934.[25]

C. Maurice (pronounced "Morris") Bowra (fig. 19) used the term "our age" to designate his own interwar, wraps-off, generation.[26] One might also apply it to the era of Bowra in Oxford. Isaiah Berlin called him "the greatest English wit of his day," and the philosopher A. J. ("Freddie") Ayer described him as "by far the most influential don in the university."[27] Bowra's specialty was ancient Greek literature, but he was most noted for his sardonic wit and "open worship of pleasure."[28] By no means debonair, he was short, pig-eyed, and neckless. Elizabeth Bowen described him as looking like the frog footman in *Alice in Wonderland* and as one who upon entering a room was always

[20] Leslie Mitchell, *Maurice Bowra: A Life* (Oxford, 2009), 182. See 160–61 for Bowra's privately circulated acid verses on "Mombotombo."

[21] Bowra, *Memories*, 107–8.

[22] Ibid., 287.

[23] 27 March 1939.

[24] Kantorowicz to Berlin, 25 October 1962: Oxford, Bodleian Library, MS Berlin 169, fol. 295. (Henry Hardy kindly called my attention to this item.) In 1951 Berlin inscribed an offprint "To EKa, with the author's warmest sentiments": IAS: Correspondence found in his offprints.

[25] Bowra, *Memories*, 286.

[26] This was taken for the title of a book by Noël Annan: *Our Age: English Intellectuals between the Wars* (London, 1990). The standard biography is Mitchell, *Maurice Bowra*, which, however, is riddled with mistakes concerning Bowra's German connections. See also Noël Annan, *The Dons: Mentors, Eccentrics and Geniuses* (Chicago, 1999), 135–69, and Bowra's *Memories*.

[27] Berlin in Hugh Lloyd-Jones, ed., *Maurice Bowra: A Celebration* (London, 1974), 16; Ayer cited by Adam Sisman, *Hugh Trevor-Roper: The Biography* (London, 2010), 37.

[28] Anthony Powell in Lloyd-Jones, *Maurice Bowra*, 92.

Figure 19. Maurice Bowra, circa 1955. (Courtesy Warden and Fellows, Wadham College, Oxford)

"delighted to see himself."[29] He spoke very loudly, although lowering sometimes to pianissimo and then back up again, so that nobody could miss his shocking pronouncements. It was said that Isaiah Berlin learned to talk very rapidly in order to get in a word edgewise.[30] Noël Annan, who heard Bowra speak often, recalled: "Echoes of [his] intonations and inflexions reverberated through Oxford and London. People who never met him used his phrases. . . . His voice had the carrying power of the Last Trump."[31] Bowra believed "that life could be about what was possible rather than what was allowed."[32] Anthony Powell recalled: "Everything about him was up-to-date. The innovation was not only to proclaim the paramount claims of eating, drinking, and sex (if necessary auto erotic), but accepting as absolutely natural open snobbishness, success worship, personal vendettas, unprovoked malice, disloyalty to friends, reading other people's letters (if not lying about, to be sought in unlocked drawers)."[33]

[29] Mitchell, Maurice Bowra, 181.

[30] Humphrey Carpenter, *The Brideshead Generation: Evelyn Waugh and His Friends* (Boston, 1990), 95.

[31] Annan, *The Dons*, 145.

[32] Mitchell, *Maurice Bowra*, 155.

[33] Powell in Lloyd-Jones, *Maurice Bowra*, 92.

One cannot write about Bowra without reporting some of his quips. He complained that he had met X, who "gave him the warm shoulder"; another acquaintance was "one of his more delible memories"; and another was "the fake's progress." When told of an acquaintance who was ill he remarked, "Where there is death there is hope." An Oxford colleague (Boase) was "a man of no public virtues and no private parts"; a vice-chancellor was one who "split infinitives until the floor was covered with them." As for a very famous Oxford philosopher, his wife was "the influence under which was her husband." Bowra complained that he was "a man more dined against than dining" and frequently made jokes about his sexuality. For him, "buggery was invented to fill that awkward hour between evensong and cocktails." While reading the London *Times*'s engagement notices in the Common Room, he remarked in a stage whisper, "Damned—I slept with them both." And most famous was his rejoinder to someone who wondered why he might be thinking of marrying a plain woman: "My dear boy, buggers can't be choosers."

Despite his public stance of coldness, Bowra did have passionate feelings for poetry. His tastes ran from his own special subject, the poetry of the ancient Greeks, through French, German, and Russian (he learned Russian as a youth), to English-language contemporaries such as Eliot and Yeats. Given EKa's own mastery of the ancient Greek poetic canon, Goethe, Hölderlin, and George, discussion of poetry, and even reading out loud, offered one basis for their friendship. The fact that Bowra had fought in the trenches in the world war offered another, and then came the common zest for gossip (preferably pungent) and quips. Few in the George circle were adept at verbal volleying; the wittiest among them was Gundolf, but even he was not capable of off-the-cuff, off-color aphorisms. Consequently, the Oxford don and the German visitor soon came to appreciate how much they enjoyed each other's company.

Also, being practiced in such things, they became lovers. Because "pederasty" was illegal in England, Bowra avoided propositioning anyone who might possibly blackmail him. (He was so careful that he bypassed the subject in his memoirs of 1966.) But he had much experience in anonymous homosexual "cruising" before EKa arrived.[34] As for EKa, even after he entered into his affair with Baby he did not abandon homosexuality. A passage in a letter he wrote in 1928 to Wilhelm Stein lamented that the sculptor Fueter was looking for a female model since this now seemed more suitable for current tastes than sculpting "youths." As he concluded, "It's gradually becoming too undangerous here!"[35] Later EKa lamented the lack of "an erotic atmosphere . . . and especially a joy-boy atmosphere" in New York, acknowledging that perhaps he missed it because "the places I go to are not the right ones."[36] He left Oxford in July 1934

[34] Annan, *The Dons*, 165.
[35] 23 November 1928: Stein papers.
[36] Kantorowicz to Bowra, 25 February 1939.

and Bowra quickly came to visit him in Heidelberg, where he was staying with Baby.[37] Then, after the Oxford fall term, Bowra arrived in Berlin to see EKa and they lived in EKa's apartment for the period between Christmas and New Year's.[38] A passage in a letter from Kantorowicz to Bowra of 1943 reminisces about talks they had on their "honeymoon."[39]

EKa's social life in Oxford did not distract him from his research agenda. On the contrary, he was extremely productive during his six-month stay, and the work he did would prove fundamental for his subsequent career. He pursued four different projects. One, on "the cult of Saint Edward the Confessor," was never finished.[40] But he did make good progress on a second project, the relations between Frederick II's chancellor Petrus de Vinea and England in terms of diplomatic history and the transformation of the letter-writing style of the English chancery. The project must have been on his mind since 1930, when he had planned a volume containing registers of new documents pertaining to Frederick and he also pointed to underresearched connections between the Sicilian and English courts in the *Ergänzungsband*. Once in England he located relevant unpublished documents in London and Oxford, and when he returned to Germany he saw this work to completion, publishing an article, "Petrus de Vinea in England," in an Austrian historical journal in 1937.[41] The contents are primarily of interest to specialists in medieval Latin epistolary style (*ars dictandi*), but the article otherwise deserves mention because it displays what became the author's signature habits of pursuing minute details and producing footnotes of enormous length. It has been customary to call this Kantorowicz's "second manner."

Kantorowicz's third project in Oxford concerned liturgical chants. We have seen that he thrice adduced the ceremonial acclamation "Christus vincit, Christus regnat, Christus imperat" in KFII and that he returned to it in the *Ergänzungsband*. Then he took careful note of a pathbreaking article of 1930 by Percy Ernst Schramm on German imperial coronation liturgies.[42] From Schramm he learned that the "Christus vincit" triad was chanted in numerous medieval coronation rites. His particular interest in the Sicilian rite gave him material for a paper he agreed to deliver to Oxford's "Mediaeval Society," presided over by the prominent medievalist and Regius Professor of History, F. M. Powicke. The

[37] Bowra, *Memories*, 290–91.

[38] Kantorowicz to Beate Salz, 22 December 1934: Eckhart Grünewald Archive.

[39] 19 November 1943, edited in Lerner, "Letters by Ernst Kantorowicz Concerning Uxkull and George," 171.

[40] Mentioned in Kantorowicz to Percy Ernst Schramm, 7 April 1934, without further detail: Schramm papers.

[41] "Petrus de Vinea in England," *Mitteilungen des österreichischen Instituts für Geschichtsforschung* 51 (1937): 43–88; reprinted in Kantorowicz, *Selected Studies*, 213–46.

[42] Schramm, "Die Ordines der mittelalterlichen Kaiserkrönung: Ein Beitrag zur Geschichte des Kaisertums," *Archiv für Urkundenforschung* 11 (1930): 285–390.

match was perfect because the topic concerned a specific case of relations between the three "Norman realms" of Normandy, England, and Sicily, a subject of evident interest to English medievalists and perhaps most of all to Powicke, who in his own research had been concerned with relations between England and Normandy. (One should notice some symmetry: Powicke was a disciple and friend of Charles Homer Haskins, whose *Normans in European History* had given the title and guiding principle to Kantorowicz's Frankfurt lecture series of that name.[43]) EKa's thesis must also have pleased his audience, for he argued that a Sicilian coronation ritual descended from Normandy via England. In the Petrus de Vinea work influences ran from Sicily to England; in the liturgical chant lecture they ran the other way.

Before EKa gave his talk to the Oxford Mediaeval Society he wrote to Schramm that he was working in the area of coronation liturgy that Schramm had opened up and that he had come upon the Norman-English-Sicilian dimension by chance. He assured him that he was limiting himself to the "Anglo-Sicilian special question" because he did not want to anticipate any of Schramm's work; the liturgy paper was incidental to him just as the Edward the Confessor and Petrus de Vinea projects were.[44] But he changed his mind after his return to Germany. Instead of putting the "Christus vincit" triad aside he decided to expand his research into a short book. This aimed to consider the use of the triad in ceremonial ruler acclamations—*laudes regiae*—some of which were found in coronation rites and some elsewhere. Since Schramm was working on the subject of coronation rites proper he was not poaching. We will follow the fortunes of Kantorowicz's work in this area in subsequent chapters. Here it suffices to say that after constant roadblocks to publication a monograph was published in English in 1946 by the University of California Press. Although twelve years had passed, EKa acknowledged its origins with a dedication to his Oxford friends: "AMICIS OXONIENSIBUS."[45]

In a letter to Schramm of April 1934 he wrote that aside from his occasional occupations with "Edward the Confessor," "Petrus de Vinea," and the "Anglo-Sicilian special question" of coronation liturgies, he was working on "[his] matters." A statement in his curriculum vitae of July 1938 confirms that this was the "Interregnum" book he had mapped out in Frankfurt: "There [in Oxford] I was in [a] position to continue my researches on the german 'Interregnum' (1250–1308)." Put another way, he was continuing to work on a topic that would evolve into an important part of *The King's Two Bodies*. The only

[43] F. M. Powicke, "Charles Homer Haskins," *English Historical Review* 52 (1937): 649–56. On Powicke see Richard W. Southern, *History and Historians: Selected Papers of R. W. Southern*, ed. R. J. Bartlett (Oxford, 2004), 144–67. EKa and Bowra came to make jokes about him: in a letter to Bowra of 24 November 1954, EKa refers to him as "Pickwick."

[44] 7 April 1934: Schramm papers.

[45] Ernst Kantorowicz, *Laudes Regiae. A Study in Liturgical Acclamations and Mediaeval Ruler Worship* (Berkeley, 1946), x.

surviving evidence from the Oxford phase is the title of a lecture that he gave at New College and St. John's College (where A. L. Poole was a fellow): "Secularization of the Middle Ages." We will see that he moved ahead with this theme when he returned to Germany.

The most distinguished medievalist EKa met in Oxford was Marc Bloch. The convergence is notable because the two were among the greatest medieval historians of their age. (A French historian later referred to Kantorowicz as "the Marc Bloch of beyond the Rhine."[46]) Moreover, both were Jewish and both served in their respective armies in 1916. Before the meeting Bloch had no high opinion of Kantorowicz. In 1928 he reviewed KFII in the leading French historical journal, the *Revue historique.* He granted that it was "agreeable to read, sometimes moving," but he did not care for the biographical format, the "panegyrical" tone, and the nationalist stance. Remarkably he also found the research "entirely lacking." Bloch reviewed the *Ergänzungsband* in the *Revue historique* four years later. This time he was friendlier. Given the apparatus of "copious and clearly presented references" he considered it "a precious instrument of research." But he did wonder about the extent of the author's knowledge of French, for he found the volume lacking in coverage of the relevant French literature.[47]

Although a face-to-face meeting might not have seemed auspicious, F. M. Powicke brought the two men together when Bloch was visiting Oxford in 1934. EKa wrote about it twice, first in a letter to Powicke of 1957. There he reminisced: "It was indeed together with Marc Bloch that I dined with you at Oriel. Around 10 p.m. you left us alone with a bottle of Whisky in the Oriel Common Room under the picture of Cardinal Newman (or am I mistaken?) and the two of us went along talking until long after midnight."[48] In 1961 he presented a more expansive account of the meeting in a letter he sent to the *Times Literary Supplement* in regard to a review of the English translation of Bloch's *La société féodale.* Now he wanted to set the record straight on the question of influence.

> I was slightly puzzled, though greatly honoured, by the fact that from among hundreds of scholars upon whom Marc Bloch exerted considerable influence, your reviewer saw fit to single me out by mentioning my name. It is perfectly true that I was greatly impressed by his *Rois thaumaturges.* I actually met Marc Bloch in Oxford, dining with him in 1934 at Oriel, and talked with him until far into the small hours after our kind host, Sir Maurice Powicke, had left us alone with

[46] Guy Bois, cited by Peter Schöttler, "Ernst Kantorowicz in Frankreich," in Benson and Fried, *Ernst Kantorowicz,* 144–61, at 155.

[47] On both reviews, ibid., 157–58.

[48] 27 July 1957, Powicke Papers, Bodleian Library, Oxford. Sir Richard Southern informed me of these papers and Fiona Robb located the letter in question.

> a good supply of Bordeaux and Whisky. Both of us got so excited in the course of our conversation that we did not sit down but stood in front of the fireplace to exchange our arguments and places and quotations about any relevant subject. I, too, felt that his historical scholarship was "unmistakably lit from an inward fire" so absent from the works of historians. But exactly this was a quality which, alas, I could not borrow from him. I am sure there are many others who were far more dependent on him than I was, though it be far from me to deny the great impression his studies and his personality made upon me.[49]

Kantorowicz cited Bloch's *Les rois thaumaturges* (published in 1924) once in the *Ergänzungsband* and once again in his book *Laudes Regiae*. But although *Les rois thaumaturges* was a milestone in treating aspects of "divine kingship," it concerned healing powers, and that was not EKa's subject. As for Bloch he moved in very different directions afterward. Thus the judgment can stand that the "inward fires" of both men burned apart.

The fact that EKa was willing to spend an evening talking with a Frenchman suggests a certain amount of mellowing. It may be recalled that less than twelve years earlier he had fulminated about the "revolting grimaces" and "nauseating grotesqueness" of the French. Possibly a new tolerance was conveyed to him by Bowra, who championed the poetry of Paul Valéry and had come to befriend Valéry when he received an honorary degree from Oxford in June 1931. In his *Memories* of 1966 Bowra wrote that "even now [Valéry] seems to me to have had the finest intelligence I have ever met."[50]

Intimacy with Bowra certainly exposed EKa to political attitudes much unlike those prevalent in his German world. Although Bowra never was really politically engaged, he "always tended to the Left in politics."[51] One of his friends was the Socialist Hugh Gaitskell. During the General Strike of 1926 Bowra joined with the leftist Oxford political philosopher A. D. Lindsay in seeking to find a negotiated settlement between the miners and the government.[52] Later he acted as honorary treasurer of the Oxford University Miners' Wives and Children Fund and together with another Oxford leftist, G.D.H. Cole, collected money for holidays for the unemployed.[53] When he was in America in November 1936 he got caught up in the electoral excitement and cheered for Roosevelt. "On election night, sitting by the radio, he would say, 'What of Arkansas? We've had no news from Indiana.'"[54]

[49] *Times Literary Supplement*, 7 July 1961.
[50] Bowra, *Memories*, 189.
[51] London *Times* obituary, in Lloyd-Jones, *Maurice Bowra*, 15.
[52] Bowra, *Memories*, 179.
[53] Mitchell, *Maurice Bowra*, 199.
[54] Ibid., 223.

Regarding foreign affairs, Bowra was as an early and vehement critic of Hitler. During the 1920s and early 1930s he had made frequent trips to Berlin, motivated primarily by sexual cruising. In the fall of 1932 he was together with some journalists whom Hitler had invited to his hotel to listen to his views. As Bowra later recalled, "Hitler ranted at us in his usual way, and his theme was the unity of Germany. His peroration was that it was not a political unity, not an economic unity, not a geographical unity—'but, understand, it is a spiritual unity.'"[55] He was appalled. Thus we can easily appreciate that when Kantorowicz was in Oxford less than two years later and "was liable to talk about a thing called 'secret Germany,'" Bowra found that the term "lacked substance in English."[56] The fact that EKa gradually stopped talking that way in the mid-1930s is perhaps most attributable to the influence of his English friend.

[55] Bowra, *Memories*, 284.
[56] Ibid., 290.

CHAPTER 13

"Leisure with Dignity"

IN 1937 ERNST KANTOROWICZ PUBLISHED AN ESSAY ENTITLED "The Return of Learned Reclusiveness in the Middle Ages."[1] Originally it was meant to have been a contribution to a second volume of a Festschrift for Ludwig Curtius, but the publisher withdrew the volume after setting it in type because it had too many contributions by Jews.[2] Given that it already was "printed," however, EKa ordered offprints to be made with their own cover so that he could distribute them to colleagues and friends. The piece did not engage in scholarly debate. Instead it expatiated on the revival of a classical ideal: Ciceronian *otium cum dignitate*: "leisure with dignity." Although "loneliness is the wise man's lot," in the ancient world this principle did not mean avoiding society: the philosopher could be found in the marketplace or at a banquet. During late antiquity philosophers took to reclusiveness, yet still for the sake of finding this-worldly wisdom. The next step came with Christianity: reclusiveness (i.e., monasticism), for the sake of leading an ascetic life dedicated to attaining other-worldly blessedness. Kantorowicz identified Abelard as the first to return to reclusiveness as a means for pursuing a life of learning, but he acknowledged that Abelard's reclusiveness remained monastic or ascetic and that when he spoke of pursuing philosophy he ultimately meant theology. The main actor in Kantorowicz's story was Petrarch, the admirer of Cicero, who sought to live as a philosopher, scholar, and poet away from the madding crowd and whose solitude was to be spent to be in comfortable withdrawal. Petrarch wished to partake of simple but good-tasting food in a landscape of "blue heavens, mountains, trees, flowers, and brooks." Thus it was he who bequeathed to posterity the ideal of

[1] *Die Wiederkehr gelehrter Anachorese im Mittelalter* (Stuttgart, 1937), reprinted in Kantorowicz, *Selected Studies*, 339–51. The essay is short enough to obviate the need for page citations.

[2] EG, 141 (referring to a "third" volume inasmuch as the first volume was accompanied by one of plates). See also Kantorowicz to Fritz Saxl, 22 February 1938 (Warburg Institute Archives, London): "die Anachorese, die ja offiziell nicht existiert und nur in den paar Freiexemplaren vorliegt." The page proofs, including EKa's emendations, stamped 7 January 1937, are in LBI, box 3, folder 14. This folder contains an English translation, doubtless part of the author's efforts around 1939 to gather works for publication in England or America.

"the learned hermit" surrounded by books in a "refined-lonely, cerebral, and beautiful *otium cum dignitate*."

It takes little to see that Kantorowicz's Petrarch stood for himself at the time of writing. His commitment to the ideal of unemployed, refined, scholarly reclusiveness meant so much to him that he was willing to pay for disseminating what amounted to an *apologia pro vita sua*. It seems difficult to believe that he thought he could live with dignity despite Nazi outrages, but his essay implicitly made that claim. Calling up Carpaccio's image of *Saint Jerome in His Study*, he asserted that this Jerome, engaged in his scholarship and surrounded by books, hardly needed to be guarded by a lion but only by a "tiny, alert Pomeranian dog." In fact from mid-1934 until late 1938 Kantorowicz did lead a quiet, comfortable, and productive life. But his ability to conduct research and to publish kept on being whittled down until it became impossible for him to continue on course.

Critics of Kantorowicz's political views of the 1920s and early 1930s seize on the fact that he remained in Germany "as long as possible."[3] Particularly nasty comments come from Norman Cantor, who charged that EKa stayed on in Germany as "the ideal Nazi scholar and intellectual" under the protection of "Nazi bigshots." Cantor speculated that Kantorowicz considered "militant anti-Semitism [as] just a vulgar intermediary instrument for the Nazis [that] would burn away; then he would get his suitable reward and eminence in the Hitlerian regime."[4] This is preposterous. Kantorowicz was not on close terms with any highly placed Nazis; rather, his anti-Nazism in the years in question can be documented. He and Bowra referred to "Shitler."[5] A more nuanced interpretation is that of Martin Ruehl, who sees Kantorowicz's delayed departure from Germany as stemming from his "ultrapatriotic views."[6] But this ignores the absence of patriotic expressions after 1935.

If we look at the situation without prejudice, it may be well to avoid casting stones. EKa had sufficient income to live in Germany comfortably, but this income could only be drawn in Germany and he had no way of knowing whether he could find employment in a foreign country during the Depression. His best German friends were still in the country until shortly before his departure and he had only one contact across the ocean. His ailing sister Gretel, afflicted with ALS (Lou Gehrig's disease), was living in Berlin, as was his septuagenarian mother, who had moved there in 1934. Staying in Germany was preferable

[3] The "Ernst Kantorowicz" file of the Emergency Committee in Aid of Foreign Scholars contains four documents dating from the spring of 1934, showing that a "Dr. Ernst Kantorowicz" sent his curriculum vitae to New York in the hope of finding employment in the United States. But this was "the other" Ernst Kantorowicz (1892–1944), a professor of sociology who never managed to escape from Germany and died in Auschwitz. On him, Walther and Ernst, "Ernst Kantorowicz," 216–17.

[4] Cantor, *Inventing the Middle Ages*, 95, 97.

[5] To Bowra, 29 May 1939; Kantorowicz to Bowra, 17 December 1937, expresses mordant hostility to Neville Chamberlain's foreign policy and willingness to "hand things over to Dr. Goebbels."

[6] Ruehl, "'Imperium transcendat hominem,'" 220.

from the point of view of pursuing his research and writing. His income allowed him to engage in scholarship, he was free to work in the library of the MGH, and he possessed a good private library of his own; the documents for his research were located in Germany or elsewhere in Europe. Those who believe that Kantorowicz should have made a break with all this out of political principle have never had to make such a choice.

After leaving England in July 1934 EKa stopped off to visit Paris for the first time, joining his sister Soscha on a "sight-seeing tour." The weather was too hot and he found the Parisians unendearing.[7] Then he went to Heidelberg to see Baby.[8] Maurice Bowra soon arrived and the Baroness drove EKa and Bowra around the vicinity. As Bowra recalled, "On these trips we had endless talks, in which she and I made fun of Ernst's more romantic notions."[9] Bowra stated frankly that as soon as he arrived in Heidelberg he "fell at once" for Baby. No doubt exists that at a certain point she shifted her affections from EKa to him, but just when this happened is not clear. Bowra's memoirs report that "from Heidelberg I went to Berlin," and letters from late August show that EKa was then staying in a hotel on Lake Maggiore in the Ticino district of Switzerland.[10] He definitely was traveling with Baby, for one of the letters refers to his (female) "autofriend" and the other to returning soon to Heidelberg.

In the fall EKa took up residence in Berlin, staying first with Gretel. Intent on resolving the Frankfurt situation, and evidently unwilling to swear an oath of personal loyalty to Adolf Hitler that had been required of all civil servants by a law of August 20, he submitted a request to the Prussian Education Ministry that he be awarded emeritus status on the grounds that he could not imagine being able to return to teaching and that it was pointless to apply perennially for leaves of absence. His petition was granted on November 10 by the Nazi minister with the exquisite formula: "I take this opportunity to express to you my thanks and appreciation for your meritorious academic service."[11] EKa was not receiving a special favor; the minister had no choice other than this concession because the petitioner was exempted from dismissal by the "front fighter" clause of the law of April 7, 1933. (EKa later joked that he must have been the youngest "emeritus" professor in German history.[12]) What does seem strange is that EKa's emeritus status came with regular payments of a pension (at full salary) as if he had retired at the end of a normal career. Moreover, with one interruption these substantial payments continued to be disbursed until the outbreak of war between Germany and the United States in 1941. But

[7] To Soscha Salz, 21 January 1938: Eckhart Grünewald Archive.

[8] To Hans Jantzen, 22 July 1934, from Mozartstr., Heidelberg: Frankfurt University Archives.

[9] Bowra, *Memories*, 291.

[10] To Edgar Salin, 29 August 1934: Salin papers; to Karl Hampe, 29 August: Hampe papers. EKa had vacationed in the same hotel earlier: postcard to Wilhelm Stein, 3 September 1932: Stein papers.

[11] EG, 139.

[12] William A. Chaney to David Spear, 6 August 2001: Lerner archive.

rules were rules. Ernst Morwitz, a highly placed Prussian judge and Jew who also was rescued from dismissal by the "front fighter" clause, also was paid a regular pension from the time of own "retirement" in 1935 until 1941.[13] During Christmastime EKa closed down his Frankfurt apartment. In May he moved into his own rented apartment in Berlin[14] and resided there, with interruptions for travel, until November 1938.

EKa's apartment was on the Carmerstrasse, right off Savignyplatz, a choice location in the heart of Charlottenburg. According to Bowra, "He suffered deeply from finding that as a Jew he was thought different from other Germans, and once or twice had awkward scenes in restaurants when the waiters were offensive to him, and the only thing was to leave at once."[15] A letter of his to Baby of March 10, 1935, refers to the awful atmosphere, or state of being unable to breathe, in which he was living; if she thought the mood was low in Frankfurt, in Berlin it was still lower.[16]

Nevertheless, he managed. He was at no loss for friends. Kurt Riezler and his wife had moved to Berlin and he saw them frequently. He spent time too with Morwitz, a former associate of Stefan George's. A new friend was Albrecht Graf von Bernstorff (1890–1945), an aristocrat who was destined to play an important role in his life.[17] Bernstorff was six feet six inches tall and weighed over 250 pounds. Having been one of the first German Rhodes scholars he was a staunch Anglophile; according to his one-time lover Enid Bagnold, he "knew more about England and England's upper-class eccentricities and specialties than most Englishmen." He "knew the value of the English weekend [and] the deceptive appearance of dallying."[18] He also was a liberal and a pacifist. He once told EKa that as a child he had melted down toy soldiers.[19] In keeping with these ideals he was an outspoken anti-Nazi. Early in 1934 he wrote to an English friend: "We hate and fight [the Nazi] system because it is bound to destroy and pervert Germany . . . we suffer because this gang of criminals, psychopaths, well-meaning lunatics and swashbuckling youngsters are destroying those fine qualities of which we have been proud and which have made Germany what she was before March 1933."[20] Not only did Bernstorff write such things, he was liable to say them loudly in restaurants where he easily could be overheard.[21]

[13] Groppe, *Die Macht der Bildung*, 443, n. 161.

[14] To Beate Salz, 7 May 1935: Eckhart Grünewald Archive.

[15] Ibid.

[16] Communicated to me by Eckhart Grünewald.

[17] Knut Hansen, *Albrecht Graf von Bernstorff: Diplomat und Bankier zwischen Kaiserreich und Nationalsozialismus* (Frankfurt, 1996).

[18] Enid Bagnold, "Albrecht," in *Albrecht Bernstorff zum Gedächtnis* (Altenhof, 1952), 40–42.

[19] Ernst Kantorowicz, "Der Gastfreund," in ibid., 53–56, at 56.

[20] Hansen, *Albrecht Graf von Bernstorff*, 202.

[21] Marion Dönhoff, "De Nobilitate," in *Albrecht Bernstorff zum Gedächtnis*, 48–52, at 48.

Bernstorff had served as an undersecretary in the German Embassy in London for a decade but was dismissed in 1933 because he was deemed unreliable. Returning to Germany, he became a codirector of the A. E. Wassermann Bank in Berlin. He was recruited for this position by a friend, Joseph Hambuechen, a partner in the bank who was a cousin by marriage of Ernst Kantorowicz. (Hambuechen's wife, Dorothee, was the granddaughter of a Kantorowicz; when the couple's daughter, Beate, was born in 1927, Bernstorff became her godfather.[22]) EKa may have met Bernstorff through this family connection, or else through Kurt Riezler, who had been close friends with Bernstorff ever since their joint diplomatic engagements in 1918. EKa not only socialized with Bernstorff in Berlin, often together with Riezler and Riezler's sparkling wife Kaethe, but met others through him. One was Adam von Trott zu Solz, another Anglophile and former Rhodes scholar, who a decade later was to be executed for his role in the plot against Hitler.[23]

Bernstorff often hosted guests at his country estate of Stintenburg, a few hours' drive from Berlin. In August 1936 EKa was there with Bowra, where they swam in the nearby lake while Bernstorff went deer hunting.[24] Pentecost 1937 saw a large gathering, later well remembered by both EKa and Marion Dönhoff.[25] Amidst radiant sunlight there was sailing, fishing, hunting, and always lively conversation. A photo (fig. 20) shows EKa standing in front of the stately residence in the company of Bernstorff, Dönhoff, "Jerry" Pinsent, the British commercial attaché in Berlin, and Ivone Kirkpatrick, first secretary in the British Embassy.

Kantorowicz's Berlin apartment was spacious and well appointed. He lived in three rooms, not counting kitchen and bath, without any hint of financial constraint.[26] Bowra, who stayed often with EKa in the Carmerstrasse between 1935 and 1938, conveys the atmosphere:

> Ernst, who had been deprived of his professorship at Frankfurt, moved to Berlin on the principle that the best place in a maelstrom is at the centre, and established himself in a flat near the Zoo. Here he worked out a new pattern of life. He read a lot, but never allowed it to interfere with his friends or his pleasures. He was a first-class cook, who excelled at chrysanthemum soup, bouillabaisse, ducks done in brandy, and *crêpes Suzette*. We spent much time on preparing meals, and though I was the merest tweeny [a maid who assists the cook], I greatly enjoyed

[22] Beata [Beate] Alden to Robert E. Lerner, "I do remember von Bernstorff fondly, as one of Dad's friends we liked": email, 18 February 2012.

[23] On the meeting through Bernstorff, Kantorowicz, "Der Gastfreund," 55.

[24] Bowra, *Memories*, 296.

[25] Dönhoff, "De Nobilitate," 50–51; Kantorowicz, "Der Gastfreund," 56.

[26] Interview with Walter Gross (who visited Kantorowicz in Berlin) 13 August 1994; interview with Beate Salz, 28 June 1990. The rooms and their contents appear in inventories in LBI, box 5, folder 3.

Figure 20. Relaxing at the country residence of Graf Bernstorff, 1937. EKa is standing at the right. Bernstorff is sitting at left; to his right is Countess Dönhoff; the two other men are Jerry Pinsent and Ivone Kirkpatrick. (Courtesy Hartwig Graf von Bernstorff)

> it since Ernst talked unceasingly with much fancy about the various ingredients and what must be done with them. The rest of the time was spent mostly in conversation, usually of a coherent kind, on single subjects. Politics could not be forgotten, but they were treated from unexpected angles, and Ernst would maintain that all the trouble began with Luther, or that Hitler was the only Nazi who did not believe in National Socialism, or that the most important figures in history die at the age of fifty-six.[27]

The passage is just one of numerous indications that between 1935 and 1938 Kantorowicz and Bowra were a couple. In the Christmas season of 1934–35 they stayed together in Berlin and then in Frankfurt.[28] Subsequently Bowra was in Berlin often and came to know some of EKa's friends.[29] EKa arranged in 1935

[27] Bowra, *Memories*, 294.

[28] To Beate Salz: 22 December 1934: Eckhart Grünewald Archive.

[29] Bowra, *Memories*, 292–94; letter to Bowra, 8 July 1936, tells of expecting him in Berlin around late August; Bowra then was in Stintenburg with Kantorowicz in late August. (I am grateful to Hartwig Graf von Bernstorff for the Stintenburg guest book entries.)

for him to write radio scripts on "Greek War Games and Pindar" and "England and the Olympic Idea" for transmission in Berlin in connection with the forthcoming Berlin Olympics.[30] In addition he arranged to have him write an introduction for an edition of the poems of Sappho translated into German by Ernst Morwitz. (Bowra explained in his memoirs that his German was overhauled by EKa; most likely EKa translated the radio scripts.) One evening EKa and Bowra translated together a poem by Stefan George, *Seelied*, into English.[31] The two men traveled together in Italy: Gerhart Ladner saw them in Rome.[32]

The close relationship between the two men raises the issue of the EKa-Bowra-Baby triangle. As Bowra stated in his memoirs that he "fell at once" for Baby, so Baby's daughter told me that Baby had "her eye out for him."[33] When EKa and Bowra were in Frankfurt at the beginning of 1935, Lucy von Wangenheim had recently moved there with her daughters and must have met Bowra when he was with EKa in Frankfurt around New Year's. They may have met again in Frankfurt without EKa in the following months; by 1935 she suddenly wanted to go to Oxford to study. Sometime in the spring she consulted Robert Boehringer, a leading former George disciple, about such possibilities. and the latter forwarded her questions by mail to Ernst Morwitz in Berlin. Innocently, Morwitz then passed them on to EKa, leaving him to reply to Boehringer.[34] EKa told Boehringer disingenuously that "Fräulein v. W." should make contact with "Mr. C. M. Bowra," as if he had no idea that Baby already knew him. He wrote that "Mr. Bowra is the smartest and wittiest of the younger Oxford dons," adding that if "Miss von Wangenheim" contacted him, mentioning his—EKa's—name, Bowra could "put her in touch with Oxford people." He must have been pleased by the idea that Boehringer, whom he greatly disliked, would play his part as the unwitting intermediary of a private joke. But one wonders what he thought of the fact that Baby was making inquiries about studying in Oxford behind his back.

While she was flirting with Maurice Bowra, Baby occupied herself as a translator of English novels into German. She began with Helen Waddell's, *Peter Abelard* (1935), for which an arrangement must have been made by EKa. (It will be remembered that Waddell had been the motive force behind the translation of KFII into English.) Baby's second translation was of Evelyn Waugh's *A Handful of Dust* (1936), a fact that suggests that both Bowra and EKa were acting in her service: Bowra was a friend of Waugh's; the book was published by the firm of Bondi, directed after Bondi's death by EKa's friend Helmut Küpper. (Stefan

[30] Michael Philipp, *"Vom Schicksal des deutschen Geistes": Wolfgang Frommels Rundfunkarbeit an den Sendern Frankfurt und Berlin 1933–1935* (Potsdam, 1995), 72, 75. Kantorowicz to Bowra, 6 September 1939, indicates that Bowra had met the director of the radio series, Wolfgang Frommel.

[31] William A. Chaney to Robert E. Lerner, 13 August 2010: Lerner archive.

[32] Ladner, *Erinnerungen*, 36.

[33] Interview with Arianna Giachi, 16 December 1993.

[34] To Robert Boehringer, 10 June 1935: StGA, Boehringer papers.

George would have been horrified had he known that his former house publisher was printing satirical English novels.) It seems as if EKa was still Baby's man in the summer of 1936, for he wrote to Bowra in July that he would be vacationing with her for two weeks in a Belgian seaside resort.[35] Yet in the same letter he added, "Won't you join us there in August before going with me to Berlin?" One can only surmise that he had not yet noticed the mutual amorous interest of his own two amorous attachments. Soon thereafter Bowra went to America to teach at Harvard for the academic year 1936–37. When he returned he visited Baby several times in Frankfurt; in March 1937 Graf von Bernstorff hosted Bowra, Baby, and EKa for lunch in Berlin.[36] By the autumn of 1938 at the latest Bowra and Baby were certainly engaged in an affair which they did not hide from EKa.[37] Not only did he have no hard feelings, but he never broke with either.

The departure of Baby from Germany to Oxford in October 1938 is surrounded by rather colorful stories. An English socialite, later turned novelist, Mary Wesley, told her biographer that a German refugee from Czechoslovakia named Heinz Ziegler once worked together (the implied date is late 1938) with an anti-Nazi German "Baroness" in London for the antiappeasement diplomat Sir Robert Vansittart. According to Wesley's account, Ziegler "said he would 'give the *Baronin* to Bowra' [and] in due course Maurice Bowra did indeed receive the *Baronin* at Wadham College, where she assisted him in his war work and seduced him."[38] The only truth here is that Bowra hosted Baby at Wadham College. Evidently Baby was trying to create the impression that she had gone to England as an anti-Nazi agent, and Bowra's biographer indulges it further by saying that "according to Mary Wesley, she was also in the pay of British Intelligence."[39]

Baby led Noël Annan to believe that Bowra "rescued" her from Germany.[40] But there is no truth in that either. Bowra's own account brings us closer, although it is flawed because of Baby's self-dramatization and misrepresentations. As he tells of her move to England:

> Though she was candidly anti-Nazi, her father's reputation meant that even the Nazis had some respect for her and left her alone. But a member of her family turned against her. She wished to do some job which did not appeal to the Baroness who spoke firmly against it. The young woman was extremely angry and threatened to go to the Nazis to tell them about the Baroness's long friendship

[35] To Bowra, 8 July 1936.

[36] Bowra, *Memories*, 303; Albrecht Graf von Bernstorff to Elly Reventlow (information communicated to me by Hartwig Graf von Bernstorff).

[37] As evident from his letters to Bowra of 30 September and 29 October 1938.

[38] Patrick Marnham, *Wild Mary: The Life of Mary Wesley* (London, 2006), 69, 75.

[39] Mitchell, *Maurice Bowra*, 213.

[40] Annan, *The Dons*, 166.

> with Ernst, upon which she put the worst interpretation, knowing that this might do untold damage and quite probably lead to a concentration camp. The Baroness found out just in time and saw that she must leave the country at once. This she succeeded in doing, but with almost no money or possessions . . . she bore it all with her usual courage and lack of complaints.[41]

Bowra discreetly refrained from naming the "member of the family" who supposedly caused Baby's precipitous flight, but I can report that "the young woman" was Baby's second daughter, who told me the story from her side.[42] In the spring of 1938 Arianna was nineteen and had just graduated from the gymnasium. Baby was still living in Frankfurt with Arianna and her third daughter, but by then "she clearly decided that she wanted to be with Bowra in England" and consequently had already moved out of her apartment into a pension. (A letter of EKa's of January indicates that Baby wanted to visit England then, and another letter of March refers to her being able to tell Arianna that she was going away.[43]) Arianna explained that she and her mother were on terrible terms, so much so that they hardly spoke to each other but passed notes in their respective mailboxes. And the notes got very heated. Arianna wanted to proceed to the university to study medicine, but Baby was determined that she attend a boarding school in French-speaking Switzerland. (In the fall she did send her youngest daughter to such a school.) In youthful pique Arianna wrote that "she was prepared to do anything to avoid this," and her mother used the paper as proof that her daughter was ready to report her to the Gestapo.

Although this happened in the spring at graduation time, Baby, who supposedly needed to flee immediately because of danger of arrest, left Germany half a year later. It is true that the Nuremberg laws of 1935 forbade sexual relations between gentiles and Jews on pain of imprisonment or "hard labor," but the ultimate proof that Baby was not fleeing possible arrest for that reason comes from a letter from EKa to Bowra of September 30, 1938, reporting that she had just been with him in Berlin for three weeks, "bankrupting him" because of her expensive ways.[44] Clearly she was neither in desperate flight nor fearing arrest for consorting with a Jew.

Bowra reported in his memoirs that Baby "settled first in London and then in Oxford," but though she doubtless passed through London she surely did not immediately settle there because she was living in Wadham College on October 24.[45] Evidently Bowra did not want to give the impression that she went

[41] Bowra, *Memories*, 303.

[42] Interview of 18 July 1994; Jennifer Kolpacoff Deane was present. (After I wrote what follows, confirming information has been reported to me by Eckhart Grünewald.)

[43] To Soscha Salz, 21 January 1938: Eckhart Grünewald Archive; to Lucy von Wangenheim, 27 March 1938; communicated to me by Eckhart Grünewald.

[44] To Bowra, 30 September 1938.

[45] Diary of Nigel Clive, 24 October 1938, in Mitchell, *Maurice Bowra*, 213.

to England to be with him, but that seems to have been the case. (In his memoirs she appears dignifiedly as "the Baroness," never as "Baby.") EKa knew that she had departed in order to live with Bowra in his newly remodeled Warden's cottage—Bowra's "palazzo." In a letter of October 29, 1938, he wrote lewdly to Bowra: "Did you 'enjoy' Baby? I hope you did."

For reasons that remain unclear, Baby had lost all her money. Because it apparently was unseemly for her to live with Bowra for too long, she went to London where she may have taken some sort of job. In August, however, she vacationed with Bowra, at his expense, in France. frequenting, among other locations, Monte Carlo. The two returned to England together after the signing of the Hitler-Stalin pact, staying in Paris in "an excellent hotel" and having "a memorable lunch at 'La Pérouse.'"[46] Baby's intimacy with Bowra apparently did not last much longer, but the two remained close. In 1943 he dedicated his *Heritage of Symbolism* "To "L.v.W"; later, circa 1957, he offered to introduce Lucy von Wangenheim to a visiting American.[47] Puzzlingly it was EKa rather than Bowra who supported her financially. In September 1939 he wrote to Bowra that he had hoped to persuade her to move to Berkeley because it would have been easiest to support her there, but she demurred.[48] A year later he referred in a letter to his financial stringencies caused, among other things, by the fact that he "had to support someone in London *completely*."[49] EKa was known to be financially generous—in Berkeley he sometimes helped to pay for his students' medical bills—but it is unclear why in this case he felt a sense of ongoing obligation. Whatever the answer, he remained amicable with Baby for the duration of his life. In 1939 she typed a fair copy of one of his articles for him, and in 1953 they saw each other when EKa was visiting London.[50] From 1939 until EKa's last years they stayed in regular touch by mail. By the time of his death he had saved "thousands" of letters from Baby, but Judith Kent (Soscha's daughter) burned them on Baby's request.[51]

Bowra's memoirs state that in Kantorowicz's second Berlin period he "was beginning to move away from the doctrines which he had gained from Stefan George, and regarded his own ultra-patriotic activities in 1919 as an aberration."[52] A radio talk EKa wrote early in 1935 for a lay audience shows

[46] Bowra, *Memories*, 353–54.

[47] William A. Chaney to Robert E. Lerner, 13 August 2010: Lerner archive.

[48] To Bowra, 6 September 1939.

[49] To Felix Hepner, 8 September 1940: Hepner papers 1206/1/14/7.

[50] Fair copy: Kantorowicz to Fritz Saxl, 21 October 1939: Warburg Institute Archives, London; meeting in London: interview with Arianna Giachi, 16 December 1993.

[51] Ariane Phillips (Judith's daughter) to Robert E. Lerner: email, 2 February 2014. EKa told Ralph Giesey and Michael Cherniavsky shortly before his death that he did not want the letters to be saved but apparently could not bring himself to do the destroying. (Ralph Giesey to Robert E. Lerner, email, 6 July 2004.)

[52] Bowra, *Memories*, 294.

that his move away from George's ideology was gradual but that he no longer was bent on propagandizing for it. The talk was one in a series of late-night broadcasts transmitted between October 1933 and October 1935, first from Frankfurt and then from Berlin. It was organized by the publicist Wolfgang Frommel, an admirer of George, who engaged a wide variety of contacts to contribute, including George circle personalities and noted academics.[53] The talks were meant to treat a range of cultural topics under the rubric of "the Destiny of the German Spirit." Given the times, Frommel's enterprise was daring insofar as most of his contributors were not zealous Nazis and spoke without reference to current Nazi slogans.

Frommel was daring too in including a few Jews, even though Jews were banned from speaking over the airwaves.[54] In March 1935 he recruited Kantorowicz at the suggestion of Ernst Morwitz. To circumvent the ban he arranged for a young gentile friend of his to deliver the talk under his own name and pass on the honorarium to the real author. Nevertheless, he still was taking risks, for the friend was a law student who could hardly have been thought to have had the erudition in medieval history displayed in the script he was reading. Indeed one listener who wrote in smelled a rat: "It sounded as if you had engaged a specialist in the Hohenstaufen period."[55] If the Gestapo had paid any attention it might have noticed the deception and punished the perpetrators severely.[56]

Kantorowicz's "German Papacy" (Deutsches Papsttum) was broadcast from Berlin on February 22, 1935. Without being political, the talk implicitly opposed Nazi triumphalism. "German Papacy" treated the several occasions in the Middle Ages when Germans had become popes.[57] The theme was the tension between the pontificates of German popes who had been imperial bishops and were dwarfed by their Germanness and others who were committed to universal claims and thereby lost their Germanness. For Kantorowicz the failure to unite the German and the universal was "the hopelessness—*as we know*—that sticks to all German history" (my emphasis).[58] The censor who oversaw Berlin

[53] A thorough account is Philipp, "*Vom Schicksal.*"

[54] Confusion about the date arises from an anonymous statement in Frommel's postwar journal *Castrum Peregini* 12 (1953) (under "Mitteilungen"): "Der Vortrag von Professor Dr. Ernst Kantorowicz über das deutsche Papsttum entstammt dem Jahre 1933." Although this text almost certainly was written by Frommel, a subsequent "Mitteilung" in *Castrum Peregini* 107–9 (1975): 176, doubtless also written by Frommel, explains that the talk came from a suggestion of Ernst Morwitz and was discussed by Kantorowicz and Frommel in Morwitz's Berlin apartment.

[55] Kantorowicz to Lucy von Wangenheim, 10 March 1933, communicated to me by Eckhart Grünewald.

[56] Philipp, "*Vom Schicksal,*" 195–96, 199–200.

[57] Ernst Kantorowicz, "Deutsches Papsttum," *Castrum Peregrini* 7 (1953): 7–24. (First published in *Vom Schicksal des deutschen Geistes* [Berlin, 1935], 42–57.)

[58] "Deutsches Papsttum," 19: "das Ausweglose, das—wie wir wissen—aller deutschen Geschichte anhaftet."

broadcasts in 1935 must have been nodding when he let pass a reference to German history as being mired in hopelessness.

Yet Kantorowicz still had difficulty in abandoning the ideal of a Germany that somehow was once and always German and cosmopolitan. His talk opened with an evocation of the cathedral of Bamberg. The cathedral held an imperial and a papal tomb: the tomb of Henry II, the only German emperor to be recognized as a saint, and that of Clement II, the only German-born pope to have been buried in Germany. Here alone were grounds for taking Bamberg as a marker of what could have been. And there was more. Kantorowicz alluded to the presence of four sculptures: *Frankish Rider*, *Galilean Sibyl*, *Ecclesia*, and *Synagoga*. Each needs comment. In referring to what is most often known as the "Bamberg Rider," the remarkable thirteenth-century equestrian statue attached to a column inside the cathedral, he was invoking the presence of what he had called in KFII the "knightly noble human type that must have lived in Germany." According to the biography, the Rider was "at once of cosmopolitan and yet German nature." (77) The *Galilean Sibyl* was the name sometimes given to a thirteenth-century statue in the east choir that actually represented Saint Elizabeth. Kantorowicz chose the term "sibyl" because of its aura. The Erythrean Sibyl's "he lives and lives not" were words with which he had ended his biography. He commented directly on *Ecclesia* and *Synagoga*. For him Bamberg cathedral "binds through its walls the equally noble figures of an Ecclesia not too loud in its triumph and a Synagoga in restrained sorrow."[59] The reference in 1935 to a German monument linking a "Church" (*Ecclesia*) and "Synagogue" that are portrayed with equal nobility was quietly defiant. And the same was true of the script's concluding allusion to the cathedral of Bamberg as "the Delphi of the few Germans who know of Apollo."

One notes the elegiac rather than militant tone. Kantorowicz's reverence for Stefan George had not slackened. He placed flowers on George's grave together with his friend Wilhelm Stein around New Year's 1938.[60] Two years later he wrote to Stein from Berkeley that he should do the same for him again.[61] But "German Papacy" was to be the last of his writings that would evoke the theme of a "hidden Germany."

Kantorowicz's two major scholarly engagements between the fall of 1934 and the summer of 1937 were his work on the *laudes regiae* liturgy and his book on the German Interregnum. Thorough discussion of the *laudes regiae* project must be postponed to a later chapter. Here it can be said that EKa finished a short study on the subject before the summer of 1936 but was unable to see it into print because of restrictions in Germany on publications by

[59] Ibid., 7.

[60] Kantorowicz to Stein, 5 January 1938 Stein papers.

[61] Kantorowicz to Stein, 21 December 1939: Stein papers.

Jews.[62] Percy Ernst Schramm published extracts from it in 1937 within a long article of his own, but that was hardly satisfactory.[63] We can gauge EKa's frustration from a letter he wrote in February 1938 to Fritz Saxl in London when he was desperate for publications in order to find a job outside of Germany. In this he probed the possibility of whether Saxl might be able to publish his study in a Warburg Institute series. Since he estimated that it would come to some seventy printed pages, he recognized that it probably was too long for the institute's newly initiated journal but thought that it could pass in the monographic series and was ready to have it translated into English. He pressed his case by saying that his work was "absolutely suited," but it really was not, for the Warburg Institute dealt with art history and the study treated liturgy. When Saxl declined to publish EKa attempted to go elsewhere but once more without success. In a curriculum vitae of early 1939 he reported that a book in German on "Laudes Regiae" had been "planned as a private print, but withdrawn by the publisher quite recently."[64] We owe it to his need for survival in Berkeley that a much expanded book in English followed.

It may be remembered that in Frankfurt EKa had planned a book on the German imperial interregnum of the thirteenth century.[65] But while he was in Oxford the idea of writing a book exclusively on German history faded: the Oxford evidence consists only of the title of a lecture: "Secularization of the Middle Ages." It is fairly certain that the lecture was meant to serve as an introduction to his interregnum book because of the survival of two German drafts that treat the theme of "secularization." Both bear the heading "1. Change in the Attitude toward Time" ("Wandel des Zeitgefühls"); evidently the "1." indicates the opening of a larger work. The earlier of the drafts dates from soon after June 1935, the second not much later.[66]

The drafts—similar enough to count as versions of the same piece—demonstrate remarkable evolution in the nature of Kantorowicz's historical

[62] *Laudes Regiae*, x. The German manuscript consisting of eighty-two pages and forty more of notes is in LBI, box 3, folders 25 and 26.

[63] Schramm, "Ordines-Studien III: Die Krönung in England," *Archiv für Urkundenforschung* 15 (1938) (published 1937): 305–91, at 315–16, 326–27.

[64] LBI, box 1, folder 2.

[65] The following three paragraphs draw on Lerner, "Kantorowicz and Continuity," in Benson and Fried, *Ernst Kantorowicz*, 107–10.

[66] LBI, box 2, folder 8. The drafts are distinguished as "A" and "B." A certainly precedes B, for handwritten corrections and notes for alterations in A become part of the typed text in B. Draft A cites a book published in 1935 and contains a penciled-in addition (p. 19) that refers to "Erdmann 200"—that is, Carl Erdmann's *Entstehung des Kreuzzugsgedankens*, also published in 1935. Since Kantorowicz wrote to Karl Hampe on 7 June 1935 (Hampe papers) that he was looking forward to reading Erdmann's book, draft A must be placed after that date, although not too much later. (Nothing published after 1935 is cited.) Draft B gives the impression of being done in direct continuation of A; at the latest it would have antedated the summer of 1937, when EKa turned his attentions to Valois Burgundy.

writing. While they take up roughly where KFII had ended, they eliminate narrative. Nor do they open with poetry and legend as if to announce a work of "historical representation" as opposed to "historical research." Instead they broach the issue of the continuity of government created by Frederick II's death and do so in terms of a historiographical argument: the thirteenth-century reaction against Augustinianism. Saint Augustine posited a duality: earthly time and cosmic eternity. Earthly time was unstable: life on earth was transitory, and the world itself could end at any moment. Consequently political institutions under the Augustinian impress lacked any assumption of duration. On the death of a king there was no king and hence no government until another king was elected; armies were mustered and taxation was levied ad hoc. But in the thirteenth century England and France went over entirely to the principle of dynastic continuity; armies were summoned more regularly than before; taxation became ever more an annual event. Kantorowicz set these developments against the thirteenth-century rise of Aristotelianism. Scholars at the University of Paris rejected the Christian-Augustinian assumption that the world was created in time and argued instead that it was eternal. Although the doctrine was branded as heretical in 1277 it still stuck. Consequently a new "feeling of time" underpinned trends toward institutional continuity.

The fact that Kantorowicz never advanced to a draft of "chapter 2" of his planned book may tell us much.[67] He could no longer consider writing a book that would deal in any way with Germany because it had become no longer permissible for Jews to publish books on German history. But most likely he no longer wanted to write on Germany, for the draft of chapter 1 already concentrates on institutional developments in England and France and intellectual developments at the University of Paris. Indeed he was adumbrating a section of an entirely different book that he was to complete many years later. Here is the evidence from *The King's Two Bodies*:

> To maintain that the problem of Time had the effects of an activating intellectual undertow throughout the Middle Ages and the Renaissance would probably be an understatement. . . . [W]hat had been epidemic in the thirteenth century became endemic in the fourteenth and fifteenth. . . . [O]ne presupposed continuities where continuity had been neither noticed nor visualized before; and one was ready to modify, revise and repress, though not to abandon, the traditional feelings about limitations in Time and about the transitoriness of human institutions and actions. (283)

[67] Kantorowicz to Kurt Kofka [*sic* for Koffka], 31 August 1938, http://www.regiesey.com, lists an English paper on "Charles of Anjou and the Rise of Imperialism" as the topic of a talk he was prepared to give at Smith College. This surely was a spin-off of the interregnum project, probably based on work done in Frankfurt at the time he was lecturing on the German Interregnum.

One aspect of Kantorowicz's treatment of "the problem of Time" set out in *The King's Two Bodies* that is absent in the two drafts of the mid-1930s is the notion of a middle term, *aevum*, lying between *aeternitas* (eternity) and *tempus* (time). But although EKa first introduced *aevum* in a paper of 1939 (to be discussed later), a handwritten scratch sheet attached to version "A" of "Wandel des Zeitgefühls" includes a diagram for "Aetern.," "Aev.," "Temp.," showing that he already was aware of this theme circa 1935.[68] In other words, a path that led from *Kaiser Frederick II* to *The King's Two Bodies* passed through Kantorowicz's aborted book on the German Interregnum.

In his curriculum vitae of July 1938 Kantorowicz wrote: "From then on [November 1934] I stayed in Berlin where I continued my work. But as I could not expect to have a book printed on a subject concerning German History, I began to collect documents on the history of the Dukes of Burgundy of the Valois race. As I could travel in those days, I could make use of the archives and libraries at Brussels, Paris, Venice, Mantua and other places."[69] This tells us of a second phase of the "leisure with dignity" period lasting from November 1936 until February 1938 that consisted mostly of travel. EKa had become fascinated with the fifteenth-century Burgundians as early as 1926 upon reading a study by his friend Wilhelm Stein on the paintings of Roger van der Weyden. As he wrote then: "It is just as it always is on reading a good work—one thinks that now one knows something but has ever greater hunger to learn more—all of Burgundian history, the Burgundian court and all the art—the Eycks, and the Flémalle Master, and the other works of Roger himself—one wants to know everything."[70]

Yet EKa delayed his quest for knowing more about the Burgundians for a decade. The earliest indication that he had become committed to writing a book on Burgundian history appears in a letter of September 3, 1936, to his friend, the classicist Ernst Langlotz.[71] He had recently returned from a three-week vacation in Belgium and reported that he eagerly looked for "things Burgundian." (In 1951 he reminisced in a letter to Ralph Giesey about the Van der Weyden paintings in Brussels and Antwerp, adding "I believe in Brussels."[72]) In November he went to Brussels to begin research for a new book.[73] As he wrote to

[68] The sheet also has a note: "Mommsen NA n.9," alluding to a document (on taxation) contained in an article by Theodor Ernst Mommsen that was published in *Neues Archiv der Gesellschaft für ältere deutsche Geschichtskunde* in 1935: see 50:396–97. In his letter of 22 February 1938 to Fritz Saxl, EKa refers to having discussed "the time and angel problem" with him in Oxford (in 1934), and his later discussion of the category of *aevum* indicates that it was "angelic time."

[69] CV.

[70] 23 February 1926: Stein papers. The reference is to Wilhelm Stein, "Die Bildnisse des Roger van der Weyden," *Jahrbuch der preussischen Kunstsammlungen* 47 (1926): 1–37.

[71] Langlotz papers.

[72] Kantorowicz to Giesey, 10 December 1951, http://www.regiesey.com.

[73] Franz Kantorowicz to his wife Eva, 21 November 1936: "Ernst Kanto geht einige Monate nach Brüssel zum Arbeiten": Lerner archive.

Langlotz, he had "fiddled about with small stuff . . . a very entertaining activity that pleases no one and hurts no one."[74] But now he had found something large that really engaged him.

Kantorowicz remained working in Brussels until the early spring of 1937[75] (aside from a trip to England in December to view the ceremonial of the royal abdication and pursue some research in the British Museum[76]). He lived on the Rue Royale in the heart of the city in an apartment he later described as having "a lovely view over the roofs of the Coudenberg hill to Sainte Gudule."[77] A Japanese woman who sung in the opera house lived in the apartment below and distracted him (woke him?) with her practicing early in the morning. His walk to the archives offered exercise because it was hilly. EKa later referred in print to "the excellent cuisine of Brussels" but wrote privately to Bowra of his disappointment with the nightlife.[78]

After an interval in Berlin and a short stay in Brussels in August, he set off for a longer trip in November 1937 to pursue research in Italy and Paris for several months. EKa went to Venice and Modena on the first part of his trip; then Naples for the first two weeks of December, then Rome, Mantua, and Milan.[79] At New Year's he took a break from research to be with Stein in Switzerland.[80] After brief stops in Bern and Basel, he reached Paris around January 3 and stayed there for the rest of the month.

In Paris Kantorowicz resided in a comfortable hotel on the Place Vendôme, within walking distance of the Bibliothèque nationale.[81] He worked in the library and when the library was closed he explored the city. He enjoyed visiting

[74] In addition to "Petrus de Vinea" and "Anachorese," both completed by this time, a list of topics EKa was prepared to speak on in America (to Kurt Koffka, 31 August 1938: http://www.regiesey.com) consists of "The Transformation of the Nature of time in the later Middle Ages"; "Oedipus, a Mediaeval Saint"; "Charles of Anjou and the Rise of Imperialism"; "'Imago' or 'Verbum': The Hierarchy of Senses in Mediaeval Thought"; "Charles the Bold and the Italian Renaissance"; and "Secularized Hermitage and the Cult of S. Jerome in the Renaissance."

[75] He was in Berlin in March (see above, n. 43). Later he was in Posen (an easy trip from Berlin) with his uncle Franz from 28 April until May 2 1938: postcard from Franz to his wife Eva, 2 May 1938, and postcard from Eva to Ernst and Vera Pietrkowski, 2 May 1938: Lerner archive.

[76] To Bowra, 1 October 1938, 21 June 1939; ticket to British Museum reading room for two days, stamped December 1936: LBI, box 5, folder 3.

[77] Unpublished draft of an introduction for "The Este Portrait by Roger van der Weyden": LBI, box 3, folder 15.

[78] "Este Portrait," 378; to Bowra, 25 February 1939: the lack of a "joy-boy atmosphere" in New York was "even worse than in Brussels."

[79] He was in Berlin on 11 November 1937 to receive an identification document (LBI, box 5, folder 3). CV refers to research in Venice; "The Este Portrait," Kantorowicz, *Selected Studies*, 372, n. 47, cites a document from the archives in Modena; to Heinrich and Christiane Zimmer from Mantua is dated 25 December 1937: DLA, Zimmer papers; for the rest, to Bowra, 17 December 1937.

[80] To Stein, 5 January 1938: Stein papers.

[81] The following paragraph is based on Kantorowicz to Wilhelm Stein, 5 January and 19 January 1938: Stein papers; and to Soscha Salz, 21 January 1938: Eckhart Grünewald Archive.

the Musée de Cluny, especially because of its Flemish and French tapestries. Dining out regularly, sometimes with German émigré acquaintances, he paid close attention to the cooking, partly in view of imitating it at home. In the middle of the month he had the company of Lucy von Wangenheim, who checked into his hotel in a room next to his own. (By then the two were not cohabitating.) During this stay in Paris EKa modified his opinion of the French. He wrote to his sister Soscha that he did not find the people brusque as he had four years earlier. And he was "carried away" by Paris.

The fact that Kantorowicz spent much time in Italy in order to write a book on Burgundy shows that he was aiming at a new way of studying the subject. During the reign of Duke Charles the Bold (1467–77), Burgundian emissaries frequented the courts of Italy, and emissaries from Italy sought Charles's presence in the North. For example, in 1471 the duke received ambassadors from Rome, Venice, Naples, and Ferrara in Lorraine. Milanese ambassadors to the courts of France and Burgundy regularly sent dispatches back home after 1450. EKa recognized that the letters and reports that passed back and forth were rich sources for Burgundian policy aims and Burgundian mores. Indeed this is the earliest period for which it is possible to write sustained history based heavily on diplomatic documents. Had EKa written the book he had planned it would have been pathbreaking from the methodological point of view, not to mention quite different from the rest of his oeuvre. (An article that he spun off from the project shows his alertness to archival evidence.[82]) As for the actual subject of the book, apparently it would have centered on Charles the Bold's imperial ambitions: his attempt to recreate the Carolingian "middle kingdom" and his efforts to outflank the French diplomatically by gaining Italian allies. Kantorowicz believed that Charles's imperial policy was based on reviving ancient Roman ideals, implicitly not unlike the policy of Frederick II.[83] Unfortunately, after he returned to Berlin from Paris in early February 1938,[84] he abandoned the Burgundy project because he decided that it no longer was possible to remain in Germany and he needed to find quicker publishing strategies to aid him in seeking employment abroad.

[82] "The Este Portrait," 372, n. 47; 373, n. 53; 374, n. 60; 375, n. 67.

[83] For hints see the unpublished paper, "The Dukes of Burgundy and the Italian Renaissance": LBI, box 2, folder 13. This was originally the paper listed as "Charles the Bold and the Italian Renaissance," as listed in EKa's letter to Kurt Koffka (see n. 74).

[84] In between he had checked some details in Brussels for three or four days. To Fritz Saxl, 22 February 1938: Warburg Institute Archives, London.

CHAPTER 14

Flight

Ernst Kantorowicz lost his "leisure with dignity" painfully in 1938. Upon his return from Paris his passport was taken away from him, meaning that he could no longer travel abroad for foreign research. In 1937 his "Reclusiveness" article had been withdrawn from publication because he was Jewish, and he just managed to have his "Petrus de Vinea in England" published in January 1938 in Austria before the Anschluss of March. It clearly was time to emigrate.

At first his highest priority was to prepare a number of papers for delivery in English. He had not been offered any job outside of Germany in advance. Nor was he seeking employment in England: Bowra must have made clear to him that the employment situation there was hopeless. The United States remained (for him Palestine was out of the question), and he was advised that the best strategy for finding a position there would be to embark on a lecture tour. Hence the need for a number of papers because it was best to offer potential hosts a choice of topics. Thus from the late winter to the summer of 1938 EKa engaged himself in the task of producing a set of papers in a language he had not yet fully mastered. When he felt he was ready he sought the return of his passport. That was by no means easy, but he finally succeeded on October 29. Very soon after, on the night of November 9, the Nazis unleashed their fury against Jews in "the night of broken glass" (*Kristallnacht*). EKa all but certainly would have been arrested in the morning and shipped to the Sachsenhausen concentration camp had he not been sheltered. When the danger passed he managed to obtain the necessary visas. Then, at the beginning of December, he crossed the border to Holland and from there ferried to England. Two months later he sailed for New York.

His preparations for departure owed much to the helpfulness of friends. Particularly solicitous was Theodor Mommsen, who had emigrated to America in 1936 as one of the rare Germans to leave Nazi Germany without being Jewish or having a Jewish wife. (He was a bachelor.) While slowly adjusting to the new language and culture (he decided to call himself "Ted"), he gained a research position at Johns Hopkins. This led him to encourage EKa to come to America too. In a letter of early 1937 Mommsen wrote to say that American universities had nothing to be ashamed of and that he thought EKa might well be able to find a position. He insisted that he did not want to press him, nor he did he want to underestimate the difficulties. But he made clear that he would be delighted to have EKa in the same country and that if he responded positively he would see whether he could be of help.[1] In June he sent a follow-up.[2] Now he wrote that he had won a "Sterling Fellowship" at Yale for the next academic year which would put him in a better position to help than before because Yale was more centrally located. (He joked that "Sterling" did not refer to the British currency but to the endower's name.) His proposal now was that EKa should come to visit the United States on a lecture tour to see whether he liked it, and that he would do what he could to make arrangements. If EKa was willing he should send a list of lecture titles, to which Mommsen added, "a rich menu is desirable."

EKa indicated his interest when he returned from Paris at the beginning of February 1938.[3] Mommsen, then thirty-three years old, was shy but persistent and well connected. He had come to know Julius Goldman, son of Marcus Goldman, founder of the banking firm Goldman Sachs. And Goldman in turn was close to Bernard Flexner (1865–1946), brother of Abraham Flexner, founder of the Institute for Advanced Study and himself a prominent lawyer and philanthropist. Through the Goldman connection Mommsen met Bernard Flexner and came to be an occasional guest in his home. The link became essential for EKa's future because Flexner did more to support his early career in the United States than anyone else. Flexner was able to play this role because he was an influential member on the board in New York of the Emergency Committee in Aid of Displaced German Scholars (after November 1938: "in Aid of Displaced Foreign Scholars").[4]

On February 4, 1938, Mommsen wrote from Yale to Bernard Flexner to send him some basic data regarding Kantorowicz.[5] He stated that the biography of Frederick II "had a greater popular success than any other scholarly historical

[1] To Kantorowicz, shortly before April 1937 (the letter is missing the first page that would have had a date; it is incorrectly dated to 8 May 1938 in Walther and Ernst, "Ernst Kantorowicz," 224): LBI, box 5, folder 3.

[2] 13 June 1937: LBI, box 5, folder 3.

[3] The papers of the Academic Assistance Council in London indicate that Fritz Epstein, a young historian who had been in Frankfurt in 1932–33, sought to locate Kantorowicz's address when he was in Harvard in December 1937. Perhaps Epstein knew of a job for EKa, maybe even an opening at Mount Holyoke College discussed below, but the fact that Epstein was ignorant of Kantorowicz's whereabouts in Germany indicates that EKa had not instructed Epstein to do anything for him. (Bodleian Library, Oxford, MS SPSL 508/2, file 1, ff. 298–301. By permission of the Council for Assisting Refugee Academics, as applies to all the following documents from Bodleian SPSL 508/2.)

[4] A history of the organization, which aided in rescuing Thomas Mann, Jacques Maritain, and Paul Tillich, among many others, is Stephen Duggan and Betty Drury, *The Rescue of Science and Learning: The Story of the Emergency Committee in Aid of Displaced Foreign Scholars* (New York, 1948),

[5] Emergency Committee papers.

work of the post-war period in Germany." Mommsen hoped that Flexner would ask Stephen Duggan, chairman of the board of the Emergency Committee, whether it would be possible to arrange some lectures and signed off by writing, "Please remember me to Miss Flexner [Flexner's sister] I enjoyed so much to have been in your company." (Mommsen had visited Flexner earlier at his home on Park Avenue.) Flexner promptly wrote to Duggan about the matter, adding that he thought he could raise $500 for the cause (this would be $8,300 today), and Duggan responded by requesting a private discussion.[6]

In March the Emergency Committee became engaged in seeking to place EKa in a permanent job at Mount Holyoke College. Before Duggan was ready to submit a recommendation he wanted to have assurance about Kantorowicz's qualifications. One inquiry went through Flexner's brother Abraham to E. Llewellyn Woodward, a fellow of New College, Oxford, in 1934. Responding to a cable from Princeton, Woodward cabled back: ENGLISH MODERATE PROBABLY WOULD IMPROVE THINK HIM SUPERFICIAL WOULD NOT RECOMMEND APPOINTMENT CABLING ANOTHER OXFORD OPINION." Then three days later he cabled "MY OPINION CONFIRMED."[7] This might have been the end of the matter had not Duggan drawn on his own contacts in England to make inquiries in Oxford about Kantorowicz's personality and facility in speaking English. One was Walter Adams, the director of the Society for the Protection of Science and Learning Academic Assistance Council (a new name for the organization that had placed EKa in New College in 1934); the other a former secretary of the Emergency Committee, the subsequently famous Edward R. Murrow, who meanwhile had become a foreign correspondent for CBS in England. The results, although somewhat mixed, were sufficiently satisfactory. Of the three Oxford dons reached by Adams, one, J. L. Brierly, could not remember having met Kantorowicz; another, J. L. Myers, was cool but wrote "his self confidence and absence of reserve will be better understood in an American college than here," and the third, H. L. Henderson, was entirely positive.[8] And Murrow cabled briefly: "GENERAL OXFORD OPINION KANTOROWICZ EMINENTLY SUITABLE."[9] Duggan then forwarded Kantorowicz's name and the data supplied by Mommsen to the president of Mount Holyoke.

For whatever reason EKa did not get the Mount Holyoke job. Accordingly he continued to prepare papers for a lecture tour and otherwise proceeded with his life as usual. A postcard from Eva Kantorowicz, his aunt by marriage, to her daughter Vera indicates that he came to dinner on July 5: "It is always nice

[6]Flexner to Duggan, 9 February 1938; Duggan to Flexner, 19 February 1938: Emergency Committee papers.

[7]To Abraham Flexner in Princeton, 26 March and 29 March: Emergency Committee papers. (Much later Woodward and Kantorowicz were to be colleagues at the Institute for Advanced Study.)

[8]Bodleian Library, Oxford, MS SPSL 508/2, file 1, ff. 304, 309, 312.

[9]To Duggan, 30 March 1938: Emergency Committee papers.

with him; we talked much about cooking."[10] An evocative account survives from his own pen of a very different dinner on "a hot summer night in July 1938."[11] The scene was the Wannsee villa of the painter Max Liebermann, who had died in 1935. The hostess was Liebermann's widow; the others present were her daughter and son-in-law, Kaethe and Kurt Riezler, an unidentified "diplomat" (this was Albrecht von Bernstorff, unnamed because at the time of the writing he was in Germany), and the art connoisseur Max J. Friedländer. EKa communicated the atmosphere by writing: "Runciman had started his portentous mission to Prague and under the cloudless black-blue sky of that night heavy planes were droning and announcing the thunderstorm that was about to burst over Europe." Coffee was served after dinner in the garden. When political news was exhausted, the talk turned to America because the Riezlers would soon be on their way and EKa was hoping to be there as well. This led to European paintings in American collections, and thence to a portrait in the Metropolitan Museum that earlier had been identified by Friedländer as a work by Roger van der Weyden. The discussion continued and will be returned to at the end of this chapter.

A few days later EKa received a letter from a certain Fritz Demuth, director of the Emergency Association of German Scholars Living Abroad. (This organization had been founded in Zürich but had been moved to London, where it worked closely with the Society for the Protection of Science and Learning.) Demuth wrote:

> I have been asked to suggest candidates for a post as Ordinary Professor of Mediaeval History at one of the most renowned universities in California. The post is a permanent one, salary about $9000.—. Please let me know if you would be willing to be named and if so send me a 'curriculum vitae' (3 copies) to be forwarded. A reply is urgent. (A thorough knowledge of English is necessary.)[12]

EKa was amazed. He responded immediately, expressing his keen interest in the position.[13] He was ready to send his c.v. promptly. In addition he inquired politely whether it was possible for Demuth to say which California university was meant (he assumed it was "either Stanhope or Berkeley") inasmuch as he had English friends who might have contacts that could help him. But Demuth answered that he did not know himself since he was only an intermediary.[14] Meanwhile he needed supporting letters from Anglophone referees.

[10] Postcard, Lerner archive.

[11] Holograph and typescript, filed with "The Este Portrait," LBI, box 3, folder 15. The opening of the passage is quoted *in extenso* in Sonja Asal, "Ernst Kantorowicz und Kurt Riezler," in *Mythen, Körper, Bilder:* ed. Lucas Burkart et al., 219–38 (Göttingen, 2015), at 232.

[12] 27 July 1938: LBI, box 5, folder 3.

[13] 29 July 1938, and a follow-up letter 5 August 1938: LBI, box 5, folder 3.

[14] 2 August 1938.

EKa then went to work with great energy to gain as many prominent supporters as possible. His papers include two drafts of letters addressed, respectively, to F. M. Powicke and to the former American ambassador in Berlin, "His Excellency" William F. Dodd.[15] By coincidence Dodd had been a professor of history at the University of Chicago before he took the Berlin post; Kantorowicz had not met him but had learned that Dodd knew and admired his Frederick biography. In both drafts he used similar language explaining his plight and wondering whether the recipients could see their way to recommending him to Demuth and to writing to any California friends they might have. Most likely the two men wrote at least to Demuth. (In 1939 EKa placed Dodd at the top of a list of referees for a U.S. permanent visa application.) Numerous others wrote in EKa's behalf. The list includes H.A.L. Fisher, A. L. Poole, Tom Boase, and of course Maurice Bowra. Another was George Lee Haskins, the twenty-three-year-old son of Charles Homer Haskins (who had died the year before). Haskins, who was a member of the Harvard Society of Fellows, wrote to EKa from England that he had dined with Bowra and learned that EKa was being considered for a position in California. Accordingly he wrote, "Knowing my father's very high opinion of everything you have done, I inquired whether I might be of service."[16]

In late August EKa learned that the California school with the opening was Berkeley. At that point Bowra recommended Kantorowicz to Max Radin, a prominent Berkeley law professor, and influenced his friend, the Harvard law professor Felix Frankfurter, to do the same. Radin, who had never met EKa but did know his biography of Frederick II, then wrote to the provost at Berkeley, Monroe Deutsch, praising him in the strongest terms: "[In] this particular field I think I can say that there probably is no man available who would bring more distinction to our faculty."[17] Deutsch passed this recommendation along to the chair of Berkeley's search committee, but the committee was giving precedence to a number of American candidates. The position in question was an endowed chair about to be vacated by the retirement of an American medievalist, and there were other American medievalists who might fill it. For most on the committee it seemed unnecessary to look elsewhere, let alone consider a German whose command of English was unproven. The fact that Kantorowicz was Jewish may also have militated against him. Certainty is lacking but we do have the following memo sent by a committee member, the geographer Carl Ortwin Sauer, to the committee chair: "I [seem] to detect a strain of nativism running through expressions about prospects. It may be banal to say that science knows

[15] LBI, box 5, folder 3. (This is the source of all the other evidence, dating from August and early September 1938, that underpins this paragraph.)

[16] G. L. Haskins to Kantorowicz, 2 September 1938: LBI, box 5, folder 3.

[17] Radin to Deutsch, 29 August 1938, http://www.regiesey.com. (Radin's letter refers to the communications to him from Bowra and Frankfurter.)

no frontiers of nationality or race, but I hold to this view passionately."[18] At any rate Kantorowicz's candidacy was held in abeyance.

Common sense of course dictated to EKa that he could not count on Berkeley and needed to polish his credentials for employment in every way possible. Thus when he received a visit in Berlin from his friend Percy Ernst Schramm in early August he requested a general letter of recommendation and Schramm complied.[19] EKa hoped to leave Germany in the early fall, and with that in mind he had a meeting in Berlin in late August with the German-born Gestalt psychologist, Kurt Koffka, in order to broach the possibility of speaking at Smith College, where Koffka was on the faculty.[20] Soon after, when EKa entered into correspondence with George Haskins, he indicated that he would be pleased to speak at Harvard, and Haskins indicated that that would present no problem.[21] Meanwhile he had confidence that his devoted friend Theodor Mommsen would be able to arrange something at Yale (as in fact he did).

EKa's planned lecture tour was predicated on the assumption that he would be able to travel, but this assumption began to founder after his application for the return of his passport was held up by officialdom. On August 5 he took the necessary first step by appearing at the "Emigration Advisory Office" in Berlin.[22] That went well enough: the office was willing to recommend to the police travel rights for six months (a standard length). This meant that EKa could appear at police headquarters to make formal application on August 25, having allowed sufficient time for the favorable recommendation from the Emigration Advisory Office to make its way through channels. But it could not be expected that the passport would be handed over by a bureaucrat while EKa sat there, so he went home and waited. At first it did not occur to him that there would be difficulties. A letter to Ernst Robert Curtius of September 1 alludes to his imminent departure and his lack of regret, given the destruction of the world they had known.[23] (With an elegiac tone he quoted in English lines of Wordsworth's poem "On the Extinction of the Venetian Republic": "Men are we and must grieve when even the shadow of that which once was great is passed away.") But in the following days it was becoming evident that return of his passport was being delayed. It was the worst of times because his way station was to be England and war between England and Germany seemed imminent. When Bowra was in Berlin in the first week of September he was warned by a friendly

[18] Sauer to J.S.P. Tatlock, 7 December 1938: Bancroft Library, University of California President's papers, CU-5, Ser. 4, box 17, folder 11.

[19] A carbon copy of the letter, dated from Göttingen, 10 August 1938, is in LBI, box 5, folder 3. (For an English translation see http://www.regiesey.com).

[20] Kantorowicz to Kurt Kofka [*sic* for Koffka], 31 August 1938, http://www.regiesey.com. (Koffka's wife was a stepdaughter of Georg Bondi.)

[21] George Lee Haskins to Kantorowicz, 5 September 1938: LBI, box 5, folder 3.

[22] Document in LBI, box 5, folder 3, as all bureaucratic documents referred to further.

[23] Curtius papers.

German that he had better leave soon and did so.[24] EKa spent the weekend before Munich at Count Bernstorff's country estate. Military transports were rumbling on the roads; everyone was listening intently to the radio: "London, Paris, Rome."[25] Still believing that he would be leaving soon, EKa wrote "farewell" in Bernstorff's guestbook."[26]

The culmination of the Czechoslovak crisis provoked an exchange of telegrams between Bowra and Kantorowicz. Bowra communicated his solidarity; EKa telegraphed back: "THANKS OLD BOY AND LET US HOPE TO MEET AGAIN."[27] Then, right after the crisis was resolved by Chamberlain's capitulation, EKa wrote to Bowra: "The present solution may not be too pleasant—it is anyhow *a* solution and anybody will be glad of being discharged from this unbearable tension. Though hero I too uttered (to use Blum's phrase) a 'coward sigh of relief.'" And then he added that he thought he would see his good friend "in not too far a time, as I am pretty sure of getting my papers in the next days."[28] But on the same day he felt it necessary to send a reminder to the police headquarters, and he followed that up on October 3 with a personal visit.[29]

A letter to Bowra of October 7, 1938, is a classic. Bowra had attended an Oxford festivity and had written of his regret that EKa had not been there to have tried dining on grouse. EKa answered: "The idea even would be intolerable to me that I did not like grouse after all, that I might be disappointed and be poorer with the experience made than I was before. So I must go practicing self-restraint and eating partridges and pheasants which *are* delicious now and so consoling in these days." That point made, he sympathized with Bowra's complaints about the troublesomeness of electricians and curtain hangers being in the Warden's cottage and said that he hoped to see something of the cottage "if ever I should happen to come and see you." Finally came the really important news: "There *is* a hope aloft, as Mrs. Kerlchen has put her rose tipped fingers [*Odyssey* Book 9] into my affairs at last and so I might either be killed or may succeed, both of which would please me."

Who was "Mrs. Kerlchen"? "Kerlchen" was EKa's nickname for Helmut Küpper whom EKa had known since 1923 when he had appeared in Heidelberg and EKa momentarily mistook him for Woldemar Uxkull (the two were both blonde and of roughly the same height).[30] They quickly became close (Küpper was on the periphery of the George circle), and as of 1935 they saw much of each other

[24] Bowra, *Memories*, 304.

[25] Kantorowicz, "Der Gastfreund," 53.

[26] Entry from Gutsarchiv Altenhof, Sammlung Albrecht von Bernstorff, kindly communicated to me by Hartwig Graf von Bernstorff.

[27] 28 September 1938.

[28] 30 September 1938.

[29] Kantorowicz, statement about difficulty in receiving passport dated 16 October: LBI, box 5, folder 3.

[30] Kantorowicz to Vera Peters, 16 April 1956: Lerner archive.

because Küpper had moved to Berlin to take over direction of the publishing firm of Bondi. His first wife, a White Russian named Paraskewe Bereskine, called "Baika," was a painter who was patronized by Hermann Goering. Since she did portraits of Goering's wife, the two had become friends.[31] And this is part of the story of how EKa's passport was revalidated.

Küpper's second wife told me in 1993 that on his first wife's request Frau Goering put in a good word with her husband that accomplished the deed.[32] But this account is too simple, for EKa wrote on October 7 that "Frau Kerlchen" was taking an interest in his affairs whereas his passport was revalidated only at the end of the month. On October 29 EKa wrote to Bowra that "there are lots of people pulling my strings [*sic*]," and it is little known that among them was the head of the Berlin police. The source for this is an account EKa related to his student, William A. Chaney, in the early 1940s.[33] EKa told Chaney that when he taught in Frankfurt a student who admired him happened to be the son of a Nazi police officer, Wolf-Heinrich Graf von Helldorf, and that by 1938 von Helldorf had become the head of the police in Berlin. When the former student ("a very nasty boy but useful on occasion") learned of EKa's passport difficulties he went to his father to see what could be done. Graf Helldorf then called a Gestapo officer who stood in rank directly below Himmler to find out whether it was the Gestapo that was holding up the passport. The officer knew nothing of it and sought to learn who was responsible. Upon inquiry it emerged that the person was Erhard Milch, Goering's second-in-command in the Reich Aviation Ministry. Milch's explanation was, "It's exactly people like this who make the worst propaganda against Germany when they get out," to which the Gestapo officer shot back: "It's exactly people like you who make the worst propaganda against Germany by not *letting* people out! Kantorowicz will get his passport within 24 hours!"

How would Kantorowicz have known about a conversation between a Gestapo officer and Erhard Milch? According to Chaney, EKa learned of it from Helldorf's son. Granted that Chaney first set down his account in 1988, he claimed to have remembered the wording of the story as he heard it from

[31] Helena Ketter, *Zum Bild der Frau in der Malerei des Nationalsozialismus* (Münster, 2002), 231. A portrait by Bereskine of Frau Goering with her baby can be seen on the website of the Deutsches Historisches Museum, "Die Kunstsammlung Hermann Goering," Datenblatt RMG00125. (My thanks to Thomas Gruber for this information.) Judging from the baby's age, however, this one was more likely to have been done in 1939. The friendship between Küpper's first wife and Goering's wife was the basis for Norman Cantor's slander that "Kantorowicz was close to Hermann Goering": Cantor, *Twentieth-Century Culture*, 311. EKa expressed acid hostility about Baika's Nazi connections in a letter to Bowra of 29 May 1939.

[32] Bowra offers an improbable alternative in *Memories*, 304.

[33] It appears in Jon vanden Heuvel, "The Early Life and Work of Ernst Kantorowicz" (Master's thesis, Columbia University, 1989: accessible via http:www.regiesey.com), 120–21. I own a slightly different written version by Chaney, dating from 2001, that adds minor details not present in Vanden Heuvel's.

Kantorowicz. (The present author can testify that Chaney did have an extraordinary memory.) Furthermore, a connection exists of which Chaney was not aware: Erhard Milch was a distant relative of Kantorowicz's. (EKa's first cousin, Else Kantorowicz, had married Ludwig Milch, a relative of Erhard's; if one wonders what someone of partial Jewish ancestry was doing in Goering's ministry, the answer is that Goering issued his notorious remark, "I decide who's Jewish," in reference to him.) Perhaps Milch had a personal grudge against Kantorowicz; even if not, he would have been alert to his name. To put everything together, someone prompted by Frau Goering tried to help EKa by means of influence in the Aviation Ministry, but Erhard Milch blocked the effort until a Gestapo man who was tipped off by Helldorf overruled him.

EKa was ignorant of the details of what was transpiring until the outcome. On October 11 he wrote to Bowra: "I have not yet got my chief paper—it is too awful. [I] simply waste my time as I hardly can work whilst waiting, waiting, waiting! I am very cross indeed and in a bad temper—so bad that since days I drink but Fachinger [bottled water] instead of wine without finding the taste of water too bad." Bowra tried his best to get EKa back to wine by going to the top of the British diplomatic ladder and asking the foreign secretary, Viscount Halifax, whether he might use his influence to intervene. (Halifax had shaken hands with Hitler at Munich only three weeks before.) The reply, dated October 24, was unsurprising:

> My dear Warden, thank you for your letter of October 18th. I have much sympathy with your desire to assist Professor Kantorowicz in his efforts to leave Germany. Unfortunately, however, my experience is that any foreign pressure exercised in matters such as this, which concern a German national, is resented by the German authorities and is likely to redound to the disadvantage rather than to the advantage of the person whom one is anxious to assist.[34]

Meanwhile EKa had written a strong letter to police headquarters on October 16. He pointed out that he had originally applied for the return of his passport on August 25, sent a reminder on September 30, and visited the headquarters on October 2. Now it had come to a total of seven weeks of waiting and the delay was placing his chances of finding an academic position in the United States in jeopardy. He had planned on a speaking tour in the fall but now the threat of his running into the vacation period was looming. He could only infer that there had been some mix-up and requested an immediate investigation because of the urgency. Ultimately it was the "Emigration Advisory Office" that set things rolling. On October 20 this office issued a document confirming the original favorable recommendation and claiming that the original "allegedly had gone lost." The reconfirmed recommendation still had to go through channels until finally on October 29 the police handed over the passport.

[34] LBI, box 5, folder 3, as also the documents mentioned in the succeeding two paragraphs.

Once that was accomplished, EKa cabled his contacts in the United States that he was free to come to lecture. Their responses were gratifying. On November 4 "young Haskins" wrote to him enclosing a formal invitation from the chairman of the Harvard History Department; on November 7 he received the same from the master of Pierson College at Yale; and on November 8 the same from the "Committee on Lectures" of Smith College. As soon as he gained entry visas for England and the United States he would be ready to leave.

But then came *Kristallnacht*. EKa told the main part of the dramatic story in a postwar memorial to Graf von Bernstorff.[35] He was scheduled to host a dinner for Bernstorff and Küpper in his apartment on the evening of November 10. But early that morning he received a phone call that took him out of the shower. It was Bernstorff, ringing up to say that the dinner had to be postponed. Instead EKa should come over to his apartment and bring necessities in case it might be necessary to go to Bernstorff's estate in Mecklenburg. EKa followed the instructions and then learned that during the night synagogues had been burned, Jewish shop windows smashed, and stores plundered. In the morning prominent Jews were being rounded up, and Bernstorff wanted to shelter Kantorowicz from arrest. He gave no thought to the danger he was bringing on himself, an example of the courage that would lead to his hideous murder by the SS a few days before war's end in 1945.[36]

EKa remained hidden in Bernstorff's apartment for two days, then stayed with Küpper for five, and then moved into a pension.[37] What prevented immediate departure was the gaining of visas. In his letter of October 29 to Bowra he expressed worry that he would have difficulty getting visas for England and the United States because he was Jewish. ("The foreign authorities are ambitious to accumulate difficulties over difficulties to all owners of a passport signed with a huge red J.") He hoped that Bowra might move "Prince Hal" (Halifax) to help with the granting of a visa to Great Britain. But that proved unnecessary. Bowra saw matters through for England by declaring that he would assume all of Kantorowicz's expenses while he was in that country, and EKa was able to go to the British Passport Control office in Berlin to have a temporary visitor's visa attached to his passport a day or two after November 15. Around the

[35] "Der Gastfreund," 53. Kantorowicz mistakenly dates the story to 8 November, whereas it had to have been 10 November.

[36] In a letter of 29 May 1939 to Maurice Bowra EKa wrote that he had learned from a British functionary in Washington that Bernstorff's dossier with the Nazis was likely to land him into difficulty. Recognizing that Bernstorff was in the habit of visiting Oxford, in June he told Bowra that if he should see him he should warn him not to stay in Germany: "You know how careless he is when talking about politics, and that is known, by now, also in the Nazi circles." Whether Bowra warned Bernstorff is unknown, but EKa's concern was warranted, for Bernstorff did stay in Germany and was sent to Dachau in 1940 before being murdered by the SS in Berlin in April 1945.

[37] Statements by Ernst Morwitz, Morwitz papers, New York Public Library, box 3, f. 197^{r}. (The passage was discovered and kindly copied for me by Eckhart Grünewald.)

same time his path to the American visa was smoothed by his contact with the American consul in Berlin, a friend of Bernstorff's.[38] On November 27 Franz Kantorowicz wrote from Berlin to his daughter in London that "Ernst K." had been with him and his wife the evening before and that he was ready to leave in a week or two.[39]

A week was all that it took. EKa left Berlin in the company of Helmut Küpper on the third of December.[40] Bernstorff saw them off at the train station. EKa ceded his apartment to Küpper to use as an office for the Bondi firm. By doing this he could preserve his library, which by this time had become enormous. In addition it allowed him to save an extra room in the apartment for a housekeeper to whom he felt obliged.[41] He and Küpper traveled through Holland on their way to the Channel, EKa not neglecting the opportunity to consume oysters.[42] He reached Harwich on December 4 and then made his way to Oxford.[43] He was nine months ahead of the outbreak of war between Germany and England.

Bowra hosted EKa in his newly renovated Warden's cottage at Wadham College. (Baby recently had vacated.) Bowra disposed of his own butler.[44] The dining at high table and at the cottage was excellent. The two men probably were not still lovers: in a letter of October EKa had referred to Bowra's former "buggerable days."[45] But they never tired of each other's company.

In late December EKa wrote to a correspondent that he was so preoccupied about his future that he could hardly work.[46] Yet he still managed. Tom Boase had become the director of the Courtauld Institute of Art in London and graciously scheduled him to give a talk there on an art-historical topic in January. Such an appearance would be impressive for his curriculum vitae, especially in terms of demonstrating an ability to lecture in English. The topic brings us back to the July evening at the Wannsee villa of Max Liebermann. When the talk turned to works of art in America and to a portrait that had been identified by Max J. Friedländer as a work of Roger van der Weyden, EKa (whose interest in Roger had been stimulated by his friend Wilhelm Stein) asked Friedländer whether he was sure that the portrait represented Lionello d'Este, a prince

38 Morwitz papers, box 3, f. 196^{v}.

39 Eva and Franz Kantorowicz to Ernst and Vera Pietrkowski, 27 November 1938: Lerner archive.

40 He purchased English currency in Berlin on 2 December (LBI, box 5, folder 3). On 4 December Franz Kantorowicz thought that he had already arrived in England: letter to Ernst Pietrkowski: Lerner archive.

41 Peter Pawlowsky, *Helmut Küpper Vormals Georg Bondi 1895–1970* (Düsseldorf, 1970), 36.

42 Kantorowicz to Küpper, 10 September 1949: StGA, Kantorowicz, II:1901.

43 United Kingdom Certificate of Registration: LBI, box 7, folder 7. Kantorowicz to Bowra, 27 March 1939.

44 Interview with Donald Bullough, November 1994. Bullough also knew of the excellence of Bowra's table at the cottage.

45 Kantorowicz to Bowra, 11 October 1938.

46 To Ludwig Curtius, 27 December 1938: Ludwig Curtius papers.

of Ferrara, as Friedländer had maintained. Here is Kantorowicz's narration of what followed:

> For a moment Max Friedländer hesitated before saying "Yes" and asking me whether I objected. It was my turn to hesitate for a moment before saying "Yes" and confessing that I had reason to believe the man portrayed could not be Lionello but most likely Lionello's bastard son Francesco whose name, after all, was written under the Este coat of arms on the reverse side of the panel. [Friedländer replied]: "for goodness sake, if your assumption is right the image cannot be painted by Roger! And it was I who recommended this purchase for a really extraordinary price." . . . It took me months before I found the really satisfying solution that both Friedländer and I were right. Friedländer had not been deceived by his eyes; the panel was by Roger. . . . And I was right because in the meantime I had found another portrait of [Lionello's] son which not only made it clear who the man depicted was but also where the stumbling stone was to be sought.[47]

By the time of his talk at the Courtauld Institute on "The Este Portrait by Roger van der Weyden" Kantorowicz had put everything together. Although the portrait, one of Roger's finest, was said to have been of Lionello d'Este, lettering on the reverse referred to a "francisque," a French form of the name of Lionello's bastard son. The "stumbling stone" for making it a portrait of Francesco d'Este had been that Italian genealogists had assigned Francesco's birth to a date much too late for Roger to have represented him as a man of about thirty. Kantorowicz, however, produced documents to prove that the date was mistaken and that Francesco d'Este had been born some fifteen years earlier than previously thought. Moreover, although Francesco had been born in Ferrara, he spent almost all his mature life in the service of the Burgundian court located in Brussels, where Roger lived and worked, and this explained the "francisque" in the French of Burgundian court language. Many iconographical explications and some other contemporary portraits nailed everything down. On the basis of Kantorowicz's publication of the talk in 1940[48] the Metropolitan Museum changed its labeling; some reference works on the portrait now refer to the accomplishment of "the art historian Ernst Kantorowicz." But the author wanted to go beyond a new identification for the subject of a portrait, for he believed that by eliminating the assumption that Roger had executed the portrait while at the Este court he could eliminate the assumption that Roger had spent a period of time in Italy. (He wrote to Stein that Roger was as little in Italy as Stein had been in Peru.[49]) But experts have not accepted this, his major conclusion.

[47] LBI, box 3, folder 15.

[48] "The Este Portrait by Roger van der Weyden," *Journal of the Warburg and Courtauld Institutes* 3 (1939–40): 165–80; reprinted in Kantorowicz, *Selected Studies*, 366–80.

[49] 2 July 1939: Stein papers.

EKa could not afford to live for more than a few days in London; Soscha's daughter Judith put him up in her own modest apartment.[50] He was short of cash because the pension he drew from the German government was cut off on his departure. It is difficult to know how he managed to survive. Perhaps he had saved something and smuggled out some cash; perhaps he borrowed. In any case he still had to buy a steamship ticket and make ends meet in America. A week before his departure he wrote to a friend in Germany: "Of me, there is little to report. I'm of course very much in a state of anticlimax, in a bad mood, with bad sleep, bad appetite, and bad digestion."[51] In such a state he boarded the SS *Aquitania* on January 28 to sail for the United States.

[50] Unpublished memoirs of Judith Kent: "[Ernst] came to stay with me for a few days in my shabby flat in Notting Hill in London, since he had nowhere else to go." (My thanks to Judith's daughter, Ariane Phillips, for informing me of this passage.)

[51] To Ernst Langlotz, 20 January 1939: Langlotz papers.

CHAPTER 15

"Displaced Foreign Scholar"

Ernst Kantorowicz's first months in America were difficult. His future was uncertain, he was short of money, and he did not like New York City. Even the landing was difficult. As he wrote in a letter to Baby, his "vita nuova" was leading first through an Inferno.[1] The *Aquitania* arrived on February 3, but instead of being allowed to debark in New York he was sent to Ellis Island to be detained as an "alien held for special inquiry." The problem was that his passport was stamped for a six-week stay and the officials suspected him of planning to immigrate illegally. As he admitted, they did have a right to hold these suspicions because he was bringing a crate of books and more papers than seemed reasonable. (They unpacked every last item.) Since the ship docked during a late afternoon on a Friday he had to wait until Monday for an official hearing, and he wrote mordantly that he could see the Statue of Liberty through a barred window. Although the living conditions were decent for the circumstance, he still had to sleep in a room with thirty-five others. He wrote to Baby that he worried about a bad omen and was not keen on America so far. Fortunately Kurt Riezler came to the rescue. The Riezlers, who had arrived in New York two months earlier, were waiting to greet him on the pier and he was able to wave and throw them an explanatory message. So Riezler was able to visit the American consulate to gain an extension of EKa's visa, and that was sufficient to bring him to Manhattan.

There he stayed in the Hotel Paris, built in 1931, on 97th Street and West End Avenue. The rooms were small but the rent was reasonable. The hotel was chosen by Riezler, who was living nearby with his wife and young daughter on the corner of Riverside Drive and 99th Street. The proximity to the Riezlers must have been a solace because of their company. Moreover, their apartment was luxuriously furnished with items that they had managed to rescue from Berlin and was adorned with paintings by Manet, Van Gogh, and Cézanne passed on

[1] To Lucy von Wangenheim, 5 February 1939, communicated to me by Eckhart Grünewald.

by Kaethe Riezler's father.[2] Riezler had found a job at the New School for Social Research, but the couple still had to sell a painting occasionally to make ends meet. As Kaethe put it, "we are living from wall to mouth."[3]

Even with the reasonable rent at the Hotel Paris, EKa was financially strapped. Not only was he unable to draw on his German pension, but he was making regular payments for the support of Baby in England.[4] In a letter to Maurice Bowra he wrote: "There is some vacancy at Chicago. But they are said to have no money, and that is the only thing I want."[5] Later he held forth to his Berkeley students about how he had once been obliged to live in New York "in a furnished room on $100 a month."[6] He also was disgruntled; he wrote to Bowra that "the weather is filthy and I can't stand the rapid changes from 62 to 18 degrees. It is rather awful and I cannot get rid of a cold, specially as the rooms are roaringly hot."[7] On top of that he complained of the lack of an "erotic atmosphere," or else that he did not know the right "joy-boy" places—although he granted that "the symbols of the World's Fair—pike and ball—are as indecent as they could be."[8]

He did have some contacts in addition to the Riezlers. On the first weekend after his arrival, his friend Ted Mommsen came in from New Haven (he was still at Yale) and was joined by another friend, Felix Gilbert, to show EKa the town. For Mommsen and Gilbert, neither of them nightlife lizards, that meant conventional tourism. They took EKa to the observation deck on the seventieth floor of the skyscraper in Rockefeller Center.[9] As he wrote to Bowra on 25 February, "It is beautiful to go up with the lift to the top of the Rockefeller Building. The view from there (though you detest views, and to like them may be very German) gave me for the first time an impression of what America is or [what] she produced by herself, and this is anyhow something." One weekend later he visited Mommsen at Yale, telling Bowra that "the Colleges are Oxford

[2]On Riezler during this period, Thompson, *In the Eye of the Storm*, 217–28. Kantorowicz wrote to Bowra on 25 February: "Riezi is as he always was, rather mad, but delighted to read about things nobody understands."

[3]Marion Dönhoff, "Ernst Kantorowicz," 12. Katherine Whild, the Riezlers' granddaughter, informed me that the *bon mot* ("von der Wand in den Mund") was her grandmother's: interview 27 December 2011.

[4]Kantorowicz to Soscha Salz, 18 October 1941: "Vergiss nicht, dass ich, ausser in diesen letzen Monaten, durch Jahr und Tag die Baby erhalten musste, resp. miterhalten.": LBI, box 5, folder 1.

[5]25 February 1939.

[6]Interview with Lucy Cherniavsky, 5 September 1990. She added that EKa dwelled on this so often that she was under the impression that he had lived "in a furnished room" for years rather than months.

[7]25 February 1939.

[8]25 February 1939; 13 March 1939. Benjamin Ivry, "How Ernst Kantorowicz Escaped the Nazis," *Jewish Daily Forward*, 21 June 2011, observes that Kantorowicz's letters exhibit "a fairly racy sense of humor."

[9]Interview with Felix Gilbert, 14 November 1988.

Buildings vintage 1929/30; the 'gymnasium' similar to a cathedral and the library to Windsor Castle."

Mommsen, solicitous as usual, arranged an interview with Bernard Flexner. EKa visited him in his law offices on Lexington Avenue and 51st Street and then mailed a memo of the interview for his future use.[10] This laid out his "intentions in this country." First, he would soon deliver some papers he already had been asked to read at several East Coast universities. Meanwhile he would "wait and see" whether he would be "elected by the California State University or not." Should this fail, he would try to obtain some other academic appointment but understood that his chances would be best if he published a volume of collected studies. He had in mind "a volume of about 400 to 500 pages containing [his] researches on the History of Mediaeval Thought and Education." Since he implicitly was asking whether Flexner could arrange for supporting this undertaking, he specified the subjects of the "researches" he wanted to publish.[11] Then he concluded by writing: "May I add how very grateful I am for your taking this interest in my affairs." As events will show, the two had struck a rapport.

EKa's first lecture in the United States was as a guest at a regularly scheduled class at Barnard College.[12] This came about as a result of happenstance. Bowra's friend, the Columbia University classicist Gilbert Highet, had taken EKa to lunch at the Columbia faculty club a few days after the interview with Flexner, and there he chanced to meet Eugene H. Byrne, the medieval historian at Barnard. Byrne, "a nice but dull man" (EKa's description), then invited him to take over his class and lecture to "50 Columbia girls."[13] EKa refrained from speaking on one of his specially prepared topics meant for a scholarly audience and gave a lecture on Frederick II. Yet bewilderment must have been considerable on both sides, for lecturing exclusively to "girls" would have been a novelty for Kantorowicz, and the audience probably had little understanding of what he was saying.

Shortly afterward EKa reported to Bowra that Riezler had hosted a lunch to which he had invited EKa, Gilbert Highet, and another person. As he described

[10] 15 February 1939: Emergency Committee papers.

[11] These were "the Bolognese Rhetors and Writers in the 12th and 13th Century such as Guido Faba, Pierre della Vigne and others: on Abélard and Petrarca; on the transformation of the Nature of Time in the 13th Century; on the Five Senses; on the problem of the revival of Stoicism in the 12th and 13th Century; on the question of acquiring Nobility by Education; on the Imperialism of Charles of Anjou; on the Italian Renaissance at the Court of Charles the Bold: the unprinted work of an Oxford Humanist in the early 15th century; and besides that several papers on liturgical subjects."

[12] "Memorandum by Dr. Kantorowicz," 14 March 1939: LBI, box 5, folder 3.

[13] To Bowra, 25 February 1939. Byrne and EKa had come to know each other earlier: an offprint from 1935 by the former is in the Kantorowicz offprint collection in the Institute for Advanced Study with the inscription: "With the writer's humble and belated homage."

the event, "We behaved rather frivolously not knowing that the fourth man, who was asked to meet me, was the head of the Dept. of History of Columbia, who said a quiet little prayer before lunch but did not find the opportunity of uttering another word as we were much too talkative." (The "fourth man" was Carlton J. H. Hayes, a prominent convert to Catholicism.) Kantorowicz assured Bowra that "I retained [*sic*] of telling dirty stories."[14]

During the second week of March he toured New England, speaking at Harvard, Smith College, and Yale. He wrote to Bowra that "it was a great fun altogether, travelling about like a wandering scholar and begging one's way through the country." To this he added, "People were quite generous in giving me money at Yale and Smith College; only Harvard was the great exception, as they preferred to pay nothing at all." The manuscript of the Harvard talk, EKa's first formal public appearance in America, survives and shows that he was still unsure of how to pronounce certain words. Thus he made pencil markings to indicate phonetics, for example placing an "o" over the "ou" in "moulded."[15]

The Harvard talk, to the History Department, was entitled "The Idea of Permanency and Progress in the Thirteenth Century" and was a milestone in the historiographical progress of Ernst Kantorowicz.[16] Although it was a revised version of the introductory section of his aborted book on the German Interregnum, the revisions introduced a new analytical concept and adumbrated a new analytical framework. The new concept was the significance of the thirteenth-century scholastic term *aevum*. EKa proposed that this was devised to mediate between "eternity" and "time." *Aevum* was endless time rather than the timeless time (*aeternitas*) of God or the timebound time (*tempus*) of humans. It was "angelic" (the status between God and man) because angels dwelled in it. Equipped with the concept of *aevum*, or infinite duration that was not eternal, thirteenth-century shapers of political institutions could deal more comfortably with the idea of enduring continuities in political institutions that transcended individual human lives. One can turn to the first two sections of chapter 6 of *The King's Two Bodies* to see how this proposition became a building block for the construction of Kantorowicz's famous work.

The Harvard lecture also showed EKa's turn to full engagement with the history of the Western nation-states. He opened with his customary flair by invoking an address given at Harvard for the tercentenary of 1936 by F. M. Powicke. The latter had referred to the "remarkable" English assumption of a continuously existing "community of the realm," thereby opening the way for Kantorowicz to place two thirteenth-century political innovations in juxtaposition:

[14] 13 March 1939. Kantorowicz's memo to Bernard Flexner of 15 February refers to an imminent speaking engagement at Columbia, but he had merely sent an inquiry on 14 February about the possibility of such a talk. See Russell Potter to Kantorowicz, 3 March 1939: LBI, box 5, folder 3.

[15] LBI, box 2, folder 1.

[16] The following two paragraphs depend heavily on my "Kantorowicz and Continuity," 114–16.

continuously existing institutions, and the idea of the "community of the realm" existing apart from the life of any given ruler. While he did not pursue the theme of the "community under the crown but not dependent on the crown," his emphasis on English and French examples of political continuity and his remark that the new idea of continuity is "perceivable . . . *even in the Empire*" (emphasis mine) show that he was leaving Germany behind in more ways than one.

EKa was disappointed that "nobody of importance" heard his talk at Harvard and that he was not given a direly needed honorarium.[17] At Smith, where his lecture resulted from the contact he had made in Germany the summer before with Kurt Koffka, he found "the girls very nice, the level of knowledge of my colleagues rather low." His greatest success was at Yale: "They appreciated my paper very much more as the audience was better." (His friend Mommsen must have exerted some effort in drumming up attendance.) The chairman of the Yale History Department invited him to give another paper in April and said that he would use his influence with Princeton to arrange a series of "well-paid" lectures (EKa's gloss) the following academic year. EKa was particularly pleased by this because he had heard nothing about his candidacy for the position at Berkeley. He was coming to think that American colleges and universities were "at a point of being fed up with foreign professors, which I can understand, and there is going to be some new arrangement about refugees not being granted a job."

Kantorowicz's pessimism about surviving, however, was soon allayed. Mommsen had secured an interview for him for an unfunded one-year research position at Johns Hopkins University. Within a few days after his return from New England EKa traveled to Baltimore to be interviewed by members of the Hopkins Departments of History and Romance Languages. As he wrote to Bowra, "The people are charming, don't like teaching—6 or 7 hours weekly utmost is what they do—and think of Yale and Harvard's 16 or 17 hours' work as a plebeian Yankee Weltanschauung, but they seem to like scholarly research and stamp collecting."[18] EKa was immediately offered the position, but the trick then was to find funding. At that point the rapport he had established with Bernard Flexner literally paid off for the first time. In less than three weeks the Emergency Committee in Aid of Displaced Foreign Scholars acted favorably on a recommendation for funding sent by Isaiah Bowman, the president of Johns Hopkins, awarding EKa $1,200 on the proviso that a matching amount be found elsewhere. Armed with this commitment, EKa then gained the necessary remaining $1,200 from the Oberlaender Trust of the Carl Schurz Memorial Foundation, another philanthropic organization dedicated to helping refugee German scholars.[19] The resulting sum of $2,400 was adequate for the

[17] This paragraph relies on letter to Bowra, 13 March 1939.

[18] 16 March 1939.

[19] The sequence of events pertaining to the funding is pieced together from Isaiah Bowman to Bernard Flexner, 17 March 1939; Bowman to Stephen R. Duggan (director of the Emergency

day. Consequently EKa could well write to Bowra, even before the funding arrangements had been settled: "I have found at least a 'toe-hold' which carries me on [until] something definite will be established."[20] (His good news even reached Germany, albeit garbled. Franz Kantorowicz's wife wrote from Berlin to her daughter that "Ernst K. has a position in Balmoral near New-York."[21])

Toward the end of March EKa honored a previous commitment to speak at Ohio State University where his sister Soscha's husband Arthur had gained a position in the Economics Department. He must have been happy to be reunited briefly with his sister, but he surely did not care for Columbus. Reporting to Bowra on his return, he wrote: "Columbus [is] as ugly a town as you might wish. . . . I am glad I was not offered anything at this place." Still, he acknowledged that "it must be very much nicer indeed than Kansas, Minneapolis or Dallas." The dreary Midwest was "not even funny, as it is too dull."[22]

After EKa was finished with his tours he had time for work, and high on his agenda was preparing his spoken presentation on Roger van der Weyden for publication in English. He must have worked hard since his written correspondence in English was still full of mistakes. (Before the article was published its English was touched up by T.S.R. Boase.[23]) In the finished product his style was as distinctive as it had been in German: Lionello d'Este "enjoyed love before a new disease poisoned his pleasures"; in response to the view that a supposed second portrait of Lionello gave a glimpse of the "other side of the moon"—"Who would trust the moon?"[24] When he wrote to Fritz Saxl, the director of the Warburg Institute in London, to sound him out about publishing the article in the institute's journal he explained that publications were crucial for his career in the United States and this one was most appropriate because it was "positivistic."[25]

May brought a trip to Baltimore for an apartment hunt and a linked visit to Washington, DC. In Baltimore EKa was surprised to learn that certain neighborhoods were off bounds for Jews and found this startling because in the Germany he knew Jews could move into whatever neighborhoods they pleased.[26] Regarding Washington, he wrote to Bowra that it was "a really lovely city, not

Committee), 1 April 1939; Emergency Committee, Agenda for 3 April, Supplement A; and Betty Drury (assistant secretary of the Emergency Committee) to Bowman, 4 April 1939, all from Emergency Committee papers, as well as Bowman to Kantorowicz, 29 April 1939: LBI, box 5, folder 3.

[20] 16 March 1939.

[21] Eva Kantorowicz to Vera Peters, 31 March 1939: Lerner archive.

[22] 27 March 1939.

[23] Rudolf Wittkower to Kantorowicz, 22 June 1940: LBI, box 3, folder 15.

[24] "The Este Portrait," 366, 367, 368.

[25] 21 October 1939: Warburg Institute Archives, London.

[26] Interview with Robert Benson, 5 November 1990; interview with Ralph Giesey, 2 August 1991. The fact that Kantorowicz reported this years after the event independently to two of his students indicates that it must have made a great impression on him.

in the least Broadwayish, devoid of empty tins, broken engines, sheet-iron and all the iron remainders and rubbish which make American cities so squalid and poisoning."[27]

The highlight of EKa's stay in Washington was befriending Justice Felix Frankfurter, who a few months earlier had been appointed by President Roosevelt to the United States Supreme Court. Frankfurter, an Anglophile, had been a visiting professor of law at Oxford in 1933–34 when he developed a lasting friendship with Maurice Bowra.[28] EKa had met him briefly when he was in Oxford in 1934, but it was the Bowra connection that allowed him to write in advance to request an interview.[29] In particular he had concerns about how to gain the immigration visa necessary for his employment at Hopkins.

Frankfurter generously offered EKa some of his time and took the opportunity to stage an improbable event. Being aware of Kantorowicz's reputation as a biographer, he brought him together with Francis Hackett, the author of a popular biography of Henry VIII that had inspired the film *The Private Life of Henry VIII*. Rather incredibly, Frankfurter led EKa and Hackett into the hallowed Washington courtroom of the Supreme Court, placed himself and EKa on two of the judges' chairs, and sent Hackett to the dock. Then EKa charged Hackett with having invented his sources and having omitted evidence of Henry's sexual strength—or as EKa phrased it, of "how often he could." Frankfurter issued the judgment, but lamentably it is unrecorded.

The next day Frankfurter invited EKa to lunch and listened to his concerns about obtaining an immigration visa. Unfortunately he could pull no strings but only specify the rules. Otherwise the conversation was lively. As EKa wrote in his mischievous manner to Bowra: "Felix Frankfurter was delightful. I did not remember him being so nice and so cheerful as he is. . . . [W]e exchanged all the bad experiences we and anybody had made with you. So it was a delightful lunch."[30] A few weeks later Frankfurter sent a brief message to EKa about his impending trip to England: "My dear Kantorowicz—I shall be staying with his Wardenship [Bowra] and so we shall drink your health and your absorption of America and her red-tape ways."[31]

The "red-tape ways" were making Kantorowicz ever more desperate. On May 11 he had taken a barge to Ellis Island in order to have his permission to remain in the United States on a temporary visa extended to August 29.[32] But that was merely a stopgap measure to last him until he could gain an immigration visa, and by late June he was no closer to that goal. He needed to apply

[27] 29 May 1939.
[28] Mitchell, *Maurice Bowra*, 222–23.
[29] 7 May 1939: LBI, box 5, folder 3.
[30] 29 May 1939. This is also the source for the mock trial of Francis Hackett.
[31] 11 June 1939: LBI, box 5, folder 3.
[32] LBI, box 5, folder 3.

from outside of the United States but was not allowed to enter Canada without a declaration from an American consul in Canada that he would be prepared to issue it, yet consuls would not issue such a declaration if the applicant were not already in Canada. Still hoping that he could move the American consul in Montreal to issue a provisional acknowledgment of his suitability without a personal appearance, he prepared a list of references and a new curriculum vitae, both dated June 22. The list of references was gilt-edged, leading off with former ambassador William E. Dodd and Justice Frankfurter. The c.v. was very impressive too. It even stated untruthfully that Kantorowicz "lectured in Oxford at the request of the Warden of Wadham College in 1936/37" and taught in Oxford again in 1939.[33] How did he hope to get away with this? We have the answer in a letter to Bowra of 21 June:

> I should like to have another letter of yours (with official heading) saying that I conducted lectures and classes at the request of your college in the Winter 1938/9 as I did in 1936/7, my subject being Mediaeval European History . . . dated—as your other letter was—April 16, 1939. The addition of 1936/7 is *essential*, as they want proofs of my having lectured during the last two years. And '36/7 would fit in very well, as I have a date-stamp: "December 1936," from Dover, in my passport, when I came to England in order to witness the abdication of Windsor. If you can send this letter with the "Clipper" then I could have it within a few days; and I need it rather urgently.[34]

Sure enough the Kantorowicz papers in New York include a letter from the warden of Wadham College, dated April 16 1939, that stated what EKa had requested from Bowra in June.[35] Fine von Kahler long ago had remarked that Kantorowicz was "famous for his illegal ways."

The consul in Montreal remained unmoved, but while EKa was trying to settle matters contingent on moving to Baltimore, he was bowled over to learn that he was being offered the job at Berkeley for which he had applied almost a full year earlier. The matter had dragged on because the final decision lay with Robert G. Sproul, the president of the University of California, and Sproul had a motive for delaying a decision. Namely, the open position, an endowed chair, came with an enormous amount of money that Sproul had his eyes on. Since there was no overwhelmingly superior candidate, he waited until the last minute and then announced that he would fill the position with a one-year trial appointment and draw as little from the funds as possible so that he could use the greater part for purposes to be determined. With all the talk about refugees not being hired in the United States in preference to Americans, a desperate foreigner who might be supported in part by philanthropic funds was the

[33] Ibid.
[34] 21 June 1939.
[35] LBI, box 5, folder 3.

obvious person who might accept whatever was offered at a date as late as June. Consequently Sproul wrote to see whether the Emergency Committee would be willing to assume a good part of Professor Kantorowicz's salary were he to be appointed.[36] Bernard Flexner took over and signaled agreement, also checking pro forma with Isaiah Bowman of Hopkins about whether he was willing to release Kantorowicz. Bowman of course acceded, writing that "[Kantorowicz] is a charming man and will make a substantial addition to any university; we would not stand in his way for one moment."[37] The Berkeley appointment was now settled.

Two weeks' worth of correspondence had been passing through the mails without EKa's knowledge before he found out that he had landed the Berkeley job. On June 29 he wrote to Flexner: "From Miss Drury [the assistant secretary of the Emergency Committee] who was kind enough to ask me to come and see her yesterday afternoon I learnt that—if I may say so—the Pacific salmon at last rose to the bait. It seems unnecessary to tell you how glad I am."[38] To this he added, "It was, obviously, in a good stellar hour that you started taking my fate into your helping hand, and I feel rather poor at not being in a position to do anything else than to take your hand and to say: I thank you." It was then not on his mind that he was not being offered a regular position, as the original message the year before specified, but only a temporary one. Instead he was thinking only of his total salary for the coming year, and he politely but firmly wrote that this required "consideration without sentiments; it is not that I am really greedy although knowing very well that—in using Byron's words—'ready money is Aladin's [*sic*] lamp.'"[39] (He was flamboyantly quoting Byron's *Don Juan*.)

Kantorowicz's point was that although $2,400 had already been raised for him by the consortium of the Emergency Committee and the Oberlaender Trust, California should be obliged to add to that since the university still had all the funds from the endowed professorship at its disposal. Thus he almost cheekily proposed a contribution of $3,600 in consideration of the fact that the endowed chair had been assigned $9,000. As he wrote to Flexner, "I would not think it advisable to be thought of as being 'very cheap' and thus to create a precedent unfavorable to possibly occurring later dealings."[40] Yet the implied total of $6,000 would amount to upward of $93,000 today, quite a sum for a

[36] Sproul to Charles J. Liebman (President of the Refugee Economic Corporation in New York), 12 June 1939: Emergency Committee papers.

[37] Bowman to Flexner, 23 June 1939: Emergency Committee papers.

[38] Kantorowicz to Flexner, first of two letters of 29 June 1939: Emergency Committee papers.

[39] Kantorowicz to Flexner, second of two letters of 29 June 1939: Emergency Committee papers.

[40] Ibid. See also Betty Drury to Flexner, 5 July 1939, Emergency Committee papers, reporting that Kantorowicz thought then that California should put up $2,400: "At that, they will be getting off cheaply, he points out; the Chair he will be filling carries with it normally a stipend of $9,000. He does not see how the University can object to paying $2,400. (I can, however.)"

temporary trial position. When EKa learned that the Emergency Committee had a rule of not contributing to a salary in excess of $4,000, he retreated and conceded that he would be delighted to receive that much. The result was that he earned $4,000 for the year: $2,000 from the consortium of the Emergency Committee and the Oberlaender Trust (as of his Berkeley appointment on August 1 he had already drawn $400 allotted to him on account for his position at Hopkins from the consortium[41]), and $2,000 from the University of California.[42] This was still a respectable amount.

A problem that remained was gaining the necessary immigration visa. Having a letter of appointment from Hopkins, which he had not yet put away, EKa was able to apply for a "nonquota" visa, but he still needed to travel beyond the United States to make the application. Mexico did not come under consideration because the borders at that time were closed, and Canada was not an option because of the bureaucratic circularity previously mentioned. That left Cuba, but EKa lacked the cash for the fare: whatever remained from the $400 he had drawn on account from his funding consortium was insufficient. Fortunately his position at California began officially on August 1, with the result that the university issued him an advance of $300 as of August 1 so that he could fly from New York to Havana with a return to Miami, and from there pay for land travel to San Francisco and Berkeley.[43]

While waiting for the advance (and confirmation from the Cuban government that he would receive a visa to enter that country!), EKa spent a few days in late July with his sister and brother-in-law on Martha's Vineyard. There the Salzes had rented a small house for the summer. Unhappy with New York's "sticky sultriness," he must have been pleased by the sea breezes and opportunities for swimming. After returning to New York in the first days of August, he made his way to Havana. He was glad to escape; in July he had written to Wilhelm Stein, "I don't like it here and look forward to moving to the lovelier, or supposedly lovelier, California."[44] His economizing had led to a loss of weight. In late May he had written to Bowra: "I am getting very thin and am loosing [*sic*] my precious little belly entirely. I have lost about 5 kilo and had to go to the saddler to have three new holes made into my belt. And almost all my trousers are hanging down to the ground."[45]

[41] Kantorowicz to Wilbur K. Thomas (director of the Oberlaender Trust), 14 July 1939: Emergency Committee papers.

[42] The total salary of $4,000 for 1939–40 appears on a schedule of the history of Kantorowicz's annual salaries drawn up in connection with the loyalty oath controversy. (Bancroft Library, Neylan papers.) The contribution from the consortium is mentioned in a letter from Monroe Deutsch to Bernard Flexner, 31 May 1940: Emergency Committee papers.

[43] The sum of $300 is added in pen by Betty Drury: Kantorowicz to Drury, 29 July 1939: Emergency Committee papers.

[44] 2 July 1939: Stein papers.

[45] 29 May 1939.

In Havana it took Kantorowicz two days to obtain the necessary visa. Then, on August 10, he went to Miami to embark on a cross-continental train trip, a journey that lasted for five days.[46] Most of it was spent on the *Argonaut*, a Southern Pacific train running from New Orleans to Los Angeles designed for economy travel. "Near to El Paso," he typed a letter to his mother's brother in Switzerland, indicating that he had already traversed "an immense number of states for over one hundred hours." Debarking in Los Angeles, he made his way to the San Francisco Bay.

[46] For the trip to Havana and subsequent train travel, Kantorowicz to Felix Hepner, 15 August 1939, 4 January 1940: Hepner papers 1206/1/14/2, 3.

CHAPTER 16

"Without Any Desire for Europe"

The fall term at Berkeley began on Monday, August 21 (classes started a week later), and was accompanied by a brief editorial in the *Oakland Tribune*: "The announcement of the University of California that Dr. E. Kantorowicz will fill a chair in medieval history for the coming year means that another great scholar has been added to the faculty. Professor Kantorowicz is noted for his definitive work on Frederick II, German King (1215–1250)." The statement lacked strict accuracy in reporting that Ernst Kantorowicz had been "added to the faculty," for he had been hired as a one-year visitor. It was true that he was a great scholar, but that was not going to ensure his remaining at Berkeley for more than a year.

Upon arriving EKa found an apartment in a building meant mainly for students, 2424 Ridge Road, one block north of the campus. After his recent difficulties he felt content from the earliest days. On September 6 he wrote to Bowra: "The place is charming, my apartment is very nice, the work is not too irksome, the professors are nice men so far, the lectures are going on quite decently and the climate is wonderful." Furthermore, the food was "much better than in 'America,' i.e., New England and New York—it is really good." And then there were the coeds. Before he had arrived he assumed that he would be "whispering secrets about Charlemagne into the ears of short Filipinos,"[1] but now he knew better: "The nicest girl in my class is called Miss Quinn. She is very pretty indeed, but so are about 5,000 on the campus. Never in all my life have I seen so many nice and well groomed, well bred, well grown girls gathered in one spot."

Three letters written around Christmas might fit under the rubric "euphoric state." EKa wrote to his uncle Felix Hepner in Switzerland that he was "positively happy." The climate was "like paradise" and San Francisco was one of the most beautiful of cities; its location on the water made it comparable to Constantinople and Naples.[2] To Felix Frankfurter, he wrote that "I praise almost every day I am allowed to spend here . . . the view of the Bay reminds me

[1] To Wilhelm Stein, 2 July 1939: Stein papers.

[2] To Felix Hepner, 4 January 1940: Hepner papers 1206/1/14/3: Wiener Library, London.

of Naples . . . the food is excellent, the wine not too bad . . . the students are charming, receptive, grateful and handsome."[3] To Wilhelm Stein he wrote that he did not miss the "'cosmic' subtlety" of the Regensburgerstrasse (the address in Berlin of the George standard-bearer Ernst Morwitz).[4]

Another passage from the letter to Stein bears quoting at length:

> Only since I've been here in the West have I been feeling really comfortable and completely at home, without any desire for Europe, aside from human contacts. This here is not "America"; it is somehow seventeenth-century Spain or Mediterranean, with a touch of China—enormously charming because of this variety, and life passes with Neapolitan ease, thanks to the divine climate. Even now I breakfast and have lunch on the veranda, eat strawberries, and look either left to the mountains or right to the sea. What would you otherwise want, my friend! . . . The students have something sunny about them, as we hardly know in Europe. They are completely unencumbered, completely pagan; only a few are baptized, for here that's not a custom; accordingly they smell of fresh air [*ganz unmufflig, vielmehr gut gelüftet*] and enjoy learning things that give them pleasure; and otherwise they take pleasure in their pretty limbs, [they are] eager for knowledge and have animal vitality—a combination that amuses me indescribably and somehow tickles me continually deep in the pit of my stomach so that I'm actually always delighted as soon as I walk into the classroom or speak with the children [*Kindern*] who do have some knowledge but with gaps that we would consider unimaginable. So it's all an endless play with people, books, and intellect that makes me appear to myself very old and terribly young at the same time.

Berkeley had a heavier teaching load than EKa had known in Frankfurt. During the regular academic year he was required to teach an undergraduate survey, an upper-level lecture course, and a two-hour graduate seminar. (But he did not need to grade exams—graduate students were paid to do that.) The survey was a yearlong course called Medieval Institutions. (This was an inherited course title; when he taught it he told the students that it really was about "medieval thought and ideas.") For his upper-level topics he chose The Normans in European History (fall) and The Dawn of Humanism and Renaissance (spring).[5] Preparing lectures took virtually all his time during his first year. Quite likely both upper-level lecture courses were versions of what he had given in Frankfurt, but even if so he needed to translate his German into English. At the end of the first semester he wrote that he had been "staggering from

[3] To Frankfurter, 16 December 1939 [typed mistakenly as "1936"]: Frankfurter papers.

[4] 21 December 1939: Stein papers.

[5] On Kantorowicz's first-year teaching assignments, see the exchange between Herbert E. Bolton (the department chair) and Kantorowicz, 24 July 1939 and 29 July 1939: Bolton papers. EKa offered six topics for the upper-level lectures and wound up with the two mentioned.

one day to the next."[6] Still in need of money, he took the opportunity of doing some extra teaching during an intersession term running from late May until the end of June. For this he was allowed to repeat the first half of his Medieval Institutions and The Dawn of Humanism and Renaissance. There was only one serious disadvantage: for five days a week he was required to start teaching at nine in the morning.

Kantorowicz always lectured from a written script because he never wanted to leave anything to chance; consequently most of his Berkeley lectures can be consulted today. They are typed with very few abbreviations: The Dawn of Humanism runs to 237 pages. Although English was still not entirely second nature to him, he always wanted to be stylish. Thus we find such phrases as "the motor of history rattling through the centuries," and epigrams such as "Renaissance and Humanism are but the secularization of the Medieval World."[7] He developed themes instead of offering uninterrupted narrative. At the start of the spring course he told the students in Medieval Institutions that he would be discussing "not so much the historical facts as the development of the political-religious ideas of these five centuries."[8] With consummate elegance he stated, "It is my intention to discuss first of all some leading ideas which are the keyboard, so to speak, on which the sonata of the Middle Ages is played." Individual lectures were rigorously organized and artfully constructed. The Dawn of Humanism series moved from "Papal Sovereignty," to "Imperial Sovereignty," to "Popular Sovereignty," and from Bologna (law), to Chartres (Platonism), to Paris (Aristotelianism). The lecturer announces his overarching thesis briefly at the beginning: "not rediscovery but secularization," and ends with a full cadence: "We may confidently say that the Renaissance as well as Humanism originated from a religious movement."[9]

Although Kantorowicz wrote to Felix Frankfurter that his first semester of teaching was "great fun," and to Stein that he was "delighted to walk into the classroom," the question arises as to whether the feeling among his students was mutual. The evidence regarding his reputation as a teacher in his first year at Berkeley is limited. In February 1940 all his colleagues in the History Department were asked to comment on his case for a permanent position.[10] Teaching seldom came up, but when it did the brief remarks went both ways. One mid-rank colleague had no animus, expressing his "high admiration for K. as a man

[6] To Stein, 21 December 1939. "One day to the next" also in Kantorowicz to Fritz Saxl, 21 October 1939.

[7] Lecture texts for course on The Dawn of Humanism and Renaissance (spring term, 1940): LBI, box 9, folder 15.

[8] LBI, box 9, folder 2.

[9] Ibid., 1, 230.

[10] The responses are contained in a memorandum of C. D. Shane, chair of the Budget Committee and professor of Astronomy, dated 26 February 1940 (Budget Committee papers, Bancroft Library.)

and as a gentleman." But he had reservations about retaining him as a teacher of undergraduates "because of the inability of some students to understand him." Nevertheless, a junior colleague reported that "[he] knows some of K.'s students and finds they hold him in high esteem. Three of them appeared at U.C.L.A. to hear his paper" (a reference to a talk EKa gave at the annual meeting of the Pacific Coast Branch of the American Historical Association).[11]

In the lack of any direct student comment, the professor in charge of gathering information located a student, Peggy Bray, on his own. As he wrote: "This opinion was obtained through her father, Professor Bray, without his informing her of the reasons for his questions. Miss Bray thinks that K. is a real scholar. In his teaching he exhibits a bad accent but one gets used to it quickly. She considers him one of the most effective and inspiring teachers she has had."

Peggy Bray's mention of a "bad accent" raises a question. Surely EKa did have an accent, but whether it was so strong as to impede comprehension is doubtful. Surviving notes taken by a student in the Medieval Institutions course offer no indication of difficulty in understanding—the notes are fluent and contain no dashes for gaps in comprehension.[12] Thus it seems most likely that Peggy Bray was referring to EKa's highly eccentric mode of delivery—his "peculiar sing-song."[13] In the United States this was a prominent part of his public persona. The story is told that when lecturing in Berkeley he once noticed some students whom he had never seen before and after class asked who they were. The answer was that they were studying Chinese and their instructor had told them to listen to Kantorowicz to help them master the Chinese third tone. Some people found the intonation irritating. Yakov Malkiel wrote that "while his English vocabulary was more than adequate and his syntax caused no difficulty, his intonational curve . . . never lost its obtrusively foreign contour, to the point of distracting auditors hypersensitive to pitch."[14] The historian Louis Gottschalk, who was a visitor at Berkeley during the summer session of 1942 and became a friend, spoke of Kantorowicz's "extraordinarily unpleasant voice and inflection."[15] But his graduate student William A. Chaney insisted that "the semi-chanted rhythm . . . was mesmerizing, and his students loved it!" For Chaney, "EKa was one of the greatest lecturers [he] ever heard."[16]

[11] In his letter of 21 December 1939 to Wilhelm Stein, EKa tells of organizing a handful of students to be at his talk in UCLA to serve as a "claque."

[12] George T. Romani's notes for Medieval Institutions, intersession 1940, are in the Northwestern University Archives: Romani papers, box 2, folder 2.

[13] Diary of William T. Hutchinson (UCSC), entry for 11 April 1945: "He has a most peculiar 'sing-song' intonation."

[14] Malkiel, "Ernst H. Kantorowicz," 155, n. 5.

[15] Louis R. Gottschalk to William T. Hutchinson, 14 May 1945: UCSC, Presidential papers, box 7, folder 8.

[16] Chaney to Robert E. Lerner, 27 May 2010. When I heard Kantorowicz speaking in conversation in Princeton in the spring of 1961 I was both fascinated and bewildered.

Later we will return to Kantorowicz's teaching at Berkeley. Here we can look at other aspects of his first year. EKa always found it easy to ingratiate himself with those for whom he felt the motivation. From the vantage of his future at Berkeley the most important new friend was Monroe Emanuel Deutsch, vice president and provost since 1931. Deutsch, sixteen years older than EKa, had begun his career as a student of Classics. He earned a Ph.D. degree from Berkeley in 1911, spent the following year studying in Europe, and then ascended the academic ladder to become professor of Latin at Berkeley in 1922. Before Deutsch moved into administration (without any known hindrances arising from the fact that he was Jewish) he had written several scholarly books, most of them revolving around the career of Julius Caesar. Given that he was a cosmopolitan intellectual, it is not surprising that he and EKa quickly developed a rapport. Four months after EKa arrived in Berkeley, he informed Felix Frankfurter that "Deutsch is a delightful man, and I am glad to see quite a lot of him, as he and Mrs. Deutsch chaperon me in the kindest way."[17] In the spring, when EKa desperately needed help to stay on, Deutsch wrote to Bernard Flexner in New York supporting a second subvention from the Emergency Committee and providing a testimonial.[18]

Another early friend was Max Radin. He was one of those eastern European Jews who rose by his merits to the academic heights. Radin came to the United States. with his parents when he was four, gained a B.A. degree from New York's City College in 1899, a Bachelor of Law degree from New York University in 1902, and a Ph.D. degree from Columbia in 1909. He joined the Berkeley law faculty in 1919 and took an endowed chair in 1940 (then a rare distinction). Radin and Deutsch were on good terms. When EKa's name first was bruited as a possible appointment in August 1938, Radin wrote to Deutsch: "I myself do not know Kantorowicz personally, but of course I know his work. He is one of the two or three greatest medievalists in the world."[19] Despite the disparity in age—Radin was EKa's senior by fifteen years—the two became close friends in Berkeley. *The King's Two Bodies* is dedicated to his memory, and an account of a conversation with him opens the book. When Radin died in 1950 EKa wrote to his cousin Elise Peters: "I really loved Max as I did very few men."[20]

A third friend was Robert H. Lowie, professor of anthropology at Berkeley from 1925 to 1950. Born "Löwe" (doubtless still earlier the family name was Levy), he came to the United States from Vienna at the age of ten and rose in the same manner as Radin. He gained his B.A. degree from City College in 1901 and his Ph.D. degree from Columbia in 1908; he joined Berkeley's Anthropology Department in 1917 and became full professor in 1925. An ethnologist

[17] 16 December 1939 [typed mistakenly as "1936"]: Frankfurter papers.
[18] 31 May 1940: Emergency Committee papers.
[19] 29 August 1938, as posted by Ralph Giesey, http://www.regiesey.com.
[20] To Elise Peters, 22 June 1950: Lerner archive.

who did field work among American Indians, his presence in Berkeley together with that of Alfred L. Kroeber made the Berkeley department one of the most distinguished in the country. Of the three men mentioned, Lowie was the only one who conversed with EKa in German. Within weeks of EKa's arrival the two were discussing how some words came easily to them in German but not in English, and vice versa.[21]

Mention of Lowie brings us to EKa's travails in attempting to remain in Berkeley. In his letter of December to Stein he wrote: "I don't think that anything can tempt me away from here and I would only submit to force." But he did recognize that his chances of gaining a permanent position were uncertain. He wrote to his cousin Franz that he had received a one-year job "on a trial basis."[22] Maneuvering in academic politics was not his forte; as he wrote to Stein, he hoped that others would take up his cause in concert with their own "university-political" goals. This was a shade too cynical; it will be seen that Lowie and Deutsch favored him without any "political" goals other than supporting excellence. Support of excellence, however, hardly seems to have been on the minds of most of the other men who had a role in deciding whether he would be staying in Berkeley after his first year. President Robert Sproul wanted to let him go him for budgetary reasons and his colleagues in the History Department were largely indifferent, aside from those who were hostile.

A brief look at the membership of the department will give some indication as to why EKa seemed out of place. During the early twentieth century the department was small and insignificant. Around 1910 an observer is said to have remarked, on seeing the chairman of the History Department walking with his colleagues, "There goes a fake giant surrounded by real pygmies."[23] The hiring of Herbert E. Bolton in 1911 was meant to add inches. Bolton was a first-rate Americanist with a national reputation, known for the "Bolton thesis," which argued for the influence of the Spanish borderlands on the development of the United States.[24] He became chair in 1919 and served in that capacity until his retirement at the end of EKa's first year, 1939–40. In 1932 he served as president of the American Historical Association. He was a conscientious administrator but was driven in hiring policy by a fixation that the history of North and South America had to be studied and taught together. Because this notion had little following elsewhere, this commitment meant that Bolton hired from a limited pool of his own students or disciples. Unfortunately the "Boltonites"

[21] Kantorowicz to Lowie, 10 October 1939: Lowie papers.

[22] Franz Kantorowicz to Vera Peters and her husband, letter fragment probably of autumn 1939: Lerner archive.

[23] Robert Nisbet, *Teachers and Scholars: A Memoir of Berkeley in Depression and War* (New Brunswick, NJ, 1992), 151.

[24] Albert L. Hurtado, *Herbert Eugene Bolton: Historian of the American Borderlands* (Berkeley, 2012).

were characterized by mediocrity.[25] The only Americanist hired by Bolton who was a scholar of some distinction was a Pulitzer Prize winner, Frederic Paxson. But Paxson had won his Pulitzer in 1925, well before he came to Berkeley, and while he was in Berkeley from 1932 until 1947 he raised no rafters.

With Bolton and Paxson the American wing of the department at least had two historians of national reputation, but the European wing had none. Robert J. Kerner, a historian of Slavic Europe was productive, with several books to his credit, and was active in the profession. But in terms of the interests of the day his geographical emphases were peripheral, and even then he had never written a major study. The appointment in 1933 of James Westfall Thompson, a medievalist who had been full professor at the University of Chicago, might have made a difference had he been younger. Thompson (known sotto voce as "James Windfall Thompson" because he had married an heiress) had been lured to Berkeley by the offer of the newly created and extremely well-endowed Sidney Hellman Ehrman chair in European history. (The chair paid an annual nine thousand dollars whereas the president of the university made only eleven thousand.) But in 1933 Thompson was sixty-four and he retired according to regulations in 1939 at the age of seventy, although he continued to play a role in departmental politics until his death in 1941.

Unfortunately for EKa, both Thompson and Kerner had no use for him. Thompson, the author of a book entitled *Feudal Germany* (a misnomer because medieval Germany avoided feudalism), may have regarded EKa as a scholarly rival. Certainly in February 1940 he "urgently recommended" the appointment of the very junior Lynn White for the Ehrman chair.[26] (White was a former Haskins student who then was teaching at Stanford.) Kerner opposed EKa's career at Berkeley from the start and never relented. One Berkeley witness described him as "inordinately vain and quick to be resentful or jealous of colleagues."[27] He was the local favorite for the Ehrman chair, which he coveted; it was said that he had "virtually appointed himself to it."[28] In August 1939, when EKa was on his way to California, Kerner thanked the dean of Berkeley's College of Mining: "The splendid letter which you wrote to Professor Bolton suggesting my name for the Sidney Hellman Ehrman Professorship touched me

[25] Henry F. May, "Comments," in *History at Berkeley, A Dialogue in Three Parts*, ed. Gene Brucker et al., 23–32, at 24 (Berkeley, 1998); David A. Hollinger, "Afterword," in ibid., 35–50, at 37–39.

[26] Memorandum of A. R. Robb to President Robert Sproul, 7 February 1940 (Bancroft Library, President's papers CU-5, Ser. 4, box 17, folder 11). Sometime after Thompson's death in 1941 EKa and Lynn White were given the assignment of cataloging Thompson's books and found that his method for writing his two-volume *A History of Historical Writing* was to rip out pages and paste them into his manuscript, a particularly strange custom for someone who earlier had written an essay on *The Importance of Libraries in the Preservation of Culture*: interview with Ralph Giesey, 2 August 1991.

[27] Nisbet, *Teachers and Scholars*, 171.

[28] Ibid.

deeply. . . . It would indeed be a very great honor for me to be appointed to this chair, which I regard . . . as the best in this country."[29] Since EKa had been hired temporarily with the understanding that he could possibly take the Ehrman chair, Kerner was immediately hostile.

A third senior Europeanist in the department was William A. Morris, a constitutional historian of medieval England. In 1940 he was sixty-five, recovering from some mild strokes, absorbed in his own unobtrusive technical scholarship, and indifferent to a German scholar whose research did not impinge on his own. Still another medievalist on the roster of the history faculty was Paul B. Schaeffer, who had studied at Harvard with Charles Homer Haskins and been at Berkeley since 1932. Schaeffer was a dedicated teacher and by all accounts a well-loved man: an "old-fashioned gentleman-scholar-bachelor." But he never published more than one short article and some revisions in a survey textbook. Reportedly he told people, "Why should I publish? There's too damned much published already."[30] He had de facto tenure and was not petty. Thus he did not chafe at EKa's presence. (In subsequent years the two were neither rivals nor friends.) But EKa would never expect any help from an assistant professor who preferred classical music over departmental affairs.

As far as the History Department faculty was concerned, there was no objection to keeping Kantorowicz on for another "probationary" year, with the Ehrman chair excluded. In December Chairman Bolton recommended to the president such an appointment for 1940–41. No immediate action was needed, but an interdisciplinary Committee on History conferred the following month as to whether Kantorowicz should be granted a permanent appointment. All members who were present when the vote was taken voted in the negative. Their rationale (and it must be said it was a plausible one) was that "considering the lapse of time since his last important scholarly production (1927–31), the committee feels a permanent appointment should be based on his performance here, and that no reliable judgment on it can be expected for another year."[31]

Robert Lowie, who belonged to the committee, was not notified of the meeting. When he got wind of the outcome he was furious and fired off a sizzling letter to President Sproul.[32] The words might have set the paper ablaze. Lowie wrote that he "deplored" the decision: "In my opinion Professor Kantorowicz is intellectually superior to any permanent member of our History Department; he represents a different order of intelligence and scholarship." Moreover, he was certain that "[Kantorowicz] is an excellent teacher, lively in exposition,

[29]To Dean Frank H. Probert, 7 August 1939: Bancroft Library, Robert J. Kerner papers, C-B 1057, carton 1.

[30]Interview with Norman Rich, 14 January 2010.

[31]Memo of "Committee on History: Lowie and Bolton absent," 26 January 1940 (Bancroft Library).

[32]29 January 1940: Lowie papers.

humorous, and thoroughly human." He had learned from one of the members who had voted against the permanent appointment (evidently Frederic Paxson, who soon would become a Kantorowicz supporter) that although the committee had considered the favorable letters that had come from England the previous year, they had dismissed them as being prompted by charitable sentiments toward a refugee. Lowie rejected this as "an insult to the distinguished scholars in question." He also had learned that the committee had considered only a few reviews of *Kaiser Friedrich der Zweite*, without taking into account what he considered to be a fair sample. Hence he was sending with his letter some of the reviews that the committee had ignored. Expressing his own opinion, based on his own reading and many reviews, he stated that "Kantorowicz's book is universally recognized as a work of literary distinction and of original ideas. For a man of thirty-two (in 1927) it seems an amazing feat of scholarship. . . . His retention is important in the interests of the *University*, his departure would be a grievous loss."

Lowie continued with a blistering indictment of the History Department. He charged that "instead of enthusiastically urging Dr. Kantorowicz's permanent appointment, [the Department] is bent on his elimination. It concedes—ungraciously—that he is of full professorial stature, but alleges that it can get more *value* out of any typical American-born scholar." He could only conclude that "the Department is opposed to the appointment of brilliant scholars and favors commonplace men who can be set at Departmental chores." (Two days later Lowie wrote to Paxson, charging the History Department with "crass provincialism, fatuity, and malice."[33])

Perhaps cowed, President Sproul charged the head of Berkeley's Budget Committee with polling the members of the department for their opinions as to whether EKa should receive a permanent appointment.[34] (We have already reviewed the few remarks about Kantorowicz's teaching.) Four were unreservedly favorable. Frederic Paxson was one, evidently having been brought over to EKa's camp by Lowie. Another was George Guttridge, an associate professor whose field was eighteenth-century English history. He stated that "[Kantorowicz] is brilliant without being shallow." Two others leaned to the favorable but lukewarmly. A seventh "knew nothing about Kantorowicz," and the remaining three leaned toward the negative. Of these, two were the senior Europeanists, Kerner and Morris. Morris believed that "Kantorowicz will continue to produce but doubt[ed] [that] he will attain a topmost standing in his field."

The polling being nonbinding, it remained for the department to vote. After a delay of more than a month, EKa was invited to give a public lecture. Herbert Bolton introduced him by saying, "We have much enjoyed and immensely

[33] 1 February 1940, as posted by Ralph Giesey at http://www.regiesey.com.

[34] For the detailed memorandum of C. D. Shane, n. 10 above.

profited by Dr. Kantorowicz's genial and stimulating presence amongst us."[35] The talk was accessible, a lecture with slides on "Charles the Bold and the Italian Renaissance in Flanders." Afterward Bolton wrote to Sproul that it "made a good impression" and concluded, "I recommend that he be made Professor of History on permanent appointment." Apparently Bolton did this with the department's backing, although whether a formal vote was taken is unclear. Bolton wrote that he was not asking for EKa to receive the Ehrman chair, which he understood Sproul wanted to hold in reserve, but proposed that he be retained with interim funds until Morris retired and a full professorial position was vacated.[36]

Everything seemed promising until Sproul suddenly turned off the lights. Sometime around the middle of May he called EKa in for an interview and informed him that for budgetary reasons he was being let go—no permanent position, no one-year position, nothing. Bolton and Monroe Deutsch attempted to intervene on EKa's behalf, urging that he be retained for one more year, but Sproul was adamant. Deutsch wrote to Kantorowicz on May 28: "It is with the very deepest of regret that I am writing to tell you that I did take up with the President the question of your reappointment, and he said that he felt that he had definitely stated that there would not be a reappointment. It was his feeling that at the interview which you had with him he had given a final and definite answer."[37]

Deutsch's bleak message coincided with black news from overseas. German armies were overrunning northern France. To gain a sense of how EKa must have felt, we may note some of his earlier expressions about the war. His letter to Maurice Bowra of September 6, 1939, shows him invigorated by the outbreak of hostilities. He was gratified that Chamberlain's appeasement policy had finally ended, and he offered a German insider's advice about propaganda tactics. Leaflets being dropped on Germany should address "Deutsche Patrioten" rather than "Deutsche Männer und Frauen" and should say that the really "patriotic" German had the duty to desert. In sum he thought (quite unrealistically) that it would not be too hard "to 'seduce' many Germans if the proper words were found."

Together with the excitement, however, came concern. For one, EKa was worried about Baby: "Is she in a camp?" He was also worried about anti-Nazi friends he had left behind in Germany. He wished that he himself were "not so

[35] I infer that the chair of the meeting (9 April 1940) was Bolton, for the text of the introduction is in the Bolton papers of Bancroft Library. The presenter was careful to say that "Dr. Kantorowicz is with us *this year*" (my emphasis).

[36] I have the quotations from Bolton's letter from David H. Wright, "Kantorowicz in Berkeley," ms., April 2002, 7. Otherwise see Kantorowicz to Bernard Flexner, 29 May 1940: Emergency Committee papers: "a public lecture which must have been quite successful as it induced the Department to change their minds and to recommend me for a permanent full professorship."

[37] LBI, box 7, folder 2.

far off in these horrible days," wondered what country might be involved next, expressed the hope that Hitler had "no more trumps in his hand," and added prophetically, "nor Stalin who, after all, most likely holds the last trump."

As German troops overran Poland, EKa became glum. On September 22 he wrote to Edgar Salin in Basel about the "madness," pronouncing that the war had "been forced on the world by the fates coldly and remorselessly." He conceded that he perhaps was not able to see things as they were but nevertheless ended his remarks with the bitterest of lines: "Putting aside the unpredictable, I take the chances for England and France to obtain their war goals to be hopeless; the century of German wars is not over by far."[38] In a letter of December to Wilhelm Stein in Bern he wrote that he now thought that the outlook for "England etc." seemed somewhat better than before. Nevertheless, he feared that even if there were to be an English victory it would be Pyrrhic because it would have enormous costs: "The consequences cannot be foreseen—politically, economically, constitutionally, intellectually."[39]

In December 1939 EKa received a visit from Adam von Trott, whom he had met in Berlin through Count Bernstorff. Von Trott had attempted a few months earlier to solicit interest in Washington for building contacts between the U.S. administration and Nazi opponents like himself in order to bring down the regime (he was in favor of a compromise peace), but Bowra, who had known him in Oxford, thought him a double agent and warned Felix Frankfurter of this, who in turn blocked Trott from seeing Roosevelt.[40] EKa, however, had nothing against Trott, who was on the West Coast on his way to China, and was pleased to spend some time talking with him. Trott told him that he ultimately was going back to Germany, where he planned on working to undermine the regime, adding that "some of us might be killed." EKa warned him against this, but Trott became a leading member in the conspiracy of 1944 to assassinate Hitler and was hanged with a wire hook after its failure.[41]

In late May 1940, as Belgium surrendered, EKa wrote to Bernard Flexner in New York to inquire into the possibility of receiving a second grant from

[38] Kantorowicz to Edgar Salin, 22 September 1939: Salin papers. For the entire German letter, Lerner, "Letters by Ernst Kantorowicz Concerning Uxkull and George," 168.

[39] 21 December 1939: Stein papers. See also letter of 16 December 1939 to Felix Frankfurter: "a war the outcome of which cannot be but bad, also for an England that comes out victorious": Frankfurter papers.

[40] Giles MacDonogh, *A Good German: Adam von Trott zu Solz* (Woodstock, NY, 1992). Regarding Bowra and Trott, Mitchell, *Maurice Bowra*, 214–17.

[41] "Might be killed": EKa reported this conversation to William A. Chaney: interview 10 February 2010. Also Kantorowicz to Maurice Bowra, 24 September 1944: "That Adam von Trott has been executed by the Nazis is not surprising. He went to Germany with the purpose of 'undermining.'"; Kantorowicz to Ernst Langlotz, 15 September 1945 (Langlotz papers): "Adam von Trott visited me here in Berkeley in the winter of 1939/40. He was determined, regardless of my advice against it, to go to Germany and there to work against the Nazi regime in a crucial position, which he then did." (All the foregoing is hitherto unknown evidence regarding von Trott's commitments.)

the Emergency Committee.[42] Most of the letter consisted of an account of his misfortunes in Berkeley, but he could not refrain from closing with his view that England would fall after France and that the United States would be overrun with a new wave of scholars—"from Holland, from Belgium, but also from England." He worried that "the competition is bound to increase gigantically and every university in this country [might] expect to get an Oxford Regius Professor for little money."[43]

Otherwise EKa's report to Flexner of his Berkeley travails included some frank lines. He understood that he had never had a realistic chance of receiving the Ehrman Professorship because "the regents" (he refrained from blaming Sproul) did not want to bestow the chair on a man of forty-five, thereby creating the likelihood that for twenty or twenty-five years the opportunity would be lost of hiring someone better. Regarding the possibility that antisemitism had played some role, he granted that "antisemitism is practically unknown on the campus." (Indeed, in a letter to his uncle of early January he had written "antisemitism is hardly noticeable here; at any rate I have not yet experienced it."[44]) Yet because the donor of the chair, Sidney Ehrman, was Jewish it would not have looked right to others if a Jew received the chair. Monroe Deutsch, another Jew, might have attempted to exert his influence, "yet Dr. Deutsch's hands were tied up in my special case." The point was telling.

EKa wrote in the same letter: "I cannot quite conceal my own disappointment, the more so as I just succeeded in getting my 79 years old mother to Switzerland, where I have to sustain her." Actually he thought he had succeeded in getting his mother to Switzerland, but he was wrong.[45] The complicated story is as follows. After the financial disaster of 1931 Clara was able to retain the Holstein estate because she let an entrepreneur build greenhouses on the land to grow cucumbers and split the income 50–50. But this solution proved inadequate: the land was auctioned in 1933 and the villa in 1935.[46] (It is now a hotel

[42]To Bernard Flexner, 29 May 1940: Emergency Committee papers.

[43]On 17 June EKa thought that "the fall of England was imminent"; if the English and French fleets survived, a new campaign might possibly be launched from Canada: to Felix Hepner: Hepner papers 1206/1/14/6.

[44]Kantorowicz to Hepner, 4 January 1940: Hepner papers 1206/1/14/3. Albert L. Hurtado, "False Accusations: Herbert Bolton, Jews, and the Loyalty Oath at Berkeley," *California History* 89 (2012):, 38–56, absolves Herbert Bolton, the chairman who hired EKa, of antisemitism.

[45]The following account of EKa's activities on behalf of his mother depends primarily on letters to Felix Hepner of 15 August 1939, and 4 January, 16 March, and 17 June 1940, as well as a carbon copy of a letter from Hepner's daughter in Zürich to EKa of 8 March 1940: Hepner papers 1206/1/14/2–6.

[46]*Chronik von Malente-Gremsmühlen* (Husum, 2008), 105. (EKa was in Posen on 1 December 1935. In a postcard of that date to Vera Pietrkowski he called the trip a "family outing": Lerner archive. There may have been macabre humor in the description, for Beate Salz believed that he went to Posen to bring back his father's remains from the Holstein property, which had just been sold: Salz's written comments are in the Eckhart Grünewald Archive.)

where the Kantorowicz family arms [!] can still be seen over the front door.) Clara then went to live with her daughter Grete in Berlin. (Grete's husband was no longer alive.) When EKa left Germany for England in 1938 he had been forced to leave his mother behind because he lacked the means of obtaining the substantial financial guarantees for her to be issued an entry visa into England or the United States. He intended to support her in Berlin by assigning funds to her from his university pension which he could not draw himself since he was not in Germany.[47] At first this could not be done because the German government discontinued the payments, but he challenged the ruling and in November 1939 the bureaucracy reinstated them and even disbursed the arrears.[48] Thus there was now money for his mother's upkeep, but given the situation of Jews in Germany this obviously was not a long-term solution. In the summer of 1939 he tried to obtain an English visa by means of contacts he had with English officials in Berlin, but bureaucratic obstacles could not be surmounted, and when war came in September that course of action was eliminated.

EKa wrote regularly to his mother, and she to him, but none of these letters are known to survive.[49] But two letters that Clara Kantorowicz wrote to her brother Felix in November and December 1939—written in a cultivated and firm hand—are extant and offer insight into her situation.[50] Jews were placed on reduced rations. Clara wrote that "Ernstl" had sent her a package to supplement her allowances, but that it had been opened and confiscated. Curfews for Jews meant that she was lonely in the evenings because she was living alone. (Grete had died shortly before February 20, 1939.[51]) She would have liked to have listened to the radio, but Jews had been prohibited from owning them. As she wrote, "I am very sorry about this because I enjoyed listening to the concerts. . . . How nice it would be particularly now in the lonely evenings to hear some music—I'm always at home from six in the evening at the latest—I wouldn't feel sooo alone."[52]

Once the English route was cut off, escape via Switzerland became the only possibility. This seemed feasible for a while because Felix was living in Switzerland and could help. In fact he succeeded in getting his sister a visa number,

[47] To Ernst Langlotz, 20 January 1939, referring to Helmut Küpper being granted power of attorney: Langlotz papers.

[48] Helmut Küpper to Kantorowicz, LBI, box 5, folder 3; Felix Hepner, 16 March 1940. It is unclear what Clara lived on until the payments that began in November 1939; her granddaughter Beate Salz reported that her sale of the entire Holstein property in 1935 brought her some income: interview of 28 June 1990.

[49] See letter sent by Clara Kantorowicz to the twin children of her brother, 23 November 1939, in which she laments that "a letter from Ernstl is again due—the last from him came on the tenth" and also tells of letters she received from Boston and New York: Hepner papers 1206/1/13/7. That Clara sent letters to EKa is indicated by Kantorowicz to Soscha Salz, 18 October 1941: LBI, box 5, folder 1.

[50] 30 November 1939, 4 December 1939: Hepner papers 1206/1/13/8, 9.

[51] Gertrud Kantorowicz to Soscha Salz, LBI, box 5, folder 1.

[52] 4 December 1939: "man fühlte nicht sooo allein!"

and he generously agreed to post the exorbitant 10,000 Swiss Franc guarantee (roughly $30,000 today) demanded by the canton of Vaud. The plan was to have Clara live near him until she could move to the United States. (Beate Salz, her granddaughter, was scheduled to become an American citizen in the fall of 1940, and relatives of citizens moved to the top of the list for entry permits.) But there was still the matter of living expenses in Switzerland, especially since no one could be certain about how long Clara would have to stay. Felix could not afford this commitment and EKa's pension could not serve because German marks could not be exported. Thus EKa's American salary alone came into play. (He wrote to Felix that Soscha was unable to contribute—she and her husband had run up debts in order to surmount their own emigration hurdles.) During the winter and spring of 1940 EKa believed that he could pay for his mother's expenses: he was drawing income and hoped to receive a permanent appointment. By March he had already started making payments on account to Felix Hepner. In May everything seemed so certain that Clara shipped some luggage with her clothing to Switzerland in advance of her arrival.

In view of all this it is only surprising that EKa did not raise his voice more in his letter to Flexner, for we have seen that he thought his mother already was in Switzerland, and without a new subvention he would have no income to support her. To move ahead of the chronology, on June 17 he called everything off. By then he had reason to believe that he would gain a new one-year contract, yet that gave no assurance of steady income afterward. Moreover, the German conquest of France had led the United States to limit the entry of refugees, meaning that Clara might have to stay in Switzerland for much longer than first thought. So EKa asked Felix to arrange for shipping his mother's luggage back to Berlin (where he still was able to pay for her), promising that he was not giving up but saying that he needed to see how events would play out before he pursued a specific plan.

Bernard Flexner did rescue EKa. By 29 May it was too late to pursue the option of finding another academic position. Consequently on Monroe Deutsch's recommendation EKa requested Flexner's help in subsidizing a position as "research associate" at Berkeley. As he ended his letter of May 29, he was "compelled to write once more as a petitioner and to raise the unpleasant question whether the Emergency Committee in co-operation with the Oberlaender Trust would be prepared to grant me, once more, the sum allowed to me during the last year."

Flexner had a great liking for him and quickly set the wheels in motion for approving a grant from the committee. That happened in late June.[53] Funds from the Oberlaender Trust never materialized, but Flexner creatively appealed to none other than Sidney M[yer] Ehrman. It is time to explain that Ehrman

[53] Emergency Committee agenda considering application for renewal by Ernst Kantorowicz, 27 June 1940; telegram from Flexner to Deutsch, 28 June 1940: Emergency Committee papers.

was a wealthy San Francisco lawyer whose endowment of a professorship in European history in memory of a deceased son was a token of the interest that he took in Berkeley affairs. Flexner did not know him, but he had a colleague, a banker named Fred M. Stein, who did. Accordingly with Flexner's prompting Stein wrote to Ehrman to inquire "whether some local money [could] be raised" to supplement Kantorowicz's income.[54] Stein apologized for troubling Ehrman when everyone was preoccupied by the world situation but excused himself by saying "this is not personal; this is communal." Ehrman's prompt reply was that he was "heartily in favor" of helping to keep Kantorowicz at Berkeley.[55] He had met him on several occasions, had entertained him at his home, and had found him "delightful." He added that "from all I have heard he is outstanding as a scholar and teacher and has been very popular with his students." Thus he wrote: "Please let me know as soon as you can what funds you will have available and I shall at once go to the bat [*sic*]." Ehrman was barred by university regulations from contributing directly to EKa's income, but he directed that $3,000 from unspent funds from his chair (not yet filled) be combined with the Emergency Committee's $1,200 to produce a respectable total income for a research associateship at Berkeley of $4,200.[56] As a result, EKa could live well enough and even be free for pursuing his own scholarship.

[54] Fred M. Stein to Sidney Ehrman, 7 June 1940: Emergency Committee papers.

[55] Ehrman to Stein, 11 June 1940: Emergency Committee papers.

[56] The full roster of salary payments to Ernst Kantorowicz, compiled in 1950 and now in the Neylan papers in the Bancroft Library, shows an entry of $1,200 for 11 July 1940 and another of $3,000 for 17 July 1940. In the summer term of 1940 EKa did teach the first half of the survey course on Medieval Institutions, but whatever supplemental income he received is not recorded in the roster of payments.

CHAPTER 17

Laudes Regiae

In the course of seeking support for a research associateship in June 1940, Ernst Kantorowicz laid out his agenda. His intention was to publish three books: "1) Burgundian Studies; 2) a book on a liturgical subject; 3) Studies in Mediaeval learning."[1] This was a highly ambitious program, and only one of the three planned books came into being. Yet the rubrics allow us to follow EKa's scholarly engagements from the time of his arrival in the United States until the end of his research year.

The planned "Burgundian Studies" book was a will of the wisp. We have seen that EKa dedicated himself to research on Valois Burgundy from 1936 until 1938 at a time when he was barred from writing on German history. But the only publication that resulted was the spin-off on Roger van der Weyden. Aside from that we know that a second study, "Charles the Bold and the Italian Renaissance," was already finished when he left for America, for he gave it as a lecture at Yale in March 1939. But then he deferred the Burgundy project. In April 1941 he announced his intention to complete "during the summer . . . a work entitled 'Charles the Bold and the Italian Renaissance' which will be a volume of some 150 to 200 pages."[2] Nevertheless, such a volume never appeared.

Although EKa never published the lecture on Charles the Bold it is possible to read a version of it in manuscript. He was parsimonious. After having given the lecture twice (the second time in Berkeley in 1940) he drew it out of his files for delivery in 1960 on the occasion of an exhibition of Flemish art in the Detroit Museum of Art.[3] As he wrote then to his student Michael Cherniavsky, "There is lots of moss grown on it and nobody will recognize it, not even I myself."[4] The surviving manuscript shows that the lecture was

[1] To Herbert Bolton, 7 June 1940: Bolton papers.

[2] Monroe Deutsch to Bernard Flexner, 2 April 1941: Emergency Committee papers.

[3] "The Dukes of Burgundy and the Italian Renaissance," Detroit, 1 November 1960: LBI, box 2, folder 13.

[4] 4 July 1960: Lerner archive. See also Kantorowicz to Leonardo Olschki, 15 September 1960: "the old Burgundy lecture for the exhibition in Detroit," in Anke Dörner, *La vita spezzata: Leonardo Olschki, ein jüdischer Romanist zwischen Integration und Emigration* (Tübingen, 2005), 331–33.

more accessible than many of his others, especially because of its use of slides. It begins with reference to the received view of fifteenth-century aristocratic Burgundian culture as a world of chivalry—of "white unicorns and white palfreys." But while Kantorowicz accepted this for the reign of Philip the Good, he rejected it for that of Philip's son, Charles the Bold. According to his analysis, Charles's reign contrasted with Philip's owing to his ambitious goal of advancing Burgundian dominance on the continent by challenging France on every front, including Italy. To gain influence with various Italian polities, Charles sought the presence of ambassadors: "The ducal court was swamped with Italians." Of these a number were exponents of "Renaissance Humanism." One was Bernardo Bembo, a Venetian rhetorician who stayed at Charles's court for four years. Such men brought with them copies of Roman classics and contemporary Humanist works, helping to shift the culture of Charles's main residence of Brussels away from medieval chivalry. Roman thought contributed in turn to Charles's new ideal of imperialism. In conclusion EKa contrasted a medal of Philip the Good with one of Charles the Bold, the style of the former being "Burgundian or Gothic" and the latter "classical." All told, "It no longer was the colorful splendor of Burgundian chivalry, it was the universal fame and the laurel of Caesars that Charles longed for. And in this longing the doctrine and princes of the Italian Renaissance were his teachers." The piece, uncharacteristically free of technical terminology, but hardly fluff, displays the author's interest in relationships between rhetoric and rulership and advances an original, convincing, and well-documented argument.

The planned "book on a liturgical subject" actually did appear. According to the preface the author had begun the project in Oxford in 1934, and a German version was "ready for the press" in 1936 but "conditions made publication impossible."[5] By the time EKa decided to leave Germany in 1938, he knew that he needed to have articles ready to publish in English. Hence he turned to his liturgical materials and finished a draft of an article he showed to Bowra on his way from England to America that he called his "liturgical song." This would have been one of the "several papers on liturgical subjects" that he listed as part of his research agenda in his memo of February 1939 to Bernard Flexner.[6] It must then have been nearly finished, for when EKa was in Cambridge in March he introduced himself to the Harvard historian of religion, Arthur Darby Nock, with the intention of seeing whether Nock might publish this piece.[7] As for the

[5]Ernst H. Kantorowicz, Laudes Regiae: *A Study of Liturgical Acclamations and Medieval Ruler Worship* (Berkeley, 1946).

[6]To Bernard Flexner, 15 February 1939: Emergency Committee papers.

[7]To Maurice Bowra, 13 March 1939: "I was very successful with your friend Nock as he, probably, is going to publish my liturgical song." This turned out to be an article with a rather more formidable title: "A Norman Finale of the Exultet and the Rite of Sarum," *Harvard Theological Review* 34 (1941): 129–43. The article shows relations to work begun in Oxford in 1934 that later issued into chapter 6 and appendix 2 of the book *Laudes Regiae*. EKa revised the version of the paper that he

other papers on liturgical subjects, the time had come in 1940 for putting them together with what he had already written in German to produce a book in English. EKa worked on this project throughout the second half of 1940, writing new material and translating the old. In December he wrote to Édouard Roditi, a younger friend: "These damned laudes turned out to be much more wearisome than even you and I had expected them to be; they are also much longer than I wanted to have them, about 350 typewritten pages; and the footnotes were more than hell. But I am finished now and turned the book down [*sic*] to the Berkeley Press."[8]

That was in 1940. Before looking at the book, *Laudes Regiae*, itself, we can look to see why it took another six years to come out. In November 1940 EKa asked Frederick Paxson, who had become department chair that year, by letter about publication procedures. Inasmuch as the main question was whether publication by the University of California Press would be feasible (the book's frequent quotations of liturgical acclamations required complicated typesetting), Paxson forwarded EKa's letter to President Sproul. The latter then responded reassuringly to EKa in December. Perhaps wishing to make amends for his peremptory action of the spring, Sproul wrote: "If you do decide to have the book published by our Press, I shall be glad to do everything that I can, personally, to expedite its passage through the machinery."[9]

Initially the book did move along swiftly. EKa submitted it in December; by January 16, 1941, it had been approved for publication by a faculty committee of three historians who oversaw the "University of California Publications in History."[10] But then "the machinery" got jammed. In the spring EKa learned that despite Sproul's earlier assurance, the book was being held up for publication because of the lack of "necessary funds."[11] Sometime thereafter it was determined that because the author was not a permanent member of the Berkeley faculty the book could not be published without an external subvention of

---

submitted to Nock on the basis of useful criticism by George La Piana (Harvard Divinity School), to whom Nock sent the piece for review: Kantorowicz to La Piana, 22 October 1940 (La Piana papers, Andover-Harvard Theological Library). The view taken in the article that the "finale" probably migrated from Sicily to Normandy has now been replaced with the argument that it migrated from Normandy to Sicily: Thomas Forrest Kelly, *The Exultet in Southern Italy* (New York, 1996), 74. Another close relative of *Laudes Regiae* is Kantorowicz's "Ivories and Litanies," *Journal of the Warburg and Courtauld Institutes* 5 (1942): 56–81. The two works even repeat the phrase "have clearly an apotropaeic or exorcizing character" (*Laudes Regiae*, 38; "Ivories, 64"). Kantorowicz worked on this article in the fall of 1941, as can be seen from his presentation of a version of it for the Berkeley Colloquia Orientalia on 26 November. Later he did not deem either "A Norman Finale" or "Ivories and Litanies" important enough to be included in his *Selected Studies*.

[8] 12 December 1940: Roditi papers, box 9: UCLA archives.

[9] 18 December 1940 (the letter refers to Paxson having passed along EKa's letter of November 9): LBI, box 7, folder 2.

[10] From the front matter of *Laudes* Regiae.

[11] To Bernard Flexner, 4 May 1941: Emergency Committee papers.

$1,200 (the equivalent of $16,700 today). EKa wrote of his quandary to Bernard Flexner in June 1942, saying that he was not in a position to "mobilize" such funds and inquiring whether he might be able to receive support from the Carnegie Foundation.[12] Nothing came of that, and internal correspondence within the Emergency Committee, dated August 3, 1942, referred to "Ernst Kantorowicz's need for $1,200." But the committee "did not have such a large sum as that to place at the disposal of any one author."[13] Financial barriers must have continued to comprise the "unfortunate concatenation of circumstances" to which the author delicately referred in the preface to the book that was published in 1946. Since he said nothing about its having been published with a subsidy, it appears as if the author's long-delayed permanent appointment to the rank of full professor did wonders for alleviating "unfortunate circumstances."

Concatenations of a different sort led to the creation of a noteworthy book. EKa knew from his work on Frederick II that the motto "Christus vincit, Christus regnat, Christus imperat" (Christ triumphs! Christ reigns! Christ commands!) appeared on the gold seal of the boy king of Sicily before he reached his maturity.[14] Even though the motto was irrelevant to the thought or policy of the mature emperor, who preferred "Roma caput mundi" for his gold seal, EKa dilated on it in his supplementary volume of 1931.[15] There he mentioned that the same words appeared on coins issued by the Norman kings of Sicily and by Louis IX of France. He also speculated hesitantly about possible origins in Quintilian. The step from the biography to the supplementary volume gives a sense of how Kantorowicz's mind worked. The association of kings with "Christ the ruler" was an aspect of medieval ruler worship, a subject of abiding interest to him. Moreover, the appearance of the slogan on coins of the Norman kings and a French king who had inherited Normandy impinged on a newly developing theme, "The Normans in European History."

Another concatenation stemmed from his belief, expressed picturesquely in KFII, that the Christus vincit triad had been used as a chant accompanying the child Frederick's coronation as king of Sicily. In fact solid evidence for that was lacking, but nonetheless his fascination with Schramm's article of 1930 on coronation liturgies led him to pursue the liturgical use of the triad. As we have seen, he first engaged himself with this in order to offer something appropriate for his hosts in Oxford in 1934. The book of 1946 reports that chapter 6 concerning coronation liturgies in the three "Norman realms" of Sicily, Normandy, and England originated "as a paper to the Mediaeval Society in Oxford presided over by Professor F. M. Powicke." Chapter 6 appeared fittingly toward the end of the published book because it did not deal with the heart of the subject. Instead

[12] 15 June 1942.

[13] Betty Drury to Stephan Duggan, 3 August 1942: Emergency Committee papers.

[14] KFII, 20.

[15] *Ergänzungsband*, 14.

it concentrated on the Norman interrelations, expressing a debt for the underlying idea to Charles Homer Haskins (157, n. 157).[16] It shows how the earliest documented liturgical appearance of the Christus vincit triad in the three Norman lands came from eleventh- and twelfth-century Normandy, where it was chanted on feast days (166). From Normandy it crossed over to England. One of several proofs could be found in a document of 1188: "[clerici] qui cantaverunt *Christus vincit* die Pentecoste ante regem" (clerics who sung *Christus vincit* on Pentecost before the king) (174).

The quoted passage demonstrates that the acclamation now was used to hail the monarch, and EKa went further by pointing out that it became part of the English coronation ritual. He even argued plausibly that the first instance was for the coronation of William the Conqueror on Christmas Day 1066 (178). The Sicilian kingdom takes a back seat in this account but is not entirely missing, for Kantorowicz argues from two pieces of evidence (actually both quite tenuous) that the *laudes* were also used for coronations in twelfth-century Sicily (158, 166). (He did draw back cautiously from the passage found in KFII that the Christus vincit triad was chanted during the coronation of the child Frederick II in Palermo, without referring to his earlier self-confidence [161].) Working on the assumption of twelfth-century Sicilian usage, he felt able to say that the idea would have come from England. Voilà: "The liturgical unity of the three Norman states becomes more and more visible" (179).

We have seen that EKa wrote to Schramm from England in 1934 that his research on the Norman *laudes* was merely incidental and that he did not want to anticipate any of Schramm's own work, but that back in Germany he conceived of writing a book on lauds that contained the Christus vincit triad, some of which belonged to coronation rites and some not. Rather than tracing the evolution further, we may now look at the finished English-language product. The first chapter takes off from the initial Frederick II research by treating the Christus vincit legend on coins. The motto "IC XC NIKA" (Jesus Christ Conquers) had been used on coins by Byzantine emperors since the eighth century and was appropriated in the twelfth by the Norman king, Roger II, who wished to show that he had replaced the Byzantines. This precedent easily led to the full slogan "Christus vincit, Christus regnat, Christus imperat" inscribed on the gold seal of Roger's grandson, the child Frederick II (7–10). Although Frederick, with his ambitions for Roman universality, replaced "Christus vincit" with the motto "Roma caput mundi" when he began to rule on his own, "Christus vincit" migrated elsewhere. Louis IX appropriated it in 1266 for his first gold coinage, and thereafter it appeared on many other French coins as well as those of copy-cat European polities.

Always keen on pointing to implications and ramifications, EKa observed that the motto on French coins played its part in the miraculous cure of the

[16] Relevant page numbers from the book appear in parentheses.

"king's evil." As he had read in Marc Bloch (5, n. 13), French kings sometimes used the coin with "Christus vincit" to "touch" for the cure, implying that they ministered for Christ (5). In late-medieval Cologne the Christus vincit triad was equated with the city's patrons, the "three kings," and in late-medieval Aachen it was altered to "Christus vincit, Christus regnat, Karolus Magnus imperat" to point to the association of Charlemagne with Aachen (2–3). He also found a "well-calculated reference" to the coin device in the fact that Guillaume de Nogaret, the first minister of Philip the Fair, opened his speech of 1308 demanding the suppression of the Knights Templar by intoning the words "Christus vincit, Christus regnat, Christus imperat" (4). A researcher of the twenty-first century would of course resort to cyberspace for retrieving instances, but EKa, with no search engine, found that the triad on French coins was appropriated by John Calvin to "justify military action in the name of Christ." (His reference is to 20, 1, no. 3942, in Calvin's *Opera omnia.*)

As much as EKa delighted in displaying nuggets, he designed his first chapter primarily to score a major historiographical point. Although he might have preferred to demonstrate filiation from coins of Norman Sicily to coins of France, the Sicilian coins ceased being minted in the late twelfth century and the French ones started being minted more than half a century later. But Kantorowicz found that the Christus vincit triad was so widely known in the twelfth century in regions distant from Sicily that it had become material for parody. An example was a passage from the French satirist Walter of Châtillon on the power of money: "Nummus vincit, nummus regnat, nummus imperat" (6). Certainly Walter of Châtillon and others who wrote similarly were not studying inscriptions on Sicilian coins. So how did this happen? EKa's answer was that "it was not the coin, but the litany which must be considered the source of these jests" (7). More specifically, a Gallo-Frankish liturgical acclamation began with the words "Christus vincit, Christus regnat, Christus imperat" (9). Kantorowicz's use of numismatics for insights into the history of medieval rulership was sufficiently new, but his turning to liturgy was even more so. As he wrote in the preface to *Laudes Regiae*, the evaluation of liturgical sources, then "in its first phase" (viii), needed to be cultivated; historians should no longer "deal cheerfully with the history of mediaeval thought and culture without ever opening a missal" (ix).

Most of *Laudes Regiae* deals with the central liturgical occurrences of "Christus vincit." Although EKa offered some of his findings in his German book of 1936, he wrote the two crucial chapters (2 and 3) in Berkeley in 1940. Essential for their composition had been his ability to examine original liturgical manuscripts when he was in Paris early in 1938 as well as his "extravagant use" of Berkeley's Inter-Library Loan services (xi). Seeking the origins of the Christus vincit triad, EKa first raised the possibility of a connection between classical rhetoric and Christian liturgy. Quintilian was intriguing: he wrote of the rhetorical power of clauses that omit conjunctions by means of the example "hic regnat, hic imperat, hic sola [scil. eloquentia] vincit" (22). But EKa thought it improbable "that an early liturgist should have drawn on Quintilian's work" (23). Perhaps the combination of the verbs *regnare*, *imperare*, and *vincere* was sufficiently well known for a liturgist to have drawn on it, but even that seemed far-fetched. Instead, EKa proposed that the ultimate source for what he was seeking lay in East Roman secular acclamations, for "it is more likely that the liturgical tricolon originated in the crowds in the Byzantine theater, circus, or streets, rather than in the studio of a liturgist who checked Quintilian's *Institutio oratoria*" (28).

We need not follow the skein of details by which the author moved from Byzance to place the first western lauds in Carolingian Francia and date them to between 751 and 774 (54). It need only be emphasized that the significance of this location and dating was very great. It meant that the lauds, chanted in the liturgy to acclaim the ruler, originated as part of a Carolingian program of ruler worship—a program meant to enhance the legitimacy of a new royal dynasty by ceremonial anointment and the casting of the monarch as a new David. If Christ "conquered, reigned, and commanded," he evidently was Christ the King, and intoning the words during a coronation ceremony implicitly allowed the ruler to assume the mantle of Christian kingship. Here is Kantorowicz's thesis statement: "[T]he laudes are among the earliest Western political documents in which the attempt was made to establish in the secular-political, as well as in the ecclesiastical, sphere a likeness of the City of God. The mediaeval equivalent of ancient ruler worship is the liturgical homage to the ruler. We may safely call it the 'Mediaeval Ruler Cult'" (62). Kantorowicz drew on the specialized bibliography of "liturgiology" for the purposes of writing history and was one of the earliest historians to do so.[17]

The remaining central chapters of *Laudes Regiae* (3 and 4) treat with deep learning the various occasions and contexts in which the lauds were sung in the Frankish and German realms, and then the ecclesiastical occasions—acclamations to bishops and popes. Emphasizing interplays in installation and coronation ceremonies between secular and spiritual realms, Kantorowicz wrote of "papal laudes imperialized" and "imperial laudes papalized." The reign of Innocent III saw the "imperial pope" gaining supremacy over the German emperor even from the liturgical point of view (144–45). Chapter 4 closes with a strong statement concerning periodization: Christ conceived of as king had once supported the prestige of the monarch, but by the end of the Romanesque age (roughly the early thirteenth century) a new image of Christ began to prevail—"more human and intimate . . . by no means imperial or royal" (146). As the author concluded: "[T]he triumphant phrases of *Christus vincit,*

[17] But a cluster of superb medievalists of the same generation were aware of one another's work. See Schramm, "Die Ordines" (as cited in chap. 12, n. 42, above); Gert Tellenbach, "Römischer und christlicher Reichsgedanke in der Liturgie des frühen Mittelalters," *Sitzungsberichte der Heidelberger Akademie der Wissenschaften*, 1934, Abhandlung I, and Carl Erdmann, "Die Entstehung des Kreuzzugsgedankens (Stuttgart, 1935), 326–35.

Christus regnat, Christus imperat lost their substance and became unreal too. They fell into oblivion or were used as magic words. . . . [A]s a consequence the whole performance of singing the ancient laudes to the ruler was to be discarded" (146). Readers familiar with *The King's Two Bodies* will recognize this periodization of "Christ-Centered Kingship."

Laudes Regiae ends with a satyr play. The final chapter, "The Laudes in Modern Times," points out how recent popes and dictators had begun to require their congregations to sing the old songs, "somewhat like a caricature of a former life" (180). For example, the lauds appeared in a Fascist hymnbook: "*Christus vincit, Christus regnat, Christus imperat* . . . DUCI BENITO MUSSOLINI italicae gentis gloriae, pax, vita, et salus perpetua" (186). In March 1939 the newly installed Pius XII smiled from his balcony as the throng below broke into an "old, and yet new, chant" (185). We can picture EKa reading the following in the *New York Times* in his small room in the Hotel Paris on March 3, 1939, and saving it for future use: "Suddenly and apparently spontaneously the whole crowd was singing. The noble notes of the hymn with the chorus *Christus vincit, Christus regnat, Christus imperat* rolled up to the sky with an intensity and volume of sound that moved even skeptical observers" (185, n. 223).

Despite its disconnected genesis, *Laudes Regiae* is well organized. Chapters proceed directionally. Another compositional strength lies in clear-cut statements about major points. But from the literary point of view esotericism is a problem. While proposing to offer a case for a neglected category of source material to make it seem less "a magic thicket of prayers, benedictions, and ecclesiastical rites" (vii), Kantorowicz leaves a thicket with brambles. Aside from his Latin title, he presents untranslated Latin at length (sometimes to the extent of complete pages) and also includes some untranslated Greek. Chapter 2 opens with a quotation in French from a fin de siècle poet, Rémy de Gourmont, to express a point that the author then proceeds to discount. Particularly challenging is the proliferation of undefined technical terms: "asyndetic clauses," "doxological phrases" "praeconium," "Déesis group," and "*euphemia* of the basileus." Readers would have had to go to an unabridged dictionary or scratched their heads. EKa might have explained that "tricolon" denotes a sentence composed of three clearly defined parts, usually independent clauses, such as "we cannot dedicate, we cannot consecrate, we cannot hallow this ground." By using "tricolon" and "triad" interchangeably, he implicitly strengthened his point about "the close connection between rhetoric and liturgy." But by assuming his audience was as learned as he was, he was wrapping himself in his esoteric "second manner," hardly appropriate for his colleagues in the Berkeley History Department and indeed most other groundlings.

A review of the book, written by an excellent medieval intellectual historian, F. Edward Cranz, appeared in *Speculum*.[18] This opened by announcing

[18] *Speculum* 22 (1947): 648–51.

Kantorowicz's "double contribution": "Not only has he clarified many of the obscure points in the history of a particular liturgical form . . . but he has also used this history to throw light on more general political and ecclesiastical developments." From there Cranz engaged in sure-footed summary and occasional demurrer before concluding that *Laudes Regiae* "show[ed] what rich results the liturgy yields when it is interpreted with the insight of a great historian." Later, in 1959, on the occasion of a reprinting, one of Germany's most prominent medievalists, Herbert Grundmann, reviewed it for the *Historische Zeitschrift* and praised it lavishly.[19] Grundmann was delighted about Kantorowicz's "astounding judiciousness and resourcefulness," his "comprehensive knowledge of disparate sources and secondary literature," and his "critical acumen and perceptive understanding." According to him, Kantorowicz proceeded "as if with a divining rod through what at first sight seems monotone but is really polyphonic, observing from where and why each liturgical sequence occurs and what political and cultural changes each one points to."

Probably most gratifying to EKa was a communication he received from Percy Ernst Schramm, whose work of 1930 had showed him the way:

> You have assembled so much that there can scarcely be addenda. Absolutely overwhelming is your exposition of how the laudes and the litanies were interrelated, how this stood in contrast to both antiquity and Byzantium, and how an independent tradition developed in Rome. No one will be able to doubt the origin of the laudes in the Frankish realms. For me it is particularly important that again and again you emphasize their character as a political declaration: as the State becomes visible in images, so it becomes audible in the laudes.[20]

And yet the book never became very well known, nor did Kantorowicz's claims for the importance of the liturgy ever make as great an impact on scholarship as his later use of legal sources did. In an article on "The Anglo-Norman Laudes Regiae" of 1981, H.E.J. Cowdrey lamented that "liturgical sources do not receive from historians the attention that is their due."[21] Committed scholars will continue to read Kantorowicz's *Laudes Regiae* with admiration, but most medieval historians still "deal cheerfully with the history of mediaeval thought and culture without ever opening a missal."

The projected volume to be called "Studies in Mediaeval Learning" would have lacked the continuity found in *Laudes Regiae* had it ever appeared. This is evident from the list of titles that EKa specified to Bernard Flexner in February 1939—"that he had not been able to publish in Germany" and that he wanted to prepare for an English-language audience. The three that he did produce were a study on the Bolognese rhetorician Guido Faba, another called "Anonymi

[19] *Historische Zeitschrift* 188 (1959): 116–19.

[20] 14 August 1947: Schramm papers.

[21] *Viator* 12 (1981): 39–81, at 39.

'Aurea Gemma,'" and a third listed in the letter to Flexner as "On the Transformation of the Nature of Time in the Thirteenth Century."

The point of departure for the article concerning the thirteenth-century rhetorician Guido Faba was a manuscript discovery Kantorowicz had made in the library of New College when he was in Oxford in 1934. In a letter of April 2, 1941, from Monroe Deutsch to Flexner reporting on what Kantorowicz had accomplished during that academic year, Deutsch states: "The medieval history [journal] 'Speculum' has in press an article of his entitled "Guido Faba's Years of Training."[22] The expression "in press" may have come from EKa and may have come from a misunderstanding of the English usage, for the editor of *Speculum* declined to publish the article in August.[23] But in June 1942 he was able to write to Flexner that his article, "An Autobiography of Guido Faba," was soon to be "born" in *Mediaeval and Renaissance Studies*,[24] and it was indeed published in that journal in 1943.

EKa probably first became aware of Guido Faba as a result of his work on rhetoricians for KFII and candidly admitted in his article that "[he] was not a man of genius." The article first laid out Faba's tenuous claim to fame as a rhetorician and then reviewed the sparse biographical data. Kantorowicz's contribution was to revise the data for the earlier part of Faba's career on the basis of an autobiographical section he found in a prologue to a rhetorical treatise. (EKa appended an edition of the text.) Most likely the editors of *Speculum* rejected the piece because it lacked general interest. Placing the word "autobiography" in the title made it potentially more interesting, but the alteration was merely cosmetic, for Kantorowicz was indifferent to treating the brief autobiography as a rare specimen of the genre.[25]

The article is noteworthy for its learned pyrotechnics. Fava's prologue is written in frightfully difficult periphrastic and allusive prose, and one marvels at how Kantorowicz deciphers it. For example, he coyly considers its reference to working in a smithy as perhaps implying some punning on *faba* and *faber* (smith) before rejecting that to demonstrate by means of an exquisite erudite reference that "smithy" was Bolognese student slang for the study of law. EKa's soon-to-be good friend Lynn White wrote in appreciation: "You had told me that there was some nice detective work in it, but the article exceeded all expectations."[26] Rita Copeland observes that Kantorowicz's decoding "rivals the

[22] Emergency Committee papers.

[23] Samuel Hazard Cross to George Lee Haskins, 5 August 1941: Benson papers, box 20. (Jost Phillip Klenner located this letter.)

[24] 15 June 1942: Emergency Committee papers.

[25] See now Rita Copeland, "Medieval Intellectual Biography: The Case of Guido Faba," in *Through a Classical Eye*, ed. Andrew Galloway and R.F. Yeager, 110–24 (Toronto, c. 2009).

[26] 3 January 1944: LBI, box 7, folder 5. (It is noteworthy that Kantorowicz, who saved few incoming letters not needed for bureaucratic reasons, saved this one.)

most arcane exercises of Arthur Conan Doyle."[27] Yet the empirical results consist only in revised biographical data concerning a limited period in the life of a Bolognese rhetorician of no great importance.

Related to the article on Guido Faba is "*Anonymi 'Aurea Gemma,'*" published in 1943. EKa's penchant for esoteric titles here is at its extreme. "*Laudes Regiae*" at least was followed by an explanatory subtitle, whereas "*Anonymi 'Aurea Gemma'*" has no subtitle and gives hardly any inkling of the subject matter. (EKa would do this again with "Christus-Fiscus" and—Pelion on Ossa—"ΣΥΝΘΡΟΝΟΣ ΔΙΚΗΙ.") If one is tempted to read this piece one learns that it intends to prove that the ascription to a certain Henricus Francigena of a twelfth-century Bolognese rhetorical treatise, *Aurea Gemma* (Golden Gem), is incorrect. This may be EKa's most egregiously old-fashioned scholarly article, almost bizarrely so for a man who a decade before had railed against the "Bonzen." It begins by showing that prologues are often separated in manuscripts from the works they were meant to introduce, then it offers a *stemma* of four manuscripts to clarify filiations, and it concludes that *Aurea Gemma* was written by "Anonymous." Five appendices carry editions. Aside from technical proficiency, all that separates this piece from the desiccated is the florid prose. Here is a specimen: "The reader was led, so to speak, through the peristyle of a solemn and beautifully couched preface, in which the secret of the allegorical title was disclosed, before he was to approach the shrine of Eloquence on whose altar, of course, he would find nothing but the arid and bony rules of the *dictamen prosaicum*" (254). It is worth noting that EKa liked both "Guido Faba" and "*Anonymi 'Aurea Gemma'*" well enough to indicate at the end of his life that they should be included in his *Selected Studies*.

The paper listed in the letter to Flexner of 1939, "On the Transformation of the Nature of Time in the Thirteenth Century," was of an entirely different order. The first American version that dates back originally to Kantorowicz's planned book on the German Interregnum was the talk EKa gave at Harvard in March 1939: "The Idea of Permanency and Progress in the Thirteenth Century."[28] Then, in late December 1939, EKa gave a reduced version of the Harvard paper at the annual convention of the Pacific Coast branch of the American Historical Association held at UCLA. Because this talk was limited to twenty minutes it was streamlined and "Progress" was deleted from the title. As in the case of the Harvard version, the manuscript survives and permits us to see transformations. Probably because the talk was meant for an audience of historians in all fields, it captures attention by positing two larger claims to significance. One is methodological. Kantorowicz proposes that developments in philosophy and theology can have bearing on political and constitutional history. The second concerns the origins of nation states. The presupposition behind the concept of

[27] Copeland, "Medieval Intellectual Biography," 110, 114.

[28] The following two paragraphs depend on my "Kantorowicz and Continuity," 116–17.

the nation-state is that nations or peoples can have a permanent political existence apart from the life of a king. This became ever more explicit in thirteenth-century political practice. Tying his propositions together in the body of his short paper, Kantorowicz establishes the realities of the new political practice and then proposes to account for them with reference to thirteenth-century philosophical and theological discussions about time, especially the scholastic concept of *aevum*—infinite duration.

The initial footnote of the Pacific Coast paper refers to "the generous offer" of the editor of the *Pacific Historical Review* to publish the spoken presentation substantially as it was delivered. But it could not be published without footnotes. So EKa worked on plugging in the notes in the spring; then he sent the article to the editor of the *Pacific Historical Review*, one Louis K. Koontz, around the end of May. But Koontz (the author of a monograph on *The Virginia Frontier, 1754–1763*) indicated in a letter of June 6 that he would not be honoring his offer.[29] As he said, "With the crowding amount of material on the Far West and the Pacific Area that we now have on hand, it does not seem possible in the immediate future to use in the *Review* your interesting paper." Despite these diplomatic words, it seems more likely that editor Koontz looked quickly at the manuscript and concluded that since it bristled with Latin technical terminology and distinctions between timelessness and endlessness it had no place in a journal that featured the Far West and the Pacific Area. But the pages he rejected were to become with little change part of one of the most applauded historiographical works of the twentieth century. EKa put the Pacific Coast paper aside once he decided to devote his energies to *Laudes Regiae* and returned to it when writing *The King's Two Bodies.*

[29] 6 June 1940: LBI, box 2, folder 11.

CHAPTER 18

Fight for Employment

Ernst Kantorowicz, earlier a full professor at Frankfurt, had to struggle for employment at Berkeley from the winter of 1939 until the spring of 1945. We have seen that he wrote in June 1939, "the Pacific salmon at last rose to the bait." But subsequently the salmon kept wriggling. For three successive academic years Kantorowicz faced unemployment until he was rescued at the last minute by one-year appointments. For the academic year 1943–44 the salmon actually wriggled off the hook: EKa did not even gain a one-year appointment but supported himself by teaching for the army. In 1944–45 came another one-year appointment at Berkeley, but this one was made on the presumption that he would then move a year later into the chair of William A. Morris. That was no guarantee, but in May 1945 Kantorowicz finally reeled in his salmon with news of the award of a tenured full professorship.

"The perils of Ernst" begin with a letter from Monroe Deutsch to Bernard Flexner of April 2, 1941.[1] Deutsch reported that "on conferring with the President on Monday it became clear that there was no possibility for the appointment of Dr. Kantorowicz for the coming year on the University budget. This is, I assure you, a source of very deep regret to me as well as to the President, since we have a very high regard for him as a scholar and a man." As Deutsch observed, "While to be sure Dr. Kantorowicz's appointment was but for the year, it was clear that he entertained hopes that he would be reappointed." Nevertheless, President Sproul's decision was firm. Thus Deutsch "[hoped] that the grant made him for 1940–41 [by the Emergency Committee] may be renewed for the year 1941–42." Matters then moved swiftly in EKa's favor. Deutsch received an agreement from Sidney Ehrman to authorize an allotment for him from the Ehrman funds that still were lying fallow, and the Emergency Committee came through on April 16 with a grant of the same amount as the year before.

Although EKa was provided for (he was made "lecturer in history" with an income of $3,000) he felt it proper in early May to write to Flexner as follows: "I admit that this solution is very welcome to me. Nevertheless I cannot quite

[1] Emergency Committee Papers.

conceal my disappointment. Things should have turned out more favorably for me at this university. The deadlock, however, which hampered my permanent appointment last year, is practically unchanged." [2] He then went on to note that the Ehrman Professorship was the only vacancy but was not available for him: he had garnered the information that it was likely to be conferred, starting the year after, on "a scholar of Modern History who will not be elected from this campus." (This was an allusion to the imminent appointment of Raymond J. Sontag, on which more later.) He thought that Frederick Paxson, his department chair, and Monroe Deutsch wanted to retain him until another professorship fell vacant, implicitly the professorship of Morris, who at the time was sixty-six. Yet EKa was uncomfortable with that because it meant depending on Emergency Committee funds. As he wrote with dignity, "[Y]ou may believe me that I greatly dislike the idea of remaining a burden to my friends instead of earning my livelihood. After all, I am not that incapable, neither corporally nor intellectually, and there is no reason why the Emergency Committee should be doomed to support me for another year." He had in the meantime "finished a book on the relationships between mediaeval liturgy and politics," but for the last five months it had just been sitting at the press. He hoped to write much more so that he might be more saleable, but his reappointment came with teaching duties that would necessarily limit his scholarly output. To which he added that "all our plans may be upset by the political events in Europe and their reflections in this country. [The Germans had just taken Yugoslavia and Greece.] I am quite prepared to become a soldier once more."

The war situation in Europe was particularly grim for EKa because his mother was still in Berlin. After the fiasco of the previous spring, the new plan was to have Clara Kantorowicz travel immediately via Switzerland and France to Lisbon, and thence directly or indirectly to the United States. Travel costs and bureaucratic fees would be enormous. Hence EKa wrote to Clara's brother Felix in March and then again in April to return the money he had sent him the year before.[3] The second request was urgent: Felix should send back the money "as soon as possible" (underlined), as it was "bitterly needed." From the spring to the fall of 1941 EKa and Soscha (who now was able to offer some financial contribution) were engaged in trying to manage a rescue. Aside from finding the cash, they faced bureaucratic hurdles posed by the U. S. government on the grounds that immigrants might be Gestapo spies.[4] Then new hurdles were raised in July: in response to the U.S. government's ordering of the closing of all German consulates, the German government reciprocated by demanding the closing of U.S. consulates. This made gaining a visa possible only by going

[2] 4 May 1941: Emergency Committee papers.

[3] 16 March 1941, 24 April 1941: Hepner papers, 1206/1/14/8, 9.

[4] For U.S. immigration policy in this period, David S. Wyman, *Paper Walls: America and the Refugee Crisis, 1938–1941*, 2nd ed. (New York, 1985).

to another country first, or, as EKa hoped, perhaps by application to the U.S. Embassy. Added to all this was the fact that Clara was no longer capable of traveling alone; arrangements had to be made for her to travel with her cousin by marriage, Gertrud Kantorowicz, who also was still in Berlin.

Inquiries were being sent to the State Department and forms were being filled out when suddenly in the autumn of 1941 the situation of the Jews in Germany took a dreadful turn for the worse. In September they were required to wear the yellow star. They also were forbidden to board public transportation vehicles until all non-Jews had boarded first, and they were forced to stand if all seats were taken. Most frighteningly, *Aufbau*, the Jewish-German newspaper published in America, reported that Jews in some German cities were being deported to the East.[5] EKa and Soscha now went into emergency mode. In mid-October they spoke to each other on the long-distance telephone (the first time they had heard each other's voices since the summer of 1939).[6] Then EKa telegraphed a contact from the George circle, Silvio Markees, who was living in Basel: "Lacking funds. Swiss journey almost impossible, but Visa USA perhaps available through embassy. Please inquire publisher [Helmut Küpper] and cable answer whether mother Gertrud affected by new measures." Around the same time a telegram reached EKa from Zürich, where friends of Gertrud Kantorowicz were working on her behalf: "Gertrud needs guarantee 20,000 Francs at Swissbank can Lisel Pietakowsky procure them please wire Zürich GREIGTUSTR 22." Although he was a master at deciphering medieval rhetorical codes, EKa was baffled by the address and wrote to his sister on 18 October: "GREIGTUSTR is definitely garbled. Do you have any notion of what this could mean?" Still, he telegraphed "Greigtustrasse 22" to say: "Are doing our best." In fact the name was cipher for Freigutstrasse ("G" for Gertrud replacing "F" and the "TU" reversed).

"Lisel Pietakowsky" was EKa's second cousin Elise Pietrkowski (née Kantorowicz). She was the widow of Edmund Pietrkowski, a lawyer who had risen to become a member of the board of IG Farben before being dismissed as a Jew and moving to Zürich, where he died in 1936. Since Edmund had maintained business relationships with Emil Barell, the director of the Zürich pharmaceutical firm Hoffmann-La Roche, there was some reason to suppose that Elise had money. But she had spent most of what she had to pay for travel in the summer of 1941 from Zürich through France to Lisbon to Havana (for bureaucratic reasons the only route for her to enter the United States), and thence to Berkeley. Thus EKa wrote to his sister: "I called Lisel immediately, who naturally also didn't have the money, but immediately wrote to Barell [he had emigrated to New York in 1940] whether he could take over the guarantee."

[5] *Aufbau*, 3 October 1941, headline story: "Schwere Tage in Deutschland."
[6] The following paragraph depends on EKa to Soscha Salz, 18 October 1941: LBI, box 5, folder 1.

EKa wrote four letters to Soscha during the fall of 1941 regarding their efforts to rescue their mother, not counting additional telegrams.[7] During this time they could read in *Aufbau* such headlines (in German) as "The Expulsions in the Reich" (October 24) and "Deportations Continue" (October 31). Details in this correspondence extend to many names of relatives and friends who might help (Barell did not), as well as specifications about bureaucratic requirements, potential travel routes, and, above all, sums of money for fees, guarantees, and travel and living expenses. On October 18 EKa wrote: "With regard to the other $500 I can only contribute a part; I can't raise it all. I can borrow 200 dollars from the bank, but then don't know how I could have money ready for Mama's stay in Havana, and for the long and expensive trip from Havana. If you could make $300 and the bond available, that would open a possibility. But I am completely at the end of my finances. . . . Moreover the future [for me] all seems so uncertain that I can't be without a reserve, which I don't currently have."

When the question arose of Soscha contributing to costs necessary for the trip of Gertrud Kantorowicz (a close friend), EKa wrote in the next letter: "For the time being neither you nor I can take part in this action financially because we'll both need all available funds for Mama, and I'm absolutely against fragmenting your means and mine instead of using them for *one* purpose, namely Mama." Since Gertrud was a well-known personality, a poetess who had been a protégée of Stefan George and mistress of Georg Simmel, he added with painful frankness: "Many more people are interested in Gertrud, understandably, than in Mama. . . . That even to me Gertrud's passage appears objectively more important than that of a woman of 80 years, you may believe. But please hold on to what you have only for Mama. You will need it."

EKa never stopped emphasizing the priorities. On December 3 he wrote: "If you have money available for [Gertrud] (and by this I mean not such as is necessary for Mama, that is to say, not YOUR personal money) then it would be easiest to give this too to the 'Joint' [The American Jewish Joint Distribution Committee]. I'll let you know as soon as I know myself. For Gertrud it will always be easier to raise money than for Mama. And we will still need a lot more for her." He learned, for example, that "the boat travel from Lisbon to Cuba costs $450 at the minimum. They say though that if one takes a higher class, that costs about $600 and more, the journey would not only be more comfortable but one would be more likely to get a place. But considering what will come after that it will be hard to afford this easing for Mama." Even expenses for communicating between Berkeley and Columbus, Ohio, were adding up: "I had a telephone bill of over 50 dollars [$765 today] and paid $30 cash for telegraphing. I can't sustain this much longer, just as little as you." But at least Clara was sending telegrams from Berlin proving that she had not been deported. EKa's

[7] After 18 October come letters of 23 October, early November (undated), and 3 December: all LBI, box 5, folder 1.

letter of December 3 is the last in the series. He ended it by saying, "I would be glad if once in our lives we had written such long letters about more pleasant things." The correspondence ends there because in December news trickled in that the German government had banned legal exit in October.[8]

To return to EKa's employment problems, during the spring of 1942 the question arose again: would he be rehired? The decision rested with President Sproul. A story about him was recounted by Wallace Stegner: "Once a visitor came into his office for an appointment and heard Bob's voice booming away in the inner office. 'Sit down,' the secretary said, 'he'll just be a few minutes, he's talking to New York.' 'It seems so,' says the visitor, 'but why doesn't he use the telephone?'"[9] Booming-voiced Bob was an energetic and efficient administrator yet one who always looked at his account books and ruled by his rule book.

This time he moved early to absolve Berkeley of any responsibility for Kantorowicz's future. In March he wrote to Frederic Paxson that although he would "welcome an arrangement which would keep Dr. Ernst Kantorowicz on the campus," he was not certain that he would be able to offer him any appointment.[10] As he summed up his position: "I should be glad to have Dr. Kantorowicz stay as long as he wants to, provided his salary comes from some source other than our general funds and provided he understands fully that we are not incurring an obligation, either legal or moral, by retaining him." Paxson would have understood that the situation differed from that of the previous two years because the Ehrman chair had been filled. Raymond J. Sontag, hired away from Princeton, had taken the chair in the fall, leaving no surplus from the allotted funds.

That left the Emergency Committee, and Kantorowicz's friends swung into action for him in May, before the annual decision making in June. Monroe Deutsch wrote to Stephen Duggan requesting a renewal of the grant that Kantorowicz had been given for the previous three years.[11] Duggan replied by asking whether any additional funds might be available and whether there was any chance of a permanent appointment, to which Deutsch was forced to answer that "at this time no additional funds are in sight," and that "at a time of financial stringency it is impossible to predict permanence of appointment for him."[12]

Not wishing to leave everything to Deutsch, EKa wrote to Bernard Flexner to give a full account of his situation and to ask for Flexner's vote.[13] He apologized for "the all too well known petition" but added, "I simply do not know

[8] Wyman, *Paper Walls*, 205.

[9] Wallace Stegner, *Angle of Repose* (New York, 1971), 195.

[10] 14 March 1942: LBI, box 7, folder 2.

[11] Letter of 7 May 1942, mentioned in Duggan to Deutsch, 11 May 1942: Emergency Committee papers.

[12] Duggan to Deutsch, 11 May 1942; Deutsch to Duggan, 20 May 1942: Emergency Committee papers.

[13] 15 June 1942: Emergency Committee papers. By the time EKa wrote this letter a positive decision had already been made: see Flexner to Kantorowicz, 2 July 1942: LBI, box 7, folder 2.

what else I can do in the present moment." Aside from the fact that the Ehrman funds were no longer available, the new wartime situation meant that the federal government was curtailing funds to the University of California. The war added another complication in his own case, for he was now listed as an "enemy alien," a classification that made it impossible for him to be considered for a permanent appointment. Reckoning with the possibility of becoming unemployed, he said that he "tried to volunteer and join the army because I thought I could be useful in a staff. But being an enemy alien, I am not entitled to volunteer." He also looked into "other defense work" but was "barred for the same reason." Thus, as he wrote with quiet eloquence, "although I do not consider it very satisfactory to be the civilization for which others fight, I see no way to playing any active role in this war." Kantorowicz assured Flexner that much as he liked Berkeley he was not committed to staying; he intended to do all he could to find another position that would free him from having to rely on the Emergency Committee. He was even planning to travel to the meeting of the American Historical Association to be held that winter in Baltimore. But meanwhile he could only conclude by asking Flexner "to intercede once more with the Emergency Committee on [his] behalf."

Once more the vote was favorable, but the maximum grant remained $1,200, less than half of what EKa had been making the previous year. Given that $1,200 in 1942 amounted to about $16,000 today and that EKa had written to his sister the previous fall that he was "completely at the end of his finances," it is clear that the Emergency Committee grant by itself was barely satisfactory. EKa's chairman, Paxson, apparently recognized that by appealing to Sproul for a supplement of $800. The response is lost, but a second letter by Paxson indicates that Sproul had dismissed an appeal based on "human considerations." Paxson answered with polite force. It was not "human considerations" he had in mind but the best interests of the institution: "In Kantorowicz we have on the campus a man of recognized competence in the field of Mediaeval History. . . . I have been, and I continue to be, of the opinion that Kantorowicz would buttress the field with dignity and strength. There will never be many large classes in Mediaeval History, or many advanced students qualified for the study. With a promise of continuity, however, I believe that he would build up a respectable and intelligent following."[14]

It seems unlikely that Sproul would have yielded had Paxson not been able to recruit a powerful ally: Raymond J. Sontag, a man much to be reckoned with. Berkeley's hiring of Sontag for the Ehrman chair had been a coup. Previously he had taught at Princeton for seventeen years, rising in 1939 to become Henry Charles Lea Professor of History and chairman of the department. Later Berkeley would recruit professors from the Ivy League frequently, but in 1941 this was a rarity. Sontag had all-around strengths. He was well-published and highly

[14] 27 June 1942: Bancroft Library, President's papers.

visible in his prestigious field, modern European diplomatic history. He also was articulate and a man of great presence, qualities that made him a superb lecturer. Not least, as his elevation to the chairmanship at Princeton indicates, he could be counted on to engage in departmental and university affairs. Unlike his predecessor, James Westfall Thompson, who in effect had come to Berkeley to draw a huge salary and retire, Sontag, forty-four at the time of his appointment, was in his prime. Sproul understood that he had come to Berkeley to stay and was unlikely to cross him.

"Ray" Sontag immediately became a supporter of Ernst Kantorowicz in whom he recognized quality. Thus he marshalled his persuasive powers in writing to Sproul on the same day as Paxton.[15] He began by insisting that "the middle ages and the renaissance are the essential foundation for the study of later European History. It is impossible for an institution to be really strong in European history without this foundation." But Berkeley at present was lacking distinction in the medieval field. He acknowledged that Paul Schaeffer was a fine teacher but noted that "he has not fulfilled his undoubted scholarly promise." He neglected to mention William Morris, perhaps because Morris was limited to English constitutional history, or because he was soon to retire. Sontag refrained from overselling. He granted that "an exile should not be kept on unless he is clearly much better than any available American scholar." In principle one should look over the entire field before making a choice. But this route was not presently viable for Berkeley, and Kantorowicz was already there. In Kantorowicz's favor were the facts that "his scholarship has won international recognition; his knowledge has an unusually wide range, extending through the renaissance; [and] his special field, medieval intellectual history, is the most important and most difficult." Therefore he concluded: "If possible, he should be given the full professorship he deserves. But even the present set up is better than losing the one man here who is nationally known as an able scholar in an essential field. If we cannot buy the top man available in the country, we should certainly keep Kantorowicz in one way or another."

What was Sproul to do? Clearly he had little choice other than to write to Paxson: "In the light of your letter of June 27 and a letter of the same date from Professor Sontag, I am willing to recommend and to justify an appropriation of $800 from University funds toward a salary for Professor Kantorowicz for the academic year 1942–43."[16] Thus the third fight for a one-year continuation was won.

Before we turn to the fourth installment, we may report the awful story of the final years of Clara and Gertrud Kantorowicz.[17] Gertrud was intrepid. In the

[15] 27 June 1942: http://www.regiesey.com.

[16] Sproul to Paxson, 30 June 1942: LBI, box 7, folder 2.

[17] I depend primarily on Angela Rammstedt, "'Wir sind des Gottes der begraben stirbt . . .': Gertrud Kantorowicz und der nationalsozialistische Terror," *Simmel Newsletter* 6 (1996): 135–77.

spring of 1942 she engineered a plan to cross into Switzerland illegally, leading a brigade comprising herself and four other women. The youngest was sixty-three, Gertrud was sixty-five, and EKa's mother, "Tante Clärchen," was eighty. The troop managed to travel without their yellow stars and with forged documents from Berlin to the Swiss border near Bregenz. There they waited in a small town for a prearranged signal under a dubious pretext ("vacationing") for several weeks while their ration cards were expiring. A French general had recently escaped from German imprisonment into Switzerland in the same general area, and the border was being heavily patrolled. Finally the signal came on May 6, 1942, that the elderly ladies could cross at night with some guides supplied by Gertrud's contacts. But only one crossed safely while the other four were caught. Of these one immediately swallowed poison and another was transported to "the East," never to be heard from again. The remaining two were Gertrud and Tante Clärchen. Transported from camp to camp, they ultimately were taken back to Berlin where Gertrud so impressed some Gestapo officers with her cool dignity that they decided to bend the rules: although the women were "criminals" and should accordingly have been punished by shipment to the East, it was decided to send them to the "privileged" prison-city of Theresienstadt.[18] They went by train on July 6, 1942, on an "aged-people's transport" of one hundred deportees.

EKa learned of this appalling turn of events in the fall. On October 3 Gertrud's sister-in-law Eva, then a refugee in England, wrote to her daughter Vera and her son-in-law who were living in Stockton, California: "We know now that Tante G. has come with Clara . . . to Th.-town [*sic*]. Will we ever see her again? We still hope!"[19] Since Vera and EKa saw each other regularly, Vera would have told him of this immediately. Some months later Gertrud managed to send a letter or postcard that reached Eva and her husband Franz (Gertrud's brother), and Eva relayed it to her California family with the request that they send it on to "Ernst Kanto."[20] In this communication Gertrud, who was a trained nurse, reported that she was tending to Clara. Finally in a communication to her brother, a copy of which reached EKa on an uncertain date, Gertrud

---

(This is reprinted with few changes as "Flucht vor der 'Evakuierung': Das Scheitern der Damen Kantorowicz, Hammerschlag und Winter," in *Der abgerissene Dialog: Die intellektuelle Beziehung Gertrud Kantorowicz—Margarete Susman oder Die Schweizer Grenze bei Hohenems als Endpunkt eines Fluchtversuchs*, ed. Petra Zudrell, 11–70 [Innsbruck, 1999].)

[18] Maria Wunsch to Franz and Eva Kantorowicz, 12 November 1945: LBI, box 5, folder 1: "She [Gertrud] was unchanged despite all the strains and the frightful uncertainty of the situation—so calm and composed that she impressed even the Gestapo." (Wundsch was a nurse in Berlin who was permitted to see the detainees. Her extraordinarily moving account, written in the direct aftermath of the war, deserves to be published in entirety.)

[19] Lerner archive.

[20] 9 September 1943: Lerner archive. An enormous delay in the letter reaching Eva is indicated by the fact it refers to Clara as being alive, whereas she died on 10 February 1943.

endeavored to be cheerful about herself: "It goes well with me as ever." But she was obliged to report that "Tante Klar" had died of heart failure, albeit without pain and "attended by all of us as if she were a princess."[21] The date of Clara Kantorowicz's death was recorded at Theresienstadt as February 10, 1943,[22] corresponding to a poem written by Gertrud, bearing "10. Februar 1943" as an epigraph. One line reads: "how quietly we kiss the beringed finger."[23] Did EKa blame himself for the tragedy? His correspondence is eerily silent on the matter, but a doctoral student, Robert Benson, reported that when he once innocently asked EKa about his mother, the frightful answer came back: "Mother? I had no mother."[24] Otherwise EKa's bitterness was most fully expressed in a statement reported by William Chaney: "As far as Germany is concerned they can put a tent over the entire country and turn on the gas."[25]

The year 1943 was a difficult one in other respects.[26] The financial situation at Berkeley was much worse than it had been previously. With war mobilization in full gear, the number of students had declined sharply and the state legislature had cut the budget by 20 percent. In March Paxson submitted a budget request that included a slot for Kantorowicz as full professor, but without response. In May John D. Hicks, a prominent newly hired American historian, wrote to Sproul, saying that "Modern History without medieval support is like a man on a ladder with the ladder being pulled out from under him,"[27] and the chairman of the Department of Oriental Languages wrote: "I can speak for all the members of the Department in stating that having [Kantorowicz] as a colleague on this campus has stimulated all of us immeasurably." Sproul, however, replied to the latter that he was "very sorry that Dr. Kantorowicz should be among the first of our war casualties."

Quite likely, EKa understood in the spring of 1943 that his future for the coming academic year was grim. In May he wrote to his acquaintance, the art historian Edgar Wind, who was then teaching at the University of Chicago,

[21] The letter, LBI, box 5, folder 1, is published in Rammstedt, "'Wir sind des Gottes der begraben stirbt,'" 156.

[22] *Gedenkbuch: Opfer der Verfolgung der Juden unter der nationalsozialistischen Gewaltherrschaft in Deutschland 1933–1945*, 4 vols. (Koblenz, 2006), 2:1626.

[23] Gertrud Kantorowicz (who died of disease on 19 April 1945) wrote poems in Theresienstadt on scraps of available paper that survived the war. They were rescued by a survivor and sent to Franz Kantorowicz, who had them privately printed in 1947: "Verse aus Theresienstadt." A critical edition, based on the holographs now in the LBI (box 5), is Philip Redl, ed., *Gertrud Kantorowicz: Lyrik* (Heidelberg, 2010). See p. 158 for the poem in question.

[24] Johannes Fried, "Einleitung," in *Ernst H. Kantorowicz, Götter in Uniform*, ed. Eckhart Grünewald and Ulrich Raulff (Stuttgart, 1998), 38.

[25] Interview, 10 February 2010.

[26] Most of the details in this paragraph are taken from David H. Wright, "Kantorowicz in Berkeley" (ms., April 2002), 8.

[27] 20 May 1943: Hicks papers, carton 10.

testing the possibility of getting a job there.[28] To do what he could to polish his credentials he completed one of his most important articles, "The 'King's Advent' and the Enigmatic Panels in the Doors of Santa Sabina," published in 1944 in *The Art Bulletin*.[29] The main intention was art-historical. He was certain, almost smug, about his proposed decoding of the iconography of two carved wooden panels on the doors of the church of Santa Sabina in Rome (c. 430). For him his readings could not be held in doubt—they were "the only possible and consistent explanations." Yet critics immediately took issue with this: relevant correspondence in the Kantorowicz papers shows that experts proposed well-informed grounds for rejecting both of his iconographic readings.[30]

But the critics' demolitions need not concern us, for the importance of the article lies in an extended exposition that sets the stage for an iconographical interpretation that can be read separately with wonder. In this Kantorowicz reviewed Hellenistic, Roman, and Early Christian evidence as if it had a composite coherence. In other words he was foreshadowing a historiographical development of the later twentieth century by treating what is now termed "the world of late antiquity." And the extended exposition itself is a flamboyant specimen of his engagement with what he called "political theology." This demonstrates influences of late-Roman imperial ceremonials and imagery of ruler worship on early Christianity, and a ricocheting between sacred and secular within Christianity. The Roman imperial advent—the ceremonial entrance into a city—lay behind the imagery of Christ's advent into Jerusalem on Palm Sunday, and that in turn offered a pattern for "advents" of Christian rulers. Furthermore, it demonstrates a dependence on the prophecy of Malachi, "Behold I send my angel before thy face, who shall prepare the way before thee," that underpinned a Christian theme of "eschatological" advent. Kantorowicz's erudition is simply astonishing. He had drawn on numismatics before, but now, with the aid of the *Art Bulletin*'s generosity in reproducing images, he was able to display and comment on large numbers of coins, as well as amulets, sarcophagi, wall paintings, and manuscript illuminations. To which may be added a vast repertoire of primary written evidence spanning cultures and centuries. Liturgy sings out. Angels flutter. The bibliographical apparatus is so extensive that its length outstrips the text. That a historian of such quality should have had to worry about employment seems incredible.

But the ax did fall. On June 2 EKa received a letter from Paxson reporting: "It has recently come to my knowledge that the President is not going to find

[28] Wind to Robert Maynard Hutchins, 25 May 1943: Wind papers, Bodleian Library, box 1, 8. (Jost Philipp Klenner called my attention to this letter.)

[29] Reprinted in Kantorowicz, *Selected Studies*, 37–75.

[30] See LBI, box 3, folder 23. Two prominent critics who presented weighty objections were Richard Delbrueck and Rudolf Berliner.

himself able to offer you a position in the University after June 30."[31] The rest reads like a genuine farewell. Paxson was "deeply grieved." He had developed a great respect for Kantorowicz's scholarship, "which would be an ornament to any department of history," and he had "an even deeper appreciation of the dignity and courage and tact with which you have met a situation of greatest difficulty."

Paxson's fine words were heartfelt, but they paid no bills. EKa responded cordially but could not suppress his bitterness.[32] He wrote: "It was good of you to let me know that *Roma locuta est* and that President Sproul is equally interested in both Mediaeval History and my person. I gathered the fact from the program in which Course 125, though still found in the proofs, ceased to figure." He observed that he had "not received any official notification as to the state of affairs—three weeks before my contract with this University expires." Then he added: "This way of dealing with a person who is not criminal, but merely defenseless, strikes me, to say the least, as unfair. It tops all the humiliating experiences I have gone through these years." His letter assumed that the end had really come. Kantorowicz expressed appreciation for the "friendly feelings shown to me by almost all members of the Department and in the first place by Mr. Bolton and you; you may be sure that I shall not forget either the one or the other."

EKa waited until the expiration date of his one-year contract before writing to Sproul to protest how he had been treated: "To-day is July the first. An official notification from the part of the Administration of this University is not in my hands. My conduct, as far as I am aware, does not make it self-evident that a dismissal without notice should be the appropriate form to end a connection which has lasted four years."[33] Sproul's reply was restrained and perfectly correct.[34] He pointed out that he had written to Paxson the year before about EKa's status, stipulating that he was not incurring an obligation, "either legal or moral." He enclosed a copy of the letter in question and observed further that EKa's status as "Lecturer" was well known to be "honorable but impermanent"; "failure to make similar provision for the year 1943 is not to be considered, therefore, as in any sense a dismissal." Sproul apologized for having offended Kantorowicz, but "plead[ed] in extenuation, 1) that it has never been the custom of the University to send such notification to Lecturers, and 2) that I thought, in accordance with the enclosed letter, that the chairman of the Department would have told you of the impermanence of your status." And that was that.

Or so it seemed. EKa was not rescued this time by the Emergency Committee and was stricken from the rolls of the University of California. But a deus

[31] LBI, box 7, folder 2.
[32] 5 June 1943: ibid.
[33] 1 July 1943: ibid.
[34] 5 July 1943: ibid.

ex machina came in the form of a new instructional program instituted by the United States Army. Three days after EKa had the news from Paxson about not being rehired, he received a letter from Raymond Sontag about the army program and an offer to join.[35] Sontag was the overseer of the program scheduled to be taught on the Berkeley campus and could assign appointments. Accordingly, he proposed that Kantorowicz teach four sections of the Modern History and Contemporary Politics course and serve as assistant and exam reader for all seven sections of the course. The term was to last for three months, beginning in mid-June, and would net EKa a total of $600. Were such duties and remuneration to continue for a year, the income on a prorated basis would be adequate.

The "Army Specialized Training Program" (ASTP) lasted for three terms of eleven weeks, meaning that EKa was employed by the U.S. government from June 1943 until March 1944. Indirect evidence suggests that his salary was increased: a ledger of payments indicates that he received a total of $2,400 for the period in question. The program's purpose was "to identify, train and educate academically-talented enlisted men as a specialized corps of Army officers." EKa mordantly called it the "Gauleiter program" meant to prepare future American occupiers to become the equivalent of regional Nazi officials.[36] Students took intensive courses on the campuses of land-grant universities. They were expected to complete the program in eighteen months, upon which they would receive a four-year bachelor's degree and a commission. EKa's responsibilities were to teach history. From June through August he lectured on Modern History and Contemporary Politics; from September through December on German History; and from December through March on Italian History.

In March 1944 the army abruptly terminated the ASTP and EKa again was without a job. But Frederic Paxson and Raymond Sontag were looking out for him. In March Paxson wrote to Sproul to make a renewed case.[37] He explained that after consultation with his colleagues he was specifically recommending that Kantorowicz be appointed as a permanent full professor as of the beginning of the academic year 1945–46 and that he be carried over during the intervening time with a one-year appointment. He argued that such action would solve two problems. William Morris was obliged to retire as of July 1, 1945, and his courses in English constitutional history were a "must" for the department. (The two-term sequence in medieval English constitutional history was then required for students majoring in "Jurisprudence"—that is, those who planned to go on to law school.) In addition George Guttridge wanted to be relieved of some courses he was teaching in early-modern Europe in order to devote himself entirely to his preferred fields of modern England and the British Empire.

[35] 5 June 1943: ibid.

[36] Interview with Norman Rich, 14 January 2010; interview with William A. Chaney, 10 February 2010.

[37] 20 March 1944: President's papers, Bancroft Library.

Paxson proposed that Kantorowicz was specially fitted to fill in for both areas. In addition he avowed that he "is so competent a mediaevalist that friends from off campus, consulted with reference to the Morris retirement, have declared him to be the best mediaevalist now at large." He allowed that Robert Kerner doubted the wisdom of appointing "exiles" and closed deftly by saying that he himself had the same doubt "until I came to know this exile."

Even stronger than Paxson's letter was one sent to him by Sontag that he passed along to Sproul. [38] The well-connected Sontag had already written to two prominent medievalists in order to gain their views of Kantorowicz. They were Lynn White, who had left Stanford to become president of Mills College, and Joseph R. Strayer, Sontag's successor at Princeton as Henry Charles Lea Professor and chairman of the Department of History. White and Strayer were the greatest American-born medieval historians of the mid-twentieth century. Sontag wrote to Paxson that "they both agreed that it would be foolish to look elsewhere when we have the best medievalist in the country on our campus." He quoted Strayer as saying that "California would be crazy to look for another medievalist. . . . Kantorowicz is better than anyone you can bring in from outside." Sontag then gave his own view: "The range and depth of Kantorowicz's knowledge amazes me. I have read articles by him printed in the last year on art, on humanism, on theology, and on constitutional history . . . he has been ranging over the whole field of history, and earning the applause of a most difficult audience." Sontag believed that Kantorowicz was Morris's "logical successor." Since he recognized that a shortage of money would be an issue until the chair was actually free, he made a startlingly generous proposal: "I am willing to offer up to a thousand dollars, contingent on the pledge of an equal amount by other contributors—and I am willing to try to get the balance from others."

Sproul now referred the Kantorowicz matter to the Berkeley Budget Committee.[39] On April 19 this committee recommended a lectureship for EKa because of the History Department's urgent need for certain courses but called for an outside review before considering a permanent appointment. Meanwhile Paxson had recruited six graduate students to write in behalf of EKa, thereby producing two pages of encomia. After further behind-the-scenes correspondence, Sproul asked an ad hoc committee to review Kantorowicz's credentials for a permanent professorship. Sontag (a member of the committee) elicited a letter from Lynn White that opened with a breathtaking statement: "Kantorowicz would be an ornament to any historical faculty in the world."[40] White then entered into specifics. In regard to KFII he wrote:

[38] 21 March 1944: Bancroft Library, Frederick Logan Paxson papers, BANC MSS Z-R1.
[39] Wright, "Kantorowicz in Berkeley," 8.
[40] White to Sontag, 3 June 1944: http://www.regiesey.com.

> When it first appeared, it was widely criticized as being "too subjective" and "impressionistic," by which I suspect the historical guild meant that it committed the unforgivable sin of being readable and interesting. But I remember Haskins' remark in 1929 that "while other people were talking about writing a biography of Frederick, Kantorowicz wrote one."[41] When, in 1931, the *Ergänzungsband* was published in Berlin containing the notes which had been omitted from the original, it was evident that this biography rested upon a prodigious scholarship, and even the dullest of pedants was convinced of Kantorowicz's technical capacity.

Lynn White was highly gifted at writing testimonials. Here is another splendid passage: "He has a happy facility for starting an article with some apparently inconsequential item and then letting the implications of it fan out until, at the end, not only is one convinced that he has established the fact which he starts out to establish but also one's understanding of the Middle Ages as a whole has been expanded." More choice phrases follow: "as beautifully put together as a good string quartet"; "it is a rare scholar who can lick the antiquarians at their own game." By way of aside White remarked that Kantorowicz knew a "whopping lot" about the Court of Burgundy. All told, his conclusion was that "in my none too humble estimation, Berkeley could be committing a major blunder [if it] let him go."

The ad hoc committee recommended unanimously in favor of a permanent full professorial appointment. But even then Sproul dragged his feet. (In 1944 Berkeley had shifted provisionally to a fall term that began in November.) On July 4 he wrote Paxson that he could not act on the Kantorowicz matter without a complete survey of the needs of the History Department. Paxson complied by polling all the members he could locate and submitted a seven-page, single-spaced report on July 15 that was favorable to the appointment. Another month then passed without anything having been decided. But on August 15 EKa heard very discouraging rumors. This emerges from a letter he wrote to Monroe Deutsch requesting a private conversation: "I do not wish to indulge in a 'Historia calamitatum'. But things have become most involved and I confess that I am at the end of my reserves in every respect. May I call on you some time in the near future?"[42] EKa was referring to Abelard's calamities (which were dire indeed), but unlike Abelard's his were soon relieved. Three weeks after this letter of desperation to Deutsch, Frederic Paxson wrote to EKa that while the president was unable to make any commitment for the longer term, he had authorized a one-year lectureship for the coming year.[43] The reason

[41] Haskins wrote the same in print. See his review of *Frederick the Second* in the *American Historical Review* 37 (1932): 533: "produced a book where others have only planned and hoped to produce one."

[42] Monroe E. Deutsch papers, Bancroft Library, BANC MSS C-B 1054.

[43] 8 September 1944, LBI, box 7, folder 2.

offered was that a pressing need existed for someone to teach medieval English constitutional history. Because Morris was already taking leave for the spring term before his formal retirement beginning in the summer, and also because a course in the Renaissance needed to be taught owing to a leave granted to George Guttridge, President Sproul had decided to ask Kantorowicz to teach these courses, as well as others that yielded a full load.

In his letter of September 1944 Paxson felt bound to write, doubtless on Sproul's insistence, that the new lectureship was authorized "entirely 'without prejudice' to future action respecting the Morris retirement." But a careful appraisal of the situation indicates that the "Battle of Berkeley" (Lynn White's term) was really over.[44] Even if Morris was to be on leave in the spring, Kantorowicz was asked to take both of his constitutional history courses, strongly indicating that he was being tagged for teaching them in the future. Moreover, his assignment to teach Guttridge's Renaissance course was exactly what Paxson had recommended to Sproul in March for the longer term since it freed Guttridge to teach the courses he preferred. In other words, EKa's one-year assignment was to teach everything that would legitimate a permanent position. The ever-cautious Sproul must have demanded the "without prejudice" clause because he always wanted to keep his options open, but the temporary step of September 1944 was an obvious harbinger.

It would have been a terrible imposition on EKa had his set of assignments for 1944–45 not been aimed toward permanence. At the time he had an allergy to English constitutional history. Shortly after he received the news of his new teaching schedule he wrote to Maurice Bowra, "Unfortunately I shall have to lecture during the next semesters [on] English Constitutional History of which I know nothing and in which I am not very interested."[45] To William Chaney he remarked that he felt "as if he were teaching the subject as if in teaching the Second World War he made the central figure Hore-Belisha and never mentioned Winston Churchill."[46] Even while he was soldiering through the assignment nothing was fixed. On May 7 Paxson wrote to Deutsch that if Kantorowicz was going to be appointed he needed to be listed in the catalog, and if not he should be informed promptly. What finally tipped the balance was that EKa now was being courted by the Committee on Social Thought at the University of Chicago. On May 17 Louis Gottschalk of Chicago was visiting Berkeley and let Paxson, Sontag, and others know that an offer of a full professorship was being discussed. Then when Gottschalk returned he reported Paxson's statement that "if Chicago makes him an offer, we shall try to persuade him to stay here."[47]

[44] White to Kantorowicz , 6 June 1944, ibid.

[45] Bowra papers, 21 September 1944.

[46] Chaney to Robert E. Lerner, 13 August 2010: Lerner archive.

[47] Louis R. Gottschalk to William T. Hutchinson (chairman of the Chicago History Department), 17 May 1945 (UCSC: Presidential papers, box 7, folder 8).

Ultimately, such an offer never was made because of determined resistance to it by Chicago's History Department.[48] Nevertheless, its initial possibility brings this chapter on "the perils of Ernst" to a happy end. Inasmuch as EKa had published very little between his *Ergänzungsband* of 1931 and his arrival in Berkeley, the reluctance of many to make him a permanent full professor was understandable. And of course the tendentious nature of his biography of Frederick II was a real issue. Although the appearance of articles in English in the early 1940s and especially the acceptance of *Laudes Regiae* for publication as of January 1941 by a committee of Berkeley historians should have turned matters in his favor, budgetary pressures associated with the war created new grounds for delaying a permanent appointment. But as the war was being won and Kantorowicz's reputation as scholar and teacher continued to grow, ever less reason existed for holding him at arm's length. Fortunately he had well-placed allies who pressed his case, foremost among them being Deutsch, Paxson, and Sontag. Robert Sproul, of course, was the person who made the decisions, and while he does not appear to have harbored malice, he was strong-willed and obsessed with a need for caution. Whenever there was a possibility for delaying, he delayed as long as he could. In May 1945, however, the time was over when he learned that Kantorowicz might be hired away by a prominent rival institution. We will let EKa have the concluding, baroque, words. In a letter to John Nef of the University of Chicago he wrote: "[I]t so happened that the intrinsic unity of Macrocosmos and Microcosmos has manifested itself at a time when I did not expect it. Our Macrocosmos (President Sproul) has left, several weeks ago, for Russia. Before leaving, he cleared his desk on which he found papers referring to Microcosmos (myself)—the humble petition of the History Department, renewed for the fifth or sixth time, concerning my permanent appointment. And thus—so to speak, under the pressure of Stalin—Macrocosmos nominated Microcosmos."[49]

[48] For an account of the copiously documented Chicago episode, including many estimates of Kantorowicz's scholarship as of that time, Janus Gudian, *Ernst Kantorowicz* (Frankfurt, 2014), 154–67.

[49] 31 May 1945: UCSC, Nef papers, box 25, folder 11.

CHAPTER 19

"Hyperborean Fields"

One might have thought that the five and a half years of uncertainty about employment in Berkeley and concurrent dismaying news from Europe, military and personal, would have made Ernst Kantorowicz continually depressed or morose. But this would be far from the truth. Granted frequent bad moments, on the whole he was happy. When he wrote to Bernard Flexner with hat in hand in 1940, he assured him that his second semester at Berkeley had "abounded in work and pleasure." Heinrich Zimmer, who visited him in the spring of 1941, reported that he was "very cheerful."[1] Later, in 1945, EKa wrote to a friend in Germany that he had not been directly affected by the war, for he had been living "in distinctly hyperborean fields" (beyond the north wind in a region of perpetual sunshine).[2] In another letter he wrote of his fortunate situation more fully: "We're stranded! But of all the shores on which we could have been stranded, this at any rate is the pleasantest. . . . Externally we live in an endless flowering that knows no winter and only a few weeks of rain. There's a circle of friends that brings the needed stimulation, and, given that several are 'Heidelbergers,' one can understand 'every word.'"[3] The previous chapter treated EKa's most dramatic bad moments. This one will treat the atmosphere of endless flowering that knew no winter.

The remark about "Heidelbergers" referred to three German émigrés who arrived in Berkeley in successive years: Walter Horn, Manfred Bukofzer, and Leonardo Olschki. Although one of EKa's friends from the time of his arrival was the Viennese-born Robert Lowie, they probably did not "understand each other's every word" in the sense of EKa's statement just quoted, for Lowie had been living in America for most of his life, and his area of scholarship, ethnology, was unrelated to EKa's own interests. But Horn, Bukofzer, and Olschki,

[1] Heinrich Zimmer to Max Kommerell, early summer 1941, in Maya Rauch and Dorothee Mussgnug, "Briefe aus dem Exil: Aus der Korrespondenz von Heinrich Zimmer 1939–1943," *Heidelberger Jahrbücher* 35 (1991): 219–43, at 236.

[2] To Ernst Langlotz, 15 September 1945: Langlotz papers.

[3] To Ludwig Curtius, 9 February 1948: Ludwig Curtius papers.

all with Heidelberg credentials, spoke EKa's language in both senses of the expression.

Walter Horn, born in 1908, was the son of a Lutheran minister.[4] He studied in Heidelberg before gaining a doctorate in art history in Hamburg under the direction of Erwin Panofsky. After an interval of four years in Florence he emigrated to the United States in 1938: even though his father was a minister he was one-quarter Jewish and hence unemployable in Germany because of the Nazi racial laws.[5] In 1939 Horn became a visiting lecturer in Berkeley. The next year he gained a tenure-track appointment and subsequently remained at Berkeley for the rest of his life, aside from three years in the army from 1943 to 1946. Horn's academic interests were next door to EKa's. His dissertation treated the iconography of a twelfth-century Romanesque façade. As early as EKa's second term in Berkeley he and Horn gave guest lectures in each other's courses.[6] A photo of a cookout arranged by EKa in Berkeley c. 1943 (fig. 21) shows Horn ostentatiously hugging a girl who was not his wife. (He was counted as one of Berkeley's premier philanderers.)

The musicologist Manfred Bukofzer, born in 1910, studied in Heidelberg and Basel, where he received his doctorate after the Nazi takeover.[7] In 1941 he arrived in Berkeley where he taught in the music faculty until his premature death in 1956. He was the author of a musicological appendix to EKa's *Laudes Regiae* and called "one of the great musicologists of his generation."[8] In addition he was a wide-ranging intellectual. He had studied philosophy in Heidelberg with Raymond Klibansky, and one of his publications was on "Hegel's Aesthetics of Music." Because he and EKa were both experts on the liturgy of feet-washing, EKa joked that the two might go to Telegraph Avenue on Holy Thursday and compete with the shoe-shine boys; they would charge ten cents for washing feet and throw in a rendition of the liturgy for another five.[9] EKa sometimes called him affectionately "Bukofze Monthclub."[10]

Of all the German scholars who landed in Berkeley, Leonardo Olschki, an expert on the medieval literature of Italy, was the one with whom EKa was

[4] *Dictionary of Art Historians*, http://www.dictionaryofarthistorians.org/hornw.htm. The statement there, however, that "Horn's strong opposition to National Socialism forced him to emigrate to the United States" does not tell the whole story.

[5] For the fact (unknown to many) that Horn was one-quarter Jewish, see Kantorowicz to Wilhelm Stein, 21 December 1939 (Stein papers): "besonders nett übrigens ein junger deutscher Kunsthistoriker mit 25% Beimischung namens Horn."

[6] Kantorowicz to Wilhelm Stein, 21 December 1939: Stein papers.

[7] David D. Boyden, "In Memoriam: Manfred F. Bukofzer (1910–1955)," *Musical Quarterly* 42 (1956): 291–301.

[8] Ibid., 293.

[9] Interview with William Chaney, 22 December 2011.

[10] Ihor Ševčenko, email, 12 January 2009. (Ševčenko wrote: "You may find this information useful.")

Figure 21. Cookout in Berkeley, circa 1943. EKa is at far right. Next to him is Walter Horn's wife, and next to her is Dorothee Franchetti; Walter Horn is hugging girl in center. (Lerner archive)

closest.[11] The two referred to each other as "the Firm" (*die Firma*). Olschki was the son of the prominent (Jewish) German-Italian book dealer and publisher, Leo S. Olschki. A sister married a Finzi of Ferrara, a name best known from Giorgio Bassani's novel *The Garden of the Finzi-Continis*. Leonardo was born in Verona in 1885 and grew up speaking German at home and Italian elsewhere; it was difficult to say whether German or Italian was his native language because he spoke both languages fluently from youth. After pursuing studies in Florence, Rome, Munich, Strassburg, and Heidelberg, he received his doctorate at Heidelberg in 1906 and subsequently habilitated there in 1913. Remaining in Heidelberg, he rose to become Ordinarius in 1924, in those days an extraordinary distinction for a Jew. Excluded from the Heidelberg faculty on "racial" grounds in 1933, Olschki was able to gain employment at the University of Rome in the same year and remain teaching there until 1938. Emigrating to the United States in 1939, the one-time Heidelberg full professor found life difficult. In answer to a questionnaire regarding the extent of his knowledge of English he wrote: "enough for make me understood." After a succession of short-term jobs, and for a time no job at all (in 1941 his wife, from one of Berlin's wealthiest Jewish families, supported both of them by working in a leather factory), Olschki gained an appointment with EKa's help as research associate for a year

[11] On Olschki's career, Arthur R. Evans, Jr., "Leonardo Olschki, 1885–1961," *Romance Philology* 31 (1977): 17–54, and Dörner, *La vita spezzata*. Further information provided by Olschki's nephew, Bernard Rosenthal: interview, 5 December 2008. For Adele Finzi, née Olschki, Bernard Rosenthal, *Autobiography and Autobibliography* (Berkeley, 2010), 6–8.

(1944–45) in Berkeley's Department of Oriental Languages. (He had written on Marco Polo.) Unemployed again in 1945 (he described himself then as "an academic without academy"), he waited in Berkeley until 1948 to gain another paid position, now as lecturer in the Department of Oriental Languages, but was fired in 1950 for refusing to sign the controversial loyalty oath. Olschki was a truly remarkable scholar. He published articles and books in Latin, Italian, German, French, and English that ranged over a span of subject matters from the library of Lorenzo da Ponte, to the Romanesque façade of the Cathedral of Modena, to "the Columbian nomenclature of the Lesser Antilles." The central work of his Heidelberg period was a pioneering history of scientific literature from the Middle Ages to Galileo that ran to three volumes, each of some five hundred pages.

Although Olschki and Kantorowicz were together in Heidelberg in the 1920s, they hardly knew each other then.[12] (Olschki was far removed from the George circle.) But once they were refugees in the United States it became natural for them to be in touch. In 1943 they shared the common assignment of teaching in the Army Specialized Training Program, Olschki's service being at the University of Oregon. When the program was terminated in 1944, EKa helped bring him to Berkeley. From then until Olschki's death in 1961 the two continually stimulated each other's research. Specific convergences were that both were medievalists particularly attuned to symbolic meanings inherent in words and images and that both were engrossed (perhaps obsessed) by Dante.[13] They were kindred spirits in their Greek and Latin erudition, in their penchant for displaying their ready wit, and in their clever multilingual word plays. (A choice Olschki specimen relates to names he gave to a secondhand car that gave him trouble. First he named it "Galileo." Why? "Eppure si muove" [But it does move]. And when it broke down, he named it "Luther": "Hier stehe ich, ich kann nicht anders" [Here I stand, I can do no other.][14])

One other member of EKa's German-speaking set, although not associated with Heidelberg, was the Viennese born Otto Maenchen-Helfen, who was forced to flee Austria in 1938 because his wife was Jewish.[15] (So many Austrian refugees were on a boat carrying them to the United States in June 1938 that they called it "the Juneflower.") Once in America he found a teaching position at Mills College in Oakland, where he stayed from 1940 to 1947 before moving to Berkeley to become professor of art from 1947 until his retirement in 1962. Like so many other of EKa's friends in the Berkeley years, he was a man

[12] EKa mentions this in passing in a letter to Karl Hampe of 16 April 1933: Hampe papers.

[13] Olschki published nine different contributions to Dante studies. EKa's appreciative review of his *The Myth of Felt* (devoted to solving the "Veltro" crux) appears in *Romance Philology* 4 (1951): 281–84. EKa thanks Olschki for "fruitful criticisms" of his Dante chapter in the preface to *The King's Two Bodies*.

[14] Interview with Ihor Ševčenko, 18 November 2008.

[15] The best biographical sketch is *Neue Deutsche Biographie* 15 (1987): 636.

of diverse interests. Primarily an expert on Chinese art, he was best known for his work on the history and culture of the Huns. (He had spent some time as a student in the Soviet Union and had traveled through central Asia). He knew Greek, Latin, Russian, Chinese, and Japanese, as well as German and English. A scintillating wit, he once observed that the motto placed under the buffalo on the American nickel coin should really be "E pluribus nullum."[16]

A formal venue for EKa's coming together with some of his polyglot, polymath German friends was the Berkeley-sponsored Colloquium Orientologicum.[17] This was a society of Bay Area scholars interested in matters Asian who met regularly to present papers and exchange information, insights, and views. It was founded in 1939 by the German émigré Ferdinand Lessing, a professor of Sinology and chairman of the Department of Oriental Languages. Working closely together with him and soon the driving force was Peter A. Boodberg, another Sinologist, who took over as chair of the Oriental Languages Department in 1940. EKa was good friends with Boodberg, yet another remarkable émigré personality.[18] He was of Baltic German descent, born in Vladivostok as the son of the commanding general of czarist forces in the Pacific area. He learned Chinese in Harbin and left for the United States in 1920, studying at Berkeley and then rising through the academic ranks. Olschki (himself no ignoramus) called him "one of the most amazing scholars I ever met."[19] Boodberg was said to have had knowledge of the principal ancient and modern Indo-European, Semitic, Hamitic, Altaic, Sinitic, and Malayo-Polynesian languages. Students and friends appreciated his Russian accent and the "artistic strain in Pjotr Alekseevitch" that extended to appreciation of the poetry of Gerard Manley Hopkins.

EKa once quipped that the Berkeley Colloquium Orientologicum should really have been called the "Colloquium Ornithologicum" because of all the "rare birds" in attendance.[20] Ihor Ševčenko, who arrived in Berkeley from Europe as a junior faculty member in 1949, could not remember a single native-born American in the group.[21] Although EKa was hardly an Orientologist he hastened to join because he so much enjoyed the give-and-take of humanistically infused intellectual discussion.[22] In the fall of 1941 he spoke on a recent book,

[16] Kantorowicz to Maurice Bowra, 18 May 1949: Bowra papers.

[17] See the account in Malkiel, "Ernst H. Kantorowicz," 206–7.

[18] Biographical data depends on *University of California: In Memoriam, July 1975.*

[19] Leonardo Olschki to Meyer Schapiro, 29 October 1946: Schapiro papers, Columbia University Rare Book and Manuscript Library.

[20] Evans, "Leonardo Olschki," 41.

[21] Interview, 18 November 2008

[22] The records of the Berkeley Colloquium Orientologicum are in the Bancroft Library, University Archives, CU-64.1. (Stephanie Di Notto located this material for me.) In chronological order EKa's papers are "Methodological Aspects [sic] of an Historian on Mr. Teggart's Book on China Rome" (30 Oct., 27 Nov. 1941); "Liturgica Illustrata" (26 Nov. 1941); "Reception of the Kyrios" (26 May 1943); "Epiphany and Coronation" (25 Oct. 1944); "Synthronos: Throne Sharing with the

Rome and China: A Study of Correlations in Historical Events, and eviscerated it. Subsequently he spoke on matters Byzantine (which passed the "oriental" test), using the opportunity to preview material for publication. When Leonardo Olschki arrived in 1944 to join Boodberg, Maenchen-Helfen, and Kantorowicz (and of course others), the candlepower increased. The sessions were semipublic, and an observer later wrote of the interchanges of scholars "whose far-reaching interests and lively wit made [the Colloquium] a forum that was perhaps unique in Berkeley history."[23]

We may move to EKa the lecturer to undergraduates. For the period under consideration his courses covered enormous territory both chronologically and geographically. For the first years, before he taught in the Army Specialized Training Program, he moved by steps to teaching four terms of Medieval Thought and Institutions (the name changed from Medieval Institutions), three of them running from 300 to 1300, and a fourth devoted to Byzantium from 300 to 800. We have seen that for the army he taught intensive courses over a one-year period on Modern History and Contemporary Politics, German History, and Italian History. And then, to earn his full professorship, he moved into two terms of English Constitutional History, and one term each of Renaissance and Reformation. In other words, he taught a stretch from 300 to 1600, with outliers for the army courses into the twentieth century.

Granted that he sometimes repeated a given lecture course or shifted lectures from one discontinued series into a new one, the labor involved was huge. As mentioned earlier, Kantorowicz typed out all his lectures. Most, with handwritten revisions and addenda, are preserved in the Leo Baeck Institute in twenty-two ring binders adding up to some six thousand pages.[24] The lectures are typed on 6″ × 9½″ sheets, smaller than the standard American 8½″ × 11″. Ralph Giesey explains the reason: "He never carried a briefcase into class: he entered smiling, nodded and made some greeting to the class, plucked the lecture from his pocket, seated himself at his desk, and began to speak."[25]

Browsing through the lectures today, one can see that they not only were dazzling in their insights, juxtapositions, and sometimes even new knowledge but also were works of art, structurally and rhetorically. The army course on the history of Italy begins:

> In July 1871 an unimportant petty prince from the Franco-Italian borderland of Piedmont-Savoy, carried on the crest of a wave of romanticism and liberal

---

Deity" (6 Dec. 1945); "Roman Coins and Christian Rites" (28 April 1948); "Oriens Augusti" (4 Jan. 1950). The records contain summaries of most but not all of these papers.

[23] Yakov Malkiel in the Boodberg necrology, *University of California: In Memoriam, July 1975*.

[24] Robert L. Benson, "Kantorowicz on Continuity and Change in the History of Medieval Rulership," in Benson and Fried, *Ernst Kantorowicz*, 202–10, at 203.

[25] Ralph Giesey, typed introduction to the lecture texts for Kantorowicz's course on The Normans in European History: LBI, box 9, folder 4.

idealism, held his entry into the city and settled in the large, low, ochre-colored summer palace of the popes on the Quirinal Hill, parts of which had been built by Bernini in the seventeenth century.

Often the lectures were laced with irony. Not wishing to suppress his displeasure about lecturing on English Constitutional History, EKa opened his series thus:

> I cannot introduce a course on English Constitutional History better than by quoting the somewhat discouraging words of Bishop Stubbs, whose Constitutional History of England, first published in 1874, has given milk—sometimes dried milk—to generations of historians. Says the bishop: "The history of institutions cannot be mastered without an effort." I am sorry for you, and for myself, that indeed such an effort cannot be spared to either you or me.

With that out of the way, he presented a less mordant introduction for the first substantive lecture:

> It is always safe to start and, if you can, to conclude a course of lectures with a quotation from Homer or the Bible, Dante or Goethe, depending upon whether you lecture on Greek or Church, Italian or German history. It goes without saying that Shakespeare is to be bothered in a course dealing with Constitutional History.

(Since Kantorowicz was starting with Roman Britain, the play of Shakespeare he "bothered" was *Cymbeline*; for *The King's Two Bodies* it was *Richard II*.)

A rhetorical pinnacle comes in the introduction to the course on The Reformation (here we must remember that he was speaking in the winter of 1946):

> That otherwise so thrilling spectaculum of the birth and gradual growth of the new-born appears here, metaphorically spoken, not as the joyful self-manifestation of "the new life", but as travails, travails on end. . . . All that rolled off in the most torturous way of tortured minds, of endless persecutions, endless hatred, endless cleavages, endless impact of heresy and witchcraft, until it reached its maturity in the fold of a nation which itself is one of the most tortured and at the same time self-torturous nations of Europe, that of Germany. If the Italian Renaissance leaped like another Pallas Athena in full armor from the head of Zeus, who, to our knowledge, did not suffer considerably from the pangs of childbirth, the German Reformation took place under conditions which far surpassed all that had been promised to Eve in the [*sic*] Genesis, ch. III, v. 16: "Unto the woman he said I will greatly multiply thy sorrow and thy conception; in sorrow thou shalt bring forth children."

Once past his introductions, EKa loved to present detail in all its wriggling variety. In an early manifestation of the Medieval Institutions course he referred to the simple little letter "i" being responsible for dividing Christianity in the fourth century between Arians and Athanasians: Jesus was either *homoiousios* (god-like) or *homoousios* (god-equal). Elsewhere he brought in his own research: Diocletian took *Sol invictus* to be Jupiter, Constantius Chlorus to be Hercules; the emperor as *Sol invictus* might be represented with a nimbus because that was the sign of the radiant sun: hence the origin of the Christian halo.[26]

Norman Rich, who attended Kantorowicz's lectures in the early 1940s, reported that "far from being a showman like Sontag, he sat at a desk and read from a meticulously typed script in his sing-song. Then he took questions with a cigarette in his mouth. I was always afraid that the cigarette would drop out. It doesn't sound very exciting but it *was* because the exposition was so brilliant."[27] Another Berkeley eyewitness has written: "Entering promptly, faultlessly dressed, Kantorowicz brought into the classroom an almost tangible aura of intellectual excitement and anticipation. . . . Nothing was alien to this agile mind, roaming freely over the centuries as it unfolded the drama of man."[28]

EKa's graduate seminars of course were not scripted. The seminars were held in his home. They began at 8 p.m. and continued until 11, "after which the work was over and more informal conversations began."[29] EKa placed a gallon of wine in the middle of his living room for participants to share as they liked.[30] The method was that of the German seminar: choosing one primary source in the original language for a term, and digging deep into it. Students delivered papers on various aspects, and discussion ensued. (Norman Rich has written that "we discussed and argued with him."[31]) Some of the seminar texts were the "Book of Ceremonies" by the Byzantine Emperor Constantine Porphyrogenitus (read in Latin because none of EKa's students knew enough Greek), Liudprand of Cremona's account of his legation to Constantinople, the "Norman Anonymous," and Dante's *Monarchy*.[32] When EKa gave the *Monarchy* seminar in the

[26] I draw here on George T. Romani's notes on Medieval Institutions, Northwestern University Archives: Romani papers, box 2, folder 2. Kantorowicz's research fascination with *Sol invictus* appears in "Dante's Two Suns" (1951).

[27] Interview with Norman Rich, 14 January 2010.

[28] Sayles, "The Scholar and the Loyalty Oath," 27–28.

[29] Robert Benson, a participant in the seminars of the later 1940s, as quoted in Ekbert Fas, *Young Robert Duncan* (Santa Barbara, CA, 1983), 258.

[30] Interview with Norman Rich, 14 January 2010, who states that the jug was moved back and forth across the floor.

[31] Norman Rich, review of Alain Boureau, *Kantorowicz: Stories of a Historian*, in *Central European History* 35 (2002): 612.

[32] There is no known list of EKa's seminar topics. My knowledge of the first two comes from William Chaney; of the third from the introduction to George Williams, *The Norman Anonymous of 1100 A.D.* (Cambridge, MA, 1951); and of the fourth from Gene Brucker to Robert E. Lerner, 29 July 1989: Lerner archive. Ralph Giesey reports that the text for the seminar given in the autumn of 1949 was the "Book of Ceremonies," meaning that EKa gave a seminar on this text a second time since Chaney would have taken the one to which he referred earlier. (For Giesey's reference see http://www.regiesey.com.

summer term of 1949, he assigned a Catholic priest the job of defending, as "devil's advocate," the Tridentine Church's branding of the treatise as heretical and was amused that he took up the role of prosecuting Dante with great enthusiasm.[33]

Throughout the Berkeley years EKa had a coterie of admiring students, undergraduate and graduate. Report has it that he could be seen on the campus, "surrounded by one group of students, who delivered him to another group, who then escorted him to a local restaurant for food and conversation."[34] Some of the graduate students who were closest to him during the war years were William A. Chaney, Norman Rich, and George H. Williams. All these became professional scholars and authors of books.[35] Right after the war another Williams, Schafer ("Spike") Williams, arrived to join the graduate student group. Predictably the doubling of Williamses led to witticisms. Because George Williams did research on the Norman Anonymous he was called "Anonymous Williams," whereas Spike Williams, who worked on the decretals of "Pseudo-Isidore," was called "Pseudo-Williams." One evening when George had not yet arrived Spike rose to say, "Have no fear! Pseudo will go and find Anonymous!"[36]

Another graduate student was Luis Weckmann, a Mexican descended from a prominent Bavarian family. Weckmann came to Berkeley in 1944 to write a doctoral dissertation and received a topic from EKa: Alexander VI's bull of 1493 apportioning the new world between Spain and Portugal. EKa put himself out for the visitor, helping him to place the bull in its medieval canon-law context, to compare it to other charters according to methods of the MGH, and to see that Pope Alexander's grant, made by the issuer as a feudal overlord, descended from an idea manifested in the forged Donation of Constantine. This was the first doctoral dissertation that EKa oversaw, and he was so proud of it that he wrote an introduction to the Spanish version that appeared as a book in 1949.[37] (Weckmann later became a diplomat, with portfolios to the United Nations, Israel, Germany, and Italy.)

EKa was more than extraordinarily conscientiousness as an academic supervisor; he also chose to become friends with some of his favorites. A case in point is that of William ("Bill") Chaney. He entered Berkeley as a transfer

[33] To Elise Peters, 25 June 1949: Lerner archive.

[34] Gene Brucker to Robert E. Lerner, 29 July 1989: Lerner archive.

[35] Chaney, *The Cult of Kingship in Anglo-Saxon England* (Berkeley, 1970); Williams, *The Norman Anonymous of 1100 A.D.*; also Schafer Williams, *Codices Pseudo-Isidoriani* (New York, 1971). All these books originated from work with Kantorowicz. Norman Rich's titles are in modern German history.

[36] William A. Chaney, "Schafer Williams, A Memoir," in *In Iure Veritas: Studies in Canon Law in Memory of Schafer Williams*, ed. Steven B. Bowman and Blanche E. Cody, xii–xiv (Cincinnati, 1991), at xiii.

[37] Luis Weckmann, *Las Bulas Alejandrinas de 1493 y la Teoría Política del Papado Medieval* (Mexico City, 1949), with introduction in English by Kantorowicz.

student from the College of the Pacific in 1941 at the age of eighteen, gained his B.A. degree in 1943, and stayed as a graduate student until 1949, when, with the support of Kantorowicz and Maurice Bowra, he was elected to the Harvard Society of Fellows.[38] Chaney wanted to be a medievalist and had the requisite languages. This partly explains EKa's interest in him, but the two spent many hours in conversations that extended to more than shoptalk. EKa reminisced with Chaney about many aspects of his earlier life. In 1943 or 1944 he presented the twenty- or twenty-one-year-old with a copy of Bowra's *Heritage of Symbolism* with a Latin inscription. That led to their talking one evening about a translation Bowra presented in the book of a poem by Stefan George. Chaney, who knew German, offered his opinion that the translation was both more accurate and more sensitive than the one in a recent book of George's poems translated into English by one of George's leading disciples, Ernst Morwitz. To which EKa responded that he was glad to hear Chaney say that because he and Bowra had spent one evening making that translation together.

Kantorowicz always welcomed the conversation and conviviality of favored students outside of class and insisted on their calling him "EKa." The previously mentioned cookout photo dating from roughly 1943 shows him with a group mainly of students. During the war years he was obliged to observe a curfew as an "enemy alien" that kept him at home after 8 p.m.[39] Norman Rich, George Williams, and one or two others came for visits to keep him company. They brought cheap "Mission Bell" wine ("Make Mission Bell mine/because Mission Bell's fine"), and EKa was very grateful—for the company and even for the wine, since he was short of cash.[40] (Raymond Sontag told Rich that Kantorowicz didn't have much money but "wine was really necessary for him.") There were also parties for students at EKa's home that could go on until the morning hours.

In addition to socializing with colleagues and students, EKa maintained contacts with a rather large number of relatives who migrated successively to Berkeley or environs. The earliest to come, indeed before EKa, around the year 1938, was Bernhard Pietrkowski (born in 1910), who Americanized his first name to Bernard and his second to Peters. ("Pietrkowski" was too troublesome to spell over the telephone.) His presence together with EKa's in the same place was coincidental. He was not a blood relative but a nephew of Elise Kantorowicz's owing to her marriage to his uncle Edmund Pietrkowski. Curiously enough he was at first a longshoreman and then a physics student of J. Robert Oppenheimer's. But even though he came to be at the university, he and EKa had no interest in each other.[41] He is mentioned here only because he arranged

[38] Kantorowicz to Bowra, 27 April 1949.

[39] To Bernard Flexner, 15 June 1942, Emergency Committee papers.

[40] Interview with Norman Rich, 14 January 2010.

[41] My information about Bernard Peters comes from his son, Tom F. Peters, and his cousin, Beata Alden. Bernard Peters spent several months in Dachau in 1933 because of his politics and

for his father, Georg Pietrkowski/Peters (born in 1874), and his mother, Eva, to come from Germany in June 1940 to join him.[42] These two did play a role in EKa's life—in their own right and as a result of their attracting others. Georg, who in Germany had been a physician, had intellectual leanings and took an interest in EKa's work. EKa knew his interests well enough to present him in 1942 with an offprint of a review article, "Plato in the Middle Ages," and sent him other offprints from Princeton in the 1950s. When EKa reported the death of Max Radin in 1950 to Elise Peters, he wrote, "Georg too will be very sad."[43]

The presence in Berkeley of Georg and Eva Peters then became a magnet for the arrival in the summer of 1941 of their niece, Dorothee Franchetti (born 1900), together with her six children. To do full justice to Dorothee's career would take a chapter in itself. She was the daughter of Edmund Pietrkowski and Elise Kantorowicz, whose combined wealth at the time of her upbringing was very great. Her first husband, Joseph Hambuechen, known as "Beppo," also was wealthy, being the adopted son of James Loeb, a partner in the banking firm Kuhn, Loeb & Co., and later the founder of the Loeb Classical Library. Hambuechen was advanced by Loeb to become a banker, a copartner of the A. E. Wassermann Bank in Berlin. He and Dorothee were married in 1927, moved from Berlin to a suburb of Zürich a few years later, and had five children before they were divorced in 1937. Dorothee then promptly married a half Italian-Jewish, half-German baron, Luigino Franchetti. Once more there was wealth, for certain. Luigino descended from Rothschilds; his father had owned the most opulent palace on Venice's Grand Canal, the Ca' d'Oro, and was able to buy paintings by Giorgione, Tintoretto, and Van Dyck. Luigino, a gifted pianist, had been educated in Eton and Oxford, where he had been friends with Clive Bell and Prince Felix Yussopov (among others).

In the 1930s he bought the spectacular palace of Bellosguardo on the outskirts of Florence with his Rothschild wealth, and by the time of Dorothee's arrival Luigino's mother, Marion von Hornstein (from a Bavarian noble family and the sister-in-law of the portrait painter Franz von Lenbach), had refurbished the palace in grand style and ran it as a luxurious *pensione*, with chosen paying guests and a *table d'hôte*. In 1940 Prince Rupprecht, the titular crown prince of Bavaria, stayed for a while in Torre di Bellosguardo with his wife and children. Bernard Berenson would come from time to time. (Luigino once asked Berenson how he was feeling and got the reply, "I'm a little giú"—Italian for "down"—to which Luigino responded, "I know that, but I asked you how you were feeling.") Dorothee bore a child by Luigino in 1938. Then, in the

was forced to leave America in 1949 after he was named as a communist sympathizer by Oppenheimer in secret testimony before the House Un-American Activities Committee. See Kai Bird and Martin J. Sherman, *American Prometheus: The Triumph and Tragedy of J. Robert Oppenheimer* (New York, 2005), 116–17, 395–97.

[42] Tom Peters to Robert E. Lerner, 11 November 2011.

[43] Kantorowicz to Elise Peters, 22 June 1950 (Lerner archive).

summer of 1941, Beppo, the father of the first five, called his former wife on the long-distance telephone (he was now living in New York) to tell her to "get those children out of Europe NOW." So she flew with all six of her children to Lisbon, where she waited for her mother Elise, who had been in Zürich, to join her. Elise had to pass through occupied France by train, and they waited for her with some worry, but she did arrive and, with the financial support of Hambuechen, mother, grandmother, and six children boarded a Pan-American clipper for a transatlantic flight to Bermuda and thence to New York. A photo in a New York newspaper displays the "Italian Baroness Dorothee Franchetti" and her six children soon after they had stepped off the clipper.[44]

In Berkeley Dorothee bought a spacious house, large enough for all her children, her mother, and a governess, as well as for Luigino and his mother, who arrived in Berkeley at the end of the war. For a time Dorothee attended EKa's lectures (she can be seen in figure 21); in 1947 she lent EKa money to enable him to buy a house. And of course she gave dinner parties. Among the guests might be the composer Ernest Bloch, or the conductor Pierre Monteux, both friends of Luigino's, or Olga Schnitzler, once the wife of the Viennese playwright Arthur Schnitzler. (Olga was a Berkeley character with substantial frontage who was known for her many shawls and who often could be seen striding down Telegraph Avenue with a cape partly draped over a gold-crested walking stick.) Another frequent guest was EKa. He was good with children (so long as they were not babies). In May 1945 Dorothee organized a surprise party for EKa's fiftieth birthday at her home, with large numbers of people, young and old.

The cook on that occasion was Dorothee's mother, Elise Pietrkowski/Peters, known as "Lieschen." Aside from his sister Soscha, this was the relative whom EKa loved best. Her father, Nazary Kantorowicz, the director of a large chemical firm, was among the richest men in Posen at the time of her birth in 1878. Her husband, Edmund, whom she married in 1898, was a lawyer who assumed the direction of the firm after his father-in-law's retirement and who subsequently joined the board of directors of IG Farben. In 1905 a spacious villa in the latest art-nouveau style was designed in Posen for the families of Nazary and Edmund by Alfred Grenander, a noted architect who had designed the Berlin subway stations.[45] Lieschen's money, however, ran out after she and her husband were forced to leave Germany as a result of the Nazi takeover and her husband's death in 1936. She remained in Zürich until the summer of 1941 when she met her daughter in Lisbon. In Berkeley she served as Dorothee's cook, descending greatly in status. But this did nothing to lessen her liveliness.

[44]Most of this paragraph depends on an unpublished memoir written by Beata Alden, Dorothee's eldest daughter, now available in the Leo Baeck Institute; the anecdote about Luigino and Berenson comes from Tom Peters.

[45]The Kantorowicz villa is described in Georg Swarzenski, "Alfred Grenander," *Moderne Baukunst* 4, 12 (1905): 131–40.

EKa's affection for Lieschen was unbounded. They were joking partners. In 1947 he sent her the rear part of a turkey to celebrate her naturalization as an American citizen and consequent divorce from her earlier world of "von Hintenburg" (*hintern* is German for rear end). A year later, after she moved to Italy with her daughter, EKa sent the following message to her on the occasion of her seventieth birthday:

> So now on Monday you will officially enter "old age"—there's no denying that. Yet, just as March 21 is the official beginning of spring but by no means signifies the real thing, so your seventieth birthday is not the May of your old age, and until you arrive in "the prime of your senility" you still have plenty of time to maintain your customary deportment. Let me embrace you very tenderly and lovingly. Let me wish that the burdens don't become too heavy and always remain endurable. And let me wish further that you remain "necessary" as before for others, and yourself avoid becoming a burden.[46]

In 1949, when she returned for a short visit, he wrote:

> For me, being together with you is always a sort of return to a natural condition which lies three generations behind us. . . . Everything else, with the exception of Soscha, is, in Gundolf's language, educational experience, but you two are still primal experience.[47]

The last family member to be mentioned is Vera Pietrkowski/Peters. She was EKa's mistress. It may be recalled that when he was in his teens his father did not want him to "start anything" with his first cousin. At the time he obeyed, but Vera was his first cousin once removed, being the daughter of his uncle Franz. She was born in Posen in 1907 and, to the initial displeasure of her parents, married her second cousin Ernst Pietrkowski (son of Lieschen and brother of Dorothee) in 1928. The couple lived in financial comfort in Berlin until the Nazi takeover in 1933. Ernst had a degree in plant pathology and was able to pursue his research in that area on a four-hundred-acre farm about sixty miles from the capital, while holding down a job as a division chief in a Berlin bank. But as soon as the Nazis took power he was "denounced" by someone who coveted his property. Supposedly he had made a defamatory remark about Goering. Thus he was arrested in July 1933, taken into SS captivity, first in the downtown Columbia House, and then at the Tempelhof airport, and subjected to unspeakable brutalities: "knifed and whipped."[48] (Others arrested by the

[46] 25 June 1948: Lerner archive. Even when she became older, EKa could not leave off joking about Lieschen's age. When she was eighty-two, he addressed her as "dearest Lolitachen (counting from 100 backwards)"; and when she was almost eighty-four he wrote, "It's already really hot here, over 80°, but that doesn't bother me; you are also over 80": 1 October 1960, 8 May 1963: Lerner archive.

[47] 23 May 1949.

[48] Details of Ernst Pietrkowski's arrest and imprisonment by the SS are in postwar indemnification papers regarding Ernest Peters: Lerner archive. The detail comes from an interview with Eva Peters-Hunting, 26 June 2001.

Nazis in this period were tortured to death.) After two weeks in SS prisons he was released; a limousine sent by his father (still a director of IG Farben) picked him up and drove him out of Germany. Ernst recuperated in Zürich for several months; then, reunited with his wife and young daughter, he entered into a succession of far-flung wanderings—France, Cyprus, England—until the family arrived in Stockton, California, in January 1940. There Ernst, with the new name of Ernest Peters, had located a job with a large potato company.[49]

The move to California was unrelated to EKa's presence in California, but given that Berkeley is only fifty-six miles from Stockton, the Peterses saw EKa often. Letters to Vera from her parents in England repeatedly send regards to "Ernst Kanto."[50] The Peters couple lent EKa a painting by Lyonel Feininger, *Normannisches Dorf*, which had been a gift from Vera's once wealthy father. Ernest Peters was diagnosed with multiple sclerosis in 1942 and after a while could no longer walk the potato fields. When it became clear that he was unable to function in an outdoor job he became an accountant, while Vera took up nursing to help with the finances. (For financial reasons they took back the Feininger and sold it for $3,000[51]—in 2004 it was auctioned by Sotheby's for $1,240,000.)

Vera had long admired EKa. She had saved a letter and a postcard he had sent her from as far back at 1935, as well as a letter he sent her from Berkeley in September 1939 when he learned that she was in Stockton.[52] Vera Peters (fig. 22) was an attractive woman. In 1940 she and EKa became lovers.[53] She was careful to keep the relationship a secret from her husband and thus had EKa send intimate letters to her at the Stockton post office, General Delivery, but when he wrote letters without intimacies he sent these to her home so that she could leave them lying around and maintain the fiction that they were just good friends.[54] (He once referred to these as his "official letters."[55]) Vera owned a car and could drive away for assignations. They often accompanied each other to Carmel, where they stayed with two of EKa's German friends, Arthur and Leni

[49] Interview with Vera's daughter, Eva Peters-Hunting, 26 June 2001. Also email message from Beata Alden, 11 November 2011 (potato company), and a trove of letters, mostly from Eva (née Mühsam) and Franz Kantorowicz to their daughter Vera dating from the 1930s: Lerner archive. (The letter collection is so vast that to master it properly would be a research project in itself.)

[50] Franz Kantorowicz to Vera, late summer 1940: "es ist doch schön, dass ihr so nah bei einander seid"; Franz to Vera, September 1940; Eva Kantorowicz to Vera, 18 March 1941, late April 1941; Eva to Vera 28 July 1941.

[51] Interview with Eva Hunting, 22 February 2013.

[52] 18 February 1935; postcard of 1 December 1935; 23 September 1939: Lerner archive.

[53] Vera to EKa, 23 September 1962 (Lerner archive): "Dazu hast Du mich 22 Jahre zu gut gezogen oder erzogen."

[54] Interview with Eva Hunting, 22 February 2013. On Vera's request Eva Hunting destroyed EKa's personal letters after Vera's death but kept the others, some 160 letters and postcards, which she generously passed along to me. (The collection includes another 50 letters from Vera to EKa, which Vera retrieved after EKa's death.)

[55] To Vera, in a "General Delivery" letter that was misplaced into the wrong batch, 1 August 1953: Lerner archive.

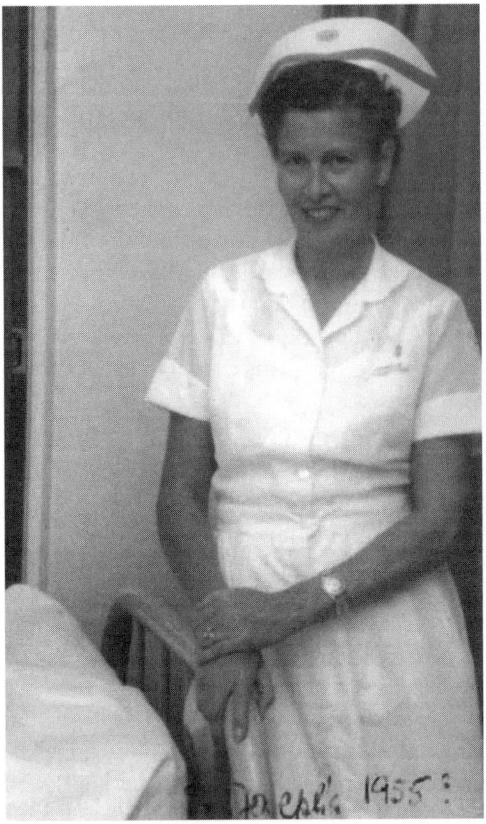

Figure 22. Vera Peters, circa 1955. (Lerner archive)

Lehman, who were among the few who knew of the relationship.[56] Sometimes they went together to Lake Tahoe.[57] According to Ihor Ševčenko, who knew certain aspects of the Berkeley scene very well, Walter Horn kept an apartment far from campus for trysts with his numerous conquests and lent EKa a key.

Vera Peters was not an intellectual, and that fact probably enhanced her appeal. Lucy Cherniavsky observed that EKa's attitude toward women was that "they were guilty until proven innocent."[58] They were guilty if they were bluestockings or tried to be rivals to men. Instead he preferred women with whom he could relax and have a good time. Vera also had a nice sense of humor. Once when they were together at a restaurant a waiter referred to her as EKa's "kid sister," which prompted her to address him in a subsequent letter as "Brother,

[56] Ralph Giesey to Robert E. Lerner, 19 May 2009.

[57] Interview with Lucy Cherniavsky, 5 September 1990.

[58] Interview of 5 September 1990.

Cousin, or whatever."[59] At Carmel EKa and Vera would go walking and at Lake Tahoe swimming. In September 1951, when he was about to leave the West Coast for Princeton, they had what they assumed would be their last tryst. They checked into separate rooms in a hotel in San Francisco and parted after midnight. At 1 a.m. Vera wrote a wistful note that tells as much about him as it does about her:

> EKa—There is no sense trying to say very much. Especially as you abhor romanticism and I apparently did a good job to cover up. Or maybe that is what I call the feeling-repellent substance you forgot to put around me, when you "formed" your "Gebild aus Menschenhand" [creation by human hand]. Though imperfect, I want to thank you for doing this "creative" work. And a lot of other things, I have to thank you for—You wouldn't understand, therefore the generalization. I hope that some of it will help in having a different aspect towards life or the shell thereoff [*sic*] and help making a go of what I am about to begin. Nevertheless—with too much affection and love—Vera.[60]

The fact that EKa saved this note (along with many other later ones from Vera) until his death suggests that he was not quite as heartless as Vera portrayed him. Moreover, his resettling in Princeton by no means ended the relationship; rather it continued until his death. (Shortly before then he made Vera his primary heir.) For Vera's part, she told her daughter in reference to her still loving her husband: "They say one cannot love two men at the same time, but I did."[61]

[59] 9 December 1959.

[60] 15 September 1951, from the Clift Hotel.

[61] Interview with Eva Hunting, 22 February 2013; also Ralph Giesey to Robert E. Lerner, 6 July 2004.

CHAPTER 20

"Scarcely Wants to Go to Germany"

In 1930 Ernst Kantorowicz had offered his "here I stand" in Halle: "a real belief in something like a German mission . . . yes, a fanatical belief in today's threatened nation." About a decade later he told a favorite student in Berkeley, "as far as Germany is concerned they can put a tent over the entire country and turn on the gas." There are continuities aplenty in Kantorowicz's thought and career, but not in this regard.

To be sure, the hatred took a while to develop. The allusion in the "German Papacy" broadcast of 1935 to "the hopelessness—as we know—that sticks to all German history" expressed frustration rather than hostility. And private expressions before the war are directed against "Shitler." EKa's letters to Bowra castigate Chamberlain for giving in to "Shitler." For example, on March 16, 1939, a day after German troops marched into Bohemia, he wrote to Bowra with dripping irony, "My idea is to re-baptize the name of the Wilhelmsplatz in Berlin and call it Chamberlain Square, erecting in front of the Propaganda ministerium two monuments, one for Houston Stewart, the other for Neville, both with the dedication: 'A grateful nation to the founders of Greater Germany.'" He was encouraged that the audience in Baltimore watching a newsreel shared his sentiments: "Chamb is booed more than Shitler—I never heard such a noise."[1]

After war broke out EKa wrote mordantly about the aggressive lust of his compatriots: "Europa once more is being raped by a bull."[2] That was in December 1939, but with the German victories of May 1940 he forsook irony: "I can scarcely manage to concentrate on anything other than the awful announcements of victories that keep streaming in."[3] Forthrightly he wrote to Bernard Flexner of "the nightmare in Europe, from which I suffer more than I can tell

[1] 9 March 1939. On 27 March he wrote: "It might be useful for distinguished English to sign their letters—according to German Heil Shitler's—with some phrase such as 'Hang Chamberlain' just in order to demonstrate that the writer was still an honest man."

[2] To Wilhelm Stein, 21 December 1939: Stein papers.

[3] To Albrecht von Bernstorff: Gutsarchiv Altenhof, Sammlung Albrecht von Bernstorff, vol. 41, no. 78. The date can only be approximated because the top of the letter is missing.

you."[4] EKa had no reason to write to Flexner what he thought of the Germans, but Norman Rich, who spent many evenings with him, reported that by 1942 "the entire Nazi business had transformed Kantorowicz into a bitter and even passionate critic of Germans in general.[5]

Unfortunately the texts for Kantorowicz's army lecture series on Modern History and Contemporary Politics do not survive and those for the German history series are incomplete. But we do have a lecture in the latter series in which EKa discoursed on what he posited as a centuries-old German fascination with political prophecy. Thus "When the piper [Hitler] came he baited the youth. He made them believe he was the 'redeemer' foreseen and promised for centuries."[6] In this context EKa cited Schiller's line, "every nation has its day in history but the day of the German is the harvest of all times," for the third time in his public career, but now he changed Schiller's "is" to "will be" to make him most explicitly a political prophet. Whereas he had adduced Schiller in his Halle address of 1930 and his "Secret Germany" lecture of 1933 with zealous approval, now he brought forth the quotation as a specimen of how Germans had been hoodwinked.[7]

On the day of Germany's surrender in May 1945 Kantorowicz skipped his regular lecture in his Renaissance class to comment on the event and its significance.[8] Postwar newspaper reports informed him about frightful Nazi atrocities, and these were most difficult to bear because they entirely discredited his earlier proclamations of faith in "the dogma of the worthy future and honor of the nation." His specific reactions can be found in letters exchanged with prewar German friends. One was Ernst Langlotz, who had remained teaching in Bonn. Certain that Langlotz had little to do with the "brown plague" (*die braune Pest*—a play on *die schwarze Pest*, or Black Death), EKa referred in September to the Nazi regime as a "monstrous obscenity" and pronounced that "the worst grotesquerie of the world saw to it that in Hitler excrement was made flesh."[9] He wrote too that "the disclosures about the concentration camps [and] the marauding of the freed slave laborers [are] a Brueghel-like witches' sabbath that defies the imagination." (He did not yet know the worst: a passage in the letter refers to "Belsen, Dachau, Theresienstadt" but not to the liquidation camps in the East.) In 1946 he reestablished contacts with Marion Dönhoff and received from her what he described as "a shocking report about

[4] 29 May 1940: Emergency Committee papers.

[5] Rich, in *Central European History* 35 (2002): 612.

[6] LBI, box 8, folder 2.

[7] The about-face in the citing of Schiller has been noted previously by Eckhart Grünewald and Ulrich Raulff.

[8] Interview with Lucy Cherniavsky, 5 September 1990.

[9] Langlotz papers.

the years from 1940 to 1945 that makes one (and listeners when it is read aloud) freeze."[10]

In his letter of 1945 to Langlotz EKa wrote that returning to Germany was for him "of course entirely unthinkable." In a letter of September 1946 to Edgar Salin he assured him: "Reunion with a few friends would be the only thing that might draw me to Germany. I wrote to Reinhardt, the Greek expert, a little while ago, to say that I can no longer lecture in Germany because it makes no sense to plant my own unreality, in which I necessarily live here, into a completely differently ordered unreality presumably found now in all European countries, and certainly in Germany."[11] He was toying with the idea of traveling to Europe in May 1950 but wrote to Helmut Küpper that it was likely to be too expensive. ("For me travel has never yet been cheap; I'm too old to travel uncomfortably and to cram myself into an in-between deck without distress.") And if he did go he "would scarcely want to go to Germany."[12]

EKa was acutely aware of his own deracination—his "own unreality." He had become an American citizen in January 1945 but had done this only for bureaucratic convenience. That he had no illusions is clear from a passage in a letter to Salin: "Lloyds offers no insurance for what stands before this country; it probably is preferable in many respects to today's Europe, but it's no longer 'the land of dreams.'"[13] In a letter to Küpper of 1949 he expressed annoyance with a "particularly stupid" report that he had become "fully American" and expressed his tug of feelings in a felicitous bitter-sweet passage:

> You must know who Gisela Werbezirk is, the actress? A really witty person. After she had been in New York for a while she met an acquaintance. "Are you happy, Mrs. Werbezirk?" She reflected for a bit and then replied: "Happy—? Yes! Glücklich—? Nein!" ["Glücklich" means "happy" in German.] That goes, mutatis mutandis, for every one of us here—and I myself am still stranded on the most pleasant of the coasts![14]

Returning to EKa's concern about postwar news from Germany, he was aware that living conditions were distressing and sought to help friends with gift packages. In his letter reestablishing contact with Langlotz he wrote: "My dear good friend, all the things I have to ask you—thousands, questions without end!! And what I would give for an hour with you. But most important:

[10] Kantorowicz to Edgar Salin, 30 November 1946: Salin papers. Dönhoff published an account of her experiences in the war years, especially during the Russian invasion of East Prussia, as *Namen die keiner mehr nennt* (1962). A copy she gave to EKa bore the inscription (in German): "for EKa, who understands all of this."

[11] 13 September 1946: Salin papers.

[12] 10 September 1949: StGA, Kantorowicz, II:1901. (The quotation about being "too old to travel" is from the same letter.)

[13] 13 November 1945: Salin papers.

[14] 10 September 1949.

can I send you something? And what? And how? I know of course that there's nothing you couldn't use."[15] Particularly affecting is a passage from a letter of May 1947 to Friedrich Baethgen, who then was fifty-seven:

> I was happy to hear from him [a Berkeley colleague] that you are doing well "so far," although he gave a deplorable description of the cold under which you suffered, and the many woolens you had to pack yourself up in, and then still freeze. Should I send you some clothing? There is a type of CARE package with blue navy cloth including buttons, thread, needles, lining, etc. There is even shoe leather with all the materials, in case you have someone who can make you some shoes. On that subject, it occurs to me: have you received the package with socks, tea, and so forth? A whole lot of packages went out to you, CARE as well as other kinds of shipments.[16]

(Charles Jelavich, who had taken courses with EKa in the Army Specialized Training Program, still remembered in 2012 visiting Baethgen in Berlin in 1946 with a parcel sent by EKa.[17])

The letters from this period also feature reflections on the political situation and show that EKa was developing a critical stance regarding American foreign policy in relation to the German question. In his letter of September 1946 to Salin he referred to the "grotesque incapacity" and "self-righteous ways" of the Western occupation powers. He was particular taken aback by a speech made in Stuttgart on September 6 by Secretary of State James F. Byrnes which assured Germans that U.S. troops would remain in Germany as long as Russian troops remained in the Russian zone. The speech led EKa to fear that "it simply serves to invite a German MacArthur," that is, a high military commander who would oversee a long-term American occupation. His view of the situation comes out more clearly in a letter written a week later to Langlotz that laments a hardening of the cold war.[18] Byrnes had promised American help in rebuilding Germany, and EKa "wanted to hope" that this foretold an improvement in the German situation. But he found the speech clearly "political" and implicitly sided with a strong criticism of it by Henry Wallace for its anti-Soviet position which led to Wallace's being fired by President Truman. As EKa went on to say, "In this country the hovering problems are treated with the much too simple and diplomatically impossible formula of 'for or against Russia.' Nothing good can come of that."

EKa surely was not sympathetic to the Russians. In writing in May 1947 to Baethgen, who then was professor in Berlin, he advised his friend to think

[15] 15 September 1945: Langlotz papers.

[16] Baethgen papers: 4 May 1947.

[17] My thanks to Charles Jelavich's son Peter for passing on this information: email message 14 July 2012.

[18] 20 September 1946: Langlotz papers.

seriously of taking a different job in the West, "crossing the Elbe in the opposite direction from the Ottonians." The reason was, as EKa wrote presciently, that "it could come to a blockade that one ought better avoid"; if Baethgen were caught in that "from Berlin, strategically, there is only *one* line of withdrawal: direction Siberia." But propping up Germany militarily against the Russians was not to EKa's liking. In the same letter he observed critically an American tendency to extend military bases and appeared to be saying that if there was indeed going to be a blockade of Berlin it would be the West's fault.

The most remarkable incident relating to EKa's dealing with former German friends was his engagement in the denazification proceedings concerning Percy Ernst Schramm.[19] To gain a full sense of the story one must go back to August 1938 when EKa was desperately trying to leave Germany and seeking people who might write in his behalf in order to obtain a teaching position in the United States. We have seen that he and Schramm were friends with overlapping research interests. They had been together in Heidelberg in the 1920s and maintained cordial relations during the next decade. By then Schramm had become Ordinarius at Göttingen. Since he knew EKa's personality and scholarship he was an obvious person to write an open letter of recommendation. The only question was whether he would do this, given that writing favorably about a Jew in the Germany of 1938 was somewhat risky for a German professor: even if the letter was meant for reading beyond the borders, a possibility always existed that word of it might leak out back home. Yet Schramm accepted the assignment and wrote a strong letter.[20]

Schramm wrote that he had known Kantorowicz for a good dozen years and had read more or less everything that he had written. He referred to the great success of the Frederick biography and singled out the supplementary volume as "remain[ing] a storehouse of information for all research concerning the medieval German empire." He went on to point out that Kantorowicz had been appointed to his full professorship in Frankfurt without having habilitated and that his pedagogical gifts then had become as highly recognized as his scholarly ones: "He placed great emphasis on attending to his students." The letter then became rather daring. Schramm wrote that Kantorowicz's pedagogical commitments made it "particularly painful" for him to surrender his Frankfurt position, one "that from the outside view was so successful and belonged so much to his very being that he felt empty without it." Had these words been read in Nazi Germany they would have raised questions about Percy Ernst Schramm's reliability: was he really saying that it was a pity that a Jew had been forced out of his job?

[19] A full-scale biography of Schramm and appraisal of his work is Thimme, *Percy Ernst Schramm und das Mittelalter*.

[20] 10 August 1938: carbon copy in LBI, box 5, folder 3.

More daring followed. Schramm indicated that he had not broken with his Jewish friend. To the contrary he was fully apprised of all EKa's scholarly work ever since he had left Frankfurt; moreover, he had included parts of an unpublished article by Kantorowicz in a recent article of his own. (Everyone knew why Kantorowicz was unable to publish.) He knew too that EKa had written a collection of scholarly essays and believed that it was "in the interest of scholarship that it be published as soon as possible." After referring to Kantorowicz's knowledge of English, he ended as follows:

> I must emphasize that the conversations I have held with Kantorowicz through the many years of our acquaintance have brought me an intellectual exchange that I value and that at the same time allows me to feel certain that Kantorowicz would fit in with and enrich any new circle of intellectually lively people because he is an upstanding and solid person whose departure from here will be seen only with regret by his many friends.

Schramm sent EKa a copy of the letter (standard German procedure), and EKa saved it. Thus when Schramm faced grave difficulties of his own EKa was ready to reciprocate. The problem was Schramm's Nazi past, which raised the possibility of his being barred from returning to his professorship in Göttingen after the war. Certain points were not in dispute. He had belonged to the Nazi paramilitary organization, the Sturmabteilung (S.A.), from 1934 until 1938, and he became a Nazi Party member in 1939 although he withdrew in the same year. During the war he was the official staff historian of the Wehrmacht. (In the 1960s he published two volumes based on these experiences, leading Erwin Panofsky to refer to him as "Hitler's Thucydides."[21]) But one could always present extenuating circumstances, and postwar "denazification" boards, staffed by Germans, granted themselves latitude in making decisions.

In October 1946 Schramm was required to fill out a questionnaire about his past by a denazification board in the British zone.[22] When his wife informed EKa he immediately offered to be of help in writing a letter in Schramm's behalf.[23] For some reason Schramm declined the offer, and initially all seemed well because in January he was cleared by the German board. But matters did not rest there, for in March the British military government overruled the board's decision. According to the new ruling Schramm was to be barred from returning to his professorship because of his memberships in the S.A. and the Nazi Party, and also because "his record indicates that it is undesirable that he should be in a position to influence German youth." The rector at Göttingen, who had counted on Schramm's return, decided to challenge the ruling and

[21] Thimme, *Percy Ernst Schramm und das Mittelalter*, 532.

[22] For a narrative of the events, see ibid., 489–94.

[23] See the extract of a letter from Kantorowicz to Frau Schramm in Schramm's statement to the "Denazifizierungsausschuss" of 3 December 1946: Staatsarchiv Hamburg, Familie Schramm, L 247.

wrote immediately to EKa and Hans Rothfels (a prestigious émigré professor at the University of Chicago), asking whether they could engage themselves "to clear the international estimation of Prof. Schramm's personality and scientific work."[24]

Three days later Schramm sent a similar plea to Kantorowicz and Rothfels, providing all the information that might help them to advance his cause, and a list of scholars, mainly in the United States and Britain, he thought might write for him too.[25]

EKa quickly swung into action. He and Rothfels consulted by mail about mobilizing a letter-writing campaign in Schramm's favor and agreed on respective assignments.[26] EKa then recruited several others to write letters[27] and submitted a notarized three-page, single-spaced letter himself. With near symmetry, as if Clio were Euclid, EKa wrote on behalf of Schramm in Schramm's darkest hour as Schramm earlier had written in behalf of EKa.

The symmetry is not perfect because Kantorowicz wrote at greater length and with greater intensity.[28] He began with his own experience:

> The last time I met Dr. Schramm was in the gloomy summer of 1938. Shortly before the pogroms were started in Germany and before I emigrated to the United States, Dr. Schramm had the courage to visit me in my home Berlin-Charlottenburg. On that occasion he wrote a letter on my behalf recommending me for appointment to the University of California. (See Document I.) I know that Dr. Schramm wrote a great number of similar letters to American and English institutions in order to recommend his emigrating Jewish friends and to alleviate the difficulties caused to them by the Nazi régime. I should also mention that it was at Dr. Schramm's request that I visit him in Göttingen, in 1937 or 1938, dining there with him and his family in his house. I wish to add that, whereas many German scholars avoided in those years the quotation of works of Jewish authors, Dr. Schramm took the risk to cite even an unpublished study of mine . . . openly disclosing the fact that he was still in personal contact with Jewish scholars and friends.

EKa then moved to Schramm's scholarship. In this regard his purpose not only was to establish the indisputable point that Schramm was "outstanding

[24] R. Rosemann to Kantorowicz and Hans Rothfels: ibid.

[25] LBI box 7, folder 3.

[26] Rothfels to Kantorowicz, 23 April 1947, 28 April 1947: LBI box 7, folder 3.

[27] According to Thimme, *Percy Ernst Schramm und das Mittelalter*, 492, n. 26, letters on behalf of Schramm by Gray Boyce (then the medieval historian at Northwestern University who had known Schramm since 1933) and Monroe Deutsch are in Staatsarchiv Hamburg, Familie Schramm, L 247. EKa was probably the one who elicited the Boyce letter and surely the one who elicited Deutsch's. Indirect evidence suggests that he recruited others, or at least attempted to do so.

[28] Kantorowicz, "To Whom it My Concern," 27 May 1947: Staatsarchiv Hamburg, Familie Schramm, L 247.

and internationally recognized" but, more important in the present context, to advance the equally indisputable point that his historiographical accomplishments were "supra-national." In fact this point was as indisputable as Schramm's outstanding international recognition. EKa wrote with full warrant that Schramm by no means limited himself to German history but had written basic studies concerning the English, French, and Spanish royal coronations; he had even planned a history of European coronations "from the beginning to the present" that was "to cover the wide and difficult area of comparative constitutional history of Europe." In sum "the general character of Dr. Schramm's work . . . as well as the topics which he has studied, exclude almost *a priori* a narrow nationalistic approach or militaristic outlook on the part of the author. In the approximately 3000 pages of Dr. Schramm which I have read, I have not found one utterance betraying a nationalistic or militaristic spirit."

EKa went on to maintain, quite accurately, that during the Nazi period Schramm had promoted international collaboration among European historians and that he had supported the careers of non-German students. Giving an example of the latter, he referred to Schramm's investment in the career of the Slavic scholar George Ostrogorsky: when Ostrogorsky "was still a poor student at Heidelberg, he owed part of his livelihood to the support, and his early career to the recommendations of Dr. Schramm." Still another point was that Schramm's doctoral students never worked on Nazi-favored topics. All told, EKa's letter was overwhelmingly strong in answering the charge that Schramm's record demonstrated that "he should not be in a position to influence German youth." On the contrary Schramm's return to his professorial chair was "almost imperative with regard to the problem of educating and re-educating German students for sober and scholarly work."

The question is whether EKa went further in two passages than was necessary. He stated that Schramm's willingness to help Jews "made it evident that [he] was not a pupil of Nazism," and in his last paragraph he wrote, "Percy Ernst Schramm has never to my knowledge demonstrated a nationalistic or militaristic attitude in speaking, writing, or teaching." But he did know that Schramm had been a member of the S.A., a point about which he kept silent, and he brushed aside the party membership as a "smoke-screen." Here is not the place to consider at length Schramm's political record during the Third Reich, but some salient points will show that EKa's two quoted passages teetered on falsehood. Schramm enthusiastically welcomed the Nazi takeover of Germany in 1933. As an exchange scholar in Princeton he went out of his way to give talks in Princeton and New York aiming to persuade his listeners of the virtues of the new regime. He argued that Germany was experiencing a healthful revolution that not only negated the possibility of a communist takeover but worked for social justice; as for the antisemitic policies, these were secondary matters and affected only a part of the Jewish population.[29] On October 18, 1938, after the Munich pact, he wrote in a diary: "80 million—without shedding of blood. Neither Bismarck nor the Maid of Orléans could have done that, but only someone who unites the capabilities of both. One feels too fulfilled to go to work."[30]

Obviously EKa could not have known what Schramm had written in letters to others or in notes to himself, and most likely he did not know about Schramm's public statements of 1933 in support of the Nazi regime. Moreover, he guarded himself in his last paragraph with the qualification "to his knowledge." Unquestionably Schramm's record was full of ambiguities; all the positive details that EKa presented were true, and another, of which EKa was unaware, was that in a book published in 1943 Schramm cited approvingly a statement of his great-grandfather regarding the nineteenth-century emancipation of Hamburg's Jews: "For we all, Jews as well as Christians, are citizens of Hamburg . . . and truly the emancipation of the Jews is not an act of indulgence but an act of justice."[31] Still, to say categorically that Schramm could not have been considered a "pupil of Nazism" was going over the line, and it is hard to doubt that EKa must have known that.

Since the letter would have been very strong even without the two dubious statements, the question arises as to why he went as far as he did. One answer seems clear. "Loyalty" (*Treue*) was always one of his watchwords, and Schramm was a friend who earlier had incurred some risk in proving his friendship. We may also turn to a passage in EKa's letter: "Within the 'Republic of Scholarship,' which still exists, Schramm appears as a clear-cut figure." For EKa the precedence of the "Republic of Scholarship" had become a credo. At least partly as a result of his alienation from "*Deutschtum*" and his indifference to his American citizenship, the "Republic of Scholarship" extended a new loyalty that rose above the merely personal. Despite whatever Nazi record Schramm may have had, he was a "clear-cut figure" of the "Republic," and there really was no danger of his indoctrinating the youth in anything other than coronation rites and iconology. As it turned out, the British military officials accepted the University of Göttingen's appeal, and Schramm returned to pursuing a very fruitful scholarly career. The likelihood that EKa's strong letter played a signal role in the outcome seems great.

Norman Rich has written that EKa's anti-Germanism "became somewhat more moderated in the postwar years,"[32] but this seems true only to a degree. In the course of his first postwar trip to Europe in the summer of 1953, he

[29]Thimme, *Percy Ernst Schramm und das Mittelalter*, 340–41, also Joist Grolle, *Der Hamburger Percy Ernst Schramm—ein Historiker auf der Suche der Wirklichkeit* (Hamburg, 1989), 24–25—Grolle's short book offers an excellent weighing of Schramm's political record.

[30]Grolle, *Der Hamburger Percy Ernst Schramm*, 30–33.

[31]Ibid., 37, citing Schramm, *Hamburg, Deutschland und die Welt* (Munich, 1943).

[32]*Central European History* 35 (2002): 612.

felt obliged to spend a few weeks in Germany because he had research and publication matters to attend to and because he did really want to see some old friends. In Munich he stayed with Helmut Küpper, in Bonn he saw Ernst Langlotz, and in Frankfurt he went walking in the Palmengarten with Baby's estranged daughter Arianna.[33] He found the condition of the German cities frightful because they still were in ruins—"they looked like excavations in Ostia or Delos."[34] But even had the cities been rebuilt he would have felt alienated. As he wrote to his cousin Lieschen, "Germany is now as foreign to me as the once foreign Greece has become familiar. I wish to have nothing more to do with this place and as soon as I'm finished with the 'business' part of my trip I probably will never again come back."[35] On his next trip to Europe in 1955 he in fact did not go back. Although his attendance at an International Historians' Congress in Rome gave him the opportunity to meet with his two closest German medievalist friends, Friedrich Baethgen and Schramm, he did not venture north of Trastevere.

Business at the Monumenta did dictate two short stays in Munich in 1958 and 1961. In 1961 he was in Munich for a day and a half. He wrote on his return that he had first run into German tourists in Greece and when he heard their language he almost canceled his planned trip. Going through with it after all, he met with three colleagues in Munich: "It wasn't so bad and I forgot where I was."[36]

[33] Interview 16 December 1993.
[34] To Vera Peters, 1 August 1953: Lerner archive.
[35] To Elise Peters, 25 July 1953: Lerner archive.
[36] To Eva Kantorowicz, 29 September 1961: Lerner archive.

CHAPTER 21

"Land of Lotus-Eaters"

THE FOUR YEARS FROM JUNE 1945 UNTIL JUNE 1949 were probably the happiest in Ernst Kantorowicz's life. He considered himself to be in a "land of lotus-eaters."[1] Although he complained that "a janitor earned as much as he did,"[2] he moved into a house of his own and became absorbed in new matters such as gardening. He went regularly to Carmel for sun and crawfish and to Lake Tahoe for fishing and swimming. He engaged with numerous conversation partners, and he acquired a number of new advanced students for whom he felt affection and in whom he invested much time. Conviviality was unending, as was scholarly work.

Buying a house was a major event. The building near campus in which EKa had an apartment was sold in the summer of 1946, obliging him to find a new place. With housing scarce in postwar Berkeley, he took an apartment in the Berkeley Hills, at 193 The Uplands. But the location was inconvenient. As he wrote to Ernst Langlotz, "I had to move, could only find in the overfilled Berkeley something far out, and that demands endless time driving about each day."[3] ("Driving" here meant public transportation; Kantorowicz got a U.S. driver's license only later in Princeton, after the introduction of automatic transmission.) Writing to Edgar Salin, he complained similarly that his new location cost him travel time of two hours per day.[4] Two years later he decided to buy a small house at 1421 Euclid Avenue (fig. 23). He had no money for a down payment, but his cousin Dorothee put up all the cash and he agreed to pay off his debt in monthly installments. From his point of view the arrangement was fortunate because "it is my accumulating pension . . . I save compulsorily 500 dollars a year." (When his student Michael Cherniavsky expressed amazement that he had enough money to buy a house, he answered, "Well, Michael,

[1] To Edgar Salin, 13 September 1946: Salin papers.
[2] Interview with Vera Peters, 11 August 1989.
[3] 20 September 1946: Langlotz papers.
[4] 13 September 1946.

Figure 23. EKa's house on Euclid Avenue in Berkeley, now sadly overgrown. At the left is his addition: the new "wing" for his "palazzo." (Photo by Callum Lerner-Thomas)

not everyone is a refugee."[5]) Given that the house was located within moderate walking distance of campus (a bus also stopped nearby), and that smaller houses in that vicinity were marketable, he believed that even when he died at age fifty-six "there would be no risk for Dorothee."[6] (EKa joked continually about dying at fifty-six, the age at death of Frederick II, as well as of Julius Caesar and Nietzsche.[7]) Moreover the house was pretty and had a fine view of San Francisco Bay and the Golden Gate Bridge.

EKa took to house owning (a first for him) with enthusiasm. He paid for building an addition,[8] for walls facing the street, and for painting the exterior of the house. A black cleaning lady—"the woman I love"—came three times a week for two hours.[9] Even though a Japanese gardener came once a week for two hours, EKa discovered that he liked to work in the garden himself. In April 1949 he wrote to Bowra: "My garden is quite pretty now with Iris and Roses under the Scotch Broom, which is an ocean of yellowness"[10] In May he wrote to

[5] Lerner interview with Lucy Cherniavsky, 3 March 1991.

[6] To Elise Peters, 23 May 1949: Lerner archive.

[7] E.g., letter to C. M. Bowra, 27 April 1949: "I may go to Italy & Greece at the age of 56 hoping to die there."

[8] To Elise Peters, 25 June 1948 (Lerner archive): "I have to go to my treadmill of the Summer Session in half an hour in order to earn the new 'wing' for my palazzo—prostitution, but not the first building erected on such a foundation."

[9] To Helmut Küpper, 31 October 1949: StGA, Kantorowicz, II:1902 . In a letter of 1947 Kantorowicz had complained about having to do housework by himself because of the difficulty of getting help: to Friedrich Baethgen, 4 May 1947: Baethgen papers.

[10] 27 April 1949.

Lieschen: "The garden is in continual bloom, gives me pleasure, and distracts me much too much from my work. This 'bug' has really gotten to me. The tigridias will soon be in bloom and I'm very curious about them." So keen was he on aerating the soil that he imported earthworms from Ohio and kept an eye on them: "The earthworms are doing wonderfully well and have become quite improbably large."[11] In November 1949 he wrote to Bowra: "Rain began to fall two days ago and my garden has lost its glamour. Only the earthworms from Ohio are happy and are making love in my corpse [why his corpse is unclear], as it were, in dead earnest."[12]

In terms of hobbies, however, gardening still took second place to cooking. With a centrally located house of his own EKa could give dinner parties as often as he liked. The stories about these parties are legion: three days—one for shopping and planning the menu, one for cooking, one for cleaning up.[13] A menu might be as follows: "chrysanthemum soup with shrimp and scallops and spinach, then the so-quickly made chicken breasts with saffron rice and persimmons and strawberries."[14] I once asked EKa's colleague in Princeton, Kurt Weitzmann, whether Kantorowicz really served chrysanthemum soup; the answer: "Yes, he did. Once he invited me to dinner and actually had chrysanthemums on the table, and he took the flower and put the petals in his and my dish!"[15] When EKa served a roast, "his exquisite carving, accompanied by an intricate and witty historical monologue, would have done credit to the grand chef of the Palace."[16] A familiar story is of EKa preparing a dinner while on vacation at Lake Tahoe. Staying at a cottage owned by Otto Maenchen-Helfen and his wife Anja, he was busily going about his work in the kitchen when he looked for something in the cabinets and could not find it. So without a word he went upstairs and descended with a tin of truffles. When an amazed onlooker inquired, "EKa, do you always travel with truffles?" he responded, "Doesn't everyone?"[17]

Three other kitchen stories are less noted. EKa maintained a rivalry on the culinary front with Margherita Rosenthal, Leonardo Olschki's sister. According to Margherita's son Felix, both would tell guests that they had "just whipped something up" when they had spent three days slaving over it. One morning when Felix was out driving with his mother she asked if they might stop off

[11] To Elise Peters, 23 May 1949: Lerner archive.

[12] 8 November 1949.

[13] Interview with Homer Thompson (Institute for Advanced Study): April 1989.

[14] EKa's report of a menu to Elise Peters, 8 November 1956: Lerner archive.

[15] Interview, 3 May 1989.

[16] Sayles, "The Scholar and the Loyalty Oath," 28.

[17] The full version of this story was told to me by Lucy Cherniavsky, 3 March 1991. A confirmation is Kantorowicz to Michael Cherniavsky, 4 July 1960 (Lerner archive), apropos Cherniavsky's visit to a doctor: "you should have asked him to stuff your liver with truffels [*sic*] so that you too would 'never travel without truffels.'"

briefly at EKa's house because she knew he'd be preparing a meal around that time; she wanted to see what the special ingredient was that he put into his bouillon. So they went in and EKa was indeed stirring the stock pot. Knowing that his rival was looking over his shoulder, he nonchalantly threw in a walnut and she left thinking that she had finally learned his secret. But it was a ruse.[18] I heard another cooking story from Michael Cherniavsky's wife. Once at a dinner party EKa served kidneys and Lucy was struck by the finesse with which he made them. So later she asked how he managed to eliminate the faint odor of urine that kept her from preparing kidneys herself: "Do you do something to eliminate the traces of urine?" To which EKa replied: "On the contrary my dear, I usually put in some of my own."[19] EKa loved organ meats. He prided himself on his "riz de veau [sweetbreads], à la Maison."[20] A one-time Berkeley student recalled being on a bus when Kantorowicz stepped in on his way home. But then he said to the driver: "Oh, but stop, I forgot my brains."[21]

Putting aside organ meats, fresh seafood was a Kantorowicz specialty, and this coincided with two more hobbies: crawfish trapping and fishing. The former was one of his activities when he visited friends in Carmel, as he customarily did at the end of spring semesters. The friends were Germans, Arthur and Helene ("Leni") Lehman, brother and sister. Arthur was lucky enough to sell his property in Germany and export his money just in time to use it for buying a house in Carmel and pursuing investment strategies there. EKa's cousin Eva (daughter of Vera), who sometimes as a teenager accompanied him to Carmel, remembered that conversations with the Lehmans ranged over a wide variety of topics—but always including what would be good to cook for dinner.[22]

EKa's letters make a fuss most of all about trout. In April 1949 he wrote to Bowra, "At present I am living on Salmon-Trout, most likely the best fish I have tasted, which has the rather noble complex of making love exclusively in sweet water."[23] A month later came, "I am going up to the mountains next weekend—Monday will be a Holiday—with three or four students, and hope to fish enough trouts to convince those Americans how good a truite bleue is."[24] (For those who might wonder, *truite bleue* is trout freshly caught and poached in bouillon with the "blue" slime still on it.) After EKa left California he returned in the summer of 1952 to wrap up affairs and added a trip to Lake Tahoe. Writing to his student Robert Benson, he reported about his fishing: "I got a number of 9–10 inchers, fat and heavy brown brook trouts, which the Strasbourg cook of the

[18] Interview with Felix Rosenthal, 24 February 2002.

[19] Interview, 3 March 1991.

[20] Kersten, "In vino dignitas," 120.

[21] Interview with Wilder Bentley, Jr., 1 September 2012.

[22] Email message from Eva Hunting, 13 May 2012.

[23] 27 April 1949.

[24] To Bowra, 18 May 1949.

hotel prepared exactly the way one treats those darlings in Europe—*en bleu*."[25] This was the sort thing that EKa felt driven to mention in his letters.

In the Berkeley years he went often to Lake Tahoe and did not shrink from swimming in ice-cold waters. When there he often stayed in the cottage of the Maenchen-Helfens. Anja (née Anna Aronsohn) was a lively sparring partner. She was from Vienna and was a Freudian psychologist, analyzed by Anna Freud. An article she published in 1936 dealt with "aggression from fear of castration," and one of 1946 was "A Case of Superego Disintegration."[26] The sparring arose from EKa's contempt for Freudianism. In 1956 he wrote to Lieschen, "I wanted 'out' and nothing but 'out' . . . and until today I have no desire to return again to the womb, which apparently is psychoanalytically not at all good."[27] When he wrote to Bowra of the "complex of Salmon-Trout making love exclusively in sweet water," he added, "I shall consult Anja about it and might take to it myself."[28] But Anja was not ready to serve as a consultant. Once at Lake Tahoe EKa saw her opening a can of Campbell's soup and said that he could never be psychoanalyzed by such a person. To which she shot back that she would never take him on.[29]

This story, as well as numerous others, was told to me by Lucy Cherniavsky, wife of Michael, a fact that leads easily to the subject of EKa's relations with his students. Some who appeared in Berkeley after the end of the war were as important to him as his coeval friends. Before seeing who they were it is necessary to make some exclusions. Ulrich Raulff, in his scintillating account of the dispersal of the George circle after the "death of the Master," places Ernst Kantorowicz at the center of a group of Bay Area poets who constituted the "Berkeley Renaissance," which later issued into the "Beats."[30] These poets were Robert Duncan, Jack Spicer, and Robin Blaser.[31] All attended Kantorowicz's lectures in the years between 1947 and 1950 and were enthralled.[32] Some of his observations influenced their thought and their poetry. Duncan once said that Kantorowicz was one of only two teachers who deserved a place in his biography and specified further: "Robin Blaser, Jack Spicer, and I, as poets, are all variously students of Kantorowicz and share through his teaching the sense of creative

[25] 22 July 1952: Benson papers.

[26] http://psyschoanalytikerinnen.de/oesterreich_biografien.html#Maenchen.

[27] 30 November 1956: Lerner archive.

[28] 27 April 1949.

[29] Interview with Lucy Cherniavsky, 16 September 1990. Anja's sense of humor can be seen in a "synopsis" of a play by Tennessee Williams that EKa relayed to Bowra in a letter of 26 June 1962: "Act I: the hero sleeps with his mother; Act II: the hero sleeps with his brother; Act III: the hero kills himself when he hears that he was an adopted child."

[30] Raulff, *Kreis ohne Meister*, 337–38.

[31] Raulff also mentions Kenneth Rexroth, but Rexroth never had anything to do with Berkeley.

[32] Faas, *Young Robert Duncan*, 258–59, 272, lists the many undergraduate courses given by Kantorowicz that Duncan took.

ground in history that is also poetry."[33] Robin Blaser agreed: "Kantorowicz was of enormous importance to all three of us."[34] Examples of the influence run to specific images as "The Kingdom of Jerusalem" and EKa's view, expressed in his lectures on Dante and Petrarch, that a true poet holds an "office."[35] One study of the Berkeley poets finds another influence in Kantorowicz's "cold rigor, melodrama, and a certain overdependence on tradition."[36] It even turns out that the very term "Berkeley Renaissance" derives from the Kantorowicz influence: Duncan said that "when Spicer and Robin and I were Kantorowicz's students, in poems assuming medieval and Renaissance learning . . . we called ourselves the Berkeley Renaissance."[37]

But these men hardly "studied medieval history" with Kantorowicz, for they did no more than listen to his undergraduate lectures.[38] Moreover, however much they may have admired him, he did not admire them. The witnesses I interviewed who were contemporaries had no doubts. Margaret Bentley Ševčenko emphasized that EKa was not—and could not have been—attracted by the circle around Robert Duncan: "[EKa] was fastidious and Duncan was dirty; Duncan didn't take baths."[39] Lucy Cherniavsky reported that although EKa usually had the highest respect for poets, he did not respect these three because he could not endure slovenliness.[40] In the words of Norman Rich, "EKa didn't like this group." Spicer wanted to be an insider but was too pushy; as EKa expostulated to Rich "he called me EKa!! without my permission."[41] Also regarding Spicer, EKa's cousin, Beata Alden, wrote to me: "I was in an EKa class with Jack Spicer, who was a dirty, sandalled youth who lounged in class, and was heartily disapproved of by the elegant, immaculate EKa."[42]

[33] Ibid., 41, 281.

[34] Lewis Ellingham and Kevin Killian, *Poet Be Like God: Jack Spicer and the San Francisco Renaissance* (Hanover, NH, 1998), 20. See also Robin Blaser, *The Fire: Collected Essays* (Berkeley, 2006), 13, 51–52, et passim.

[35] Faas, *Young Robert Duncan*, 230, 273.

[36] Ellingham and Killian, *Poet Be Like God*, 21.

[37] Ibid., 79.

[38] Interview with Ralph Giesey, 2 August 1991: "Spicer and Duncan may have heard EKa's lectures but neither of them had ever been in his seminars"; interview with William Chaney, 25 June 2010: "lecture classes, never the seminars." Blaser's statement that Spicer and Duncan took Kantorowicz's graduate seminar on Constantine Porphyrogenitus (Ellingham and Killian, *Poet Be Like God*, 328) is almost certainly mistaken. Not only were Spicer and Duncan undergraduates when the course was given in the autumn of 1949 (EKa occasionally made exceptions on that score), but it required Latin, which neither of them had.

[39] Interview, 27 August 1996.

[40] Interview, 27 April 2012.

[41] Interview, 14 January 2010. In the same interview Rich recalled that Spicer once asked someone in EKa's circle for wine, and when the prankster gave him vinegar instead he did not know the difference.

[42] Email message, 10 May 2011.

An example of the "Berkeley Renaissance" lore that has grown up is a statement attributed to Blaser. Supposedly after EKa's "last lecture before he left to teach at Princeton," he tapped Duncan, Spicer, and Blaser on their shoulders and said, "I would take you three with me, but you are all poets."[43] Yet in the spring of 1950 EKa was not counting on leaving Berkeley and never broached a possibility of going to Princeton, let alone bringing students there. The lore about EKa and the poets has a somewhat larger significance than might first appear because it makes him comfortable with manifest homosexuals. But Ralph Giesey reported that EKa made fun of homosexuals.[44] The specific evidence not only refutes Raulff, who drags in Allen Ginsberg (influenced by Duncan), but also William A. Percy, Jr., who wrote in the *Encyclopedia of Homosexuality*, "[Kantorowicz] taught at Berkeley from 1939 to 1951, where he fitted into the gay scene, notably befriending the poet Robert Duncan."[45] If one is sufficiently determined one might try to "queer" Ernst Kantorowicz, but surely not by this route.

Most prominent among the new group of students who were indeed "retained" were Michael Cherniavsky and Ralph Giesey. The judgment is easy to make because EKa named these two to be his literary executors. Michael Cherniavsky (fig. 24) was born of émigré Russian Jewish parents in 1922 in Harbin (Manchuria) and raised there until the Japanese occupation of 1931 led the family to resettle in Tientsin.[46] The family continued to speak Russian but Michael was educated in British schools. In 1939, when he was ready to go to college, the United States seemed the obvious place, especially since there were relatives who could find a school for him in or near New York. But on the way from Tientsin to the East Coast he stopped off in Berkeley, where there was a contact, and he liked it so much that he enrolled in the University of California. Although he had intended to study mathematics, within a year or two he fell under the spell of Ernst Kantorowicz and switched to history. In 1942, soon after the war broke out, he volunteered for the U.S. Army. As his wife reminisced, "He wanted to fight Hitler, so they sent him to fight Japan." He returned in late 1945 and received his B.A. degree in June 1946. After that he earned an M.A. in history in 1947 and a Ph.D. in 1951. Because Kantorowicz recommended that he work in Russian history, his research supervisors were Robert Kerner and Peter Boodberg.

Several contemporaries thought that Michael considered EKa to be a surrogate father (until 1948 his actual father was still living in Tientsin) and that EKa took up the role. (Those who are thinking of the relationship between Stefan

[43] Ellen Tallman, "Stories with Robert Duncan," in *Robert Duncan and Denise Levertov*, ed. Albert Gelpi and R. J. Bertholf, 63–70 (Stanford, 2006), at 64.

[44] Interview, 2 August 1991.

[45] Wayne R. Dynes, ed., *Encyclopedia of Homosexuality* (New York, 1990), 658. This passage is cited by Raulff, *Kreis ohne Meister*, 338, n. 183. (I once discussed this passage with Percy and he expostulated: "You're not going to take Kantorowicz away from us gays.")

[46] The following account is based primarily on interviews with Lucy Cherniavsky.

Figure 24. EKa and Michael Cherniavsky, circa 1950. (Photo by Bernard Rosenthal, Lerner archive)

George and Kantorowicz will want to know that in 1942 Kantorowicz was fifty-three and Cherniavsky twenty—the difference in age almost matched.) Michael already did household jobs for his favorite professor before he left for the army, and when he departed he left his clothes and belongings with him. Remarkably EKa gave him a cyanide pill to wear around his neck in the event of his finding himself in a situation in which suicide was preferable to suffering.[47] In the later 1940s Michael and a few other young men would go on trips with EKa for fly-fishing in the high Sierra where they would camp for days. After he became a graduate student Michael took all of EKa's seminars and consulted with him about his doctoral dissertation. In the spring of 1951, while still in Berkeley, he sent the following telegram to EKa on the East Coast regarding a legal ruling concerning the aftermath of the Berkeley loyalty oath controversy: VICTORY FULL REINSTATEMENT BRAVO MICHAEL.[48] When Michael served as EKa's first research assistant at the Institute in Princeton in 1951–52, EKa wrote of the

[47] Interview with Ellen Hurwitz, 8 August 2000.

[48] LBI, box 1, folder 14.

"symbiosis going very well."[49] Dauril Alden, a Latin American historian whose student career overlapped with Cherniavsky's, remembered him as being "the brightest graduate student he ever knew at Berkeley."[50] Yet we will see that Michael had difficulty in writing and a tendency toward depression. (In 1973 he committed suicide.)

EKa's relationship with Ralph Giesey gradually became even closer than that with Cherniavsky. Toward the end of Giesey's life (he died in 2011) he wrote to me in regard to preparing the many letters he had received over the years from Kantorowicz for Internet publication: "It is an emotionally moving experience for me, as I can almost hear him speaking the words of his that I am reading."[51] The final part of his acknowledgments in the book published in 1960 that grew out of his doctoral dissertation reads: "One person's influence has been paramount from first to last. . . . With the deepest respect for him as mentor, and affection as friend, I dedicate this work to Professor Ernst H. Kantorowicz."[52]

Ralph Giesey was born of a working-class family in Detroit in 1923. His father was a mechanic; some observed that it seemed a bit strange that one of EKa's most prominent students was so "American"—"born and raised in Detroit on a diet of baseball and apple pie."[53] He obtained a bachelor's degree from Wayne State University in 1944 and then entered the navy, where he rose to become a junior lieutenant. He preferred not to talk of his wartime experiences, but he did let it be known that his ship in the Pacific at one time had come under kamikaze attack.[54] The incessant booming of the ship's battery damaged his hearing so badly that for many years before he died he was virtually deaf.

Upon his discharge Giesey returned to Detroit and received a master's degree from Wayne State in 1947. In the fall he entered Berkeley on the GI Bill. Shortly before his death he began to place installments of what he termed "Ekaica: Varia on Ernst H. Kantorowicz" on his website. This included copies of all the letters that EKa had sent to him, as well as assorted letters pertaining to EKa, and several of EKa's unpublished writings. Giesey's also planned "Reminiscences about Ernst H. Kantorowicz" but he finished only a brief "Prologue" and an introductory "Relationship with Eka" before his death. Yet "Relationship" still tells much. Giesey explains that when he entered Berkeley to pursue graduate studies he expected to work in modern European history (emphasizing France), with a minor field in early modern. Needing a course for his minor requirement, he signed up for one on the Reformation. And then at the end of that semester: "I revised my Ph.D. program drastically: early modern history

[49] To Elise Peters, 12 December 1951: Lerner archive.
[50] Interview, 29 September 2005.
[51] Email message, 27 June 2009.
[52] Ralph E. Giesey, *The Royal Funeral Ceremony in Renaissance France* (Geneva, 1960), ii.
[53] Gordon Griffiths to Robert E. Lerner, 3 April 1994.
[54] Donald Weinstein, email message, 11 May 2011.

(still mainly France) became my major field, medieval and ancient history my minor ones. Such was the impact on me of Eka's lectures on the Reformation."

Giesey goes on to explain that in the following semester (spring 1948) he took a seminar course given by Kantorowicz on historiography—one that was required of all Ph.D. candidates:

> Early on I raised a question about the theory of a certain historian . . . and he asked me to make a special report on that author's work at the next meeting. He was delighted by my report . . . and at semester's end he queried Michael Cherniavsky . . . in this fashion: "and what courses is Giesey planning to take next semester?" That, Michael told me, was Eka's way of asking me to join his seminar.

Thereafter Giesey took all of EKa's graduate seminars and immediately was catapulted into the rank of a favorite student. He was strong-boned and handsome. EKa awarded him the nickname of "chevalier."[55] Giesey was utterly dedicated. So captivated was he with EKa's ways that he took up cooking and a preference for wine. He was the "boutillier" (wine supplier) at many a social gathering. Giesey was the person who discovered EKa's body in Princeton on the morning after his death.

A third individual who sometimes is mentioned together Cherniavsky and Giesey as being among the most favored Kantorowicz students from the later Berkeley years is Robert Benson.[56] Doubtless EKa and Benson were close. But even though Benson worked directly under EKa's guidance along lines closest to EKa's own research interests, EKa ultimately distanced himself from him and did not name him as a literary executor. "Bobby" Benson, born in 1925 in Portland, Oregon, served in the air force from 1943 to 1945. From 1946 to 1950 he was an undergraduate at Berkeley. He began as an English major[57] and joined the "Berkeley Renaissance" set, attending evening meetings in a dilapidated boardinghouse on Telegraph Avenue where a group of protohippy young people under the leadership of Robert Duncan would explore the poetry of Ezra Pound and other modernists.[58] But Benson quickly fell under the influence of EKa and changed his major to history. Most unusually EKa admitted him into his graduate seminar in the spring semester of 1948 when he was a sophomore. The special circumstances were not only that he was very bright, dedicated, prepossessing, and conversationally scintillating, but that he was extremely gifted

[55] Kantorowicz to Giesey, 8 December 1952: "Dear Ralph, Chevalier, and Friend," http://www.regiesey.com.

[56] A useful biographical sketch is Richard A. Jackson, "Robert L. Benson," *Majestas* 5 (1997): 5–22.

[57] Interview with Margaret Bentley Ševčenko, 27 August 1996.

[58] The ambiance of the "Throckmorton Manor" is well described in Fass, *Young Robert Duncan*, 210–11. See also Ellingham and Killian, *Poet Be Like God*, 14. Benson's participation emerges from Fass, 277, 285.

in languages: he knew Latin and German well. From then through the fall semester of 1949 he took all four graduate seminars that EKa offered.[59]

Benson's linguistic gifts are worth further comment. A student of his wrote: "It is not just that he knew French, German, Italian, and Latin . . . but how well he knew them."[60] The distinguished German medievalist Horst Fuhrmann was more specific: "Benson strove in every language—whether German, English, or even Italian—to find, after pausing for thought, the exactly telling word."[61] Benson's German was so good that he wrote and lectured in it effortlessly. Indeed in 1972 he was offered a position as Ordinarius at the Free University of Berlin, which he turned down. Furthermore, he was the only one of EKa's "second group" who shared his interests in poetry, and that meant that he took immediately to reading and quoting the poetry of Stefan George in the original. (I have in my possession a four-line poem by George that Benson had jotted down off the cuff from memory.) Understandably, then, EKa liked him very much in the early days. But there were going to be problems. Above all, Benson was an inveterate procrastinator, and that was a trait that EKa would come to find more and more troublesome.

A good number of other students clustered around Kantorowicz in the late 1940s, most of whom took his seminars and socialized with him but did not choose medieval history as their main field. Some of their names are Joseph ("Yossel") Rubinstein, Adam Parry, Morton Meyer, John Leddy Phelan, and Robert Colodny. If one asks, where are the women, the question is not quite apt because female graduate students were rare at that time. That said, some women did follow his courses. In addition to his cousin Beata Hambuechen, who studied with him for a time, there was Barbara Jelavich, the daughter of a Berkeley English professor, who subsequently made an excellent reputation as a scholar of Balkan history. Another was Betty Weigel, who went on to pursue graduate work in medieval history in England. A warm and charming letter she wrote to Kantorowicz from England in 1950 shows that she was quite witty. She apologized for being pregnant (EKa let everyone know that he hated babies) and ended by saying that when she recently was in Italy she often noticed "Christus vincit! Christus regnat! Christus imperat!" scrawled on walls, but that "on the whole Christ got much less space than the hammer and sickle."[62] It is noteworthy, however, that Betty Weigel addressed EKa in this letter as "Mr. Kantorowicz," showing that she had never been admitted to the inner circle. One can see a double standard: EKa had no trouble having a few women in his seminars but they were not in his in-group.

[59] Ralph Giesey, "Reminiscences about Ernst H. Kantorowicz," http://www.regiesey.com.

[60] Jackson, "Robert L. Benson," 18.

[61] Horst Fuhrmann, "Ein Amerikaner in München: Robert L. Benson," in *Menschen und Meriten: Eine persönliche Portraitgalerie*, ed. Fuhrmann, 319–26 (Munich 2001), at 321.

[62] 13 October 1950: LBI, box 6, folder 3.

Without question he liked to look at girls—those who "take pleasure in their pretty limbs." In December 1939 he wrote to Felix Frankfurter that he had to beware of becoming a "polygamist"—"the only possible solution for a praeceptor of many extremely good looking and well groomed girl students."[63] Margaret Bentley Ševčenko stated outright that "EKa had a great interest in females" and that he "liked little girls."[64] Michael Cherniavsky grumbled to his wife that EKa was "an old goat," and to others that he was a "Bock" (Billy Goat).[65] In 1956 he lectured at Vassar to "many very young girls," but he complained that he could not see them because he was showing slides: "It would have been better had I asked for the lamp to be turned around."[66]

Nevertheless, as much as EKa liked looking at girls he was very selective about having young women as friends. Not surprisingly he ruled out the unsophisticated. Robert Benson's first wife was a "bobby-soxer,"[67] and perhaps not coincidentally Benson divorced her in 1949. At the other extreme, he did not care for obtrusively intellectual women. And that left rather few. He had a warm and affectionate relationship with his young cousin Beata Hambuechen (he called her "Beatnik"), but that was a special case, especially since Beata was the granddaughter of his favorite relative Lieschen Peters. Another exception was blue-eyed Lucy Dukes, "beautiful and fiery,"[68] who married Michael Cherniavsky. Lucy (fig. 25), a Jew from Hungary raised in Vienna, came to the United States in 1939 and found a job in Berkeley working for Erwin Rosenthal, a refugee book-dealer who needed a bilingual secretary. The Rosenthal connection led to EKa. (Erwin's wife Margherita was the sister of Leonardo Olschki.)

EKa took to Lucy immediately, especially because she was lovely to look at and was no bluestocking: she danced the czardas. EKa was intrigued by the fact that she bore the same first name as his former lover, Lucy von Wangenheim, and that her husband often called her "baby."[69] She audited some of EKa's courses but always insisted that she was a dilettante. He enjoyed speaking with her in German and poking fun at her Viennese accent; he taught her how to cook. In turn she helped him with little things around the house. (Although when she volunteered to help with the cooking for dinner parties she was allowed only to cut the parsley.) Lucy met Michael Cherniavsky through EKa in 1946. But when they decided to get married EKa was furious. On one account he exclaimed: "Michael, this is the end!"[70]; as Lucy put it "he almost disowned them." The reason was: "A scholar does not marry; Petrarch didn't." Gradually

[63] 16 December 1939: Frankfurter papers.

[64] Interview of 27 August 1996.

[65] Interview with Lucy Cherniavsky, 27 April 2012; interview with Ihor Ševčenko, 12 April 1991.

[66] To Vera Peters, 16 May 1956: Lerner archive.

[67] Interview with Lucy, 27 April 2012.

[68] Ihor Ševčenko, interview of March 2000.

[69] Interview of 5 September 1990.

[70] Bernard Rosenthal, email message to Robert E. Lerner, 1 June 2012.

Figure 25. Lucy Cherniavsky. (Courtesy Eva Cherniavsky)

he relented and came to accept the Cherniavskys' marriage since it did not interfere with Michael's work.

The only other young woman in Berkeley who equaled Lucy in EKa's affection was Margaret ("Margie") Bentley, an undergraduate history major. Born in 1931, she was famously good-looking and came from a noted Berkeley family: her great-grandfather was a leader of the Methodist Church on the West Coast and her father, Wilder Bentley, was a noted printer of limited editions. EKa had known her since she was twelve by means of the Rosenthal connection. (Her father was a publisher and Erwin Rosenthal was a book dealer.) Margie had grace and wit and was an outstanding student. She was elected to Phi Beta Kappa in her junior year and graduated from Berkeley in 1950 with "highest honors."[71] "She never got anything but an 'A.'"[72] After Ralph Giesey divorced his Detroit wife (or maybe even before then) he fell in love with Margie, and the two became a couple. The relationship did not last long, but Ralph always felt

[71] http://news.harvard.edu/gazette/2002/02.21/02-sevcenko.html.
[72] Interview with Wilder Bentley, Jr., 1 September 2012.

close to her and she reciprocated even after she married another man. Giesey wrote after her death, "She was my oldest and dearest friend."[73]

By the time of her affair with Ralph Giesey Margie had become a peripheral member of the EKa group. Once, in 1949, at a party that included the Cherniavskys, a newcomer by the name of Ihor Ševčenko (pronounced "Igor Shevchenko") was present. Margie had broken her leg, which was in a cast; Lucy remembered that Ševčenko came over to say: "Miss Bentley is so pretty; if only she could walk."[74] She of course did again walk and will remain in this story later as Ševčenko's wife, but it is best now to turn to Ševčenko. He was born in Poland in 1922 of Ukrainian parents. (At the end of the First World War his father had served in the Interior Ministry—the police branch—of a short-lived Ukrainian state.) From his earliest years Ševčenko was trilingual, speaking Ukrainian, Polish, and Russian. At the Adam Mickiewicz Gymnasium in Warsaw he learned Latin and Greek. Ševčenko graduated just before the Germans shut down the gymnasium, and because Polish universities were closed he continued his studies at the University of Prague, where he received a doctorate in classics and ancient history in 1945. During the war instruction at the university in Nazi-occupied Prague was in German; Ševčenko mastered that language perfectly and later conversed in it with Kantorowicz in preference to English. In 1946, while living in a camp in Germany for displaced persons, he wrote to George Orwell asking whether he could translate *Animal Farm* into Ukrainian. Orwell agreed and even wrote a special introduction for it. (Orwell's original English went lost and is now available in a retranslation from Ševčenko's Ukrainian.) Soon after, in the fall of 1946, Ševčenko went to Belgium to pursue a second doctorate, this time in Byzantine studies, at the Catholic University of Louvain. Now studying and writing in French he received his Louvain doctorate in 1949. Then in the fall of 1949 he managed to make his way to Berkeley to take up a temporary junior teaching post in ancient and Byzantine history. English thus became the sixth modern language that he learned to speak fluently.

Given his cosmopolitan background (he had also translated Rilke into Ukrainian) and research interest in Byzantium, Ševčenko inevitably entered the Kantorowicz group. Some people have thought of him as a student of EKa's but he was not. As he wrote to the present author, "Nobody in Berkeley days or Princeton ever thought of me as a 'Schüler von Kantorowicz.' If I really had been a Schüler, maybe I would have turned into the author of an epoch-making book."[75] Indeed he "stood up" to EKa in a manner unlike that of the acolytes. He told me in his inimitable manner: "I was an obnoxious young man, post-Marxist and pre-Annales, and EKa did not know what hit him."[76] Independently, his

[73] Email message, 6 July 2004.
[74] Interview 4 May 2012.
[75] Email message, 12 January 2009.
[76] Interview 28 August 1996.

one-time wife, Margie Bentley, reported that "EKa was always a little bit afraid of Igor—he knew things that EKa did not know."[77]

In addition to being learned and brash, Ševčenko was tall, with charismatic bearing, and very much the ladies' man. He was uninhibited in talking to me about his amatory prowess. He remembered being instructed by Walter Horn shortly after his arrival in Berkeley: "Only with 'A' students."[78] Margie Bentley was an 'A' student, so she was permissible by the Horn rule. In short order "Shev" swept her off her feet, ending her affair with Giesey. But there was scandal: Ševčenko was married. He had left a wife behind in Europe, the daughter of a Ukrainian poet who had died in the Gulag. The original plan was for her to join him until he had made his way in the United States. So the liaison between Ihor and Margie was something of a local sensation. Bernard Rosenthal remembered that his mother once found the teenage Margie sitting insouciantly on Ihor's lap in her house and was quite upset about it. (Sometime in the early 1950s Ševčenko legally discarded his first wife and married Margie.)

Ševčenko took over EKa's classes in 1950–51 after EKa ceased teaching because of his refusal to sign the loyalty oath. (Since Ševčenko was not an American citizen taking the oath was not required, which satisfied all concerned.) EKa was influential in seeing to it that he received a grant for 1951–52 at the Byzantine studies center at the Dumbarton Oaks Institute in Washington, DC, with Margie nearby, pursuing a master's degree at Johns Hopkins. But his scandalous behavior made it impossible for him then to return to Berkeley for an ongoing position.[79]

This chapter may conclude by moving beyond the young people in EKa's entourage. Two contemporaries were particularly important to him in the later 1940s, aside from the European émigré colleagues treated earlier. One was the brilliant and irrepressible Lynn White, the medievalist student of Charles Homer Haskins. White had risen from assistant to full professor at Stanford from 1937 to 1943 and then became president of Mills College. His dissertation, published in 1938, concerned "Latin Monasticism in Norman Sicily," a subject of interest to Kantorowicz. But even more appealing must have been his subsequent turn to the history of technology, for it emphasized an East-West program then unheard of in American medieval historiography. As White wrote in an extraordinarily original article on "Technology and Invention in the Middle Ages," published in 1940, it was necessary to "smash the conventional barriers between Greek and barbarian, Roman and German, oriental and occidental; for mediaeval technology is found to consist not simply of the

[77] Interview 27 August 1996.

[78] Email message, 12 January 2009.

[79] Kantorowicz to Michael Cherniavsky, 28 June 1952 (Lerner archive): "I do not believe that Sev's chances [for a job at Berkeley] are too good. Walther [*sic*] Horn gave me some dope about Sev's stupid behavior." (Since EKa surely knew about Ševčenko's alliance with Margie Bentley, it appears as if he may have been involved in more than one scandal.)

technical equipment inherited from the Roman-Hellenistic world modified by the inventive ingenuity of western peoples, but also of elements derived from three outside sources: the northern barbarians, the Byzantine and Moslem Near East, and the Far East."[80] White's future work in this area would make him widely recognized as a "founding father of modern technological and ecological history."[81]

In the course of 1944 EKa and White began to socialize: "Mrs. White" in a letter of January 1944 became "Maude" in a letter of June. Later EKa and White saw each other as often as possible, given the busy schedule of a college president. (White wrote in the letter of June, "The college seethes with activity . . . but I am determined not to be involved in its seething all day every day."[82]) EKa's ultimate testimonial to his admiration came in a letter to Maurice Bowra of June 1962:

> Clarendon Press just published a book by a friend of mine, Lynn White, *Medieval Technology and Social Change*, which no doubt you received and which you *must* read. It is, to my opinion, the best book on mediaeval problems (mine included) that I have read in twenty years. . . . I found it so fascinating that I even read it in bed, and over-read my sleeping drugs so that I could not fall asleep. . . . Lynn White [is] the only American I know with whom you can speak without "relativating" your talk.[83]

EKa's friendship with White allows response to the proposition that as a European émigré he felt "marginalized" in America.[84] Certainly Kantorowicz never became "one of the boys"—he never spent time jockeying in academic politics or addressing local clubs. But then again he would not have done that had he remained in Europe. Although most of his closer friends in Berkeley were Europeans, he had always preferred to socialize with cosmopolitans and people of broad cultural interests. Among the regulars at the lunchtime "history table" at the Berkeley Faculty Club in 1941–42 were Bolton, Paxson, and Sontag but not EKa.[85] But if he was not particularly close to any members of the department (as he had not been with his Frankfurt history colleagues), he was on perfectly civil terms with most of them. Sontag is an example (until a falling out over the loyalty oath). A letter of June 22, 1950, reports a dinner with the Whites and Eka's department chairman, John D. Hicks.[86] To this it must be

[80] *Speculum* 15 (1940): 141–59, at 143.

[81] Radkau, *Max Weber*, 76.

[82] 6 June 1944: LBI box 7, folder 5.

[83] Circa 27 June 1962 (first page missing).

[84] Anthony Molho, "Exile and the Values of Western Civilization: German Jewish Historians and American Studies on the Renaissance," in *Power, Gender, and Ritual in Europe and the Americas: Essays in Memory of Richard C. Trexler*, ed. Peter Arnade and Michael Rocke 317–37 (Toronto, 2008).

[85] Nisbet, *Teachers and Scholars*, 186.

[86] To Elise Peters: Lerner archive.

added that Kantorowicz was a regular attendant at professional meetings and built contacts with American medievalists with related interests.

Kantorowicz did not feel "marginalized" by his admiring flocks of students, and he spent much time with his favorites, only one of whom, Michael Cherniavsky, came from a European background. He even attended the annual banquets of Phi Alpha Theta, the undergraduate history honors club, and on one occasion (June 1949) gave the after-dinner talk complete with deadpan introduction:

> I am far from being a professional after-dinner speaker, nor do I find it humorous and funny at all to be set to work tonight instead of being allowed to enjoy peacefully my wine and listen to the performance of one of my rhetorically far better equipped colleagues. . . . [It was] recommended [that I] start with a praise of the predecessor's speech. Now the last after-dinner speaker I heard at a Phi Alpha Theta dinner was Mr. Guttridge; his speech, as all of you would admit, was beyond praise, so I cannot praise it. [Another] suggestion was to compare banqueters with flowers. I rather liked that idea. . . . I liked to think of Mr. Kerner as a violet, modestly hidden away in the cold southwestern corner of Wheeler 30.[87] [This barb about a known enemy who had been "almost pathologically eager" for the job of chair in 1947[88] must have caused embarrassed laughter.]

In treating EKa's life in Berkeley we have lost sight of Maurice Bowra, who was his closest friend. The two had not seen each other between early 1939 and late 1948. In the first years of Kantorowicz's emigration they maintained a regular correspondence, but around 1943 it began to slacken. In 1944 EKa wrote to Bowra, "Only the soldiers go on writing letters and letters and these one should answer; so there remains little time for other correspondence."[89] Between 1944 and 1948 no letters from Kantorowicz survive in the extensive Bowra collection. But the friendship was recharged when Bowra came to the United States to lecture at Harvard in 1948–49 and stayed in Berkeley for a month during the holidays. Later EKa reported his delight to Helmut Küpper:

> My correspondence with him was also dormant, at most one letter per year, as it was as with all of you—the written contact was lost. Then, last Christmas, Maurice was here and stayed for almost a month—the brightest point of my ten years in America. We missed each other at the airport; his taxi then arrived at my house a few minutes before mine so that he was waiting for me on the steps. From this

[87] "Postal Stamps and the Historian," http://www.regiesey.com. Ralph Giesey's heading places the talk at a dinner of the History Graduate Students' Association, but the text refers to Phi Alpha Theta. Kantorowicz's presence at another such banquet in the late 1940s is indicated by Boyd F. Hill to Kantorowicz 21 May [194?] in the Cherniavsky papers: "Dr. Kantorowicz, the banquet will be held at Veneto's—S.F. May 21 7:30 p.m. Transportation will be furnished for you."

[88] John D. Hicks, *My Life with History: An Autobiography* (Lincoln, NE, 1968), 275.

[89] 21 September 1944, Bowra papers.

first moment of greeting it was as if we had seen each other just days before. It was scintillating, as it's scintillating only with Maurice, and it was four o'clock when we went to bed.[90]

This quotation indicates that Bowra at first lived in EKa's house. But that did not last for long: for most of the time he lived in the nearby apartment of Kantorowicz's cousin, Lieschen. Her granddaughter Beata remembered this clearly, although she did not recall the reason given.[91] And whatever it was, it probably was not the real one, for EKa's house had three bedrooms and two baths. EKa and Bowra all but certainly had once been lovers, but the decision to move Bowra to a relative's apartment, with whom he had no common fund of interest (Beata reported that Bowra "was polite and utterly uninterested in us ladies"[92]), leads to the conclusion that whatever had been the case in the past, EKa and Bowra were now just very good friends.

In Berkeley Bowra got to know all of EKa's friends at social functions—Olschki, Bukofzer, Horn, Radin, the Maenchen-Helfens ("the Ottochens"). As he wrote at the time, he heard "all sorts of Europeans . . . talking their own languages."[93] EKa also introduced him to his younger set, but with them there was less socializing. Lucy remembered Bowra but only vaguely; Vera's daughter Eva recalled that she at first could hardly understand Bowra because of his "Oxfordese"; when Ralph Giesey wrote in 1963 to inform Bowra about EKa's death, he addressed him as "My Dear Sir Maurice." William Chaney did become acquainted with Bowra rather well, but this was only when he spent some time in Oxford. Chaney remembered Bowra telling him that when he was in America in 1936–37 the word had spread that he was willing to accept an appointment in the United States, and universities started bidding against one another. To which Bowra added: "I began to wonder how long I could hold out against money like that, but I finally decided that I couldn't give up the corruption, ill will, and intrigue of the old world and went back."[94]

Except for a brief time shortly before EKa's death, the two were never together again in the United States. But the Christmas visit ensured the endurance of their friendship. In April 1949 EKa wrote to Bowra with somewhat uncharacteristic wistfulness, "America is again as poor as it was before your arrival," and signed off, "It must be, or have been, your birth-day second half of April; so do take even more love than normally from E."[95]

[90] 10 September 1949: StGA, Kantorowicz II 1901.
[91] Emails to Robert E. Lerner, 27 January 2009, 11 May 2012.
[92] Beata Alden, email to Robert E. Lerner, 27 January 2009.
[93] Mitchell, *Maurice Bowra*, 225.
[94] Chaney to Robert E. Lerner, 4 September 2010.
[95] 27 April 1949.

CHAPTER 22

The Fundamental Issue

If the four years from June 1945 until June 1949 were among the happiest in Ernst Kantorowicz's life, the succeeding fourteen months were among the most dreadful. He had supposed that he would be remaining in Berkeley for the rest of his career. Everything was going well. Earlier he had been engaged in a bitter fight at the University of Frankfurt, but who would have thought that anything like that would happen again? But in June 1949 a bitter controversy broke out at the University of California. Driven by principle, Kantorowicz strode right into it and then involved himself in struggle until late August 1950, when he was defeated and fired.

The California loyalty oath controversy arose from a tactical decision made by President Robert Sproul.[1] America was obsessed about communism. Czechoslovakia had fallen in 1948. Communist armies were sweeping over the Chinese mainland in 1949: Beijing fell without a fight in January, Nanjing in April. Within the United States concern about spying and "subversion" was mounting. In December 1948 Whittaker Chambers led House Un-American Activities Committee investigators to a "pumpkin patch" where microfilms of government secrets were hidden. The Smith Act trials began in New York on March 7, 1949; the Judith Coplon espionage trial began in April. A California Un-American Activities Committee threatened to pass legislation in the state that would strike at "disloyalty" in the state university system. The chairman, Jack Tenney, declared that "you can no more coexist with communism than you can coexist with rattlesnakes." Concerned about the possibility of the legislature interfering directly in the university's affairs and possibly curtailing financial support, Sproul decided to wave the flag and ask the Board of Regents

[1]Unless otherwise indicated, my narrative of events and quoted passages derive from George R. Stewart, *The Year of the Oath: The Fight for Academic Freedom at the University of California* (Garden City, NY, 1950); and David P. Gardner, *The California Oath Controversy* (Berkeley, 1967). Bob Blauner, *Resisting McCarthyism: To Sign or Not to Sign California's Loyalty Oath* (Stanford, 2009), now the richest study (with some inaccuracies), came to my my attention after initially writing this chapter—I have been able to draw on it only in one instance.

to introduce an enhanced loyalty oath to be signed by all university academic employees.

At the board's meeting in March Sproul's motion passed unanimously. The enhancement was crucial. Hitherto all employees had been required to swear an oath saying: "I will support the Constitution of the United States and the Constitution of the State of California, and I will faithfully discharge the duties of my office according to the best of my abilities." No one had ever found this offensive, but not so the enhancement that read: "I do not believe in, and I am not a member of, nor do I support any party or organization that believes in, advocates, or teaches the overthrow of the United States Government by force or by any illegal or unconstitutional means." This was a political test of employment. And that was the reaction of the Academic Senate of the university, northern section (representing the Berkeley and Davis campuses) when it convened in special session on June 14, 1949, to consider the new requirement. Hitherto an attendance of two hundred was rare;[2] now some four hundred professors consisting of about half the faculty were present. As Sproul presided, Edward Tolman, a highly distinguished member of the Psychology Department, rose to present a motion that upheld the loyalty of the members of the Senate to the country and the state, raised issues of academic freedom and tenure, and called for the addition to the original oath to be stricken.

Soon another distinguished faculty member, whose mere personal appearance lent him enormous gravity, rose to read a prepared statement. Here is an eyewitness account:

> Of all the incidents of the Year of the Oath, perhaps none made a more profound impression upon those who experienced it than the speech of a once German scholar. . . . Speaking as in a strange rhythmical incantation, high-pitched with fervor . . . he told of the imposition of oaths in the early days of Hitler's power. His theme was always: "This is the way it begins. The first oath is so gentle that one can scarcely notice anything at which to take exception. The next oath is stronger!" The time to resist, he declared, was at the beginning: the oath to refuse to take was the first oath.

And here are some of EKa's actual words:

> History shows that it never pays to yield to the impact of momentary hysteria, or to jeopardize, for the sake of temporary or temporal advantages, the permanent or external values. . . . The new oath, if really enforced, will endanger certain genuine values the grandeur of which is not in proportion with the alleged advantages. . . . It is a typical expedient of demagogues to bring the most loyal citizens, and only the loyal ones, into a conflict of conscience by branding non conformists as un-Athenian, un-English, un-German. . . . I am not talking about

[2]Nisbet, *Teachers and Scholars*, 104.

> political expediency or academic freedom, nor even about the fact that an oath taken under duress is invalidated the moment it is taken, but wish to emphasize the true and fundamental issue at stake: professional and human dignity. It is a shameful and undignified action, it is an affront and a violation of both human sovereignty and professional dignity that the Regents of this University have dared to bully the bearer of this gown into a situation in which—under the pressure of a bewildering economic coercion—he is compelled to give up either his tenure or, together with his freedom of judgment, his human dignity and his responsible sovereignty as a scholar.[3]

A young and subsequently prominent economist, Walter D. Fisher, remembered the speech forty plus years later.[4] He had been innocent of politics; his father had been a bank president and chairman of the Illinois Commerce Commission. But at the June 1949 meeting he was spellbound by Kantorowicz's intensity and struck by the argument "that the Hitler regime got started that way—little oaths leading to bigger things." This convinced Fisher to become a "nonsigner" and he held to this position until he was severed from the university in August 1950. In June 1949 the fact that Ernst Kantorowicz was even attending a faculty meeting was remarkable. Gordon Griffiths, an assistant professor of history, wrote in a memoir: "I noticed with astonishment that Professor Kantorowicz . . . was walking up to the front of the auditorium to speak. He had never until then taken any part in academic or any other kind of politics in America."[5] Indeed, for as long as EKa had been at Berkeley he had avoided committee work as much as possible and paid no attention to university affairs. He liked to quote a remark attributed to the king of Saxony when forced to abdicate in 1918, "Make your mess by yourselves."[6] But now he was throwing himself into the fray and soon would be attending meeting after meeting.

After much discussion the Senate members passed by an overwhelmingly favorable vote a substitute motion to replace Tolman's. Instead of requesting deletion of the new disclaimer, this stated that it should be "deleted or revised" and called for an advisory committee of Senate members "to consult with the President of the University with a view to working out such a solution." Six days later the Academic Senate of the southern section of the faculty passed an identical resolution, calling for its own advisory committee. The northern committee made its recommendation to President Sproul before then. This

[3] Complete text given in Gardner, *California Oath Controversy*, 34–36, and in Kantorowicz, *The Fundamental Issue*, 4–6.

[4] Interview with the author, 6 December 1990.

[5] Gordon Griffiths, "Venturing Outside the Ivory Tower: The Political Autobiography of a College Professor" (typescript, c. 1990s), 63. (A copy of this memoir is in the Library of Congress; another was generously made available to me by Dauril Alden.)

[6] Kantorowicz to Leonardo Olschki, 19 December 1958 (Olschki papers). (The colorful colloquial German is "Macht Euch Euren Dreck alleene.")

favored complete deletion of the new disclaimer but conceded that if necessary for public relations new language should be provided that eliminated reference to "belief" and read: "I am not under any oath, nor a party to any agreement, nor as a member of any party or organization am I under any commitment that is in conflict with my obligations under this oath [the constitutional pledge]." Then, when the matter came before the Board of Regents at its meeting of June 24, the board voted unanimously in favor of a resolution that adopted the "public relations" addition to the original oath proposed by the northern advisory committee and added: "I am not a member of the Communist Party." This was "*the oath*" that Ernst Kantorowicz would never sign.

EKa wrote to his cousin Lieschen on June 25 that "the Regents held to an oath anyway, and with that the whole dance will start over again. You can see that my days are filled."[7] Indeed on June 27 he attended a first meeting of "nonsigners" at the Berkeley Faculty Club. (He and many others had remained in Berkeley because they were teaching during the summer.) This group agreed that the new oath was no better than the old and that the advisory committee had been directed only to consult rather than to make recommendations in the name of the faculty. A few weeks later, however, President Sproul plowed ahead and mailed a copy of the regents' oath to every faculty member with the request that it be signed and notarized "no later than October 1." The implication was that the annual appointment letter would not be sent until receipt of a signed copy of the oath. And indeed by late July it became clear that only those who had returned signed copies to the administration (about half of the Berkeley faculty) were receiving appointment letters. In reaction to this, on July 25 a group of six nonsigners, one of whom was Ernst Kantorowicz, sent a letter to the Senate members of the northern section asking them to withhold their signatures until the next plenary meeting of the Senate scheduled for September.

In July EKa was uncharacteristically optimistic. On the 14th he wrote to Ernst Langlotz in Germany that Americans were happily celebrating the Goethe bicentennial even though hardly anyone knew who Goethe was. But "the name somehow has a German-friendly ring." Then he added:

> For the most part this sentiment is of course determined by politics—the Russian fear and the fear of Communism. The first is well-founded; the second is a phantom, greatly exploited by the Republicans, that now is haunting even the universities. We are in the midst here of a hard fight about an anti-communist oath which was meant to be forced on the faculty from above and which the academic senate resisted with astonishing unanimity. It is interesting to see how far such questions let themselves be fought out by purely parliamentary means within the University, and I've seen here on a small scale how true battles over

[7] Lerner archive.

principle can be carried on without leaving behind resentments. How would all of that fare in Germany![8]

At the full meeting of the Senate of the northern section on September 19 President Sproul announced that failure to sign the oath would not in itself trigger severance from the university; then the faculty voted to "request the privilege of affirming [its] loyalty to the principles of free constitutional government by subscribing voluntarily to the oath of loyalty sworn by officers of public trust of the State of California." That vote implied that there should not be any other oath, but in their meeting of September 30 the regents did not rescind their controversial oath, conceding only that pending further negotiations letters of appointment could be sent to nonsigners. EKa did not wait for the outcome of further negotiations but on October 4, calculatedly after the initial deadline of October 1, he mailed to the president a signed and notarized copy of the constitutional oath together with a letter stating that he "could not conform to the demands of the Board of Regents to sign a political oath."[9] The letter was the one in which he wrote that "my political record will stand the test of every investigation," for he had "twice volunteered to fight actively with rifle and gun, the left-wing radicals in Germany." Then he went on to inform Sproul that "[nevertheless] my respect for the University of California and its tasks is such that I cannot allow myself to believe that the base field of political inquisition, which paralyses scholarly production, should be in the range of its activities."

An English department member who experienced the events of "the Year of the Oath" wrote: "We went to oath meetings, and talked oath, and thought oath. We woke up, and there was the oath with us in the bright cheeriness of the morning. . . . We discussed the oath during lunch at the Faculty Club. And what else was there for subject matter at the dinner table? Then we went to bed and the oath hovered over us in the darkness, settling down as a nightmare of wakefulness."[10] John D. Hicks, the chairman of the History Department, was a moderate who spent much time and energy endeavoring to negotiate agreements; later he wrote in his memoirs that it "was the most traumatic experience of my life."[11] EKa had been granted a "sabbatical in residence" for the academic year 1949–50 and hence had a reduced teaching schedule. He had looked forward to this released time in order to pursue his scholarship, but now his work was continually interrupted by meetings and his mind preoccupied by tactics. His surviving papers include folders full of minutes of meetings, drafts

[8] Langlotz papers.

[9] Submission of constitutional oath is established by President's papers, Bancroft Library-University Archives, CU-5, ser. 4, box 39. The letter is reproduced in Kantorowicz, *The Fundamental Issue*, 6–7.

[10] Stewart, *The Year of the Oath*, 9.

[11] Hicks, *My Life with History*, 278.

of memoranda, scores of letters, forms, and jottings pertaining to the oath. Toward the end of the controversy he wrote to Helmut Küpper: "The affair cost me a year of my working life and it didn't improve my health either."[12]

Throughout the fall of 1949 both Academic Senates of the university met several times and advisory committees of the respective sections met with the Board of Regents. Semantic jockeying came into play regarding whether the university should be dedicated to the *objective* of eliminating Communists from the faculty, or to a *policy* of eliminating Communists as already embodied in the oath. At a meeting of the Senate of the northern section of November 7, Gordon Griffiths, who had become Kantorowicz's aide de camp,[13] offered a strongly worded resolution that passed by a vote of 148 to 113. (It was late in the hour and most of the attendees had left for home.) This insisted that "the power of the Regents must be exercised not only with due regard for those principles of freedom of thought and association which constitutionally limit the power of all public officials, but also with deep respect for the essential nature of a University as an institution peculiarly dedicated to freedom of mind."

With the regents holding to the oath throughout the fall, a group of Berkeley nonsigners organized informally and met regularly on Friday evenings at the Faculty Club. According to an observer, "This courageous and highly idealistic, though loquacious, group exercised a not inconsiderable influence on general faculty opinion and helped to direct the conscientious objections of its own members along co-operative and strategic lines."[14] The leader was Edward Tolman and Kantorowicz was a prominent presence. Joseph Tussman, then a young member of the Philosophy Department opposed to the oath, remembered him as "very idiosyncratic, and sometimes uncooperative, but still a stalwart asset."[15] Edward W. Strong, associate dean of Berkeley's College of Letters and Science in 1950, stated in an interview of 1988: "Kantorowicz was undoubtedly the most militant of the non-signers."[16]

During the spring semester EKa was so preoccupied with politics that his notes for teaching a graduate seminar on historical methods include the following:

"Committee on Un-Athenian Activities"

a. persec. for "un-x" activities recurrent everywhere.
b. complete absurdity—"x" is a generalization or creation of our imagination.
c. cd. be reversed: "Un-American" to persecute; Socrates *true* Athenian," heretics with poverty ideal "true medieval men."
d. self-righteousness, narrowness.[17]

[12] 22 July 1950: StGA, Kantorowicz, II:1903.
[13] Interview, 25 March 1994.
[14] Stewart, *The Year of the Oath*, 35.
[15] Interview, 23 March 1992.
[16] http://sunsite.berkeley.edu/uchistory/archives_exhibits/loyaltyoath/symposium/strong.html.
[17] Cherniavsky papers, box 8, series 9, FF2.

Without narrating here all the complex details of the oath affair, it may be said that Kantorowicz's militancy was particularly pronounced during a stage of the controversy in the late winter of 1950. The issue of compelled signing had come to a head as a result of the dominance of a group on the Board of Regents led by John Francis Neylan, a prominent San Francisco lawyer and once an advisor to William Randolph Hearst. On February 24 the Neylan group forced through a resolution whereby the regents announced that "as trustees for the people of California, they [needed to] safeguard the freedom of the University against ruthless, fanatical and subversive minorities in the body politic, such as the Communist Party." Consequently they required all academic employees to submit a signed oath containing the original wording of June on or before April 30, with the stipulation that those who did not comply "[would] be deemed to have severed connection with the University as of June 30, 1950."[18] In other words, the regents were announcing their intention to abrogate the principle of academic tenure. (President Sproul now changed sides and voted nay.)

The *San Francisco Chronicle* carried a headline: "Loyalty Oath or No Job, Cal Professors Are Told." In a desperate attempt to save the situation by finding a compromise to bring to the regents, a constituted faculty committee held an emergency meeting with the nonsigners' organization that was attended by some two hundred people. Nearly everyone who spoke supported resistance. Kantorowicz, however, went further and called for mass resignations. Decades later a molecular biologist remembered him rising and saying, "Here's a card. If you put your name on the card—if there are two hundred people, two hundred cards collected, any of those people on that list will resign when the first man is fired."[19] The memory was reliable for we know that on the next day, February 28, Kantorowicz circulated a proposed declaration to the following effect:

> We, the undersigned, solemnly declare that unless at the next meeting of the Regents on March 27 the proposed special oath of loyalty is revoked, we the undersigned shall immediately and automatically discontinue to discharge our duties in offices and classrooms. If any member of the teaching staff, including teaching assistants, be dismissed on or by July 1, 1950, for the sole reason of not having signed the oath, section 2, the resignation *in corpore* will follow immediately and automatically.[20]

EKa wrote in the same declaration, "The faculty as a body corporate, should meet ultimatums with ultimatums, alternatives with alternatives, deadlines

[18] The full resolution is the Leonardo Oschki papers (Getty Library), with Olschki's marginal exclamation points and question marks.

[19] Interview with Howard Schachman, Regional Oral History Office, Bancroft Library, 2000–2001.

[20] Many drafts of the text and the final version in a letter to Edward Strong are in LBI, box 7, folder 1.

with deadlines. We have to stop building treacherous 'golden bridges' which can only lead to defeat and disaster." One history of the oath controversy concludes, "Although the [Kantorowicz] proposal gained little support, the fact that it was made at all and by a scholar of international repute, was indicative of the gravity of the situation."[21]

EKa's determination led to a clash with Raymond Sontag. After the latter had played a crucial role in 1944 in helping him gain his permanent appointment, the two had maintained a good friendship. He and his wife once gave a gift to EKa, an out-of-print book on English constitutional history, with a card that read: "With all good wishes, Dora and Ray."[22] Sontag's devout Roman Catholicism had not been an issue, but he had become a cold warrior, and his politics placed him on the opposite side from Kantorowicz regarding the oath. Soon after EKa's call for mass resignations the two had a meeting that produced sharp disagreement, and a day later EKa felt compelled to write a follow-up letter.[23] This referred to "that not quite pleasant, but at least quite honest and sincere conversation of yesterday afternoon." EKa wrote: "It makes little difference whether a man is Christian or not so long as he bears in his heart an image of *humanitas* which is unshakable and uncompromising. . . . You may include me with those you have castigated for scholarly pride, or you may call my 'idealism' Jewish or German. But I am, or try to be, both as Jew and as German also an 'eternal anti-Barbarus,' no matter whether the Barbarianism be brown or black or red and emerges in the ugliness of Mr. Stalin, Mr. Hitler, or Messrs. Neylan et consortes." Later, when Norman Rich asked EKa for a recommendation for a job working in Washington, EKa replied, "Better you than Sontag."[24]

The debates of late February and early March revealed that most members of the Berkeley faculty were moderates who hoped that the regents would rescind the requirement of the oath for the sake of the nonsigners but were supportive of the principle of eliminating Communists from the university. Motions in favor of both goals passed overwhelmingly by a mail ballot when the votes were counted on March 22. The nonsigners were very disappointed that only 136 people (11 percent) voted against one of the motions that included the words "all future letters of acceptance of salary and position will contain a statement that the person concerned accepts such position subject to the University's policies embodied in the Regents' resolution of . . . June 24 1949 excluding members of the Communist Party from employment in the University." But while those who favored this motion hoped it would mollify the Neylan group on the Board of Regents it did not: a roll-call vote of the regents taken on March

[21] Gardner, *California Oath Controversy*, 121.

[22] The book was Charles H. McIlwain, *The High Court of Parliament* (New Haven, 1910). The copy, with the card still in it, is in the library of the Institute for Advanced Study, Princeton.

[23] Carbon in LBI, box 6, folder 3.

[24] Interview, 14 January 2010.

31 on a motion to rescind the oath resulted in a tie of ten to ten, which meant that the requirement for signing the oath, or now "an equivalent statement," stood unchanged.

Consequent on the March 31 outcome Sproul sent a mimeographed request to the nonsigners asking for compliance. EKa's answer of April 6 was: "I shall not under any condition yield to pressure, compulsion, intimidation, or duress, and therefore shall not take an additional oath to the standard oath that I had the pleasure to sign, and hand over to you, on October 4th 1949."[25] The fact of the March tie, however, postponed a showdown, for it led alumni to lobby for compromise. These efforts succeeded beyond expectation. On April 21 the board voted to rescind the requirement of signing the non-Communist oath by a count of twenty-one to one. (The sole negative vote was that of L. M. Giannini, president of the Bank of America, who had said before the vote, "I want to organize Twentieth Century vigilantes, who will unearth Communists and Communism in all their sordid aspects," and that "if we rescind this oath flags will fly from the Kremlin."[26]) For the moment it seemed as if the controversy was over. The *San Francisco Chronicle* carried a banner headline on April 22: REGENTS ACCEPT PEACE PLAN—DROP UC OATH.

But all was not over, for the decision entailed a quid pro quo. Anyone who had not signed the original oath and who refused to comply with a requirement to disavow in writing before May 15 membership in the Communist Party "or any other organization which advocates the overthrow of the Government by force or violence" was to be dismissed unless he or she petitioned for review of his or her case by a standing faculty committee on privilege and tenure of either the North or the South. Such review was to be based on interviews. The respective committee would establish the petitioner's reasons for lack of compliance and seek to ascertain whether the person had any relations with the Communist Party. If lack of compliance was based on legitimate conscience and no association with communism was found to exist, a favorable recommendation was to be forwarded to the president of the university. The credentials of the seven members of the northern committee on privilege and tenure were impeccable: all had signed the oath required by the regents on June 24, and all had supported the regents' policy of excluding Communists from the university.

It is impossible to listen in to Ernst Kantorowicz's hearing in late May because formal transcripts were banned. In 1990 I asked Charles Muscatine, who went before the northern committee, whether he had any information about EKa's appearance, but he did not. He did say that he found it hard to picture because "EKa was a pretty fierce character," but he thought he might have been temperate in this instance because speaking with fellow faculty members was

[25] LBI, box 6, folder 3.

[26] Stewart, *The Year of the Oath*, 94, 97.

understood to be a courtesy.[27] Ralph Giesey reported that the procedures were rather pro forma: "Questions were set up in such a way as to lead to satisfactory answers."[28] We do know the outcome of the interview: EKa was one of forty-seven faculty members who were recommended favorably by the relevant committee in its report to the president of June 13. In reference to Kantorowicz's specific case the committee pointed out that he already had sworn that he had never been a Communist during his naturalization procedures in 1945 and added that he "has a violent hatred of any form of totalitarian government and is abnormally sensitive to anything which reminds him of his experiences in Germany." The committee was "convinced that he is not a member of the Communist Party and has no commitments which conflict with his responsibilities with respect to impartial scholarship and the free pursuit of truth."[29]

The two committees recommended favorably in sixty-four out of sixty-nine cases concerning members of the Academic Senate. (Five faculty members of the northern section and one in the southern refused to discuss their views with the respective committees and consequently were recommended unfavorably.) The committees also examined eighty-one non-Senate academic employees (mostly teaching assistants) and recommended favorably in fifty-eight cases. (One such case was that of Ralph Giesey, who later signed the oath on EKa's urging: "because it's a matter of your livelihood."[30]) When President Sproul submitted these recommendations to the Board of Regents, many of the regents were displeased because they had not expected to see so many favorable recommendations. They thought the committees must have been too soft. Nevertheless, the work had been undertaken on the implicit assumption that the recommendations would be accepted. Not only had the regents' concession of April 21 implied as much, but in the entire history of the university the Board of Regents had never rejected any recommendation by any constituted committee on privilege and tenure. Consequently at their June meeting the regents temporized. They found no difficulty in voting unanimously to terminate 157 non-Senate academic employees for whom President Sproul had found sufficient grounds for not rehiring. (These numbers were swelled by the fact that many teaching assistants had not been scheduled to be rehired and thus saw no point in adhering to required procedures.) But the regents decided to postpone a decision on the cases of 62 Senate nonsigners who had been recommended favorably until their next meeting, scheduled for July.

[27] Interview, 6 December 1990.

[28] Interview, 2 August 1991.

[29] Report to the President of the University of California from the Committee on Privilege and Tenure (Northern Section), June 13, 1950. (Bancroft Library, Loyalty Oath Digital Collection.)

[30] Blauner, *Resisting McCarthyism*, 148. The same pattern was followed by some of EKa's other students or disciples.

That decision was made on June 23, 1950. On June 25 North Korean troops invaded South Korea, and on June 27 President Truman ordered U.S. air and sea forces to support the South Korean government. On June 29 Truman sent in ground troops. The fact that the country now was literally at war with communism did not bode well for the future of the nonsigners. Recognizing this, Edward Tolman presented a statement at the Friday evening nonsigners' meeting held on the 29th. With great dignity he urged remaining holdouts not to "jeopardize themselves and their families" unless they were firmly determined to do so. Those with futures before them were "likely not only to be fired, but also to be smeared in the public press"; they were likely to find it difficult to gain appropriate new employment; they were likely to earn insults from former colleagues and friends for being "stiff-necked malcontents." (As indeed already was happening.) He himself was soon to retire anyway. He did not need to worry too much about economic security, and he was pleased with the idea of getting a book finished. Thus he found himself able "to indulge in the sin of self-righteousness and in the luxury of an untrammeled conscience." Others, however, should not feel bound to sacrifice their lives. In conclusion he "merely wish[ed] to state, as perhaps some comfort to whatever number of you feel that you must do likewise, that I myself am going to remain a non-signer." Yet he would "continue to feel friendship and respect for any others of you whose circumstances or reasoning makes it seem desirable and right to you that you should sign."[31] Tolman's generous statement recognized realities: twenty-two out of sixty-two gave in during the succeeding days. (By the end of the summer the total number of nonsigners had dwindled to thirty-one.)

EKa presented his own view that he might be fired or forced to resign in a letter to an acquaintance of June 30, full of sting:

> "Les dieux ont soif." The Regents will not be satisfied by the small-fry hecatomb [sacrificial oxen] of 157 miscellaneous employees, but will want to have their steak dinner from among the 62 professors who have not signed. Since my anti-Communist record is such that it would please even the Hearst Press, I may not be dismissed, but may be forced to resign in case some innocent colleagues are penalized. It is a dirty mess.[32]

The nonsigners who were left established a formal Group for Academic Freedom on July 6. Kantorowicz wrote a manifesto seeking support from alumni.[33] EKa's department chairman, Hicks, was guardedly optimistic about the outcome of the July Board of Regents meeting when he wrote to a colleague

[31] Bancroft Library, Tolman papers. (Christina Bobek located this item for me.)

[32] Kantorowicz to Albert M. Friend, 30 June 1950 (Dumbarton Oaks archives).

[33] A carbon of a statement "To the Alumni and Other Friends of the University of California" is in LBI, box 6, folder 2. EKa's authorship is evident from a locution ("the specific task to keep a watchful eye") and the citation of Max Radin.

on the East Coast: "The President has recommended the retention of all men cleared by our Committee on Privilege and Tenure. If his recommendation is accepted, as I believe it will be, we should be pretty well out of the woods."[34] In reference to the only History Department member who was a nonsigner (Gordon Griffiths had surrendered earlier), he added, "I suspect that Kantorowicz could have several jobs if our Regents were so crazy as to dismiss him."

The next regents meeting was dramatic. Many members of the board—state politicians, captains of industry—had never bothered to attend meetings before the controversy had broken out. One was Lieutenant Governor Goodwin ("Goodie") Knight, who had no interest in higher education and had never attended a board meeting from the time he was elected in 1946 until February 1950. Now, like several others, he made it his business to participate in order to display his anticommunist credentials. An observer wrote while the events were unfolding, "These regents seem ready to come running, like small boys to a fire, when a University issue becomes a burning political issue."[35] Nineteen regents were present at the meeting of July 21, with their number nearly evenly divided. Governor Earl Warren led the group that supported acceptance of the favorable recommendations regarding Senate nonsigners; John Francis Neylan led the opposition. Concurrently the North Koreans were pushing back American forces and threatening to drive them into the sea. This allowed Neylan to emphasize the need for recognizing the communist threat. Had all twenty-four regents been present the outcome would have gone against the nonsigners, but the absence of five resulted in the vote going the other way—ten to nine. But after the votes were counted Neylan announced that he was changing his vote to aye so that he could move for reconsideration at the next meeting.

Neylan's notification that he would move to reconsider had the effect of barring letters of appointment and salary checks to be sent to the nonsigners on the first of August. A letter from Kantorowicz of August 2 to Theodor Mommsen, then in Princeton, takes note of this:

> We are already thrown out *de facto*. On August 1 we received neither salary nor the annual so-called contract. Sproul, cowardly as always, did not send out the contracts promptly and now our old friend Neylan, the Hearst attorney, has held up further employment until the next meeting in August. He will have the majority at this next meeting, and with that the nonsigners are fired. I don't see how matters can take a different turn. I don't know yet whether I'll let myself be

[34]John D. Hicks to Chester McArthur Destler, 13 July 1950: Hicks papers, carton 14. (Jost Philipp Klenner located this item.) Hicks had written to Sproul on 12 July, reemphasizing that Kantorowicz had been naturalized in 1945 and thus at that time swore that he was not a member of the Communist Party; moreover, "Kantorowicz has repeatedly expressed himself as being not only non-Communist, but also bitterly anti-Communist." (Bancroft Library, President's papers, kindly communicated to me by Randolph Starn.)

[35]Stewart, *The Year of the Oath*, 112.

thrown out or still resign before then. Probably the former, in which case I can say with Olschki "Californiam vadi iterum eici."[36]

Olschki's learned irony played on Christ's saying (Apocryphal Acts of Peter), "Romam vado iterum crucifigi" (I go to Rome to be crucified again); in his version it meant "I went to California to be thrown out again." Both Olschki and Kantorowicz had been forced to leave Germany (in Olschki's case also Italy); on August 25, 1950, they indeed were "thrown out of California." By then Neylan had gained his necessary votes. Discussion at the regents meeting arose regarding the question of whether anyone believed the remaining nonsigners were Communists or whether the real issue was maintaining discipline. Regent McFadden of the Neylan faction (an ex officio member of the board by virtue of his presidency of the State Board of Agriculture [*sic*]) conceded the latter by responding: "No Regent has ever accused a member of the faculty of being a Communist. . . . The question has become, should any discipline whatever be enforced in the University, on its employees, or shall each be allowed to settle his own standard of employment?" In regard to the question whether the board would be acting in bad faith if it rejected recommendations based on a procedure it had set in motion itself, another member of the Neylan faction simply stated: "I don't think anybody could arrive at an intelligent decision . . . by a mere hearing." And then the regents concluded their business by voting twelve to ten to dismiss the nonsigners.

Once the new semester began a student group that supported the fired professors painted black the "Big C" (a rock that overlooks the campus) "in memoriam for academic freedom."[37] *LIFE* magazine published an article in its October 2 issue that was surprisingly sympathetic to the fired professors. This displayed several photos of Edward Tolman packing and leaving the campus, as well as one of the photogenic EKa sitting at his desk. The accompanying caption read: "Historian Ernst Kantorowicz, 55, has been at California for 11 years, has written four books of medieval history. Polish-born, now a U.S. citizen, he was wounded in 1918 [*sic*] in Munich battling Communists. He too refused to sign: I would not accept a compromise."[38] Outraged, an insurance broker in Philadelphia wrote to Kantorowicz: "Whether you are or are not a Communist or have Communistic leanings may be debatable, but for sure, you have demonstrated that you are something less than a 100% American. . . . Patriotically yours."[39]

In October EKa chose to make his own case by bringing out a pamphlet: *The Fundamental Issue. Documents and Marginal Notes on the University of*

[36] 2 August 1950: Lerner archive. The letter was stuck in a book loaned by Mommsen to Karl F. Morrison before Mommsen's death, and Morrison generously passed a copy on to me.

[37] Bancroft Library, Loyalty Oath Digital Collection.

[38] *LIFE*, 2 October 1950, 46.

[39] Irvin R. Barton, 2 November 1950: LBI, box 6, folder 3.

California Loyalty Oath, adorned on the title page with the university's motto: "Fiat Lux." He paid for the publication out of his own pocket: $425 ($4,100 in today's equivalent.)[40] Already in his statement of June 1949 he had identified the "fundamental issue" as "professional and human dignity." Now he wrote: "What the fundamental issue is has been obvious to me from the minute the controversy started," naming it as "the dignity of the profession." On the same page he also quoted an unsigned "Group for Academic Freedom" statement of August that he probably had written himself: "The issue is not Communism but the welfare and dignity of the University." The appearance of the word "dignity" twice in succession was not coincidental. In *The King's Two Bodies* Kantorowicz states that "it would be a mistake to understand the word Dignity only in its moral or ethical connotations, that is, as something contrary to 'undignified' conduct." Instead he explains that in addition to its moral connotations Dignity (with a capital D) pertains to offices or corporations that never die: "the Dignity never perishes, although individuals die every day."[41]

In *The Fundamental Issue* he did not waste much space discussing the regents' insistence that they were fighting communism.[42] For him the demand for taking an oath was "tom-foolery," and at any rate the charge "Suspect of Communism without self-signed affidavit" had effectively been changed on August 25 to that of "Non-conformity to the Board of Regents." In his view aside from creating an "academic abattoir" the regents were acting in violation of the faculty's dignity. He noted that Regent Ehrman had stated at a board meeting that professors are "merely employees of the Board of Regents." But Ehrman neglected to see that just as judges are the court, and ministers, together with the faithful, are the church, so professors, together with students, are the university. As Kantorowicz wrote, "One can envisage a university without a single gardener or janitor, without a single secretary, and even—a bewitching image—without a single Regent. The constant and essence of a university is always the body of teachers and students." Furthermore, the university teacher is a professional whose "whole being depends on his conscience." He went on in white heat: "Only the culpably naïve ignorance on the part of the malevolent Regents, not knowing what a scholar's life and being is, could venture to break the backbone of the academic profession—that is, its conscience—in order to 'save the University,' nay, to dismiss a scholar for that very conscience that makes him a scholar." The pamphlet continues by presenting considerable detail as to how

[40] Invoice from Parker Printing Company, San Francisco, 31 October 1950: LBI, box 6, folder 5.

[41] K2B, 383–87.

[42] After a preface and before the body of his presentation, Kantorowicz reproduced three documents: his statement delivered at the faculty meeting of 14 June 1949; his letter to President Sproul of 4 October 1949; and an eloquent and moving letter sent by Walter Horn to Sproul on 23 August 1950 explaining why he had decided to sign at such a late date. (Horn wrote that he had just been called up for service in Korea and could not allow himself "to expose my wife and my son to the consequences of being denied continuance of my civilian occupation upon return from military duty.")

the regents had connived deceitfully to obtain their goals by abrogating tenure. Finally come anaphoric cadences:

> [I refused to sign] because I refused to act under duress, work under the threat of supervision by vigilantes [or] yield to compulsion, intimidation, and economic pressure . . . because I refused to buy and sell my academic position and scholarly dignity at the price of my conscience and conviction; because I was shocked by, and disgusted with, the lack of honesty, decency, fairness, and the tendency to pettifogging and trickery which those responsible for the procedure against the Faculty have shown from beginning to end.

It is customary to assume that Kantorowicz's unbending, outspoken opposition to the University of California loyalty oath was a dramatic swerve away from the far-right-wing politics of his *Volkswehr* and Weimar days. For the most part this is true. We have seen that he expressed regret in his noncompliance letter to Robert Sproul for having joined "the white battalions," recognizing that in doing so he had helped prepare "the road leading to National Socialism." In *The Fundamental Issue* he used the image to indict the self-proclaimed patriotism of the Neylan-faction regents by referring acidly to "what generation of vipers [Matth. 23:33] can originate from 'White Battalions' once they don the brown shirt." While repeating that he was not and had never been a Communist, he zealously opposed those who manufactured the non-Communist oath in order to exploit what he considered to be unreasoned hysteria. For him "the fear of Communism [was] a phantom." Since he did not consider it "the fundamental issue," he refrained from debating the rights of Communists. But in March 1950 he opposed the Senate motion that included the words "proved members of the Communist Party are not acceptable as members of the faculty." On this matter he sided with those who opposed political tests for academic appointment on the grounds that "professional fitness to teach or engage in research should be determined by an objective evaluation of the quality of the individual's mind, character, and loyalty, and not by his political or religious beliefs or lawful associations."[43] Kantorowicz's support of the position that "so long as the Communist Party in the United States is a legal party, affiliation with that party in and of itself should not be regarded as a justifiable reason for exclusion from the academic profession" put him about as far left on the issue of academic freedom as it was possible to go. In that regard "left of him was only the wall."

But why then did he say in the preface to his pamphlet "I am genuinely conservative"? It has been argued that his insistence on "the constant and essence of a university [being] always the body of teachers and students" is a "mythopoetic vision," supposedly "an eternal presence of genius minds," akin

[43] Statement of faculty minority as Gardner, *California Oath Controversy*, 137–38.

to his earlier belief in the "Secret Germany."[44] But, while clever, this argument goes too far. The genuinely mythopoetic "Secret Germany" had no beginning, whereas Kantorowicz knew that the university began as a body of teachers and students in the twelfth century. Moreover, the membership of the "Secret Germany," being transcendental, could only at best be inferred in the here and now, whereas the membership of the university was empirical—tangible, and identifiable by rosters. Nevertheless a continuity of conservatism in Kantorowicz's thought is surely observable since the reverence for sacrosanct professions displayed in the pamphlet is a reverence he had displayed before. In April 1933, in requesting leave from the University of Frankfurt, he had emphasized "the dignity of the University Professor, founded solely on inner truth." Taking that view further, a statement in the drafts of 1935–36 for the aborted interregnum book alludes to the special "spiritual" qualities that link professors and judges to clerics.[45] Clearly, then, Kantorowicz's statement at the faculty meeting of June 1949 identifying "three professions that are entitled to wear a gown: the judge, the priest, the scholar" was a long-held belief. The author of *The Fundamental Issue* develops his argument that professors do not serve at the pleasure of the regents because they *are* the university by means of a contrast between professors and employees such as janitors or gardeners: professors have certain vested rights in the institution they both serve and constitute which gardeners and janitors, who serve the comforts of the institution, do not. Although Kantorowicz referred to "human dignity" in his statement of June 1949, he did not use the term in his pamphlet, perhaps because he now was referring strictly to the sacred dignity of elites.

It remains to conclude the loyalty oath story. On August 31 Kantorowicz and nineteen other nonsigners (some called them "never signers") retained a top-flight San Francisco lawyer, Stanley Weigel (who took no pay), to sue the regents for reinstatement. The case was heard in late December by a California district court of appeals. When the lawyer for the regents conceded that the loyalty of the petitioners was not the issue, the presiding judge revealed her position by responding, "The issue then is that they were naughty boys and girls because they didn't obey the teacher and sign?" On April 6, 1952, by which time EKa was at the Institute for Advanced Study in Princeton, the court handed down a unanimous decision in favor of the petitioners based on a mandate of the state constitution that the University of California was to be independent of all political influence. We have seen that Michael Cherniavsky telegraphed EKa: "BRAVO." But this reaction was premature because the losers carried the case to the California Supreme Court. The crowd at the hearing was the largest that

[44] Mario Wimmer, "Kantorowicz's Oaths: A Californian Moment in the History of Academic Freedom," *Österreichische Zeitschrift für Geschichtswissenschaften* 24 (2014): 117–48, esp. 121. Unfortunately this article is marred by numerous factual errors.

[45] "Wandel des Zeitgefühls"—version "A," insert after 9; version "B," 13. (LBI, box 2, folder 8).

had ever appeared in the court's chambers. After long deliberation the court upheld the decision of the district court on October 17, 1952, and ruled for reinstatement. The only effect for EKa was that this entitled him to severance pay for the period between July 1, 1950, and the date when he had accepted appointment in Princeton. Perfectly content at the Institute, he submitted his resignation from the California faculty on December 17, 1952.

One might think that Kantorowicz had won a victory in principle, but that was not so. The Supreme Court's ruling in favor of the nonsigners was based on the following statement: "We need not discuss the numerous questions raised by petitioners with regard to alleged violation of their civil rights and impairment of contract because we are satisfied that their application for relief must be granted on the ground that state legislation has fully occupied the field and that university personnel cannot properly be required to execute any other oath or declaration relating to loyalty other than that prescribed for all state employees." This referred to the fact that after the regents voted for the dismissal of the nonsigners, Governor Warren had called for the California legislature to adopt a loyalty oath to be submitted to every employee of the state. (Warren may have been addressing the nonsigners' repeated complaint that it was unfair for academic employees to be singled out, but he may also have been polishing his own anticommunist credentials in view of the fact that he was running for reelection.) The legislature then quickly adopted an oath to be taken by all, and this was more far-reaching than the regents' oath dictated to the University of California faculty. The new oath stipulated that the signer did not currently advocate the overthrow of the government of the United States or the State of California by force or violence or other unlawful means, and also that the signer had not been a member of any party or organization that advocated such things for the past five years, and also that he or she would not join such a party or organization for the length of his or her service to any public branch of the state. Those nonsigners who had been reinstated and wished to have their jobs back were required to take this oath, and strangely enough all of them did. Perhaps they reasoned that at least they were not being treated differently from others, but perhaps they had simply been worn down.

CHAPTER 23

Advanced Study

A DEFT TURN OF PHRASE IN A LETTER SENT BY THE GERMAN émigré philologist Paul Friedländer to J. Robert Oppenheimer, the director of the Institute for Advanced Study in Princeton, may serve as an opening for this chapter. Friedländer had been recruited to write in support of EKa for an appointment at the Institute, and he did so in October 1950 with the words: "Professor Ernst H. Kantorowicz at Berkeley, one of the non-signers of the loyalty declaration, is a man of the highest caliber of historical research. His studies are very advanced indeed."[1] EKa, as is well known, did receive that appointment.

He did not move immediately. During the fall of 1950 he remained in Berkeley because until the late summer it was uncertain whether he would be fired, and by the fall it was too late for him to find another position. As in the Frankfurt summer of 1933, he offered an advanced seminar in his home without remuneration.[2] He also remained immersed in matters concerning the loyalty oath; he continued to attend meetings of the nonsigners group—the Group for Academic Freedom—aimed at pursuing legal remedies.[3]

Above all, he expended his energies on writing and disseminating his pamphlet concerning the oath controversy, *The Fundamental Issue*. In late September he sent a draft to his friend Monroe Deutsch, retired as provost of the Berkeley campus, to learn whether Deutsch might have something to contribute or correct on the basis of his long experience. When Deutsch gave the pamphlet his imprimatur,[4] EKa had it printed and sent out copies to a stunningly large number of addressees. (He had ordered 1,000 copies and 800 cards reading "With the Compliments of the Author.") Most of those to whom he sent the pamphlet, aside from former students, were people in high places or scholars

[1] 7 October 1950: LBI, box 7, folder 2 (carbon copy).

[2] Robert L. Benson, "Norman Cantor and 'the Nazi Twins,'" in Benson, *Law, Rulership, and Rhetoric* (Notre Dame, IN, 2014), 319; Faas, *Young Robert Duncan*, 281.

[3] Kantorowicz to Vera Peters, 1 January 1951: Lerner archive, refers to his attending a meeting of the group in the Shattuck Hotel.

[4] LBI, box 6, folder 3.

of reputation. A bulging folder in the Kantorowicz collection in New York includes dozens of thank-you letters, mostly with congratulatory remarks, from such as President Hutchins of the University of Chicago; Felix Frankfurter; Gray Boyce, chairman of the History Department at Northwestern; Oswald Veblen; and Arthur Schlesinger Jr.[5] Felix Frankfurter remarked that despite "the miserable business," he must have had a certain *gaudium certaminis* (joy in the battle).[6]

But EKa was looking forward to working on his scholarship full time. In the midst of the Oath tumult in May 1950 he had attended a weeklong symposium and read two papers at the Byzantine Studies Center at Dumbarton Oaks. He was happy to meet and talk shop with leading Byzantinists whose work intersected with his own. (The group consisted of "Grabar from Paris, L'Orange from Oslo, Alföldi from Budapest, now Bern, and myself as 'full blooded American!'"[7]) He also was dazzled by the center's rich library in the Byzantine field. EKa struck up a friendship with the center's director, Bert Friend, who extended an invitation to return for a full term as visiting professor in the spring of the following year.[8] Not knowing what would be happening in Berkeley, he was delighted to accept. On the basis of his short experience he considered a stay at Dumbarton Oaks "a rare feast."[9] Later, when he knew the Berkeley outcome, he was delighted even more. He left for the East at the end of January 1951 and remained in Washington until June. It was an excellent time. The Dumbarton Oaks complex, set in quietly elegant Georgetown, had opulent gardens. EKa lived in a comfortable cottage, utilized the center's specialized library (he called it "enchanted"[10]), gave two papers, and interacted with specialists. While in the East he took the opportunity to visit Princeton and New York. He was relaxed because he knew his future was secure: before he had left he had learned that he had gained a permanent position at the Institute for Advanced Study.

Kantorowicz owed a debt for garnering that appointment above all to two men, Theodor Mommsen and Erwin Panofsky. Mommsen was devoutly loyal and tireless when need arose to act in his behalf. It was he who had urged EKa to come to America in 1938, who had used his influence to put him in touch with Bernard Flexner, who had arranged an appearance at Yale, and who had been the intermediary for his offer of a fellowship from Johns Hopkins. Having helped rescue EKa in 1938–39, he set about doing the same in 1950. Now he was associate professor of history at Princeton. Émigré Germans located in Princeton, whether at the university or the Institute, knew one another, and one

[5] Ibid.

[6] 13 November 1950: ibid.

[7] To Helmut Küpper, 22 July 1950: StGA, Kantorowicz, II:1903.

[8] Correspondence with Friend: 20 May, 31 May, 15 June, 3 June, 15 July (all 1950), and 5 January 1951: Dumbarton Oaks Archives.

[9] To Friedrich Baethgen, 14 December 1950: Baethgen papers.

[10] To Ernst Langlotz, 28 June 1951: Langlotz papers.

of Mommsen's friends was the renowned art historian Panofsky, who also was the most influential member of the Institute's School of Historical Studies. Thus in the late spring of 1950 Mommsen conversed with Panofsky about whether it might be possible for Kantorowicz to gain an appointment. As yet there seemed no urgency, but in July when EKa came to see that he might be fired, Mommsen wrote "quite openly" to Panofsky, who was vacationing in Maine, and followed that up with a long-distance telephone call. Panofsky soon told Mommsen that he was supporting Kantorowicz but that appointment procedures could only move forward in October.[11]

Panofsky's decision to support EKa was by no means predetermined, for until the spring of 1950 Panofsky had associated him with right-wing positions he abhorred. In a letter of 1948 to Fritz Saxl he referred to Roger van der Weyden and Italy, "despite Kantorowicz, Kaiser and Reich."[12] Gerhart Ladner's memoirs are particularly informative.[13] During the fall term of 1949 Ernst Robert Curtius was a visiting member at the Institute and so was Ladner. A position at the School for Historical Studies had become available, and Panofsky as well as Oppenheimer wanted to fill it with Curtius. But the latter declined and recommended Kantorowicz. Panofsky then consulted with Ladner, whom he knew to be a friend of EKa's, to learn more. He explained that he harbored great reservations because of the biography of Frederick II. Specifically he called attention to a spine-chilling passage wherein the author unapologetically defended Frederick II's edict that Sicilians not be permitted to marry foreigners for the sake of the purity of their blood. Ladner maintained that Kantorowicz was writing only from the viewpoint of the thirteenth century (given the passage, this was a lame defense) and heartily recommended Kantorowicz's subsequent works. Complementing this account is one I heard from Felix Gilbert, who told me that when Mommsen broached Kantorowicz's name as a possibility for the Institute Panofsky telephoned him with alarm to ask whether Kantorowicz was "dangerous."[14] Gilbert reassured him, and so did Harold Cherniss, a classicist in the School of Historical Studies who had known EKa when he taught at Berkeley from 1946 to 1948.

Panofsky's about-face arose from his admiration for Kantorowicz's steadfastness in the loyalty-oath crisis. An ardent civil-libertarian, Panofsky had kept abreast with affairs in Berkeley because his son Wolfgang was on the physics faculty there.[15] In September 1950 he wrote to Erich Auerbach that Wolfgang had signed the oath, which had made him and his wife furious, but that

[11] Mommsen to Kantorowicz, 13 July 1950; 21 July 1950: LBI, box 7, folder 2.

[12] Dieter Wuttke, ed., *Erwin Panofsky, Korrespondenz 1910 bis 1968*, 6 vols. (Wiesbaden, 2001–14), 3:913–14. After Kantorowicz's death, Panofsky wrote to Richard Salomon that he initially had been worried about him, "because of George and Frederick II" (ibid., 5:393).

[13] Ladner, *Erinnerungen*, 37.

[14] Interview, 14 November 1988.

[15] Wuttke, *Erwin Panofsky*, 3:17.

when the regents broke their word in the summer, Wolfgang had "decently resigned."[16] And in the same letter he told of how he was officially nominating the *filius praecentoris* (son of the cantor). Mommsen wrote to EKa in October that "Pan" was lobbying for him "fantastically," especially against those who thought that an appointment should be made in some other field.[17] Mommsen had sent Panofsky the complete list of Kantorowicz's writings in early August, so Panofsky must have informed himself about the more recent scholarship in order to wage his campaign.

Voting took place in November. A plenary session of the Institute's faculty was convened by the Institute's director, J. Robert Oppenheimer, on November 14. The group consisted of five members of the School of Historical Studies and seven of the School of Mathematics. Panofsky had written a position paper in favor of Kantorowicz which had been circulated in advance. Now he read it to the assembled group.[18] He explained that the School of Historical Studies might have taken one of many directions but surely needed a medieval historian. The school had looked for candidates in many fields but could find only one person, a medieval historian, whom it "could support with confidence and enthusiasm." And that was Ernst Kantorowicz. He then quoted a letter from Felix Gilbert stating that Kantorowicz was "the best mediaeval historian now active." To emphasize EKa's suitability Panofsky wrote:

> His work and interests transcend the field of mediaeval history as commonly defined in time and space and in subject-matter and method. In time they range from the later phases of classical antiquity to the fifteenth and sixteenth centuries; in space they embrace both western Europe and the Byzantine and Islamic East; in subject-matter and method they treat complicated problems of many facets by viewing them from all the various angles from which his familiarity with widely different specialties and techniques enables him to illumine all of them.

After specific details came the conclusion: "Besides the professional ability so fully attested by his accomplishments, Ernst Kantorowicz recommends himself to us by the quality of mind, easier to sense than to define, which enlivens whatever it touches."

A vote was not taken immediately in order to leave a few days for anyone to inform himself independently if he so wished. Then the faculty voted unanimously in favor on November 20, although one mathematician, displeased with Kantorowicz's stance in the Berkeley oath controversy, declined to vote. It only remained for the Board of Trustees to approve the recommendation. An arch conservative, Admiral Lewis Strauss, attempted to block the appointment but relented when it became clear that he was alone in his opposition and then

[16] Ibid., 3:70.

[17] 19 October 1950: LBI, box 7, folder 2.

[18] "Ernst H. Kantorowicz": IAS, Kantorowicz faculty file.

joined to make the vote unanimous.[19] EKa received a formal invitation on December 29, rounding out what had been a very eventful year.

His letter of acceptance, addressed to Oppenheimer on January 4, 1951, expressed deep gratitude:

> Your letter of December 29 has certainly lit up the otherwise so gloomy outlook for 1951, at least within the purely personal sphere, and after the low of the paralyzing "Year of the Oath" this invitation fills my spirits again with new buoyancy and gives my desire to work a new impetus. In fact, I am looking forward impatiently to settling down peacefully in Princeton. The terms you have outlined to me open up a new perspective of my life as a scholar, and it seems almost unbelievable to me that in future no classwork or semester routine shall compel me to break off my own work in the midst of a sentence and that instead I shall be able to finish all my unfinished studies and sail, once more, freely and like a young adventurer on that vast ocean of historical problems.[20]

The Institute appointment necessitated EKa's return to Berkeley from the East for the summer of 1951 in order to sell his house, wrap up his affairs, and prepare for his move. Since he had already visited Princeton, he knew its attractions. In June he wrote to his friend in Germany, Ernst Langlotz, that "[Princeton] is a charming small city of only 8,000 [*sic*] inhabitants, entirely set in gardens and meadows, but still only fifty minutes away from New York. . . . So I'm quite satisfied with the outcome of this battle."[21] Writing to Helmut Küpper aboard the train en route to Princeton, he confessed that he was leaving California with a somewhat heavy heart, especially because of the many friends he had there. But he was hoping to find new ones in the East. For that reason, and with the feeling that he was traveling into the wilderness, he was "bringing along beads and little mirrors as bartering objects to exchange with the 'natives.'"[22]

He felt very comfortable at the Institute from the start. He was widely admired. A passage from the memoirs of George Kennan sums that up: "A bachelor, an aesthete, and a man of ineffable Old World charm, Eka, cozily installed in his home on Alexander Street, was an essential feature of the Princeton of the 1950s."[23] A month after his arrival, the "old world charmer" wrote to Küpper that his situation pleased him more than he thought it would.[24] He found the town "enchantingly pretty"; the "entire atmosphere thoroughly agreeable."[25]

[19] Kai Bird and Martin J. Sherwin, *American Prometheus: The Triumph and Tragedy of J. Robert Oppenheimer* (New York, 2005), 383.

[20] IAS, Kantorowicz Faculty File, box 18.

[21] 28 June 1951: Langlotz papers.

[22] 21 September 1951: StGA, Kantorowicz, II:1905.

[23] George F. Kennan, *Memoirs*, vol. 2 (Boston, 1972), 16.

[24] 31 October 1951: StGA, Kantorowicz, II:1905.

[25] To Vera Peters, 16 April 1951; to Elise Peters, 12 December 1951: Lerner archive.

Figure 26. Ernst Kantorowicz at his desk at the Institute for Advanced Study. In 1957 EKa wrote to Vera: "Here are two photos. Keep one, or keep both, or keep neither. For me they show, as photos almost always do, a 'foreign gentleman' with whom I'm not on speaking terms." (Lerner archive)

His dwelling was a picturesque small wooden frame house dating from the first half of the nineteenth century on Alexander Street, near enough to the Institute to walk. At first he lived on the ground floor and someone else on the second. Short of space, he built a little wine cellar in a linen closet.[26] In December 1951 he wrote that the "overperson" was complaining about commotions after 11:00 at night, a time when "normal" people should be asleep.[27] A source of gratification during his first months was that Helmut Küpper arranged to send to him the enormous collection of books that he had left behind in Europe. The weight was two and a half tons. EKa wrote to his cousin Lieschen that "it's like the birth of quintuplets when only one was expected, but I have the diapers ready—that is the bookshelves."[28] By arrangement Küpper labeled the crates according to subject, so that those containing "literature" went to his home and the others to his office where there was ample space (fig. 26).

[26] To Maurice Bowra, 11 October 1951.

[27] To Elise Peters, 31 October 1951, 12 December 1951; to Vera Peters, 15 December 1951: Lerner archive.

[28] Kantorowicz to Elise Peters, 12 December 1951.

He did not have to barter "beads and little mirrors" to make new friends. In short order he became excellent friends with Erwin Panofsky. EKa and "Pan" were roughly the same age, came from similar wealthy Jewish-German backgrounds, and matched each other as devastatingly witty savants. (EKa wrote an elaborate Latin poem for Panofsky's Irish setter—"Canis Panis"; when Panofsky read EKa's paper on "The Dukes of Burgundy and the Italian Renaissance," he wrote "Veni, legi, vicisti"—"I came, I read, you conquered."[29]) EKa's notes for a Berkeley seminar on historical method dating from 1948 to 1950 indicate that he had already read some of Panofsky's writings and regarded him as a paragon in the field of art history.[30] Knowing from Mommsen that Panofsky had played a decisive role in gaining him the Institute appointment, he wrote to thank him a day after he had sent his acceptance letter to Robert Oppenheimer, saying how much he looked forward to working at his side.[31]

A German art museum director recalled that when he visited Panofsky at his home and Kantorowicz was there, one of the two might cite the beginning of a line of poetry and the other would complete it; they might also explore the names of all those in world history who earned the sobriquet "the Great," commenting on the aptness of the award in each case.[32] Panofsky's wife Dora was also an art historian and intellectual (coincidentally she was a cousin of Leonardo Olschki's wife), and when EKa visited the Panofskys she was part of the company. (The husband and wife team went by the name "Pandora.") After EKa died Pan wrote to his student William Heckscher saying, "Eka's sudden death is an irretrievable loss. He was probably our closest friend in Princeton and—apart from yourself—the only one with whom a conversation in the form of a Mozart trio could be conducted."[33]

An even more famous person with whom EKa gained friendship at the Institute was the director, J. Robert Oppenheimer. Although the two hardly knew each other before then,[34] in Princeton they developed a warm relationship. Oppenheimer, who had studied between the wars in Göttingen, could read German effortlessly[35] and liked to keep up with the work of the Institute's eminences. Consequently EKa gave him offprints of his articles. Oppenheimer authorized payments for EKa's European travel expenses, even including EKa's vacation time on the Greek islands. Kantorowicz's letters sent regards to "Robert's" wife and children. The two could even indulge in erudite pranks.

[29] Wuttke, *Erwin Panofsky*, 3:245–47; 4:771.

[30] Cherniavsky papers, box 8, series 9, FF2.

[31] Wuttke, *Erwin Panofsky*, 3:119.

[32] Gert von der Osten to Panofsky, 4 November 1963, in Wuttke, *Erwin Panofsky*, 5:404.

[33] Wuttke, *Erwin Panofsky*, 5:394–95.

[34] Kantorowicz to Oppenheimer, 4 January 1951: "The very casual acquaintance we once made, at the beginning of the oath controversy, in the house of our unforgettable friend Max Radin": IAS, Kantorowicz faculty file, box 18.

[35] Interview with Kurt Weitzmann, 3 May 1989.

An unknown person played a joke by writing a letter of application in French for a visiting position at the Institute in the name of N. Boileau, but this was a French poet who lived from 1636 to 1711. In support of Boileau's "candidacy," EKa wrote to Oppenheimer recommending one of his verses, "Allez, vieux fous, allez apprendre à boire./On est savant quand on boit bien: /Qui ne sait boire ne sait rein" (one who doesn't know how to drink knows nothing) and concluded, "It will not be quite easy to live him down, especially since he is already dead."[36] Persuaded by the recommendation of the "Faculty in Parapsychology," Oppenheimer wrote to "Dear Dr. Boileau," addressing him at "Pluto College" in "Transtygia, and offered him a position from 1959 until 1984."[37]

Very serious, on the other hand, was the notorious incident of April 1954 concerning Oppenheimer's clearance for working in the government's Atomic Energy Commission. When charges were lodged that he was a "security risk," Oppenheimer decided to stand for a hearing. EKa then wrote to him: "I greatly admire your decision to take a stand. . . . I would have acted in exactly the same way. I know from experience on a far inferior scale how much of your nerves and your health will be demanded by this ordeal, but I can assure you that one recovers, especially when in the end all works well."[38] All did not work out well, however, and Oppenheimer was stripped of his clearance. The faculty of the Institute remained silent throughout the closed hearings on the instructions of Oppenheimer's lawyers, but when the outcome was announced EKa helped lead a successful effort to have the entire faculty (including John von Neumann, a leading supporter of the hydrogen bomb project that Oppenheimer had opposed) agree to a public statement in Oppenheimer's behalf. The signers expressed "complete confidence in [his] loyalty to the United States, his discretion in guarding its secrets and his deep concern for its safety and welfare." EKa had stood against the red scare in Berkeley and now he opposed it again.[39]

A third name that bears consideration in treating EKa's friends at the Institute is George Kennan. The friendship with Kennan is noteworthy because he came from a different background from most of those with whom Kantorowicz socialized (he was a midwesterner), because he was not one to make puns in Latin and Greek, and because he had a reserved personality: his middle name was "Frost" and some called him "frosty." But after Kennan retired from government service and joined the Institute in 1955 he and Kantorowicz took each

[36] 23 February 1959: IAS, General, box 40.

[37] Oppenheimer to "Dr. Nicholas Boileau-Despreaux," 23 February 1959: IAS, General, box 40.

[38] 13 April 1954: Oppenheimer papers, Library of Congress, Washington, D.C. , MSS 35188, box 43.

[39] A letter of E. Llewellyn Woodward, a faculty member of the Institute then on leave, to Kantorowicz of 22 June 1954 makes clear that EKa was an organizer of the pro-Oppenheimer statement: Cherniavsky papers, box 8, series 9.

other's measure and were mutually impressed. Kennan was heading toward the completion of his first work of history, *Russia Leaves the War*, and asked EKa whether he would "care to look over" a draft. Here is Kennan's account:

> He took the typescript home and read, at least, great parts of it. Then he asked me to dinner, alone at his home. Being not only a gourmet but an accomplished cook, he prepared . . . a marvelous meal for the two of us, served it with the best of wines, and then, seating me in the living room over coffee and brandy, took out the typescript and said: "Now, my friend we will talk about what you have done." Whereupon he proceed to subject the piece . . . from the standpoint of technique and taste in historical writing, to the most searching, useful, and unforgettable criticism. This, I thought, was the mark not just of a great scholar but of a great gentleman.[40]

In 1957 Kennan gave a series of lectures for the BBC, published the following year as *Russia, the Atom, and the West*. The lectures argued for détente: "Until we stop pushing the Kremlin against a closed door, we shall never learn whether it would be prepared to go through an open one." Kennan even proposed that U.S., British, and Russian troops be withdrawn from Europe. Predictably given the cold war atmosphere the lectures were sharply attacked. Dean Acheson averred that "Mr. Kennan has never, in my judgment, grasped the reality of power relationships, but takes a rather mystical attitude toward them."[41] Kennan, who was easily bruised, was quite upset by the reaction, and EKa endeavored to console him: "I meant to write to you . . . to tell you how highly I thought of your BBC Lectures. Somebody had to say the things you said, and even if the boomerangs from this country will not have been pleasant to you, they did not do any good to the antagonists either. You did the right thing." Kennan was grateful and thanked EKa for his "kind and understanding note."[42]

Kantorowicz's other Institute friendships were too numerous to be treated here in any detail. Suffice it to mention the Hellenist Harold Cherniss, the German-born Byzantine art historian Kurt Weitzmann, and the German-born mathematician and theoretical physicist Hermann Weyl. EKa spent a particularly great amount of time with old friends who lived in Princeton: Theodor Mommsen and Erich Kahler (who divorced Fine in 1940 and now was married to a charming and vivacious Viennese woman). Mommsen was the person in Princeton whose interests were closest to EKa's, and they constantly exchanged

[40] Kennan, *Memoirs*, 2:16–17. Kantorowicz to Kennan, 12 January 1957, offers criticisms of what Kennan had termed the "conclusions" to his next book, *The Decision to Intervene*, signing "affectionately": Kennan papers, box 30, folder 1. Kennan heeded some of EKa's advice changing his title from "conclusions" to "epilogue" and greatly curtailing the final section.

[41] Cited by Brian Urquhart, "A Contest in the Cold," *New York Review of Books*, 17 December 2009, 54.

[42] 8 March 1958: 13 March 1958: Kennan papers, box 30, folder 2.

ideas and bibliographical tips. When Mommsen left Princeton in 1954 to accept a professorship at Cornell, EKa was very annoyed with him.[43]

In addition to the permanent faculty of the Institute, dozens of others were there regularly, either as "members" for a term or two or just to pass through for a brief time. EKa was gregarious, but he soon came to complain about "visititis." In 1955 he wrote to Leonardo Olschki, "I'm going to stay at home for Christmas, unfortunately overrun by visitors just as this entire semester. Starting with the new year I've decided to check out, so to speak, and the capable Margie [Ševčenko] is going to tell everyone that I am presently in Alaska, phone "Klondike 3–4556."[44]

EKa offered a seminar for Princeton graduate students in the fall of 1955 to fill in for the recently departed Mommsen. As at least once before it was on Dante's *Monarchy*; this time the topic made particular sense because he was working simultaneously on the Dante chapter of *The King's Two Bodies*.[45] He gave another seminar for graduate students in the spring of 1956 and in the fall of 1962 (interrupted by illness). But he was not a campus presence and did not attract a new following. Instead he remained close with some of his Berkeley protégés. Robert Benson came to do graduate work at Princeton and became EKa's de facto student for his degree. In addition he was able to employ his favorites one at a time to be his research assistants. First came Michael Cherniavsky (1951–52), then Benson (1952–53), and then Ralph Giesey (1953–55). EKa hired Margie Ševčenko for the year after Giesey. Although she had gained a master's degree at Johns Hopkins she decided that she was not meant for scholarship and did not proceed to a doctorate. But EKa had a special fondness for her; he even referred to her (whether she knew it or not) as his "daughter."[46] During her term as his assistant he wrote to Maurice Bowra: "I still have Rhodes cigarettes, and I do not mind it that my present assistant, Margie, adores them because she is unusually pretty and therefore may do what she wants."[47] Since she was bright and capable and had some knowledge of the field he was happy to employ Margie for practical purposes as a secretary. He dictated letters to her. Once she needed to speak to a reservation clerk at the Princeton Inn because EKa was having Michael and his wife Lucy as guests. Margie called to say that she wished to make a reservation for "Professor and Mrs. Cherniavsky." To which the clerk asked, "How exactly do you spell that name?" So she spelled it and then instructed that the bill should be charged to "Professor Kantorowicz"—"How exactly do you spell that name?" Finally the

[43]Interview with Alice Kahler, 18 March 1989.

[44]19 December 1955: Olschki papers.

[45]To Vera Peters, 2 November 1955: Lerner archive; to Leonardo Olschki, 8 December 1955: Olschki papers.

[46]To Vera Peters, 16 April 1951: Lerner archive.

[47]To Bowra, 11 November 1955.

clerk needed to know who was calling, so she said, "Mrs. Ševčenko"—"How exactly do you spell that name?"[48]

EKa developed a different daily routine in Princeton from Berkeley since he no longer needed to teach classes.[49] He rose at what he told people was "eight o'clock and ninety minutes," and worked at home in the mornings—according to Ladner from ten until two. (In the fall of 1953 he took over the whole house on Alexander Street, which meant that he could equip himself with a home office.) After a light lunch he usually went to the Institute to attend to his correspondence and official business. He would leave around five to go shopping for dinner and then return home to read or socialize—in both cases until very late hours. After the evening meal he never did any scholarship. As Ladner pointed out, this routine shows how much a scholar can accomplish on the basis of just four working hours, but hours of intense concentration.

In his first two years EKa had to rely on others with whom to go shopping since he had no automobile and the shopping district on Nassau Street was too far for carrying packages. For long he had been leery of driving because he was uncomfortable with the stick shift. (He had bad memories of the Fiat he drove in 1927.) But in the fall of 1953 Ralph Giesey volunteered to sit next to him while he gained practice driving with an automatic transmission. (He wrote to Bowra that the day of his death "may be approaching quickly because I have finally bought a car and an accident is bound to occur and prevent me from aging."[50]) At first Giesey "bit his knuckles," but EKa caught on quickly because it was so easy. In November he bought a Chevrolet and in December found that he could drive even in heavy traffic "without jitters."[51] This simplified his daily life and also allowed him to drive to Trenton to buy furniture for the house on Alexander Street. He also went to New York often but in doing so availed himself of the easy train connection.

EKa broke his Princeton routine in the summers. For the first and third of them after his Institute appointment he returned to California. He chose to live in Berkeley in the summer of 1952 as a matter of convenience because he preferred a location that was cool and had a good library. And he was able to see Vera and go trout fishing in Lake Tahoe. In 1954 he avoided Berkeley because he did not want to spend all his time seeing people he was obliged to see and felt oppressed by many bad memories.[52] Instead he remained in Princeton working through July and went to Lake Tahoe for August and to Carmel for the first two weeks of September. Fishing and swimming were his passions. He liked to joke about the first:

[48] Kantorowicz to Michael Cherniavsky, 17 April 1962: Lerner archive.

[49] To Vera Peters, 15 December 1951; Ladner, *Erinnerungen*, 39.

[50] To Bowra, 12 November 1953.

[51] To Vera Peters, 8 December 1953, 21 December 1953: Lerner archive.

[52] To Vera Peters, 18 April 1954: Lerner archive.

> The trouts followed me in streams and lakes as though I were a reincarnation of Saint Francis and therefore lovingly refused to take the hook though not despising the bait. Only a few heretics were stupid enough to be lured by the devil and I am glad that those dirty communists have been eradicated in Neylan's waters. I had them boiled *en bleu* at Tahoe Taverns, a punishment which foolishly had not been applied to the Albigensians by our predecessor Innocent III.[53]

Kantorowicz had made tentative plans to go to Europe for the summers of 1950, 1951, and 1952 but for different reasons these never materialized. In 1953 he did take the trip and it was a long one, extending from early May until the beginning of September.[54] He sailed for England on the *Queen Elizabeth* on May 6 and stayed there for ten days, mostly with Maurice Bowra at the Warden's cottage of Wadham. In Oxford he also had a reunion with Baby, not having seen her for fourteen years. Then he crossed the Channel to France and spent a day in Paris with Ralph Giesey, who was completing a Fulbright year, in order to discuss his research and "brief him" about his coming responsibilities as his assistant at the Institute. From France he sailed to Naples to see the Olschkis.

The major goal of the trip was to introduce himself to Greece, the land of his dreams. He journeyed by ship from Naples to Athens, where the American School in Athens became his headquarters. He visited all the major mainland sites and stayed for a week on the island of Mykonos. Taking a side-trip to Istanbul he wrote to Vera that he found it strange to be having a "reunion with his youth" and to be meeting friends from his First World War days "who then were twenty and now are sixty." Ever since EKa had seen the Greek temple at Paestum and Roman copies of Greek statuary in Naples in 1924, he had decided that "the divine Hellas" resonated with him more than any other culture. He seems quite seriously to have believed that his "Mediterranean ancestry" had something to do with it. The Jewish Kantorowicz wrote that Greece was his "patria." (He never set foot in Israel.) For him Greece now even outranked Italy: "How can you enjoy 'panels' when you can see things in three dimensions? Everything in Italy seems thin and derivative compared to Greece." His week on Mykonos had given him "the leisure to absorb the Greek world from within."

Some of his effusions make the customarily ironic EKa sound almost adolescent. He wrote to Michael: "[Greece] is overwhelming—not only the 'heroic' or Arcadian landscape, but what man *made* of it and how he brought life to it without 'Burma Shave' or 'Coca Cola' signs." And to Vera: "Greece was exactly

[53] To Robert Benson, 22 July 1952: Benson papers.

[54] The following account relies on letters or postcards (all from 1953) from Kantorowicz to Ralph Giesey, 19 April, 29 April, 7 June, 25 July, http://www.regiesey.com; Michael Cherniavsky, 7 June, 21 June (Lerner archive); Vera Peters, 23 April, 22 June, 1 August (twice) (Lerner archive); to Elise Peters, 11 July, 25 July (Lerner archive); Ernst Langlotz, 29 August (Langlotz papers); Robert Oppenheimer, 24 September (IAS).

what I needed. One is so close there to the origins as one is far from them in America and one realizes what is offensive when one sees that people can live *with* time and not, as in America, attempt to live *against* time."

After seven weeks in Arcadia, EKa came back to the real world, spending some days in mid-July for research purposes in Rome, Siena (to study the "allegory of good government" fresco for *The King's Two Bodies*), and Bologna. Then he went to Germany, as we have seen because of a sense of obligation, and afterward to Basel to evaluate an uncompleted book manuscript on "The Essence of Greek Art" by his cousin Gertrud. (He admired it, and the manuscript was published in 1961.) Then he spent two weeks with Bowra on Lago Maggiore, footing the bill.[55] Knowing that he would be returning to America from Rotterdam on August 28, he chose to spend his last week in Holland, visiting museums and swimming at a North Sea beach.

Kantorowicz's second postwar trip to Europe transpired in the summer of 1955 and was caused by financial necessity. Or at least so he told Vera. He had enjoyed himself during the summer of 1954 on the West Coast, delighted about "the combination of heights and sea level."[56] But going to California meant that he had to pay all the costs, whereas if he went to Europe the travel costs would be reimbursed by the Institute and he could write off from his income tax returns his living expenses as research expenses.[57] He had a plausible scholarly excuse, attending the Tenth International Congress of Historical Sciences, held in Rome from September 4 to 11. But he was not going to skip Greece. Leonardo Olschki wished him the best for his trip and that "bedbugs and sirocco would spare him."[58]

He sailed the mid-Atlantic on the *Cristoforo Colombo* for Naples in early August and immediately took a smaller ship to Athens, where he met up with Bowra.[59] The two went to the island of Rhodes and then spent eight days on Hydra, off the southern Peloponnese, where they were guests of Patrick Leigh Fermor and his wife Joan, née Monsell—the latter an attractive aristocratic woman for whom EKa had a special liking. A photograph depicts guests on the Leigh Fermor's flagstone terrace: Cyril Connolly and "Paddy" in the background, Bowra sitting in a chair looking pleased with himself, and a shirtless sun-browned Kantorowicz playing chess with Joan.[60] (One cannot tell who is winning.) EKa recalled later to Bowra that he had "flirted with her a little."[61]

[55] Bowra to Felix Frankfurter, 12 September [1953]: Frankfurter papers.

[56] To Vera, 30 September 1954: Lerner archive.

[57] To Vera, 7 August 1955, 26 March 1957: Lerner archive.

[58] Olschki to Kantorowicz, 16 July 1955: Olschki papers.

[59] To Vera, 7 August 1955.

[60] Itinerary in Kantorowicz to Kurt Riezler, 4 September 1955: LBI, box 7, folder 5. Photo reproduced in Charlotte Mosley, *In Tearing Haste: Letters between Deborah Devonshire and Patrick Leigh Fermor* (New York, 2008) (with incorrect dating).

[61] To Bowra, 11 November 1955.

Figure 27. In Vatican procession, September 1955: supporter of throne and altar with handkerchief in vest pocket. (Lerner archive)

EKa spent more than a week at the end of August with Helmut Küpper on the island of Ischia off the Neapolitan coast before going to Rome for the International Congress, the first such meeting since 1936. He gave no paper, and although he claimed to have had business there, it is unclear what it was. He termed the meeting "a 'Fair' (including Vanity Fair)."[62] Nevertheless. it enabled him to spend a long evening at a trattoria with Friedrich Baethgen and Percy Ernst Schramm. The three agreed that it was just as it had been when they were together in Heidelberg thirty years before.[63] EKa was hoping to meet with Kurt Riezler as well. He wrote from Rome to his friend, who was lying in a hospital in Munich, but the letter came back with the notations: "Addressee deceased"; "return to sender." Riezler had died of cancer.[64]

Initially EKa had thought that he would not visit the Vatican: he was annoyed that Pius XII had excommunicated Juan Perón but not Hitler.[65] Yet while on board the *Cristoforo Colombo* he met a highly placed Vatican official who offered to bring him to a papal ceremony, an invitation he could not resist. Afterward he sent to Michael and Lucy Cherniavsky a photo showing the pope being carried aloft on the *sedia gestatoria* amid a large crowd (fig. 27), on the reverse of which he wrote: "Look at the man half-covered by the *gestatoria* carrier

[62] To Riezler, 4 September 1955.

[63] To Percy Ernst Schramm, 9 January 1956: Schramm papers; to Friedrich Baethgen, 25 May 1956: Baethgen papers; Schramm in *Erasmus* 18 (1966): 455.

[64] To Riezler, 4 September 1955; to Bowra, 11 November 1955.

[65] To Elise Peters, 26 June 1955: Lerner archive.

with spec's. He is a supporter of throne and altar, escorted by papal guards."[66] (He could have said: "the nattily dressed sunburned man with handkerchief in vest pocket.") Kantorowicz wrote to Erich Kahler that when others sank to their feet he was delighted until he realized that this was not meant for him, and to Marion Dönhoff: "I now know how a Hellenistic ruler must have felt when his subjects acclaimed him and prostrated themselves before him; I miss this a little in Princeton."[67]

From Rome EKa went to Sicily, where he stayed in Palermo and visited the Greek ruins of Selinunte and Segesta. He wrote to Vera that people took him for an American because of his bad Italian accent and asked whether he knew one of their relatives from Brooklyn. He noted too that he had spent almost all of his trip on islands. Now he would be returning (by air, for the first time) to his "Ivory Tower"—"also an island."[68] And there would be little keeping him from finishing a book he had started long before and for which he was to become most famous.

[66] Lerner archive.

[67] To Kahler, 12 September 1955: StGA, Akte Kantorowicz; to Dönhoff as in Janus Gudian, *Ernst Kantorowicz* (Frankfurt, 2014), 179.

[68] 25 September 1955: Lerner archive.

CHAPTER 24

The King's Two Bodies

Ernst Kantorowicz thought of the scholarly articles he wrote during his American career as *Kabinettstücke*, by which he meant well-crafted gems, kept in collectors' cases—gems dazzling to the connoisseur but too subtle in their austere beauty to be appreciated by the uninitiated. An article of his of 1953 bears a title in Greek, ΣΥΝΘΡΟΝΟΣ ΔΙΚΙ, without any subtitle. He wrote twenty-three such articles between 1945 and his death in 1963. (His statement that at the Institute "one is paid for being, not doing" was just a quip.[1]) Thus to hold each article up for examination would be an undertaking that would go too far beyond the reasonable limits of an already long book. The concept of the cabinet-gem, however, is useful for introducing Kantorowicz's masterpiece, *The King's Two Bodies*, because this book can best be seen as an assemblage of such gems under one cover: the cabinet of Dr. Kantorowicz.

The composition of *The King's Two Bodies* extended from 1945 to 1955, a time when Kantorowicz was at the peak of his scholarly powers. The initial steps are recorded in the first two paragraphs of the book's preface. A conversation with his friend, the legal philosopher Max Radin, led from Radin's pointing out that in the United States the Benedictine order and other monastic congregations counted as "corporations," to F. W. Maitland's study of "The Crown as Corporation," to the legal fiction of "the king's two bodies," and thence to its role in Shakespeare's *Richard II* and to its medieval antecedents. Soon afterward Kantorowicz wrote an essay on "the two bodies" meant to be published in a Festschrift to honor Radin, but plans for this volume did not materialize; instead he took the opportunity to expand the essay into a separate publication to be offered to Radin on the occasion of his seventieth birthday in the spring of 1950. But Kantorowicz's embroilment in the California loyalty oath controversy caused delay, and Radin's death in June 1950 made him put the project aside.

He thought he had finished his book around that time. His preface is misleading because he referred to his work of 1950 as a "paper," but in August 1950 he informed Theodor Mommsen that a book called *The King's Two Bodies* was

[1] Quoted by Marion Dönhoff, "Ernst Kantorowicz," 13.

"completely finished"—only a few footnotes remained to be added.[2] Similarly he submitted a bibliography for his candidacy at the Institute that included a statement that a volume, *The King's Two Bodies*, was ready for publication. But this never happened then or in the immediately following years. Evidently he was nurturing new ideas, but his writing and dissemination of *The Fundamental Issue* came first, and then his term at Dumbarton Oaks in the spring of 1951 obliged him to concentrate on matters Byzantine. Once he was in Princeton, however, he dedicated himself to enlarging and finishing the book he had previously thought was ready for the press. He started this work in December 1951, and in February 1952 he wrote to a friend in Berkeley who had requested an article for a journal: "At present I am frightfully busy at getting a book done, originally my contribution to the Max Radin Festschrift, which never appeared. To finish that seems so important to me that I would even cancel a trip to Europe which I had planned for May."[3]

A year later Joseph Strayer, the chairman of the Princeton History Department, wrote to Herbert Bailey, the director of the Princeton University Press: "Kantorowicz has nearly finished his book and from conversations with him I think it will be a good one. I certainly hope that we will try to get it."[4] Strayer's recommendation sufficed to prompt Bailey to solicit the manuscript from the author and submit it to two reviewers. These were Gaines Post, a medieval historian at the University of Wisconsin who had written some important articles related to Kantorowicz's concerns (he also was a good friend of Strayer's) and (with some impropriety) Strayer himself. Both recommended publication strongly. Strayer summed up by writing: "This is a fascinating book. Some people will swear by it, others at it, but it will not leave scholars indifferent. Also, I fear, it won't sell in large numbers."[5]

By November 1953 *The King's Two Bodies* was "enthusiastically approved" by Princeton University Press's editorial board. But it still was not finished. Kantorowicz explained to Bailey that he wanted to write one more chapter (the one on Dante) and to integrate findings from research he had done in Europe in the summer of 1953. Indeed, he said that it would take him about a year "to put on the finishing touches." Yet a year later he still was not finished. In November 1954 he wrote to Bowra that "the revision proceeds rather slowly, one has found so much stuff in the meantime; I do not believe I shall ever again write a book which demands any kind of thinking."[6] In June 1955 Kantorowicz joked to his cousin Lieschen about how long his "pregnancies" were: "They always last for

[2]To Mommsen, 2 August 1950: Lerner archive.

[3]To Vera Peters, 15 December 1951: Lerner archive; to Yakov Malkiel, 27 February 1952: Bancroft Library, Yakov Malkiel papers.

[4]21 April 1953: Princeton Press papers.

[5]19 May 1953: Princeton Press papers.

[6]28 November 1954.

years, with innumerable aborted articles coming in between."[7] Only in the fall of that year were the "finishing touches" applied. Given that everyone knew that the book would be expensive to produce and believed that it "wouldn't sell in large numbers," Robert Oppenheimer authorized a subvention from the Institute; the author also agreed to forgo royalties. *The King's Two Bodies* went into production in 1956; in November EKa wrote to Lieschen that he had become "a pure correcting institution"—a proper role for a "senile delinquent."[8] The book was announced for appearance in spring 1957, but because of the labors involved in making the very detailed index it came out in the fall. Bailey wrote to an editor from Harper's who was thinking of a paperback version that the book "would not be appropriate for paperback publication; it is an enormous scholarly work, very specialized in nature, and because it is so new I am sure we would not be willing to release it, even if by some outlandish circumstance you should want to do it."[9]

Why did it take Kantorowicz so long to write *The King's Two Bodies*? One answer is that he was learning to use sources that were new to him—legal sources. We have seen that he viewed his obligation to teach English constitutional history at Berkeley with great repugnance. Yet he dutifully went about mastering the material. He read the historiographical classics, Bishop Stubbs and "Pollock and Maitland," as well as the recent textbooks. Doing nothing by halves, he also studied the basic repertoire of charters and statutes, and the expository works by Glanville, Bracton, and Sir John Fortescue. Discussing readings in 1947 for the second half of his Berkeley course, he told his students that they should keep up with the *Handbook of Anglo-American Legal History* (1936) by Max Radin and a textbook on *The Constitutional History of Medieval England* by J.E.A. Jolliffe but implicitly that they mostly should be listening to him.[10] He observed in his preface to *The King's Two Bodies* that he had "swerved from the normal tracks of the mediaeval historian" as he already had done in his *Laudes Regiae*. In the *Laudes* he had "swerved" into the liturgy; now he was "breaking through the fences of the mediaeval law." But whereas he already had learned some liturgy for his biography of Frederick II, he needed to learn the English law from scratch, as well as commentators on the law such as Bracton and Coke.

Obviously another answer to the question of why it took Kantorowicz so long to write *The King's Two Bodies* is that the book is long (550 pages, crammed with reduced-font footnotes). As he explained in his preface (viii) it became so long because although "the original plan was merely to point out a number of mediaeval antecedents or parallels to the legal tenet of the King's Two Bodies, [the book] gradually turned, as the subtitle suggests, into a "Study in Mediaeval

[7] 26 June 1955: Lerner archive.
[8] 8 November 1956: Lerner archive
[9] Bailey to Lucille Withers, 29 April 1957: Princeton Press papers.
[10] LBI, box 9, folder 8.

Political Theology." The subtitle immediately raises the question of Kantorowicz's relation to the German authoritarian political thinker Carl Schmitt, who coined the term *Politische Theologie* in a book of that name of 1922. Granted the use of the same term, Kantorowicz was in no way thinking of either a dialogue with Schmitt or expressing an ideological debt. Schmitt's name does not appear in *The King's Two Bodies*, nor in any other of Kantorowicz's published writings, nor in any of his many hundreds of letters. Some commentators simply will not let the supposed connection go. A recent critic writes: "Kantorowicz's refusal to engage directly with Schmitt constitutes, paradoxically, his very mode of engagement."[11] But this is a conventionally unconventionable mode of argument that Kantorowicz would have ridiculed. Perhaps this critic and others who make the same assumption should know that Kantorowicz's notes for a historical methods seminar he offered at Berkeley in 1949 have "political theology" as one of many possible historical approaches to be discussed, and to exemplify it he put down the name not of Schmitt but of Joseph Strayer, who that year had published an article on "Defense of the Realm and Royal Power in France," which displayed how the French crown around 1300 drew on ecclesiastical precedents.[12]

It would be entirely mistaken to suppose that Kantorowicz was upholding "idols of modern political religions" (viii) as he had upheld in 1933 the "idol" of "Secret Germany." At a dinner party hosted by Ralph Giesey in the autumn of 1949 he insisted on his ability to write history free of the influences of his own time (a long way from the EKa of 1930), while Ihor Ševčenko argued that this was impossible.[13] Ševčenko confirmed that "EKa always maintained his own writing was not influenced by contemporary affairs."[14] Kantorowicz became attached to the term "political theology" in the early 1940s. In his introduction to a version of his medieval survey course dating from 1942 he wrote that he would be treating "not so much the historical facts as the development of the political-religious ideas of those five centuries . . . what may be called the <u>Theology of Rulership</u> or an outline of <u>Political Theology</u>." (The underlining is his.)[15] Although the preface to *The King's Two Bodies* alludes to a change in intention—an initial one intending to point out a number of antecedents and parallels to a legal tenet, and the ultimate one that resulted in a "Study in Medieval Political Theology"—a bibliography he drew up in 1950 showed that political theology was on his mind during the first phase, inasmuch as it already refers to a forthcoming book, "The King's Two Bodies: A Study in Mediaeval

[11] Richard Halpern, "The King's Two Buckets: Kantorowicz, *Richard II*, and Fiscal *Trauerspiel*," *Representations* 106 (Spring 2009): 67–71.

[12] Joseph Strayer, "Defense of the Realm and Royal Power in France," *Studi in onore di Gino Luzzato* (Milan, 1949), 4:289–96.

[13] Gordon Griffiths to Robert E. Lerner, 3 April 1994, 31 December 1994.

[14] Interview, 28 August 1996.

[15] LBI, box 9, folder 2.

Political Theology (manuscript of 300 pages—ready for the Press)."[16] The fact that the published work of 1957 turned out to have become almost twice as long as the manuscript of 1950 seems to indicate that he wanted to write much more on the subject of medieval political theology. Indeed one might say that the finished book was nearly an anthology of disquisitions concerning transmutations of Christian theological formulations into political ones.

Thus we would do best by taking the subtitle as the means for analyzing the book. When Kantorowicz writes, "We might be tempted to look here for the solution of the whole problem of the king's two bodies" (268), he gives the impression that he is concerned to see how the tenet originated. But in his introduction he assures us that this is not the case. Although Maitland had uncovered the Tudor legal fiction of Kantorowicz's title, he had not attempted to trace its origins back "into the legal and political thoughts of the Middle Ages." Kantorowicz laments that such a history has never been written but disavows any intention of writing one himself: "The present studies do not intend to fill that gap" (6). Readers of his fascinating but frustrating book know that he expatiates on a range of theological, philosophical, and legal developments that exemplify aspects of his "two bodies" theme, only to reject them as constituting the specific origins of the Tudor tenet. Toward the end of his book he comes close when he proposes:

> What apparently happened was that the English jurists failed to make a clear-cut distinction between the corporate body of the Crown and the supra-individual personage of the Dignity, and instead equated each other with the body politic.... That is to say, they fused two different concepts of the current corporational doctrines: the organic and the successional. And from this fusion of a number of interrelated corporational concepts there originated, it seems, both the "King's body politic" and the king as "corporation sole." (449)

But the hundreds of previous pages by no means lead directly to this point, and the passage still does not put everything together to show how the king's "body natural" was juxtaposed to the "body politic" and "corporation sole."

Many years earlier in his Halle talk of 1930 Kantorowicz had excluded the search for origins as a legitimate task of historiography: he saw no point in pursuing "predecessors" backward, so that "the kiss exchanged by Pope and Emperor already was in the Gilgamesh epic." Since then he had not changed his mind. He recognized that if one wanted to find the origins of a sixteenth-century theory, one at least had to pay attention to "the crucial fifteenth century," but he disavowed any intention of doing that (6). Even in citing a seemingly pivotal passage from the fifteenth-century political theorist John Fortescue, he disarmed those who thought that he might have been tracing

[16] Bibliography drawn up for consideration by the Institute for Advanced Study: Erwin Panofsky, "Ernst H. Kantorowicz": IAS, Kantorowicz faculty file, box 18.

backward by insisting that "the passage has not been adduced here in order to prove that the Elizabethan jurists 'borrowed' from Fortescue, or that his treatise was their 'source'" (8). He was not writing a linear history of ideas because such could yield "lack of tension resulting from tedious repetitions" (ix). He was not trying to solve a problem concerning the origins of an idea but displaying its "transformations, implications, and radiations" (ix). Perhaps his best formulation of what he was doing occurs when he writes: "We find ourselves involved in a tangle of intersecting, overlapping, and contradictory strands of political thought, all of which somehow converge" (381). Kantorowicz never wished to abide by historiographical orthodoxies. His book of 1927 violated the orthodoxies of the "truth-seeking historian" in numerous ways yet offered an orderly chronological presentation; his book of 1957 violates no methodological orthodoxies but purposely eschews conventions of orderly presentation. What he was writing were "Studies in Mediaeval Political Theology" (the author himself disregards the singular in the title by using the phrase "the present studies" [6]): a collection of studies, with the important qualification that they do generally relate to a theme and "somehow converge."

The first chapter starts at the point to which Kantorowicz doubles back toward the end—the Tudor legal fiction that provides the title to his book. The Elizabethan legal text, Edmund Plowden's "Reports," contain several statements such as the following:

> The King has in him two Bodies, *viz.*, a Body natural, and a Body politic. His body natural . . . is a Body mortal, subject to all the Infirmities that come by Nature or Accident, to the Imbecility of Infancy or old Age. . . . But his Body politic is a Body that cannot be seen or handled, consisting of Policy and Government, and constituted for the Direction of the People, and the Management of the public weal, and this body is utterly void of Infancy, and old Age, and other natural Defects and Imbecilities, which the Body natural is subject to.

F. W. Maitland became interested in this legal fiction because he saw it as a link between the medieval and the modern—the medieval assumption of personal royal rule and the modern one of the abstract enduring state. But Kantorowicz gave no regard to such teleology. For him the primary interest of the two-bodies fiction lay in its "crypto-theological" nature, which would allow him to use it as a point of departure for a book on political theology. He could not refrain from mentioning that the fiction aided Parliament to resort to a similar formulation when it declared that it was fighting King Charles I in the name of his body politic which had become severed from his mortal body: "fighting the king to defend the King." On this basis Kantorowicz was willing to allow that "there were great and serious advantages in the English doctrine of the King's Two Bodies." And we may be permitted to see in this brief passage a glimmer of oblique homage to Anglo-American constitutionalism. But that was a far as he went: he was not pointing forward to any modern political religion of the state, whether that was to be understood positively or negatively: "The fascination emanating as usual from the historical material itself prevailed over any desire of practical or moral application" (viii).

The book's second chapter, devoted to Shakespeare's *Richard II*, is closely linked to the first. It intends to demonstrate how the two-body fiction "scarcely belonged to the arcana of the legal guild alone" (24). Kantorowicz had been engaged with the theological-political aspects of Shakespeare's play at least as early as the spring of 1940 when he told his Berkeley students that Richard II was the "prominent type" of the "David-like king who was the *Christus Domini*—anointed of the Lord."[17] The play then entered his conversation of 1945 with Radin about the "two bodies." Although in his book he held out the possibility that Shakespeare "chanced upon the legal definitions of kingship . . . when conversing with his friends at the Inns," he did not insist on that because "the image of a twinned nature of a king . . . was most genuinely Shakespeare's own and proper vision" (25). But however one judges Kantorowicz's reading of the play, the chapter hardly contributes to the progress of the book since it restates Plowden's legal fiction in different terms. Joseph Strayer wrote in his reader's report that "the chapter on Shakespeare is out of place; it should either be dropped, or put in an appendix." Nevertheless, Kantorowicz was intent on showing how a reading of a work of literature belonged in a work of history and the chapter stayed.

Kantorowicz's treatment of medieval political postulates in terms of theological origins emerges in chapters 3 through 5, which treat "Christ-Centered Kingship," "Law-Centered Kingship," and "Polity-Centered Kingship." Here one does find chronological movement—tenth and eleventh centuries; twelfth and thirteenth centuries; late thirteenth and fourteenth centuries. These chapters are favorites with readers because of their easily graspable and quotable rubrics, as well as their original and quite convincing conceptualizations. In the first period the king was seen as having two persons because in addition to his natural person "a certain spiritual capacity was attributed to him as an effluence of his consecration and unction" (44). In the second his duality consisted in being "above and below the law"—the "father and son of Justice" (159). In this period "the ancient idea of liturgical kingship . . . gave way to a new pattern of kingship centered on the sphere of Law, which was not wanting its own mysticism" (192). Finally, the third period saw the triumph of the idea of the "body politic" parallel to the "mystical body of the Church," of which the King was "the head but still himself a common mortal" (271). So we have three studies in medieval political theology that display versions of how the mortal king shared in something mystical beyond himself.

The heart of chapter 5 is a detailed presentation of an important conceptual hinge: the spillover of the doctrine of the "mystical body of the Church"

[17] Lectures on "Medieval Foundations of Humanism and Renaissance," LBI, box 9, folder 15, p. 48.

(*Corpus Ecclesiae mysticum*) to that of "the mystical body of the polity" (*Corpus Reipublicae mysticum*). Saint Paul had used the language that the Church was the "body of Christ," but this was liturgical, and the Carolingians referred to the "mystical body of Christ," but this did not refer to the body of Church but rather to the Eucharist. Only after 1150 did the term ""mystical body of the Church" assume a "sociological sense," allowing Boniface VIII in *Unam sanctam* to refer to the Church as "one mystical body, the head of which is Christ." With the notion of the "mystical body of the Church" well established, this "easily fell prey to the world of thought of statesmen, jurists, and scholars who were developing new ideologies for the nascent territorial states" (207). Thus after the thirteenth century, the continuity of "polity-centered kingship" was "now guaranteed by the *corpus mysticum* of the realm which, so to speak, never died, but was 'eternal' like the *corpus mysticum* of the Church" (231). (It is here that those who see Kantorowicz making a contribution to the ideological foundations of the nation-state are on their strongest ground.)

After reading from page 42 to page 272 we find nothing yet that directly foreshadows, let alone comprises, the Tudor doctrine of "the King's Two Bodies." But the book's next two chapters (175 additional pages) deal more clearly with how the doctrine could have come into place. Chapter 6 treats the theoretical underpinning of the concept of "never dying." The first section of this chapter on "continuity" is not new. We have seen that Kantorowicz addressed the subject as early as 1935 with two drafts of a chapter meant for his unfinished interregnum book. Then he pursued the topic in his Harvard paper of 1939 and his "Pacific Coast" paper at the end of that year. I have shown elsewhere that extended passages from the latter, "The Idea of Permanency in the Thirteenth Century," appear verbatim in chapter 6 of the book of 1957.[18] Although the idea for treating antecedents of a specific Tudor legal fiction may have originated in a conversation with Max Radin in 1945, Kantorowicz constructed a montage consisting partly of ideas he had explored previously.

The second part of chapter 6 concerns "non-dying corporations"—the empire, the university. (Since he was working on *The Fundamental Issue* shortly after his work on the proto-*King's Two Bodies*, his concept of "the constant and essence of a university [being] always the body of teachers and students" in the former most likely was a tailored version of the late-medieval juristic view (303) of the "corporate, if incorporeal" *universitas* that "represented . . . species and individuation at the same time.") That left it to broach the formulation of the doctrine of the "king who never dies." Chapter 7 has three parts (with many subparts) treating, respectively, the postulate of dynastic continuity; fictions concerning the abstract "crown"; and the concept of the "Dignity" that pertained to the royal office, leading to the principle that "the Dignity does not die." After considering developments in France (influenced by the work of

[18] Lerner, "Kantorowicz and Continuity," 117–20.

Ralph Giesey), Kantorowicz explains that because England was endowed with a unique parliamentary system, it was only there that the fiction of the king never dying in the capacity of his "body politic" was able to take shape.

The Press readers for the book manuscript of 1953 did not know that, after reaching the Tudor king as corporation sole with a dignity that never died, Kantorowicz was going to add a chapter on Dante. They would not have been pleased, having already had reservations about the chapter on Shakespeare. I heard Joseph Strayer say, "We pleaded with him to omit the Dante chapter, but he would not listen." So the large book ends (aside from the epilogue) with an exposition of Kantorowicz's views on Dante's "opalescent notion" of *humanitas* "in all its numerous hues" (451). The chapter distills years of thinking about Dante, who was one of the major authors in the canon of Stefan George (as was Shakespeare). It is a classic expression of the "humanistic" as opposed to the "theological" interpretation of Dante. Adding a fourth term to the rubrics of chapters 4 through 6, Kantorowicz proposes that Dante stood for "man-centered kingship," as quintessentially when he had Virgil intone in his last words to the *Commedia*'s pilgrim: "I crown and mitre you over yourself." How this relates to "the king's two bodies" is obscure. We can see that the author himself was not confident about the chapter's relevance when he wrote, "Perhaps we will find it easier now, or perhaps more difficult, to understand the later definitions of English jurists" (494). Ralph Giesey, the disciple to whom Kantorowicz was closest, assured me that the Dante chapter was "absolutely central to EKa's philosophy of life."[19] It may be best to leave it at that.

Gaines Post's reader's review of 1953 proposed that *The King's Two Bodies* could be improved if it offered a "brief conclusion of 5–10 pages to draw together the principal points made."[20] But the preface of the published book states: "Only hesitatingly and rarely did the author find it necessary to draw conclusions or indicate how the various topics discussed in these pages should be geared with each other" (xi). Thus, instead of "conclusions," Kantorowicz appended an epilogue (actually a prologue placed at the end) that effectively constituted a final brief chapter by pursuing the question of whether the Tudor legal fiction had classical antecedents. The results are that indeed parallels and similarities existed but that "nothing in pagan thought would justify the diction of the king having two *Bodies*" (505). Therefore the book concludes: "The KING'S TWO BODIES is an offshoot of Christian theological thought and consequently stands as a landmark of Christian political theology" (506). Is this the thesis? Perhaps. But it remains true that in the publicity form for *The King's Two Bodies* Kantorowicz left blank the space asking for "the author's own version of the thesis of his book."[21]

[19] Letter of 25 November 1991.

[20] Princeton Press papers.

[21] Ibid.

Despite uncertainty about whether the book has a thesis, most readers consider it to be one of the greatest works of medieval history of the twentieth century. The legal historian William Huse Dunham, Jr., opened his review for *Speculum* by announcing: "Kantorowicz has written a great book. Its greatness [is] apparent on well-nigh every page," and ended by saying: "Few will care to write on any aspect of the Middle Ages without having first read this major classic." Brian Tierney wrote that the book was "of major importance for medievalists" and "brilliant." The reviewer for the *Historische Zeitschrift* called it "an absolute historical delight." Gaines Post, Joseph Strayer, and Erwin Panofsky wrote in their memoir of Kantorowicz for the Medieval Academy of America: "It is a masterpiece of art and reason in the writing of History." After the book was made available in paperback in 1981 the reviewer for *Church History* referred to it as a "monumental classic," and after it was translated into German the reviewer for the *Süddeutsche Zeitung* agreed that the book is "rightly considered a masterpiece."[22]

There also are many detractors. A frequent complaint is that *The King's Two Bodies* is located "up in the air"—that it rarely takes account of actual political events. Beryl Smalley wrote: "By the end of the book I felt as queasy as one would after a diet of jam without bread. Is it possible to study the history of ideas without relating them to their genesis in actual problems and conflicts?"[23] Walter Ullmann referred to its "thought-surgery."[24] A contemporary critic refers to it as concerning no more than "the semantics of medieval constitutionalism."[25] Others take objection to arguments in particular chapters, above all to the treatments of Shakespeare[26] and Dante,[27] and to the "two bodies" reading of an Ottonian miniature.[28] And of course the nonlinear organization is a problem for many. Among the early reviewers, H. S. Offler found that the "main stream of [the] argument [is] at times hard to follow"; Cecil Grayson regretted the lack of the "continuity that enables the reader . . . to be exactly sure where he has been"; F. M. Powicke found the

[22] Dunham in *Speculum* 33 (1958): 550–53; Tierney in *Thought* 10 (1958): 306–8; Rudolf M. Kloos in *Historische Zeitschrift* 188 (1959): 358–64; Post et al. in *Speculum* 39 (1964): 596–98; Morimichi Watanabe in *Church History* 52 (1983): 258–59; Peter Schöttler in *Süddeutsche Zeitung*, 21 March 1991, xi.

[23] *Past & Present* 20 (November 1961): 32.

[24] *Mitteilungen des Instituts für Österreichische Geschichtsforschung*, 364.

[25] Wimmer, "Kantorowicz's Oaths," 136.

[26] David Norbrook, "The Emperor's New Body? *Richard II*, Ernst Kantorowicz, and the Politics of Shakespeare Criticism," *Textual Practice* 10 (1996): 329–57; Lorna Hutson, "Imagining Justice: Kantorowicz and Shakespeare," *Representations* 106 (Spring 2009): 118–42.

[27] Charles Davis, "Kantorowicz and Dante," in Benson and Fried, *Ernst Kantorowicz*, 240–64.

[28] Konrad Hoffmann, *Taufsymbolik im mittelalterlichen Herrscherbild* (Düsseldorf, 1968), 14–41; Johannes von Müller, "Wunderliche Übertragungen: Das Herrscherbild Ottos III—eine Deutung," *Zeitschrift für Ideengeschichte* 8 (2014): 73–86. (I thank Jost Philipp Klenner for the references.)

book "unsystematic"; and Beryl Smalley minced no words in deeming its organization "baffling."[29]

A different range of criticism revolves around the fact that the book is not just scholarly but "ultrascholarly"—demanding intellectual calisthenics. Many readers are uncomfortable with its gratuitous display of arcane theological learning: for example, the parsing of the "two bodies" fiction in terms of the Christological heresies of Arianism, Nestorianism, Patripassianism, Sabellianism, Monophysitism, and Monothelitism (17–18). Similar complaints refer to the recurrent employment of untranslated Latin theological or legal terminology. (Kantorowicz also includes some Greek, in Greek characters.) And then comes the gratuitous display of recondite vocabulary—catoptromancy, geminate, caducity, chiasmus, equiparation.

The trait of enormously long footnotes is yet another problem, for the number of words in the notes roughly matches the number of words in the text. Kantorowicz's preface states that he kept "tangential problems" out of the text to keep them from "stifling the main argument," instead using notes to explore such problems in ways that "might become useful to others" (x). Yet many of the footnotes are not expansive but digressive. One example (85, n. 105) will suffice. The text adduces a sermon from the *Opus imperfectum* of Pseudo-John Chrysostom that tells of the dual nature of the ass on which Christ rode into Jerusalem, and the accompanying note gives a bibliographical reference. Most historians would have stopped there, but once the hare is up Kantorowicz is on the chase. He observes regarding the *Opus imperfectum* that "Thomas Aquinas supposedly said that he would prefer its possession to that of the whole city of Paris" and accompanies this with a citation of the statement in Latin. Then comes bibliography for the *Opus imperfectum*, and one scholar's belief that its place of origin was Ravenna; then a report that "the Palm Sunday homily of Aelfric, otherwise a paraphrase of the *Opus imperfectum*, does not contain the passage quoted here," although, on the other hand, "the ass is mentioned quite often in the writings of the Fathers." Finally the irrepressible author cannot refrain from sharing the information that "according to later legends, the holy animal died, very advanced in years and after long migration in Verona where a local cult developed." Edification abounds.

Despite all these criticisms, it can hardly be denied that the *Two Bodies* has great literary strengths. The author explains that it was his "prime ambition to produce a fairly readable text . . . to keep the reader's attention, if possible, awake instead of abandoning him to some jungle teeming with scholarly tsetse flies" (xi). And most readers are in fact kept awake by the stimulation of a firm authorial presence. The *Speculum* reviewer, Dunham, wrote that the book is "written in the grand manner with an appropriate Latinity of style; the prose

[29] Offler in *English Historical Review* 75 (1960): 297; Grayson in *Romance Philology* 15 (1961): 180; Powicke in *Medium Aevum* 28 (1959): 50; Smalley in *Past & Present* 20 (November 1961): 34.

is stately yet vigorous and refreshing"; the *Speculum* memoir judged it a "great work of literary art." Kantorowicz delights in paradoxes ("father and son of justice", "above and below the law," "perpetual necessity"), teasing out nuances, and offering instruction on fascinating matters of which no one before had any ken. The author who refers to "tsetse flies" can shoo them off by displaying occasional humor: "after thus having gained a foothold on, so to speak, firm celestial ground" (9); "certain regalian rights . . . big fish (tuna, sturgeon, and others)" (170); tomb sculpture, "the horrors of which would spoil the appetite of an inveterate ghoul" (433). And readers should be on the lookout for sly obiter dicta: "[Petrarch's] readiness to call anyone disagreeing with him an 'Averroist' has its equivalent in modern habits" (301, n. 62).

Another outstanding quality of *The King's Two Bodies*, by common consent, is the book's astonishing diversity of sources. Post, Strayer, and Panofsky praised it as "a great synthesis of art, literature, religion, theology, ecclesiology, numismatics, and political and legal thought." The employment of unusual or underutilized varieties of sources had always been a Kantorowicz trait, and in *The King's Two Bodies* he outdid himself. If one knew nothing about the book and looked first at the rear instead of the front, one might take it to be a work of art history, for there one finds reproductions of manuscript illuminations, ivory book covers, sarcophagi, mosaics, frescoes, coins, medals, seals, badges, and reconstructions of architecture, as well as reproductions of funeral effigies and tombs and one funny caricature of Louis XIV without his wig and robes.

Of course the single most impressive "new" sources in *The King's Two Bodies* are legal texts. We have seen that in his preface Kantorowicz compared his "swerving" from "the normal tracks of the medieval historian" (ix) by drawing on the law just as he had swerved in his *Laudes Regiae* by drawing on the liturgy. Studying and mastering the medieval law, however, was a more challenging and vaster project, for it meant mastering Roman law, canon law, and English common law. If one looks at the index to the *Two Bodies* one sees that references to legal citations and commentaries fill six and a half columns, and "maxims, legal" another column. Kantorowicz had to expend considerable energy just to locate his legal sources, for most of them were available only in rare sixteenth-century editions. As he wrote, "Every student laboring in the vineyard of mediaeval Law will be painfully aware of the difficulty of laying hands on even the most important authors" (ix). (Today, of course, these texts are easily retrievable.) Clearly the subject matter of the *King's Two Bodies* necessitated traveling away from "normal tracks," and the extent to which Kantorowicz did that without any previous model to imitate (for he was not writing a book on legal history) was one of his great historiographical triumphs.

The greatest triumph of the book, however, lies in its content. If it had been merely a treatment of foreshadowing of a Tudor legal phrase it now would be gathering dust. But it addresses big subjects. The Press readers and early reviewers agreed on the "bigness." Joseph Strayer wrote that "the book will be of interest to students of constitutional and legal history [and] students of political theory"; Gaines Post wrote that it would be "useful to students of medieval thought in general, as well as to historians of law and institutions"; Brian Tierney's view was that the book presented a synthesis of "a fascinating array of theological, iconographical, and above all, juristic materials concerning medieval ideas of kingship"; Peter Riesenberg averred that Kantorowicz's book was "perhaps the most important work in the history of medieval political thought," tracing "the development of the theory and symbolism of the early national states from the eleventh to the sixteenth centuries";[30] and W. H. Dunham found that it "describe[d] the totality of concepts that composed medieval Political Theology." One notices that these critics did not always exactly agree as to what the book was about—constitutional and legal history, political theory, medieval ideas of kingship, theory and symbolism of the early nation-states; medieval political theology—but they agreed that it was a major work concerning major subject matters. And if we grant that Kantorowicz had written a loosely connected anthology of "cabinet jewels" dedicated to exposing cross-currents of theology, law, and politics, it is easy to see how offering new angles on "legal history," "political theory," and "ideas of kingship" all fell within his purview.

Dunham astutely recognized that Kantorowicz "does not try to 'prove' by logic the 'influence of one idea upon another,' but that by looking at a congeries of concepts "rather than by resorting to a cause-and-consequence formula [provides] answers that convince." One can observe this best in the dominant interpretive line: "the change from the Pauline *corpus Christi* to the medieval *corpus ecclesiae mysticum*, thence to the *corpus reipublicum mysticum* which was equated with the *corpus morale et politicum* of the commonwealth" (506). Even Beryl Smalley, who was not friendly to the *Two Bodies*, implicitly agreed with Dunham that it consisted of "a number of learned, specialized papers grouped together to form chapters" and found that "any unity that the book may have comes from the cycle of mutual borrowing between Church and State of ideas and symbols to express them. . . . Kantorowicz points to the process repeatedly and I have never seen it better illustrated."[31]

Without treating the longer-term reception at any length, it may yet be noted that the book became much more popular twenty years after its appearance than it was when it first appeared and then kept up the new pace. Apparently the impetus was given by an approving reference to the *Two Bodies* by Michel Foucault in his *Discipline and Punish*.[32] Foucault said that he wished to pay "homage" to Kantorowicz, and that alone seems to have been sufficient to send many to look up a book that they never had heard of. Since then Kantorowicz's

[30] Riesenberg in *American Political Science Review* 52 (1958): 1139–40.

[31] Smalley in *Past & Present* 20 (November 1961): 31.

[32] Michel Foucault, *Discipline and Punish: The Birth of the Prison* (New York, 1977), 29. The original French, *Surveiller et punir*, was published in 1974.

work has been associated with many catch phrases: "post-modernism";[33] "new historicism";[34] "text archaeology";[35] "history of the body";[36] "Foucauldian interest in power and the body."[37] A different essay would be needed to judge the aptness of such categories. But not only "theorists" take up the book.[38] The shift to cultural history in the later twentieth century made it clear that Kantorowicz's work had much of importance to say about the rites and representations of power. Many probably do not read the book from beginning to end, but even those who read only parts must be awed by its nuances and its presentation of fascinating novelties based on an arsenal of learning. Kantorowicz's book has never become the foundation of a "school"; no one has ever tried to write another *King's Two Bodies* or anything in its mode. But it remains a scholarly best seller in several different disciplines, and in William Chester Jordan's words, "It remains a wonderfully exciting and constantly rewarding book."[39]

[33] Victoria Kahn, "Political Theology and Fiction in *The King's Two Bodies*," *Representations* 106 (Spring 2009): 77–101.

[34] Wolfgang Ernst, "Kantorowicz: *New Historicism avant la lettre?* in Ernst and Vismann, *Geschichtskörper*, 187–285.

[35] Bernhard Jussen, "The Two Bodies Today," *Representations* 106 (Spring 2009): 102–17, at 111.

[36] Stephen Greenblatt, "Fifty Years of *The King's Two Bodies*," *Representations* 106 (Spring 2009), 63–66.

[37] Graham Hammill and Julia Reinhart Lupton, *Political Theology and Early Modernity* (Chicago, 2012), 9.

[38] A treatment that one might discuss in another place is Paul Monod, "Reading the Two Bodies of Ernst Kantorowicz," *Yearbook of the Leo Baeck Institute* (2005): 105–23.

[39] Preface to *The King's Two Bodies*, seventh paperback printing (Princeton, 1997), xv.

CHAPTER 25

"EKa Is Sick of EKa"

ERNST KANTOROWICZ HAD AN OBSESSION ABOUT YOUTH and the effects of aging. Already in 1926 he wrote to Wilhelm Stein that he knew well of the "crisis of the thirty-year-old." In 1939 he regretted that he was putting on weight as a result of his age (he was forty-four). His continual joking about dying at the age of fifty-six contained an element of memento mori, and when he outlived that year and turned sixty in 1955 his concern with age became a fixation. Just two weeks after his sixtieth birthday he referred to his "senility," a term he then changed to "senile delinquency," and when he returned from Europe in the fall of 1955 he wrote of a realization that he had "become too old for sight-seeing." In June 1956 he complained that "I'm becoming very old." In February 1957 he wrote that the rights of being a sexagenarian included "pedantry, ricketiness, [and] impotence." An explicit statement about the significance of turning sixty comes in a letter to Vera Peters of July 1957: she had just turned fifty and he wrote to her that one's fifties were the best years and at sixty things "start to go downhill." Such a view darkened his mood, as can be seen in letters in which he listed the names of friends and acquaintances who had died—the deaths of Riezler and Küpper (the latter ten years younger than he was) particularly affected him. "The Archangel Gabriel's list of the living keeps on getting smaller." In 1958 he wrote that he was "in the prime of his senility." This was not just meant to be funny for in the same letter he wrote that "EKa is sick of EKa."[1]

This is not to say that he did not have his enjoyments and active engagements. In his later Princeton years until his death at age sixty-eight Kantorowicz led a very comfortable life. His many gratifications included lively conversations

[1] "Crisis": 23 February 1926: Stein papers; "putting on weight": to Stein, 13 January 1939; "senility": to Leonardo Olschki, 18 May 1955: Olschki papers; "senile delinquency": to Elise Peters, 8 November 1956: Lerner archive; "too old for sight-seeing": to Olschki, 8 December 1955; "very old": to Vera Peters, 27 June 1956: Lerner archive; "rights": to Ernst Langlotz, 4 February 1957: Langlotz papers; "downhill": to Vera 10 July 1957; "friends who had died": to Olschki, 8 December 1955, to Olschki, 21 May 1956, to Vera, 16 April 1956; "rights": to Ernst Langlotz, 4 February 1957; "prime": to Olschki, 27 December 1958.

Figure 28. Christmas card to the Kahlers, circa 1960. On the reverse: "and a happy New Year to you and Lily from EKa who is still hunting for truffles." (Deutsches Literaturarchiv, Marbach)

with friends, especially Erwin Panofsky and Erich Kahler,[2] meeting others for rendezvous in New York, and giving and attending dinner parties. He joked about his need for truffles (fig. 28). He went regularly to Medieval Academy meetings in Cambridge in April, and to Dumbarton Oaks seminars in May. He gained honors—the Haskins Medal of the Medieval Academy in 1959; an honorary degree from Lawrence College in the same year. He continued to travel—to Europe, to Lake Tahoe, and, starting in 1958, for winter vacations on the island of St. John in the Virgin Islands. He had assignations with Vera Peters on West and East Coasts. And yet for a man who had been attached to a cult of youth from the George period onward he was repelled by his signs of old age and tried his best, necessarily with diminishing success, to keep himself looking young.[3] And all this made him feel that his life's trajectory was heading downward.

[2]EKa once sent Kahler a Christmas present with the note: "Acipenseris ovaria, /Biotics for the Prostate" (the Latin means caviar). (Eckhart Grünewald archive.)

[3]Interview with Ralph Giesey, 2 August 1991.

A genuine scrape with death occurred in the autumn of 1957. Kantorowicz had always been athletic and enjoyed many sports, especially swimming (often in very cold water) and skiing. As he aged he was grateful for being in good shape. In July 1956 he boasted that his blood pressure was 128 over 80.[4] When he returned in the fall from vacationing at Lake Tahoe he wrote that it did him such good that he "felt like fifty-eight and a half" (he was sixty-one).[5] But a year later matters were not going so well. He went to an eye doctor with complaints about an ongoing headache and pain in his left eye. This doctor told him to see his internist and when the latter took his blood pressure he was startled: it had risen to 250 over 130. So the internist immediately sent him to the hospital for five days of tests. In a letter to Vera describing the stay, he inevitably commented on the food—"quite good for mass-production." Conditions were "endurable" since he was allowed to bring his own wine.[6] All the tests were negative until a final one when x-rays revealed a malfunction of his left kidney. After a cystoscopy to probe the matter further and clean out the "mud" in his urethra—"the cleaning of my plumbing"—the doctors determined that the kidney was misconnected (congenitally) to his aorta and needed to be removed. EKa feared that he soon would be "fishing trout in the Styx,"[7] but the operation was a success. The surgeon, who had seen EKa's new book in his room, commented that he was glad his patient was not a king, or else he would have had to have taken out two left kidneys.[8]

EKa then feared that he might have to marry "in order to have a cheap nanny who would wash my diapers and blow my nose."[9] But he recovered well. On December 8 he wrote to Ralph Giesey:

> I was for three weeks in the hospital where they removed my left kidney—and in the same moment there happened what the doctors hardly had been hoping for: my blood pressure went down to normal, my headaches (which I called sinus troubles) disappeared, and my impaired eyesight began to improve. Lourdes could not have worked more promptly. I am back to normal diet, and on Christmas I may have again my daily bottle of wine.[10]

Fortunately EKa's bout with the cystoscope and the knife came after the protracted labors involved in preparing *The King's Two Bodies* for publication. These had stretched out so long that they had become a constant source of irritation. In May 1956 he complained to Leonardo Olschki that "the book is

[4]To Vera, 27 July 1956.

[5]To Vera, 21 September 1956.

[6]To Vera, 29 September 1957. EKa added in this letter a sampling of his hospital menus, including his choice of beef brisket with horseradish sauce.

[7]To Robert Boehringer, 28 December 1957: StGA, Akte Robert Boehringer, II:4108.

[8]To Vera, 9 October 1957; to Leonardo Olschki, 12 October 1957.

[9]To Elise Peters, 19 October 1957: Lerner archive.

[10]http://www.regiesey.com.

beginning to spit proofs that hang out of my throat in their great length even before they've really begun. If only the sweepings [*quisquilien*] were not so complicated and boring, the continuous checking of citations, the additional supplements to notes, the forgetting of the best passages, and the hunting, hunting, and hunting in my mess."[11] In December he was still working on the proofs, and in March 1957 he was laboring on the very detailed index: "a hell of a work, not the names, of course, but the notions"; "just as boring as lengthy and difficult." He estimated that doing the index would take six weeks, but that did not include reading the proofs for the index, a job he fulfilled when he was in the hospital for tests in September.[12] In February, after the book had appeared but had yet to receive reviews, EKa wrote to Olschki: "It has become entirely foreign to me and I hardly still know why I actually wrote it and exerted so much effort over it. A single really good poem would have been so much more valuable."[13]

His spirits picked up after the appearance of *The King's Two Bodies* and after he knew that he would not yet be "fishing in the Styx." With renewed energy he took a third trip to Europe in the summer of 1958, from the beginning of June until the middle of August. First he stayed in England for two weeks, living in the Warden's cottage at Wadham College with Maurice Bowra and giving a paper at the Warburg Institute in London.[14] From there he made his way to Madrid, overcoming reluctance. He had been disinclined to go because the country was both too "black" (Catholic) and too "white" (fascist). But he wanted to see some twelfth-century manuscripts from Sicily and despaired of getting photocopies by mail.[15] In the event he had a fine time in Madrid, mainly because a student of his from the Frankfurt years, Angel Ferrari, had become a professor of medieval history at the university. Ferrari owned an automobile and was happy to show him around the city and environs. Nobody he met talked about the fascist government, although everybody complained about the priests. He thought that the civil war must have been terrible: ruins were everywhere and he had never seen so many mutilated people on the streets. The rest of the trip was different: Greece, obviously, where he met up again with Bowra and the two hopped islands like frogs from lily pads.[16]

Back in Princeton the reviews of *The King's Two Bodies* were starting to come in. Most were favorable, and EKa was pleased by those he thought discerning.

[11] To Olschki, 21 May 1956.

[12] To Vera, 19 December 1956, 26 March 1957; to Ralph Giesey, 20 March 1957: http://www.regiesey.com; to Vera, 29 September 1957.

[13] 19 December 1958.

[14] To Ernst Langlotz, 24 April 1958: Langlotz papers; Ralph Giesey, introduction to the unpublished paper "Glosses on Late-Mediaeval State Imagery," http://www.regiesey.com.

[15] To Vera, 9 April 1958; to Elise Peters, 17 February 1958; to Ernst Langlotz, 24 April 1958.

[16] To Ernst Langlotz, 24 April 1958; to Ralph Giesey 26 August 1958: http://www.regiesey.com; to Leonardo Olschki; 29 September 1958. EKa and Bowra were on Paros, Mykonos, and Rhodes; later he went by himself to Rome, Munich, and Paris.

But he latched on to those that he considered inferior: Dunham's glowing review in *Speculum* he thought "shallow" and Norman Cantor's in the *American Historical Review* "laughable."[17] A notice in the *Revue historique* by a senior Sorbonne medievalist, Édouard Perroy, annoyed him the most: "[He] gives his hostility toward every sort of 'Geistesgeschichte' free run, and accuses me of not even having organized the illustrations in chronological order."[18] He also was offended by a critical review by R. W. Southern that appeared in 1959,[19] as well as an anonymous one that appeared in the *Times Literary Supplement*, which he called "silly and superficial."[20] As late as 1962 he wrote to Stephan Kuttner, "What does your friend Beryl Smalley have against me? . . . she wrote a personally spiteful review of the Two Bodies."[21]

After the book Kantorowicz wrote only articles. Most often these were devoted to what Yakov Malkiel called "prohibitively narrow topics." Malkiel speaks for many when he acknowledges that "[Kantorowicz] knew how to render [these articles] fascinating by the discovery of hidden implications and by his consummate skill in using mutually corroborative techniques and bits of evidence [but] he cannot be entirely absolved of the charge of excessive miniaturization."[22] Yet he did what he preferred to do regardless of knowing that he was writing for a limited audience. As he wrote to Olschki, "Just as the Zille-mother in Berlin north said to her snot-nosed son: 'go down to the courtyard Karlchen and play yourself' [Geh runter in den Hof, Karlchen, und spiel Dich], so I play myself and still have fun with the nonsense."[23]

Kantorowicz's letters are full of self-denigration about one or another of the twenty articles he produced during his Institute years. Six of them he felt obliged to write in order to contribute to Festschriften for friends. Although he wanted to display his loyalty, he often complained about the "*Pestschriften*" to which he was committed. (The play on words changes "Festival-Writing" to "Plague Treatises.") Other articles arose out of lecture invitations he felt he could

[17] Cantor in *American Historical Review* 64 (1958): 81–82. The assignment of the review to the twenty-nine-year-old Cantor, whose doctoral dissertation EKa had just read the year before, was inappropriate.

[18] To Olschki, 19 December 1958. EKa's words about Perroy's review were accurate: *Revue historique* 220 (1958): 158–60.

[19] Southern in *Journal of Ecclesiastical History* 10 (1959): 105–8. See David Abulafia, "Kantorowicz, Frederick II and England," 143, who reports that Southern did not consider it to be particularly biting. Kantorowicz would not like to have read what Sir Richard wrote to me, 18 April 1995: "Your account of Kantorowicz has aroused in me a deeper criticism of his whole approach to the past than I have ever been conscious of before."

[20] To Ralph Giesey, 19 December 1959.

[21] To Kuttner, 27 February 1962. An impartial reader might find it difficult to see anything malicious in Smalley's notice.

[22] Malkiel, "Ernst H. Kantorowicz," 215.

[23] 21 May 1956. (Heinrich Zille was an illustrator who drew satirical sketches about life in working-class quarters in Berlin.)

not turn down: once he was at the Institute for Advanced Study invitations came streaming in. Several of the articles reformulate aspects of *The King's Two Bodies*; others deal with matters Byzantine in connection with EKa's regular attendance at Dumbarton Oaks; others take their points of departure from the author's extraordinary command of art-historical evidence. A published disclaimer comes at the end of an article for the Karl Reinhardt Festschrift in which the author acknowledges that he had broached a vast theme—Frederick II's debt to Hellenism—but that he laid no claim to surveying it; all he was doing was retrieving "some fruits of his reading by means of a few all-too fleetingly drawn lines."[24]

In referring to Kantorowicz's articles that deal primarily with Late Antiquity or Byzantium, Ihor Ševčenko cogently observed that they all are "basically about the same thing: about the close relationship between the divinity and the ruler, and about the vicissitudes of that relationship—'continuity by transference' from one epoch, culture, and ideology to another."[25] The same is true of some other articles, but one of them goes against the trend by breaking a link between divinity and the ruler. This is a piece on "The Legal Foundations of the Kaiser Legend" that EKa elected to write in German and published in 1957 in Germany's premier medieval history journal.[26] It implicitly reverses an approach that Kantorowicz had featured in his KFII of thirty years before. In his biography he had adduced the paradox of the "Erythrean Sibyl," "he lives and he lives not," as a prophecy that offered consolation for the emperor's unexpected death by "transfiguring" him as immortal. He even went so far as to place the German words of the paradox in bold capitals: **ER LEBT UND LEBT NICHT**. The aura of the supernatural was spellbinding.

In the article of 1957, however, he retracted this interpretation albeit without indicating that he was doing so. Having familiarized himself with legal history and having concentrated on the theme of dynastic continuity in preparing *The King's Two Bodies*, he concluded that the Sibyl's words were not to be interpreted as referring to the transfiguration of an individual but rather as a promise of continuity: the king will live through his heirs. Granted that the line became associated with a belief current after Frederick's death (and with variants for centuries thereafter) that he was miraculously suspended and someday would return to right all wrongs, Kantorowicz argued, as he phrased it to Olschki, that it was really a "German-bottled 'Le roi ne meurt jamais,' and, as so often with Germans, a great misunderstanding."[27] Although he was mistaken in

[24] "Kaiser Friedrich II. und das Kónigsbild des Hellenismus (Marginalia Miscellanea)," in Kantorowicz, *Selected Studies*, 283.

[25] Ševčenko, "Ernst H. Kantorowicz (1895–1963) on Late Antiquity and Byzantium," in Benson and Fried, *Ernst Kantorowicz*, 274–87, at 283.

[26] Kantorowicz, "Zu den Rechtsgrundlagen der Kaisersage," *Deutsches Archiv für Erforschung des Mittelalters* 13 (1957): 113–50; reprinted in Kantorowicz, *Selected Studies*, 284–307.

[27] 21 May 1956.

some of his details, his dynastic interpretation of the Sibylline line now stands as a significant debunking contribution to German history.[28] And in terms of the author's own biographical trajectory, the article is a stunning example of his shift from subjective "mythical views" to the objective study of a phrase in the context of legal sources.

The about-face displayed in the article was matched by EKa's steady resistance to reprinting KFII after the war.[29] He was powerless to block the reprinting of the English translation of 1931 because he had sold away his rights. Thus an American publisher, Fredrick Ungar, brought out a reprinting in 1957 without even notifying him. Judging from a library census, Ungar made a shrewd move. The original printing is located in 250 public libraries whereas the reprint is located in 991.[30] A reprinting of the original German was particularly desired in Germany, but in this regard Kantorowicz was able to stand his ground for a long time. After Helmut Küpper's death his widow, Ursula, replaced him as director of the successor firm to Georg Bondi, and she knew that a reprinting of the famous book would be financially advantageous. But EKa held her off after repeated requests from 1958 to 1962. In 1960 he wrote to her of an Italian scholar who recently had asserted that the book had been written under the influence of National Socialism and the "German-imperial sentiments" that led to the Second World War. Just this sort of reading made him resolve never to permit a new printing for the duration of his life. Only a rumor that Frau Küpper reported to him in 1962 made him change his mind: supposedly an East German press intended to publish a pirated edition. When he heard this news EKa relented about having the Küpper firm bring out a new printing, although he insisted this should come out together with the *Ergänzungsband*. He also stipulated that the title page with the swastika signet and the single-page preface referring to "Das Geheime Deutschland" be omitted, but he allowed the dedication to Woldemar Graf Uxkull-Gyllenband to stand. As expected the reprinting was a financial success. The first printing ran to 2,000 copies, as did subsequent runs of 1964 and 1973. (Later reprintings appeared in 1980, 1985, 1987, 1991, 1992, and 1994.) But EKa quickly regretted his decision when he received a letter from a German general expressing delight that his "deeply moving work about the great Staufer" was still in demand. His reaction was one of rage. As he wrote to Frau Küpper it was "just as he had feared": in his view the letter came from just those circles on whose account he had wanted to bar reprinting: "Most likely the meanwhile-fortunately-hanged Herr Eichmann would have been just as delighted."

[28] Christian Jostmann, *Sibilla Erithea Babilonica: Papsttum und Prophetie im 13. Jahrhundert* (Hannover, 2006), 306.

[29] The following account depends on EG, 166.

[30] I refer to listings in "WorldCat."

Eckhart Grünewald has pointed out that Kantorowicz allowed the reprinting even after he had learned that a threat from East Germany did not exist. He explained his motive to Ursula Küpper: he did not want it to seem as if he had dissociated himself from his past in the George circle.[31] Earlier testimony in this regard is a letter he wrote to Alexander von Stauffenberg in 1947. "Alex," who was one of the three Stauffenberg brothers, was a cousin and friend of Woldemar Uxkull's. He had studied in Heidelberg for a semester in 1923, where he met EKa through the Uxkull connection; a few years later he studied with Uxkull in Halle. Of the three brothers he was the only one to opt for the humanities and a professorial career; his speciality was ancient history. Otherwise he was prominent in the George circle and was one of those who stood at George's death watch in 1933. Fortunately for him, his brothers kept him ignorant about their conspiracy against Hitler. He was married to a Jewish woman and, although the marriage had gained Nazi consent (the woman, a famous aviator, was useful in serving the Luftwaffe as a test pilot), Claus and Berthold von Stauffenberg thought he still might be under surveillance.

In 1943 Alex von Stauffenberg had written a poetic cycle, *Der Tod des Meisters* (The Death of the Master), which was published anonymously in 1945. Two years later, when the mails allowed, he sent this to EKa, who expressed his great appreciation.[32] He explained that when Alex had informed him about the cycle in a previous letter he had worried that it would be too "forced" in the manner of Friedrich Wolters. (EKa hated Wolters's stentorian "priest-like" pronouncements concerning the greatness of "the poet.") But now, right from the first part of the cycle called "Death Watch" (he had kept watch too), he was drawn in and congratulated the author on "a great success." What particularly impressed him was that it was written in a straighforward style as a "report of events" without rhetorical amplificaton. The result was that it led him to reexperience what he himself had felt in the shadow of George's death; as he was sitting in the October sun it granted him a few very special hours.

But EKa had no patience with former members of the circle whom he thought were "petrified" in their public displays of reverence for the Meister and were holding to a "passé orthodoxy."[33] Ernst Morwitz was such a one, and Edgar Salin's panegyical book on Stefan George "rubbed him the wrong way."[34] His most extended criticism of circle "petrifaction" appears in a letter to Helmut Küpper regarding Küpper's younger friend Karl Josef Partsch. EKa had talked with Partsch in 1951 when he was visiting America and was appalled by

[31] EG, 165.

[32] To Alexander von Stauffenberg, 11 October 1947: StGA, Akte A. von Stauffenberg, III:1601.

[33] To Ursula Küpper, 16 December 1956, cited in EG, 158.

[34] To Helmut Küpper, 30 June 1951: StGA, Akte Kantorowicz, III:1904; to Ludwig Thormaehlen, 10 March 1956: StGA, Akte Kantorowicz, II:2201.

an "orthodoxy" he otherwise only would have expected from Salin.[35] It was "a rigidity that had not been relaxed either by war or bombardment—an inflexibility that did not stem from strength of character but weakness." Related to that was a vaunting of "hubris" that to EKa seemed entirely "Hitlerish and nationalistic": Partsch scorned American students because they could not fathom what he called "our profundities." When EKa listened to Partsch's talk about the "younger State" he felt entirely alienated.

Aside from quoting some passages from George's poetry in his army lectures, Kantorowicz never referred publicly to Stefan George in his American career and eschewed quotations from or references to George in his scholarly writings. Words from the opening lines of the introduction to the *Two Bodies* may signal his attitude: "Mysticism, when transposed from the warm twilight of myth and fiction to the cold searchlight of fact and reason, has usually little left to recommend itself. Its language, unless resounding within its own magic or mystic circle will often appear poor and slightly foolish" (note the reference to "circle"). Ulrich Raulff has detected aspects of George's influence in Kantorowicz's American writings,[36] but to pick them up one must be extremely well versed in the Meister's symbolic imagery. Had EKa distanced himself from the memory of the demigod of his youth? His second cousin Beata Alden, who knew him well in the late 1940s, believed that to be the case.[37] But aside from the letter to Alexander von Stauffenberg, another letter includes an astonishingly devout statement. Writing in 1954 to a prominent George disciple, Robert Boehringer, Kantorowicz commented on George's influence on him: "There is not a day in which I am not aware that everything that I manage to accomplish is fed by a *single* source, and that this source continues to bubble even after twenty years."[38]

Opposed to a prolongation of a "George Kreis," Kantorowicz rejected the notion that he was creating a *Kreis* of his own. In his view this was a canard. As Ralph Giesey wrote to me "he despised the notion of himself as the head of a *Kreis*."[39] Supporting evidence comes from letters to Bowra. In 1951 EKa wrote: "The boys are all right, only they write after my fashion which I do not like," and in 1961, "I hate it to be persiflaged [*sic*] by quotations on the part of my former students."[40] And yet even though Giesey insisted that Kantorowicz did not play a "guru" role with the younger people who were close to him, onlookers

[35] To Küpper, 30 June 1951.

[36] Raulff, "Apollo unter den Deutschen"; Raulff, "Ernst Kantorowicz—Die zwei Werke des Historikers," in *Nationalsozialismus in den Kulturwissenschaften*, ed. Hartmut Lehmann and Otto Gerhard Oexle, 2:451–69 (Göttingen, 2004).

[37] Interview, 30 July 1989.

[38] Quoted in Eckhart Grünewald, "Kantorowicz, Ernst Hartwig," in *Stefan George und sein Kreis: Ein Handbuch, Band 3*, ed. Achim Aurnhammer et al., 1471–77 (Berlin, 2012), at 1476.

[39] 13 July 1999.

[40] 28 June 1951; 2 December 1961.

saw remarkable devotion. Ihor Ševčenko referred to Kantorowicz's "acolytes"; Gene Brucker wrote to me that Kantorowicz "was the object of cult devotion by his student admirers and exercised an enormous influence on their lives and work"; William Bowsky, who served as EKa's research assistant in 1956–57, wrote that "EKa was capable of arousing almost fierce loyalty in his students—some of whom I tended to think of as a Kreis"; and Wilder Bentley, Margie's brother, wrote, "I used to watch the ripples go outwards from whatever crises gripped the Kantorowicz Kreis."[41]

The correspondence between Kantorowicz and Robert Benson in the Benson papers includes the following typed letter:

> *Princeton, New Jersey, 8 April 1951*
>
> *My dear Robert:*
>
> *It is with deep regret that I find myself forced, after your degrading performance last Friday night, to say that I can no longer allow you to number yourself among my disciples. Really Robert, that you should ever demean yourself by singing those vulgar cowboy songs—I could never have believed it of you. . . . I seem to feel the shade of Stefan George standing accusingly at my shoulder and saying, "Ernst, you have betrayed my teachings by letting this commoner insert himself into your kreis." Do not think that I cast you off with equanimity. On the contrary, it causes me great pain. I loved your sensitive soul, but in this shifting world STANDARDS MUST BE OBSERVED. Your scandalous flouting of them must be punished, cost me what it may.*
>
> *Yours sorrowfully,*
> *[signed] Eka.*

One might be fooled, but the three written letters "Eka" were not in EKa's hand. Some well-informed wag was playing a prank, yet one that had a soupçon of probability.

If Kantorowicz did not encourage the notion of a Kreis, Michael Cherniavsky and Ralph Giesey surely imitated him in various ways. Cherniavsky and his wife Lucy were wine drinkers before they met him, and they chose red or white wine according to the meal as most people do. But EKa favored white wine regardless of the meal and Michael came to imitating this. When he began teaching he also imitated EKa's practice of holding seminars in his home with wine provided.[42] Giesey gave dinner parties in the Kantorowicz manner. Howard Kaminsky, a colleague of Giesey's at the University of Washington, complained

[41] Ševčenko to Robert E. Lerner, 28 August 1996; Brucker, 29 July 1989; Bowsky, 14 July 1989; Wilder Bentley, Jr., email, 20 September 2012.

[42] Interview with Lucy Cherniavsky, 3 March 1991.

that "when I became friendly with Ralph [I] had to sit through interminable dinners whose program imitated EK's—a preliminary hors d'oeuvre, conversation, a first course, conversation, main course, conversation, salad, conversation, dessert, conversation."[43]

Kantorowicz of course did not pressure his admirers to imitate him, but he did meddle into the personal lives of some in a manner more reminiscent of Stefan George than the norms of American academia. By the time he moved to Princeton the cluster of his disciples consisted of Michael Cherniavsky, Robert Benson, and Ralph Giesey, all of whom served successively as his research assistants at the Institute. They all saved his letters, and along with subsequent interviews these provide ample documentation of Kantorowicz's intrusiveness.

We have seen that when Cherniavsky announced his plans to marry Lucy, EKa, who liked her a great deal, was so furious about the two getting married that he "almost disowned them." The storm subsided, but later came another assault on the couple's private life. In 1960 Lucy became pregnant and, knowing EKa's insistence that scholars should not have children, kept her condition secret for as long as she could; when she began to show she avoided seeing him.[44] After the birth of a daughter Kantorowicz had to accept the reality, but this did not hinder him from indulging in tasteless humor. When the baby was three months old the Cherniavskys were scheduled for a visit to Princeton. EKa offered them the option of staying with him but thought the Princeton Inn would be better: if they were bringing "the worm" he could easily put it in the refrigerator so that "it" could stay fresh, but all told he preferred not to pollute his ice-box with milk containers.[45] Later, in 1962, when EKa met the couple in Chicago (where Michael had taken a position on the university's history faculty), they did all they could to keep the child away from him by hiring sitters to take her elsewhere—"they didn't want to impose on him."[46]

EKa also made outrageous jokes about Lucy as a female. Once when Lucy and Michael were vacationing with him, Lucy took a shower and emerged saying that "now she was clean all over." Little did she know that this would be the basis for constant smutty remarks about where she may not have been clean, extending to a promised gift of perfume to cover "her stink." More tasteless still were remarks about her being able to help the family budget by taking up

[43] Email, 12 November 2005.

[44] Interview, 4 May 2012.

[45] To Lucy, 10 March 1961: "Ja,und bringt Ihr den Wurm mit? Ich kann ihn ganz leicht in die obere Icebox legen, damit er sich frisch hält. Aber . . . verunreinige ich ungern meine Icebox mit Milchbehältern statt mit Weinflaschen": Lerner archive. Much earlier he had made the same heavy joke about hosting his cousin Beata with her children: "I'll have to ruin my ice-box with milk bottles, which will pollute my Liebfrauenmilch and goose-liver—but what one does for the family." (To Elise Peters, 21 September 1956: Lerner archive.) To Ihor Ševčenko he remarked about Ševčenko's baby daughter, "[I] find her quite nice as babies go." 16 July 1962: Lerner archive.

[46] Interview with Lucy Cherniavsky, 4 May 2012.

whoring, and most tasteless of all a "joke" about the move to Chicago: "Has Lucy already been raped in the slums of Chicago, and did she like it?"[47] (The biographer cringes.)

EKa was concerned that Michael was insufficiently committed to his scholarly work. The concern was legitimate (his wife confirmed that Michael had trouble writing) but perhaps not the frequent reprimands. For example:

> I'm the last to spoil another person's pleasure, and especially if that person is an old friend. What I do not quite understand, however, is why a scholar's pleasure should not be, in addition to trout or salmon fishing, also his undisturbed working for four months at his desk—those irreplaceable four months during which one is not interrupted and may reap the joy of getting something done. Your annual escapes to California are something like an obsession, and especially in your situation you may find that those pleasant California summers were a loss of time which none of us can really afford. You know as well as I do that that you will need more than anything a good quantity of publications. You have to come up for promotion next year.[48]

Justifying his license, Kantorowicz concluded by saying that he was assuming "the right of a spiritual father." With such a "father" often lecturing him, Michael continually felt that he was letting him down. He did manage to publish enough to gain tenure at Wesleyan and then advancement to the University of Chicago (with an interval at Rochester, he ended his career as Mellon Professor of History at the University of Pittsburgh), but EKa offered no encouragement about what he actually did write. Cherniavsky's only book was *Tsar and People: Studies in Russian Myths* (1961), which showed a good measure of Kantorowicz's influence. It argued that a dominant theme in early Russian culture was a divinization of the ruler—"the development of a political mythology [around] an image of a . . . god-emperor" (99). Still EKa wrote to him: "It is a good book, not at all dull, a little crazy at times—but so are the Russians. . . . You will get good reviews I now believe, although you have fucked up every single Greek quotation and many of the German book titles—and you cannot tell me this is the fault of the Press."[49] Obviously this was not a way of enhancing a "spiritual son's" self-esteem.

In contrast to Cherniavsky, who wrote his dissertation under Berkeley Slavicists, Robert Benson was fully a Kantorowicz student. He took Kantorowicz's courses as an undergraduate at Berkeley and came to Princeton with Kantorowicz to do graduate work in the fall of 1951. It was understood that EKa would be his main advisor even though he needed to enroll in the History Department to gain his Ph.D. degree. (Pro forma his dissertation supervisor was

[47] To Michael Cherniavsky, 8 November 1961: Lerner archive.

[48] 6 May 1956.

[49] 22 January 1962.

Joseph Strayer.) EKa called him "Bobchen." Benson also chose to work in the field of medieval canon law just at the time when EKa was exploiting the same field for *The King's Two Bodies*, and in 1955 he wrote an unpublished paper in the area that EKa cited in his book (317, n. 9). But he never took to imitating the Kantorowicz manner as did Cherniavsky and Giesey, plausibly because he never became as close to the master as the other two.

One reason for this may have been that EKa detested Benson's wife, Joan. (Benson had divorced his first wife in Berkeley and she was his second.) Joan was a perfectly agreeable person and also quite attractive, but she was antielitist and not tony.[50] Whatever the reason, EKa had a deep aversion to her. Once when Benson came to a party without Joan, EKa turned to Lucy and said, "How nice that Bobchen is here without the goat."[51] In 1951 he wrote to Vera Peters: "Bob Benson is unfortunately weighed down by his goat who is a lead weight on his leg."[52] Joan's becoming a mother inevitably made matters worse. Benson steeled himself before the birth of the child in 1958 and thought he would inform EKa by means of a parody of scholastic legal debate: "Queritur an in utroque iure doctor esse melior est quam in uteroque iure doctor. Quidam dicunt quod sic, cui sententie accedit magister ernestus" (The question is whether it is better to be a doctor of both laws or a doctor of the law of the uterus. Some say yes, to which sentence master Ernestus agrees). But the witty parody appears on a postcard addressed to Kantorowicz that was never sent.[53] When news could no longer be withheld, Benson informed "master Ernestus" and received a reply with an awful innuendo, "Dear Papa Bobby, I hope the arrival of Miss Emily Benson was less surprising to you than it was to me."[54] Later, after Joan became the mother of two girls, EKa wrote to Michael Cherniavsky that he would not engage them later as "Lolitas" (as he would Michael's daughter!) "because I do not like the mare of that stable."[55]

EKa's aversion for Joan did not affect his support of Benson, whom he made his research assistant at the Institute during the academic year 1952–53 even though Benson then lacked a doctorate. He also supported him for a Fulbright grant to study in Munich and paved his way by writing to his old friend Friedrich Baethgen, who was then president of the Monumenta. Benson recalled that at professional meetings EKa would introduce him with the words, "I want you to meet my least promising student,"[56] which everyone understood to connote real affection. And certainly after Benson returned from Germany

[50] Interview with Lucy Cherniavsky, 3 March 1991.

[51] Interview, 27 April 2012.

[52] 15 December 1951: Lerner archive.

[53] The card, which remains in the Benson papers, lacks a date but had to have written before 1 August 1958, when the rate of two cents increased to three.

[54] 23 August 1958: Benson papers.

[55] 16 July 1962: Lerner archive.

[56] Interview with Robert Benson, 5 November 1990.

in December 1955, EKa supported him for numerous job positions. But EKa showed impatience with the length of time that Benson was taking to finish his dissertation by referring in 1957 to his *opus aeternum*.[57] By late 1959 he became exasperated. Benson had gained a job at Wesleyan University through the Cherniavsky connection after three years of teaching at Barnard College, where he had been dismissed. He still had no publications and understood that he needed to turn his dissertation into a book in order to stay at Wesleyan. But he was an egregious procrastinator. Already in December 1958, after the Barnard administration announced that it would not be keeping him, Benson wrote to EKa that he "*must*" make his revised work ready for publication.[58]

But as of November of the following year he had not accomplished that, and EKa decided that he needed an *ani calcatio*, a Kantorowicz coinage for "kick in the pants."[59] EKa decided that this should be administered by Ihor Ševčenko and wrote to Cherniavsky, "As for Bobbychen I wished I could see his *ani calcatio* administered by Ihor—at least it should go on TV. . . . [W]e shall have to make that a new Feast Day of the Holy R. Church: '*St. Roberti ani calcatio*.'"[60] The kick not yet delivered, EKa wrote to Benson in February 1960: "Dear Bobby, Should you get the *ani calcatio* that you deserve, it should leave you as an object of envy to all the less colorfully bottomed baboons of our best zoos. . . . There are perpetually openings which would be suitably filled by one of the 'less promising' students of my acquaintance had that boy only published a line or had his book in the press that was due many a summer ago. But after many a summer dies the swan."[61] Benson replied with a letter of excuses that he ill-advisedly sent special delivery. Then came the acid response: "Your Special Delivery letter got me out of bed at six a.m. Thank you for being an efficient guardian of my most important hours of sleep. . . . [T]he Baboons are waiting for you to bestow after a successful *ani calcatio* . . . the rare honor of "Baboon h. c."[62] And then another year passed and Kantorowicz wrote: "Breach of promise is nothing quite uncommon with you. How often have I . . . been promised that the manuscript of your book would go to the press at the latest within 6 weeks. This promise has been repeated annually ever since ca. 1955–56. . . . All that mess has been caused by omitting the well-deserved *ani calcatio*."[63]

[57] 3 June 1957: Benson papers.

[58] [December 1958] "Saturday afternoon": Benson papers. (Benson saved Kantorowicz's letters and carbons of many of his own; thus a dialogue is preserved.)

[59] In an unpublished paper, "Roman Coins and Christian Rites," given at Dumbarton Oaks in April 1951, Kantorowicz treated "CALCATIO COLLI"—the "stepping on or kicking the neck of the enemy."

[60] 19 November 1959: Lerner archive.

[61] 6 February 1960.

[62] 14 February 1960.

[63] 8 May 1961.

EKa genuinely cared for Benson and worried—with good reason—about the "Maximus Cunctator."[64] In January 1961 he wrote to Ralph Giesey: "About Bobby I know, as usual, very little. But he is certainly obsessed by some hysteria which prevents him from publishing his book. His is a difficult case."[65] But all his hectoring was to no avail; it only made Benson more defensive. At Christmas of 1961 EKa sent Benson a gift of wine and received a thank-you note from Joan. As EKa reported to Cherniavsky, "Bobby, she writes, feels too guilty to write to me because the MS is still on his desk and unfinished. The wine case has not been opened because Bobby feels he is not entitled to drink anything until the MS is sent off. This seems a real COUCH case of oenophobia, of lack of *ani calcatio*, and a thousand other patterns."[66] In fact EKa did not live to see Benson finish his manuscript (the book came out in 1968). To call his jabbing about a legitimate academic matter intrusiveness would not be right, but possibly he might have succeeded better had he taken a different tone; one wonders whether perhaps it was he who deserved an *ani calcatio*.

Closest of all to EKa was Ralph Giesey. EKa never directed Cherniavsky's scholarly work, and although their relationship remained friendly it became more distant after Cherniavsky went his own way with *Tsar and People* and was able to manage his own academic advancement. EKa and Benson had never been very close and their relationship ultimately became tense. On the other hand, EKa and Giesey were very close from 1948 until EKa's death in 1963. Kantorowicz was not formally Giesey's research supervisor, but he suggested his topic and mentored his project until the publication of Giesey's book, *The Royal Funeral Ceremony in Renaissance France*, in 1960. The contents were complementary to Kantorowicz's emphasis on ceremonies and ideas about the kingship that never dies.

Despite all that, Kantorowicz vigorously disapproved of Giesey's frequent marriages, which came to a total of four. Giesey married in Detroit after he left the navy. He was in his early twenties and the young woman was in her teens. Although he came to Berkeley with her, he quickly divorced her in 1949: she did not fit in and he had fallen in love with Margie Bentley.[67] Ralph's next marriage came at the end of 1951: he was then a Fulbright student in Belgium and he married another Fulbrighter. But this marriage lasted hardly more than a year (the woman asked for the divorce) and he returned single to America in 1953 (he had gained a year in France with another fellowship). EKa was hardly consoling. He wrote while Ralph was still in Europe that he was pleased to learn from a recent letter that "Hercules has cut the cord linking him to Omphale" (a learned allusion to Hercules having been forced to do menial work as a slave to

[64] To Benson, 6 February 1960.

[65] 31 January 1961: http://www.regiesey.com.

[66] 15 February 1962.

[67] Interview with Lucy Cherniavsky, 27 April 2012.

the woman Omphale, whose name means "navel"). To which he added, "Please do not get married again *before* you arrive in Princeton."[68]

The emphasized "before" was meant to indicate that EKa was confident that Ralph would marry again quite soon. But it took until 1957 for the third marriage to eventuate. Kantorowicz's response to the wedding announcement was not charming. Ralph had written that he "expected a grimace" and received what he expected. EKa's salutation was to "Dear License Collector and Bluebeard," and his letter went on to say that "I found it rather cheeky [for you] to embark on a potential third divorce while probably still being in the red for the second. In every other respect, of course, I take the stand of the psychoanalyst in the elevator: 'His problem, not mine.' May you solve yours and remain happy."[69] Writing to Vera a week later he let out all his bile: "The donkey has gotten married yet again—every change in location drives him headlong into a marriage: he escaped by a hair's breadth in Princeton and Vassar; now in Seattle he's caught, for the third time and certainly not the last. He collects marriage and divorce certificates and nothing can be done about it."[70]

Ralph's third wife, Nora, was not someone who could easily mix with the Cherniavskys and Ševčenkos, but she was a capable woman—the secretary of the University of Washington's History Department. Howard Kaminsky, a member of the department at the time, thought that Nora was "lovely and nice," adding that "her fate was sealed by K. not approving of her."[71] And K. surely did not approve of her. After he met her for the first time he wrote to Vera that "the Giesey-goat" was worse than what had come before. Later he wrote to Vera that Ralph would be coming to visit him in Princeton "thank God without the *chèvre dure*" (a play on "hard goat" and "hard goat cheese"), and after that he wrote that he hoped that his doctor would ban hard goat cheese from his diet.[72] In a postcard to Michael Cherniavsky he referred to Nora as "the squaw."[73]

The marriage lasted until the spring of 1962, when Nora insisted on a divorce. Kantorowicz's message to Ralph was as follows:

> Dear Divorcee, Although your letter sounded rather unhappy and I felt sorry for you on account of the ulcers which you have to expect popping up, I yet had to smile (a slight understatement) at your news. Thrice divorced at a relatively tender age and without being in the movie business is a good record, outstripped only by Barbara Hutton with whom you probably align—the two of you together would have quite a collection of marriage and divorce licenses to plaster the wall

[68] 19 April 1953: http://www.regiesey.com.
[69] 4 July 1955: http://www.regiesey.com.
[70] 10 July 1955: Lerner archive.
[71] Email 11 May 2011.
[72] 29 September 1957, 20 December 1958, 27 May 1959.
[73] 28 December 1958: Lerner archive.

> and produce a cozy atmosphere in the living room. Why, however, you should be depressed I do not, and probably cannot, understand. You should be used to it by now, and you still have about twenty years of marriageable life ahead of you. So you can easily make up for the loss, if a loss it be. You may have noticed that I never had any sympathies for late Mrs. Giesey III and that most of your old friends felt the same way.[74]

Shortly afterward EKa wrote to Vera that "the fourth, who will be inevitable, will be still worse than the first three put together according to [Giesey's] law of plummeting bearablenesss."[75] Indeed there was a fourth marriage and divorce, but EKa did not live to see the woman. She was a classicist, Cynthia, called "Tig" after Antigone. After Ralph died in 2011 I wrote to her to offer my condolences (she and Ralph had remained good friends). I also asked whether I could interview her regarding Kantorowicz, to get her views about his relationship with Ralph. She was very cordial but wrote back: "I have no connection with, or interest in, Kantorowicz or his work . . . and therefore must decline to be interviewed about him as I would have nothing useful to say."[76]

It needs to be recognized that the intrusiveness and nastiness was balanced by generosity and genuine warmth. EKa lent money to students, regaled them with gifts of wine, and sometimes paid their doctors' bills. In 1959, after Ralph's book was accepted for publication, it turned out that the publisher was asking for a subvention. EKa thought that Giesey should apply to a foundation but said that if all else failed he was willing to contribute $1,000 (over $8,000 in today's equivalent).[77] When Cherniavsky obtained his first teaching job at Wesleyan, EKa sent him a letter on his arrival that could hardly be surpassed for warmth:

> I am happy that they found a decent house for you, and with all the nice things you have and with Lucy's help you will get a pleasant home in a very short time. Besides, you will have to work so hard that you will hardly notice where and how you live. Your jitters will start when registration begins when you need every hour for preparing your classes, and when students deprive you of the best hours of the day. You will feel miserable when you step into your classrooms the first times, and will feel better after having become acquainted with the students and the audience and having poured your first glasses of wine to recover. Thereafter things will be rolling automatically; but the pressure will not be taken off your shoulders for years—unless you are able to repeat your courses. But then you will blush at your own notes and find that you should do it all over again. The best escape is research work which makes you forget (and neglect) your classes; but on the other

74 17 March 1962: http://www.regiesey.com.
75 1 April 1962.
76 Cynthia Gardiner, email to Robert E. Lerner, 12 May 2011.
77 To Lucy Cherniavsky, 23 July 1959.

> hand your research work will make you look forward to your classes because you will have the urge to tell them what you have found. In that way, you will enjoy again your lectures and get out of your lectures a new stimulus for research.[78]

The Cherniavskys were abroad at the time of EKa's death; Lucy remembered decades later that when they returned and Ralph called to convey the sad news, "Michael stood there and cried." As for herself, she said that "she loved the man."[79]

[78] 31 July 1952.
[79] Interview, 4 May 2012.

CHAPTER 26

Last Years

In September 1962 EKa wrote to Maurice Bowra, "I am at any time ready to leave this globe."[1] He said this in view of his belief that there soon would be a nuclear war over Cuba and was not thinking about his health. But only a month before, when he and Vera were swimming in Lake Tahoe, she noticed a bulging "pulse-beat" on the left side of his abdomen. Being a trained nurse she realized that it was a serious matter and urged him to see a doctor on his return to Princeton.[2] It was an aortic aneurysm. In November, after a useless operation, he learned that he would not be able to live very long: at most another year. To this he reacted with calm—he was indeed "at any time ready to leave this globe"—and went about his daily affairs as if nothing had changed. It turned out that the prognosis was accurate and Kantorowicz died of a ruptured aneurysm in September 1963.

Before and after the "death sentence" he worked on a succession of recondite articles, attended the annual meetings of the Medieval Academy and the Byzantine Institute at "Oakbarton Dumps," vacationed on the West Coast and the Virgin Islands, and, except for a month in the hospital, carried on earnestly with his dining and imbibing. As usual he drank enough wine and spirits to wash an elephant. After his first operation in 1957 he celebrated his recovery with a bottle of wine on Christmas. With at least one bottle per diem for the next 364 days, he celebrated Christmas a year later by sharing with Ralph Giesey "three bottles of wine and several vodkas."[3] Even after the failed operation he kept the pace. In April 1963 EKa treated Ihor Ševčenko to dinner at a restaurant where both of them drank "scorpions" and "zombies."[4] (For the uninitiated, a "scorpion" is made with dark rum, light rum, and cherry brandy, and a "zombie" with dark rum, light rum, brandy, and triple sec.) The following month at

[1] 15 September 1962.

[2] Interview with Vera Peters, 1 August 1989.

[3] To Giesey, 8 December 1957, http://www.regiesey.com; to Michael Cherniavsky, 28 December 1958: Lerner archive.

[4] Ševčenko draft letter to Kantorowicz, 1 April 1963: Lerner archive.

a Dumbarton Oaks meeting Kantorowicz downed three whiskey sours in the Dupont Plaza hotel bar, then went out to dinner with "very much Rum and very much wine," and then had "a drink or two at the hotel bar."[5] A rumor circulated once in Princeton that EKa had once been married in his earlier life; when asked about this he responded: "Yes, in those days when I still drank water."[6]

EKa's politics became ever more leftward from the postwar years until the time of his death. A poorly informed observer recently sniffed that since Kantorowicz's loyalty oath pamphlet of 1950 revealed him to be elitist, any attempt to conceive of his politics in America as having moved to the left is an "all too optimistic teleology."[7] But aside from the fact that in 1950 Kantorowicz was vigorously defending freedom of thought and association to the extent of willingness to accept Communists as faculty members, the lefter-than-thou remark can be refuted by reviewing expressions located in private correspondence and Kantorowicz's energetic defense in 1961 of a militant leftist threatened with losing his job.[8]

As early as 1948 Kantorowicz wrote to a German-born acquaintance who had just left Palestine to resettle in the United States that he was not sure whether he should congratulate him: "Basically this country represents everything that one has fought against for a lifetime." All that could be said was that "at least one can live here relatively comfortably," and that America was "still the best asylum for the roofless and homeless."[9]

For a decade and a half he was deeply worried about the possibility of nuclear war, and he held the United States responsible. In reference to the atomic tests on the Bikini atoll in 1946, he criticized the expulsion of the natives of Bikini "after thousands of years of residence" and lamented the spread of radiation poisoning, complimenting the authorities for "registering the Last Judgment with the finest instruments."[10] In 1956 he lamented how "our countrymen . . . throw H-bombs for fun into the silent ocean, poisoning the world, waves, and fish."[11] To George Kennan he wrote of the horrific possibility of "some general pulling the trigger to dump atomic bombs on China."[12] When he invited Michael and Lucy Cherniavsky for a Thanksgiving dinner he said he would prefer not to make "American Eagle" (viz. turkey) "since the farting off of 50 Megaton bombs is not to my liking and spoils my appetite."[13]

[5] To Michael Cherniavsky, 22 May 1963.

[6] To Michael Cherniavsky, 16 July 1962.

[7] Wimmer, "Kantorowicz's Oaths," 120.

[8] And see *King's Two Bodies*, 301, n. 62.

[9] To Frederick Bargebuhr, 7 February 1948. (Eckhard Grünewald called my attention to this letter: provenance Stefan George-Archiv, Stuttgart, but at present unlocatable there.)

[10] To Edgar Salin, 13 September 1946: Salin papers.

[11] To Leonardo Olschki, 21 May 1956: Olschki papers.

[12] 9 September 1958: Kennan papers, box 30, folder 2.

[13] 8 November 1951: Lerner archive.

During the 1950s he was bitterly hostile to Dwight Eisenhower and Richard Nixon. He wrote that the former was a "warlord," resembled Hindenburg so much that he should be called "Hindenhower," should be shot off at "Cape Carnival," and that "this 'general' is really one of the most stupid products of cattle-producing America."[14] He mocked the Vanguard rocket as "the U.S. flopnik."[15] In reference to the ongoing Berlin crisis he wrote in 1958 to Leonardo Olschki: "We must get used to the fact that today the main malheur no longer comes from there [the USSR] but from the incompetence of Washington. Think of the Lebanon crisis and the levity with which they sent in the Marines. Let's hope that we two will have left the world before the final crash."[16] After the U-2 incident of May 1960 he wrote of the "lies of Ike, A. Dulles, and [Christian] Herter—and then they wonder why Russians don't believe them." His antipathy for Nixon dated back to California days: "Neylan, Knowland, Nixon, Knight/ reveal Cal. State's eternal plight." The Republican victory in the presidential election of 1952 led him to write, "I was sad and disgusted and felt again like struggling against Hitler or Neylan."[17] Nixon was nothing other than a "disgusting, self-important, little toad."[18]

As for Kennedy, he wrote on the day after his inauguration that he "couldn't be worse than Eisenhower." But he changed his mind. In September 1962 he wrote to Vera: "Mr. Kennedy will have to conquer Red China after Cuba, so that he can then be guided by Wernher von Braun [the former Nazi missile scientist] to the moon." And to Maurice Bowra: "We are driving fast towards war with Cuba, which means war with Russia. . . . Like old Liebermann, I cannot eat as much as I want to vomit." (Riezler's father-in-law had said that after the Nazi takeover in Germany.) A month later he wrote in the midst of the missile crisis that "our Boston boy has been dreaming ever since his election campaign of a military invasion of Cuba, and he will not settle down before he has 'given it' to them." In the same letter he found "nauseating" the "double truth" that "our bases in Turkey are against Communism, a 'good thing,' whereas theirs in Havana are against Capitalism, and therefore a 'bad thing.'"[19]

The fullest statement of Kantorowicz's views on Cuba comes in a letter written at the height of the missile crisis:

> Kennedy can't leave his hands off Cuba. That was already the greatest weakness in his election campaign two years ago, it was the greatest disaster of his first year in office, and it may become the catastrophe of his second year—or is already. It

[14] To Elise Peters, 29 June 1960: Lerner archive; to Marion Dönhoff, 22 October 1956, cited by Kersten, "In vino dignitas," 119; to Leonardo Olschki, 19 December 1956; to Michael Cherniavsky, 29 July 1960.

[15] To Ralph Giesey, 8 December 1957, http://www.regiesey.com.

[16] 27 December 1958: Olschki papers.

[17] To Elise Peters, 18 May 1960; to Ralph Giesey, 8 December 1952: http://www.regiesey.com.

[18] To Marion Dönhoff, 22 October 1956.

[19] To Elise Peters, 21 January 1961; to Vera Peters 13 September 1962; to Bowra, 15 September 1963, 27 October 1962.

> is bad enough to have a fool as President, as Ike was, but much more dangerous to have a "wiseman" or "higher-wiseman" in this office. . . . Our leader's "highest wisdom" is more like that of Crown Prince Wilhelm: "always be tough" ("immer feste druff") on the small fish. . . . It is good for the election prospects (if also the worst demagoguery), for he has the full support of Ike, receives rejoicing telegrams from industrialists like Henry III Ford, and has the rightists with whom he's been flirting on his side.[20]

When the crisis was over he wrote to Vera: "Thanks to the political reasonableness of the Russians it seems as if we have now avoided war, and Kennedy will probably not gain the satisfaction of his real desire: the invasion of Cuba." To Michael he wrote: "I had the normal feelings of my German days in 1933 plus-plus and was about to write my farewell letters," and to Ralph: "On the whole, of course, I am pro-Mexico because their President has spoken up so nicely against the US government in connection with the Cuba crisis." After Democratic victories in the November elections he wrote to Vera that the Cuba affair had clearly proven to have been an election maneuver.[21]

During the last years of Kantorowicz's life the struggle for racial integration was continually in the news. Regarding the riots surrounding James Meredith's attempt to enter the University of Mississippi he wrote to Vera in October 1962: "I feel for the second time in my life after Hitler humiliated by the events in Mississippi. Simply abominable—Mr. Meredith should receive a Congressional Medal of Honor for Bravery." To Bowra he wrote on the same day: "I am so humiliated that I don't believe I can ever again travel on my present passport to Europe."[22] A truly searing statement comes in a letter to Erwin and Dora Panofsky (then in Europe) of May 1963 in reference to events in Alabama, when police set attack dogs against blacks: "That you missed Birmingham is good for your blood pressure. I have long been in favor of the eradication of the white race and would begin in the South, moreover happily transferring Alabama and Mississippi to the black Muslims."[23]

We have seen in an earlier chapter that Kantorowicz was active in 1954 in behalf of rallying the membership of the Institute for Advanced Study to express confidence in Robert Oppenheimer's loyalty to the United States after Oppenheimer's name had been dragged through the mud by a hearing of the Atomic Energy Commission. At that time he expressed his indignation privately but in the strongest terms in a letter to Vera: "I'm once again fully at home, whatever home means—Hitler Deutschland, Nazi California, or Stahlhelm-Soviet USA."[24]

[20] To Ernest Peters 24 October 1962: Lerner archive.

[21] To Vera, 29 October 1962; to Cherniavasky, 31 October 1962; to Giesey, 2 November 1962; to Vera 10 November 1962.

[22] To Vera 2 October 1962; to Bowra, 2 October 1962.

[23] To Erwin and Dora Panofsky, 30 May 1963: Wuttke, *Erwin Panofsky*, 5:342.

[24] 18 April 1954.

One might never have dreamt that Ernst Kantorowicz the paramilitary volunteer of 1919 against "reds" might have ended his career defending a far leftist, but that is what happened in 1961 when he came to the defense of one of his former Berkeley students, Robert Colodny.[25] At the age of twenty-two Colodny went to fight with the Abraham Lincoln Battalion in the Spanish Civil War. In the summer of 1937 he was shot between the eyes, contracting gangrene of the brain, and was expected to die. Nevertheless, he recovered and went back to fight but soon experienced a high fever and left Spain in early 1938. When he returned to the United States he was partially paralyzed and blind in his left eye. Despite his condition he volunteered for service in the Second World War and worked in Army Intelligence. After the war he enrolled at Berkeley where he majored in history and philosophy. He took courses with EKa and was a peripheral member of the set. He was good friends with Michael and Lucy Cherniavsky, also leftists, and the three worked for the Henry Wallace campaign in 1948.[26] Norman Rich remembered him well, saying he was called "the Red Menace."[27] Rich felt certain that Colodny was a Stalinist and recalled him saying: "We had to go out and shoot the anarchist bastards before we shot the Fascists." Still, he thought very highly of him, as did Ralph Giesey. The latter remembered that when Colodny refused to sign the loyalty oath as a teaching assistant and had to appear before a hearing panel, he took the opportunity of lecturing his examiners about freedom of conscience.[28]

Colodny was not rehired at Berkeley and consequently had to find a job elsewhere. To support his chances EKa wrote a general letter of recommendation.[29] He wrote that Colodny had taken or audited four of his courses and was "one of our most brilliant students and Ph.D. candidates." He specified that he was "a brilliant writer, highly stimulating in his formulations, an excellent orator and teacher whom the students liked very much," and that his "mind is very keen, his conversation always pleasant, and his company enjoyable. Having been book reviewer for one of our greater papers [the *San Francisco Chronicle*] he has read more books than any young man I know." All told, Kantorowicz concluded that he could "warmly recommend him for any teaching position in the History Department of any University." Prudently he said nothing about Colodny's politics, which he probably deemed irrelevant at any rate. But the main theme of the oath opponents in Berkeley was that none of them were Communists. So writing a letter for a man whom EKa surely knew

[25] For the basic outlines of Colodny's career, "Guide to the Robert Colodny Papers": Tamiment Library, Robert F. Wagner Labor Archives, New York University.

[26] Interview with Lucy Cherniavsky, 4 May 2012.

[27] Interview, 14 January 2010.

[28] Interview, 2 August 1991.

[29] 24 August 1950: Tamiment Library, Abraham Lincoln Brigade Archives, Collection 211, box 1, folder 17.

was a left-wing militant could have opened him to attack by the Neylan faction had the word gotten out.

Colodny held a variety of jobs until he was hired in 1959 by the University of Pittsburgh as an associate professor in the history of science. But in January 1961 he was attacked by a Pittsburgh newspaper for having signed a statement issued by the "Fair Play for Cuba Committee," as well as for having fought in the Abraham Lincoln Battalion and for having a poster from the Spanish Civil War on his office wall.[30] A Pennsylvania state representative then called immediately for an investigation of the university for harboring a subversive. When Kantorowicz learned of this he sent a letter in Colodny's behalf to Colodny's lawyer so that it could be read aloud at any hearing or be entered into the record at any investigation. Before mailing it he had it notarized under oath "so that it [would] be a little stronger."[31]

The letter, Kantorowicz's only independent public political statement he made in America between the time of the oath controversy and his death, is impassioned.[32] It begins with the author recalling the circumstances in which he knew Colodny in Berkeley. Colodny had taken his classes and he "became acquainted with him because I was startled by the brilliant examination essays he wrote, and by his ability to grasp the problems quickly, to enunciate the core of the problem, and to bring the deeper layers of a historical or philosophical problem to the surface." When the two conversed about politics "the subject would have been, in those excited days, the attitude of Senator McCarthy and of McCarthism [*sic*] in general—a fascist movement as detestable to him as it was to me." The heart of the letter deals with Colodny's engagement in Spain:

> There was in the 1930s, for most Europeans but one fiend of mankind, and that was Hitler, who then began to dwarf his satellites: Mussolini and Franco. The formation of the Lincoln Brigade and other formations of volunteers appeared as a first "Resistance Movement" against that Apocalyptic Beast of Nazism. . . . [T]he participation in that struggle on the side of the anti-Franco forces did not reflect upon the participant's feelings for or against Communism, but only his feelings against the Nazi brutes and their Fascist associates. . . . It was only after I had been in the United States for many years that I learnt to my amazement that fighting against Franco plus Hitler and Mussolini and joining the anti-Fascist Lincoln Brigade was synonymous with being a Communist. . . . About the reasons why Colodny joined the Lincoln Brigade I know nothing, since that was ten years before I met him as a student. I would doubt it, however, that it was the Communist ideology which prompted him to fight the Nazi-Fascists. But even *should* he have

[30] The case is treated by Joseph G. Colangelo, Jr., "A Slight Case of McCarthysim," *New Republic*, October 23, 1961, 13–14.

[31] To Michael Cherniavsky, 14 February 1961: Lerner archive.

[32] To Frank L. Seamans, 13 February 1961: Cherniavsky papers.

> had Communist leanings at the time, it can certainly not be considered "subversive" to fight a monster such as Hitler and his consorts; on the contrary I find it shabby to use a noble task such as that to construe *ex post* a case of "guilt by association." . . . About whether or not he belongs to the "Veterans of the Abraham Lincoln Brigade" I know nothing, but, after all a Veteran of that Brigade he *is*, no matter whether or not he belongs today to that Veteran Organisation. . . . I wish to add that I know of no "subversive" action or talk or any lack of loyalty to the United States on the part of Professor Colodny; and it is hard to imagine that he as a mature man should be teaching "subversive doctrines" at the University of Pittsburgh. I would dismiss the utterances and denunciations of the local press as baseless talk.

Most likely this letter became part of the dossier of testimony reviewed by a fact-finding committee of the University of Pittsburgh which resulted in Colodny's clearing and the acknowledgment that he was a "loyal American." After the announcement Colodny wrote to EKa to thank him for his efforts, and EKa responded by saying "I am glad you are through with it and vindicated."[33]

While he was writing for Colodny EKa was planning what was to be his last trip to Europe. He wrote to Vera as he had before that he needed to do this for "income-tax purposes."[34] He spent the summer months of 1961 in Greece. In July he made Athens his headquarters and took trips to Salonika (where for three days he was delighted by the swimming and the red mullets—even better than trout) and also to Damascus, Palmyra, and Baalbek. In August he was with Bowra for three weeks, swimming off the shores of Mykonos, Delos, and Rhodes.[35] As he wrote to Vera's mother on his return, "It was stimulating as usual in Greece and the Mediterranean is really my true and only homeland. . . . I would give all the rustling German forests for a single naked island in the Greek sea."[36] After Greece came eight days in Rome and a day and a half in Munich. He ended his trip in Paris, where he stayed for three days in a five-star hotel (probably deducting the cost from his taxes) and then sailed home.[37]

It was during the following summer that Vera noticed EKa's abdominal bulge. In Princeton his internist identified it as an aneurysm and the diagnosis was confirmed by a vascular surgeon in Philadelphia. Because it was understood that the aneurysm could rupture at any time and cause instant death, the surgeon determined that he had to go under the knife as soon as possible. EKa was chipper or at least maintained that pose. He entered the hospital in

[33] 1 July 1961, Tamiment Library, Abraham Lincoln Brigade Archives, Collection 211, box 1, folder 27.

[34] 8 March 1961.

[35] To Vera, 10 May, 28 July, 28 August 1961.

[36] To Eva Kantorowicz, 29 September 1961: Lerner archive.

[37] To Vera, 28 August; to J. Robert Oppenheimer, 10 September (IAS, Kantorowicz faculty file); to Eva Kantorowicz, 29 September.

Philadelphia with sixteen bottles of wine but remarked that he foresaw a need to have his steaks fed to him intravenously.[38] To Bowra, Vera, and Michael Cherniavsky he wrote that it was a matter of replacing a piece of artery with a nylon or Dacron tube, and since he could choose the color he would probably choose tan to match his usual sunburn.[39] Vera was in California but wrote to him regularly: she wished him a guardian angel.[40] The operation that took place on November 23 could not achieve its goal because the artery leading to EKa's sole kidney lay too close to the threatened aorta and the danger of cutting it was too great. So the surgeon stitched him up again.[41] EKa then lay in the intensive care unit for three days and remained in the hospital for another two weeks.

His internist told him that he could continue to live only for about six months to a year. The doctor explained that there would be two ways in which he might die: the aneurysm might break down and hemorrhage slowly, causing total disability and agonizing pain; or it could burst like a balloon, in which case death would come in half a minute.[42] When EKa returned home he wrote to Bowra that he had acquired a scar that "ran down the whole meridian of Greenwich from breastbone to penis," and made him "look like a Christ from the Bohemian School or by Greco or Grünewald, revolting in every respect."[43] Taking the same theme in a letter to Lieschen, he reported that he looked like "a flagellated Christ," and that he would have preferred Apollo—"but of course it is much harder to look like Apollo than like Christ and therein lies my entire objection to this cheap religion." He added that he would be going to St. John around the tenth of January to frighten the pelicans and fish with his new scar.[44] Afterward he conveyed to Vera news from the sea.[45] While snorkeling, he saw some barracudas who were polite to him, although cold-eyed. Otherwise he had lost much weight. Back in Princeton his doctor brought him a side of bacon, saying that he did not need to bother about his cholesterol count because his arteries already were as sclerotic as they possibly could be.

Many urged EKa to go to Texas for a consultation with the famous cardiac surgeon, Michael DeBakey, but he declined: perhaps DeBakey could perform unusual surgery to eliminate the aneurysm, but he did not want to spend the

[38] To Erich Kahler, 20 November 1962: StGA, Kahler papers; to Vera, 20 November 1962.

[39] To Bowra, 27 October 1962; to Vera, 29 October 1962; to Cherniavsky, 10 November 1962. Also, to Bowra, 14 November 1962: "I wish that they could replace all my 'hoses' as quickly as that: one of them is certainly deficient but I cannot remember which."

[40] 18 November 1962.

[41] To Bowra, 18 December 1962.

[42] Alfred S. Cook, Jr., M.D., to Beate Salz, 21 September 1963: http://www.regiesey.com.

[43] 18 December 1962.

[44] 12 December 1962.

[45] 11 February 1963.

rest of his life "walking around with boxes."[46] Instead he preferred to live his own way, carrying on as he always had. He wrote to Bowra that he "was alright again as far as it goes" and referred to Napoleon's mother "wandering around the Tuileries" saying "if it would only last."[47] In the spring he traveled to Cambridge, Massachusetts, for the Medieval Academy meeting and twice to Dumbarton Oaks, where he had become a member of the Board of Scholars. In May he wrote to Michael Cherniavsky that he was in the midst of preparing for himself "riz de veau aux herbes" to be drunk with "the superb 1960 Graacher Himmelreich, Wachstum Prüm, which is a good thing as Ersatz-Nymphet, gay, sparkling, amusing."[48] As he did through all his mature life (except when he was on vacation) he continued to mix hard work with his pleasures. In the spring and early summer of 1963 he completed an article ("*Constantinus Strator*") and a long book review (seven pages), full of minute detail and forthright criticism.[49]

In June Bowra came to America to receive an honorary degree from Harvard and before then to stop in Princeton to see his friend. When Bowra wrote of his plans EKa answered: "This was the best news I had in ages . . . now I have something to look forward to. . . . [W]hat is spring compared to seeing *you* here."[50] As Bowra wrote to Felix Frankfurter after EKa's death, they spent "three full and happy days [together] talking about everything under the sun"; Kantorowicz "had known . . . that he could never recover and might go off at any moment, but he made jokes about it and said it was much better than going slowly gaga."[51]

EKa spent the second half of July and most of August on St. John, the first time he had been there in the summer. He went around either in a "G-string" or entirely naked and became browner than usual. In the water he saw an "incredibly majestic" manta ray and snorkeled around a coral reef, swimming together with a "whole school of middle-sized squids." A new delicacy for him were "steaks" made from fresh turtles.[52]

Back in Princeton for three weeks he made bouillabaisse for a small gathering and brought leftovers to Alice and Erich Kahler but died before he could pick up the tureen.[53] On the evening of Sunday, September 8, he had dinner

[46] Interview with Lucy Cherniavsky, 9 September 1990; interview with Ihor Ševčenko, 12 April 1991.

[47] 13 February 1963.

[48] 22 May 1963: Lerner archive.

[49] Review of Walter Ullmann, *Principles of Government and Politics in the Middle Ages*, published posthumously in *Speculum* 39 (1964): 344–51.

[50] 13 February 1963.

[51] 1 November 1963: http://www.regiesey.com.

[52] To Vera, 28 July 1963, 25 August 1963; to Erich Kahler, 1 August 1963: Kahler papers.

[53] In 1989 Mrs. Kahler showed me the tureen, which was still with her.

with the Panofskys.[54] "Pan" reported later that it was "a particularly charming evening in the course of which he gave me an excellent tip concerning a Titian problem." Ralph Giesey picked up EKa for a "nightcap," which customarily meant more than one drink. But he had taken some pills for abdominal pains during the day and their effects were wearing off, so they had time only for a "quickie few glasses" because he needed to go home to take some more pills. Giesey accompanied him, and he was "quipping" until they got there. But when Giesey returned the next day at noon he found his mentor dead. The lights were on and Kantorowicz was lying fully clothed on the floor near his study. His doctor came over immediately and determined that he had died shortly after Giesey had left him the night before. There were no signs of his having struggled. The doctor wrote later to Beate Salz that "he died quickly, quietly, and exactly the way he had longed for." Panofsky felt the same: "He died exactly as he would have wished, without any impairment of his faculties and without protracted suffering." To which he added wistfully: "But for his friends this sudden disappearance has something unreal about it and I often catch myself on the way to the phone when I have come upon some question which only he would have been able to answer."

[54]The following relies on three accounts: Erwin Panofsky to William S. Heckscher, 7 October 1963, Wuttke, *Erwin Panofsky*, 5:394–95; Ralph Giesey to Maurice Bowra, 29 September 1963; Alfred S. Cook, Jr., M.D., to Beate Salz, 21 September 1963: http://www.regiesey.com.

AFTERWORD

Ernst Kantorowicz was not buried in Bamberg or Berkeley. Instead he left instructions in his will that he "did not wish to have any kind of funeral," that he be cremated, and that his ashes be sent to his niece Beate Salz. She was then teaching at the University of Puerto Rico and he had told her that he wanted the ashes to be scattered in a bay off the island of St. John. With grim humor he wrote somewhat earlier to Bowra: "I even decided to make a change in my will ordaining that my ashes be sent to my niece Beate in Puerto Rico together with my favorite cork-screw and that she be obliged to drill holes in my ash-box and sink it into the Caribbean Sea which henceforth should be known as the Ekaribbean."[1] Whether this actually happened is uncertain because around the time of EKa's death Beate was called away from Puerto Rico by the death of her father. But the assumption that it did happen led to an impressive jacket cover of a book on the "afterlife" of the George circle.[2] The author, Ulrich Raulff, believed that the only George disciple who created anything intellectually lasting was Ernst Kantorowicz, and hence that George's afterlife could best be illustrated visually with a photograph of a Caribbean bay which Raulff chose for his cover.

Kantorowicz's insistence that he wanted no funeral was inherent in his lifelong revulsion for religious ceremonies. Ironically this was a man who spent much of his scholarly career writing about such and who knew a good deal more about Catholicism than most Catholics. (During the pontificate of John XXIII, Kantorowicz, Gerhart Ladner, and Stephan Kuttner were among the most knowledgeable connoisseurs of Vatican II developments: all three had been born Jewish, but Ladner and Kuttner were converts.) At Berkeley he felt obliged to attend a Catholic wedding ceremony because the groom was a favored student but "he chatted through the entire service."[3] Michael Cherniavsky once referred to EKa as an atheist, whereupon EKa flared up and protested: "What have I ever said to make you think that?" Beata Alden noted that he "was certainly not an observant Jew, absolutely not a Christian . . . hated the personalized religion of post-Reformation sects, and deplored Calvin." But

[1] 15 September 1962.

[2] Raulff, *Kreis ohne Meister*.

[3] For this and the following, interview with William Chaney, 22 December 2011.

"he hankered after the Greek gods."[4] Kantorowicz came closest to expressing a credo when he wrote in *The King's Two Bodies*: "Dante achieved his 'baptism' into *humanitas* in a para-sacramental and para-ecclesiastical fashion, with Cato acting as the sponsor, and with the prophet Vergil as his Baptist—a Baptist, though, who this time unlocked to man not the heavens, but the paradise of Man" (492).

As EKa's rejection of a funeral was inherent in his distaste for religion, so his wish that there be no physical monument was inherent in his "anti-eternity complex." In 1954, before he turned sixty, Ralph Giesey and Michael Cherniavsky started a subscription to raise money for producing a portrait medal to honor his birthday. He was to receive one in gold, while subscribers could choose either silver or bronze. The two got as far as commissioning a sculptor to make a sample, but when EKa learned of what was happening he told them to call it off. As Giesey reported to Cherniavsky, "He turned vehem-eloquently against any project of commemoration and absolutely refused to cooperate in any fashion. . . . He talked about his anti-eternity complex, his desire for peace and to be left alone."[5]

But it was impossible for him to control his posthumous reputation. Medievalists paid tribute to the importance of his work from the time of his death, and the Kantorowicz boom that began in the late 1970s resulted in catapulting him into the ranks of the most noted humanistic scholars of the twentieth century. Here are some book and article titles: *The Queen's Two Bodies* (1977); "History's Two Bodies" (1988); "The Emperor's New Body?" (1996); *The King's Two Maps* (2003); "The King's Two Genders" (2006); "The King's Two Teeth" (2008); "The King's Two Buckets" (2009); *The King's Other Body* (2010); *The People's Two Bodies* (2011), "The Enemy's Two Bodies" (2012); "The King's Three Bodies" (2014). Beyond historiography some of Kantorowicz's words still resonate. In a commencement address at Stanford in 2005 the historian James J. Sheehan, then president of the American Historical Association, recalled Kantorowicz's speech of 1949 opposing the loyalty oath in which he held forth the principles of the scholar's "freedom of judgment, human dignity and responsible sovereignty." Sheehan commented that "however imperfectly and incompletely achieved, the aspirations and ideals which Kantorowicz so eloquently expressed remain no less important to remember, no less essential for those who claim the right to wear a gown."[6]

Although Kantorowicz's "desire to be left alone" would have extended to dislike for becoming the subject of a biography, he led too remarkable a life to control that either. How many noted scholars had personal careers to rival the

[4]Email, 23 December 2011.

[5]Giesey to "friends of Ernst H. Kantorowicz," 14 January 1954; Giesey to Cherniavsky, 29 September 1954: Cherniavsky papers.

[6]*Perspectives, Newsletter of the American Historical Association* (May 2005): 7–8.

drama of fighting at Verdun, skirmishing in Munich, serving as a paladin of Stefan George, speaking in opposition to Nazism, eluding *Kristallnacht*, and leading a fight against a McCarthyite Board of Regents? How many noted intellectuals moved from right to left instead of the other way around? How many were so quotable? A biography could not be helped.

Index

Page numbers in italics indicate figures.